War and American Popular Culture

A Historical Encyclopedia

Edited by M. Paul Holsinger

Greenwood Press
Westport, Connecticut • London

Library of Congress Cataloging-in-Publication Data

War and American popular culture : a historical encyclopedia / edited
   by M. Paul Holsinger.
      p.   cm.
   Includes bibliographical references and index.
   ISBN 0–313–29908–0 (alk. paper)
      1. United States—History, Military—Encyclopedias.   2. Popular
   culture—United States—History—Encyclopedias.   3. War and society—
   United States—Encyclopedias.   I. Holsinger, M. Paul, 1938–   .
   E181.W26   1999
   973—dc21   98–12141

British Library Cataloguing in Publication Data is available.

Library of Congress Catalog Card Number: 98–12141
ISBN: 0–313–29908–0

First published in 1999

Greenwood Press, 88 Post Road West, Westport, CT 06881
An imprint of Greenwood Publishing Group, Inc.

Printed in the United States of America

The paper used in this book complies with the
Permanent Paper Standard issued by the National
Information Standards Organization (Z39.48–1984).

10 9 8 7 6 5 4 3 2 1

Contents

	Preface	vii
	Acknowledgments	ix
1.	Colonial American Wars, 1565–1765	1
2.	The American Revolution	12
3.	The War of 1812	45
4.	Indian Wars East of the Mississippi, 1783–1845	55
5.	The Texas Revolution and the War with Mexico, 1836–1848	62
6.	The Civil War	74
7.	Indian Wars West of the Mississippi, 1862–1890	148
8.	The Spanish-American War and the Philippine Insurrection	178
9.	World War I and the 1920s	194
10.	World War II	223
11.	The Korean War	336
12.	The War in Vietnam	357
13.	The United States Military since 1975	429

Index	441
About the Editor and Contributors	477

A photo essay follows page 222

Preface

War and American Popular Culture: A Historical Encyclopedia looks closely at many of the most significant representations in popular culture that deal with this nation's various wars. In the following pages, attention is focused on works of fiction—both novels and short stories—poems, songs, plays, outdoor dramas, motion pictures, and radio and television presentations. There are entries on paintings, photography, cartoons, sculpture, public memorials, toys, comic books, dime novels, and even slogans and posters. There are also articles about some of the writers, photographers, songwriters, and other artists who created them.

In recent years, there have been many attempts to define popular culture. To some, it is little more than a description of those things that the "masses" of uneducated Americans enjoy. Others think of popular culture exclusively in relation to its commercial possibilities. According to some students, if a work is produced to make large amounts of money, it qualifies as "popular." If, conversely, an author, poet, artist, musician, or sculptor is simply expressing his or her innermost feelings, irrespective of how much financial gain might be realized, then, by definition, the work cannot be deemed popular. A "popular" work must appeal to the majority in a community, expressing its thoughts or meeting its needs so that, in theory at least, its members will be willing to pay for it. The entertainment value of a particular piece becomes all-important. Though there is more to be said for this definition than for one based on class distinctions, it has also been rejected for use in this encyclopedia.

"Popular culture," as defined in the following pages, is admittedly a simplistic concept. It is limited neither by its appeal to a particular class nor its economic success. If an item was embraced by "the people"—the same American people to whom Abraham Lincoln referred in his Gettysburg Address—it has been considered worthy of inclusion. When Lincoln talked about a government of, by, and for the people, it is obvious that he was being all-inclusive. Neither gender, social status, educational background, nor cultural tastes make one less a ''person'' than anyone else.

In these pages, readers will find articles that look closely at representative works of popular culture spanning the history of the European settlement of the present United States from the first Spanish settlements in Florida in 1565 through the American military presence overseas in the late 1990s. Though every effort has been made to be as chronologically comprehensive as possible, the topics that appear on these pages are undeniably tilted toward the past sixty years. A glance at the various entries will quickly reveal that there are more dealing with World War II, the Korean War, the Vietnam War, and the several ''small wars'' in which the United States has been engaged since 1975 than there are for the entire period up to 1941. This has been done unabashedly, in the belief that Americans today are far more attuned to the modern era than they are to the past. Stress has also been placed on ''new'' materials as opposed to the old, which are more readily available for use by interested readers in general libraries, video stores, reading anthologies, and other sources than those that are not.

I have included a bibliographic reference or two at the end of each entry in the hope of encouraging interested readers to delve more deeply. Space alone has dictated their small number, as it has in the inclusion of only four or five sources at the conclusion of each chapter introduction. There are tens of thousands of sources for the many items in this volume; a comprehensive list would have more than doubled its size and made the cost prohibitively expensive. Instead, I have tried to make sure that those that do appear are among the best available. All the cited references are perceptive interpretations, and in most cases, they are representative of the latest scholarship. They should be viewed only as a start to a detailed study of a given war, however, and never as the final word.

Throughout the encyclopedia, cross-references to topics discussed elsewhere have been highlighted in boldface. Readers are encouraged to examine the various examples for their relation to, or differences from, the topic being discussed.

War and American Popular Culture is a practical reference tool that seeks to pull together, from many different sources, information about how we as a people have mythologized our warring past. It has also, however, been designed to be read rather than to collect dust on a shelf in a library reference collection (whether big or small). If I and the volume contributors have succeeded in accomplishing both goals, the thousands of hours spent will be well worth the effort.

Acknowledgments

This volume, like the overwhelming majority of books everywhere, owes much to many different persons. To name them all individually would take far too much space and would, even then, risk the possibility of inadvertently omitting someone who (even if only in a small way) made an important contribution to this project.

Despite such a caveat, there are a number of people who must not be overlooked. The Board of Trustees of Illinois State University granted me a sabbatical leave during the spring semester of 1997, which provided close to four uninterrupted months in which to complete the research and finalize the manuscript for this study, for which I am grateful. The librarians of Illinois State's Milner Library Inter-Library Loan division repeatedly, and always expeditiously, obtained copies of long-out-of-print novels, plays, and other sources whenever I needed them. Brian Braye and his staff at Illinois State's Graphics Production Offices professionally helped to prepare the illustrations for use. The Bloomington and Normal (Illinois) Public Libraries—two of the best small public libraries in the United States—provided access to surprisingly good collections of popular cultural materials. Participants on H-Net-PCAACA, the joint Internet web site of the Popular Culture and American Culture Associations, gladly answered queries and clarified particular points. Though their names appear elsewhere throughout the pages of this work, the nearly three dozen other high school, college, and university colleagues who, freely and enthusiastically, contributed one or more entries were indispensable.

In recent years, it has become almost obligatory to give special thanks to one's spouse for some (real or imagined) gift of time, encouragement, or love. This volume is no exception. My wife, Nancy, who has somehow put up with my whims and peculiarities for nearly forty years, unquestionably made this work a reality by constantly keeping me on track, especially at times when it seemed the project would never be finished. She gave me time, love, and untold encouragement, to be sure—and a few words here will never repay any of those gifts—but she also did much more. A brilliant editor in her own right, she repeatedly proofread every entry, kept asking the "right" questions about what we were trying to say in each, encouraged rewrites, and always forced us to make sure that, in every case, what was said was not only precise and careful, but also always readable. Later, eschewing the many computerized indexing programs, she systematically created by hand the useful, detailed index that appears at the back of the volume. Her name fails to appear on the front cover or on any of the title pages, but it certainly should. This volume would have been completed had she never looked at even one word, but it would have been a much less capable work than it is now. If it has value, a large part of the credit is hers.

Finally, I need to acknowledge the influence, if not the input, of three young men who have not yet read a word of this study: Jordan Alexander Holsinger, Lucas Paul Holsinger, and Elijah Christopher Holsinger, my three grandsons. As this is being written, in the early fall of 1997, Jordan is six; Luke, four; and little Eli, barely two months old. None of them has even the most remote idea of what war is about. Hopefully, in the years ahead, their understanding will continue to come from books such as this one rather than having to learn first-hand. If the future allows Jordan, Luke, and Eli—and all Americans—to live in peace, with war only a vague memory, they will be blessed.

.

Colonial American Wars, 1565–1765

War was a constant of American life long before the first European conqueror landed on the shores of the New World. For many years, the Native American tribes had frequently gone on the warpath against each other. When soldiers and settlers from Spain, France, England, and the Netherlands arrived, however, military strife and violence became even more commonplace. The first conflict occurred within months after the settlement of Florida by troops from both Spain and France. Determined to control the territory, Spanish commander Captain-General Pedro Menéndez de Aviles and his men left their newly established settlement at St. Augustine in 1565 to attack, capture, and then indiscriminately massacre the French garrison at Fort Caroline, just to the north of present-day Jacksonville. Soon the Spanish were at war with several of the surrounding Indian tribes as well, and the pattern for nearly all white–Native American relations for the next 330-plus years was thus established.

The arrival of explorers, and then colonists, from Britain and, in the far north, others from France only accelerated the slaughter. The white settlers, believing that they were especially blessed by God to conquer and occupy the land, found the various Indian tribes troublesome. French soldiers under Samuel de Champlain set out to make war on the Iroquois Confederation as early as the spring of 1609, less than a year after the settlement of Quebec. The British began to kill the Powhatan peoples within a few years after they created Jamestown, their first settlement in North America, and the religiously inclined Puritans believed there was nothing wrong with killing hundreds of Pequeot men, women, and children in the mid-1630s. Given their firm belief in the efficacy of solving problems militarily, the white settlers soon were also at war with each other as they fought for control of the valuable land and its wealth of raw materials along the St. Lawrence River and the other navigable waterways of New England. Champlain and his small contingent of fellow Quebecois, for instance, were captured by enemy forces under Lewis Kirke and taken in chains to England in 1629 in what was to be but the first of thousands of face-offs between the two nations.

International rivalries abroad brought about seemingly permanent warfare in North America. In 1689, the so-called King William's War, fomented by the newly crowned William I in England against the forces of France's Louis XIV, spread quickly to the New World. Under the leadership of Louis de Buade, the Count Frontenac, French troops and their Huron Indian allies, out of Quebec and the newer settlements at Montreal and Three Rivers, ranged almost as far south as Albany, New York, wreaking havoc everywhere they went. In the dead of winter 1690, sixty British and Dutch settlers, including a number of women and small children, were killed, and another ninety were taken prisoner when the French attacked the almost defenseless settlement of Schenectady. The English quickly retaliated. The Maine-born Sir William Phips and his fellow New Englanders turned on Canada with a fury and, though they failed by only the slimmest of margins to capture the citadel in Quebec, the quick response became a symbol of the many future British-French confrontations. Indeed, during the remaining eight years of King William's War in North America, the two national powers took turns engaging in bloody raids that brought terror to the many settlers living on both sides of the border.

The English and the French were at war again from 1701 to 1713 as a part of the so-called Queen Anne's War (an offshoot of the War of the Spanish Succession in Europe), and then again from 1740 to 1748 during King George's War (when the two enemies fought around the world as a part of the European War of the Austrian Succession). Throughout North America, supporters of the two nations vied for control of the land and sea. After the French built what was supposedly the world's most impregnable fortress, at Louisbourg on the coast of Cape Breton Island, the New Englanders attacked and captured it in 1745. Even earlier in that same war, British colonial troops under the command of the founder of Georgia, James Oglethorpe, also launched an attack on France's ally, Bourbon Spain, in Florida. Its failure impelled the Spanish to attempt to capture Savannah and the small colony in Georgia in 1743, but Oglethorpe, though outmanned by his enemy, was able to force a stalemate in battles off St. Simons Island.

Of all the colonial wars, certainly the two most famous were the bloody, but limited, King Philip's War of 1675–1676 and the far greater French and Indian War, from 1754 to 1763. Philip, the son of Massasoit (the Wampanoag chieftain who befriended the first Pilgrim settlers), tried for years to unite the many Indian tribes throughout New England against the white settlers. When the war that bears his name erupted in January 1675, the numerically stronger New Englanders had an opportunity to destroy the last vestiges of Native American opposition to their control. The bloodletting was at times horrendous—in December 1675, for instance, more than 600 Narragansett Indians were burned to death when the New Englanders set fire to their enclosed fortifications. The Indians also killed at will, frequently destroying small white settlements, and occasionally taking prisoner such women as Mary Rowlandson, whose account of her captivity became one of the most renowned of all such narratives through the years of Indian warfare (see *A True History of the Captivity and Restoration of Mrs. Mary Rowlandson*). In the end, the European settlers were victorious; Philip's Indian allies were hunted down, captured, enslaved, and ultimately slaughtered. The chief himself was finally ambushed and killed in August 1676. His body was drawn and quartered, and his severed head was proudly displayed in Plymouth for many years afterward.

The French and Indian War and the British victory over the French in Quebec paved the way for an independent United States of America less than two decades later. Unlike earlier encounters between the two nations, however, the conflict began in the woods of Pennsylvania and only later spread worldwide. The story of that war (as well as many of the earlier conflicts between the British and the French) has been told again and again, but probably nowhere better than in the writings of nineteenth-century American historian **Francis Parkman**. It is a tale of military men such as France's Marquis de Montcalm, Great Britain's James Wolfe, and even the twenty-two-year-old George Washington. The brave and foolhardy General Edward Braddock, who dramatically marched his combined English-American army toward western Pennsylvania's Fort Duquense only to have it ambushed and horribly slaughtered by the French and their Indian allies, is also there (see **"Braddock's Defeat"**), as is the French attack on New York's Fort William Henry in 1757, which later became the basis for James Fennimore Cooper's *The Last of the Mohicans*.

Braddock's defeat (and death) gave the British no choice but to fight their old enemies, the French, yet their ultimate victory caused more problems than it solved for the world's great colonial power. The removal of the French threat in North America after the 1763 Treaty of Paris opened the door for American colonials to demand more control of their own destinies. British attempts to prevent further problems in the west resulted in anger and bitterness from the potential white settlers and in the bloody "Pontiac's Rebellion," which was led by an Ottawa chieftain who had been angered by white incursions on Indian lands. However, like most white-Indian conflicts, no matter how fierce, it was the technologically advanced Europeans who won and the natives who lost. Chief Pontiac, who was seen by many as a tragic figure, was assassinated in 1765, and thus the trans-Appalachian frontier was opened even wider.

The end of the French and Indian War left the financially strapped British with an enormous national debt, which they tried to repay as quickly as possible. The stamp acts, demarcation lines, and other policies approved by Parliament were logical and, in most cases, certainly not excessive, but to the American colonials, being taxed "without representation" seemed an unforgivable affront, and soon the American Revolution loomed on the horizon.

See:

Hamilton, Edward P. *The French and Indian Wars: The Story of Battles and Forts in the Wilderness*. Garden City, NY: Doubleday, 1962.

Leckie, Robert. "The Colonial Wars." *The Wars of America*. New York: Harper, 1992, 3–82.
Maslowski, Peter. "A Dangerous New World, 1607–1689"; "The Colonial Wars, 1689–1763." In *For the Common Defense: A Military History of the United States of America*, eds. Allan R. Millett, and Peter Maslowski. New York: Free Press, 1984, 1–46.

"BRADDOCK'S DEFEAT" (Folksong). On July 8, 1755, General Edward Braddock and more than 1,400 British regulars and American frontiersmen were ambushed on the banks of the Monongahela River in western Pennsylvania. In the ensuing slaughter, Braddock was mortally wounded after having five horses shot out from under him. More than 75 percent of his men became casualties. Young George Washington, one of the highest-ranking Americans present, had two horses killed but escaped unharmed. The French and Indian War had begun in earnest.

It was not long before an anonymous folksinger recounted the battle in song. "Braddock's Defeat," a ballad of a dozen or more stanzas, takes its listener through the battle and then follows the British and Americans as they make their way in retreat. Some of the lyrics are extremely vivid. When the troops crossed the Monongahela, for instance, "men fell in the river till they stopped up the flood / And the streams of that river ran red down with blood." One of the most intriguing parts is an account of Braddock's death. The song avers that the general was not killed by a French or Indian sharpshooter but by a colonial volunteer, who was angry because Braddock had "cut down" his brother for shooting at his foes while standing behind a tree instead of out in the open like the British regulars. Washington, seeing what is about to occur, begs the man not to kill the general, but when he cannot change the man's mind, he turns away and lets his commanding officer be shot. Whether there is any truth in this version of the battle will never be known.

See:

Hamilton, Charles, ed. *Braddock's Defeat: The Journal of Captain Robert Cholmley's Batman*. Norman: University of Oklahoma Press, 1959.

M. Paul Holsinger

"CHIEF LOGAN'S LAMENT" (Speech). Chief Logan (or Tachnechdorus, his given Mingo Indian name) lived on the west bank of the Ohio River near present-day Steubenville, Ohio, in the days immediately before the American Revolution. A longtime friend of white men in the region, Logan went on the warpath in 1774 after his mother, brother, sister, and several cousins were massacred by frontiersmen living near his village. The chief, his Mingoes, and a large number of Shawnees, whom he had recruited, descended on small white settlements from the Allegheny to Cumberland Gap, killing and massacring at will. Soon, the entire frontier was ablaze in what became known as Lord Dunmore's War.

When the Indians had finally been defeated, Logan refused to attend a meeting to draw up a peace treaty. Instead, he sent a representative with a short message. "I appeal to any white man to say," Logan's speech began, "if ever he entered Logan's cabin hungry, and he gave him not meat; if ever he came cold and naked, and he clothed him not." Though he readily admitted that he had "killed many" and "glutted my vengeance," now, he added sadly, "who is there to mourn for Logan?—Not one."

As early as February 1775, the *Virginia Gazette* in Williamsburg published a copy of the chief's words, and they were reprinted throughout the colonies. Thomas Jefferson was so taken with Logan's speech that in 1784 he included it in his *Notes on the State of Virginia*, where he challenged his readers to find any "single passage" in "the whole orations of Demosthenes and Cicero" or "any more eminent orator" in Europe "superior to the speech of Logan, a Mingo chief, to Lord Dunmore, then governor of this state." Though subsequent research has found an almost verbatim statement by another Indian leader in 1754, Logan's speech became a staple oration in classrooms across the country during the nineteenth century, when countless American schoolboys were forced to memorize "Chief Logan's Lament."

Logan, ironically, saw none of this. Growing increasingly despondent and drinking heavily, he became, according to one observer, "an abandoned sot." In 1780, after leaving the protection of the British in Detroit during the American Revolution, he was murdered during a quarrel.

In 1821, Joseph Doddridge wrote a play, *Logan, the Last of the Race of Shikillemus, Chief of the Cayuga Nation*. Popular for many years, it was still being performed with some regularity throughout the United States until at least 1868, when yet another copy of the drama was published.

See:

Public Library of Fort Wayne and Allen County. *Logan, Shawnee Chief.* Fort Wayne, IN: Author, 1954.

M. Paul Holsinger

CROSS AND SWORD (Outdoor Drama). The symphonic dramas of Paul Green may have been seen by more Americans than the works of any other single playwright in U.S. history. From June 1937, when his famous outdoor drama, *The Lost Colony*—the story of the first English settlements in the New World—premiered on the Outer Banks of North Carolina, to the summer of 1977, when *Lone Star*, the last of his fourteen symphonic works, opened in Galveston, Texas, Green gained world renown.

Cross and Sword: A Symphonic Drama of the Spanish Settlement of Florida is an epic play based on the Spanish founding of St. Augustine, Florida, in 1565, and one of the most important of Green's historical dramas. First produced in 1965 at the specially constructed Anastasia Island Amphitheatre near St. Augustine and the Spanish-built Castillo de San Marcos, the nation's oldest fort,

Florida's official state play is still staged nightly each summer, to the delight of thousands of tourists. Focusing on the life of the expedition's leader, Captain-General Pedro Menendez de Aviles, the outdoor drama centers its attention on the Spanish defeat of the French Huguenot forces north of present-day Jacksonville and their subsequent near-destruction at the hands of local Indian tribes. Menendez's decision to go to war with those tribes, even though he would have preferred peace, is dramatized. His victory and return to Spain to report to his king mark the end of this extremely popular play.

Though Green's Menendez de Aviles is a far more sympathetic character than actual historical facts would suggest—for example, he readily slaughtered unarmed French prisoners on more than one occasion with no mercy—*Cross and Sword* is generally fair in its assessment of the earliest European history in what is today the southeastern United States.

See:

Kenny, Vincent S. *Paul Green.* New York: Twayne, 1971.

M. Paul Holsinger

***THE LAST OF THE MOHICANS* (Novel-Films).** James Fennimore Cooper published his most critically acclaimed work, *The Last of the Mohicans: A Narrative of 1757,* in 1826. The second of five "Leatherstocking Tales," which chronicle the story of Natty Bumppo, or Hawkeye, as he is more commonly called, the novel quickly became extremely popular both in the United States and in Europe. Though his first successful book, *The Spy* (1821), had an American Revolutionary background, and both *The Pathfinder* (1840) and *The Deerslayer* (1841) feature Natty Bumppo on the colonial frontier occasionally fighting Indian tribesmen, none of Cooper's books is more stirring or exciting in its depiction of war than *The Last of the Mohicans*. Few novels more readily qualify as an American classic; today dozens of versions are available for purchase at all reading levels.

Set at the time of the successful French attack on New York's Fort William Henry, its plot centers on the attempt of Hawkeye and his Indian allies, Chingagook and Uncas, to save a young British officer and the two daughters of the fort's commander from capture and torture at the hands of the Huron Indians. The evil and lascivious Magua, leader of the Hurons, makes a swinish enemy, and his death at the end of the story has had readers cheering for more than 170 years.

There have been at least nine different cinematic adaptations of Cooper's *Last of the Mohicans* since 1911. French director Maurice Tournier's version (Associated Producers, 1920), starring Wallace Beery as the evil Magua, is still recognized as one of the best. Perhaps an even better production (United Artists, 1936) features Randolph Scott as Hawkeye and Bruce Cabot as Magua. Called by *Variety* "undoubtedly the finest film version of any Cooper tale" (September 9, 1936, 3), it still remains, more than sixty years later, a fine, if not an exceptional, film. The newest attempt (20th Century–Fox, 1992), directed by Michael Mann and starring British actor Daniel Day-Lewis as Hawkeye, borrows freely from Philip Dunne's 1936 screenplay, which was one of Mann's childhood favorites. Once again Hawkeye, the seminal frontiersman, continues to embody the very essence of American independence and adventure. He outruns, out-shoots, outpaddles, and outtracks everyone—British, French, and Indians. Though some critics were appalled by Mann's sanitized recreation of the past, the cinematography is exceptionally beautiful and there is more than enough brutal and bloody warfare to please the viewing public. *The Last of the Mohicans* was 1992's top-grossing movie, earning nearly $72 million in box office re-ceipts.

See:

Edgerton, Gary. " 'A Breed Apart': Hollywood, Racial Stereotyping, and the Promise of Revisionism in *The Last of the Mohicans.*" *Journal of American Culture* 17.2 (1994): 1–20.

Suzanne Broderick

THE LIGHT IN THE FOREST (Novel-Film). Conrad Richter's young adult novel, *The Light in the Forest* (the Newbery Award winner for 1953), tells the story of True Son, a white boy raised among the Tuscarawa Indians of central Ohio during the French and Indian Wars. After eleven years of captivity, True Son (or, as his white parents originally named him, John Cameron Butler) is forcefully sent east from the only home he remembers to live with his parents in western Pennsylvania. Feeling fully native, he hates everything he encounters. The Butlers try their best to reach out to their son, but, in their attempt to "cleanse" him of all Indian corruption, they only alienate him more. When his Tuscarawa cousin comes east to help True Son escape his "captivity," the two teenagers scalp the boy's white uncle and return to their village in triumph. Once back, however, True Son comes to see that the Indians do act savagely and that white society, for all its faults, does have a number of redeeming qualities. This ambiguity comes full circle when, shortly afterward, the boy is allowed to accompany a Tuscarawa war party. He is given the opportunity to help ambush and massacre a boatload of white settlers, but he warns them away instead. Ostracized by his Indian father and the other members of the tribe, the youngster finds himself, at the novel's end, caught between two worlds and unable to return to either.

An adequate screen adaptation of Richter's novel, *The Light in the Forest* (Walt Disney Pictures, 1958), was filmed with a young James MacArthur as True Son. Directed by Herschel Daugherty, it does a reasonably good job of retelling the story, but, as so often occurred in the early Disney movies, the end is sugarcoated and quite unlike the book's grim conclusion.

In 1966, Richter published a follow-up to *The Light in the Forest*, which he called *A Country of Strangers*. Also set in the 1760s, it focuses on a young female captive, Mary Stanton (Stone Girl), who is also forced to return to white society. She leaves behind an Indian husband and her child, only to be rejected by everyone, including her parents, who treat her as little more than a servant. She saves her younger sister (who previously despised her) during an Indian attack on the white settlement, but, when John Butler (True Son) suddenly appears, she readily deserts "civilization" to return to the forest with him. With so much in common, the two young people determine to begin a new life together.

See:

Gaston, Edwin W. *Conrad Richter.* Boston: Twayne, 1978.

Randal W. Allred

THE MATCHLOCK GUN* (Children's Novel).** Few authors of American historical fiction have been so renowned for capturing both time and place as was Walter D. Edmonds. Nearly all his many works, including the popular Revolutionary War saga for adults, ***Drums Along the Mohawk, are characterized by careful attention to historical detail. Edmonds also gained considerable fame during his career for writings designed primarily for young readers. *Two Logs Crossing, Wilderness Clearing*, and *In the Hands of the Seneca* are all well-crafted stories of life in colonial America. None of his works for junior readers, however, is more famous than *The Matchlock Gun.*

Set in 1756 during the French and Indian Wars, *The Matchlock Gun* is a fictional account of the real-life story of a young Dutch boy from a farm near Albany, New York. Ten-year-old Edward Van Alstyne saves the lives of his mother; his baby sister, Trudy; and himself from marauding Indians by firing the ancient Spanish blunderbuss that his great-grandfather brought from Holland years before. Though their cabin is destroyed and his mother is badly wounded, Edward is responsible for killing three braves and wounding a fourth. When his father, who has been with the militia, arrives home, he finds the boy, his mother, and his baby sister huddled on the ground outside the charred remains of the farmhouse surrounded by the men he has slain.

Awarded the prestigious Newbery Medal as "the most distinguished contribution to American literature for children" in 1942, *The Matchlock Gun* has never gone out of print. With the careful, evocative sketches drawn by Paul Lantz throughout its pages, it is as exciting today as it was when it was first written, more than fifty years ago.

See:

Wyld, Lionel D. *Walter D. Edmonds: Storyteller.* Syracuse, NY: Syracuse University Press, 1982.

M. Paul Holsinger

***METAMORA* (Drama).** Unquestionably one of the most popular plays of the mid-nineteenth century, *Metamora or The Last of the Wampanoags*, by John

Augustus Stone, was based on the life and death of the Indian chief who led his people against the white settlers of New England during the so-called King Philip's War of 1675. From its first performance in New York, on December 15, 1829, until at least the middle 1880s, it was invariably the hit of any season, wherever it was staged. When the great American actor Edwin Forrest offered a $500 prize for "the best tragedy, in five acts, of which the hero, or principal character, shall be an aboriginal of this country" (Moody, 199–200), a panel of judges that included the poet William Cullen Bryant selected Stone's work to receive the prize. Forrest became "Metamora," and that fictional Indian chieftain became synonymous with Forrest for the rest of his life.

Far from the cruel, rebellious monster described so vividly by such New England Puritan leaders as Cotton Mather, however, Stone's Metamora is a doomed and tragic figure who fights to protect his family and fellow tribe members from grasping, avaricious white settlers. Many viewers expressed great sympathy for the chief. So famous, in fact, did the image of Metamora become that at least four cities—in Indiana, Ohio, Michigan, and Illinois—were named for the Indian "hero" in the years before the Civil War.

Sadly, Stone benefited little from his drama's great success. Feeling despondent after the failure of several subsequent attempts at playwriting, he committed suicide in 1834 by drowning himself in Philadelphia's Schuykill River.

See:

Moody, Richard. "Metamora or The Last of the Wampanoags." In *Dramas from the American Theatre 1762–1909*, ed. Richard Moody. Cleveland, OH: World, 1966, 199–204.

M. Paul Holsinger

PARKMAN, FRANCIS (Author). Over a span of forty-one years in the mid-nineteenth century, Francis Parkman published a majestic eight-volume narrative history of the colonial wars between the French and English for European control of the North American continent. For years he was recognized as the greatest American historian because of these books, in which he glorifies "great men" and their exploits far more than the common farmer or citizen soldier who also sought to tame the wild frontier.

As a young man, Parkman made numerous voyages on foot and canoe to the edge of the frontier, which in the 1840s was little different than it had been two centuries before. His most daring adventure, an overland journey to the Pacific Northwest, resulted in one of the greatest firsthand accounts of the nineteenth century, *The Oregon Trail*, which was published in 1849. By the time he began to write his study of the French-English conflict, however, he was nearly blind, partially crippled, and suffering from severe damage to his nervous system. Though he could often only work for five-minute intervals, he insisted on using original manuscript sources, which had to be read to him. At times this meant that he wrote no more than six lines a day.

His first historic publication, *History of the Conspiracy of Pontiac* (1851), chronicled the end of the great struggle between the British and their French and Indian enemies. Subsequent works recorded the century and a half prior to 1763, but each treated the subject in the same manner as *Pontiac*—as a series of dramatic events controlled by a group of fascinating characters. Certainly that is true of the often-brilliant *Montcalm and Wolfe* (1884), one of the most exciting and popular histories of the French and Indian War ever written.

Latter-day historians have often noted that Parkman's histories, though intensely readable and romantic, are also "old-fashioned" and woefully inadequate by today's scholarly standards. Nevertheless, as long as readers continue to care about the nation's past, Parkman's literary classics, with their beautiful prose, will probably remain popular with students of North American history.

See:

Doughty, Howard. *Francis Parkman*. Cambridge, MA: Harvard University Press, 1983.

Colin L. Hopper

PONTEACH; OR THE SAVAGES OF AMERICA **(Drama).** Robert Rogers, the famous ranger of the French and Indian War, who is featured prominently in Parkman's *Montcalm and Wolfe*, Kenneth Roberts's 1937 novel *Northwest Passage*, and King Vidor's film of the same name, was also an important author in his own right. His five-act play *Ponteach; or The Savages of America*, published in 1766, not only offered the first account of Pontiac's rebellion west of the Appalachians after 1763 but also was the first drama written by an American to feature Native American characters. Surprisingly, it is Pontiac the great Ottawa chieftain and the Indians who receive the most compassion. British traders are seen as venal as they take pride in cheating or even killing the Indians with whom they trade. "Ponteach"—the phonetic spelling of the chief's given name used by Rogers and many other Americans of that day—is viewed as a magnanimous and generous lover of liberty and freedom, and his Indian allies as brave, "noble savages." Though Rogers does not deny that many settlers died in the war led by the chief, he lays the blame more on Pontiac's subordinates than on the chief himself, whose death is portrayed as both sad and unnecessary.

Ponteach was controversial from the movement it was first published. Several critics accused Rogers of hiring someone else to author his play—a claim that the eminent American historian Allen Nevins argued was probably true. Most of the play's characters are little more than badly formed stereotypes, the plot is melodramatic, and Rogers' blank verse is frequently extremely awkward. Though the play was reissued on a number of occasions throughout the nineteenth century, there seems some question of whether it was ever staged until the mid-1970s, more than two hundred years after its initial publication. Certainly, however, dozens of similar works throughout the remainder of the eighteenth and most of the nineteenth centuries were based on the formula that Rogers (or whoever the play's author might have been) created.

In 1977, Arthur Lejaren used parts of the drama's text to write *Ponteach: A Melodrama for Narrator and Piano*.

See:

Jones, Eugene H. *Native Americans as Shown on the Stage, 1753–1916*. Metuchen, NJ: Scarecrow, 1988, 4–21.

M. Paul Holsinger

A TRUE HISTORY OF THE CAPTIVITY AND RESTORATION OF MRS. MARY ROWLANDSON (Captivity Narrative).

Mary Rowlandson's account of her capture and imprisonment by a combined force of Narragansett and Nipmuck Indians during King Philip's War in 1676 is the earliest and most influential example of America's first literary genre: the Indian captivity narrative. Published in both America and England under differing titles in 1682 but best known as *A True History of the Captivity and Restoration of Mrs. Mary Rowlandson*, it became, in a day when few persons read books of any kind, an international best-seller. Its success ensured the proliferation of thousands of similar books, fiction and nonfiction alike.

Rowlandson's text, which lies firmly in the ideological tradition of New England Puritan sermons and devotional texts, established many of the conventions to be found in the captivity narrative genre: the demonization of one's captors into inhuman "others"; the focus on the physically afflicted body as a medium of spiritual growth; and, most important, the rhetorical conceit of the text as a moral and religious primer for God's subjects.

In the years that followed, other captivity narratives, such as John Williams's *The Redeemed Captive, Returning to Zion* (1707) and James E. Seaver's *A Narrative of the Life of Mrs. Mary Jemison* (1824), achieved a level of renown comparable to, but not exceeding, that of Rowlandson. Many famous works of early American fiction, including James Fenimore Cooper's **The Last of the Mohicans**, are captivity narratives. The twentieth-century cinematic Western has helped the theme to survive: a notable recent example is Kevin Costner's Academy Award–winning (Best Picture of 1990), **Dances with Wolves**. Scholars have seen the captivity narrative's influence in other genre films as well, such as Vietnam prisoner of war rescue movies like 1985's **Rambo: First Blood, Part II**.

See:

Castiglia, Christopher. *Bound and Determined: Captivity, Culture-Crossing, and White Womanship from Mary Rowlandson to Patty Hearst*. Chicago: University of Chicago Press, 1996.

Philip L. Simpson

2

The American Revolution

Long before the first "shots heard round the world" were fired by the British in Lexington, Massachusetts, on April 19, 1775, the seeds of revolution were growing throughout the thirteen American colonies. The conclusion of the so-called French and Indian War in 1763 left Great Britain with an astronomical public debt as well as the possibility that it might have to post troops in the colonies for the foreseeable future. With thousands of potential settlers poised to pour into the trans-Appalachian frontier, there was a real threat of further Indian wars. To solve both problems, Parliament quickly enacted legislation that, for the first time, placed a significant tax on American colonists. A proclamation was also issued that drew a line down the crest of the mountain ranges from the Canadian border to northern Georgia. White settlers were forbidden to go west of this "proclamation line," and all the territory in that area was officially declared "Indian Territory."

Such seemingly logical solutions, far from bringing about the desired results, only served to make matters worse. Pioneers ignored the arbitrary line and pushed deep into the West, inevitably coming into conflict with Indians such as those led by the famous Ottawa chieftain Pontiac. At the same time, the settlers in the East, who were bitter about being taxed "without representation," refused to pay the hated stamp taxes and, on more than one occasion, protested violently. In Massachusetts, for instance, the newly formed Sons of Liberty, led by Samuel Adams, attacked the home of the colony's official stamp officer and later ransacked and pillaged the mansion of the royal governor. In other colonies, similar mobs were often as brutal and uncontrolled.

For the next ten years, tensions between the British and their colonial charges steadily heightened. After 1768, King George III was persuaded to authorize sending troops to Boston to quell the unrest caused by yet another series of taxes levied by Parliament. Two years later, on March 5, 1770, an angry mob in that city pelted British troops with ice and snowballs liberally laced with oyster shells. No one knows who fired the first shot that evening but, whether from fear for their lives or not, the British regulars opened fire on the crowd, and the resultant **Boston Massacre** marked a milestone on the path toward American independence. When, three years later, the British granted the British East India Tea Company a monopoly on the sale of tea in the colonies, the Sons of Liberty openly, and with the support of most Bostonians, boarded company ships lying in the harbor and systematically threw overboard hundreds of thousands of dollars worth of the precious commodity. Angered by this obvious refusal to recognize the power of Parliament, the British soon attempted to increase their control by enacting a series of laws that Americans almost instantly called "intolerable." Martial law was declared in Massachusetts; the right of the people to maintain their own law courts was now denied; and troops were quartered in individuals' homes.

In 1774, the First Continental Congress was called to consider what to do about the escalating crisis. Though the majority of delegates were anxious to find a peaceful solution to the problems, many men by this time were not. In Massachusetts, Sam Adams and his Sons of Liberty already had the upper hand. Guns and other ammunition were stockpiled in case war could not be avoided, and patriots (see *The Minute Man*) in every village and town began forming to fight for American freedom whenever called. Meanwhile, in Virginia, men were inveighing against British tyranny; Patrick Henry declared, "[A]s for me, give me liberty or give me death." It would only take a spark to set off a full-scale conflagration.

That spark came in April 1775. Massachusetts military governor General Thomas Gage sent hundreds of British troops to Lexington and Concord to seize the many caches of guns and ammunition that were rumored to be hidden there. When the British found groups of minutemen, who had been warned of their coming, waiting in each town and refusing to disperse, it was probably inevitable that bloodshed would occur. No one will ever know who fired the first shot, but, with the deaths of colonials at the hands of "enemy" troops, the American Revolution began.

From one end of the colonies to the other, word about the killing of American citizens quickly spread. After chasing the British back to Boston, volunteer regiments started to fortify the hills across the river from the city. General Gage and his military commander, General William Howe, had little choice but to try to drive the new enemies from the heights. Though the patriots, as they readily called themselves, did great damage to the British red-coated soldiers (killing more than 200 and wounding another 800), they ultimately lost the Battle of Bunker Hill to overwhelming odds. Now there was no going back. Within a few weeks, the Second Continental Congress met and named forty-three-year-old George Washington of Virginia to be the tiny nation's first commander of troops.

American fortunes ebbed and flowed almost daily during the early years of the conflict. After Vermonter Ethan Allen and his Green Mountain Boys captured New York's Fort Ticonderoga and brought its large siege guns into Boston, Washington mounted them to overlook the city and thus forced the British to withdraw. The elation of such a great success, however, was soon tempered by numerous defeats. Two different expeditionary armies sent against the British in Canada failed to capture the citadel at Quebec; they retreated in the spring of 1776 minus their commanding officer, General Richard Montgomery, who was killed during the attack on that city. When the war had not been won by January 1, 1776, hundreds of other patriots simply returned to their homes, unwilling to fight a lengthy war. Washington, buoyed by the announcement of the Declaration of Independence in July, fought on, only to be defeated badly on Long Island. Though he and his men were able, on Christmas night, to row across a partially frozen Delaware River to surprise the British-hired Hessian troops at Trenton, New Jersey—one of the general's greatest victories of the war—more defeats followed. By the time the ragtag American Army staggered into winter quarters at Valley Forge, just outside Philadelphia, in the winter of 1777, there were many—including even Washington, from time to time—who seriously considered that the best course of action might be to negotiate peace with as much honor as possible.

Then came the biggest British blunder of the war and probably the most significant American victory. In the summer and fall of 1778, the British Army planned a three-pronged attack in the colony of New York that, had it been successful, might very well have won the war. Luckily for the patriots, however, one thing after another went wrong. One of the three armies scheduled to leave New York City and head up the Hudson River failed to do so. A second, smaller force driving through the Mohawk Valley was forced to turn back to Canada after barely winning the Battle of Oriskany against the embattled settlers of the region. The main force, led by General "Gentleman Johnny" Burgoyne, was at first successful, but was eventually cut off and defeated at Saratoga. The French, watching from the sidelines, now threw their backing and military might behind the Americans, and the tide slowly began to turn.

The British were nowhere near defeat, however. In December 1778, they captured Savannah, Georgia, and shortly afterward, the rest of Georgia fell into their hands, as did Charleston, South Carolina. As a result of that capture, more than 5,500 American troops surrendered, making it the worst defeat in U.S. military history up to the Japanese victory in the Bataan Peninsula in 1942. At Camden, South Carolina, General Horatio Gates turned and fled the field as the British attacked, and by 1780, it looked as if the entire South would soon fall to the king's troops and their Tory allies.

In the midst of seeming despair, everything once again was suddenly reversed. When the new American commander in the southern states, Nathaniel Greene, split his small army in two parts, Great Britain's Lord Cornwallis was forced to do likewise. Late in 1780, more than 1,000 "over-the-mountain men" from

Tennessee and the Carolinas met and slaughtered over 1,200 Tories at the Battle of King's Mountain. Several weeks later, at Cowpens, South Carolina, on January 17, 1781, the Americans scored an even greater victory when they stood and killed or captured more than 900 British and Tories, with the loss of only 12 of their own number. Now, with French help on both land and sea, Washington turned to the South to strike what he hoped would be the final blow. Cornwallis, who had been mauled throughout the Carolinas, retreated into Virginia only to be caught against the Chesapeake Bay at Yorktown. When it became clear that the Royal Navy would be unable to rescue him and his men, they stood and fought—and lost. On October 19, 1781, the British surrendered. Though there continued to be bloody confrontations for more than a year, especially in places as far removed as the Ohio Valley frontier and the colony of South Carolina, the Revolution became history. The Treaty of Paris, signed in 1783, not only gave the new nation its freedom but also deeded to it more than a million square miles of territory.

There remained many unanswered questions, not the least of which was whether a nation born out of violence against legitimate government and common law could possibly remain free or independent for very long. Only time would tell.

See:

Bobrick, Benson. *Angel in the Whirlwind: The Triumph of the American Revolution.* New York: Simon and Schuster, 1997.
Draper, Theodore. *A Struggle for Power: The American Revolution.* New York: Times Books, 1996.
Fleming, Thomas. *Liberty! The American Revolution.* New York: Viking, 1997.
Ward, Harry M. *The American Revolution: Nationhood Achieved, 1763–1788.* New York: St. Martin's, 1995.

ALICE OF OLD VINCENNES **(Novel).** *Alice of Old Vincennes* (1900), Indiana-born Maurice Thompson's tale of the Old Northwest during the years of the American Revolution, was one of the early twentieth century's most popular works of historical fiction. The book's heroine is twenty-year-old Alice Rousillon, a waif raised in the small Wabash River settlement of Vincennes, Indiana. When the Revolution brings war to the area, beautiful Alice quickly sides with the American forces, and even sews the town's first U.S. flag after it is captured by George Rogers Clark. She falls in love with a young Virginian, Lieutenant Fitzhugh Beverley, but the two soon have to face the recapture of the town by the British under the notorious Henry Hamilton and his Indian allies. Though Hamilton's aide, Captain Farnsworth, also falls in love with Alice, her loyalty to the American cause remains strong, and when Clark returns from Kaskaskia, in the Illinois country, and recaptures the fort, she is there to run "her" flag up the flagpole once again.

Thompson, a Crawfordsville, Indiana, lawyer, was a soldier in the Confederate Army during the Civil War. After taking up writing, he also became (long before his first book, *Hoosier Mosaics*, appeared in 1875), a well-respected and widely published author. *Alice*, unquestionably his most popular work, appeared less than twelve months before his death. Cresting at number ten on the best-seller charts in its first year, the book reached number two by the end of 1901. Though undeniably a piece of romantic fiction, it continues to capture both time and place with some skill.

See:

Otis B. Wheeler. *The Literary Career of Maurice Thompson*. Baton Rouge: Louisiana
    State University Press, 1965.

M. Paul Holsinger

AMERICA (**Silent Film**). D. W. Griffith, who is recognized by many film historians as the greatest director in the history of motion pictures, is best known for his famed 1915 Civil War–related drama, *The Birth of a Nation*. Nine years later, however, he turned his attention to the era of the American Revolution. Though *America: The Sacrifice of Freedom* (Griffith, 1924) is certainly not as well respected nor highly praised as the director's classic, it remains, nearly seventy-five years after it was made, worthy of serious attention by scholars and motion picture fans alike.

Sponsored by the Daughters of the American Revolution (DAR), *America* was intended to evoke a nationalistic, flag-waving fervor among its viewers, and the critics certainly thought that it succeeded. One reviewer, for instance, said it would "stir the patriotic hearts of the nation as probably no other picture ever has done" (*New York Times*, February 22, 1924, 20:1). Griffith pits good American virtue against British evil. Neil Hamilton and Carol Dempster are convincing as the hero and heroine, and Lionel Barrymore is a quintessential, smirking Tory villain as he and his Indian allies massacre innocent men, women, and children. The director, who was already renowned for his marvelously detailed battle scenes, reenacted for the cameras a number of major events from the Revolution, including Paul Revere's immortal ride, the "shot heard round the world" at Lexington, the minutemen at Concord Bridge, the battle of Bunker Hill, and the final defeat of the British at Yorktown. As befits the movie's chauvinism, the evil Barrymore is killed in the end, and patriot goodness wins the day. Long after the film had ceased to be popular, the DAR convinced public schools across the nation to show cuts from *America* in their history classes, and from the mid-1920s to the late 1940s, millions of school-aged children saw all or part of Griffith's work.

After the film's initial success with American critics, Griffith, who was always the entrepreneurial showman, arranged to have it widely circulated in Great Britain. First changing some of the most virulent procolonial scenes and titles, he renamed the revised production *Love and Sacrifice* and made even more money on the film.

See:

Quirk, Lawrence. "America." Chapter 4 in *The Great War Films from The Birth of a Nation to Today.* New York: Citadel, 1994, 32–35.
Simmon, Scott. *The Films of D. W. Griffith.* New York: Cambridge University Press, 1993.

M. Paul Holsinger

ARUNDEL (**Novel**). In the summer of 1775, the Continental Congress, frustrated by Quebec's refusal to join the patriot cause, sent two different American armies, led by Generals Richard Montgomery and Benedict Arnold, to attack that British stronghold. In the spring of the following year, the campaign ended in defeat. Kenneth Roberts's historical novel *Arundel* skillfully brings those days back to life for new generations of American readers.

Roberts, a feature writer for the *Saturday Evening Post* during the 1920s, was encouraged by his friend, novelist Booth Tarkington, to consider writing a fictional work of his own about the American Revolution. Though already a dedicated scholar of that period—his later, three-volume documentary study of the march to Quebec remains an important historical source—Roberts was initially dubious of his ability to write fiction. He soon proved, however, to be one the nation's best-loved and most successful novelists.

Critically praised when it was first published, in January 1930 at the beginning of the Great Depression, *Arundel* initially sold only a minimum number of copies. Later, however, after the success of many of Roberts's other novels in the mid-1930s, the book's sales mounted. The novel's hero, Steven Nason (who was drawn in part from the real-life adventures of a maternal ancestor), serves as a scout for Arnold and his men. That premise permits Roberts to give his readers an exciting account of not only the Canadian campaign in general, but also, more significantly, the failed battle for Quebec in December 1775, which sealed the fate of the American forces.

Arundel was revised in 1933, 1936, and then again in 1956, when some of the long, detailed background that the author had originally included was cut. One critic in 1930 accurately called *Arundel* "a really fine and stirring historical novel" (*New York Times*, January 12, 1930, 8). Perhaps that explains why it remains in print today, nearly seventy years after it first appeared.

See:

Harris, Janet. *A Century of American History in Fiction: Kenneth Roberts' Novels.* New York: Gordon Press, 1976.

M. Paul Holsinger

BOSTON MASSACRE (Event-Engraving). Soldier-civilian tensions in Boston started as early as October 1768, when British troops, who were poorly paid and outfitted, arrived to maintain order in that Massachusetts city. On March 5,

1770, a group of frightened soldiers of the Twenty-ninth Regiment opened fire on a mob of men and boys who were taunting them and throwing stones. Five men were killed, and seven others were wounded. Captain Thomas Preston, commander of the British contingent, and six of his men were charged with murder. Defended in court by John Adams and Josiah Quincy, two of the colony's most respected attorneys, all were acquitted (though two soldiers were found guilty of manslaughter). Four civilians accused of firing from the customhouse windows were also tried in December 1770, but they, too, were acquitted.

After the "massacre," colonial opinion against the British was quickly inflamed with broadsides and pamphlets such as *A Short Narrative of the Horrid Massacre*, which was first published in 1770 by a partisan committee chaired by James Bowdoin along with Joseph Warren and Samuel Pemberton. The document included eyewitness interviews of military men, citizens, and others who testified about their experiences on March 5. Not to be outdone, Samuel Adams, one of the most ardent propagandists of the Revolution, commissioned the famed silversmith Paul Revere to make an "eyewitness" engraving of the massacre for publication. Though *The Boston Massacre*, which Revere "borrowed" from an original design by Henry Pelham, oversimplifies more than an hour of street fighting into one compact scene of British regulars killing supposedly innocent civilians, its appearance in the *Boston Gazette*, on March 12, 1770, helped to fuel tensions in the city against the "foreign murderers."

Media coverage of the Boston Massacre had little impact in the American colonies outside Massachusetts, but the event was commemorated on its anniversary in Boston and throughout the new state for many years afterward. A plaque now marks the site of the massacre, and there are also monuments on Boston Common and in the Old Granary Burial Ground, where the victims were interred, to be joined later by such luminaries as Sam Adams, Paul Revere, James Otis, and John Hancock.

See:

Fleming, Thomas I. "Verdicts of History I: The Boston Massacre." *American Heritage* 13.1 (1966): 6–11, 102–111.

Martin J. Manning

BUNKER HILL, OR THE DEATH OF GENERAL WARREN (Drama). John Daly Burk came to Boston from Ireland in 1796. Less than a year later, on February 17, 1797, *Bunker Hill, or The Death of General Warren: An Historic Tragedy* was performed for the first time at that city's Haymarket Theatre. Though not the earliest play to focus on the years of the Revolution, it became unquestionably the most popular and best-known of its day. Over the next several years, it was staged repeatedly and, by the beginning of the nineteenth century, it had become a patriotic theatrical staple throughout the northeast.

Not everyone appreciated *Bunker Hill*; for instance, President John Adams, who was a close associate of the thirty-four-year-old commander of the Massachusetts provincial militia at the battle, thought it a slur on Warren's life. Historically, the drama is also hopelessly inaccurate. Burk invented a number of scenes that never occurred, but since all the British are portrayed as stereotypically pompous and every colonial as brave and high-spirited, it was easy for viewers to leave the performance full of renewed patriotic fervor.

Burk never lived to see his play gain the full popularity that it ultimately enjoyed. He was killed in a duel in Virginia eleven years after *Bunker Hill*'s first performance.

See:

Moody, Richard. "Bunker Hill or the Death of General Warren." In *Dramas from the American Theatre, 1762–1909*, ed. Richard Moody. Cleveland, OH: World, 1966, 61–69.

M. Paul Holsinger

"CHESTER" (Song). William Billings, one of the most popular and prolific composers in the American colonies before the outbreak of the American Revolution, wrote both the music and the first stanza of "Chester" in 1770 and published them that year in a collection of his tunes titled *The New England Psalm-Singer*. The first notable American to write both lyrics and music for patriotic songs, Billings added four flag-waving, anti-British stanzas to "Chester" in 1778 and published the revised piece in *The Singing Master's Assistant*, one of six different collections of his songs written during the war years. With its stirring martial music, it soon became the most popular American patriotic tune of the Revolution. It was sung so widely in the Continental Army's camps and by those forces going into battle that many early nineteenth-century students of music dubbed it "America's 'Marseillaise.'"

With lyrics affirming that "New England's God forever reigns," "Chester" was easily adaptable in churches throughout the region. Virtually every anthology of religious songs in the early years of the nation's history reprinted it. "Let tyrants shake their iron rods and slav'ry clank her galling chains," it proclaimed proudly, "We fear them not, we trust in God." Though its popularity waned in the years after the Civil War, the bicentennial celebration of American Independence in 1976 saw bands throughout the nation playing Billings's famous song once again.

See:

Ewen, David. "From Fuguing Tunes to Martial Tunes: William Billings." Chapter 1 in *Great Men of American Popular Song*. Englewood Cliffs, NJ: Prentice-Hall, 1970, 1–7.

M. Paul Holsinger

COMMON SENSE **(Essay).** Shortly before the outbreak of the American Revolution, Thomas Paine met Benjamin Franklin in London and, with his support, emigrated to Pennsylvania. As a contributing editor of the new *Pennsylvania Magazine*, Paine wrote widely on many subjects, both political and non-political, but it was his fifty-page pamphlet *Common Sense* that made him famous. Published anonymously in January 1776, it produced a greater sensation than any political treatise ever circulated in the thirteen colonies. Calling for separation from Great Britain as the only sensible move, it quickly sold more than 500,000 copies in less than six months. Newspapers throughout the colonies printed parts, if not all, of Paine's arguments on behalf of American independence. It is hard to imagine that any colonial who could read did not consider his views. Certainly, *Common Sense* had a great impact on the resolve of thousands of Americans to take up arms in their battle for independence in the years after 1776.

Paine was a man of action as well as words, and shortly after the publication of *Common Sense*, he enlisted as a private in the colonial army. As he watched more and more men grow discouraged by the repeated defeats during 1776, he authored a second famous statement of belief under the title, *The American Crisis*, in which he wrote, "These are the times that try men's souls." When General George Washington saw Paine's words, he supposedly had them read to his troops just before the battle at Trenton. Some historians believe that they were, in large part, responsible for the American victory in that encounter. After the war and throughout the nineteenth century, millions of American school children read and memorized large segments of Paine's writings.

Common Sense and *The American Crisis* are two of the most influential and successful propaganda pieces in this nation's history, but Paine, who was a freethinker, fell out of favor in the United States, which he had helped to create. He returned to Great Britain in 1787 and in 1792 moved to France, where he became a member of that revolutionary country's National Convention. With help from President Thomas Jefferson he came back to the United States in 1802 only to find that most Americans had either forgotten his importance to the patriotic cause or now had a negative opinion of him. He died seven years later in New York, poverty-stricken, sad, and embittered.

See:

Aldridge, A. Owen. *Thomas Paine's American Ideology*. Newark: University of Delaware Press, 1984.

M. Paul Holsinger

"CONCORD HYMN" (Poetry). There are few places more prominent in the history of the American Revolution than the village squares at Lexington and Concord, Massachusetts, where, on April 19, 1775, the minutemen made their stand against more than seven hundred British regulars who had been sent to seize stores of patriot arms in those towns north of Boston. No one knows who fired the first shot at Lexington, but the British line soon began to shoot at, and then charge with bayonets, the assembled rebels. Eight Americans were killed and another ten wounded before the British marched on, thus beginning the American Revolutionary War.

During the 1837 dedication of a memorial honoring the two battles, a pamphlet that included "Hymn, Sung at the Completion of the Concord Monument," a poem by the renowned local resident Ralph Waldo Emerson, was distributed to the crowd attending the ceremonies. The sixteen-line poem paid homage to the deeds of the American revolutionaries, painted the British as "foes" in a veil of dark shadows, and, through the use of mystical metaphors, envisioned the human spirit rising from the ashes of the past to be revitalized in this new nation. It concluded with hope that the monument, which was dedicated to those who lost their lives and to all those Americans who fought for freedom, would remain a symbol for future generations.

The most famous lines of Emerson's poem come at the end of the first stanza:

> By the rude bridge that arched the flood
> Their flag to April's breeze unfurled
> Here once the embattled farmers stood
> And fired the shot heard round the world.

The "Concord Hymn," and especially that fourth line, soon resounded in grammar schools throughout the United States. Thousands of children, imbued by their teachers with flag-waving patriotism, memorized and then dutifully recited the piece for years after it was penned.

See:

Porte, Joel. *Representative Man: Ralph Waldo Emerson in His Time*. New York: Columbia University Press, 1988.

Eric D. Sweetwood

DEAREST ENEMY (Musicals). *Dearest Enemy*, a 1925 musical written by Herbert Fields with music by Richard Rodgers and lyrics by Lorenz Hart, was one of the few Broadway plays before the award-winning *1776* to take place during the American Revolution. Set in 1776 just before the pivotal Battle of Long Island, it is both a lovely romantic comedy and the story of how the beleaguered colonial troops were saved from total destruction at the hands of the British army. In the play, General Howe, the enemy commander, and his staff stop at the home of Mrs. Robert Murray. A supporter of the patriot cause, she delays them long enough to give rebel forces under General Isaac Putnam time to reach George Washington and save his army from disaster. At the same time, however, the Murrays' niece, Betsy Burke, finds herself falling in love with Howe's aide, Sir John Copeland, and the two make plans to wed. When Copeland becomes convinced that his love has signaled the enemy, he angrily breaks off their relationship; having discovered his error, however, he returns at war's end, to claim Betsy as his bride.

Though Rodgers and Hart had worked together on several earlier plays beginning in 1920 with *Poor Little Ritz Girl*, *Dearest Enemy* was their first major success. After tryouts in Akron, Ohio, and Baltimore, Maryland, in summer 1925, it opened on Broadway on September 18, 1925, where it ran for 286 performances, finally closing on May 22, 1926. Highlighted by such songs as

"Here in My Arms" and "Bye and Bye," the play's success started the young songwriters on a collaborative career that eventually made them two of the greatest names in musical theater.

On November 26, 1955, NBC-TV produced a generally well-received made-for-television special of *Dearest Enemy*. Adapted by William Friedberg and Neil Simon, the new version featured the famed actress Cornelia Otis Skinner in the role of Mrs. Murray, while Hollywood stars Anne Jeffreys, Robert Sterling, and Cyril Ritchard took the parts of Betsy, John Copeland, and General Howe respectively.

Twenty-one years later in the spring of 1976, the play was revived for yet another month-and-a-half run at the Goodspeed Opera House in East Haddam, Connecticut.

See:

"Dearest Enemy." In David Ewen, *New Complete Book of the American Musical Theater*. New York: Holt, Rinehart, and Winston, 1970, 107–108.

Rodgers, Richard. *Musical Stages: An Autobiography*. New York: Random House, 1975.

M. Paul Holsinger

"THE DEATH OF COLONEL CRAFFORD" (Folksong). In late May and early June 1782, nearly 500 regular Army troops and frontier militiamen under the command of Colonel William Crawford moved offensively against the pro-British Delaware and Wyandot Indians near present-day Sandusky, Ohio. The campaign was a total disaster. Almost 150 men died battling the Indians on June 4 and 5. The army's retreat soon turned into a rout as dozens of bands of soldiers sought to escape the fate of their comrades. Many, including Crawford, failed even there and were captured, tortured, scalped, and eventually burned at the stake by the victors.

Some months after the debacle, an unknown author composed a nineteen-verse poem, "The Death of Colonel Crafford," that described (not always accurately but in great detail) the campaign and the fate of the men. It became a popular folksong and was soon heard throughout the Old Northwest. Like many unlettered colonials, the poet spelled almost every proper name phonetically (Crawford, for instance, became "Crafford"; the British Indian agent Simon Girty was called "Girtee"). The description of the gore that accompanied the Indian victory was vivid: "The scalps of their heads while alive they did tear / Their bodies with irons red hot they did sear." Eventually, the men's bodies "fry" in the Delawares' fires.

The poem unjustly attacked Girty's role in the American defeat and in Crawford's heroic death. Though in reality he tried to ransom the colonel and protested his torture almost to the point of being killed himself, the writer had him stand idly by throughout the entire event, apparently enjoying the brutality. The last stanza called for revenge against the British and their Indian allies:

From east to west, let it be understood
Let everyone arise to revenge Crafford's blood

And likewise the blood of those men of renown
That was taken and burnt at Sandusky town.

See:

Downes, Randolph C. *Council Fires on the Upper Ohio: A Narrative of Indian Affairs in the Upper Ohio Valley until 1795.* Pittsburgh, PA: University of of Pittsburgh Press, 1940, 273–275.
Eckert, Allan W. *The Frontiersmen: A Narrative.* New York: Bantam, 1980.

M. Paul Holsinger

THE DEVIL'S DISCIPLE (Drama-Film). *The Devil's Disciple*, by Irish playwright George Bernard Shaw, has been, for more than a hundred years, one of the most famous dramas ever written about the American Revolution. Set during General John Burgoyne's 1777 invasion of northern New York State, which culminated in the great colonial victory at Saratoga, it tries to understand how one of the world's most powerful and greatest armies could have been defeated by a mob of largely untrained farmers. Shaw's knowledge of both U.S. geography and U.S. history borders on the hopeless (*The Devil's Disciple* is set "south of Boston" in a small town in New Hampshire, a colony where neither Burgoyne nor any of his men were engaged), but his play leaves no doubt that the arbitrary (and often cruel) British rule was no match for the determined bravery of its colonial foes.

Though the playwright puts dozens of characters in his mythical town, only two are vital: Dick Dudgeon, the "Devil's disciple," and Reverend Anthony Anderson, the town's Presbyterian minister. Dudgeon, who is supposedly a skeptic, in the end proves almost Christ-like in his willingness to give up his life on a British gallows if it will save Anderson. On the other hand, the minister, who is an open advocate of turning the other cheek, becomes the rebels' leader in defeating the enemy and forcing them to head toward Saratoga and their ultimate defeat.

The Devil's Disciple premiered in Albany, New York, on October 1, 1897, under the direction of the renowned Anglo-American actor Richard Mansfield. It was an instant success and, after only one performance, Mansfield (who played Dick Dudgeon) moved the play to New York City. There it ran for another sixty-four performances, packing the house each evening before finally closing in early 1898. Shaw's royalties from the play far exceeded any that he had earned previously, and his renown, at least in the United States, assured him lasting fame.

More than sixty years later, Hollywood attempted a big-screen version of *The Devil's Disciple* (United Artists, 1959). With an emphasis on action rather than, as Shaw intended, on ideas, the film's screenplay, by John Dighton and Roland Kibbee, pits the two main characters against each other until, in a last dramatic episode, Reverend Anderson (Burt Lancaster) saves the day—and rescues Dick (Kirk Douglas) from the encroaching British army. Critics were not particularly pleased with the Guy Hamilton–directed picture, faulting the pacing and the, at times, awkward shifts in style. Only Sir Lawrence Olivier, who gave one of his typically strong performances in the small role of General "Gentleman Johnny" Burgoyne, got unqualified praise.

See:

Pearson, Hesketh. *G.B.S.: A Full-Length Portrait.* New York: Harper and Row, 1942.

M. Paul Holsinger

DOOLITTLE, AMOS (Engraver). Artist and patriot Amos Doolittle immortalized the spirit of a "new" nation during and immediately after the thirteen colonies' revolt against British rule in 1775. Through his art, Doolittle shared the stories of key events and important individuals and became one of the new nation's most significant shapers of popular cultural attitudes.

Apprenticed early in life to the silversmithing trade, the young Doolittle turned to engraving and moved to New Haven, Connecticut, shortly before the outbreak of the Revolution. While there, he joined a local militia group, the Governor's Foot Guards, and with them he participated in several engagements during the subsequent war. It was with his engraver's tools, however, that he made his most lasting impact on the winning of American freedom. In 1775, shortly after the beginning of the conflict, Doolittle engraved four copper plates depicting different aspects of the "Battle of Lexington and Concord." Though they were inaccurate in a number of specifics, Doolittle's art directly influenced thousands of Americans, who gained their conception of those two early military engagements by looking at his four prints. Only Paul Revere's etching of the 1770 **Boston Massacre** was more famous during the war years.

See:

Whitehill, Walter N. *In Freedom's Cause: Amos Doolittle's Engravings of the Battles of Lexington and Concord.* Chicago: R. R. Donnelly, 1975.

James E. Drainer

DRUMS (Novel). In March 1925, Charles Scribner's and Sons published *Drums*, thirty-six-year-old James Boyd's first fictional work. Instantly successful and widely praised by some critics as "the finest novel of the American Revolution which has yet been written," it quickly went through four printings during the first month and, by the end of 1925, it had sold more than 50,000 copies. It remained a steady seller until at least the beginning of World War II.

Set largely in North Carolina during the Revolution, Boyd's book is far more realistic in its attention to time and place than earlier historical romances. Though *Drums* tells the story of Johnny Fraser, the son of a Loyalist Scotch-Presbyterian minister in the future state, it also carefully shows how a national American identity was forged through the years of the war. At first completely loyal to King George and the British Crown, young Johnny is sent by his father to Edenton, the colonial capital, so that he can become a "gentleman" and rise above the common riffraff of the region. Eventually, his journeys take him to England as a junior clerk in a London countinghouse and then, as the war becomes a bloody reality at home, to Scotland and a life-changing meeting with the dynamic John Paul Jones. Fraser joins the crew of the *Bonhomme Richard*, where he fights bravely in the great sea battle that Jones and his men won against the enemy man-of-war *Serapis*. Returning to North Carolina a total convert to the cause of liberty and freedom, Johnny fights with the loyal militia at the Cowpens, one of the pivotal battles that helped wrest the southern states from British control.

Boyd was a fine historian, which shows in the wealth of detail that he gleaned from colonial newspapers, official state records, and the published letters of a number of North Carolina's major revolutionary leaders for inclusion in *Drums*. As a result, everything rings true. With dozens of paintings and pen-and-ink sketches by the famed artist N. C. Wyeth illustrating its pages, it has justifiably remained continually in print for more than seventy years.

See:

Whisnant, David E. *James Boyd*. New York: Twayne, 1972.

M. Paul Holsinger

DRUMS ALONG THE MOHAWK (Novel-Film). Walter D. Edmonds's *Drums along the Mohawk*, a historical novel that attempts to retell the events of the Revolutionary War in upstate New York's Mohawk Valley, was originally published in 1936. Immediately popular, by the following year it was listed as the nation's fifth best-selling book, and by 1939, it had gone through thirty-one printings. The story centers on two newlyweds, Gil and Lana Martin, and the many crises that they face throughout the war years as they seek to make a life for themselves. A fine historian as well as a writer of fiction, Edmonds was always careful with the detail that he included in all his many books; this is particularly evident in *Drums along the Mohawk* and may explain why the novel has remained in print for more than sixty years.

Darryl Zanuck purchased the movie rights to Edmonds' novel even before it became a best-seller. Two years later, after a bevy of screenwriters, including William Faulkner, had tried their hand at transforming it into a Hollywood motion picture, parts of the story were finally filmed. Directed by John Ford and starring Henry Fonda and Claudette Colbert as Gil and Lana, *Drums along the Mohawk* (20th Century–Fox, 1939) distorts the complex role that the Mohawk Valley played in the Revolution by compacting virtually the entire series of valley campaigns and Indian raids during the war into just the summer of 1777. Since the Mohawk region was far too built up by 1939 to pass for colonial New York, the entire picture was shot on location in the high country near Cedar City, Utah. As he was to do later in almost all his many great western classics, Ford depicted Indians as merciless savages, with no indication that it was often the American pioneers' antipathy and suspicion that initially forced many of the tribes associated with the Iroquois Confederation to join the British rather than the rebellious settlers.

Most viewers did not care about the inaccuracies, and *Drums along the Mohawk* became one of America's most popular films. It was rereleased in 1947 for a second successful run. Today, it has become a regular staple of many late-night and Sunday afternoon television broadcasts throughout the country.

See:

O'Connor, John E. "A Reaffirmation of American Ideals: *Drums along the Mohawk* (1939)." In *American History/American Film*, ed. John E. O'Connor and Martin A. Jackson. New York: Ungar, 1979, 97–119.

M. Paul Holsinger

"FREE AMERICAY" (Song). "Free Americay" was one of the most popular songs in the thirteen colonies during the years of the American Revolution. Written by Joseph Warren, a prominent Boston patriot leader, and set to the well-known tune, "The British Grenadiers," it emphasized that the colonies were now, and would forever remain, free. It left no doubt what would happen if any power attempted to abridge that liberty:

> Should Europe empty all her force
> we'll meet her in array
> And fight and shout, and shout and fight
> for free Americay

The thirty-four-year-old Warren did just what the song urged. Appointed a major general in the Massachusetts provincial militia, he was killed at the battle of Bunker (Breed's) Hill outside Boston in June 1775 after telling his men as they readied themselves to meet the advancing British regulars, "I hope I shall die up to my knees in blood."

Warren was adamant in his song that in the end, the patriot cause would triumph, and eventually, the new nation that it was creating would be a dominant power throughout the world:

> Some future day shall crown us the masters of the main
> Our fleets shall speak in thunder to England, France and Spain
> And the nations o'er the ocean spread shall tremble and obey
> The sons, the sons, the sons, the sons, of brave Americay.

See:

Cary, John H. *Joseph Warren: Physician, Politician, Patriot.* Urbana: University of Illinois Press, 1961.

M. Paul Holsinger

FRENEAU, PHILIP (Poet). No one deserves the title "Poet of the American Revolution" more than Philip Freneau. Though it was his political satires lampooning British military officers, Loyalists, and even King George that were most popular during the war, his ballads, which were written for the masses and printed in newspapers and pamphlet form, found a wide and appreciative audience.

Born in New Jersey, Freneau graduated from Princeton University just before the outbreak of the Revolution. In 1778, he was captured while serving in the New Jersey militia. His temporary imprisonment on an enemy prison ship led to his famous poem, "The British Prison Ship," and caused him to turn, full time, to political writing. In doing so, Freneau made no attempt to be subtle or to leave any doubt as to where he stood on the issues of the day. His 1779 neoclassical mock-epic, "George the Third's Soliloquy," for instance, is filled with invective against the British monarchy. On the other hand, "To the Memory of the Brave Americans, under General Greene in South Carolina, Who Fell in the Action of September 8, 1781" is a paean of praise to the American cause. Excellent as well (due in large part to his love of the sea) are his ballads of naval warfare such as, "On the Death of Captain Nicholas Biddle."

It was not, however, until several years after the war's end that the best of Freneau's work was collected and published. In 1786, Francis Bailey, the editor of one of the many newspapers in which Freneau's poems had appeared, printed a volume of Freneau's poetry under the title, *The Poems*. The book, which was a best-seller for its day, contains most of the poet's best satires and ballads that deal with the American Revolution. That poetry, at its best, remains today graceful, exuberant, controlled, and always readable.

See:

Nickson, Richard. *Philip Freneau: Poet of the Revolution.* Trenton: New Jersey Historical Commission, 1980.

Christine DeLea

THE GLORY OF COLUMBIA (Drama). Historians of the theater have long agreed that William Dunlap, more than anyone else, deserves the title "Father of American Drama." Painter, poet, theater manager, designer, playwright, and historian of the American stage, no one else in the United States produced more original plays before the end of the nineteenth century.

Of all his works, none was longer-lasting than *The Glory of Columbia*, which became one of the most famous dramas in the history of the American stage. In 1798, Dunlap had produced a shorter play entitled simply *Andre*, from which he now borrowed whole scenes, in many cases verbatim, to create this more successful work. For at least fifty years after its first performance on July 4, 1803, the play was a sellout whenever and wherever it was performed. The five acts, which are spectacularly patriotic in their character, tell, in sweeping panoramas, virtually the entire history of the Revolution. The last scene pictures General George Washington and the victorious American forces at Yorktown crushing the British foe in battle.

The Glory of Columbia (subtitled *Her Yeomanry!*) is certainly not great theater, but the tens of thousands of American playgoers who saw it in the early days of the nation's history cheered its flag-waving, melodramatic conclusion.

See:

Moody, Richard. "The Glory of Columbia: Her Yeomanry!" In *Dramas from the American Theatre, 1762–1909*, ed. Richard Moody. Cleveland, OH: World, 1966, 87–93.

M. Paul Holsinger

INDEPENDENCE DAY (National Holiday). On July 4, 1776, the Second Continental Congress, meeting in Philadelphia, approved Thomas Jefferson's draft of the Declaration of Independence. The first signatures, including those of John Hancock, Benjamin Franklin, and Jefferson, were placed on the document on that day, but it was not until Monday, July 8, that independence was officially declared to the large crowd gathered in front of the city's Independence Hall. According to John Adams's eyewitness report, bands played, bells rang, and muskets were fired all day and all night. The following day, General George Washington had the declaration announced to the army.

In 1777, Philadelphia made the Fourth of July a holiday. It was not until 1783 that Boston first celebrated the Fourth as Independence Day—it had previously honored March 5, the day of the **Boston Massacre**, as a day more appropriate to the revolutionary events of the war years—but by the time the Constitution was drafted, nearly every American city and state had begun to concentrate on July 4 as worthy of special recognition. The reading of the Declaration of Independence along with other patriotic speeches, often from leading politicians, became the order of the day. Parades with marching bands and musical entertainment also were common long before the Civil War. When or where the first fireworks were added to the celebrations will probably never be known, but since it had long been customary for cannons and other guns to be shot off on the Fourth, the transition to those more colorful symbols was easily made, perhaps as early as the 1820s.

See:

Myers, Robert J. "Independence Day." Chapter 28 in *Celebrations: The Complete Book of American Holidays*. Garden City, NY: Doubleday, 1972, 188–205.

M. Paul Holsinger

JANICE MEREDITH **(Novel–Silent Film).** Paul Leicester Ford was both a historical scholar of note and a fine novelist. Among his many works was an excellent ten-volume collection of the writings of Thomas Jefferson and one of the nineteenth century's most detailed studies of the life of General George Washington. When *Janice Meredith*, Ford's famous historical novel about the era of the American Revolution, was first published in 1899, it was an instant success. Its sales throughout 1900 remained strong, as thousands of American readers rushed to purchase copies. Hundreds of young women were so taken by the book cover's picture, showing the vivacious heroine's long curl of hair tossed over her right shoulder, that they began to style their hair the same way.

Janice, though part of an aristocratic, Loyalist family from the Philadelphia area, is firmly supportive of the patriotic cause. Even before the start of the war, the young teenager falls in love with one of the family's English bond servants, who then runs away to join Washington's army. The two lovers' romance is often star-crossed, but by war's end, he is a general in the Continental forces and able to win Janice's hand in marriage.

Janice Meredith, or, as it was sometimes called, *The Beautiful Rebel* (Cosmopolitan, 1924), also became a major silent film. Though far less historically comprehensive than Ford's novel, critics lauded it as "a brilliant achievement" and the best historical romance ever put on film. Starring Marion Davies (financial backer William Randolph Hearst's love interest at the time) as Janice, the movie featured such other well-known performers as the Ziegfield Follies' W. C. Fields (as a drunken British sergeant) and the cowboy hero Ken Maynard (as Paul Revere). Hearst was determined to include in the picture filmed versions of virtually every major event from the Revolutionary War. Not only is there a long scene of Washington and his men crossing the Delaware, there are also images of the Boston Tea Party, Patrick Henry's famous "Give me liberty or give me death" speech to the Virginia House of Burgesses, Revere's ride, the battles of Lexington and Concord, the severe winter at Valley Forge, the battle of Yorktown, and, finally, Cornwallis's surrender to Washington immediately after the British defeat.

See:

DuBois, Paul Z. *Paul Leicester Ford: An American Man of Letters, 1865–1902*. New York: Burt Franklin, 1977.

M. Paul Holsinger

JOHNNY TREMAIN (Young Adult Novel–Film). Esther Forbes won the 1943 Pulitzer Prize in biography for her superbly researched study of Revolutionary War–era Boston, *Paul Revere and the World He Lived In*. That same year, using much of the same material, she wrote *Johnny Tremain*, the only young adult work of her long career. Instantly successful, the novel won the Newbery Medal as the nation's best book for children. Never since out-of-print, it continues to be a favorite for old and young alike.

Johnny, who is fourteen when the tale begins in 1773, is an orphan apprenticed to a Boston silversmith. After his hand is severely burned, he goes to work delivering newspapers for one of the city's leading revolutionaries. Samuel Adams, John Hancock, Joseph Warren, and dozens of other patriots become as much a part of the boy's life as young friends his own age. Though he fights at neither Lexington nor Concord, Johnny (now barely sixteen in April 1775) does act as a spy for the patriot cause. In the novel's final chapter, Tremain reaches Lexington the day after the battle only to find his best friend wounded and dying from the first British volley on that village's green. Taking his gun, he then pledges to fight until America's independence has been won.

Fifteen years later, Forbes's story was adapted into a full-length color movie under the title *Johnny Tremain and the Sons of Liberty* (Walt Disney Pictures, 1957). With a screenplay by Tom Blackburn, the Robert Stevenson–directed film sticks fairly closely to the book and remains one of the better children's pictures dealing with the era of the Revolutionary War.

See:

Gemme, Francis R. *Forbes' Johnny Tremain*, ed. Joyce F. Jones. New York: Monarch, 1966.

M. Paul Holsinger

THE KENT FAMILY CHRONICLES (Novels). John Jakes published his first book while still a student at DePauw University. Dozens of others followed, ranging from science fiction to musical plays, but before the early 1970s, he did little to distinguish himself. Then, in 1973, Pyramid Books, a large paperback-publishing house, awarded Jakes a contract to write a projected series of novels focusing on the early history of the United States. The next year saw the appearance of *The Bastard*, the first segment of what eventually was to become the "American Bicentennial Series." Enormously popular, it was followed sequentially in rapid order by *The Rebels* (1975), *The Seekers* (1975), *The Furies* (1976), *The Titans* (1976), *The Warriors* (1977), *The Lawless* (1978), and finally, *The Americans* (1980). Beginning in 1753 with the birth of the illegitimate son of a young French woman and an English nobleman, the saga covers nearly every major historical theme in the history of the United States through 1890, including any number of wars after the Revolution. None of the eight books sold less than 3.5 million copies; the entire series sold more than 40 million. The Kent Family Chronicles, as they became better known, made Jakes a world-renowned author. Few American writers of fiction have ever been so widely read.

Only the first two volumes in the series deal with the Revolution—the others cover the periods 1794–1814, 1836–1852, 1860–1862, 1864–1868, 1869–1877, and 1883–1890, respectively. In *The Bastard*, Phillippe Charboneau or, as he becomes known in America, Philip Kent, joins the cause of freedom in the early 1770s and is at Concord in April 1775. By the time he fights at Breed's Hill and elsewhere during *The Rebels*, Kent's life has changed for good; he and his young family have become, in every way, fully American.

The Bastard was made into a widely syndicated television movie in 1978, and *The Rebels* followed in 1979. The two four-hour films, each shown over two different nights, were crammed full of both Hollywood newcomers and veteran actors. Though neither is memorable in any way, they were tremendously successful with viewers.

See:

Jones, Mary Ellen. *John Jakes: A Critical Companion.* Westport, CT: Greenwood Press, 1996.

M. Paul Holsinger

LIBERTY BELL (Artifact). In 1751, the city of Philadelphia ordered a bell for its new State House from London's White Chapel foundry. "Proclaim liberty throughout the land unto all the inhabitants thereof," taken from the twenty-fifth chapter of Leviticus, was inscribed on its outer rim. Delivered the following year, the bell cracked the very first time that it rang. After two recastings, it was finally placed in the State House tower, and for the next several decades it pealed to summon Pennsylvania Assembly members to their meetings. According to some accounts, the bell also rang out on July 8, 1776, to announce the passage of the Declaration of Independence by the Second Continental Congress, then meeting in the hall. In 1835, it cracked a second time while tolling for the death of Chief Justice of the United States John Marshall. Attempted repairs were unsuccessful, and the bell was heard only once more, on Washington's birthday, February 22, 1846.

The bell has survived numerous potential disasters. It was almost returned to England for credit towards the purchase of a second bell in 1753. In 1777, to prevent the British army from capturing and melting it down, it was removed from Philadelphia and hidden in Allentown, Pennsylvania. By 1828, it was considered of such little value that it was given as scrap metal to a contractor. However, when he discovered that the cost of removing it would be more than its scrap value, he returned it to the city. Not until 1839, when a Boston abolitionist group gave the bell its now universally recognized formal name, did the "Liberty Bell" begin to seem historically significant. Even then, it was not safe; seven years later, there were more proposals to recast it.

The Liberty Bell was removed from the tower of the old State House (or, as it was by then being called, Independence Hall) in 1852, its 100th anniversary year. For the next 125-plus years, it was displayed in various locations on the first floor of the building so that visitors could see it up close and touch it. In 1976, now finally recognized as one of America's most sacred symbols of freedom, it was permanently moved during the nation's bicentennial celebrations to an especially built enclosure directly in front of Independence Hall, where today, millions of tourists see it every year.

See:

Boland, Charles M. *Ring in the Jubilee: The Epic of America's Liberty Bell.* Riverside, CT: Chatham, 1973.

Kent Berger

LIBERTY SONGS (Songs). Between 1765 and 1775, American patriots composed and had published dozens of so-called liberty songs protesting the British interference in colonial affairs. Using the music from a then-popular British patriotic air, "Hearts of Oak," Pennsylvania's John Dickinson wrote the lyrics to the first highly popular one of the early years in 1768. Entitled simply, "The Liberty Song," it called for "brave Americans all" to "rouse your bold hearts at fair Liberty's call." "In freedom we're born and in freedom we'll live," it added and, several stanzas later, it paraphrased Benjamin Franklin: "By uniting we stand, by dividing we fall."

Published first in Philadelphia as a broadside and reprinted on July 7, 1768, in the *Pennsylvania Gazette* and the *Pennsylvania Journal*, "The Liberty Song" also soon appeared in New York and Boston newspapers and swept through the colonies within months. Patriots happily sang the lyrics while marching, at political demonstrations against the taxation policies of the British Crown, and even at dedication ceremonies for so-called liberty trees. Not to be outdone, the Loyalists parodied it with bitter verses attacking the cause of liberty.

It was not long before other liberty songs made their way into the popular culture of the day. About 1770, Joseph Warren wrote "The Massachusetts Liberty Song," the first piece to envision a united America as a future great nation. "The Glorious Seventy-Four," an anonymous 1774 Virginia song, attacked British prime minister Lord North and claimed that liberty for the colonies was "Heaven's decree." It emphasized that Americans, if necessary, were more than willing "to fight . . . for freedom with swords and with guns."

Liberty songs set the stage for American opposition to British rule. When independence finally did become a reality, clearly one of the major factors in swaying popular opinion toward such drastic action were songs such as those of Dickinson, Warren, and their colleagues.

See:

Bowman, Kent A. *Voices of Combat: A Century of Liberty and War Songs, 1765–1865.* Westport, CT: Greenwood Press, 1987.

M. Paul Holsinger

McCREA, JANE (Historical Figure). Of the hundreds of men, women, and children slaughtered by various Indian allies of the British during the Revolution, none was more famous than twenty-three-year-old Jane "Jenny" McCrea (or McCrae, as the family more often spelled its last name). Ironically, the young McCrae was the fiancée of a Tory officer, Lieutenant David Jones, who was serving with General John Burgoyne's forces during their ill-fated campaign of 1777. Fearful of marauding Indians, most of Jenny's family moved south to the safety of Albany, New York, but anxious to see her fiancé again, she did not accompany them. It was a bad decision: roving Wyandot Indians captured and, according to local legend, raped her. Scalping and then mutilating her body, they took her long, black, floor-length tresses to the British general for payment.

The story of the death of the beautiful young woman spread widely. Poets such as Francis Hopkinson soon portrayed Burgoyne as a monster saying:

I will let loose the dogs of Hell
Ten thousand Indians, who shall yell
And foam and tear,
and grin and roar
And drench their moccasins in gore.

George Washington, understanding the propaganda value of the young woman's death, refused to let the story die, and subsequently, dozens of dead British and Hessian soldiers at Saratoga were found with pieces of paper pinned on their chests that read: "For Jane McCrae."

Jane McCrae's death was, according to historian Fairfax Downey, "one of the most compelling stimulants to recruiting the American army ever knew." After the war, an unknown poet penned "The Ballad of Jane McCrea," a maudlin narrative account of the killing of the hapless young woman. Quickly turned into a folk song, it became widely popular, especially as the frontier moved West. In 1803, American artist John Vanderlyn also visually re-created the slaughter in *The Death of Jane McCrea*, one of today's most reprinted paintings dealing with the Revolutionary War.

See:

Cortesi, Lawrence. "The Tragic Romance of Jane McCrea." *American History Illustrated* 20.2 (April 1985): 10–15.
Downey, Fairfax. "The Scalp." Chapter 1 in *Indian Wars of the U.S. Army (1776–1865)*. Derby, CT: Monarch, 1964, 11–19.

                                                        M. Paul Holsinger

THE MINUTE MAN (Memorial). Daniel Chester French became one of America's most renowned sculptors in the years before his death. Best known for his monumental, larger-than-life–sized marble Abraham Lincoln, which is the centerpiece of the Washington, D.C., Lincoln Memorial, French gained his first national fame in his hometown of Concord, Massachusetts, while still in his early twenties. In 1870, a local resident, Ebby Hubbard, set aside $1,000 for a monument to honor the one hundredth anniversary of the Battle of Concord. The town fathers awarded young French the commission and asked him to produce a bronze image of Captain Isaac Davis, one of the first Americans to be killed by the British at Concord Bridge.

In Boston during the winter of 1873–1874, French created a statue that represented a man of local farmer stock determinedly stepping forward, with one hand on his plow and the other holding his rifle. After he had his figure completed in plaster, French sent the model to be cast from ten melted-down cannons, which had been donated for their bronze. With President Ulysses Grant in attendance, *The Minute Man* was unveiled near the original battle site on April 19, 1875, accompanied by a reading of Ralph Waldo Emerson's famous **"Concord Hymn,"** the first stanza of which appears on the pedestal. A copy of the statue shown at the Philadelphia Centennial Exposition the following year brought French international recognition.

The Minute Man soon became every American's image of the nation's volunteer citizen-soldiers. In 1925, it was featured on a commemorative postage stamp issued to honor the 150th anniversary of the famous battle. Perhaps even more visible were the hundreds of millions of **War Savings Stamps** sold by the government from 1942 to 1945 to raise money for war matériel during World War II. Every one of the stamps prominently featured a picture of French's *Minute Man*, and the symbolism of the average citizen, doing whatever was necessary to save the nation, was lost on no one.

See:

Richman, Michael. *Daniel Chester French: An American Sculptor.* Washington, DC: Preservation Press, 1983.

Jeffrey W. Stout

OLIVER WISWELL (Novel). Kenneth Roberts wrote some of the best historical fiction in America. Though he was a serious scholar of early American life, it was his novels that made him so popular among readers in the 1930s and 1940s. His stories covered the broad sweep of early American history from 1755 to 1815, but his specialty was unquestionably the American Revolution. *Arundel* and *Rabble in Arms* look at the patriot side of that conflict; *Oliver Wiswell*, published originally in 1940, examines the "other side"—that espoused by the Loyalists (or Tories) who chose to reject the colonists' cause and fought, instead, on the side of King George III.

Oliver, a student at Yale in 1775 when the war begins, is forced to take sides. Although the young woman he loves is from a staunchly patriotic family, he strongly believes that revolution is not the way to gain justice and soon finds himself spying, and then fighting, for the British. Roberts follows Wiswell throughout the entire Revolutionary War—the first scenes are set just before the Battles of Lexington and Concord, and the latter ones, just after Yorktown. He and his Tory associates fight in Boston, then Long Island, and, still later, in defense of Fort Ninety-Six, South Carolina. At war's end, Wiswell and his sweetheart are forced to emigrate to the future Canadian province of New Brunswick to begin a new life under British rule.

No other popular writer in the United States had presented such a compassionate view of the Loyalists before *Oliver Wiswell* appeared. Roberts offers a sympathetic picture of their cause based on a wealth of documentary and other manuscript evidence. Though nearly 800 pages long, the novel was highly praised by critics as "bold," "brilliant," and "magnificent." The public agreed; it was a best-seller in both 1940 and 1941. Still in print, *Oliver Wiswell* offers readers an unconventional view of the American Revolution, and it does so with skill and adept storytelling.

See:

Bales, Jack. *Kenneth Roberts: The Man and His Works*. Metuchen, NJ: Scarecrow, 1989.

M. Paul Holsinger

"PAUL REVERE'S RIDE" (Poetry). During the last half of the nineteenth century and the early years of the twentieth, millions of American schoolchildren learned to recite by memory the famous first stanza of Henry Wadsworth Longfellow's poem:

> Listen my children, and you shall hear
> Of the midnight ride of Paul Revere
> On the eighteenth of April in Seventy-Five
> Hardly a man is now alive
> Who remembers that fateful day and year.

Longfellow was already internationally known when, in 1860, he wrote those first lines as part of "Paul Revere's Ride" and published them in his latest volume of poetry, *Tales of a Wayside Inn*. The poem became instantly popular; Revere's image as a patriot leader was resurrected; and across the United States, the bravery of the famous horseman rallying the minutemen to battle became entrenched as historical fact.

Longfellow had long believed that writers had a duty not to create history but to perceive and provide insight into what had really happened. His version of the Boston silversmith's ride, however, falls short of such a goal. Though Revere did make Lexington and was able to warn, among others, John Hancock and Samuel Adams of the coming of the British, when he attempted to ride on, he was captured only a few miles outside town. It was another rider, Samuel Prescott, who actually reached Concord—a well-known fact by 1860—yet Longfellow had Revere spreading the word of alarm there as well.

"Paul Revere's Ride" contained a number of other historical inaccuracies, but the romantic and patriotic fervor evinced by the poem was perfect for the days of the era of the Civil War, and it never waned in its popularity. Longfellow's paean to American intrepidity still remains one of the nation's most beloved works.

In 1975, just in time for the two-hundredth anniversary of the famous ride, John Biggs wrote a chorale with full instrumental ensemble, *Paul Revere's Ride*, based on Longfellow's version of the tale.

See:

Arvin, Newton. *Longfellow, His Life and Work*. 1963. Reprint. Westport, CT: Greenwood Press, 1977.

James E. Drainer

PITCHER, MOLLY (Subject of Legend).

> "Moll Pitcher she stood by her gun
> And rammed the charges home, sir

> And thus on Monmouth's bloody field
> A sergeant did become, sir!

As it is with most schoolyard rhymes, facts often become blended with myth. For many years, Americans who sought to discover the "real" Molly Pitcher got an instant answer: "Molly Pitcher" was Mary Ludwig Hays, a young wife who, at the Battle of Monmouth, New Jersey, on June 28, 1778, not only carried water to the hot, tired patriot troops on the battlefield, but when her husband William was wounded, also fired his cannon at the advancing British.

There is little about the life of Mary Hays, however, that is not in dispute. Genealogists, for instance, doubt that Molly's maiden name was Ludwig or even that her family was German; she was probably Irish, though that can neither be proven nor disproven. There also seems to be no evidence that George Washington or any other officer ever gave her a sergeant's commission. Certainly another cherished belief, that the men of Hays's battery were so appreciative of her that they began to call her "Captain Molly," is false. That nickname, historians have shown, belongs exclusively to another cannon-firing "Molly," Margaret Cochran Corbin, a Pennsylvanian whose husband was killed at the Battle of Fort Washington in November 1776. Wounded herself when she stepped forward to take his place, she later settled near West Point, New York, where she became the first American woman to receive a military pension.

Persons continually confuse the two "Molly Pitchers," for obvious reasons. Probably the term was never intended to refer to any one person but was rather a generic name given to any woman who carried water to thirsty soldiers on duty. Due to the plethora of incorrect or suspect information, it is impossible to know the truth, but that should not diminish the importance of women like Hays or Corbin. Certainly the legend surrounding them has become one of the nation's most popular.

See:

Aikman, Lonelle. "Patriots in Petticoats." *National Geographic Magazine*, October 1975, 474–493.

Christine DeLea

RABBLE IN ARMS (Novel). Called "one of the best historical novels produced in America" (*New York Times*, November 19, 1933, 8), when it first appeared, in November 1933, *Rabble in Arms* is Kenneth Roberts's second fictional work dealing with the early years of the American Revolution. Roberts had already gained critical acclaim in 1930 with his carefully researched *Arundel*, a tale of the ill-fated American invasion of Canada at the beginning of the war. *Rabble in Arms* carries the revolutionaries' story through the Saratoga campaign of 1777.

The protagonist is young Peter Merrill, and through his memories, Roberts excitingly creates an account of flag-waving, patriotic fervor. There is plenty of bloodshed, lots of romance, and not an insignificant amount of spying by both sides, all of which increase the tension. Like all the author's historical fiction, *Rabble in Arms* is based on copious research into primary sources. Though some reviewers were concerned that Benedict Arnold was portrayed too positively, most praised the book and the reading public, even in the midst of the Great Depression, agreed.

Just before his death in 1957, the Pulitzer Award committee gave Roberts a special prize for having "long contributed to the creation of greater interest in our early American history." The recognition was well deserved.

See:

Bales, Jack. *Kenneth Roberts*. New York: Twayne, 1993.

M. Paul Holsinger

ROSS, BETSY (Subject of Legend). According to one of the most enduring legends in American history, Elizabeth "Betsy" Griscom Ross, at the behest of George Washington and members of the Continental Congress, made the first official national flag of the new United States of America in June 1776. Like so many apocryphal stories in the nation's past, there is no evidence to substantiate such a claim. Ross, a Philadelphia upholsterer, did make flags the following year for the Pennsylvania navy, but never during her long life did she say she did more.

It was Ross's grandson, William J. Camby, who, in March 1870, first put forth Betsy's name as America's most famous seamstress. Historians checked the assertion and were quickly able to show that it was untrue. Washington, they pointed out, was not in Philadelphia in June 1776. There also was no record that Congress had ever specified the need for a flag before it approved the first one in 1777. However, most Americans did not care. The romantic story soon was entrenched as fact, and Ross was transformed into an American icon.

The Ross home on Philadelphia's Arch Street, which is still standing today, became a major tourist attraction in the years after Camby made his claim. Though students of the Revolution have continued to point out that Ross's fame is based on error, the curious are still drawn to the small house where, legend asserts, the first American flag was made.

See:

Morris, Robert. *The Truth about the Betsy Ross Story*. Beach Haven, NJ: Wynnehaven, 1982.

M. Paul Holsinger

1776 **(Musical-Film).** In the mid-1950s, lyricist Sherman Edwards, a retired history teacher, conceived the idea of producing a Broadway musical about the writing of the Declaration of Independence. Edwards's idea was rejected by almost everyone, but after nearly ten years, he was able to convince playwright Peter Stone to create the much-dreamed-about production. The result was *1776*. Opening on Broadway on March 16, 1969, it was an immediate success and drew rave reviews. Though there are many serious and dramatic moments in Stone's collaborative script, a lightness predominates, and it is filled with such musical production numbers as the witty "Sit Down, John," "Momma Look Sharp," and "Yours, Yours, Yours." It won both the New York Drama Critics' Circle and the Antoinette Perry "Tony" awards as the 1968–1969 best musical. After it opened in London the following year, *1776* was also chosen as the best foreign musical by that city's theater critics. Its Broadway run lasted for 1,217 performances before it finally closed on February 13, 1972.

Later that year, many of the original New York cast and creative staff, including William Daniels in the role of John Adams, Ken Howard as Thomas Jefferson, and Howard Da Silva as Benjamin Franklin, helped transform the play into a big-screen motion picture, *1776* (Columbia, 1972). Directed by Peter Hunt, it received uniformly good reviews. Both the play and the film portray the Continental Congress during May, June, and July 1776 (including interludes with Abigail Adams and Martha Jefferson) as it moved closer to declaring independence. Edwards wanted to present these often-deified heroes as real people, and though the play stretches historical truth in places, the inclusion of such things as Franklin's acknowledgment of his illegitimate son and Abigail Adams's attempts to get her husband to "remember the ladies" mirrors factual events and breathes life into the characters.

The filmed version of *1776* has now also become a staple for television broadcast every Fourth of July as well as being a popular choice with school and community theater groups across the country. On August 14, 1997, twenty-five years after the original closed, the musical was restaged on Broadway by the Roundabout Theater Company. Restructured into two acts (from the original one), it was highly praised for its vibrant freshness by nearly all the New York critics.

See:

Fleming, Thomas. "1776." In *Past Imperfect: History According to the Movies*, ed. Mark C. Carnes. New York: Holt, 1995, 90–93.
Parish, James Robert, and Michael R. Pitts. *The Great Hollywood Musical Pictures*. Metuchen, NJ: Scarecrow, 1992, 589–592.

Christine DeLea

SIMMS, WILLIAM GILMORE (Author). American poet, novelist, critic, and editor William Gilmore Simms offered readers a glimpse of the Southern psyche in everything he wrote. Born in Charleston, South Carolina (the son of an Irish immigrant and a local Charlestonian), Simms grew up in the care of his maternal grandmother, who filled him with the idea that Southern society paralleled the natural order of God's creation. A staunch supporter of slavery, he backed South Carolina's secession from the Union in 1860 and never flagged in his loyalty to the Confederate States of America. By war's end, however, Simms had suffered greatly. His wife of many years had died, Union troops had burned his home and library, and he was destitute. Though he continued to write in an attempt to support his family, he never fully recovered and died less than five years later.

Even though he wrote about many historical eras—a number of his poems, for instance, deal with the War of 1812; a drama, *Michael Bonham* (1852), looks at the Texas War for Independence in 1836—Simms is almost always intimately connected by his writings to eighteenth-century South Carolina. *The Yemassee* (1835), probably his most famous novel, examines the bloody Indian war that ravaged the area in 1715. A seven-volume series of historical novels dealing with the American Revolution in the state, beginning with *The Partisan: A Tale of the Revolution* (1835) and concluding more than twenty years later with *Eutaw* (1856), were famous enough to have his contemporaries favorably compare him to such northern writers as James Fennimore Cooper and Washington Irving.

Using oral tradition and interviews as well as personal and formal histories of the Revolution to create his novels, poems, and dramas, Simms repeatedly projected the idea that it was the members of the coastal South Carolina aristocracy who (aided by a compliant rural middle class and loyal and courageous slaves) were responsible for all the dynamic change that occurred before, during, and after the Revolution. Historians might quibble, but his reading audience did not. Before the Civil War, no other Southern writer's works sold so well.

See:

Watson, Charles S. *From Nationalism to Secessionism: The Changing Fiction of William Gilmore Simms*. Westport, CT: Greenwood Press, 1993.

James E. Drainer

THE SPIRIT OF '76 (Painting). Archibald M. Willard was one of the nineteenth century's most prolific painters, but his fame today rests exclusively on a single work, *The Spirit of '76*. A Union Army volunteer during the Civil War, he originally sketched a prototype of *The Spirit of '76* in 1873 after remembering a group of happily marching War of 1812 veterans he had seen as a boy. Two years later, he began serious work on the eight-by-ten foot painting that was to become associated forever with his name, in the hope that he could display it at the Centennial Exposition in Philadelphia during the summer of 1876. Originally known as *Yankee Doodle*—the name *Spirit of '76* was not given to the painting until after the Centennial Exposition concluded and the work was sent on a national tour—it was completed in March 1876. Featuring three Revolutionary War patriots (an elderly man, a teen-aged boy beating drums, and a wounded soldier playing a fife) leading other soldiers off to battle, the painting seemed to many viewers the embodiment of the American spirit. Another, more gravely wounded man lying prone on the ground cheers the troops on their way, as the new American flag (which was not created until the next year) waves proudly in the background.

Willard's work soon became "America's best-known painting." Because of popular demand, he made a number of replicas; postcards featuring it circulated widely; several businesses offered free reprints to customers; and hundreds of persons (including President Ulysses S. Grant, seeing it for the first time) reportedly wept with pride at its patriotic symbolism.

Since Willard's many paintings of the famous scene are all slightly different, it is impossible to know where the original is or if it even still exists. Of the choices, most scholars favor the work owned by Abbott Hall in Marblehead, Massachusetts. It was this painting that the U.S. Postal Service used in 1976 when it designed a three-stamp commemorative strip that individually featured the men's heads on different stamps with the words "Spirit of '76" emblazoned boldly across the base of each.

See:

Gordon, Willard F. *"The Spirit of '76": An American Portrait.* Fallbrook, CA: Aero, 1976.

                                                                    M. Paul Holsinger

TRUMBULL, JOHN (Painter). John Trumbull is universally known as the "painter of the Revolution." Beginning in the days immediately following the Treaty of Paris, with the war still fresh in everyone's mind, and continuing for most of his long life, he created some of the most memorable pictures focusing on the patriot cause. Though there have been dozens of interpreters of the war years since Trumbull, no one has approached his fame or his skill.

Trumbull, the youngest child of the Revolutionary governor of Connecticut, was still in his teens when he volunteered for the Massachusetts militia at the beginning of the war. By the age of twenty-one, he had risen to the rank of colonel. In April 1777, however, he resigned from the army, and in 1780 he was accepted as a student by the famous British painter Benjamin West. It was while he was in London that he began to paint the first of his Revolutionary War scenes. A study of Joseph Warren's death at the Battle of Bunker Hill and another of General Richard Montgomery before the battlements of Quebec, during the American attack on Canada, brought him instant recognition.

In 1789, Trumbull returned to the United States, where he began to sketch from life the remaining signers of the Declaration of Independence for a painting that, when finished in 1794, was to become his most famous. In March 1817, Congress commissioned four 12-by-18 foot paintings with still other Revolutionary War themes at the then-munificent sum of $8,000 apiece. Those works, *The Surrender of Burgoyne at Saratoga, The Declaration of Independence, General Washington Resigning His Commission as Commander-in-Chief of the Army,* and *The Surrender of Lord Cornwallis at Yorktown,* were completed over the next twenty years. Some of the nation's most priceless treasures, they remain today in the Rotunda of the Capitol.

See:

Cooper, Helen A. *John Trumbull: The Hand and Spirit of a Painter.* New Haven, CT: Yale University Art Gallery, 1982.
Poch, Robert. "John Trumbull: Painter of the American Revolution." *American History Illustrated* 18.7 (November 1983): 18–27.

M. Paul Holsinger

***TRUMPET IN THE LAND* (Outdoor Drama).** The Revolutionary War often pitted neighbor against neighbor. Such was the case for a handful of peaceful, noncombatant Moravian missionaries in present-day central Ohio and the far less religious frontiersmen who lived all around them. On March 7–8, 1782, after word erroneously reached the pioneer settlements that warring Indians were using the Moravian village as a base for their attacks on the frontier, a band of irregular Pennsylvania militiamen, under the leadership of Major David Williamson, marched on Gnadenhutten, the Moravians' small town on the Tuscarawas River. The militiamen surrounded, and then systematically massacred, almost one hundred of the peaceful Christian Indians living there—men, women, and children. The story of this tragedy is told with much feeling in Paul Green's symphonic drama, *Trumpet in the Land: A Symphonic Drama of Peace and Brotherhood.*

Commissioned by the Ohio Outdoor Historical Drama Association and performed in an amphitheater built at New Philadelphia, Ohio (close to the site of the original massacre), *Trumpet in the Land* was staged for the first time on July 2, 1970. In his work, Green looks at the war years through the eyes David Zeisberger and John Heckewelder, the two missionary leaders to the Indians of the region. The plot, which spans the entire Revolutionary War era, begins almost at the moment that word arrives in the West about the war's first battles and concludes as the survivors, their homes destroyed, look to their God for "the day when men on earth, in brotherhood shall live."

See:

Adams, Agatha Boyd. *Paul Green of Chapel Hill.* Ed. Richard Walser. Chapel Hill: University of North Carolina Press, 1951.
Rodabaugh, James H. *Schoenbrunn and the Moravian Missions in Ohio.* Columbus: Ohio Historical Society, 1972.

M. Paul Holsinger

***VALLEY FORGE* (Drama).** On December 11, 1934, Pulitzer Prize–winning playwright Maxwell Anderson's *Valley Forge* opened on Broadway. Though acclaimed by most critics, who later voted it one of the year's best plays, the drama was a commercial failure and managed to last for only fifty-eight performances. Set during January 1778 at General George Washington's winter encampment outside the British-held city of Philadelphia, *Valley Forge* attempts to explore how a ragtag group of colonials, with many deserting every day, were able, not only to survive the harshness of their conditions, but also to become an effective fighting force that ultimately won independence for their new nation. Anderson does his work convincingly. In perhaps the most telling scene, a dispirited Washington, on the verge of accepting the surrender terms he has received from British Commander Lord Howe, sees his brave men, who are hungry and, in some cases, shoeless. Their faith in the cause of freedom gives him new courage to fight on to final victory.

Valley Forge centers its attention on Washington. Anderson allows an old flame to reenter his life momentarily (an unlikely, but not impossible, factual event) and attempt to dissuade him from continuing his campaigns against the British. Though he is tempted to renew his romance with her (in historical fact, Martha did not arrive at the encampment until February 1778), in the end he remains faithful to his wife and, more important, to the cause of freedom.

There were (and still remain) reviewers who find Anderson's portrait of the man later to be called "first in the hearts of his countrymen" far too earthy and his men crude and often vulgar. They are wrong, however. Anderson captures the lowest point of the Revolution with skill, and his depictions of the men are honest and unquestionably based on historical fact. Though *Valley Forge* has been largely forgotten today, its nobility and clearly enunciated patriotism make it one of America's finest and most thoughtful plays.

Besides Anderson's play, novelist MacKinlay Kantor also wrote a capable historical novel called *Valley Forge* (1975). Kantor, who is better known for his brilliant Pulitzer Prize–winning novel *Andersonville*, offers many insights into both the life and times of George Washington as well as the colonial troops who served under him.

See:

Adam, Julie. *Versions of Heroism in Modern American Drama: Redefinitions by Miller, O'Neill and Anderson.* New York: St. Martin's, 1991.

                                                              M. Paul Holsinger

WASHINGTON CROSSING THE DELAWARE (Painting). Few pictures in American history are more renowned than Emanuel Leutze's rendition of a majestic George Washington and his men rowing across the Delaware River on Christmas night, 1776, to attack the Hessians at Trenton, New Jersey. Leutze was born in Germany but came with his parents to Philadelphia at an early age. As a young man, he began painting, and he returned to Europe in 1841 to pursue his craft. It was at his Dusseldorf studio in 1850 that his most famous work, the huge (12 feet, 5 inches by 21 feet, 3 inches) *Washington Crossing the Delaware*, was completed. Even though it is highly unlikely that the general would have foolishly stood up in the boat as his men rowed him across the partially frozen river, and despite the fact that Leutze unhistorically portrayed the men holding the "Stars and Stripes" flag, which was not adopted by Congress until the following year, the work was an instant success. Awarded a gold medal in Berlin, it was displayed in the Capitol building in Washington, D.C., after it was brought to the United States in 1852. Today it hangs prominently in New York City's Metropolitan Museum of Art.

Washington Crossing the Delaware was so popular throughout America that Leutze was awarded a commission for a huge mural, *Westward the Course of Empire Takes Its Way*, in the House of Representatives wing of the Capitol building. In 1863, he established himself permanently in a Washington studio, where he often depicted other scenes from the American Revolution such as *Washington at Monmouth*, a work that is almost as famous as *Crossing*.

"The Battle of Trenton," a well-known folksong, also glorifies Washington's crossing of the Delaware and the subsequent victory by Continental troops. Written shortly after the war by an unknown author, it praises those brave men who put their lives in harm's way to conquer "the Hessian band, that dared invade fair freedom's land."

See:

Stehle, Raymond: "Washington Crossing the Delaware." *Pennsylvania History* 31 (1964): 269–294.

M. Paul Holsinger

"YANKEE DOODLE" (Song). There are almost as many stories about the origin of "Yankee Doodle" as there are persons who have ever sung its well-known lyrics. Some musicologists trace it back to the mid-seventeenth century and the Roundhead supporters of Oliver Cromwell in Parliament's battle against Charles I, but the title and famous chorus appeared originally without music as part of the libretto for Andrew Barton's 1767 New York comic opera, *The Disappointment, or the Force of Credulity*. Though its one original stanza is sung by an elderly man anxious to discover a buried treasure so that he will have enough money to continue living in an outwardly profligate way and has nothing to do with stupid bumpkins with feathers in their hats, it was not long before the British and their Loyalist supporters began to sing the jaunty chorus and a number of new verses as a slur against all rebels in the Revolution. After the Battle of Bunker Hill, however, American patriots co-opted the song as their own, laughing at themselves as they did so. Edward Bangs, a member of Harvard's Class of 1777, rearranged some of the earlier stanzas and added new ones of his own, and "Yankee Doodle" soon became one of the most popular of colonial anthems. Following the defeat and surrender of the British at the Battle of Saratoga, Continental Army fifers and drummers reportedly played the tune in triumph. According to legend, it was also performed at the time of Cornwallis's surrender to Washington at Yorktown in 1781.

The music to "Yankee Doodle" was not published in the United States until 1794, but it was already popular long before that time. When a number of new topical lyrics were penned during both the War of 1812 and the War with Mexico, the tune was automatically used. In several instances, black Union

Army troops during the Civil War marched off to battle as a band played ''Yankee Doodle,'' and as late as World War II, other songwriters were encouraging Americans to get a ''Yankee Doodle Spirit'' as they all cooperated in the nation's drive to crush the totalitarian powers of Germany and Japan.

More than two hundred years after it was written, school bands across the country continue to play ''Yankee Doodle'' at patriotic concerts. The song remains one of the nation's most enduring cultural icons.

See:

Ewen, David. *All the Years of American Popular Music*. Englewood Cliffs, NJ: Prentice-Hall, 1977, 5–7.

M. Paul Holsinger

3

The War of 1812

The clearly misnamed War of 1812, fought throughout North America almost exclusively in 1813 and 1814, was a product of the long-running Napoleonic Wars in Europe and on the high seas. For years, seamen on board American vessels were impressed into the Royal Navy to fill the void left when British crews were decimated in battles with their French counterparts. As early as 1807, the United States came close to war with Great Britain after HMS *Leopard* opened fire on the USS *Chesapeake* just outside Norfolk, Virginia, and took four sailors off the American ship, only one of whom could have been a deserter from the British navy. President Thomas Jefferson, at the end of his second term in office, was able to forestall war in 1807–1808, but his successor, James Madison, was not. On the frontier, the Indian menace to white settlement escalated and, to many in that region, it was the British, especially in modern-day Canada, and their allies, the Spanish in Florida, who were to blame. When, after the 1810 congressional elections, significant numbers of young, war-hungry westerners were elected to the House of Representatives, the possibility of armed conflict loomed even larger. As the great Native American chief Tecumseh began to organize the tribes in the West in a major attempt to drive the American pioneers from Indian lands, these so-called **War Hawks** were primed for battle.

The War of 1812 was, given all the circumstances, probably inevitable, but the straw that broke the camel's back was the tightening of the British navy blockade of American and Caribbean ports and the consequent weakening of the already tenuous southern and western farming economy. Though the reasons behind the War of 1812 or, indeed, many other U.S. wars, can never be summed up by generalizations such as insulted national pride or even economic necessity, Congress needed little persuasion to move toward war. In June 1812, the U.S. House of Representatives voted 79–49 to go to war with Great Britain; the

Senate followed suit by a 19–13 vote and, on June 18, President Madison signed the declaration of war.

American forces began the war with a series of embarrassing defeats on land, not only surrendering Detroit to a much smaller combined British-Indian force— perhaps the most disgraceful episode in all American military history—but also suffering a crushing setback in the Niagara Peninsula of Ontario when a much larger American army was driven back across the Niagara River by British and Canadian troops under the command of Sir Isaac Brock. The United States was not much more successful in the intervening years. American armies invading Canada in 1813 and again in 1814, though able to win several significant engagements, were, in the end, always forced back in defeat. When the British attacked the nation's capital in the fall of 1814, the record became more shameful when only a small contingent of U.S. Marines fought proudly at Bladensburg, Maryland, before being overwhelmed. The victorious British marched into the District of Columbia and burned government buildings, including the executive mansion. Though the news media throughout the nation (with the exception of New England, which generally opposed the war) tried to put a positive spin on the few land victories won by American commanders during the war years, only Andrew Jackson's crushing triumphs over the Creek Indians at the Battle of Horseshoe Bend, Alabama, in 1813, and later at New Orleans, were truly worthy of much pride.

If the British, in tandem with their Canadian and Indian allies, proved unbeatable on the land, such was clearly not the case at sea. The nation's first two frigates, the *Constitution* and the *Constellation*, which had been built at the time of the undeclared naval war with France in 1797–1798, won a series of great victories over the British foes. Perhaps the most renowned was the *Constitution*'s famous defeat of the Royal Navy's *Guerrière* in August 1812. The following year, Commander Oliver Hazard Perry met the enemy on Lake Erie and, in the face of a crushing British fusillade, which, early in the battle, killed almost 80 percent of his men, won the day. In 1814, a potential British attack on New York was repelled in yet another striking naval victory at Plattsburgh. That same year, when the Royal British Navy moved on Baltimore and attacked that city's Fort McHenry, its defenders, despite "the rockets' red glare, [and] the bombs bursting in air" held and eventually forced the British to withdraw. The almost unblemished record of the United States Navy was spoiled, however, in early June 1813 when the British ship *Shannon* caught the American *Chesapeake* (the same ship whose defeat six years earlier nearly provoked the beginning of the war) off Cape Cod and, in a head-to-head confrontation, destroyed it and its commanding officer, Captain James Lawrence. Only Lawrence's famous dying plea, "Don't give up the ship" (ignored by the remaining crew), gave Americans reason to memorialize the event.

The war did not officially end until the two nations signed the Treaty of Ghent on Christmas Eve 1814. Even then, the most famous land engagement, Andrew Jackson's memorable victory over vastly superior British forces at the Battle of

New Orleans on January 8, 1815, as well as the slowness of both internal and external communication, kept the two nations at war for several more months. It was not until early February that reports of Jackson's victory and of the signing of the peace treaty arrived in Washington, D.C., within days of each other. On February 17, 1815, the president finally declared the conflict at an end. During the nearly three years of war, almost 300,000 men were in uniform; 2,260 died and another 4,505 were wounded. When the conflict was concluded, there were sighs of relief but little more. The nation was ready to develop internally and had little time to glorify a near-defeat. Even though the United States did gain some land in western Florida (today's far southern parts of the states of Alabama and Mississippi) from Spain, it was hard to find much to cheer about the War of 1812. Starting off as a war of conquest, it soon became one of survival.

The War of 1812 has faded into the mists of time in most Americans' minds, and such relegation is probably justifiable. Many easily forgettable poems, songs, and plays appeared during and immediately after the fighting, but only Francis Scott Key's **"The Star-Spangled Banner"**; the newly created national icon, **"Uncle Sam"**; and, to a much lesser degree, Mordecai Noah's *She Would Be a Soldier* earned any lasting popularity. Andrew Jackson did become an overnight sensation, and he and his rough-edged "Hunters of Kentucky" (see **"The Hunters of Kentucky"**) won national praise. Thirty years after defeating the Indians in western Indiana, William Henry Harrison ("Old Tippecanoe") also parlayed his victory into the presidency of the United States in 1841, but few other military men gained more than fleeting popular support. For a nation that idealized the patriots of the Revolution, the War of 1812 was a dismal bust.

See:

Coles, Harry L. *The War of 1812*. Chicago: University of Chicago Press, 1965.
Hickey, Donald R. *The War of 1812: A Short History*. Urbana: University of Illinois Press, 1995.
Roosevelt, Theodore. *The Naval War of 1812*. 1882. Reprint. Annapolis, MD: Naval Institute Press, 1987.

"THE BATTLE OF NEW ORLEANS" (Song). Unquestionably the brightest moment for the United States Army during the War of 1812 came on January 8, 1815, at the Battle of New Orleans, when Andrew Jackson commanded a ragtag group of regulars, volunteers, Indians, pirates, and free blacks and defeated a much larger force of British regulars. The British had over 2,000 killed, wounded, or captured; American losses only amounted to about 70. The site of that historic encounter, just east of New Orleans in the suburb of Chalmette, has now become a national park. Every year, on the weekend closest to the battle's anniversary, reenactors gather to fight the conflict anew.

Though Jackson's victory has been celebrated through the years in both song and story, none has gained more renown than Jimmy Driftwood's country-and-western song, "The Battle of New Orleans." A high school principal and history teacher, as well as a fairly well-known interpreter of folk music in the 1950s, Driftwood once claimed that he wrote ''The Battle of New Orleans'' to help his students in Snowball, Arkansas, learn something about the War of 1812. Set to ''The Eighth of January,'' an old hillbilly fiddler tune which, ironically, also commemorated the American victory over the British, the lyrics are simple and direct. Beginning in Tennessee, the twelve stanzas follow each step of the campaign to Jackson's overwhelming victory against the British foe.

A first recording of ''The Battle of New Orleans'' by the writer on a 1958 RCA Victor album, *Newly Discovered American Folksongs*, was only modestly successful, but, the following April, a much shortened version was recorded by rockabilly-country star Johnny Horton. By June, it had climbed to the top of both the popular and the country-western charts, and it stayed there for nearly two and a half months. More than 2 million copies of Horton's recording were sold before its popularity finally began to fade, after more than half a year on the Hit Parade. A slightly different version also reached number two in Great Britain the same year.

See:

Chidsey, Donald Barr. *The Battle of New Orleans*. New York: Crown, 1961.
Horstman, Dorothy. *Sing Your Heart Out, Country Boy*. New York: Dutton, 1975, 235–236.

James M. McCaffrey

''HAIL COLUMBIA'' (Song). Joseph Hopkinson, son of the famous composer Francis Hopkinson, penned the lyrics to ''Hail Columbia'' in 1798 during the height of the tension surrounding the undeclared war with France. Set to the music of ''The President's March,'' a popular instrumental piece written by Philip Phile in honor of George Washington, ''Hail Columbia'' praises the ''heroes / heav'n born band / who fought and bled in freedom's cause.'' It calls on everyone to ''firm, united let us be / rallying round our liberty.'' The words continue:

> Immortal patriots rise once more
> defend your rights, defend your shore.
> Let no rude foe with impious hands
> invade the shrine where sacred lies
> of toil and blood the well-earned prize.

Hopkinson, by his own admission, purposely avoided mention of either Great Britain or France. His concern, he later wrote, was to ''get up an American spirit [that would] look and feel exclusively for our honor and rights'' (Ewen, 18).

First performed by the author's friend, actor Gilbert Fox (for whom he originally wrote the words), the song quickly gained widespread popularity as the ''favorite new federal song.'' For more than a quarter-century after its introduction, it served as America's unofficial national anthem and was heard on every ship in the navy at the lowering of the colors each night. During the War of 1812, it was sung with regularity by numerous patriotic groups, and in the Civil War, it was undoubtedly the most often-played march throughout the North. By the beginning of the twentieth century, however, "Hail Columbia," with its bombastic lyrics, had fallen into disuse; it is played today only in concerts featuring older patriotic songs.

See:

Ewen, David. *All the Years of American Popular Music.* Englewood Cliffs, NJ: Prentice-Hall, 1977, 18–19.

M. Paul Holsinger

"THE HUNTERS OF KENTUCKY" (**Folksong**). Samuel Woodsworth's popular song "The Hunters of Kentucky" (also known as "The Hunters of Kentucky at the Battle of New Orleans") was written and performed in the spring of 1822 as part of Andrew Jackson's first campaign for the presidency. In 1828, it again became the future president's unofficial campaign song, repeatedly serving to direct the electorate's attention to "Old Hickory's" skill as a military leader.

"The Hunters of Kentucky" is set to the music of "The Unfortunate Miss Bailey" (sometimes called "Miss Bailey's Ghost") which was written originally by Noah Ludlow for a comic opera, *Love Laughs at Locksmiths.* Woodsworth, whose most famous song was "The Old Oaken Bucket," had earlier written the words, and perhaps the music, for "Erie and Champlain," a paean of praise to Oliver Hazard Perry's victory on Lake Erie in 1813. Another of his war compositions, "Patriotic Diggers," encouraged Philadelphians to build fortifications to defend themselves against the feared British attack during that nation's campaign against the United States the following year. In "The Hunters of Kentucky," he accurately described the battle of New Orleans, in which the Kentuckian sharpshooters—each one "half a horse and half an alligator" according to the song's lyrics—wreaked havoc on the red-coated British army.

First published in 1822 by James M. Campbell in a book with the unwieldy title of *Melodies, Duets, Trios, Songs and Ballads, Pastoral, Amatory, Sentimental, Patriotic, Religious, and Miscellaneous. Together with Metrical Epistles, Tales, and Presentations. By Samuel Woodsworth.* "The Hunters of Kentucky" remains a classic and can be found in many folk musicians' repertoires 170 years later.

See:

Hammack, James W., Jr. *Kentucky and the Second American Revolution: The War of 1812.* Lexington: University of Kentucky Press, 1976.

M. Paul Holsinger

"OLD IRONSIDES" (**Artifact**). "Old Ironsides," the USS *Constitution,* was covered with copper sheathing on its hull fashioned by Paul Revere when it was originally built in 1797 as one of the navy's first two warships. It was reputedly so strong that cannonballs bounced off its sides. The warship's greatest fame came during the War of 1812; it never lost any of the major sea battles that it fought against the British.

The excitement caused by such feats resulted in dozens of popular songs being written to honor the ship and its crew. One of the most famous, the anonymous "Constitution and Guerriere," gives an account in its nine stanzas of the American ship's victory over the British foe on August 19, 1812. Printed originally in the *Boston Chronicle* immediately after the American triumph, it was performed publicly for the first time at a theater gala celebrating the *Constitution*'s success and attended by the ship's captain, Isaac Hull. It was sung to a jaunty popular show tune of the time, "Landlady of France," or as it was sometimes known, "A Drop of Brandy, O!"

In 1830, when the navy decided to consign the *Constitution* to the scrap heap as outdated, the young Oliver Wendell Holmes's poem "Old Ironsides" marshaled public opinion to preserve the great vessel. Completely refurbished, it saw continual duty until 1855 and then, even into the post–Civil War era, it served as a naval-training ship. Though rebuilt in 1870, "Old Ironsides," which was moored at Charlestown, Massachusetts, slowly deteriorated until the patriotic fervor of the Spanish-American War renewed interest in the old ship. Threatened with destruction yet again in the late 1920s, it was saved by a public subcription campaign aided by the appearance of a very popular and critically acclaimed silent film, *Old Ironsides* (Paramount, 1926). Set during the U.S. war with the Barbary Pirates at the turn of the nineteenth century, the picture, starring Charles Farrell and Wallace Beery, focused much attention on the famous ship.

In 1930, after its latest overhaul, the *Constitution* made one last multicity tour manned by a specially trained crew. Since that time, though still in commission as a part of the United States Navy, it has been relatively inactive. Between 1994 and summer 1997, however, the U.S. government spent more than $12 million to completely refurbish the ship, closely following the plans of its original designer, Philadelphia's Josuha Humphreys. In mid-July 1997, the *Constitution* put to sea for a short trip off Marblehead, Massachusetts, before being towed back to its mooring just outside Boston. Today, "Old Ironsides" is one of the area's top tourist attractions, drawing more than 1 million visitors every year.

See:

Martin, Tyrone G. *A Most Fortunate Ship: A Narrative History of Old Ironsides.* Rev. ed. Annapolis, MD: Naval Institute Press, 1997.

M. Paul Holsinger

SHE WOULD BE A SOLDIER (Drama). The War of 1812 had been over for less than four years when Mordecai M. Noah penned the romantic melodrama, *She Would Be a Soldier, or The Plains of Chippewa* during the spring of 1819.

Though it was not the first theatrical piece to deal with the war, it was unquestionably the most popular, being reprised repeatedly throughout the United States until at least 1868, often as the centerpiece for Fourth of July or Washington's Birthday celebrations.

Focusing on the events surrounding the American army's victory in Canada over British troops and their Indian allies at the Battle of Chippewa (July 5, 1814), the play, though somewhat contrived and silly, was one of the most flag-waving and overtly patriotic dramas to grace the stage up to that time. The army is seen as brave and magnanimous in victory, so much so that even the heroine Christine Jasper runs away from her home and, disguised as a male, prepares to fight alongside her fiancé, Lieutenant Richard Lenox. Though she is temporarily mistaken as a British spy, in the end, Christine and Richard pledge themselves to a quick marriage and lasting happiness.

See:

Moody, Richard. "She Would Be a Soldier or The Plains of Chippewa." In *Dramas from the American Theatre, 1762–1909*, ed. Richard Moody. Cleveland, OH: World, 1966, 567–574.

M. Paul Holsinger

"THE STAR-SPANGLED BANNER" (National Anthem). On the deck of a British ship attacking Baltimore's Fort McHenry, Maryland lawyer Francis Scott Key waited anxiously through the evening of September 13, 1814, to see if the beleaguered fortification had survived the massive shelling from the enemy's naval cannon. When he glimpsed an American flag still flying, he quickly began to jot down his reaction. Not allowed to land until the evening of September 16, he took a room at the Indian Queen Hotel in Baltimore and started to work even more diligently on a revised draft. By the end of the evening, he had completed the four-stanza poem that, with only minor alterations, soon became known as "The Star-Spangled Banner."

Published (probably on September 17) as a handbill by the Baltimore *American*, the poem was initially entitled simply "Defence of Fort M'Henry," with no mention of Key's name. Within a week, however, his name began to appear on all newer copies, which were issued by the *American*, the Baltimore *Patriot* and several other presses. Not until several months later was the title "The Star-Spangled Banner" used for the first time.

Set to the music of "To Anacreon in Heaven," a British drinking ditty popular in the United States from at least 1798, "The Star-Spangled Banner" was quickly turned into an extremely successful song. Whether Key intended his work to be sung to British composer John Stafford Smith's tune or not has been hotly debated for many years, but people immediately noticed how neatly the lyrics fit the music. As early as October 19, 1814, the new song, with its present title and music, was sung publicly in Baltimore.

Beginning in 1830, resolutions were introduced into Congress to make the song the official national anthem, but they continually failed. During the Civil War, however, the Union Army increasingly popularized "The Star-Spangled Banner," especially in camp settings, where patriotic soldiers frequently sat around playing it. In 1889, the secretary of the navy ordered it played on all commissioned ships at morning colors; by 1895, it was also played at every army post when the flag was lowered at retreat. As a patriotic march, it was widely performed during the Spanish-American War and, though another congressional resolution to make it the official national anthem failed in 1913, many foreign observers assumed that it was the U.S. national anthem.

In both 1927 and 1929, nationwide contests were held to find a national anthem, but none of the more than 1,000 entries was selected. Finally, in 1931, Maryland Representative J. Charles Linthicum's resolution to make Key's song the national anthem passed both the House and the Senate and, with President Herbert Hoover's signature on the bill, "The Star-Spangled Banner" finally became "America's song."

The fifteen star, fifteen stripe banner that Key saw on the morning of September 14 had been made especially for Fort McHenry at the beginning of the War of 1812 by Baltimore resident Mary Pickersgill and her daughter. Initially a huge 42 by 30 feet in size, it was the largest flag in existence in the United States. Donated to the Smithsonian Institution in 1907, it remained cramped and folded in a small case for nearly fifty years until, after being moved to the new Museum of History and Technology in the early 1960s, the "real" star-spangled banner finally was proudly displayed for millions to see every year.

See:

Svejda, George J. *History of the Star-Spangled Banner from 1814 to the Present.* Washington, DC: Office of Archeology and Historic Preservation, Division of History, 1976.

M. Paul Holsinger

UNCLE SAM (Symbol). The image of Uncle Sam (a distinguished man with a white beard; top hat; and gaudy, red, white, and blue suit); would have seemed strange to the earliest citizens of the republic. The name and image of Uncle Sam was a product of the War of 1812 and later conflicts, during which his persona was both revised and expanded.

The original Uncle Sam was a real-life meat packer from Troy, New York, named Samuel Wilson. During the War of 1812, Wilson and his brother won a contract to furnish the army with salted beef and pork. Most of the barrels were marked with the letters "U.S.," an obvious reference to the United States Army, for which they were destined. When a local workman was asked what the letters stood for, however, he reportedly replied that they must stand for "Uncle Sam," the nickname by which all Troy knew Wilson. The parallel was too good to ignore; even before the end of the war, newspaper cartoonists and amateur poets alike were using the symbol of Uncle Sam to represent the United States.

It was many years before the physical image of Uncle Sam began to look like it does today. At first, most depictions looked remarkably like earlier cartoons featuring "Brother Jonathan" (a lanky, homespun character frequently used by artists to designate the United States, especially when compared with the corpulent British "John Bull"), but by the 1840s, they frequently showed him wearing stars and stripes. Not until 1856 did a version appear with chin whiskers, but during the Civil War, the bearded Abraham Lincoln was frequently drawn by northern cartoonists in a costume similar to that of many artists' conceptions of Uncle Sam. By the late 1860s when cartoonist **Thomas Nast** created the revised prototype for *Harper's Weekly*, most readers easily accepted the "new" national symbol.

That image continued to be refined and modified for years thereafter, especially during the nation's wars with Spain in 1898 and then with Germany from 1917 to 1918. The famous "I Want You" recruiting poster for the United States Army, drawn by **James Montgomery Flagg** in 1917, brought together all the many characteristics so long associated with Uncle Sam in a definitive portrait that has varied little in the years since World War I.

See:

Gerson, Thomas I., and Flora M. Hood. *Uncle Sam.* Indianapolis, IN: Bobbs-Merrill, 1963.

M. Paul Holsinger

WAR HAWKS (Prowar Activists). From before the War of 1812 to the present day, the term *war hawks*, or simply *hawks*, has been used to describe that group of politicians and other governmental leaders who support war as a solution for American troubles. These officials believe that military action can rightfully be taken to gain territory, protect commercial interests, or enhance national pride. Originally derogatory, the term seems to have been coined by Virginian John Randolph in 1811 to describe fellow southern, western, and mid-Atlantic representatives such as future Speaker of the House of Representatives Henry Clay of Kentucky, who favored war with Great Britain.

From this beginning, the term has been used repeatedly. After the election of President James K. Polk in November 1844, public officials in favor of military intervention against Mexico to gain land for the expansion of slavery became known in the press as war hawks. When the USS *Maine* was destroyed in Havana harbor in early 1898, persons who believed that the United States ought to declare war on Spain, whether to redress the death of that ship's sailors or simply to obtain many of Spain's prime overseas colonies, were given the same title. During the Vietnam War, the American press frequently used the term to describe officials, such as Secretary of Defense Robert McNamara, who advocated heavy use of the nation's troops to stop communist aggression in South Vietnam.

Today, at the end of the twentieth century, those leaders who support a large

peacetime expenditure for this nation's military continue to earn the hawk designation. Conversely, persons in favor of nonmilitary answers to the nation's
problems have, for years, been known as "doves."

See:

Hickey, Donald. *The War of 1812: A Forgotten Conflict.* Urbana: University of Illinois
        Press, 1989, 29–51.

Steve Canon

4

Indian Wars East of the Mississippi, 1783–1845

Great Britain's decision to give the American colonists their independence, as well as millions of acres of contested land in the trans-Appalachian frontier in 1783, created an immediate crisis for the many Native American tribes that had allied themselves with the British during the American Revolution. Pennsylvania, at least as far west as Pittsburgh, was in white settlers' hands, as was much of the "bloody ground" of Kentucky, which withstood repeated raids on settlements at fortifications such as those at Boonesborough or Harrodsborough. However, west and north of the Ohio was clearly (as noted on many official maps of the day) "Indian Country," and the resident Shawnee, Delaware, Mingo, Wyandot, and other tribes were determined to keep it that way.

By 1790, violence between the many new white settlers who were pushing into the region and the Indians frequently approached full-scale war. Repeated requests for aid from the federal government were at first ignored; they were finally answered when President George Washington sent the new United States Army onto the frontier with orders to crush out Native American opposition. Everything that could go wrong, did. In the fall of the year, General Josiah Harmar, 320 Army regulars, and more than 1,000 militiamen were routed on the Maumee River in Ohio, with the militiamen turning and running at the first sign of trouble. The following year, the army, which was now under the command of General Arthur St. Clair (also the governor of the Northwest Territory), suffered an even more egregious loss when the Indians, under such leaders as Little Turtle and Blue Jacket, inflicted more than 900 casualties. Only after Washington sent his former aide, General "Mad Anthony" Wayne, and he, in turn, carefully trained his troops for battle did the tide turn. In the summer of 1794, the United States Army, aided by more than 1,500 Kentucky volunteers, faced the Indians at the Battle of Fallen Timbers, south of present-day Toledo,

Ohio. It was a significant victory. The Indians were forced to cede most of Ohio and a goodly portion of Indiana as well, and though isolated massacres continued to occur from time to time through the territory until after the War of 1812, the various tribes were never able to reclaim their former glory.

Nonetheless, the tribes did not surrender easily. The Shawnee leader Tecumseh (see *Tecumseh!*) understood that unless the Indians stopped the steady encroachment of white settlement, all their tribal lands would soon be lost. As early as the turn of the new century, he began to attempt the creation of an Indian confederation that would link tribes from the Great Lakes region with those as far south as the Gulf of Mexico. As his dream came close to reality, it became necessary for the United States, acting under the new governor of Indiana Territory, William Henry Harrison, to stop it at all costs. In early November 1811, Harrison and his men, who were camped only a few miles from "Prophet's Town" (Tecumseh's home village on Tippecanoe Creek, near today's Lafayette, Indiana), were attacked by the Shawnees and their allies. On the defense from the start, Harrison repeatedly repelled the enemy and, when the Indians finally fled in disarray, burned their village to the ground. It was his greatest victory (even though he won a number of others during the War of 1812), and his fame as "Old Tippecanoe" opened the door to the presidency in 1840.

After the War of 1812, with Tecumseh having been killed on a Canadian battlefield while fighting alongside the British and no one else capable of uniting the Native American peoples, the United States was able to use the shopworn, but clearly effective, philosophy of divide and conquer. Slowly over the next two decades, the various tribes were forcibly evicted from their homes and sent west of the Mississippi River into the newly acquired Louisiana Purchase land, which few whites then saw as worthy of settlement. Most of the Indians reluctantly accepted exile, but some did not. The Cherokees (one of the "Five Civilized Tribes"), who lived mainly in northern Georgia and the mountains of North Carolina and Tennessee, tried to fight back by using the judicial system. Though the U.S. Supreme Court, in several major cases, found in favor of the Cherokee land claims, Andrew Jackson, who was now president of the United States, refused to use the power of the executive office to carry out the Court's interpretation of the Constitution. The result was the infamous 1838 "Trail of Tears," on which thousands of Indians perished as they were driven by the United States Army on a forced trek into Oklahoma's Indian Territory.

Small bands of Cherokees refused to leave and for years hid out in the small coves and "hollows" of the Smoky Mountains. Other groups were more warlike, however. During 1832, many of the Sauk and Fox Indians who had been forced to surrender all their lands east of the Mississippi River and accept resettlement in today's Iowa returned to the new state of Illinois. Bloodshed soon occurred, and the result was the Black Hawk War. It was not much of a war. United States Army troops, buttressed with thousands of Illinois, Indiana, and southern Wisconsin volunteers (including Captain Abraham Lincoln from Sangamon County, Illinois) slaughtered their foes almost at will. At the Battle of Bad Axe in August, the army massacred hundreds of Sauk men, women, and children and forced the remainder to return to the reservations west of the river.

Only once were Native Americans able to hold their own against forces from the United States, when American troops under Andrew Jackson fought the first of three subsequent wars with the Seminoles from 1817 to 1819 with little success. When, during 1819, the government forcibly negotiated the purchase of modern-day Florida from Spain, it found itself facing thousands of its former enemies. An 1823 treaty attempted to confine the tribe on a reservation in central Florida, but when few members complied, the Second Seminole War began, in 1835. Though it seemed that the less than 5,000 Indians would pose no problem, the Seminoles eluded all attempts to corral them and fought back brilliantly. Before the United States finally ended the war in 1842, more than 40,000 troops had been sent to Florida and over $20 million had been expended, with little positive to show for the effort. A third war in the 1850s was just as ineffective, and the remaining Indians were finally left to make their homes in the Everglades swamps and backwaters.

Though Americans have long been fascinated by the Indian wars of the post-revolutionary era, there have been few popular depictions of them since it was hard, even in contemporary times, to find many official American heroes to laud or victories to champion. When men such as **Joseph Altsheler** wrote novels about the Indian Wars in the later part of the eighteenth century, his protagonists were never the nation's military leaders but rather intrepid frontiersmen fighting for their own lands. In more recent years, however, it has been the defeated Native Americans who have garnered the bulk of society's attention. Whether this will continue in the twenty-first century remains to be seen.

See:

Downes, Randolph C. *Council Fires on the Upper Ohio: A Narrative of Indian Affairs in the Upper Ohio Valley until 1795.* Pittsburgh, PA: University of Pittsburgh Press, 1940.

Downey, Fairfax D. *Indian Wars of the U.S. Army, 1776–1865.* Garden City, NY: Doubleday, 1963.

Eckert, Allan W. *Wilderness Empire: A Narrative.* Boston: Little, Brown, 1971.

ALTSHELER, JOSEPH (Author). In 1918, the nation's public librarians voted Joseph Alexander Altsheler the most popular author of books for boys in the United States, and the recognition was well deserved. Reviewers repeatedly praised his realistic portrayals of the historical past. Altsheler's descriptions of battle were especially popular. There are few works of historical fiction that so strongly capture this nation's past as his studies of such major turning points as the American Revolution, the Civil War, the opening up of Texas, and even World War I.

Of all Altsheler's works, probably those most intimately connected with him are the eight novels that comprise the Young Trailer Series depicting the late eighteenth century Appalachian and Ohio Valley frontiers. From *The Young Trailers: A Story of Early Kentucky* (1907) through *The Eyes of the Woods: A Story of the Ancient Wilderness* (1917), Altsheler took young Henry Ware and Paul Cotter. quintessential American frontiersmen, and their companions ever farther west in a quest for land.

Inspired by the writings of **Francis Parkman**, Altsheler believed, as he wrote in *The Border Watch: A Story of the Great Chief's Last Stand* (1912), that "the conquest of the North American continent at a vast expanse of life and suffering is in reality one of the world's greatest epics" (quoted in Slavick, 328). Certainly, his tens of thousands of readers agreed. City boys who had never seen the "great outdoors" could barely wait for the next Altsheler book to appear, and most of his novels stayed in print through at least the mid-1950s. Some, especially those dealing with the trans-Appalachian frontier and the Civil War, went through as many as twenty different printings, the last as recently as 1967.

Vacationing in Europe at the beginning of World War I, Altsheler and his family were trapped behind German lines. Though they eventually made their way back to the United States and he was able to use material from his experiences in a series of books about the ongoing war, he never recovered from the ordeal. Less than five years later, he died at age fifty-seven.

See:

Slavick, William, H. "Joseph Altsheler's Kentucky Frontier Epic: Manifest Destiny and the Hero." In *Consumable Goods II*, ed. Mary Lu Quinn and Eugene P. A. Schleh. Orono, ME: National Poetry Foundation, 1988, 327–337.

M. Paul Holsinger

BLACK HAWK (Indian Leader). In April 1832, Black Hawk, or Makatai-meshekiakiak, a Sac (or Sauk) Indian chieftain, led a band of approximately 400 men, women, and children east across the Mississippi River to reclaim tribal lands that had been taken by force the previous year. Thousands of United States Army and local volunteer troops, including twenty-three-year old Abraham Lincoln from Sangamon County, Illinois, marched against them. Though the Indians did manage to win several skirmishes in what soon became simply known as the Black Hawk War, in the end they were systematically driven north into Wisconsin. When they attempted to surrender, they were repeatedly rebuffed. The war came to an end when hundreds of Sauk were slaughtered on the Bad Axe River in early August.

Black Hawk was captured and taken in captivity to Jefferson Barracks, Missouri. There, in 1834, he supposedly dictated his autobiography, *Life of Black Hawk*, to an interpreter, and it was published in Rock Island, Illinois, later that year. Like the so-called confessions of Nat Turner, however, there has long been debate about whether the moving words are really those of the captive or those of a well-meaning white man. Later, Black Hawk and his son, Rolling Thunder, were taken to Washington, D.C., to visit President Andrew Jackson. During that time, John Wesley Jarvis, an important portraitist of the day, captured the two men's likenesses on canvas. That painting, one of the most famous true-to-life portraits of Native American warriors, is owned today by the Thomas Gilcrease Institute of American History in Tulsa, Oklahoma.

Never allowed to return to Illinois, Black Hawk was disgraced even in death. After his burial in Iowa in 1838, his body was dug up and his bones displayed in a local museum. Fifteen years later when the museum burned, they were destroyed. Ironically, Black Hawk is honored today throughout the area he loved. When a monumental, forty-foot-high sculpture by famed midwestern artist Lorado Taft was placed overlooking the Rock River in Lowden State Park, Illinois, in 1911, it was intended to represent every Indian in the Midwest. Local residents, however, quickly renamed it informally the Black Hawk Monument, and as that, it remains one of the state's major tourist sites today. An area community college has been named for him; there is a State Historical Site dedicated in his honor; and he is cited approvingly in the schools as an example of the American will to oppose injustice and tyranny wherever it is found.

See:

Beals, Frank L. *Chief Black Hawk.* New York: Harper, 1961.

M. Paul Holsinger

BLUE JACKET (Outdoor Drama). One of the greatest war chiefs in the eastern United States before the War of 1812 was Wey-yah-pih-her-sehn-wah or, as he was better known to white settlers throughout the Ohio Valley and Kentucky, Blue Jacket. A white man, who had been christened Marmaduke Van Swearingen by his parents, he was adopted by the Shawnees after being captured as a teenager and quickly became one of the most feared Indian leaders of the late eighteenth century. In support of the British during the Revolutionary War, Blue Jacket and his people set the frontier on fire, attacking white settlements as far south as Boonesboro, Kentucky. When pioneers poured into the Ohio Country after 1783, he continued on the warpath to protect the Shawnees' land. An American army under General Josiah Harmar was defeated in part by Blue Jacket and his followers in 1790, and the following year, he was one of the chiefs who led more than 3,000 Shawnees, Miamis, Delawares, and Wyandots to the greatest single Indian victory over the United States Army in American history. Three years later, however, after having lost the Battle of Fallen Timbers to the forces of "Mad Anthony" Wayne, he was forced to accept a dictated peace and cede all his peoples' lands in Ohio.

Since the summer of 1982, *Blue Jacket,* W. L. Mundell's outdoor drama with original music by Frank Lewin, has been staged just outside Xenia, Ohio, in a specially built, 1,200-seat amphitheater. The two-act play, which spans the thirty years from 1774 to 1803, uses Blue Jacket's experiences to give its viewers a deeper appreciation of the life and death of the Shawnee peoples. An immediate success, it has been restaged every year since its debut, attracting more than 750,000 persons during its first fifteen years.

See:

Eckert, Allen W. *Blue Jacket: War Chief of the Shawnees*. Boston: Little, Brown, 1969.

M. Paul Holsinger

TECUMSEH! (**Outdoor Drama**). Scholars have often called Tecumseh (or, more properly, Tekamthi) America's greatest Indian chief. For most of his life, he fought to keep white settlers from encroaching on the ancestral lands of the Shawnee and other Native American peoples throughout the Midwest. His efforts to unify the Indians in opposition to the power of the new United States failed, but his eloquence and political skill, combined with his prowess on the warpath, made him both feared and respected by every settler in the Old Northwest.

Each summer since 1973, Tecumseh has been honored in a sprawling outdoor musical drama staged before packed audiences at the Sugarloaf Mountain Amphitheater outside Chillicothe, Ohio. Written by Allan W. Eckert, author of the acclaimed "Winning of America" histories about the opening of the trans-Appalachian frontier, the two-act *Tecumseh!* covers nearly thirty years (1784–1813) of the great chief's life. In the process, it also details the sad destruction of the proud Shawnee, the loss of their homes, and their final defeats at the hands of General William Henry Harrison, first at the Battle of Tippecanoe in 1811, and two years later at the Battle of the Thames, where Tecumseh was killed while fighting alongside British troops in Canada.

Eckert's Tecumseh is noble and truthful, but ultimately doomed in his confrontations with the area's white men, most of whom are seen as venial and boorish. During the past quarter-century, that vision has been repeatedly presented to the more than a million theatergoing tourists and residents who have seen *Tecumseh!* while visiting central Ohio in the summer months.

See:

Gilbert, Bil. *God Gave Us This Country: Tekamthi and the First American Civil War*. New York: Anchor, 1990.

M. Paul Holsinger

UNTO THESE HILLS (**Outdoor Drama**). After years of working closely with the famous symphonic dramatist Paul Green at the University of North Carolina, in 1948 Kermit Hunter was given the opportunity by the Cherokee Historical Association to create an outdoor drama of his own. *Unto These Hills*, which Hunter completed late the following year and submitted as his master's thesis, premiered during the summer of 1950 at the specially built and, in part, publicly funded Mountainside Theatre in Cherokee, North Carolina. It has been presented to more than 100,000 persons every summer since. Only Green's *The Lost Colony* has had a longer continuous run or a larger attendance.

Unto These Hills, with music by Jack Frederick Kilpatrick, is an attempt to tell, in both word and song, the history of the Cherokee Nation and its repeated mistreatment at the hands of avaricious white men. Though the first scene is set in 1540, the majority of the drama takes place from 1811 to 1842. There are scenes that focus on the War of 1812, especially the Cherokee participation alongside Andrew Jackson at the famous battle of Horseshoe Bend in northern Alabama. Other scenes depict the United States Army forcing Cherokees from their mountain homes onto the notorious "Trail of Tears" in the 1830s. The final survival of some in their own reservation high in the Smokies during the early 1840s is also covered.

Hunter makes no attempt to be objective; *Unto These Hills* is, as might be expected, overwhelmingly pro-Cherokee. The army—and at times Jackson, too—are the villains who willingly stab friends in the back for political or military gain. Innocent Cherokee men and boys are executed to please the whims of stupid and venal officers, but in the end, justice and right triumph and the audience is left with a feeling of hope.

See:

Ehle, John. *Trail of Tears: The Rise and Fall of the Cherokee Nation.* New York: Anchor, 1989.

M. Paul Holsinger

5

The Texas Revolution and the War with Mexico, 1836–1848

More than a generation before the United States declared war on the Republic of Mexico, in May 1846, Americans, many of whom were hard-pressed financially, poured into the province of Texas, anxious to claim the large land grants being offered by the Mexican government. Led initially by such men as Stephen Austin, more than 30,000 Americans lived north of the Rio Grande River before 1836. For many years, they enjoyed complete local autonomy and home rule, and when General Antonio López de Santa Anna, the military dictator of Mexico, took away most of those freedoms, it was a great shock. Angered by the loss of what they considered "inalienable rights," many of the Texans declared their independence on March 2, 1836.

The American "Texans," like the colonial Massachusetts minutemen of 1775, took up arms even before the official declaration of independence was proclaimed. A handful of them drove the Mexican garrison in San Antonio de Bexar out and took control of that small village. Fortified behind the walls of **the Alamo**, an abandoned Roman Catholic mission, the less than 200 defenders, including such luminaries as William Travis, James Bowie (of Bowie knife fame), and former U.S. Congressman from Tennessee **Davy Crockett**, faced an army of more than 3,000 Mexicans headed by Santa Anna. Travis melodramatically proclaimed that, if necessary, "I am determined to . . . die like a soldier who never forgets what is due to his own honor and that of his country"; (McDonald, 164–165) most of the other men inside the mission's walls agreed. For thirteen days, they fought off the attacking Mexicans, but on March 6, 1836, they were overwhelmed and killed. More than half the Mexican force was also dead. Six weeks later, other Texans, commanded by General Sam Houston shouted, "Remember the Alamo" as they defeated the Mexicans at the Battle of San Jacinto, captured Santa Anna, and on April 21, 1836, forced him to recognize formally the establishment of an independent state of Texas.

For the next nine years, innumerable intersectional squabbles between the slave-holding South and the opponents of slavery's extension in the North kept the new republic separate from the rest of the United States. When the Democrats under James K. Polk won the presidential election of 1844, however, arrangements were made to annex the new state into the Union. The Mexicans were furious; many called for a war against the United States. Polk responded by sending federal troops under General Zachary Taylor to southern Texas to protect ''American'' soil.

Inevitably, Taylor's troops and their Mexican counterparts faced each other just outside present-day Brownsville, Texas, where they clashed. Though the government in Mexico City was probably correct in its belief that American forces were encamped on Mexican soil—the Texan claim to a southern boundary at the Rio Grande being, at best, tenuous—Taylor remained. When, on April 24, 1846, Mexican troops ambushed a unit of American dragoons, killing eleven and capturing most of the rest, hostilities began. In Washington, President Polk asked for a declaration of war and Congress overwhelmingly complied, approving the war resolution by wide margins in both the House of Representatives and the Senate. Thus, on May 13, the United States found itself at war once again.

The Mexican War, as it soon became known, seemed on paper to be a dangerous undertaking for the United States. Less than 6,000 American soldiers, many of them foreigners only months removed from their passage to America packed in immigrant boats, were fighting more than 30,000 Mexicans. A closer look, however, showed that despite the enemy's numerical superiority, the United States held the upper hand from the beginning. Far more technologically advanced than Mexico, the United States also had better (and newer) equipment, more modern tactics of warfare, and unquestionably, some of the brightest young military minds in history. On the staffs of General Taylor and General Winfield Scott were future Civil War leaders such as Ulysses S. Grant, Robert E. Lee, ''Stonewall'' Jackson, and William Tecumseh Sherman. Even the president-to-be of the Confederacy, Jefferson Davis, was an active participant in the conflict.

Though some Americans (such as Henry David Thoreau and Abraham Lincoln) felt that the war was little more than a poorly disguised attempt to guarantee an expansion of slavery throughout the West, thousands of volunteers rushed to join the army, whether from patriotism or the lure of excitement and adventure in exotic Mexico. American victories were not long in coming. Taylor and his men crossed the Rio Grande and soon triumphed at Palo Alto, Resaca la Palma, and Matamoros. By mid-summer, U.S. forces, now composed of a small contingent of regulars along with dozens of volunteer regiments such as the rough, undisciplined Texas Rangers, were pushing deep into the heart of Mexico. In late September, Monterrey fell to Taylor after a major three-day battle, and in February 1847, so did Buena Vista (see "**Buena Vista**"). In this latter engagement, Taylor suffered nearly 750 casualties, but he and his men were able to mete out nearly five times as much damage on their enemies. Soon other troops under Winfield Scott, a veteran of the War of 1812, moved on Vera Cruz. By March 26, it, too, was in U.S. hands. Scott then turned overland, heading for Mexico. More victories followed at Cerro Gordo, Jalapa (thanks to the leadership of Captain Robert E. Lee), Puebla, and eventually, on September 14, 1847, Mexico City itself. Members of the Marine Corps raised the American flag over the National Palace, and the war was over.

With the continual wave of U.S. victories, it is easy to make the Mexican War sound very one-sided, but clearly it was not. Mexican forces never failed to fight fiercely for their land, and on a number of occasions, they came close to driving the Americans from the field of battle. A total of 1,733 Americans died in battle (or from wounds received in combat), and another 11,500 died of disease during the war. On February 2, 1848, the American negotiator Nicholas Trist signed the Treaty of Guadalupe Hidalgo, officially ending the fighting. The United States received nearly 1.2 million square miles of territory, including all of present-day California, Utah, and Nevada; most of Arizona and New Mexico; and bits of Colorado, Texas, and Wyoming.

Even though there were many who had opposed "Mr. Polk's War," the victory gave the American people instant heroes to idolize. Just as the Revolution produced the nation's first president in George Washington and the War of 1812 gave the country both Andrew Jackson and William Henry Harrison, so now the war in Mexico patriotically pushed General Zachary Taylor to the fore. Nominated as its presidential candidate by the Whig Party in 1848, Taylor bested Democrat Lewis Cass and the Free Soil Party's Martin Van Buren in a close race in November. Winfield Scott was not as successful, however. Four years later, he too was nominated by the Whigs (Taylor having died in office in July 1850), but he was overwhelmingly defeated by Franklin Pierce and the Democrats by an electoral vote of 254–42.

The Texas Revolution (or, as some Texans say, the War for Texas Independence) and the subsequent Mexican War that resulted from it immediately produced popular poems, songs, lithographs, plays, and novels glorifying the American victories of 1846 and 1847, but most were quickly forgettable and have long vanished from sight. Only the continual memorialization of the Alamo as a sacred shrine and its defenders as bona fide American heroes has lasted.

See:

Bauer, K. Jack. *The Mexican War, 1846–1848.* Lincoln: University of Nebraska Press, 1993.
Johannsen, Robert W. *To the Hall of the Montezumas: The Mexican War in the American Imagination.* New York: Oxford University Press, 1985.
McCaffrey, James M. *Army of Manifest Destiny: The American Soldier in the Mexican War, 1846–1848.* New York: New York University Press, 1992.
McDonald, Archie P. *Travis.* Austin, TX: Jenkins, 1976.

Noti, Albert A. *The Alamo and the Texas War for Independence*. 1982. Reprint. New
     York: DeCapo, 1994.
Singletary, Otis. *The Mexican War*. University of Chicago Press, 1960.

THE ALAMO (Shrine). Later in 1835, American colonists in Mexico's northern province of Coahuila y Texas revolted, demanding separate statehood within
the Mexican republic. When Mexican dictator José Antonio Lopez de Santa
Anna led troops north to crush the rebellion, the American goal became complete political independence for Texas. In late February 1836, Santa Anna attacked the Alamo (an old mission turned fortress) and its defenders in the
militarily insignificant town of San Antonio de Bexar. Before dawn on March
6, after a thirteen-day siege, Mexican troops stormed the fort, killing all 189
defenders including such luminaries as Jim Bowie and **Davy Crockett**. The
massacre gave those under Sam Houston's command a rallying cry, "Remember
the Alamo," and, six weeks later on April 21, they defeated the Mexican Army
at the battle of San Jacinto and won their independence.

The Alamo's story has been retold hundreds of times in books, poems, songs,
and movies with varying degrees of historical accuracy. R. M. Potter's "Hymn
to the Alamo," first published in Columbia, Texas, in October 1836, became a
nationwide success. The first movie version of the siege, *The Immortal Alamo*
(Star, 1911) was shot entirely in the San Antonio area by the famed French
filmmaker George Méliès. John Wayne directed and starred in a flag-waving
and patriotic, but extremely inaccurate, epic titled *The Alamo* (Batjac, 1960),
for which a fairly faithful reproduction of the original fort was built on the West
Texas plains. *The Alamo: 13 Days to Glory* (Briggle, Hennessy, Carrothers,
1987), a three-hour NBC television special, is a star-studded rehash of the defenders' last days, replete with a number of exciting battle scenes. *Alamo: The
Price of Freedom*, which also premiered in 1987, is shown regularly in downtown San Antonio to thousands of tourists every year. Paul Francis Webster and
Dimitri Tiomkin's "Ballad of the Alamo," the theme of John Wayne's *The
Alamo*, gained instant popularity on both the popular and country-western hit
parade of best-sellers in the summer of 1960. Recorded by Marty Robbins, it
stayed on both charts for nearly two months.

To many Texans, the Alamo and its defenders have taken on mythic proportions. To be able to trace one's family back to the Texan Revolution, and especially to any man who died at the Alamo, gives one special standing in some
communities. The men's bravery in the face of certain death has been used
repeatedly since 1836 to illustrate the valiant defense of hopeless causes. During
the early days of World War II, for instance, many comparisons were drawn
between what happened at the Alamo and what was unfolding in the beleaguered
Philippines as American troops bravely battled overwhelming Japanese invaders.

A new, highly praised, epic poem, Michael Lind's 350-page-plus *The Alamo*
(1997), has recently been published. Some critics have compared it to the best
work of the famed American poet Stephen Vincent Benét.

See:

Graham, Don. "Remembering the Alamo: The Story of the Texas Revolution in Popular Culture." *Southwestern Historical Quarterly* 89.1 (1985): 35–66.

Schoelwer, Susan Prendergast, and Tom W. Glaser. *Alamo Images: Changing Perceptions of a Texas Experience.* Dallas, TX: Southern Methodist University Press, 1985.

James M. McCaffrey

"BUENA VISTA" (**Folksong**). Perhaps the most accurate song to be written about a battle in any war between the outbreak of the American Revolution and the end of the Civil War, in 1865, was "Buena Vista," a piece celebrating General Zachary Taylor's victory over the Mexican Army in February 1847. Outnumbered more than three-to-one and confronted by the desertion of a regiment of Indiana troops at the height of the action, Taylor was still able to turn the tide and seize the first great American victory of the war. Published anonymously later that year in both *Songs of the People* and the *Rough and Ready Songster*, "Buena Vista" goes into a meticulously detailed analysis of each step of the conflict from Santa Anna's boast that he would "vanquish all our host" to the final victory. Filled with dozens of "Hurrahs," the verses name off the many American war heroes as well as those states whose units acquitted themselves well in the engagement. Paying honor to the American dead, most of whom had "hearts that know no fear," the song concludes with a flamboyant, but not necessarily incorrect, assessment:

> No page in history e'er can show
> So bright a victory o'er a foe
> As we this day did proudly gain
> On Buena Vista's bloody plain.

See:

Bowman, Kent A. "Rough and Ready Singers." Chapter 5 in *Voice of Combat: A Century of Liberty and War Songs, 1765–1865.* Westport, CT: Greenwood Press, 1987, 67–89.

M. Paul Holsinger

CIVIL DISOBEDIENCE (**Essay**). *Civil Disobedience* (or, as it was originally known, *Resistance to Civil Government*) by Henry David Thoreau first appeared in print in Elizabeth Peabody's *Aesthetic Papers* (1849). Although published anonymously and largely ignored during its author's lifetime except by such fellow authors as Ralph Waldo Emerson and Nathaniel Hawthorne, it has now become Thoreau's most popular single essay. Originally it was a lecture shared with the residents of Concord, Massachusetts; not until the end of the nineteenth century did the essay begin to attract an audience, and not until after World War I did it become popular.

Civil Disobedience explains why Thoreau spent a night in jail in 1846. Because he was opposed to all forms of oppression, especially slavery, he refused to pay his Massachusetts poll tax for six years. In doing so, Thoreau was following the precedent set by Bronson Alcott, one of the most famous Transcendental thinkers of the day, who had also been imprisoned some years earlier for failure to pay his taxes. At first the local authorities ignored such rebellious behavior, but, when the Mexican War began in 1846 (in part with the aim of acquiring new American slave territories), the Concord constable arrested Thoreau and held him in Middlesex County Jail. Thoreau remained but one night; the following morning he was released after an anonymous individual paid his taxes.

The crux of Thoreau's philosophy in *Civil Disobedience* is that every individual should personally determine right from wrong. If one's higher laws come into conflict with civil law, the latter must give way. "Unjust laws exist," Thoreau wrote. "Shall we be content to obey them, or shall we endeavor to amend them?" (231).

The ramification of such an anarchical belief has been widespread. A number of diverse people, including American civil rights activists, anti–Vietnam War activists, Mahatma Gandhi, and even World War II–era Nazis have adopted Thoreau's philosophy through the years.

See:

Harding, Walter Ray. *The Days of Henry Thoreau. A Biography.* Princeton, NJ: Princeton University Press, 1992.

Thoreau, Henry David. *Walden and Civil Disobedience: Authoritative Texts, Background, Reviews and Essays in Criticism,* ed. Owen Thomas. New York: W. W. Norton, 1966, 231.

Catherine Calloway

"COLUMBIA, THE GEM OF THE OCEAN" (Song). There were few, if any American school children in the late nineteenth or early twentieth centuries who did not proudly sing "Columbia, the Gem of the Ocean" with its famous line, "The Army and Navy Forever / Three Cheers for the Red, White, and Blue." Written in a time of peace, it soon was recognized as one of the nation's most martial songs. During the Mexican War it was repeatedly played as citizens prepared to send the boys off to war. To many people, it has become, because of its military air and flag-waving patriotism, the "Army and Navy Song," and it is still heard at July Fourth celebrations nationwide.

Thomas à Becket, an actor in Philadelphia, speedily composed "Columbia, the Gem of the Ocean" during the autumn of 1843 for a fellow performer who wanted a new patriotic number to sing at a benefit performance. Returning from an engagement in New Orleans, he discovered that his "friend" David T. Shaw had published à Becket's song under his own name. Fortunately, à Becket had kept the original handwritten copy of his piece and was able to prove his authorship. In later years, however, it continued to be printed illegally by many, including several Englishmen who changed its name in their country to "Britannia, the Gem of the Ocean'' and never paid à Becket any royalties. Despite these troubles, however, he lived to see his work become one of the nation's most beloved marches, which it remains today, more than 150 years later.

See:

Lyons, John Henry. "Hail Columbia." Chapter 3 in *Stories of Our American Patriotic Songs*. New York: Vanguard Press, 1942, 23–28.

M. Paul Holsinger

CROCKETT, DAVY (Subject of Legend). No American frontiersman was more popular or famous in the early years of the nineteenth century than David "Davy" Crockett. An Indian fighter during the War of 1812, a four-term congressman from his home state of Tennessee, as well as one of the doomed Alamo defenders, Crockett has, for more than 160 years, fascinated Americans young and old alike. Though much of his earliest fame came from a self-congratulatory autobiography, *A Narrative of the Life of David Crockett of the State of Tennessee* (1834), his belief that a person ought to do what was right no matter the cost endeared him to those who admired rugged individualism. Indeed, Crockett followed his own advice. According to legend, he told his constituents that if they did not reelect him, they could go to hell and he would go to Texas, which was already in the throes of revolution against Mexico. He kept that promise and was dead less than three months later.

After his death, Crockett's fame spread around the world, with even a clipper ship taking his name. The first movie about him was *Davy Crockett in Hearts United* (New York Motion Picture Company, 1909); others followed in 1910, 1915, 1916, and 1926. On December 15, 1954, however, his name became truly legendary when ABC-TV aired the first of three Walt Disney–made short films, *Davy Crockett, Indian Fighter*. It was a fantastic success. After February, when the remaining episodes (*Davy Crockett Goes to Congress* and *Davy Crockett at the Alamo*) were shown, more than 60 million Americans had seen one or more of them. In May, the three separate productions were combined into a feature-length motion picture *Davy Crockett, King of the Wild Frontier* (Walt Disney Pictures, 1955), which captivated the entire nation.

Crockett mania swept the United States. The theme song for the expanded series, "The Ballad of Davy Crockett" by Tom Blackburn (lyrics) and George Bruns (music), reached number one on the popular music charts, and seventeen different performers made recordings of it. As late as 1991, it was rerecorded by the country band The Kentucky Headhunters and became another popular hit. Advertising tie-ins from bubble gum cards to fringed jackets and coonskin caps with Crockett's name on them sold everywhere. Davy Crockett became the image of the truly all-American leader. In 1960, it was no accident that actor-director John Wayne chose to play Davy Crockett in his larger-than-life film, *The Alamo*.

See:

Deer, Mark. *The Frontiersman: The Real Life and Many Legends of Davy Crockett.* New
    York: Morrow, 1993.

M. Paul Holsinger

CURRIER, NATHANIEL (Lithographer). Nathaniel Currier, the best-known
nineteenth-century American romantic lithographer, began his work in that field
in 1828, shortly after the lithography process was introduced. By 1834, he had
formed his own firm in New York City. With agents selling copies of his prints
in every state, Currier was soon nationally renowned. From the very beginning,
much of his work dealt with war-related themes. Three early scenes, *Perry's
Victory on Lake Erie Fought Sept. 10th, 1813; Death of Tecumseh/Battle of the
Thames, Oct. 18, 1813*; and *General Andrew Jackson/The Hero of New Orleans*
dealt with the War of 1812 and the Indian Wars. It was the War with Mexico,
however, that solidified Currier's reputation. During that conflict, a number of
his prints of the war (including the *Battle of Resaca de la Palma, May 9, 1846*
and the large *Storming of Chapultepec, September 13, 1847*), which were issued
within months of the actual engagements, were among the most popular and
best-selling of the engravings focused on the numerous American victories.

Sadly, in the years of the Civil War and after, the firm's reputation for historical accuracy suffered greatly. Currier and James Merritt Ives, his partner
after 1857, were so anxious to profit from the public's desire to know more
about the war in the South that they began to rely more on imagination than on
eyewitness accounts. *The Second Battle of Bull Run Fought August 29, 1862*,
for instance, is particularly inaccurate in its depiction of the fighting during that
bloody engagement, and *Admiral Porter's Fleet Running the Rebel Blockade of
the Mississippi at Vicksburg, April 16, 1863* is little better. Nonetheless, the
Currier and Ives prints were extremely popular throughout the northern states,
to the extent that millions of homes displayed one or more of the colorful works
in the latter years of the nineteenth century

See:

Peters, Harry T. *Currier and Ives: Printmakers to the American People.* Garden City,
    NY: Doubleday, 1953.

M. Paul Holsinger

KENDALL, GEORGE WILKINS (War Correspondent–Newspaperman).
Scholars of journalism generally recognize George Wilkins Kendall as the
world's first newspaper war correspondent. After apprenticeships at many of the
Northeast's most distinguished newspapers (including Horace Greeley's *New
York Tribune*), he moved to the South in 1832, and after a year in Mobile,
Alabama, he settled in New Orleans, Louisiana. There, he founded that city's
first major newspaper, the *Picayune*, and, over the next several years, developed

it into a national leader in obtaining information from Texas, Mexico, and other Latin American states.

In 1841, Kendall became part of the ill-fated Texas expedition to Santa Fe, New Mexico, which ended with a number of Texans dead and Kendall imprisoned in a Mexican jail. After he was released and returned home, he found himself a hero, a status that his newspaper stories only served to confirm. His account of the Santa Fe Expedition, *Narrative of the Texan Santa Fe Expedition*, was first published in 1844 and remains the only major source for that significant footnote in history.

When the war with Mexico broke out, the *Picayune* sent a number of correspondents to join the armies of Generals Zachary Taylor and Winfield Scott, but it was the now-famous Kendall who became the premier reporter with the troops. Riding with a group of **Texas Rangers**, he participated in a number of battles, including the American victories at Monterey and Buena Vista. His story to the *Picayune* about the latter battle was the first report of the success of Taylor's forces to reach the United States. He was also present during the shelling and capture of Chapultepec. Thanks to his efforts, the *Picayune* became the nation's authority on all war matters.

Immediately after the conclusion of hostilities, Kendall, along with the painter **Carl Nebel**, began work on the first full history of the Mexican War. Published in 1851, *War between the United States and Mexico, Illustrated*, offers an exciting, often firsthand, view of the campaigns and battles. Soon afterward, however, Kendall soured on publishing, sold his interest in the paper, and moved his family permanently to Texas, where for the remainder of his life, he attempted unsuccessfully to become a gentleman rancher.

See:

Copland, Fayette. *Kendall of the Picayune*. Norman: University of Oklahoma Press, 1943.

M. Paul Holsinger

MY CONFESSION (**Autobiography**). In its July 23, 30, and August 6, 1956, editions, *Life* magazine printed three installments of a newly recovered manuscript history of the Mexican War that it had purchased from a private collector. Penned by Samuel Emery Chamberlain (later a Union general during the Civil War), it was filled with dozens of watercolor scenes of such battles as those at Buena Vista and Monterrey as well as numerous depictions of army camp life. Millions of readers were fascinated at this discovery and at Chamberlain's unique account of that almost-unknown war. The manuscript, which was subsequently donated by *Life* to the United States Military Academy, and a second, even larger album of more than 150 colorful paintings of the author-artist's experiences while fighting in the war offer a unique view of a war long forgotten by most Americans. Roger Butterfield later edited the manuscript into a full-length nonfictional study titled, *My Confession: The Recollection of a Rogue, Written and Illustrated by Samuel E. Chamberlain* (1956). Unfortunately, in an attempt to make its author seem a little less raw, he rather arbitrarily deleted nearly one-third of the manuscript. In 1993, the San Jacinto Museum of History, having purchased the album of paintings for its collections, issued a large, attractive art book edition under the title, *Sam Chamberlain's Mexican War.*

Chamberlain was only sixteen in June 1846 when he volunteered and set off for San Antonio and the escalating war. He fought at the pivotal Battle of Buena Vista with the forces of General Zachary Taylor and continued moving deeper into enemy territory until the end of the fighting, more than a year later. His descriptions of the army's march and the battle at Buena Vista remain one of the best first-person accounts to emerge from the war. Though there are times when his adventures strain credulity—especially his inclusion of romantic escapades with numerous Texan and Mexican women whom he met along the way—each page offers new insights into a soldier's life in the United States Army before 1848.

Since Chamberlain's work first came to light, historians have been quick to point out that there are numerous factual errors in the manuscript (especially where he discusses events in which he did not personally participate), but that does not weaken the importance of *My Confession.* The author's often-amateurish, but nonetheless exciting, collection of watercolor prints makes his study one of the most definitive contemporary views of the War with Mexico ever put on paper.

See:

Goetzmann, William H. "Introduction." In *Sam Chamberlain's Mexican War*, ed. William H. Goetzmann. Austin: The Texas State Historical Association, 1993.

M. Paul Holsinger

NEBEL, CARL (Painter). A number of artists during and immediately after the conclusion of the War with Mexico attempted to put scenes of that conflict on canvas. Unquestionably the most accurate and most popular was the German-born Carl Nebel. America's first war correspondent, **George Wilkins Kendall**, offered Nebel the opportunity to illustrate a complete history of the just-ended war that he was putting together. In 1848, Nebel, who had traveled extensively in Mexico before the war, returned to that country and, using Kendall's detailed notes about each battle, prepared twelve major, full-color views of the *Battle of Palo Alto*, the *Capture of Monterey*, the *Battle of Buena Vista*, the *Bombardment of Vera-Cruz*, the *Battle of Cerro Gordo*, the *Battle of Churubusco*, the *Assault at Contreas*, two different scenes of the *Battle of Molino del Rey*, two other scenes featuring different parts of the *Storming of Chapultepec*, and a final view of *Scott's Entrance into Mexico* [*City*]. Historians studying his war scenes have been amazed at their accuracy. Though Nebel did (perhaps for visual effect) choose to embellish the *Battle of Palo Alto* by putting mountains in the background, his depictions unquestionably are the best studies of any American conflict done up to that time.

Nebel worked on the paintings for three years, after which he and Kendall toured Europe looking for the best watercolorists to hand-color each print. The final result was worth the effort. Even though *War between the United States and Mexico, Illustrated* (1851) was published for the then-astronomically high price of $38 to $40 a copy, it became a best-seller throughout the United States.

See:

Sandweis, Martha, Rick Stewart, and Ben Huseman. *Eyewitness to War: Prints Daguerrotypes of the Mexican War, 1846–1848.* Fort Worth, TX: Amon Carter Museum, 1989.

Tyler, Ronnie C. "The Mexican War: A Lithographic Record." *Southwestern Historical Quarterly* 76 (1974): 1–84.

M. Paul Holsinger

TEXAS RANGERS (Historical Figures). No law enforcement force in the world, with the possible exception of the Royal Canadian Mounted Police, is more famous or more renowned than the Texas Rangers. Though groups of mounted "ranging men" with special powers to protect the frontier were in existence even before the founding of the Republic of Texas in 1835, it was the Mexican War that brought the Texas Rangers to the attention of Americans everywhere.

At the war's beginning, General Zachary Taylor asked the Texan governor for several regiments of troops. The state supplied three regiments, two of which were mounted and known officially as Texas Rangers. Though Taylor felt they were "a lawless set," reporters found them fascinating and spread their fame as the fiercest, most dangerous fighting men in the United States Army. As one early correspondent zealously noted: "A Texas Ranger can ride like a Mexican, trail like an Indian, shoot like a Tennesseean, and fight like a devil" (Webb, 15). To the Mexicans, the rangers were simply *"los Tejanos sangrientos"*—the bloody Texans.

During the Civil War, most ranger units served as part of the state's Confederate Army contingents. In the war's aftermath, their image of taking on all lawbreakers at the risk of their own lives and nearly always getting their man became part of national folklore. As early as 1847, popular novels, such as Joseph Holt Ingraham's *The Texas Ranger*, began to appear. Hundreds of dime novels featuring young rangers were readily available at the end of the nineteenth century. William MacLeod Raines' *A Texas Ranger* (1911) became one of the more famous western novels in the early years of the twentieth century. Dozens of folk songs, including the still famous "The Texas Rangers," with its many stanzas recounting a bloody fight along the Rio Grande between the rangers and marauding Indians, also quickly became a part of the nation's musical heritage. The rangers have also appeared in motion pictures, though most, such as King Vidor's *The Texas Rangers* (Paramount, 1936), starring Fred MacMurray and Lloyd Nolan, are easily forgettable. *The Lone Ranger*, aided by his faithful Indian friend Tonto, thrilled millions of young boys after the

1930s, and in the late 1990s, television, too, added a paean of praise with *Walker, Texas Ranger*, featuring karate expert Chuck Norris as the quintessential ranger protecting the state from all evildoers.

See:

Samora, Julian, Joe Bernal, and Albert Peña. *Gunpowder Justice: A Reassessment of the Texas Rangers*. Notre Dame, IN: University of Notre Dame, 1979.

"Texas Rangers: Manhunters of the Old West." In *The Real West*, dir. Craig Haffner, prod. Arthur Drooker. A&E Home Video, 1994.

Webb, Walter Prescott. *The Texas Rangers*. New York: Houghton Mifflin, 1935.

M. Paul Holsinger

6

The Civil War

Scholars have argued for more than 130 years about the origins of the Civil War, or, as it is more often called in the states of the former Confederacy, the War between the States. Was it because of the South's desire to protect the "peculiar institution" of slavery or the northern abolitionists' willingness to "purge the land in blood" if it would result in an end to that monstrous social evil? Was it, instead, because of the desire of Southerners to escape the centralized "big government" and destruction of state's rights that they feared would come about under the rule of Abraham Lincoln and the newly elected Republican Party? Could the war have been prevented, or was it inevitable? Such questions will probably never be answered to everyone's satisfaction, but it is relatively easy to sketch the military parameters of the war as it developed.

The war began on April 12, 1861, with an artillery barrage on Fort Sumter in the harbor of Charleston, South Carolina. Abraham Lincoln's call three days later for troops to put down the rebellion resulted in eleven southern states (or possibly twelve—there were Missourians who sat as congressmen in the Confederate Congress, even though technically, that state never seceded) leaving the Union and becoming part of the so-called Confederate States of America. With Virginia as one of the eleven and Richmond as the seat of government for the new nation, it was logical that federal troops would attempt to quell the rebels within miles of their own border. On July 21, Union commander Irvin McDowell and his men met the rebels a few miles from the tiny crossroads of Manassas Junction, Virginia, near a stream called simply Bull Run. Though the "Yankees" seemed destined to win the battle and the war, Southern troops on the verge of defeat rallied behind Virginia Military Academy's Brigadier General Thomas Jackson, who was described by a fellow officer as standing "like a stone wall" (Catton, 1961, 456), and before the day was done, the federal army was routed. Men turned and, in panic, ran the twenty miles back to Washington, D.C. Any thought that the war was destined to be short and relatively bloodless had quickly disappeared.

During the next year, the Confederacy fought a defensive, but successful, war in the East. When newly selected Union commander George McClellan pushed his Army of the Potomac to the peninsula below the Yorktown battlefield (of American Revolutionary War fame) and began to move forward toward Richmond, he was blocked and turned back repeatedly by forces under Robert E. Lee. McClellan's men adored him, but he cautiously spent far more time discussing strategy and planning battles than actually fighting them. A frustrated President Lincoln finally replaced McClellan, but things did not improve. Marching on Richmond from the north, General John Pope got as far as the site of the previous year's Battle of Bull Run, only to be outflanked and badly mauled by Lee, Jackson, and the Confederate Army. The Union men turned and once again ran back to the capital in disgrace.

In the West, however, the Union troops proved far more effective when, after sparring with each other for months along the strategically important Mississippi River, the two sides met in battle early in 1862. In February, Ulysses Grant attacked and captured Fort Henry on the Tennessee River (on the 6th) and Fort Donelson down-river (on the 16th). With the Confederate defeat at the latter fort came more than 12,000 prisoners of war. General Albert Sidney Johnston, who was called by many at the time the South's most distinguished military mind, moved to stop the advancing northern forces, but on April 6–7, 1862, when the two sides met on the battlefield near Shiloh (Pittsburg Landing), Tennessee, federal troops won one of their greatest victories of the war. The dead and wounded on both sides numbered more than 25,000, a figure greater than the total of all the men who had died or been wounded in the American Revolution, the War of 1812, and the War with Mexico combined. It was clear that the North had in Grant a leader who would fight and win. On the other side, Johnston, who was badly wounded on the first day of the fighting, bled to death on the field of battle.

In September 1862, Robert E. Lee and the Army of Northern Virginia turned north and moved across the mountains and into the green fields of western Maryland. It was a daring but, in the end, unsuccessful move. On September 17, McClellan, back in command of Union troops, met the "Johnny Rebs" at the small town of Sharpsburg, Maryland, and, on insignificant Antietam Creek, held the field and forced Lee and his men to retreat. It was the bloodiest single day of the war, and more than 13,000 rebels were lost at such now revered sites as "The Dunker Church," "The Bloody Lane," and "The Cornfield." Though McClellan failed to pursue the beaten Confederates as they retreated into Virginia, Lincoln, feeling buoyed by the victory, issued the famous Emancipation Proclamation, which effectively freed the slaves throughout the Confederate States.

Lee was in no way defeated, however, and in December, he and his army slaughtered thousands of Union troops at Fredericksburg, Virginia. The following spring, they continued to drive their Union counterparts from the field of battle. At Chancellorsville in May 1863, Lee and Jackson routed their Northern enemy. Though Jackson was shot and mistakenly killed by his own men on the evening of May 5, Lee now made the fateful decision to invade the North a second time. The result was the same as his first foray, but the bloodshed was even worse. On July 1–3, 1863, the Confederacy reached its high-water mark on the beautiful fields of Gettysburg, Pennsylvania. After the failure of a final attempt to salvage the battle, which was rapidly slipping from his grasp—the famous Pickett's Charge against the entrenched Union troops on Cemetery Ridge—Lee had no choice but to retreat back to Virginia.

In the West, the story followed similar ups and downs for both sides, but ultimately it was Grant who turned the tide, in favor of the North. The fortified city of Vicksburg, Mississippi, which was key to the control of the entire Mississippi River above New Orleans, fell to the general in early July 1863. Grant's triumph at the same moment that Lee was admitting defeat in Pennsylvania marked the beginning of the end for Southern dreams of independence.

Early in the conflict, the Civil War was wrapped in glory and romance. Patriotic poetry abounded, and songs extolling the virtues of each side were sung gleefully and with evident pride. Those songs soon were stilled, however, and replaced by lyrics that wondered wistfully when "this cruel war" would ever end. Disease ran rampant among Northern and Southern troops alike; twice as many men died of pneumonia, dysentery, malaria, and typhoid fever as were killed in actual battle. Battlefield surgeons, who were always overworked and never provided with adequate supplies, often were forced to act as little more than butchers. Both the Blue (North) and the Grey (South) soon found themselves running short on troops, and for both sides, coercion was the only answer. The Confederate States, as early as April 16, 1862, made every white male between the ages of eighteen and thirty-five eligible to serve in the army for three years. Later, men up to the age of forty-five became eligible, and still later, as desperation set in, the age increased to fifty. The North followed suit with a conscription act in March 1863 that made all men between the ages of twenty and forty-five liable to be drafted or, as some called it, "grafted" into the army. Neither law was popular, and thousands of men looked anxiously to find a way to avoid military service and the all-too-real possibility of facing capture, dismemberment, or death.

The last year and a half of the war saw a systematic crushing of both Southern defenses and Southern pride. Fighting "above the clouds" on Chattanooga's Lookout Mountain, Union troops won one of their most famous victories, while in Georgia, the important railhead at Atlanta fell to the forces of William Tecumseh Sherman. In fall 1864, Sherman and his armies turned toward Savannah and the sea, burning a path across Georgia and later the Carolinas, and refusing to stop until the South laid down its arms in April 1865. Grant, who was ordered east by Lincoln to take command of the often-battered, but never beaten, Army of the Potomac, moved on Richmond with a vengeance. In some of the most destructive fighting of the war—at the Wilderness, Cold Harbor, Petersburg, and finally Richmond (which fell in early April 1865)—Grant wore down the weary Confederate troops. When Lee finally sued for peace, a week after Richmond fell, he had only 8,000 troops left under his command who were even capable of continuing the fight.

Though most historians are content to mark the end of the war as Palm Sunday (April 9), 1865, the day of Lee's surrender outside the small village of Appomattox Court House, Virginia, a number of other rebel units continued to fight well into the summer of 1865. The last men did not lay down their arms until late June. No one knows exactly how many men actually died during the four bloody years of war, but unquestionably, at least a half-million were killed. In the South, more than one-third of all men in uniform died in the war. A minimum of one million on both sides of the battle lines were wounded. In American history, no other conflict, including even World War II, comes close to such destruction.

The North "won" and the South "lost." The Union was preserved; the institution of slavery was ended at last. In defeat, however, the Southerners were, if anything, drawn even more closely together. They talked proudly about their "Lost Cause." They furled their conquered banners and placed them away as reverential—nearly sacred—emblems of a war they wished they had won. Blaming both the Republican Party and the new freedmen for its fate, the South became "solid" in its hatred of things Northern. For the next nearly one hundred years, it stood aloof and unyielding in its dual policies of Democratic Party membership and segregation.

In victory, the North, did little to heal the wounds caused by the war. Imposing the harshly conceived Reconstruction on the South, Republican politicians for more than twenty years eagerly "waved the bloody flag" whenever their control of the nation was threatened. They repeatedly reminded voters that it was a Southern sympathizer, John Wilkes Booth, who martyred Abraham Lincoln only days after Lee's surrender and that the Southerners' actions had caused their fathers, husbands, and sons to die on battlefields hundreds of miles from home. As long as such rhetoric survived, there was little hope that the country could ever be brought back together.

For more than one hundred years, the Civil War has fascinated Americans perhaps more than any other military conflict. Thousands of books, both fiction and nonfiction, have been written about various aspects of the combat. There seems no end to such volumes or their popularity among readers; Charles Frazier's 1997 novel **Cold Mountain** topped the *New York Times* best-seller list for many weeks. On any given week, hundreds of Civil War "re-enactors" try to understand better what the war was all about by recreating the fighting of individual battles before appreciative audiences (see **battlefield reenactments**).

Even computer simulations prominently feature the Civil War and offer students of the era an opportunity to plot strategy afresh and possibly, this time, let the South emerge victorious.

What is often forgotten in the midst of such pro–Civil War fervor is that this was truly a "brother's war." That, above all other facts, makes it this nation's most regrettable military experience. No wars are ever "good wars," despite attempts to convince the public otherwise, but the conflict that the North called the Civil War and the South, the War between the States, despite all the honor we have accorded it, was one of the worst. During the war, brothers occasionally fought and killed each other. Families, especially in the border states, were torn apart, and the enmity still has not fully healed. That, perhaps, is the war's saddest legacy of all.

See:

Catton, Bruce. *The Centennial History of the Civil War*. 3 vols. Garden City, NY: Doubleday, 1961–1965.
———. *The Coming Fury*. Garden City, NY: Doubleday, 1961.
McPherson, James M. *The Battle Cry of Freedom: The Civil War Era*. New York: Oxford University Press, 1988.
———. *For Cause and Comrades: Why Men Fought in the Civil War*. New York: Oxford University Press, 1997.
Woodworth, Steven, ed. *The American Civil War: A Handbook of Literature and Research*. Westport, CT: Greenwood Press, 1996.

ACROSS FIVE APRILS (Young Adult Novel–Film). Irene Hunt's *Across Five Aprils* (1964) has been accurately called, not only "an intriguing and beautifully written book" (*New York Times Book Review*, May 10, 1964, p. 8), but also "a touchstone of Americanism in children's literature" (Alberghene, 106). Set in southern Illinois during the four years of the Civil War and based heavily on the memories of the author's grandfather, Hunt's work is a brilliant re-creation of time and place.

Happy and united before the outbreak of hostilities in April 1861, nine-year-old Jethro Creighton and his large farming family are ripped apart by the ensuing events. Two brothers join the Union Army, but Bill, the most thoughtful of the boys and certainly young Jethro's favorite, heads south into Kentucky to join the forces of the Confederacy. Thus the family is caught in the middle of the conflict and hated by neighbors on both sides; their barn is burned to the ground and their well is poisoned. After his father suffers a debilitating heart attack (quite early in the story), Jethro is forced to become the man of the house, now having to look after his mother, two sisters, and an older brother's children as well.

Though this is a home-front story, the war is never far away. Letters from the front lines often contain depressing news: Jethro's brother Tom is killed at Shiloh; his brother John almost dies at Chickamauga; a cousin deserts; the fiancé of his fifteen-year-old sister Jenny is critically wounded at Gettysburg. Bill literally disappears from the family's lives forever. *Across Five Aprils* is a perceptive and moving minor work of art, and its portrait of a family in chaos during the Civil War is carefully developed. The "brother's war" has rarely been as clearly described in a work of junior fiction.

A generally well-crafted film adaptation called, inexplicably, *Civil War Diary* (New World Entertainment, 1990) and starring Todd Duffey as Jethro, is available. Written and directed by Kevin Meyer, it remains reasonably faithful to Hunt's novel with the exception of several ill-conceived scenes that twist the plot into silly melodrama with a "happily-ever-after" conclusion.

See:

Alberghene, Janice M. "Irene Hunt's *Across Five Aprils*: Let Your Conscience Be Your Guide." In *Touchstones: Reflections on the Best in Children's Literature*, ed. Perry Nodelman. West Lafayette, IN: Children's Literature Association, 1985, 106–112.

M. Paul Holsinger

"ALL QUIET ALONG THE POTOMAC TONIGHT" (Song). There has always been dispute over the authorship of the Civil War's most popular early song, "All Quiet along the Potomac Tonight," or as it was originally called, "The Picket Guard." Most musical scholars accept the fact that Ethelinda Eliot Beers wrote the song's lyrics. Troubled by the incongruity of newspaper headlines reporting, "All Quiet along the Potomac Tonight," while news items noted the deaths of isolated sentries, the Massachusetts resident drafted "The Picket Guard" and sent the five-verse poem to *Harper's Weekly*, which published it on November 30, 1861. Almost immediately, musician–theater entrepreneur John Hill Hewitt, the "Father of the American Ballad," set her words to music, and the new composition soon became a favorite on both sides of the Mason-Dixon Line.

There is, however, a second version of the work's inception. According to Lamar Fontaine, a member of the Second Virginia Cavalry, CSA, he penned the words to "All Quiet along the Potomac" early in the summer of 1861. Grief-stricken at the death of his best friend while on guard duty, he sat down the next day and wrote the poem. Since Hewitt was also a Virginian and several of the first copies of sheet music had a Southern imprint, Fontaine's claim is often cited as preeminent, even though as early as 1868, one of the New South's strongest supporters, Joel Chandler Harris of the *Atlanta Constitution*, rejected it in favor of Mrs. Beers's.

The common soldier, of course, cared little about authorship. The maudlin verses about a lone picket marching his assigned route while thinking about his wife Mary and his small children at home in their trundle beds only moments before being shot had great appeal to enlisted men in both armies who understood that they, too, could face a similar fate at any time.

See:

Harwell, Richard B. "Richmond Is a Hard Road to Travel." Chapter 6 in *Confederate Music*. Chapel Hill: University of North Carolina Press, 1950, 79–85.

M. Paul Holsinger

***ANDERSONVILLE* (Novel-Film).** MacKinley Kantor's brilliant novel *Andersonville* (1955) won the Pulitzer Prize for fiction in 1956. The sympathetic tale about the infamous Confederate prisoner-of-war camp at Andersonville, Georgia, during the last months of the Civil War looks closely at the horror and inexplicable violence that made that small area of the rural South the war's darkest corner. Though some reviewers thought it both too biased toward the Union and too long (at 767 pages), most found the author's command of the facts surrounding Andersonville impressive. There is no doubt that *Andersonville* ranks among the small handful of exceptional fictional studies that focus on the war years.

Kantor introduces dozens of characters but tells the full story of only a few: Ira Claffey and his daughter Lucy, the Confederate Army surgeon Harrell Elkins, who eventually marries Lucy; the savage Tebbs family; and a number of Union prisoners inside the stockade walls, especially a cultivated Jew, Nathan Dryfoos. Claffey, Lucy, and Elkins strive to lead their lives humanely in order to counter the sheer chaos of the camp, but nothing they do can take away the instant agony that the lack of food, drugs, doctors, and proper sanitation imposes on the more than 30,000 prisoners who are squeezed into the less than twenty-six-acre campsite.

After a number of failed attempts to turn Kantor's work into a full-length motion picture, John Frankenheimer directed *Andersonville* (Turner Pictures, 1995), a made-for-television film shown initially on the TNT cable television network. Based very loosely on the novel, the plot follows men of a Massachusetts regiment who are captured at the Battle of Cold Harbor, Virginia, in June 1864 and taken to the notorious prison camp. Frankenheimer's visual image of Andersonville offers a human landscape that is bleak and wretched, where prisoners prey on others and sadistic guards try to blunt their own misery through brutality. Out of the ruin of the men's lives, however, rise acts of nobility in the human spirit: starving men, for instance, share their food in order to save their comrades' lives. Although there are a few factual errors, the production is characterized by close historical research and realistic cinematography. The acting is finely tuned, and *Andersonville* is a compelling drama and appallingly true to life.

In 1998, a new National Prisoner of War Museum honoring this nation's more than 800,000 POWs from the American Revolution to the Persian Gulf War was dedicated at Andersonville—close to the old prison camp's cemetery with its 12,000 Union army graves. Money for the $5.8 million project was raised by the sale of federally-issued commemorative coins, private donations, congressionally-approved funds, and contributions from the state of Georgia.

See:

Hesseltine, William B. "Andersonville Revisited." *Georgia Review* 10 (1956): 92–100.

Randal W. Allred

THE ANDERSONVILLE TRIAL (Drama). At the end of the Civil War, as the horrors and massive deaths suffered by Union prisoners at the Confederate prisoner-of-war camp at Andersonville, Georgia, became known, pressure built to bring camp commandant Henry Wirz to trial. In summer 1865, after lengthy testimony from Wirz and a number of ex-Confederate officials as well as many former prisoners, Wirz was convicted of war crimes and executed—the only person on either side of the conflict to die for such offenses.

In the mid-1950s, Saul Levitt used testimony from the hearings to create *The Andersonville Trial*, a powerful drama about conscience and duty during wartime. In 1957, a shortened version was presented to a limited television audience, and on December 29, 1959, a full-length production opened on Broadway. Directed by José Ferrer and starring George C. Scott in the pivotal role of Lieutenant Colonel N. P. Chipman, the United States judge advocate general responsible for prosecuting Wirz, the play met mixed reviews. When it closed, on June 1, 1960, after only 179 performances, it was rated a "failure" by New York City's drama critics.

At the time, some compared Wirz's unsuccessful defense—"I was only doing what I was ordered to do by my superiors"—to that of many of the Nazi war criminals at Nuremberg, and thus, little more than an aberration. In 1970, however, after media reports of the massacre by the United States Army of Vietnamese civilians at My Lai and its officers' similar defense, *The Andersonville Trial* was restaged for the PBS *Hollywood Television Theatre*. With Scott now directing, this version was uniformly praised and received an Emmy award as the year's outstanding single program in drama or comedy. Levitt won a second Emmy for outstanding achievement in drama adaptation.

See:

Morsberger, Robert E., and Katharine M. Morsberger. "After Andersonville: The First War Crimes Trial." *Civil War Times Illustrated* 13 (July 1974): 30–41.

M. Paul Holsinger

"THE BATTLE CRY FOR FREEDOM" (Song). In the summer of 1862, after President Abraham Lincoln issued a call for 300,000 more troops, the Chicago-based songwriter-publisher George Root sat down and wrote one of the most popular marching songs of the Union Army. Introduced at a war rally on July 24, "The Battle Cry of Freedom" became an overnight success. After its introduction in the East by the famous Hutchinson Family Singers, more than 350,000 copies of sheet music were sold. Years later, veterans remembered being ordered to sing the rousing lyrics as they marched into battle.

"The Battle Cry of Freedom," or, as it was often called, "We'll Rally Round the Flag, Boys,'' was filled with overtly patriotic fervor. It echoed the Lincolnian concept of the Union in such lines as: "We are springing to the call from the East and from the West/ . . . And we'll hurl the rebel crew from the land we love the best," and "We will welcome to the ranks the noble, true and brave/ . . . /And although he may be poor, he will never be a slave." Lincoln, himself, was said to be particularly pleased with the song and, at least on one occasion, sang it with a theater audience in Washington, D.C.

Southern adaptations soon were written as well. Championing the freedoms to hold slaves and to secede from the Union, Confederate soldiers sang such anonymously penned lyrics as the following two verses:

> Meet the Yankee hosts, boys
> With fearless hearts and true
> Shouting the battle cry of freedom
> And we'll show the dastard minions
> What Southern pluck can do.
>
> Our rights forever
> Hurrah! Boys Hurrah!
> Down with the tyrants
> Raise the Southern star.

See:

Epstein, Dena J. "The Battle Cry for Freedom." *Civil War History* 4 (1958): 307–318.

Randal W. Allred

BATTLEFIELD REENACTMENTS (Events). What began in the late 1950s as local preparations for the upcoming Civil War Centennial (1961–1965) turned into a nationwide hobby that involves more than 40,000 enthusiasts. Battlefield reenactments are probably the most visible and significant manifestation of the American Civil War in America's popular culture today, and the reenactors are found in every state in the Union and in a number of foreign countries from Austria to Australia.

The origins of reenacting probably date back to the veterans' reunions and other commemorative events in the latter years of the nineteenth century. In the early 1960s, the groups were inappropriately dressed and carried anachronistic weapons, but after the centennial, those units that remained spawned a cottage industry dedicated to providing true-to-life reproductions of Civil War uniforms, weapons, and other items to satisfy the need for authenticity. Not only must uniforms and weaponry be made to exact standards, but tents, shoes, coffeepots, styles of beards, and even such items as playing cards, period newspapers, and tobacco pipes are also expected to be like those of the 1860s.

These "living historians" restage battles all over the United States (especially in the East), which often draw crowds exceeding 50,000. Nearly 13,000 reenactors took part in the 125th anniversary celebration of the Battle of Gettysburg in 1988, and many of them later served as extras in such films as *Glory, Get-*

tysburg, and ***North and South***, a made-for-television mini-series. Age, gender, and race are not barriers to becoming a reenactor. Recently, for instance, entire African-American units were formed to recreate the parts played by their ancestors during the war.

It is often the realism of the hobby that attracts and holds reenactors. Most reenactors are typically not scholars, but they read voraciously on the Civil War, researching the elements of their individual outfits with meticulous zeal. One enthusiast recently expressed the allure: "One can read of past events, or view photos and paintings, but actually sensing in a small way through one's participation how things really looked and felt, can bring a knowledge as few other things can" (Allred, 6).

See:

Allred, Randal W. "Catharsis, Revision, and Re-enactment: Negotiating the Meaning of the American Civil War." *Journal of American Culture* 19.4 (Winter 1996): 1–13.

Hall, Dennis. "Civil War Re-enactors and the Postmodern Sense of History." *Journal of American Culture* 17.3 (Fall 1994): 7–11.

Randal W. Allred

"THE BATTLE HYMN OF THE REPUBLIC" (Song). "The Battle Hymn of the Republic" by Julia Ward Howe became, before the end of the Civil War, perhaps that war's most well-known song. Howe, an abolition activist and poet, was returning to Washington, D.C., in 1861 after reviewing a Union Army parade when several of her friends began singing the then-popular abolitionist marching song, "John Brown's Body Lies a-Mouldring in the Grave." Many soldiers along the road cheered, and a fellow traveler asked Howe why she did not write better words for "that stirring tune." Awakened from sleep that evening, she arose, found a "stub of a pen," and quickly composed poetic lyrics that, she later intimated, came directly from heavenly revelation:

> Mine eyes have seen the glory of the coming of the Lord
> He is trampling out the vintage where the grapes of wrath are stored
> He hath loosed the fateful lightening of His terrible swift sword
> His truth is marching on.

The succeeding verses were filled with equally powerful Christian imagery.

Mrs. Howe sent the untitled poem to the *Atlantic Monthly*. Editor James T. Fields featured it on page one of the February 1862 issue with its now-accepted title. Within two months, it was set to the music of "John Brown's Body" (as Howe apparently hoped it would be), and the words and music were published together in the late spring. Though at first many Union soldiers disliked the strongly worded proabolitionist lyrics, "The Battle Hymn of the Republic" grew steadily in popularity after Lincoln's Emancipation Proclamation made the freeing of the South's slaves an important component of the war. By 1865, not only were military bands playing it with regularity, Northern troops were also singing it everywhere they went.

There have been several attempts through the years to adapt Mrs. Howe's story to the screen. One of the most fascinating is a silent picture entitled simply, *The Battle Hymn of the Republic* (Vitagraph, 1911). Though it is overwhelmingly melodramatic and presents Howe in almost goddess-like terms, it became tremendously popular after the producer arranged for full-sized orchestras to play the title song in large city theaters where it was shown. When the United States entered World War I, the film was shortened slightly and used to recruit new volunteers.

During the last 135 years, "The Battle Hymn of the Republic" has become one of the nation's most popular patriotic songs, and its lyrics have lent themselves to dozens of book and film titles. Millions of people, who may know nothing about its composer or background, nonetheless instantly recognize the Mormon Tabernacle Choir's famous recording of the song.

See:

Hall, Florence Howe. *The Story of the Battle Hymn of the Republic.* 1916. Reprint. Freeport, NY: Books for Libraries Press, 1971.
Ream, Debbie Williams. "Mine Eyes Have Seen the Glory." *American History Illustrated* 27.6 (January/February 1993): 59–64.

Randal W. Allred

THE BATTLE OF ATLANTA (Painting). Cycloramas were enormously popular in the United States and Europe in the latter years of the nineteenth century. Though these gigantic paintings-in-the-round could highlight any number of epic events, in the United States the subject was almost always one of the major battles of the Civil War. Gettysburg, Shiloh, Lookout Mountain, Bull Run, Vicksburg, and the battle between the *Monitor* and the *Merrimac* were all, at one time or another, featured in such artwork.

One of the most famous, and certainly the largest of all, was the 42-by-358 foot cyclorama of the Battle of Atlanta, which was produced in 1885–1886 by William Wehner's American Panorama Company in Milwaukee, Wisconsin. *The Battle of Atlanta*, as it was initially called, took the combined efforts of three landscape, six figure, and three animal painters to complete. Though it is anything but an artistic masterpiece, there was a definite attempt to achieve historical accuracy. **Theodore Davis**, the famous *Harper's Weekly* artist who had been with Sherman's forces during the Atlanta campaign, was recruited to take the Milwaukee team to the battlefield and show them actual placements of the scenes from a specially constructed forty-foot-high platform. The completed study, which was seen from the perspective of the Union lines, was first displayed in 1886 in Minneapolis before touring a number of Northern cities.

Though popular, *The Battle of Atlanta* was not a financial success. By the time it arrived in Atlanta in 1892, the owners were so financially strapped that the painting was sold for only $1,000 to pay off the company's bills. It was then donated to the city of Atlanta and displayed in a specially designed building. During the 1930s, a number of wood and clay figures (now replaced by fiberglass and plastic ones) were added in the foreground as part of a Works Progress Administration project to employ out-of-work artists and craftsmen. Today, having been completely refurbished, carefully showcased in a new home, and renamed simply the *Atlanta Cyclorama, The Battle of Atlanta*, remains a fascinating example of historical painting.

See:

Catton, Bruce. "The Famous Cyclorama of the Great Battle of Atlanta." *American Heritage* 7.2 (1956): 33–45.

M. Paul Holsinger

BEADLE AND ADAMS DIME NOVELS. Inexpensive volumes of escapist fiction (known in England as ''penny dreadfuls'') had been popular with the public since the 1830s, but in June 1860, the New York publishing house of Beadle and Adams created a new American literary form by issuing cheap novels in a continuous series at the cut-rate cost of ten cents each. Known as dime novels (even when later priced at five cents), these sensationalist offerings generally consisted of 30,000 to 50,000 vivid words printed on cheap pulp paper with a lurid color cover. While facing stiff competition from other dime novel publishers such as Street and Smith, George Munro, and Frank Tousey, Beadle and Adams issued more than 5,200 dime novels (including some 2,109 reprints) in thirty-nine different series during the years 1860–1893.

The typical tale was filled with action and adventure; there was even some humor and romance, but there was never a dull moment. American war stories were especially popular, ranging chronologically from conflicts with the Pequot Indians in the mid-seventeenth century to the Battle of Wounded Knee 250 years later. In addition, Beadle and Adams published many stories of the French and Indian War, American Revolution, War of 1812, Mexican War, and Civil War, usually with a bold, enticing title, such as *The Sea King; or, The Two Corvettes: A Thrilling Sea Romance of John Paul Jones, the Ocean Scourge* (1873).

Dime novels were especially popular during the Civil War, when millions of Beadle and Adams books were shipped to both Union and Confederate camps, where they were read avidly during lulls in the fighting.

See:

Johannsen, Albert. *The House of Beadle and Adams and Its Dime and Nickel Novels.* Norman: University of Oklahoma Press, 1950.

James Deutsch

BIERCE, AMBROSE (Author). During the Civil War, Ambrose Bierce saw action as both an enlisted man and an officer in the Ninth Indiana Volunteer Infantry. Noted for his grimly realistic war stories, he became not only a journalist, political satirist, and short story writer, but also an arbiter of literary taste for many years, writing primarily for William Randolph Hearst's *San Francisco Examiner*. At the end of his life, he disappeared into Mexico, apparently seeking adventure with Pancho Villa's army, and thus opening the door to a legacy of myth and conjecture regarding his uncertain death. This last episode of his life was dramatized in *The Old Gringo* (1989), with Gregory Peck playing the elderly Bierce.

In addition to a volume of short stories, *Tales of Soldiers and Civilians* (1892), half of which deal with the Civil War, Bierce also wrote a number of columns and essays concerning the war years. All his stories are noted for their black humor, irony, and frequent cynicism as they address the unusual and fantastic. The best-known and most anthologized is "An Occurrence at Owl Creek Bridge," a story in which Union soldiers execute a Southern spy for espionage. As he awaits death, the young man fancies that the hangman's rope has broken and that he has escaped through the woods to his home. Then the rope tightens, and his neck breaks. A French-made, Robert Enrico–directed filming of "Occurrence" won an Academy Award as the best live action short subject of 1963; Charles Vidor also directed a 1932 Hollywood version.

Bierce's "Parker Adderson, Philosopher," "One of the Missing," "Chickamauga," and "The Mockingbird" were all made into thoughtful motion pictures during the 1960s. Other excellent, if at times almost too realistically bloody, stories by the author include, "A Son of the Gods," "Killed at Resaca," "The Coup de Grace," and "The Affair at Coulter's Notch."

See:

Guelzo, Allen C. "Bierce's Civil War: One Man's Morbid Vision." *Civil War Times Illustrated* 20 (November 1981): 36–39, 42–45.
Wilson, Edmund. "Ambrose Bierce on the Owl Creek Bridge." Chapter 14 in *Patriotic Gore: Studies in the Literature of the American Civil War.* New York: Oxford University Press, 1962, 617–634.

Randal W. Allred

***THE BIRTH OF A NATION* (Silent Film).** D. W. Griffith's monumental *The Birth of a Nation* (Epoch, 1915) is one of America's most famous and influential motion pictures. It is also one of the most controversial. Based on Thomas Dixon's best-selling novels about the supposed evils of Reconstruction, *The Clansman* (1905) and *The Leopard's Spots* (1906), the 185-minute film was, at the time, one of the longest-running pictures ever made. Overwhelmingly successful, it not only guaranteed the viability of full-length features but also helped to create the "star system" for the new industry's actors and actresses.

The screenplay focuses on the relationships between two disparate families, the Pennsylvania Stonemans and the Camerons from South Carolina. Temporarily brought together before the Civil War by their two sons' friendship at West Point, the ensuing "Irrepressible Conflict" quickly tears the families apart. Ben Cameron (Henry B. Walthall) and Phil Stoneman (Robert Harron) become important opposing military leaders who clash in some of the most famous battle scenes (employing thousands of extras) ever filmed.

At the end of the war, Father Stoneman (a thinly veiled representation of the famed Thaddeus Stevens) has become a leader of Radical Republicanism. Bringing his family to South Carolina during Reconstruction, he helps the Negro-dominated legislature to legalize miscegenation and "equal marriage." Only after he realizes that his salacious mulatto protégé wants his daughter, Elsie (Lillian Gish), does Stoneman finally realize the "error of his ways." At the climactic moment, the Ku Klux Klan, led by its founder, the gallant Ben Cameron, rides to the rescue and saves the Northern family from an uncontrollable Negro mob. They are, however, unable to save Cameron's younger sister (Mae Marsh); rather than succumb to the sexual desires of yet another villainous black fiend, she jumps to her death.

The film's impact on American culture was immense. Its demonization of the newly freed Negro as the rapacious dupe of Yankee carpetbaggers and the savage defiler of Southern white womanhood helped reinforce racial prejudice at the very moment when significant numbers of African-Americans were moving north. Racial tensions caused by the movie helped to spur the rebirth of the Ku Klux Klan on Stone Mountain, Georgia, late that same year; the tensions did not subside for decades to come. In New York alone, more than 3 million people saw the movie during the first ten months. It caused such a stir—the National Association for the Advancement of Colored People (NAACP) protested; there were pickets at many theaters; riots broke out in several cities—that President Woodrow Wilson commented that Griffith's film was "like writing history with lightning" (Jacobs, 4).

In *The Birth of a Nation*, Griffith demonstrated for the first time the power of the American motion picture to create myth and influence culture. Starting with the film's release in 1915, it has become clear that the representation of history often has more cultural impact than the events themselves.

See:

Carter, Everett. "Cultural History Written By Lightning: The Significance of *The Birth of a Nation* (1915)." In *Hollywood as Historian: American Film in a Cultural Context*, ed. Peter C. Rollins. Lexington: University Press of Kentucky, 1983, 9–19.

Jacobs, Lewis. *The Rise of the American Film*. New York: Harcourt, Brace, 1939.

Martin, Jeffrey B. "Film Out of Theatre: D. W. Griffith, *Birth of a Nation*, and the Melodrama *The Clansman*." *Literature/Film Quarterly* 18 (1990): 87–95.

Randal W. Allred

THE BLUE AND THE GRAY (Television Miniseries). On November 14, 1982, CBS-TV began its dramatic eight-hour miniseries, *The Blue and the Gray*, a show that publicists claimed was "the most ambitious project ever undertaken by the network" (*Newsweek*, November 15, 1982, 121). Based very loosely on "There Was a Young Soldier," a chapter in noted historian Bruce Catton's

Reflections on the Civil War (1981), the $17.6 million series unsuccessfully tries to create a panoramic view of events ranging from John Brown's raid in 1859 to Robert E. Lee's surrender six years later. Starring Stacy Keach as Union Army spy Jonas Steele and John Hammond as John Geyser, a Virginia artist employed by **Harper's Weekly** during most of the war, the series also features Gregory Peck as Abraham Lincoln and dozens of character actors and actresses in both real and fictional roles. Hundreds of Civil War reenactors valiantly march around the landscape, shoot at each other for hours on end, and often die bloodily (see **battlefield reenactments**). Although supposedly set in such disparate locales as the Shenandoah Valley of Virginia; Gettysburg, Pennsylvania; and Vicksburg, Mississippi; the production was filmed entirely in Arkansas.

The Blue and the Gray's main emphasis is the "brother's war," a term that has become engrained as a sobriquet for the entire Civil War era. The lives of the Geysers and their Pennsylvania cousins, the Hales, interact repeatedly on and off the battlefield. Both families lose members to the bloodshed, but in the melodramatic end, they come together to live happily ever after. Though some scenes, especially the recreations of the shelling of Vicksburg and the fighting during the 1864 Battle of the Wilderness, are reasonably good, the acting is uniformly wooden and the teleplay by Ian McLellan Hunter is frequently embarrassing.

Like so many made-for-television historical dramas, *The Blue and the Gray* was extremely popular with the viewing public when it was first shown. Historians and other film critics were far less positive. Though the Pulitzer Prize–winning Civil War historian James McPherson did, inexplicably, call the series twice as good as **Gone with the Wind** (*People's Weekly*, November 12, 1982, 150), the majority of critics agreed with William C. Davis's assessment that the entire series was a "positively stupid fictional story, filled with clichés" (Davis, 198). Others panned the films' lack of authentic costuming, awkwardly choreographed battle scenes, and anachronistic tactics, and though the series is readily available today on VHS, it is best ignored.

Ironically, the real John Geyser's story is far more interesting than anything put on the screen. Union Army volunteer Geyser joined the Seventh Pennsylvania militia immediately after the bombardment of Fort Sumter and served on active duty until fall 1863, when he was transferred to Veterans' Reserve because of the illnesses he incurred as a soldier. During that time he kept a sketchbook which he filled with dozens of scenes of life in the field. Although Geyser's work is not as panoramic as *The Blue and the Gray* tries to suggest, his art remains an invaluable record of what the war was really like for thousands of boys in blue.

See:

Cassidy, John M. "The Civil War and Television: The Blue and the Gray." Chapter 9 in *Civil War Cinema: A Pictorial History of Hollywood and the War between the States*. Missoula, MT: Pictorial Histories Publishing Company, 1993, 153–166.

Davis, William C. *The Cause Lost: Myths and Realities of the Confederacy.* Lawrence: University Press of Kansas, 1996, 198.

Randal W. Allred

"THE BONNIE BLUE FLAG" (Song). Harry Macarthy's "The Bonnie Blue Flag" was the second most popular song in the Confederate States of America; only **"Dixie"** had a greater popularity. After seeing the blue flag with one white star that South Carolina adopted after seceding from the Union, and even before the war actually began, Macarthy, a British-born vaudevillian then living in Arkansas, composed a first version of the piece. Written to be sung to the tune of the lilting "The Irish Jaunting Car," "The Bonnie Blue Flag" was introduced in spring 1861 by the performer during a show in Jackson, Mississippi. Later, when he sang it to a large gathering of soldiers in New Orleans, their enthusiasm ensured its success. In spite of its contrived rhymes, uneven meter, and wretched syntax, the impact that it had on the average soldier with its call to stand strong for Southern rights at all costs can never be underestimated.

Union supporters were quick to parody "The Bonnie Blue Flag." "The Stars and Stripes," for instance, attacked Southern "traitors" and their "arrogance" in replacing the Union flag. After Appomattox, Macarthy supposedly altered his original lyrics to stress the need for national unity. In "Our Country Flag," he wrote:

> We're still the "Band of Brothers" that proudly once unfurled
> The Bonnie Blue Flag, whose "single star" was sung around the world
> But now that war no longer reigns, let the cry be heard afar
> Hurrah for our country's flag, yes each and every star.

See:

Harwell, Richard B. "The Story of the Bonnie Blue Flag." *Civil War History* 4 (1958): 285–289.

Randal W. Allred

THE CIVIL WAR (Documentary Series). It is estimated that more than 39 million Americans saw all or part of Ken Burns's *The Civil War* when PBS broadcast the series in September 1990. This sweeping eleven-hour documentary offered viewers a chance to look at the Civil War in a new way: as epic drama. Critics were overwhelmingly praiseworthy. The nationally-syndicated columnist, George Will summed up the majority opinion when he wrote: "Our Iliad has found its Homer.... [Burns] has made accessible and vivid for everyone the pain and poetry and meaning of the event that is the hinge of our history" (A23).

By telling the stories of the people involved and connecting their faces and voices with the various battlefields on which they fought, were wounded, and often died, Burns brings the war home to people in a way that high school and college textbooks cannot. His documentary is an artful combination of period photographs, panning camera shots of the battlefields as they appear today, and the songs and voices of the people who lived through the war and its aftermath. Narrators read from diaries, letters, and speeches of the time, but theirs are not the only voices the audience hears. Burns also invited contemporary historians, most notably Shelby Foote and Barbara Fields, to tell about the war.

Throughout the series, Burns pulls together accounts from both sides and from people in all walks of life: Northerners and Southerners, blacks and whites, foot soldiers and generals, poets, and wives. It is this weaving together of various voices that allows Burns to captivate, rather than bore, his audience.

See:

Henderson, Bruce. "The Civil War: 'Did It Not Seem Real?' " *Film Quarterly* 44.3 (Spring 1991): 2–14.
Toplin, Robert Brent, ed. *Ken Burns's "The Civil War": Historians Respond.* New York: Oxford University Press, 1996.
Will, George. "A Masterpiece on the Civil War." *Washington Post*, 20 September 1990, A23.

Leslie Kennedy Adams

COLD MOUNTAIN (Novel). Charles Frazier's *Cold Mountain* (1997) is unquestionably one of the finest and most unique novels ever written about the Civil War. Unlike Michael Shaara's Pulitzer Prize–winning **The Killer Angels**, to which it has been favorably compared, there are almost no lengthy depictions of military encounters or bloody battlefield engagements. Though Frazier's brief description of the Battle of Fredericksburg is taut and almost hauntingly brilliant, the great bulk of his story focuses on the Southern home front, especially during the last months of the war. Based loosely on stories told by the author's great-grandfather, *Cold Mountain* is at once both an account of a dramatic escape from the horrors of the war and one of the most intensely beautiful love stories imaginable. Sweeping praise poured from the critics, who seemingly could not think of enough superlatives. Within weeks, it climbed the best-seller lists in the United States, and in November 1997, it received the National Book Award for fiction.

A Confederate Army volunteer named Inman from the mountains of North Carolina is *Cold Mountain*'s protagonist. Mortally wounded during the Battle of Petersburg, Inman miraculously survives, and as he slowly improves, the thought of having to return to the battle lines becomes intolerable. Sneaking out of his sick bed in an army hospital in Raleigh, Inman heads west toward home, desperately trying to reach the young woman he loves. During the next several months, he repeatedly is forced to elude the often-murderous members of the Home Guard, who are determined to capture, or kill, not only federal troops, but also every suspected army deserter they can find. On more than one occasion, Inman comes within inches of being killed. Tension builds continuously, and not until the very end do readers learn whether he has managed to survive.

Frazier's vivid description of rural North Carolina in the mid-nineteenth century and his portraits of some of its many poor white inhabitants know no equal in American literature. His careful picture of life long ago—based on intense historical research in time, place, and even spoken word—has already become one of the most evocative novels in American literature.

See:

Donahue, Deirdre. "In the Grip of 'Cold Mountain.' " *USA Today*, 16 October 1997, D1.

Giles, Jeff. "Gold Mountain." *Newsweek*, 28 July 1997, 64–65.

M. Paul Holsinger

CONFEDERATE BATTLE FLAG (Symbol). After the formation of the Confederate States of America in February 1861, the new government set about establishing all the things that delineate an independent country. For their national flag, leaders came up with a design featuring three horizontal bars of red, white, and red, with a circle of white stars on a blue field in the upper left corner. During the chaos of the first major land battle of the war near Manassas, Virginia, it was difficult to distinguish the new flag from the red, white, and blue U.S. banners. To counter this confusion, General P.G.T. Beauregard pushed for the adoption of a new flag, one that would not be easily mistaken when carried into battle. The new banner featured a blue St. Andrew's cross on a blood-red field. White stars, again representing the states of the Confederacy, were placed on the cross. For the rest of the war, soldiers in General Robert E. Lee's Army of Northern Virginia made wide use of this flag.

The Confederate battle flag today is unquestionably a symbol of valor in a lost cause, but to many Americans, its use by such racist groups as the Ku Klux Klan has made it seem even more a symbol of racial divisiveness. During the height of the civil rights movement in the 1950s, for instance, Georgia added the design of the Confederate battle flag to its state flag as a visible protest against the U.S. Supreme Court's mandate to integrate the nation's public schools. The government of South Carolina, in the early 1960s, started to fly the battle flag over its capitol in Columbia for the same reason. Though the governors of both states have, in recent years, sought to remove the offending symbol, the majority of white legislators and voters have repeatedly rejected such a move. In fall 1997, the football coach at the University of Mississippi begged students not to wave the battle flag at games because it was hurting the possibility of recruiting many of the best players in the state. When they refused, the school's president was forced to create a policy forbidding the carrying of "sticks" of any kind, including flag staffs, to future home games.

The battle flag has become one of the most commercialized symbols. For years it has adorned every type of commodity that can be sold in the South, from canned vegetables to the bumper stickers mounted on a myriad of pickup trucks.

See:

Morello, Carol. "Rebel Banner Roils Ole Miss Anew." *USA Today*, 23 October 1997, 3A.
Robbins, Peggy. "Fight for the Flag." *Civil War Times Illustrated* 35.5 (1966): 32–38.

James M. McCaffrey

***CONFEDERATES* (Novel).** Though Australian Thomas Keneally will probably always be best known by most readers for *Schindler's List*, his famed documentary novel about the Holocaust, in 1980 he also authored one of the most skillful fictional accounts about the American Civil War ever written. Literary critics lauded *Confederates* for its "stunning impact of reality" (*Newsweek* 96 [September 15, 1980]: 89) and called it (quite accurately) "the best Civil War novel since *The Killer Angels*" (*Library Journal* 105 [September 1, 1980]: 1752). It is a powerful, perceptive work of art, and a book to be savored by anyone interested in America's wars or its popular culture.

Set in Virginia and Maryland during the summer and fall of 1862, *Confederates* looks closely at the intersecting histories of a number of persons, ranging from the real General Thomas "Stonewall" Jackson to the fictional Dora Whipple, a widowed nurse spying for the North. Of all the characters in the novel, however, the most appealing (and, perhaps, most important) is Private Usaph Bumpass, a Shenandoah Valley farmer and volunteer in the Army of Northern Virginia's Stonewall Brigade. It is hard not to empathize with him. While undeniably devoted to the Southern cause, he is far more concerned about his friends in the frontlines and his beautiful wife, Epheptha, who, he suspects, may be cheating on him with any number of men at home. He has a burning desire to live, not so much so he will see a glorious, free, new nation, but so he can return home to his marriage bed once again.

Keneally is a master wordsmith who paints a brilliantly accurate portrait of the "real war" as it existed for men at the bottom like Usaph Bumpass. They march, they fight, and far too often, they die horrific deaths as cannon balls blow them to bits. Though any number of skirmishes are vividly described, it is the Second Battle of Bull Run in August 1862 and the even gorier Battle of Sharpsburg (Antietam) in September that dominate the book. By the end of the tale, nearly every one of Usaph's friends has been killed or maimed; he survives, but with his left arm mangled and never fully usable again.

Keneally pays tribute in a concluding "bibliographical note" to the many sources from which much of his factual material came. He has used them all with a deft skill.

See:

Quartermaine, Peter. *Thomas Keneally*. New York: E. Arnold, 1991.

M. Paul Holsinger

"THE CONQUERED BANNER" (Poetry). During the Civil War, Abram Joseph Ryan, a Roman Catholic priest, served as a Confederate Army chaplain.

Stationed first in Tennessee, and at war's end in Augusta, Georgia, he suffered with the troops in their humiliating defeat. He returned to the parish ministry and, in his sorrow, soon began to write poetry, much of it glorifying the men who fought and died for the South. "The Conquered Banner," his most famous work, made him, overnight, the most popular poet in the former Confederacy.

"Furl that Banner—furl it sadly," begins the third of the poem's seven stanzas, as Ryan recognizes and reluctantly accepts the defeat of what so many Southerners were already calling their "Lost Cause." The old flag, though "wreathed around in glory" and "holy," represented the past, and not the present or the future. It would "live in song and story" but must never more be flown. Just as "its people's hopes are fled," so, too, must the flag itself now be replaced.

Ryan's poem had just the opposite effect on most Southerners. "The Conquered Banner" was almost immediately set to music and the poem was sung reverently throughout the region. The Confederate flag, particularly the bright red and blue battle flag, became mythologized as a sacred symbol worthy of use as a banner of defiance against all who refused to accept Southern ways. "The Conquered Banner" became perhaps the most demanded poem throughout the region. It was read repeatedly at ceremonies honoring the Confederate dead and was almost an obligatory part of most United Confederate Veteran meetings for many years. In the post–civil rights era of the latter 1990s, with its politically correct calls to remove, once and for all, the Confederate flag from public view, Ryan's poem ironically continues to intrude on change.

See:

Heagney, Harold J. *Chaplain in Gray: Abram Ryan, Poet-Priest of the Confederacy.* New York: Kenedy, 1958.
Lawrence, Vera B. *Music for Patriots, Politicians, and Presidents: Harmonies and Discords of the First Hundred Years.* New York: Macmillan, 1975.

M. Paul Holsinger

COOKE, JOHN ESTEN (Author). Confederate officer, biographer, and popular novelist John Esten Cooke came from a distinguished Virginia family. One cousin married General J.E.B. Stuart and another was a Confederate general, while an uncle (General Philip St. George Cooke) was in the Union Army. Cooke served on the staffs of both "Stonewall" Jackson and Stuart during the war, seeing action in a number of major engagements. After the war, Cooke wrote popular historical biographies of both Jackson and Robert E. Lee. Though praising the military prowess of Jackson, he was at first highly critical of Lee on the battlefield. In repudiation of his views, a number of Southern writers began a sanctification of the general that continues to this day. Properly chastised, Cooke, whose *Wearing of the Gray* (1867) is an often-exciting memoir of his own experiences in the Army of Northern Virginia, changed his views and became a strong proponent of Lee's greatness.

Cooke's renown comes from his novels, many of which focused on the Civil War from a Southern viewpoint. *Surry of Eagle's Nest, or The Memoirs of a Staff-Officer Serving in Virginia* (1866), *Mohun, or The Last Days of Lee and His Paladins* (1868), *Hilt to Hilt, or Days and Nights on the Banks of the Shenandoah in the Autumn of 1864* (1869), and *Hammer and Rapier* (1870) all combine realistic battle scenes with highly sentimental and romantic features of plot, character, and style. They became best-sellers throughout the South when first published and remained popular for many years afterwards.

See:

Beaty, John Owen. *John Esten Cooke: Virginian.* 1922. Reprint. Port Washington, NY: Kennikat, 1965.

Randal W. Allred

THE COPPERHEAD (Drama). In 1918, Lionel Barrymore took fifteen curtain calls for his performance in the lead role of *The Copperhead* by Augustus Thomas. Based on Frederick Landis's 1910 novel, *The Glory of His Country*, the play ran for 120 performances and was so successful that its star was brought to Hollywood. The silent film version of *The Copperhead* (Paramount, 1920) was, if anything, an even greater critical, international success.

In both drama and film, Barrymore plays Milt Shanks, a small-town Illinoisian who, even before the secession of the states of the future Confederacy, enrages his fellow townsfolk with his openly pro-Southern sentiments. When the Civil War begins, he declares himself a conscientious objector to avoid the conflict and is ostracized by the patriotic Northerners. Forty years later, though his wife has died despising him for his cowardice, he realizes that his granddaughter, whom he loves above all else, is being branded because of his acts. Revealing at last that President Abraham Lincoln had named him a special agent to infiltrate the Southern-sympathizing Copperheads and pledged him to lifelong secrecy, he saves her reputation and dies an honorable man in the eyes of his neighbors.

There is little today to recommend *The Copperhead*, with its numerous melodramatic scenes. Three generations ago, however, millions of Americans found themselves captivated by its tense and exciting twists of fate.

See:

Peter, Margot. *The House of Barrymore.* New York: Knopf, 1990.

M. Paul Holsinger

THE CRISIS (Novel–Silent Film). *The Crisis* (1901), by the American author Winston Churchill, was one of the early twentieth century's most successful works of historical fiction. A sequel to *Richard Carvel*, the novel combines a traditional old-fashioned plot with the polished prose and sophisticated psychological introspection of modern fiction.

In 1858, Stephen Brice, a blue-blooded Bostonian, and his recently widowed mother come to the proslavery city of St. Louis, Missouri, so that he can join the law practice of his father's friend Judge Whipple, an implacable abolitionist. Brice meets Virginia Carvel and her father at a slave auction, where he impulsively uses his savings to buy (and free) a slave girl in order to save her from the New Orleans brothels. Though he falls in love with Virginia, she at first cruelly spurns the morally even-tempered Yankee in favor of her dissipated and reckless cousin, Clarence Colfax. Brice encounters Abraham Lincoln and becomes a confirmed member of the Republican Party. After Lincoln's call for troops in April 1861, he eventually enters the Union Army and twice saves the life of Colfax, now a Confederate officer, even though both times he realizes that his rival will likely marry Virginia.

Churchill brings *The Crisis* to a choppy and melodramatic end. The Confederate Colonel Carvel is unceremoniously killed in battle. Virginia, after spirited resistance through most of the story, finally admits that she loves Stephen, and they are married. More than half the other essential characters are left unaccounted for, but the author's wit and rich narrative style make the novel a fine read. Clearly pro-Union (the North appears to have an overwhelmingly righteous fund of virtue throughout the novel), the book became a runaway best-seller, going through thirty-four editions. A silent film, *The Crisis* (Selig, 1916), was also based on Churchill's story, but when it opened, the same week that the United States declared war on Imperial Germany and entered World War I, audiences stayed away in droves, and it was declared a financial, if not artistic, failure.

See:

Schneider, Robert W. *Novelist to a Generation: The Life and Thought of Winston Churchill.* Bowling Green, OH: Popular Press, 1976.

Randal W. Allred

CYCLORAMA OF THE BATTLE OF GETTYSBURG (Painting). The most famous single painting dealing with the Civil War, the *Cyclorama of the Battle of Gettysburg*, is the work of the French artist Paul Philippoteaux, who came to the United States in 1882 intent on producing a huge study of the great three-day battle at Gettysburg. After touring the battlefield, having panoramic camera shots taken from a number of angles to help him accurately interpret the surrounding scenery, and corresponding with Union Generals Winfield Scott Hancock and Abner Doubleday (who had led troops in the battle), he returned to his Paris studios and began the monumental task. When he and his five assistants finished, in summer 1883, Philippoteaux returned to America, displaying his great work first in Chicago and then in Boston, where tens of thousands of visitors paid as much as fifty cents each to see it.

After its last showing, in 1892, the *Cyclorama* was crated and stored away. Only good fortune saved it for later generations. In 1910, Newark, New Jersey, merchant Albert Hahne purchased the painting so that he could display sections of it in his department store. To his surprise, a new generation of Americans, who had never seen the work when it was originally on display, seemed awed. After the widow of Confederate General Pickett praised the work's emotional impact, Hahne realized that it had commercial potential. He bought land on the Gettysburg battlefield, erected a specially designed building, and, just in time for the fiftieth anniversary of the battle, during summer 1913, reassembled Philippoteaux's gargantuan (25-by-375 foot) canvas in its entirety. Once again, it was a huge success, and it remains so today, more than eighty years later.

See:

Thomas, Dean S. *The Gettysburg Cyclorama.* Gettysburg, PA: Thomas Publications, 1989.

M. Paul Holsinger

DAVIS, THEODORE (Artist). Theodore Russell Davis was informally trained in art by **James Walker**, one of the nation's most renowned war artists. Davis typified the "special artist," who was hired by popular magazines and newspapers to illustrate the Civil War. In 1861, he started illustrating the war for *Harper's Weekly* and thus became one of the most popular and prolific interpreters of battlefield scenes. He covered a number of major campaigns and was the only field artist to accompany General William Tecumseh Sherman's march to the sea.

Davis spent most of his time in the field living with the troops. Although he was not known for front-line heroism like fellow illustrator **Alfred Waud**, Davis found himself under artillery fire several times. On two different occasions he was wounded while sketching battles. In 1868, he wrote a very lively description of the life of a special artist for the New York *Evening Mail*: "Total disregard for personal safety and comfort; an owl-like propensity to sit up all night and a hawky style of vigilance during the day; capacity for going on short food; willingness to ride any number of miles horseback just for one sketch, which might have to be finished at night by no better light than that of a fire." The total body of Davis's realistic Civil War sketches and paintings make such a statement even more meaningful.

After the Civil War, Davis spent a brief period illustrating Reconstruction activities in the South and accompanying Generals Winfield Scott Hancock and George Armstrong Custer in their campaigns against the Indians in the west. His illustrations were published primarily in *Harper's*, in an association that lasted for his entire twenty-three-year career as an illustrator. Davis later became a historical consultant on the Civil War for a number of publishers.

See:

Johnson, Peter. *Front Line Artists.* London: Cassell, 1978, 42–45, 51–53.
Thompson, William Fletcher, Jr. *The Image of War: The Pictorial Reporting of the American Civil War.* 1960. Reprint. Baton Rouge: Louisiana State University Press, 1994.

Michael Brown

"DIXIE" (Song). Though it became the most popular marching song of the Confederate States of America during the Civil War, "I Wish I Was in Dixie's Land"—or, more simply, "Dixie"—was never intended as anything but a minstrel show piece to be sung by actors in blackface performing on the vaudeville stage. Composed by Ohioan Daniel D. Emmett in spring 1859, while he was in New York City with Bryant's Minstrels (one of the more renowned groups of its day), it quickly spread through the United States. It is impossible to determine when "Dixie" was first heard in the South, but it soon became enormously popular everywhere in the region. In early February 1861, it was played at Jefferson Davis's inauguration as president of the new Confederate States of America (CSA), and with the outbreak of war, the CSA adopted it as its unofficial national anthem. Though the lyrics were written in crude, almost offensive, dialect, it was hard for Southerners not to get excited about taking their stand "to lib [live] and die in Dixie." Such a situation displeased the pro-Union Emmett. "If I had known to what use they were going to put my song, I will be damned if I'd have written it," he later stated (Bowman, 94).

Countless variations of the song emerged. Indeed, the Daughters of the Confederacy have discovered at least twenty-two different versions, perhaps the most renowned of which was by Brigadier General Albert Pike. Throwing out the original comedic dialect, this Mexican War veteran, whose poetry was already well known throughout the South, made "The War Song of Dixie" far more martial in tone. His eight verses contained such lines as, "Swear upon your country's altar / Never to submit or falter" and the wonderfully forgettable, "Strong as lions, swift as eagles / Back to their kennels hunt these beagles!" In another version, Maria Louisa Eve of Georgia promised: "For Dixie's land and Dixie's nation / We'll stand and fight the whole creation."

Since the end of the Civil War, "Dixie" has become an integral part of American popular culture. At the same time, it still remains a battle cry of Southern defiance against perceived interference by the federal government. Sung with pride by many people throughout the South, perhaps only the **Confederate battle flag** today remains a more visible symbol of the region's racist past.

See:

Bowman, Kent A. *Voices of Combat. A Century of Liberty and War Songs, 1765–1865.* Westport, CT: Greenwood Press, 1987.

Harwell, Richard. "God Save the South: Dixie and Its Rivals." Chapter 4 in *Confederate Music*. Chapel Hill: University of North Carolina Press, 1950, 41–63.

Long, Roger. "Uncle Dan and 'Dixie': Music that Moved the South." *Civil War Times Illustrated* 20 (April 1981): 13–17.

Randal W. Allred

THE FIRST READING OF THE EMANCIPATION PROCLAMATION OF PRESIDENT LINCOLN (Painting).

Few American paintings are more accurate in their historic recreation of events than Francis Bicknell Carpenter's large depiction of Abraham Lincoln and his cabinet on July 22, 1862, when the president announced his decision to emancipate the slaves. Carpenter, an already significant New York portraitist, came to Washington, D.C., in early 1864 specifically to prepare a work focusing on that already-famous milestone. Buoyed by the backing of the renowned abolitionist Illinois Congressman Owen Lovejoy, the artist met Lincoln and, for nearly the next six months, sketched the president and his cabinet members both from life and from photographs specially commissioned by **Mathew Brady Studios**.

Allowed to paint in the White House's state dining room, where he often worked through the night, Carpenter meticulously captured the scene on that memorable day in its most intimate detail. When *The First Reading of the Emancipation Proclamation of President Abraham Lincoln*, as he called the work, was completed, it was put on display in the White House and became an overnight success. Even before Lincoln's assassination, the picture toured the Northern states, and it was on display in Pittsburgh, Pennsylvania, the night the president died.

Carpenter was never fully satisfied with his work and continued to retouch it for the next decade. Still, so popular did it become that the New York publishing firm of Derby and Miller bought the rights to issue an engraving of the painting, and for many years, their work was a best-seller at the then-enormous price of ten dollars. Cognizant of his work's fame, in 1866 Carpenter wrote and published a detailed anecdotal study, *Six Months at the White House with Abraham Lincoln: The Story of a Picture*, recounting many episodes in the two men's brief relationship.

In 1878, Congress officially purchased the original painting for permanent display in the Capitol, where today, it is seen by millions of tourists every year.

See:

Holzer, Harold, Gabor S. Borett, and Mark E. Neely, Jr. "Francis Bicknell Carpenter (1830–1900): Painter of Abraham Lincoln and His Circle." *American Art Journal* 16 (Spring 1984): 66–89.

M. Paul Holsinger

FORBES, EDWARD (Artist). Edward Forbes was commissioned in 1861 as a staff artist for *Frank Leslie's Illustrated Newspaper*. He followed Union troops from the Second Battle of Bull Run until the siege of Petersburg (during fall 1864), drawing some exceptionally accurate battle scenes for his employer as well as dozens of pictures of life in the camps before and after engagements. He was at Cedar Mountain in August 1862 and at Antietam in September of that same year, and his pictures of both battles rival the work that **Alfred Waud** was doing simultaneously for *Harper's Weekly*. After Grant was given command of the Army of the Potomac, Forbes followed him into the Wilderness. Though Forbes retired from the battlefield after Petersburg, his work is some of the strongest to come from the war.

The best of Forbes's many sketches were collected in 1876 and printed as a set under the title, *Life Studies of the Great Army*. Later that year, the series won an award for excellence at Philadelphia's famed Centennial Exposition. Forbes prepared an illustrated history of the war for children, *An Artist's Story of the Great War* (1890), and the following year published his reminiscences, *Thirty Years After, An Artist's Story of the Great War*. This latter, entertaining study is heavily illustrated by even more of his artwork from the front.

See:

Hodgson, Pat. *The War Illustrators*. New York: Macmillan, 1977, 84–89.

Thompson, William Fletcher, Jr. *The Image of War: The Pictorial Reporting of the American Civil War*. 1960. Reprint. Baton Rouge: Louisiana State University Press, 1994.

M. Paul Holsinger

FRANK LESLIE'S ILLUSTRATED NEWSPAPER (Weekly). In December 1855, under the pseudonym of Frank Leslie, an English wood engraver named Henry Carter founded a weekly that became not only one of the most important journals reporting the Civil War but also one that set the tone for all other illustrated American papers that were to follow. *Frank Leslie's Illustrated Newspaper*, which was modeled on the famous London *Illustrated News*, pioneered the use of large and lively illustrations as well as prompt and timely coverage of the news events of the day. By often stressing the sensational side of the news, Leslie was able to build his circulation steadily, and by early 1861, his newspaper had more than 200,000 subscribers. To ensure excellent pictorial contents, he employed some of the country's top young artists, such as **Thomas Nast, Alfred Waud**, and Charles Parsons. So outstanding was their work that occasionally a drawing appeared alone rather than accompanying an article.

When the war started, *Leslie's*, like its major competitor *Harper's Weekly*, was a moderate paper opposed to suppressing the South by armed conflict. By mid-1861, however, it was solidly pro-Union and kept a dozen or more correspondents in the field to cover the major campaigns. Its articles and political analyses were always solid. No newspaper's artwork was livelier. During the war, the works of more than eighty different artists were featured in the paper's pages, and full-page and even oversize engravings from the battlefields attracted the continuing attention of a wide audience.

As the war dragged on, however, *Leslie's* was unable to remain competitive with the larger and better-funded *Harper's*. By the end of the war in 1865, its circulation was down to 50,000, a figure that remained reasonably steady until its ultimate demise in 1922.

See:

Huntzicker, William E. "Frank Leslie (Henry Carter)." In *American Magazine Journalists, 1850–1900*, ed. Sam G. Riley. Vol. 79. *Dictionary of Literary Biography*. Detroit: Gale Research, 1989, 209–222.

Mott, Frank Luther. "Leslie's Weekly." Chapter 26 in volume 2 of *A History of American Magazines, 1850–1865*. Cambridge, MA: Harvard University Press, 1938, 452–465.

Randal W. Allred

FRIENDLY PERSUASION (Novel-Films). In 1945, many of Jessamyn West's short stories about a nineteenth-century Quaker family in southern Indiana were brought together into a full-length novel. Popular from the moment of its publication, *The Friendly Persuasion* almost called out for motion picture adaptation. William Wyler, working from a screenplay by Michael Wilson with West's collaboration, did just that. *Friendly Persuasion* (Allied Artists, 1956) was nominated for a host of Academy Awards, including best picture. Though it failed to win that honor or any of the other Oscars for which it was nominated, Wyler received the Cannes Film Festival Golden Palm Award in 1957.

In the story, it is 1862 and Jess and Eliza Birdwell (Gary Cooper and Dorothy Malone) and their three children live an almost idyllic life, far removed from the war, even though non-Quakers in the area have been sending their sons to the Union Army since Lincoln's first call for troops. Everything changes dramatically when Colonel John Morgan's Confederate cavalry crosses the Ohio River from Kentucky, pillaging the local farms and spreading terror. The oldest son, Josh, who was movingly played by the Oscar-nominated (as best supporting actor) Anthony Perkins, finally decides that he must take up arms against the enemy. It is a vain and losing effort. Though Josh does kill several Confederate soldiers, including one hardly older than himself, the enemy passes through the area scathed, but victorious. Jess and Eliza also have encounters with rebel troops and learn that even the best efforts at peaceful solutions often fail.

In 1975, *Friendly Persuasion* was remade as an ABC-TV movie starring Richard Kiley as Jess and Shirley Knight as Eliza. This version puts far more stress on another part of West's novel (how the Birdwells risk their lives to help two runaway slaves) than on the war itself, but it is no less effective. Later retitled *Except for Me and Thee*, it, like its predecessor, is thoughtful and extremely well acted.

See:

Cassidy, John M. "Many Are the Hearts: Family Struggles on Film." Chapter 4 in *Civil War Cinema: A Pictorial History of Hollywood and the War between the States*. Missoula, MT: Pictorial Histories Publishing Company, 1993, 61–68.
Shivers, Alfred S. *Jessamyn West*. Boston: Twayne, 1975.

M. Paul Holsinger

FRIETCHIE, BARBARA (Subject of Legend). Poets have never been averse to creating "facts" from myth. That is exactly what John Greenleaf Whittier did in the case of ninety-year-old Barbara Frietchie, who supposedly risked her life to wave the U.S. flag defiantly at the Confederate forces of Stonewall Jackson as they passed her home in Frederick, Maryland, in September 1862.

"Shoot, if you must, this old gray head/But spare your country's flag," she melodramatically says. "Barbara Frietchie" was first published in the October 1863 edition of *Atlantic Monthly* and became an instant success. It was reprinted—and still is—in nearly every patriotic anthology. School children across America were forced to memorize it, and Frietchie became revered as one of the Civil War's bravest and most famous women.

Though Frietchie was a real person who lived in Frederick at the time of the Confederate invasion, historians have found no evidence to support Whittier's dramatic narrative. Before his death, even the poet acknowledged that the tale he told was "probably incorrect." Despite that disclaimer, however, numerous artistic recreations, such as W. J. Morgan and Company's 1896 lithograph, "Barbara Frietchie," all of which were based on Whittier's poem showing the brave Mrs. Frietchie gallantly waving her flag in front of a surprised Stonewall Jackson and his rebel troops, were widely in circulation before the end of the century.

Early in the twentieth century, strange variations of Frietchie's story also began to gain popularity. Clyde Fitch, for instance, wrote the enormously popular, but hopelessly inaccurate, *Barbara Frietchie, the Frederick Girl, a Play* (1899). Four silent movies, all using the heroine's name in their titles (Vitagraph, 1908; Champion, 1911; Metro-Goldwyn-Meyer, 1915; and Producers-Regal, 1924) also turned history on its head. The M-G-M film, featuring the beautiful thirteen-year-old Mary Miles Minter playing the heroine as a vivacious Southern girl, got the best reviews. In its script Barbara angrily shreds a Union flag before dying accidentally from a Confederate bullet. *My Maryland* (1927), a musical comedy based on Fitch's play, was also produced.

The real Frietchie home, now rebuilt in Frederick, Maryland, has been a tourist attraction for years. Many persons climb dutifully to Barbara's second-story bedroom to look down at the rebel troops as she supposedly did more than 135 years ago.

See:

Hassler, Warren. "Barbara Frietchie: Fact, Fiction, or Both?" *Civil War Times Illustrated* 22 (October 1983): 12.
Spears, Jack. *The Civil War on the Screen and Other Essays*. South Brunswick, NJ: A. S. Barnes, 1977, 14–16.

                                                                    M. Paul Holsinger

THE GENERAL (Silent Film). In April 1862, James J. Andrews, a spy for Union General Don Carlos Buell, led a group of twenty two men deep into Georgia to destroy the Western and Atlantic Railroad, which ran between Atlanta and Chattanooga. Andrews and his men stole a locomotive, *The General*, in the small town of Big Shanty and raced northward. A crew gave chase, and after the stolen train ran out of fuel, all the enemy raiders were captured. Andrews and seven of his men were hung; the rest either escaped from prison or were exchanged within the next year.

The famous silent screen comedian, Buster Keaton, used the story of the Andrews Raid to make *The General* (Buster Keaton Productions, 1926), his masterpiece as an actor-director and, to some critics, one of the greatest films ever made. Basing his script on William Pittinger's contemporary, nonfictional account of the raid, *The Great Locomotive Chase* (1863), Keaton fashioned, not only one of the screen's classic comedies, but also one of its least typical. Though full of wonderful pantomime and visual gags, the production also includes mammoth battle scenes and a tender romantic subplot involving *The General*'s brave conductor, Johnnie Gray (Keaton), and the love of his life, Annabelle Lee (Marion Mack). Shot exclusively in and around Cottage Grove, Oregon, it was one of the most expensive silent motion pictures ever made, at a cost of well over $750,000. More than 3,000 actors were employed, including hundreds of Oregon national guardsmen who convincingly portrayed Union and Confederate soldiers. The destruction of a locomotive falling from a specially built trestle in a climactic scene cost $42,000 to shoot—the single most expensive episode in all silent films.

When the comedy was released in 1927, critics hated it. Many attacked it for suggesting, even obliquely, that seeing men die in battle was funny. Others, expecting a typical Keaton film with huge laughs and dozens of pratfalls, walked out of the theater. Not until the 1960s was *The General* rediscovered by an admiring audience; it was subsequently selected by the American Film Institute as one of the fifty greatest films of all time.

In 1956, Walt Disney Studios retold the story of the Andrews Raiders in the serious, noncomedic *The Great Locomotive Chase*, starring Fess Parker and Jeffrey Hunter. More historical and truer to the real-life adventures of James Andrews and his men than was Keaton's *The General*, it is also, unfortunately, far less brilliant.

See:

Cassidy, John M. "Comedies and Keaton: *The General* and Other Humorous Hostilities." Chapter 2 in *Civil War Cinema: A Pictorial History of Hollywood and the War between the States*. Missoula, MT: Pictorial Histories Publishing Company, 1993, 17–29.

Randal W. Allred

"GETTYSBURG ADDRESS" (Speech). On November 19, 1863, President Abraham Lincoln gave perhaps the most famous speech in the history of the United States, a 272-word statement of ideological belief that has come to be known worldwide as the "Gettysburg Address." It was barely four months since the bloody battle that had surrounded the small town of Gettysburg, Pennsylvania, the previous July. More than 8,000 bodies, hurriedly buried on the field where they fell, were finally formally interred in the new national cemetery. As president, Lincoln was asked to provide some "dedicatory remarks" in the ceremony. His speech, lasting scarcely three minutes—a drastic contrast to the preceding formal, two-hour "oration" given by former U.S. Secretary of State Edward Everett—was praised by some of the reporters who heard it, yet seemed to many others at the time hardly worthy of such an important occasion. However, Lincoln's address—which was filled, not as Everett's was, with specific references to the battle and the men who died in it, but rather with eternal truths about the American system of government itself—forced, not only his listeners, but also the tens of millions who have read it since, to understand the Civil War in terms of such truths as justice, equality, and compassion.

Many of the most widely quoted phrases in American life come from the "Gettysburg Address." In calling for "a new birth of freedom," for instance, the president clearly emphasized that the United States was a "nation under God." Perhaps more significantly, he provided the essential summation of American republicanism; this was, he said, "a government of the people, by the people, and for the people." For such a principle, it was worth fighting and even dying.

As Lincoln predicted, the world has never forgotten what happened at Gettysburg—the battle is undeniably the most researched and analyzed engagement of the entire Civil War, if not of all American history—but his belief that "the world will little note nor long remember what we say here" was in error. Even before his death, Lincoln's "Gettysburg Address" was being memorized and quoted by schoolchildren and orators alike. After his assassination, it was enshrined as one of the two or three most important documents and statements of belief in the nation's past, and it will remain so indefinitely.

See:

Holzer, Harold. "A Few Appropriate Remarks." *American History Illustrated* 23.7 (November 1988): 36–46.
Kunhardt, Philip B. *A New Birth of Freedom: Lincoln at Gettysburg.* Boston: Little, Brown, 1983.

M. Paul Holsinger

GLORY (Film). *Glory* (Tri-Star, 1989) has been hailed by some critics as perhaps the best Civil War movie ever made. With a discriminating eye for detail, director Edward Zwick and screenwriter Kevin Jarre attempt to tell the story of one of the earliest all-black regiments in the Union Army, the Fifty-fourth Massachusetts Infantry, and its struggle to achieve recognition and legitimacy in the face of overwhelming racism. Based heavily on the letters of the regiment's white commanding officer, twenty-five-year-old Robert Gould Shaw, the film also draws on non-fiction material from Peter Burchard's *One Gallant Rush* (1965) and Lincoln Kirstein's *Lay This Laurel* (1973). Though events unfold through Shaw's eyes, the real heroes of *Glory* are the often-unknown and otherwise faceless African-American men on the battlelines.

Returning to Boston from the Battle of Antietam, the wounded Shaw (Matthew Broderick) is offered command of the new Fifty-fourth Regiment. The brainchild of the famous black activist Frederick Douglass and Governor of Massachusetts John Andrew, the regiment is composed of a wide spectrum of African-Americans, both free men and runaway slaves, the educated and the illiterate. The members of the unit, who include a former slave (Denzel Washington), a middle-class businessman (Morgan Freeman), and a learned Emerson scholar (Andre Braugher), have to prove themselves repeatedly. Even without proper equipment or arms, their training is more rigorous than that of most white troops. When they are thrust into battle on the South Carolina coast (their first time), they roundly defeat the rebel forces. In the film's climactic scenes, which are set on July 18, 1863, during the Union Army's suicidal frontal assault on Fort Wagner (one of the several forts guarding Charleston harbor), Shaw and his troops volunteer to lead the attack. Though as a result, he and over 60 percent of his men died, their bravery and heroism encouraged Union leaders to recruit additional African-American units. The more than 100,000 such men may, in the end, very well have turned the final tide of battle in favor of the North.

Glory is starkly realistic and unerringly authentic with respect to uniforms, period tactics, architecture, and locations. Most of the extras were Civil War battle reenactors (see **battlefield reenactments**), including a number of African-American students from the University of Central Arkansas. Nominated for five Academy Awards, the film won three: best supporting actor (Washington), best cinematography, and best sound.

See:

Cullen, Jim. "A Few Good Men: Glory and the Search for a Just War." Chapter 5 in The Civil War in Popular Culture: A Reusable Past. Washington, DC: Smithsonian Institution Press, 1995, 139–171.
McPherson, James M. "Glory." In Past Imperfect: History According to the Movies, ed. Mark C. Carnes. New York: Holt, 1995, 128–131.

Randal W. Allred

GODS AND GENERALS (Novel). In 1975, Michael Shaara's brilliantly told documentary novel about the Battle of Gettysburg, *The Killer Angels*, won the Pulitzer Prize for fiction. Looking closely at the intersecting lives of men such as the South's Robert E. Lee and Medal of Honor–winner Joshua Chamberlain of Maine, Shaara pulled his readers into the minds and hearts of his characters. Long before his account reached Pickett's climactic charge on the Federal lines at Cemetery Ridge, they understood, not only who these men were historically, but also why they acted as they did. So popular was the book that Civil War buffs longed for a "prequel" that would illuminate in a similar way the story of the war's earlier days. Shaara was never able to fulfill such wishes, but eight years after his death in 1988, his son Jeff did so with aplomb. *Gods and Generals* (1996), which was written, according to the younger Shaara, primarily for those persons who never liked history and who learned about the American past in textbooks, instantly received critical accolades. One of the *New York Times'* most notable best-sellers for many months, it continues to sell widely in a modestly priced edition.

Covering the almost five-year era from November 1858 to June 1863, *Gods and Generals* skillfully integrates biographical and psychological glimpses of dozens of men and women into a compelling account of the pre-Gettysburg years. Shaara focuses the bulk of his attention, however, on only four military leaders: Confederate Generals Robert E. Lee and Thomas "Stonewall" Jackson and distinguished Union officers Joshua Chamberlain and Winfield Scott Hancock. Though undeniably fiction, Shaara's account is so carefully researched that each of these four men "comes alive" in the book's nearly 500 pages. He re-creates a number of specific engagements, often with the skill of a dramatist. Readers are drawn onto such Virginia battlefields as Manassas, Fredericksburg, and Chancellorsville along with the thousands of men in blue and gray. Though all of Shaara's leading men are intrepid, it is the doomed Jackson, who was killed by his own men following his greatest victory at Chancellorsville, who is the most tragic. The depiction of his death is perhaps the most moving part of a work that is emotionally draining throughout.

Jeff Shaara is an excellent storyteller and *Gods and Generals* a fine work of fiction. **Mort Künstler**, one of the nation's most renowned artistic interpreters of the Civil War, called it a masterpiece when it first was published. That may be an overstatement, but it is not far from the truth.

See:

Hooper, Brad. "*Gods and Generals* [Review]." *Booklist*, 15 April 1996, 1395.

M. Paul Holsinger

GONE WITH THE WIND (Novel-Film). *Gone with the Wind*, a monumental historical romance about life during the Civil War and Reconstruction in Georgia by Margaret Mitchell, won the 1937 Pulitzer Prize for fiction. Readers loved it even more than the critics. The stores could not keep enough copies in stock, and it quickly became one of the best-selling novels of all time. Published in 1936, it chronicles the perseverance of Scarlett O'Hara, a plucky antebellum heroine, who survives the war, Sherman's destruction of Atlanta, famine, romantic disappointment—and three husbands along the way. As a flawed, yet strong, protagonist, Scarlett may well appeal to the reader in search of a complex, tenacious, female character, but the book as a whole furthers a horribly romantic ideal of a lifestyle founded on slavery, complete with racial stereotypes of African-American women as "mammies" and "pickaninnies." Yankees and, later, carpetbaggers are consistently seen as villainous Northern opportunists come to pillage Tara, Scarlett's home. Her determination to succeed at all costs can be viewed as a metaphor of the (white rebel) South, whose vow is to "rise again." Scenes depicting Scarlett's fervent attachment to the land (which she defends with her life) clearly tie her to an intensely personal, and very traditional, Southern patriotism.

Made into an enormously successful motion picture starring Vivien Leigh, Clark Gable, Leslie Howard, and Olivia de Havilland, *Gone with the Wind* (Selznick, 1939) was the top-grossing film of the year. Some of its scenes from the war, especially the panoramic view of wounded Confederate soldiers at the Atlanta rail yards and the even more famous burning of the city, have become classics in Hollywood filmmaking. The winner of the Academy Award for best picture, *Gone with the Wind* also earned nine others, including awards for Leigh (best actress, for her portrayal of Scarlett) and Hattie McDaniel (best supporting actress, as Scarlett's "Mammy"), the first such award ever given to an African-American.

In late 1991, Alexandra Ripley published *Scarlett: The Sequel to Margaret Mitchell's Gone with the Wind*, an 823-page novel that, despite horrid reviews ("a seriously awful book" [*New York Times Book Review*, October, 27, 1991, 21]; "excruciatingly dull" [*New York Review of Books*, December 19, 1991, 24]), became an immensely popular best-seller with more than 20 million copies in print. In November 1994, CBS spent more than $45 million to bring this new volume to the television screen. The resulting eight-hour miniseries was, however, little more than a bad soap opera.

Today, Scarlett lives on in American popular culture through dolls, museums, web sites, and a plethora of memorabilia, including theme quilts. While Tara was fictional, many Georgian antebellum mansions draw on its mystique, as do such places as Georgia's Tara Mobile Home Park. There are even tentative plans for a $50 million *Gone with the Wind* country theme park.

See:

Bridges, Herb. *Gone with the Wind: The Definitive Illustrated History of the Book, Movie, and the Legend*. New York: Simon and Schuster, 1989.

Cullen, Jim. "Screening the Book: The Civil War of Margaret Mitchell's *Gone with the Wind*." Chapter 3 in *The Civil War in Popular Culture: A Reusable Past*. Washington, DC: Smithsonian Institution Press, 1995, 65–107.

Harmetz, Aljean. *On the Road to Tara: The Making of Gone with the Wind*. New York: Harry N. Abrams, 1997.

Harwell, Richard, comp. and ed. *Gone with the Wind as Book and Film*. Columbia: University of South Carolina Press, 1983.

Kerstin Ketteman

"GRAFTED INTO THE ARMY" (Song). Though there were songs such as **"We Are Coming, Father Abra'am,"** which praised the president's call for troops to preserve the Republic, it was hard to find anyone who liked the idea of forcing men to fight for their country. Even as the death toll mounted on both sides and the United States continually needed more men, the government specifically avoided a draft. When it could no longer put off the necessity of taking nonvolunteers, however, Congress finally passed the Conscription Act, in March 1863. For the first time in the nation's history, American men by the thousands were suddenly "grafted" into the army.

In Northern cities such as New York, rioting led by angry mobs violently protested the new law. Editorials railed against the new policy, and even songwriters, capitalizing on the public's frustration, rushed out songs criticizing the law's consequences. Though there were dozens of such numbers, clearly the most famous was "Grafted into the Army" by the popular and prolific composer, Henry Clay Work.

Work's lyrics, which are humorously sung by "our Jimmy's" widowed mother, contain numerous plays on words and malapropisms, but there are serious, underlying notes as well. Since all her sons except the youngest have already been killed "way down in Alabarmy," the distraught mother laments of her youngest's son's conscription: "I thought they would spare a lone widder's heir / but they grafted him into the army."

Jimmy's tale, however, has a happy ending. Shortly after the conclusion of the war, an obscure writer named William A. Field published "He's Got His Discharge from the Army. A Companion to 'Grafted into the Army.' " In this sequel, Jimmy's mother proudly sings:

> My Jimmy's got home
> I am ever so glad. . . .
> He behaved himself well and was a brave lad . . .
> [and] he got his discharge from the army.

See:

Silber, Irwin *Songs of the Civil War.* New York: Columbia University Press, 1960, 303–
    305.

M. Paul Holsinger

***HARPER'S WEEKLY* (Newspaper).** Subtitled "A Journal of Civilization," *Harper's Weekly* (1857–1916) was perhaps the most popular Northern newspaper during the Civil War. Capitalizing on copious illustrations (and numerous ads to pay the bills), this brainchild of Fletcher Harper became a huge success, sending more artists and correspondents to the front lines than almost any major journal. Each issue was fronted with engravings of combat scenes or the generals who were leading the North's troops into battle. Some of the most famous illustrators of the day, such as **Alfred Waud** and his brother William, **Theodore Davis**, Robert Weir, and Andrew McCallum, drew for *Harper's* on a regular basis.

An excellent example of the journal's wartime emphasis can be found in its April 12, 1862, issue, which featured more than two full pages of large illustrations of naval action in Pamlico Sound, North Carolina, and along the Mississippi; a large centerfold of the Battle of Winchester, Virginia; and yet another full-page picture of life under the decks of the famous Union ironclad ship *Monitor.* Also included were battle reports from several different battlefronts, political cartoons by **Thomas Nast** and Henry L. Stephens, and even a poem by the editor of the rival *Atlantic*, James Russell Lowell.

Initially, *Harper's* was, at best, a moderate paper, which opposed Lincoln's effort to preserve the Union by force. Soon after the firing on Fort Sumter, however, the paper turned solidly pro-Union; even as Northern troops were being badly beaten in the field, its editors were predicting a total Union victory. The public was repeatedly excoriated for lacking the "backbone" to support the war effort enthusiastically. When Lincoln ran for reelection in 1864, *Harper's* played a major role in helping to sway popular opinion on his behalf.

While *Harper's* regularly published fine American literature, including original work by such renowned writers as Henry James, William Dean Howells, and Owen Wister, it also remained an important guide to the nation's military adventures throughout the nineteenth century. In 1898, during the Spanish-American War, for instance, the weekly put such correspondents as **Richard Harding Davis** (who was at one time the magazine's editor), John Fox, Jr., and John R. Spears into the field to guarantee expert coverage.

See:

Mott, Frank Luther. "Harper's Weekly." Chapter 29 in volume 2 of *A History of American Magazines, 1850–1865*. Cambridge, MA: Harvard University Press, 1938, 469–487.

Randal W. Allred

THE HEART OF MARYLAND (Drama). The popular playwright David Belasco tried for nearly six years to bring *The Heart of Maryland* to Broadway. When it finally opened, on October 22, 1895, New York theater critics disliked almost everything about this Civil War play—even the leading actress's newly dyed red hair. The melodramatic story line and the many improbable scenes, including one in which the heroine hangs on the clapper of a huge bell to prevent it from ringing, were especially condemned.

Such reviews, however, did not discourage theatergoers. *The Heart of Maryland*, which is set during the Confederate invasion of Maryland in 1863, became one of the great popular hits of the 1890s. During its first year, it played for 229 consecutive performances before beginning a grand tour of East Coast cities that lasted until spring 1897. Still going strong, it then opened for a third season later that year in San Francisco, after which it played in dozens of cities across America for nearly another year before finally closing in spring 1898. Impresario Charles Frohman, who had at first refused to stage the play, now took it to London, where it played for 100 additional shows. Audiences were so taken by the melodrama that they paid more than $1 million to see it. Belasco's fame rose precipitously, and he soon became independently wealthy.

The critics' assessment of *The Heart of Maryland* was probably correct. Like so many other dramas of the day, it has a beautiful Southern belle (Maryland Calvert) who is in love with a Union Army officer (Alan Kendrick). A treacherous double agent (Colonel Fulton Thorpe) almost manages to have Kendrick executed so that he can "have his way" with the heroine, but, thanks to her bravery and resourcefulness, Alan is saved. Just before the curtain falls, General Robert E. Lee intervenes, Thorpe's duplicity is revealed, and the two lovers are able to pledge their love to each other without fear of retribution.

See:

Hughes, Glenn, and George Savage. "Introductory Note, *The Heart of Maryland.*" *The Heart of Maryland and Other Plays by David Belasco*. Princeton, NJ: Princeton University Press, 1941, 171–172.

Timberlake, Craig. *The Bishop of Broadway: The Life and Work of David Belasco*. New York: Library Publishers, 1954.

M. Paul Holsinger

HOMER, WINSLOW (Painter). Winslow Homer, one of America's greatest painters, is intimately connected in most people's minds with scenes of the sea. In the early 1860s, however, he was also one of the Civil War's best combat artists. As early as 1858, the twenty-two-year-old Homer had his own studio in Boston, but after the already prestigious *Harper's Weekly* accepted one of his drawings, he moved to New York City. In March 1861, he sketched the inauguration of Abraham Lincoln, and after the outbreak of the war, the magazine made him one of its first regular artists in the field.

Homer experienced war for the first time in October 1861, when he traveled with the Sixty-first New York Volunteers through the Peninsular Campaign as well as the Battles of Fair Oaks, Seven Pines, the Wilderness, and Malvern Hill. He was good friends with illustrator **Alfred Waud**, with whom he collaborated on a number of illustrations for *Harper's*. In late 1862, Homer returned to his studio and began painting the series of large pictures of the war, which was to make him famous. When his *Home, Sweet Home*, a clear yet simple oil view of life in a Union Army tent "city," was displayed at the National Academy of Design in New York in 1863, it was an immediate success. *The Sharpshooter on Picket Duty* is one of his best. Originally published by *Harper's* in November 1862 as a black-and-white drawing, the colored painted version, which was exhibited for the first time in early 1864, shows a young Union marksman balancing carefully on a pine branch and taking aim at an invisible enemy somewhere in the distance.

The Civil War was fertile ground for Homer. From his visits to the front, he produced a number of covers for *Harper's*, many paintings, and two popular series of lithographs: *Campaign Sketches* (1863) and *Life in Camp* (1864). A strong opponent of slavery, Homer also frequently featured African-Americans in his Civil War works; his paintings and illustrations of black army teamsters from the Civil War are among his best and most popular.

See:

Simpson, Marc. *Winslow Homer: Paintings of the Civil War*. San Francisco: Fine Arts Museum of San Francisco, 1988.

Wood, P., and K. Dalton. *Winslow Homer's Images of Blacks: The Civil War and Reconstruction Years*. Austin: University of Texas Press, 1988.

Michael Brown

THE HORSE SOLDIERS (Novel-Film). During April 1863, Colonel Benjamin Grierson led the First and Second Illinois Cavalry deep into Confederate-held Mississippi on one of the most successful raids of the Civil War. When the sixteen-day trek was completed, the railway system between LaGrange, Tennessee, and Vicksburg lay in ruins, leaving that latter city, which was on the Mississippi River, cut off from adequate supplies and easy prey to the Union troops then besieging it. *The Horse Soldiers*, Harold Sinclair's exceptional 1956 historical novel, is a careful fictional retelling of that famous event, which one contemporary reviewer accurately called "a well-conceived, masterly novel of men, guts, and guns" (*New York Times*, February 19, 1956, 4). Though the author changes some of the facts to fit his plot more tightly and creates several individuals who have no real-life parallel, the book's prose is both reflective and detailed as it follows the fortunes of a brigade of Union cavalry under the leadership of the tough and worldly wise man whom Sinclair chooses to call Colonel Jack Marlowe.

Director John Ford and coproducers-screenwriters John Lee Mahin and Martin Racklin subsequently transformed Sinclair's story into a full-color, big-screen, combat-laden production. *The Horse Soldiers* (Mirisch/United Artists, 1959) highlights the conflict between Marlowe (John Wayne) and one of his officers, Surgeon Major Henry Kendall (William Holden). While the colonel is concerned with the integrity of the mission, Kendall cares more for the well-being of the men, and the two clash frequently. A subplot unique to the film in which both men fall in love with the same young Southern belle (Constance Towers) only detracts from Sinclair's original taut plot. The unauthentic uniforms, seemingly taken straight from the costume closet of one of Ford's earlier movies featuring the cavalry and Indians of the Far West, also weaken the picture's authenticity. Shot on location around Natchitoches, Louisiana, and in California's San Fernando Valley, the scenes of combat are well staged, and despite the caveats, *The Horse Soldiers* is good, swash-buckling fun.

See:

Place, J. A. "The Horse Soldiers." Chapter 12 in *The Western Films of John Ford*. Secaucus, NJ: Citadel Press, 1974, 174–185.

Randal W. Allred

JOHN BROWN'S BODY (Poetry-Drama). Published in 1928, Stephen Vincent Benét's epic, *John Brown's Body*, competes with *Battle Pieces* by **Herman Melville** as the most significant poetic work written as a result of the Civil War. Based in part on a close reading of such important studies as *Battles and Leaders of the Civil War* (1884) and John G. Nicolay and John Hay's famous 1887 biography, *Abraham Lincoln: A History*, it was awarded the Pulitzer Prize for poetry in 1929, even though many literary critics had initially found it flawed in their reviews.

Each section of the poem's eight books offers varying pictures and stories of the war. Several representative characters appear: Clay Wingate of Georgia, Jack Ellyat of Connecticut, and the two women (Sally Dupré and Melora Vilas) who love them. Other sections are devoted to John Brown as an evocation of the war and to the trials of President Abraham Lincoln. Book 7 concentrates entirely on the Battle of Gettysburg.

Benét's reputation has suffered in recent decades due to his dated sentimentalism and "common man" style, but the noted American author Hervey Allen was correct in his assessment at the time of publication, that *John Brown's Body* was "poignantly and exhaustingly alive . . . offer[ing] its audience . . . a vicarious experience" (*Yale Review*, 18 [Winter 1929]: 391). Though the poem's pacing is not chronological (the war is abruptly wrapped up in Book 8), Benét treats the conflict with respectful awe. His use of various verse forms not only provides readers with a broad experience of the flavor and mood of the times but also captures that era's democratic vision. *John Brown's Body* is a work of art, which engenders renewed appreciation with each rereading.

During the 1952–1953 theater season, actor-director Charles Laughton adapted *John Brown's Body* into a multifaceted presentation featuring three of Hollywood's more famous stars: Tyrone Power, Judith Anderson, and Raymond Massey. Opening on Broadway on February 14, 1953, with a twenty-voice chorale and a number of dancers, the drama was enthusiastically praised by every New York critic but, apparently, was too literate for the majority of theatergoers and closed after only sixty-five performances.

See:

Fenton, Charles A. *Stephen Vincent Benét: The Life and Times of an American Man of Letters*. Westport, CT: Greenwood Press, 1978.

Randal W. Allred

"JUST BEFORE THE BATTLE, MOTHER" (Song). Throughout the Civil War, hundreds of maudlin songs about young soldiers' love and concern for their mothers or mothers' yearning for their sons on the battlefield poured from presses in both the North and South. One of the most famous was "Just before the Battle, Mother" by George Root. Published by Root in 1862, it offers the reassurance that, even in the hellish environment of war, at least one lonely soldier thinks "most" of his mother. The song became a universal favorite, especially with the Union troops; carried to England by the Christy Minstrels, it became immensely popular in that country as well. Reportedly more than 1 million copies of the sheet music were sold.

Even in their melancholia, Root's lyrics did not miss a chance to take a swipe at northerners whose sympathies lay with the Confederacy. The narrator writes to his mother:

> Tell the traitors all around you,
> That their cruel words we know
> In every battle kill our soldiers
> By the help they give the foe.

Southerners also sang the piece widely, either in its original form or in a biting parody baiting the Yankee troops:

> Just before the battle, mother
> I was drinking mountain dew
> When I saw the Rebels marching
> To the rear I quickly flew
> Where the stragglers were flying
> Thinking of their homes and wives
> 'Twas not the Rebs, we feared, dear mother
> But our own dear precious lives.

During the election campaign of 1864, radicals in the Republican Party designed a parody to fit Root's music. "A Voice from the Army" not only condemns the Democrats as warmongers but also promises "[W]e'll not forget those traitors / When this bloody war is through."

See:

Silber, Irwin. *Songs of the Civil War*. New York: Columbia University Press, 1960, 121–122.

Randal W. Allred

THE KILLER ANGELS (Novel). Michael Shaara's *The Killer Angels* (1974), a brilliantly introspective retelling of the battle of Gettysburg, won the Pulitzer Prize for fiction in 1975. Looking closely at such men as the Confederacy's Robert E. Lee, James Longstreet, and Lewis Armistead and Northern officers like Josuha Chamberlain and John Buford, Shaara puts readers in the midst of the battle's three bloody days of fighting. Lean in its style like the works of Ernest Hemingway, and at times, broodingly psychological like the war stories of Stephen Crane, *The Killer Angels* captures time and place far better than the spate of recent works about the war years. There are few sections in American war fiction more exciting, for instance, than the author's taut re-creation of the successful attempt of Chamberlain and his Maine Volunteers to retain control of Little Round Top on the last day of the battle. Hailed by Civil War enthusiasts as perhaps the most authentic recent novel to deal with the war, *The Killer Angels* has also become the most popular.

Almost twenty years after its publication, *The Killer Angels* was adapted into a six-hour, made-for-television motion picture. Shown initially on the TNT Cable television network (and later released in a cut-down four-hour version to commercial theaters), *Gettysburg* (Turner/Neufeld-Rehme, 1993) features Martin Sheen as Lee, Tom Berenger as Longstreet, Jeff Daniels as Chamberlain, Richard Jordan as Armistead, and Sam Elliott as Buford. A "magnificent, awe-inspiring re-creation,'' in the words of Leonard Maltin, it received high praise for its close attention to historical detail and meticulously accurate uniforms, weapons, and tactics. Director Ronald Maxwell used more than 3,000 battlefield reenactors from all around the United States and forty-two different Civil War cannons in the making of his film. Photographed in part at Gettysburg (the first picture to be granted that right by the U.S. National Park Service) by Kees Van Oostrum, one of Hollywood's more famous cinematographers, the visual quality is often breathtaking. Daniels makes Joshua Chamberlain, who was awarded one of the first Medals of Honor, come alive, and most reviewers praised his strong performance. Civil War students, on the other hand, found both Sheen's Lee and Berenger's Longstreet far less faithful to the novel's excellent and accurate depictions. The hackneyed Hollywood phrasing used throughout the film is also disconcerting.

If *Gettysburg* clearly fails to capture the emotion and drama of *The Killer Angels*, it is, nonetheless, a fine addition to the roster of motion pictures about the Civil War's most pivotal battle. VHS copies of it are readily available for home rental.

In 1996, Michael Shaara's son, Jeff, authored a "prequel" to his father's famous novel that covers the years from 1858 up to July 1863. *Gods and Generals* provides readers of *The Killer Angels* with carefully sketched accounts of the often-harrowing wartime experiences of many of the same men who are prominently featured in that original work.

See:

Hartwing, D. Scott. *A Killer Angels' Companion*. Gettysburg, PA: Thomas, 1996.
Jorgenson, C. Peter. "Gettysburg: How a Prize-Winning Novel Became a Motion Picture." *Civil War Times Illustrated* 32 (November–December 1993): 40–49, 92–93, 113.

Randal W. Allred

"KINGDOM COMING" (Song). Many years after the Civil War, George Root, the co-owner of the famous Chicago music publishing firm of Root and Cady, remembered vividly the day when Henry Clay Work came to his offices with the manuscript of "Kingdom Coming." Ostensibly based on the Union's capture of the Georgia Sea Islands, where slaveholders had panicked and run, leaving their charges behind, Work's song capitalized on that picture and impressed the older businessman. It was, he said, "full of bright good sense and comical situations in its darky dialect" (Bolcom), and he agreed to publish it. Several days later on April 23, 1862, it was introduced on the Chicago stage by the original Christy Minstrels and became one of the great popular hits of the war.

The slave who is supposedly singing the peppy song regales his audience with stories about his master who ran away as soon as he saw "smoke, way up the ribber, where de Linkum gunboats lay," and the cruel overseer locked up "in de smoke house cellar, wid de key trown in de well." The chorus adds the rollicking words:

> De massa run? Ha, ha!
> De darkey stay? Ho, ho!
> It mus' be now de kingdom comin'
> in de year of Jubilo.

So popular was "Kingdom Coming" that the public begged for more such songs. In 1863, Work obliged with "Babylon Is Fallen," a piece that focuses on the Union's decision to recruit African-American soldiers for its ranks. Staunchly supporting the position of radical abolitionism, it gained Work a continued fame that was to crest with his most famous—and most hated—piece, **"Marching through Georgia."**

See:

Bolcom, William. *Who Shall Rule This American Nation? Songs of the Civil War Era.* (Nonesuch H-71317) Liner Notes.

Heaps, Willard, and Porter W. Heaps. *The Singing Sixties: The Spirit of Civil War Days Drawn from the Music of the Times.* Norman: University of Oklahoma Press, 1960, 268–270.

M. Paul Holsinger

KÜNSTLER, MORT (Artist). Almost from the moment that Mort Künstler graduated from Pratt Institute, in the early 1950s, his illustrations for magazine articles and book covers made him one of the highest paid and most widely respected artists in his field. By the 1970s, he began to attract the attention of serious collectors, and after a 1977 one-man show of his works, his popularity spread nationwide.

No contemporary American artist's name is more intimately connected with the visual interpretation of American history than Mort Künstler. His works, many of which now hang in some of the nation's most prestigious art collections, focus on the broad spectrum of American historical life. There are paintings of the nation's many wars, including the British surrender after the Battle of Yorktown during the American Revolution, the charge of the Rough Riders up San Juan Hill during the Spanish-American War, the shooting down of a German aerial balloon by Eddie Rickenbacker (America's top air ace during World War I), and a Japanese kamikaze attack off the coast of Okinawa in World War II. A book of these and dozens of other historical paintings, *The American Spirit*, was issued to much critical acclaim in 1986.

During the 1980s, Künstler turned his attention exclusively to portraying the men and events of the Civil War years. In 1982, for instance, it was his artwork that CBS-TV used as an integral part of its *The Blue and the Gray* miniseries. Before 1992, when he became the first artist ever allowed to have a one-man exhibition of his original paintings on the grounds of the Gettysburg National

Military Park, more than one hundred major works dealing with the war flowed from his brushes. There are paintings of the opening cannon shots on Fort Sumter; depictions of hand-to-hand combat at the battles of Shiloh, the Wilderness, and Spotsylvania Court House, and still other works featuring the last moments at Appomattox for the defeated Confederate Army. A retrospective of many of the best of these paintings was published along with a text by the famed Pulitzer Prize–winning historian James M. McPherson as *Images of the Civil War* (1992). The next year, another volume, *Gettysburg: The Paintings of Mort Künstler* (1993), featured dozens of Künstler's paintings about the war's most pivotal battle. Issued as a companion to *Gettysburg*, the made-for-television movie Turner Pictures had adapted from the popular novel about that battle, *The Killer Angels*, it added to the artist's acclaim from Civil War "buffs."

It is easy to exaggerate the impact that works of art may have on their viewers but it does not go too far to claim that the historical paintings of Mort Künstler are among the best ever produced by an American artist. Intensely accurate and based on careful historical research, they capture, better than any painter since **John Trumbull**, the reality of military events in the past.

See:

Doherty, M. Stephen. "Biography of the Artist." In *The American Spirit: The Paintings of Mort Künstler*, ed. Henry Steele Commanger. New York: Harry N. Abrams, 1986, 219–235.

M. Paul Holsinger

THE LAST MEETING OF LEE AND JACKSON **(Painting).** One of the most copied icons of the defeated Southern cause, *The Last Meeting of Lee and Jackson*, or, as it was known originally, *The Heroes of Chancellorsville*, is a monumental painting of Confederate Generals Robert E. Lee and Thomas "Stonewall" Jackson astride their horses following the South's great victory at Chancellorsville, Virginia. The work of Everett B. D. Julio, the original oil painting measures a huge 12 feet, 10¾ inches by 9 feet, 7 inches.

Completed by the young artist at his studios in St. Louis in 1869, the painting failed to bring Julio the fame or fortune he was seeking. Lee refused the artist's offer of the painting as a gift, and when he attempted to sell it throughout the South, he found no buyers. In several cities, lotteries proposed to raise the necessary capital for the work failed. Julio's dream of becoming a great artistic chronicler of the history of the Confederacy came to a crashing end. When he died, at age thirty-six, worn out from his battle for financial solvency, the *Last Meeting* was sold to satisfy his debts.

Only belatedly was the high quality of Julio's work recognized, and today, prints of it can be found in almost every biographical study of Civil War leaders. Considered by critics to be one of the truly great heroic works of American martial art, the original painting now has a place of honor in the Museum of the Confederacy in Richmond, Virginia.

See:

Pennington, Estill C. *The Last Meeting's Lost Cause.* Spartanburg, SC: Hicklin, 1988.

M. Paul Holsinger

THE LITTLE SHEPHERD OF KINGDOM COME **(Novel-Films).** John Fox, Jr., was a capable war correspondent whose reports from Cuba during the Spanish-American War appeared regularly in ***Harper's Weekly***. Later, he sent back a number of fine accounts from Manchuria reporting on the Russo-Japanese War. It is as a novelist, however, that Fox is more often remembered. In the early years of the twentieth century, *The Little Shepherd of Kingdom Come* (1903) and *The Trail of the Lonesome Pine* (1906) both were hugely popular and endeared him to the American reading public, which clamored for his stories.

The Little Shepherd of Kingdom Come, a romantic tale set in Kentucky during the Civil War era, was a runaway best-seller. Within a year, it sold more than 1 million copies, making it probably the first American-published novel to do so. It tells the story of young Chad Buford, an isolated shepherd in the valley of Kingdom Come Creek, high in the Cumberland Mountains of Kentucky. When the war breaks out, he has to choose sides. Though a benefactor and the girl he loves both encourage him to support the South, he eventually throws his loyalty to the Union and later returns with federal troops to occupy the valley. Chad loses most of his friends as a result but knows that he has done the right thing. Eventually, he comes to see that he really loves his childhood sweetheart, and at war's end, they marry and settle far away from their former home.

In 1911, Fox's tale was dramatized by Eugene Walter and had a successful run on Broadway. There have also been at least three film adaptations of *The Little Shepherd of Kingdom Come*: (Samuel Goldwyn, 1920; First National, 1928; and 20th Century–Fox, 1961). The first version starred Jack Pickford; eight years later, Richard Barthelmess (probably the country's leading male romantic film star at the time) took the role of Chad. The most recent Cinemascope remake starred singer Jimmy Rodgers. Unfortunately, however, all three movies are bland and often deadly dull.

See:

Titus, Warren I. *John Fox, Jr.* New York: Twayne, 1971.

M. Paul Holsinger

THE LITTLEST REBEL **(Drama-Films).** On November 14, 1911, Edward Peple's four-act play, *The Littlest Rebel*, opened on Broadway with Mary Miles Minter (soon to be one of America's most popular silent film stars) in the role of seven-year-old Virgie Carey and the well-known William Farnum as her father. When the war begins, Carey becomes one of General Lee's most important spies, forcing his wife and little Virgie to take charge of the plantation and the always-happy slaves. When Mrs. Carey sickens and then dies, the captain sneaks through the lines to bury her and take his daughter to safety in Richmond. Arrested by Union troops who have been searching for him for months, he is granted a safe conduct pass by the enemy commander, Lieutenant Colonel Morrison, who has long been enchanted by Virgie's spunkiness. When Carey is captured a second time, however, both he and Morrison are sentenced to die, but at the last moment, Virgie intervenes with General Grant to save them. In 1914, shortly after its New York run, *The Littlest Rebel* was also made into a popular silent movie and novelized by E. S. Moffat (though his name appears nowhere except in Peple's foreword to the new book.)

After World War I, the play was forgotten until Darryl Zanuck cast the multitalented seven-year-old Shirley Temple (just recently voted the world's most popular film star) as Virgie in a clearly modified, musical version. The "new" *The Littlest Rebel* (20th Century–Fox, 1935) was scripted by Edwin Burke. Costarring with the great tap dancer Bill "Bojangles" Robinson (Uncle Billy), Shirley sings, dances, and charms even Abraham Lincoln, who dramatically pardons her father (John Boles) and Colonel Morrison (Jack Holt) in a typically happy ending.

The Littlest Rebel was a smash success, not only in the United States, but throughout the world. In Germany, even the Nazis, who had earlier banned all Temple films, showed this one enthusiastically. It received critical acclaim, and some students of motion pictures believe it to be the best work of Temple's fabled career. Seen today, however, it is simply embarrassing. Cloying and saccharine, the production is made even worse by frequent scenes featuring happy-go-lucky slaves who readily accept their lot and gaily sing and dance their lives away.

See:

Edwards, Anne. *Shirley Temple: American Princess*. New York: Morrow, 1988.
Spears, Jack. *The Civil War on the Screen and Other Essays*. South Brunswick, NJ: A. S. Barnes, 1977, 60–61.

M. Paul Holsinger

"LORENA" (Song). Sung to a lilting, sentimental melody by J. P. Webster, "Lorena" was arguably the best-loved song in the Confederate Army. Predating the war by four years, the lyrics by Webster's brother, Reverend H.D.L. Webster, mention nothing of war but concentrate, instead, on the agony that he felt after a woman he loved and to whom he had proposed married a more successful lawyer instead. Though never intended to appeal to troops on the battlefield, the mournful lament that "the years creep slowly by . . . since last I held [your] hand in mine," sentimentally touched thousands of homesick soldiers, even though the final stanza promised a reunion of the two sweethearts only after death. It was sung so often around campfires throughout the South that at times, it almost appeared to be a new national anthem. In response to the millions who found the piece so moving, the Websters later wrote "Paul Vane; or Lorena's

Reply'' in which the young woman promised that, although they were now separated, ''our souls could not be torn apart, dear Paul / They're bound together still.''

So popular did ''Lorena'' become during the war years that hundreds of Southern girls, several pioneer settlements, and even a steamship were named for the song's heroine. Lorena, Mississippi, and Lorena, Texas, still exist, as does the small town of Lorena, Kansas.

See:

Heaps, Willard, and Porter W. Heaps. *The Singing Sixties: The Spirit of Civil War Days Drawn from the Music of the Times.* Norman: University of Oklahoma Press, 1960, 235–236.

Randal W. Allred

''MARCHING THROUGH GEORGIA'' (Song). The announcement in late December 1864 that General William Tecumseh Sherman and his Union forces had split the Confederacy by marching from the burning ruins of Atlanta to the port city of Savannah, Georgia, was greeted in the North by tumultuous praise. Within days after Sherman had telegraphed President Lincoln to offer him Savannah as ''a Christmas gift,'' songwriters throughout the Union were penning lyrics to honor the audacious campaign. Undoubtedly the most popular of these was Henry C. Work's ''Marching through Georgia,'' which was published in early 1865. Southerners soon came to hate the five-stanza piece perhaps more than any other Yankee song written during the war years, but its popularity throughout the North was boundless.

''Marching through Georgia'' had an upbeat martial melody and patriotic lyrics that glorified the prowess of Sherman and his men in despoiling the land of its slaves and the foodstuffs needed to keep the rebellion alive. According to Work, ''the darkeys shouted when they heard the glorious sound,'' the now freed Union prisoners of war (POWs) ''wept with joyful tears / When they saw the honored flag they had not seen in years,'' but the ''saucy Rebels,'' ''treason'' personified, ''fled before us, for resistance was in vain.'' Though such phrases expressed what many Northerners clearly believed, Sherman personally disliked the song. Shortly before his death, the retired general told a reporter: ''If I had thought when I made that march that it would have inspired anyone to compose such a piece, I would have marched around the state'' (Bowman, 137).

Despite the hatred that it engendered, ''Marching through Georgia'' became an accepted classic in American patriotic music. Enthusiastically played by military bands through at least World War II, it remains a standard for secondary school, college, and university bands in the latter days of the twentieth century.

See:

Bowman, Kent A. *Voice of Combat: A Century of Liberty and War Songs, 1765–1865.* Westport, CT: Greenwood Press, 1987, 136–137.

Randal W. Allred

MARY CHESTNUT'S CIVIL WAR **(Autobiography).** Mary Boykin Miller Chestnut was the daughter of one of South Carolina's most outspoken proslavery governors and U.S. senators, James Miller, and the wife of another senator and one of the state's most wealthy men, James Chestnut, Jr. Far more important, she authored the most famous "diary" of life on the Southern home front to be written during the Civil War. Because of her family's social and political standing, Mrs. Chestnut was in Montgomery, Alabama, for the inauguration of Jefferson Davis; in Charleston, South Carolina, when Fort Sumter was attacked; and in Richmond, Virginia, while her husband served as an aide to Davis. She met most of the major military and administrative leaders of the Confederacy, and her insights into their character, coupled with her comments about life in the beleaguered South after 1861, make fascinating reading. Of the thousands of published collections of letters, journals, and diaries written in the South during the Civil War era, Chestnut's study, known for many years simply as *A Diary from Dixie*, has been, since its first printing in 1905, the most valuable in providing readers with a feminine perspective of the impact of the war.

Chestnut's work actually is not so much a diary as a collection of many different sources that focus on its author's memories of the past. It was not until 1881–1884, fully twenty years after most of the events about which she wrote, that Mary Chestnut took some of the journal entries she made during the war years and combined them with other notes and personal reminiscences to create the published work that everyone came to call her diary. In 1981, C. Vann Woodward edited a definitive version of her writings. Using all Chestnut's many journals, her other manuscripts, and the 1880s "diary," he created a monumental, 900-page, definitive account. *Mary Chestnut's Civil War* was an instant success and the 1982 Pulitzer Prize for history that it earned was unquestionably deserved.

See:

Woodward, C. Vann. "Introduction." In *Mary Chestnut's Civil War*, by Mary Boykin Chestnut. New Haven, CT: Yale University Press, 1981, xv–lviii.

M. Paul Holsinger

"MARYLAND, MY MARYLAND" **(Song).** After James Ryder Randall, a twenty-two-year-old teacher in a small college near New Orleans in spring 1861, read about the riots that took place in his hometown of Baltimore when volunteers from the North attempted to march through that city on their way to answer Lincoln's call for troops, he immediately sat down, almost in a fury, and wrote a nine-stanza poem calling on his fellow Marylanders to rise up against Union tyranny. The *New Orleans Delta*, one of the area's more influential newspapers, published "My Maryland" on April 26, and its fame soon spread. In Baltimore, Jeannie and Hetty Cary, two young sisters, realized that, with only a few minor changes, the lyrics perfectly fit the German folk air "O Tannenbaum." Charles Ellerbrock provided a formal arrangement, and the

Southern-sympathizing firm of Miller and Beacham published the new song, with its emotional plea for the state to secede from the Union and repel "the despot's heel" now on its shore.

Randall's lyrics left no doubt where he stood on the question of loyalty to Abraham Lincoln and the United States. After pleading for Maryland to rise up and join the other Confederate States of America, he triumphantly predicted:

> She is not dead, nor deaf, nor dumb
> Huzza! She spurns the Northern scum—
> She breathes, She burns! She'll come! She'll come!
> Maryland, My Maryland!

Northern sympathizers, of course, found such sentiments repellent and quickly offered a number of entirely different versions. One of the more popular was the Philadelphian songwriter Septimus Winter's "Answer to My Maryland," which included such lines as: "The Rebel horde is on thy shore . . . / Arise and drive him from thy door." A year later, at the time of Lee's invasion of the state, an anonymous, but extremely contentious, wag added yet another parody:

> The Rebel feet are on thy shore . . .
> I smell 'em half a mile or more . . .
> Their shockless hordes are at my door
> Their drunken generals on my floor
> Now what can sweeten Baltimore?
> Maryland, my Maryland!

Randall continued to write poems for the Confederate cause during the war, some of which became very popular throughout the South. During the later nineteenth century, he also became one of the South's more respected minor poets. Nothing he did, however, came close to the popularity of his first, most famous work. Today, having being modified to remove some of its more offensive prorebellion pleas, "Maryland, My Maryland" is the official song of that state.

See:

Harwell, Richard B. *Confederate Music.* Chapel Hill: University of North Carolina Press, 1950, 52–56.

M. Paul Holsinger

MATHEW BRADY STUDIOS (Photographers). The most important, and perhaps most brilliant, collection of visual images to come from the Civil War were the more than 3,500 photographs attributed to the Mathew Brady Photographic Studios between 1861 and 1865. Though it is now clear that Brady, who was legally blind when the war began, took few of the photographs himself (as most scholars initially gave him credit for doing), there is no way to overstate the importance of his company to the history of American warfare.

From the moment when Fort Sumter was attacked, the war became Brady's obsession. Although he took pictures of nearly all the important political and military figures (including most of the definitive poses of President Abraham Lincoln), it was on the battlefield that his studio's most significant work was done. An astute businessman, he quickly hired some of the best photographers in America—men like Timothy O'Sullivan and Alexander Gardner—and signed them to contracts that allowed him to claim credit for the prints they made. Though most of the photographers left before the war's end to become business rivals, the Brady Studios played the most important role, at least in the Northern states, in the creation of a permanent photographic record of the war.

Many public exhibitions were held at Brady's two studios. Besides bucolic campfire scenes, hundreds of images of death and gore from the battlefields were displayed. There were pictures of vast piles of corpses, dead horses, and wrecked wagons, all of which forcefully helped to bring home the chaos of war. It is hard to look at such devastating photos as those taken immediately after the Battle of Antietam on the "Sunken Lane" without being deeply moved. The Brady Studio's many shots and their impact on those who saw them were equivalent to the nightly scenes of body bags and endless carnage in Vietnam that were viewed on television by millions of citizens in the late 1960s.

Brady hoped to convince Congress to buy his prints at the end of the war, but his pleas went unheeded. As a result, much of the huge collection was divided and sold to pay off his debts and those of his studio. Some wound up in private hands; the majority eventually did become the property of the United States. Reproductions of some of the most famous of these have been used to illustrate books about the Civil War almost from the first day of peace in 1865. Every student of the war years is indebted to Mathew Brady for providing one of the most valuable visual records that exists for any of America's numerous conflicts.

See:

Horan, James D. *Mathew Brady: Historian with a Camera*. New York: Bonanza, 1950.

Randal W. Allred

MELVILLE, HERMAN (Poet-Writer). Herman Melville, who is today best known as the author of *Moby Dick* (1851), strongly believed "Secession, like Slavery, is against Destiny" (Robertson-Lorant 493), and incorporated this belief into his writing about the Civil War. Between February and July 1866, *Harper's New Monthly Magazine* published several of his war poems. These, plus some of Melville's other Civil War poetry and a prose piece he wrote about the problems of Reconstruction, were published in August 1866 as *Battle-Pieces and Aspects of the War*. Although *Harper's* reviewed the book favorably, it was dismissed or ignored by most other magazines and sold fewer than 500 copies in the following nine years. Considered a failure at the time, *Battle-Pieces* is now thought by many critics to rank, along with *Drum-Taps* by **Walt Whitman**, as the best poetry to come out of the war.

Melville has been called the "Brady of Civil War verse." His poetry reflects the modern technologies of war, gunboats, torpedoes, artillery, and the ironclad battleships. However, his concerns are not all mechanical. He writes of ordinary soldiers on both sides, slogging through mud and dodging shrapnel. He also presents Confederate soldiers as human beings who were misguided, but not evil. Some of Melville's views of the war were shaped by a visit he made to the front when he went on a scouting party with the Massachusetts Second Cavalry and helped to capture a half-dozen of Mosby's Raiders. Elements of his feelings about the war are reflected in such poems as "The Conflict of Convictions," "Sheridan at Cedar Creek," and "The March to the Sea."

See:

Garner, Stanton. *The Civil War World of Herman Melville.* Lawrence: University Press of Kansas, 1993.
Robertson-Lorant, Laurie. *Melville: A Biography.* New York: Clarkson-Potter, 1996.

Sally E. Parry

MEMORIAL DAY (National Holiday). Who first had the idea of setting aside a special day to remember the dead of the Civil War will probably never be known. In 1966, however, Congress officially proclaimed that the honor should go to Henry C. Welles, a druggist from the village of Waterloo, New York. During the fall of 1865, he suggested that the graves of Union Army dead in his hometown should be decorated with flowers, which was done for the first time the following May. Though there were earlier memorials both in the North and South, none appears to have called persistently for a systematic decoration of graves.

The idea of creating a national holiday to honor the dead soldiers of the Civil War (and later, all wars), is usually credited to General John A. Logan of Illinois. Logan, who commanded the Army of Tennessee under fellow Illinoisian Ulysses Grant, was the national commander of the Grand Army of the Republic (GAR), the national organization of Union Army veterans in 1868. Though it is also debated who was responsible for convincing him of the idea's merits—some suggest it was Mrs. Logan; others opt for the GAR's adjutant general, N. P. Chipman—Logan set aside May 30, 1868, as a special day of recognition and ordered every GAR post to spread flowers on the graves of their dead comrades. The practice caught on; in 1873, New York made it a state holiday. Soon most other states in the North followed suit, and Memorial Day, or Decoration Day, as it was often known for many years, was established.

Before 1971, Memorial Day was always celebrated on May 30 (though there appears to be no special significance to that particular date). Its coming marked the informal beginning of summer for millions of Americans. Many communities celebrated with picnics, parades, and even fireworks. In that latter year, however, Congress made the day one of several "Monday-only" holidays. Most states have opted to acquiesce in that decision, officially observing Memorial Day on the last Monday of every May no matter what the specific date might be.

See:

Myers, Robert J. "Memorial Day." Chapter 24 in *Celebrations: The Complete Book of American Holidays*. Garden City, NY: Doubleday, 1972, 159–164.

M. Paul Holsinger

***MISS RAVENAL'S CONVERSION* (Novel).** Hailed as the first work of American literary realism, *Miss Ravenal's Conversion from Secession to Loyalty*, a heavily autobiographical novel by John W. DeForest, was begun in 1864 while the author was a Union Army captain in Virginia's Shenandoah Valley. When Harper published the book three years later, the largely female, middle-class audiences were shocked to find a traditional sentimental romance coupled with uncompromisingly realistic scenes of battle gore and bloodshed. It was the latter that caused DeForest the most problems. To many readers, the battlefield horrors seemed inappropriate for the family drawing room. The book was poorly edited, and it soon vanished from public view. Only after its "rediscovery" seventy years later did it gain critical acclaim.

DeForest's novel tells the story of Southern belle Lillie Ravenal. She admires a young New Englander, Captain Edward Colburne, but after the war begins, she marries another Union officer, the dashing, yet immoral, Colonel [later General] John Carter. After his death in battle, she realizes that she loves Colburne, and they marry with the promise of a happy life ahead. Though *Miss Ravenal's Conversion* is clearly a love story, it is far more a story of war. DeForest does not try to spare his readers' sensibilities; one of the more horrific scenes describes an Army field hospital filled with "great pools of clotted blood amidst which lay amputated fingers, hands, arms, feet, and legs" (292). It was one thing for most Americans to read about war's supposed glories; it was quite another to consider the realities of everyday life and death.

Like John Bunyan in *Pilgrim's Progress*, DeForest uses allegory throughout his tale. Justifying the war as part of God's plan for America's redemption, he attempts to show, especially through Lillie's gradual education and conversion from supporting Southern sentiments to her embrace of more virtuous Northern tenets, that only through grief, deprivation, or chastening can persons' lives really be altered. The famous novelist William Dean Howells admired *Miss Ravenal's Conversion*, calling it "the best novel suggested by the Civil War" and DeForest one of "the masters of American fiction" (Turner, v). Sadly, at the time, few others agreed.

See:

Schaefer, Michael. *Just What War Is: The Civil War Writings of DeForest and Bierce*. Knoxville: University of Tennessee Press, 1997.
Turner, Arlin. "Introduction." In *Miss Ravenal's Conversion from Secession to Loyalty*, ed. John W. DeForest. Columbus, OH: Charles E. Merrill, 1969, v.

Wilson, Edmund. "The Christening of American Prose Style: John W. DeForest." Chapter 15 in *Patriotic Gore: Studies in the Literature of the American Civil War.* New York: Oxford University Press, 1962, 669–742.

Randal W. Allred

NAST, THOMAS (Artist). Undeniably the most famous political cartoonist in American history, Thomas Nast is renowned for his denunciatory caricatures of New York City's infamous William Marcy "Boss" Tweed. He was also the creator of the prototype for **Uncle Sam**, as well the Republican elephant and the Democratic jackass. During the Civil War, Nast was one of the most important artistic propagandists. President Abraham Lincoln reportedly noted on one occasion that "Thomas Nast has been our best recruiting sergeant. His emblematic cartoons have never failed to arouse enthusiasm and patriotism" (Keller, 13).

The son of a German regimental musician, Nast came to the United States with his parents in 1846. Frank Leslie, the publisher of *Frank Leslie's Illustrated Newspaper*, recognized his talent and hired him at age fifteen. The cartoons that made him famous began appearing in *Harper's Weekly* in 1859. Nast became a regular for *Harper's* early in 1862, and, for the rest of the war, his artwork supporting Lincoln and the Union often graced that magazine's front cover. His cartoons and other illustrations of fighting men on the battlefields of the South and women grieving on the home front were seen by millions.

Nast's artistic efforts always pictured Southerners as brutes capable of rape and pillage and Union men as saviors of the poor and downtrodden. During the presidential election campaign of 1864, the artist, who was an unabashed Republican Party supporter, worked hard for Lincoln's reelection. For at least the next twenty years, while continuing to espouse the "Grand Old Party" (GOP) and its programs, he remained the nation's most influential political cartoonist.

See:

Keller, Morton. *The Art and Politics of Thomas Nast.* New York: Oxford University Press, 1968.
Paine, Albert B. *Thomas Nast: His Period and His Pictures.* New York: Chelsea House, 1980.

M. Paul Holsinger

NORTH AND SOUTH **(Novel–Television Miniseries).** In November 1985 and May 1986, when ABC televised its versions of novelist John Jakes' *North and South* (1982) and *Love and War* (1984)—called *North and South Book II*—the twenty-four-hour adaptation was not only the most expensive miniseries ever filmed but also the longest. The epic begins by centering its attention on the antebellum relationship between two families, the Hazards of Pennsylvania and the Mains of South Carolina. The friendship of the families' two sons, George Hazard and Orry Main, is traced from their first meeting at West Point, through the Mexican War, and into the stressful 1850s as the nation moves recklessly toward war. The 1985 production ends with the attack on Fort Sumter. Part 2 picks up the tale and carries it through the remaining war years. Both Jakes's books and the two screenplays borrow heavily from D. W. Griffith's famous film, *The Birth of a Nation* (1915), which involves two families divided by borders and ideology. In an attempt to make the stories more palatable to contemporary audiences, multiple subplots and even a steamy interracial love affair were added. Producers David L. Wolper and Robert Papazian were praised for their insistence on using meticulously researched props and authentic period costumes (which won their designers Emmy awards in 1986), but the contrived plots, token treatments of race, and idealized portrayals of Southern plantation life guaranteed that, no matter how many million viewers watched each evening, the two series would be critical disasters.

Recurring roles are played by veteran performers such as Patrick Swayze, Kirsti Alley, David Carradine, Leslie Ann Downes, and David Ogden Stiers. There are also cameo performances by dozens of other Hollywood stars, from Jimmy Stewart and Linda Evans to Las Vegas singer Wayne Newton, who appears as a sadistic Confederate commander of a prisoner of war camp. Hal Holbrook takes the role of Abraham Lincoln; Lloyd Bridges is, strangely, but not ineffectively, cast as Jefferson Davis.

Critics savaged both *North and South* films, calling them "trash" (*People's Weekly* 24 [November 4, 1985]: 9) and "a turkey of . . . prodigious dimensions" (*Newsweek* 106 [November 4, 1985]: 81). The soap opera plots, frequent casual sexual encounters, and implausibility of much of the story add credence to such claims. Nonetheless, the war scenes (especially the last several hours' examination of the Battle of Petersburg), though sometimes stilted, are, in the main, well done and bear rewatching for the close attention to authentic military detail provided by a number of battlefield reenactment units.

See:

Cassidy, John M. "The Civil War and Television: The Blue and the Gray." Chapter 9 in *Civil War Cinema: A Pictorial History of Hollywood and the War between the States*. Missoula, MT: Pictorial Histories Publishing Company, 1993, 166–169.

Randal W. Allred

"OLD GLORY" (Symbol). "Old Glory" has become synonymous with the American flag; perhaps only the nickname "Stars and Stripes" is more commonly used. There are a number of accounts of how the name came into common usage, but all center around a Salem, Massachusetts, sea captain named William Driver. In 1831, as Driver and his crew were leaving for a round-the-world voyage, a group of local citizens gave him a nine-and-a-half-by-seventeen-foot flag to fly from his mast. That flag was, he told his men, "Old Glory," and from then on he continually referred to it by that name.

Years later, after retiring to Nashville, Tennessee, the captain flew the standard from his home on nearly all patriotic occasions. When Tennessee seceded from the United States in June 1861, however, Driver, hid his prized possession inside an old comforter and kept it safe there until the Union Army recaptured Nashville, on February 25, 1862. Then, carrying his flag downtown, he raised it over the state capitol. "Thank God," he is reported to have said, "I lived to raise 'Old Glory' on the dome of the Capitol of Tennessee; I am now ready to die and go to my forefathers" (Furlong and McCandless, 204–205). As the story spread throughout the North, "Old Glory" took on national meaning. Soon soldiers and citizens alike were referring to every U.S. flag by that name.

The original "Old Glory" remained in the Driver family until 1922, when the captain's daughter gave it to President Warren G. Harding. He, in turn, donated it to the Smithsonian Institution, and it remains a part of that museum's collections today.

See:

Furlong, William Rea, and Byron McCandless. *So Proudly We Hail. The History of the United States Flag*. Washington, DC: Smithsonian Institution Press, 1981.

M. *Paul Holsinger*

PHARAOH'S ARMY (Film). In few areas of America was the Civil War more savagely contested than in the Cumberland Mountains of Kentucky. Documentary filmmaker Robby Henson's first feature production—an intimate drama based on several true stories that he heard initially from local Kentucky oral historian Harry Caudill—highlights a small part of the bitterness. Written, directed, and produced by Henson in seven weeks for the bargain-basement cost of only $275,000, and shot entirely in the Kentucky mountains, *Pharaoh's Army* (1995) centers on two individuals: Sarah Anders, a mountain wife and mother whose husband is fighting for the Confederacy, and Captain John Abston, the leader of a small, ragtag group of Union Army troops foraging for food and supplies at the Anders's hard-scrabble farm in late spring 1862. An Ohio farmer before the war, the captain (Chris Cooper) finds himself drawn to Sarah (Patricia Clarkson) and her young son. He tries to help them plow their fields and do other chores, but nothing he does can ease the hatred she feels for him and all other enemy soldiers. She can never forget the ghoulish Union sympathizers who, only a few weeks earlier, dug up her only daughter's body from its grave, leaving it to be mauled by wild animals. Reconciliation is impossible, and in the end, only bloodshed is a solution.

Praised by critics when it was first shown on PBS television stations in October 1996, *Pharaoh's Army* is at times powerful, truthful, and undeniably real in its close look at how the rancor of the so-called brother's war could, and often did, destroy the lives of persons on both sides of the lines.

See:

Schodolski, Vincent J. " 'Army' Puts a Human Face on Civil War Hardship." *Chicago Tribune TV Week*, 20 October 1996 [early ed.], 5.

M. *Paul Holsinger*

"THE PRIVATE HISTORY OF A CAMPAIGN THAT FAILED" (Short Story–Film). In summer 1861, twenty-five-year-old Samuel Langhorne Clemens (or, as he soon became far better known, Mark Twain) and fourteen of his Hannibal, Missouri, friends went to war. Organizing themselves as the so-called Marion County Rangers, they set out to join others who were loyal to the Confederate States of America in order to repel the Union Army, which was then moving rapidly into their state. It was a ludicrous enterprise. For several weeks, Twain (the unit's duly elected second lieutenant) and the others camped out, went through the motions of training, and, whenever they heard of invading Union forces, quickly retreated; they engaged in no fighting at all. One evening they did shoot and kill a suspected Union sympathizer, but his death triggered a revulsion that quickly sent most of the men home for good.

Twenty-four years later, at the urging of Robert Underwood Johnson of *Century Magazine*, Twain told of his brief war experiences in a short story, "The Private History of a Campaign That Failed," which that periodical published in its December 1885 issue. It was republished as part of a collection of the author's short stories in *Merry Tales* (1892) and has been reprinted hundreds of times since. Though Twain was seriocomic in the telling, he left no doubt that he was ashamed to have served, even for so short a time. The stranger's death, perhaps at his hands (none of the youngsters knew whose shot actually killed the intruder), spoiled "my campaign," he wrote, "and I resolved to retire from this avocation of sham soldiering while I could save some remnant of my self-respect" (Rasmussen, 45).

In 1981, Peter H. Hunt resurrected Twain's tale and, in connection with Nebraska Educational Television, directed and produced a film version under the title, *A Private History of a Campaign That Failed.* The teleplay by Philip Reisman, Jr., follows Twain's account fairly closely. Only Hunt and Reisman's decision to make all the Rangers young teens instead of older men is glaringly at odds with the original story. A re-creation of Twain's staunchly antiimperialist "The War Prayer," written in 1899, at the time when the United States was attempting to crush the Philippine Insurrection, is awkwardly tacked on to the end, but it does not detract from the author's message of the foolishness, if not immorality, of combat. Simple and uncomplicated, the picture remains worthy of attention.

See:

Gerber, John. "Mark Twain's 'Private Campaign.' " *Civil War History* 1 (March 1955): 37–60.

Rasmussen, R. Kent. "The Private History of a Campaign That Failed." In *Mark Twain A to Z: The Essential Reference to His Life and Writings.* New York: Facts on File, 1995, 370–371.

M. Paul Holsinger

***THE RED BADGE OF COURAGE* (Novel-Films).** For a number of years in the early 1890s, *Century Magazine* published installments of the monumental

Battles and Leaders of the Civil War, a supposedly definitive account of war compiled from the memories of its participants. Reading these stories, Stephen Crane found himself frustrated. "I wonder," he later wrote, "that some of these fellows don't tell how they felt in those scraps! They spout eternally of what they did but they are as emotionless as rocks" (Linton, 37). He determined to write an account from a soldier's point of view; *The Red Badge of Courage* (1895) was the result.

Young Henry Fleming, a romantic and self-conscious Union soldier, panics in his first skirmish with the enemy. Running wildly away, he wanders aimlessly, trying to justify his actions. Eventually he makes his way back to his regiment, his head bloody from accidental contact with the rifle of another retreating soldier. Surprisingly, he is hailed as a hero because of that "red badge of courage." The next day, renewed by his comrades' support, he leads a charge and earns accolades from everyone.

Crane's novel is notable for its innovations. The ironic narrative framework, the psychological realism, and the impressionistic style clearly foretell the development of modernism in literary art. Though critics have long disagreed on how to interpret it (some prefer to think of it as little more than an honest account of a young boy's coming of age under pressure; others believe that Crane was attempting a far more complex study in egotism and self-delusion), the work quickly became a classic because readers found it easy to identify with Henry's insecurity and faltering self-image. He soon became one of American literature's most widely recognized and appreciated characters.

A severely cut version of *The Red Badge of Courage* (Metro-Goldwyn-Mayer, 1951), directed by John Huston, was brought to the screen with Audie Murphy (the most decorated U.S. soldier of World War II) as Henry Fleming. Though it was nominated for a British Academy Award as one of the year's best pictures, it was a dismal commercial failure in the US, and it soon faded from view. A 1974 NBC made-for-television production with Richard Thomas in the lead (copies of which are readily available on VHS), is far more faithful to the plot of the novel.

See:

Gibson, Donald B. *The Red Badge of Courage: Redefining the Hero*. Boston: Twayne, 1988.
Linton, Corwin K. *My Stephen Crane*. Syracuse, NY: Syracuse University Press, 1958.
Schoell, William. "Red Badge of Courage." In *The Great War Films from The Birth of a Nation to Today*, ed. Lawrence Quirk. New York: Citadel, 1994, 118–120.

Randal W. Allred

RICHARDSON, ALBERT (War Correspondent–Newspaperman). Albert Deane Richardson was reporting on "Bleeding Kansas" for several newspapers before the Civil War, but once the fighting began, this daring and reckless war journalist was sent to New Orleans as an undercover agent by the *New York Tribune*. Barely escaping capture, he soon became the *Tribune*'s chief war correspondent. He was later caught attempting to run a boat past the Confederate guns at Vicksburg, Mississippi, and spent nineteen months in a prison camp in Salisbury, North Carolina. Shortly before the end of the fighting, he escaped, fled overland, and safely reached Union lines after a number of harrowing near-tragedies.

In 1865, he published an account of his war adventures in a popular book: *The Secret Service, the Field, the Dungeon, and the Escape.* An avid Republican, he also wrote a campaign biography for General Ulysses S. Grant during the presidential campaign of 1868. He did not live, however, to see the general take office. Shortly after Grant's victory, Richardson, who had avoided death at the front many times, was shot and killed by a jealous rival.

See:

Andrews, J. Cutler. *The North Reports the Civil War.* Pittsburgh, PA: University of Pittsburgh Press, 1955.

Bullard, Frederick L. "Covering the American Civil War." Chapter 14 in *Famous War Correspondents.* 1914. Reprint. New York: Beekman, 1974, 375–408.

Randal W. Allred

RIFLES FOR WAITE (Young Adult Novel). Harold Keith's *Rifles for Waite* is one of the most highly praised young adult novels ever written about the Civil War. Voted the Newbery Medal as the "most distinguished contribution to American literature for children" when it was first published in 1958, it offers a unique look at the war years. With skill and a wealth of carefully researched detail, Keith turns his attention to the bloody conflict that existed in such western areas as Missouri, Kansas, and Oklahoma—areas often ignored by most writers, for whom Gettysburg or the Union attempts to capture Richmond take center stage.

The story centers on Jeff Busey, a sixteen-year-old Kansan who leaves home in 1861 to volunteer for the Union Army. Fighting with an infantry regiment in a number of important western campaigns, he eventually is transferred to the cavalry and assigned to scouting duty. On being captured by rebel troops, he pretends loyalty to the South and eventually is allowed to join the predominantly Native American forces under General Stand Waite, the chief of the Southern Cherokee Nation. While trapped in this ruse, for more than a year, he develops a sincere appreciation for the Cherokee and the rebel cause (a common element in fiction from this period). Eventually, Jeff discovers a conspiracy on the part of a corrupt Union officer to sell Spencer repeating rifles to the Confederates. Jeff escapes and foils the plot, saving the Union forces in the process. As the novel ends, he is planning to return to Indian Territory to marry an aristocratic, part-Cherokee girl with whom he has fallen in love.

See:

Sutherland, Zena. "Harold (Verne) Keith." In *Twentieth Century Children's Writers*, ed. Tracy Chavalier. 3rd ed. Chicago: St. James, 1989, 481–482.

Randal W. Allred

SAINT-GAUDENS, AUGUSTUS (Sculptor). Artist-sculptor Augustus Saint-Gaudens produced some of America's most important works of public art. The ten- and twenty-dollar gold pieces he designed for the U.S. Treasury, for example, are considered by many to be the most beautiful coins ever minted in this country. Even more memorable are his Civil War–related sculptures.

One of the earliest, a larger-than-life-sized rendition of Admiral David Glasgow Farragut (hero of the battle of Mobile Bay), is in New York City's Madison Park. Saint-Gaudens began the eight-foot-high bronze in 1878 and dedicated it three years later. The universal praise it received soon led to opportunities to design memorials in honor of Colonel Robert Gould Shaw, commander of the famous Fifty-fourth Massachusetts Colored Regiment, and General William Tecumseh Sherman. The huge Shaw Monument, though commissioned in 1884, was not dedicated until 1897. Featuring an equestrian Shaw flanked by sixty-five exquisitely accurate, full-sized members of his company, it sits opposite the State House in Boston and is one of the sculptor's most brilliant works. The equally impressive statue of Sherman has stood in New York's Grand Army Plaza since 1903.

Saint-Gaudens's full-sized statue of General John Logan during the Battle for Atlanta stands in Chicago's Grant Park. Mounted on his excited horse, the first commander of the Grand Army of the Republic grasps a partially unfurled flag minutes before leading his troops into combat. According to Saint-Gaudens, the design was intended to embody "the very incarnation of the warlike spirit" (Reedy, 235). Ironically, peace demonstrators during the 1968 Democratic Convention brought the statue its greatest fame when, protesting the war in Vietnam, dozens hung from it during daily rallies. Pictures of the scene made the front pages of most newspapers throughout the United States, giving Saint-Gaudens a type of recognition far different than any he could have imagined when the sculpture was dedicated in July 1897.

See:

Hofferber, Michael. "Bronze Heroes: Augustus Saint-Gaudens' Civil War Memorials."
    Civil War Times Illustrated 26 (November 1987): 32–37.
Reedy, James L. *Chicago Sculpture.* Urbana: University of Illinois Press, 1981.
Wilkinson, Burke. *The Life and Works of Augustus Saint-Gaudens.* New York: Dover,
    1992.

M. Paul Holsinger

SANITARY FAIRS (Events). The U.S. Sanitary Commission, whose purpose was to improve the sanitary conditions of the Union Army and supplement government issue to soldiers, was organized in June 1861 by a group of patriotic citizens. The most lucrative source of financial aid proved to be the Sanitary Fairs, which began in fall 1863 and continued during the rest of the Civil War.

Chicago was the site of the first fair, which was organized by Jane C. Hoge and Mary Livermore. Held from October 27 through November 7, 1863, it served as the prototype for those that followed. On opening day, all businesses and schools were closed and a parade three miles long concluded at the court-house square, where opening ceremonies then commenced. Food, entertainment, and exhibitions drew thousands of onlookers. The donations included needle-work, pianos, livestock, industrial products, real estate, and the original draft of the Emancipation Proclamation from President Lincoln. Net receipts from the fair far exceeded expectations.

The Chicago fair set off a chain reaction in Northern cities large and small. Patriotism snowballed as the fairs opened, one after another. President Lincoln and his family attended the Philadelphia fair, where he gave an address. An interesting feature of the Cincinnati fair was the sale of letters, documents, and manuscripts donated by famous personalities. Several fairs, including the one in Brooklyn, even sold fans, rings, and other handicraft items that were originally made by Confederate prisoners of war in exchange for tobacco. The New York fair garnered a multitude of gifts and donations from abroad; the Pope even sent $500. At the same fair, an event that received the most attention was the "sword-voting" contest in which people paid a dollar per ballot to vote for their favorite military hero.

The Sanitary Fairs drew cities and towns together in patriotic support for a hoped-for Union victory and also raised thousands of dollars in cash and sup-plies for the United States Army as hundreds of thousands of citizens united in a common cause.

See:

Thompson, William Y. "Sanitary Fairs of the Civil War." *Civil War History* 4.1 (1958): 51–67.

Carol Moots

SCOTT, JULIAN (Painter). No Civil War artist was more honored for his heroism than the often-brilliant Julian Scott. Enlisting as a fifer in the band of the Third Vermont Regiment in May 1861, when he was barely fifteen, he soon distinguished himself for his bravery in combat. At the Battle of Lee's Mills, during the Union Army's Peninsular Campaign against Richmond, the following spring, he risked his life repeatedly in the face of heavy Confederate fire to rescue his wounded comrades. So impressive was the feat that he was awarded the Medal of Honor, making him the first person in American military history to earn such a citation for an individual act of battlefield bravery. Severely wounded several weeks later in a skirmish outside the Confederate capital, he was permanently disabled and, in April 1863, honorably discharged from the service.

By that time, Scott had already begun to gain fame for his many drawings of Union soldiers at war. Partially crippled, he insisted on rejoining the Northern army as a combat artist. There he made dozens of sketches detailing, not only everyday army life, but also many highlights of the bloody conflict itself. Re-turning to New York City after General Lee's surrender in April 1865, he continued to put down, on both paper and canvas, his memories of the war. He was one of the first artists to combine photography and art to guarantee that his military scenes would be as realistic as possible. Working from pictures taken during the war as well as from many that he carefully posed himself, he was able to create some of the most stirring and most believable paintings to come from the era.

Today, Scott's works are found in museums and galleries throughout the United States, including the Smithsonian Institution in Washington, D.C. One of the best, *Colonel Robert Potter at the Battle of Burnside's Bridge, Antietam*, is part of the permanent collection of the U.S. Military Academy at West Point. Another work, a huge, ten-by-twenty-foot representation of the Third Vermont Regiment at the 1864 Battle of Cedar Creek in Virginia's Shenandoah Valley, is permanently displayed in the Vermont State Capitol in Montpelier.

See:

Titterton, Robert J. *Julian Scott: Artist of the Civil War and Native America.* Jefferson, NC: McFarland, 1997.

M. Paul Holsinger

SECRET SERVICE (Drama). William Gillette was one of the late nineteenth century's most astute actor-playwrights. Of his many plays, the most popular was *Secret Service: A Drama of the Southern Confederacy*, a four-act drama that premiered on Broadway in October 1896. The play tells the story of Lewis Dumont, a Northern spy posing as a Confederate officer in Richmond, Virginia, early in the Civil War. While stealing information from the South and sending it to the Union Army outside the city, Dumont (played originally by Gillette) falls in love with a loyal Virginian, Edith Varney. She returns that love and, when she discovers his true identity, offers to shield him so that he can escape. With a gentlemanly flourish he refuses, melodramatically opting to go to prison instead. Edith promises that she will wait for him, and the play ends with a hope for happier days ahead.

Viewed today, *Secret Service* seems dated and a little silly, but audiences at the end of the last century loved it. During its initial run, the play went through 176 performances, and over the next twenty years, it was brought back again and again to ever-increasing popularity. By 1915, it had been staged more than 1,700 times, making it the most popular drama ever put on the New York stage up to that time.

There were two screen adaptations of *Secret Service* (Paramount, 1919; RKO, 1931). The first was a stagey melodrama, and the second, which starred the extremely popular Richard Dix, was slow moving and old-fashioned.

See:

Quinn, Arthur Hobson. "Secret Service." In *Representative American Plays from 1767 to the Present Day*, ed. Arthur Quinn. 7th ed. New York: Appleton, 1953, 547–549.

M. Paul Holsinger

SHENANDOAH (**Drama-Film**). Bronson Crocker Howard, the first professional playwright in America who was neither a theater manager nor an actor, has been called "the dean of American Drama." His 1889 work, *Shenandoah*, a "typical" Civil War romance involving a Northern soldier and a young Southern beauty, may be the best drama focusing exclusively on the Civil War era ever written.

At its 1888 Boston preview, *Shenandoah* failed badly, but with changes, it began packing in audiences wherever it was shown. One of the central scenes that never failed to bring down the house used a live horse to re-create Sheridan's ride to rescue his troops in the Shenandoah Valley in 1864. William Dean Howells, the great American novelist, was charmed "from the first moment to the last" by the play. Other reviewers were equally enthusiastic. It initially ran for 250 performances, with regular renewals and good press for more than fifteen years. In the midst of the Spanish-American War, the martial spirit of the performances was so great that the New York *Dramatic Mirror* seriously suggested that a recruiting station be set up in the theater to enlist volunteers.

An epic screen version of *Shenandoah* (Kalem, 1913) was made, which originally ran for almost four and a half reels (fifty-four minutes). Filled with many panoramic shots and reminiscent of D. W. Griffith's later ***Birth of a Nation*** (1915), it was finally pared to only three reels on the assumption that movie audiences would be unwilling to sit for nearly an hour.

See:

Moody, Richard. "Shenandoah." In *Dramas for the American Theatre, 1762–1909*, ed. Richard Moody. Cleveland, OH: World, 1966, 567–574.

M. Paul Holsinger

SHENANDOAH (**Song-Film-Musical**). "Shenandoah," a popular song of the Civil War, provided the inspiration for the movie *Shenandoah* (Universal, 1965), which starred James Stewart as Charlie Anderson, a proud farmer who does not want his six sons to leave their farm in Virginia's Shenandoah Valley to fight for the South. He and his family oppose slavery but do not believe that the escalating Civil War is "their war," even when battles are being fought nearby and his daughter marries a Confederate officer.

All complacency is destroyed when the Rebels kill three family members and the youngest son is taken prisoner by the Yankees. The family's search for the boy and his efforts to get back home provide much of the drama in the beautifully photographed and sentimental film, which many critics saw as a warning about the futility and waste of war. *Shenandoah*, which also starred Doug McClure and Katharine Ross, was released during America's involvement in the Vietnam War, another conflict that pitted brother against brother. Directed by Andrew V. McLaglen, the picture was a box office success and clearly struck a chord with audiences.

James Lee Barrett, who wrote the screenplay for *Shenandoah*, also wrote the libretto for a musical version with music and lyrics by Gary Geld and Peter Udell. *Shenandoah* the musical opened on Broadway in 1975 starring John Cullum, who won a Tony award for his role as Charlie Anderson. It ran for 1,075 performances before finally closing.

See:

Cassidy, John M. "Many Are the Hearts: Family Struggles on Film." Chapter 4 in *Civil War Cinema: A Pictorial History of Hollywood and the War between the States.* Missoula, MT: Pictorial Histories Publishing Company, 1993, 68–76.

Sally E. Parry

SHERIDAN'S RIDE (**Poetry-Painting**). No single event caught the imagination of the public in the Northern states more forcefully than the famous twenty-mile ride of General Philip Sheridan during the Battle of Cedar Creek in Virginia's Shenandoah Valley on October 19, 1864. This turning of defeat into victory epitomized to many Americans the meaning of courage. The famous gospel hymn "Hold the Fort," which was written in 1874 by P. P. Bliss and sung at thousands of Protestant camp meetings for more than a hundred years, was supposedly inspired by Sheridan's message to his beleaguered forces: "Hold the fort. I am coming."

Long after the war was over, Sheridan's famous ride remained one of the greatest of all war-related stories. Much of the credit belongs to Thomas Buchanan Read, one of the late nineteenth century's most famous poets and painters. He was in Cincinnati when he saw Thomas Nast's picture of Sheridan on the front cover of the October 31, 1864, edition of *Harper's Weekly*. Several hours later, Read completed "Sheridan's Ride." Recited that same night at a local opera house by his close friend James Murdoch, the new poem's fame spread quickly. Within a week, it was published in Horace Greeley's *New York Tribune*. Though **Herman Melville** wrote another poetic account of the famous ride in 1866, Read's was the one most Americans took to heart. School children were required to memorize it, amateur theatrical companies performed it, and reunions of veterans insisted on having it read to their gatherings. It has continuously been in print; recently, a children's book publisher issued a glossy version, filled with many pictures.

In 1871, Read's equestrian portrait of the charging Sheridan also became an overnight success. Originally commissioned by the Union Club of Philadelphia, it was so popular that Read made sixteen additional copies, one of which was owned by Sheridan himself. Though there were a number of other artistic interpretations of the ride, Read's was unquestionably the best known and most praised.

See:

Ford, Harvey S. "Thomas Buchanan Read and the Civil War: The Story of 'Sheridan's Ride.' " *Ohio State Archeological and Historical Quarterly* 56 (1947): 215–226.

M. Paul Holsinger

"SHERMAN'S MARCH TO THE SEA" (Song). Union General W. T. Sherman's notorious march from the ruins of burning Atlanta to the Atlantic Ocean port of Savannah, Georgia, in the fall and early winter of 1864 was hailed by Northerners as one of the truly great moments of the entire Civil War. Though Southerners were appalled at the Union forces' destructiveness, the general's telegram to President Lincoln announcing the latter city's capture seemed to everyone on both sides of the battle lines to signal the beginning of the end of a conflict that had taken too many lives.

After reading about the general's great success in a newspaper smuggled into his Columbia, South Carolina, prison cell by a loyal Negro slave, Lieutenant Samuel H. M. Byers composed a poem in its honor. Another prisoner, Lieutenant J. C. Rockwell, set "Sherman's March to the Sea" to music (though the number was sung more often in latter years to the old Irish melody, "Rosin the Bow," to which the lyrics fit almost perfectly). The completed song was then smuggled out of the prison and taken to the Union Army, which was hurrying toward South Carolina; it quickly became popular. When Byers and Rockwell were freed after Sherman captured Columbia, they supposedly heard their rescuers happily singing their new composition. More than 1 million copies of the sheet music were eventually sold. Though Henry Work's **"Marching through Georgia"** (which also dealt with the notable victory) became even more renowned, Sherman always claimed that he liked the Byers-Rockwell song better. Ironically, Lieutenant Byers, who had accepted five dollars for his rights to the song, never received any other remuneration.

"Sherman's March to the Sea" (the title and lyrics gave the campaign its popular nickname) was memorized by Union schoolboys in the years after the war. Its five stanzas offer a short and simple account of the fighting in Georgia. From the moment when "a rider comes out of the darkness" yelling "Boys! Up and be ready / For Sherman will march to the sea" until the successful culmination of the campaign, the narrative account is inspiring and patriotic. The Union wins, "the traitor flag falls," "and the stars on our [the Union] banners shone higher / when Sherman marched down to the sea."

See:

Heaps, Willard, and Porter Heaps. *The Singing Sixties: The Spirit of Civil War Days Drawn from the Music of the Times.* Norman: University of Oklahoma Press, 1960, 345.

M. Paul Holsinger

SHILOH **(Novel).** The Nobel prize–winning American author William Faulkner thought Shelby Foote's 1952 novel *Shiloh* to be "the damnedest book I have ever read [but] one of the best." Though unusually short (less than 150 pages) and unbalanced in point-of-view (there are seventeen different narrators), it is also brilliantly written and historically accurate, even in the most minute detail. Foote is one of the nation's finest storytellers. His repeated appearances in the

1990 Ken Burns–produced PBS miniseries *The Civil War* captivated millions of American viewers; his three-volume *The Civil War: A Narrative History* (1958) has long been recognized by many critics as the best written study of the military side of the war for modern readers. Those same characteristics shine through on every page of *Shiloh*.

It is a nineteen-year-old Southerner, Lieutenant Palmer Metcalfe, an aide to General Albert Sidney Johnston, who both opens and ends the narrative. As the battle near the tiny village of Pittsburg Landing, Tennessee, begins, the young Louisianan sees no reason to doubt that Confederate forces will annihilate Grant's northern army, yet by the last pages, which find him weary but miraculously unharmed, he is left to admit that the Confederates have been badly "whupped." In between those two sections, Foote lets his reader hear from various participants, including a Union captain, a young Confederate rifleman, a cannoneer from Minnesota, a scout with Colonel Nathaniel Bedford Forrest's rebel cavalry, and all twelve members of a rifle squad from Indiana. Their accounts, when combined into a whole, provide an eclectic, but comprehensive, view of the Shiloh battlefield during the first week of April 1862.

There is no attempt to spare readers the horrors of combat. Ohioan Walter Fountain is blown to bits by an exploding rebel cannonball shortly after writing his wife a love letter, and Private Luther Dale from Mississippi retreats with only a bloody stump where his left arm had been. Bodies are piled in heaps, one on top of the other, in common, unmarked graves, with no attempt made to identify the dead

Some years ago, Foote claimed that novelists and historians seek the same thing but go about reaching it differently (219–225). In *Shiloh*, he sought to tell the story of that famous 1862 battle and did so admirably. It may not be, as many critics have said, "the best novel of the Civil War," but it qualifies unquestionably as one of the best.

See:

Foote, Shelby. "The Novelist's View of History." *Mississippi Quarterly* 17 (Fall 1964): 219–225.

Phillips, Robert L. *Shelby Foote: Novelist and Historian.* Jackson: University of Mississippi Press, 1992.

White, Helen, and Redding S. Sugg, Jr. *Shelby Foote.* Boston, Twayne, 1982.

M. Paul Holsinger

"SOMEBODY'S DARLING" (Song). "Somebody's Darling," one of the most popular sentimental songs written during the Civil War, was penned early in the war by a young woman from Savannah, Georgia. Marie Ravenal de la Coste brought her poem to musical publishers in her home city. They, in turn, sent a copy to the South's most famous composer and balladeer, John Hill Hewitt, hoping that he would set it to music. After he did so, the new song became an instant hit, and the demand for sheet music far exceeded the supply.

The four verses of de la Coste's poem tell the tearfully sentimental story of a young unknown soldier, "somebody's darling," who is brought into a hospital ward and surrounded by others who have been "wounded by bayonets, sabres and balls." Soon, "still and cold," he is destined only for a "wooden slab over his head," but listeners are cautioned to remember that "somebody's watching and waiting for him / Yearning to hold him again to her breast." "Drop on his grave a tear," the final verse requests, and carve on his marker: "somebody's darling is slumbering here."

No single song written during the Civil War had more musical settings than "Somebody's Darling." Though Hewitt's tune was always the most popular, the lyrics were set to another Southern version by A. C. Matheson and to fully eight different melodies in the North as well.

See:

Silber, Irwin. *Songs of the Civil War.* New York: Columbia University Press, 1960, 121, 145–147.

M. Paul Holsinger

STONE MOUNTAIN MEMORIAL. In 1915, the United Daughters of the Confederacy awarded noted sculptor Gutzon Borglum the commission for a massive carving of Robert E. Lee on the side of Stone Mountain outside Atlanta, Georgia. Overwhelmed by the size of the granite outcropping, Borglum soon persuaded his benefactors to allow him to carve, not only an enormous, full-length image of the great Confederate general, but also additional portraits of Stonewall Jackson and Jefferson Davis. Over the next several years, he continued to expand his vision, at times projecting as many as 2,000 figures in the finished composition. By 1917, he had scaffolding covering more than 500 feet of the mountain and planned to extend it to almost a ½ mile wide and 800 feet high.

Work was halted during World War I, and Borglum did not return to the mammoth project until 1923. By that time, expenses had drastically risen, and the Ku Klux Klan (KKK), which had been reborn on Stone Mountain in 1915, dominated the memorial association. Though Borglum completed a twenty-one-foot-high head of Lee to great acclaim in 1924, he was fired the following year and replaced by a Southerner, Augustus Lukeman. At the behest of the KKK, Lukeman stupidly blew up his predecessor's work and started anew. When his efforts were terminated in 1928 for lack of funds, there was nothing but "an ugly scar" on the mountain.

Not until 1963 did the state of Georgia, which was now in control of Stone Mountain, finally bring in two sculptors, Walker Hancock and Roy Faulkner, to complete some of the original plans. In 1970, the basic central section envisioned by Borglum, a 90-by-190-foot-high equestrian portrait of Lee, Jackson, and Davis riding together, was dedicated. Today the memorial has become a major tourist attraction in the Atlanta area. One can only speculate how much greater it could have become had Borglum, who went on to create the great stone faces on South Dakota's Mount Rushmore, been allowed to make his grandiose dreams a reality.

See:

Freeman, David. *Carved in Stone: The History of Stone Mountain*. Macon, GA: Mercer University Press, 1997.

M. Paul Holsinger

"STONEWALL JACKSON'S WAY" (Song). Joel Williamson Palmer, a war reporter for several New York newspapers, accompanied the Army of Northern Virginia to Maryland in fall 1862 and was at the fateful battle of Antietam (Sharpsburg). Filled with awe at the commanding presence of Virginia's General Thomas "Stonewall" Jackson, Palmer penned words of praise to that officer and his "way" in battle. Jackson's forcefulness, his ability to motivate his troops no "matter if our shoes are worn[,] . . . [no] matter if our feet are torn," his religious piety, and his understanding of his enemies all receive lavish glorification. Palmer leaves no doubt that Jackson's troops will succeed because "the foe had better ne'er been born / That gets in Stonewall's way."

The poem became so popular that within a few months, it was transformed into a rollicking march by the Confederate forces. Until Jackson's untimely death the following year, after the battle of Chancellorsville, it was apparently sung with regularity. Possibly set originally to the music of Stephen Foster's "Camptown Races," today the song is more often heard with a different tune whose author is unknown.

See:

Harwell, Richard B. *Confederate Music*. Chapel Hill: University of North Carolina Press, 1950, 75–77.

M. Paul Holsinger

"TENTING ON THE OLD CAMP GROUND" (Song). Walter Kittredge wrote "Tenting on the Old Camp Ground" in 1863, shortly after receiving his draft notice to serve in the Union Army. Though he was later exempted (rheumatic fever suffered as a boy made him physically ineligible) and never fired a shot, his plea for peace and an end to "this weary war" remained one of the best and most popular of all Civil War songs.

Before the war, Kittredge was a member of one of the several Hutchinson Family singing groups that toured the United States. When his new composition was rejected by a publisher who wanted a more martial air, it was natural for him to offer it to his former colleagues. Asa Hutchinson, the leader, was instantly enthusiastic about "Tenting," and after the singers presented it in a series of concerts, he persuaded one of America's largest sheet music publishers to print copies. It was a huge success, earning Kittredge and Hutchinson (who split the royalties) the then-munificent sum of more than $1,000 each within less than two years. Though melancholy in places ("we are tired of the war on the old camp ground / many are dead and gone'') and totally black in others (''we've been fighting today on the old camp ground / many are lying near / some are dead and some are dying / many are in tears''), the song mirrored the growing antiwar sentiment.

Some Northerners found Kittredge's sentiments too depressing, and a number of variations were written to counter its negativity. ''We're Tenting on the Old Camp Ground'' by J. W. Turner even tried to inject an upbeat tone (''our hearts are light and joyous ever / we think of home / we talk of friends / and happy times together''), but his variation failed to gain any appreciable popularity.

''Tenting on the Old Camp Ground'' had appeal on both sides of the lines. Union troops sang its often hopeless words wistfully as they waited for the next battle, and Rebel soldiers found Kittredge's lyrics expressive of their often-demoralized feelings in the latter days of the war.

See:

Heaps, Willard, and Porter W. Heaps. *The Singing Sixties: The Spirit of Civil War Days as Drawn from the Music of the Times.* Norman: University of Oklahoma Press, 1960, 159–162.

Randal W. Allred

"TRAMP! TRAMP! TRAMP!" (Song). As the Civil War stretched on and thousands of men on both sides were captured and imprisoned under frequently unsanitary, overcrowded conditions, those on the home fronts worried endlessly about them. Songwriter George F. Root was quick to focus on that anxiety. Written in 1863 and published the following year by the author's own Chicago firm of Root and Cady, ''Tramp! Tramp! Tramp! or The Prisoner's Hope'' expresses a Yankee captive's feelings:

> In the prison cell I sit, thinking mother dear, of you
> And the bright and happy home so far away
> And the tears they fill my eyes, spite of all that I can do
> Though I try to cheer my comrades and be gay.

There is no doubt that already ''the boys are marching.''

> [Soon] they will come
> And beneath the starry flag
> We shall breathe the air again
> Of the free land in our own beloved home.

So universally popular was Root's song that Southerners wrote their own words. In one version, Union forces at some unspecified battle were ''driven back dismayed'' while ''the Rebel yell went upward to the sky.'' It was impossible to avoid the always pervasive gloom, however: ''In the cruel stockade-pen / Dying slowly day by day / For weary months we've waited all in vain,'' the lyrics intone. Only the Almighty appears to hold the answer: ''But if God will speed the way / Of our gallant boys in gray / I shall see your face, dear mother, yet again.''

See:

Silber, Irwin. *Songs of the Civil War*. New York: Columbia University Press, 1960, 13–14.

Randal W. Allred

VIZETELLY, FRANK (War Correspondent–Newspaperman). Some of the most accurate, on-the-scene depictions of the American Civil War, from both sides of the battle lines, were done by English artist Frank Vizetelly. In May 1861, the *Illustrated London News* sent him to the United States to draw and report on the growing war between the North and South. Initially attaching himself to the Union Army, he witnessed the disastrous First Battle of Bull Run. His picture of the "stampede" of the Northern troops, which showed them in disarray, was subsequently printed in the *News* along with his comments about "this disgraceful rout for which there is no excuse" (Cochran, 454), helped convince many British observers of the seeming inability of the Union to win. Vizetelly remained with the Northern forces for the next year and a half, observing and sketching scenes in Virginia, along the Mississippi River, and finally in Memphis, Tennessee, after that city was captured by Union troops.

After being denied official correspondent's credentials in 1862, Vizetelly secretly worked his way across the Potomac River and joined General Robert E. Lee's Army of North Virginia. He stayed in the South for the rest of the war; he was in Vicksburg, Mississippi, during that city's siege and in Charleston, South Carolina, when it was shelled by Union batteries. Though his illustrations were always done for the *News*, a number of Vizetelly's works also wound up being published in Northern periodicals after they were intercepted and seized from a blockade runner on its way to London.

After the war, Vizetelly returned to England, where his drawings were used to illustrate Heros von Borcke's *Memoirs of the Confederate War for Independence* (1866). Like many of today's best news photographers, he continued to follow wars wherever they occurred. This eventually proved to be his undoing; in 1883, he and an entire garrison of British troops were massacred in Egypt.

See:

Cochran, Robert T. "Witness to a War: British Correspondent Frank Vizetelly." *National Geographic*, April 1961, 452–491.

Hoole, William Stanley. *Vizetelly Covers the Confederacy*. Tuscaloosa: University of Alabama Press, 1957.

M. Paul Holsinger

WALKER, JAMES (Artist). James Walker was one of the most prominent contemporary painters of battlefield scenes during both the Mexican and Civil Wars. Born in Great Britain but raised in New York during most of his early years, Walker became trapped in Mexico City at the outbreak of the U.S. war with Mexico in 1846. After being liberated the following year, he joined the United States Army as an interpreter and soon began portraying some of the major events of the war on canvas. Though predominantly a landscape artist, his paintings of the Mexican War remain among the handful of carefully rendered views from that conflict. Congress purchased his huge *Storming of Chapultepec*, which was completed around 1857, for permanent display at the Capitol.

Walker's paintings of the Civil War come in all shapes and sizes, though he is best known for panoramic scenes of several of the major engagements after 1863. A huge re-creation of the Battle of Lookout Mountain, for instance, was commissioned by Union General Joseph Hooker and, though it was later adapted into a considerably smaller version, remains one of the most significant artistic views of that important battle in the West. Walker's most famous work captures the last minutes of General George Edward Pickett's charge at Gettysburg on July 3, 1863. Within days after General Robert E. Lee and his Confederate troops retreated south, Walker visited the battlefield with Colonel John Badger Bachelder, the official congressional historian of the battle. He walked the fields and interviewed a number of participants before he started to paint. Not until 1868 was the work (formally called *The Battle of Gettysburg: Repulse of Longstreet's Assault, July 3, 1863*), completed. Engraved copies were issued in 1870 and circulated widely throughout the United States.

See:

McNaughton, Marian R. "James Walker–Combat Artist of Two American Wars." *Military Collector and Historian* 9 (1957): 31–35.

M. Paul Holsinger

THE WARRENS OF VIRGINIA (Drama-Films). One of the most popular plays of the early twentieth century was William C. deMille's *The Warrens of Virginia*. Remotely based on the 1865 capture of one of deMille's grandfathers, the drama, like so many of the era, features a young Southern heroine (Agatha Warren), the daughter of a Confederate general, and her sweetheart (Ned Burton), who fights for the North. Captured (purposely in order to mislead the rebel officials into thinking that the false documents he is carrying are real) and sentenced to die, he is spared at the last minute by Lee's surrender and melodramatically reunited with his beloved. Staged on Broadway by the great director David Belasco, the four-act production opened in December 1907 to smash reviews and continued playing for well over a year before going on tour for several more months. Included in the cast were deMille's younger brother, Cecil (later to be one of Hollywood's most famous movie directors), and a young Canadian, Gladys Smith, who was just now beginning to use her new stage name of Mary Pickford.

The Warrens of Virginia (Lasky Pictures, 1915) was made into one of the most realistic war films of its day. Directed by Cecil DeMille (who, unlike his brother, always capitalized the "D" in his family name), and starring Blanche Sweet as Agatha and House Peters as Ned, the motion picture emphasized the suffering brought on by war rather than its glory. One of the most dramatic scenes shows a desolate field covered with corpses, which lie, supposedly, as they fell in battle. With photography by Alvin Wyckoff, one of the great innovators in the new, but rapidly expanding, field of cinematography, the film, though overshadowed by D. W. Griffith's *The Birth of a Nation*, remains one of the best silent movies to deal with the Civil War. A remake of *The Warrens of Virginia* (Fox, 1924) directed by Elmer Clifton, on the other hand, has little to recommend it.

See:

Higashi, Sumiko. *Cecil B. DeMille and American Culture: The Silent Era.* Berkeley: University of California Press, 1994.

M. Paul Holsinger

WAUD, ALFRED (Artist). Alfred Rudolf Waud was arguably the most popular and talented artist working for *Harper's Weekly* during the Civil War. He started his war work for the *New York Illustrated News* in July 1861, producing several front-page pictures for that periodical. Late that year, he joined illustrator **Theodore Davis** as a field artist for *Harper's*. To Davis, a fine artist in his own right, Waud was the best illustrator of the Civil War. In 1862, a reporter for the London *Daily Telegraph* described him as "blue-eyed, fair-bearded, strapping and stalwart, full of loud cheery laughs and comic songs, armed to the teeth, jack-booted, gauntleted, slouch-hatted" (Hodgson, 82).

Particularly known for his battle scenes, Waud was not afraid of being close to the action. He was shot at several times during his attempts to observe and draw the battle lines. He was also popular with members of the military; they liked his aggressive demeanor and desire to be at the front lines, and they allowed him free access to the battles. Early in the war, he accompanied General Irvin McDowell's march on Richmond and quickly sketched the battle at Bull Run before retreating Union soldiers forced him to flee. General George Gordon Meade was so impressed with Waud's keen eyesight that he used him as an observer on occasion. He was the only correspondent Meade allowed to accompany his advance at Raccoon Ford. He also was the sole artist to go ashore with the troops during the capture of Fort Hatteras in North Carolina.

Waud's most popular and extensive works were produced while he was with the Army of the Potomac. He was the most prolific of the Civil War artists, producing over 340 drawings for the *Illustrated News* and *Harper's*. After the war, he returned to the South to chronicle Reconstruction, and continued sketching and illustrating for the remainder of his life.

See:

Hodgson, Pat. *The War Illustrators.* New York: Macmillan, 1977.
Ray, Frederic E. *Alfred R. Waud: Civil War Artist.* New York, Viking, 1974.

Thompson, William Fletcher, Jr. *The Image of War: The Pictorial Reporting of the American Civil War*. 1960. Reprint. Baton Rouge: Louisiana State University Press, 1994.

Michael Brown

"WE ARE COMING, FATHER ABRA'AM" (Song). When the Union Army failed to crush the rebellious Confederacy after more than a year of fighting, President Abraham Lincoln (in summer, 1862), was forced to issue a call for 300,000 more volunteers. In response, James Sloan Gibbons, a New York Quaker abolitionist, quickly penned "We are Coming, Father Abra'am." "Sturdy farmer boys . . . from Mississippi's winding stream to New England's rocky shore," the martial poem promised the president, would soon be joining the fight, glad for the opportunity "our Union to restore."

The words, which were printed originally in William Cullen Byrant's *New York Evening Post*, were at first attributed to that famous editor-poet. The poem quickly became popular and was reprinted so many times with Bryant's name as author that he was finally forced to issue a public disavowal, specifically giving credit to Gibbons.

Songwriters, including Stephen Foster, rushed to set the verses to music, but the version that became the best known and most sung was written by Luther Orlando Emerson, a composer of Protestant religious hymns. Confederate writers soon gave a different slant to "We Are Coming." One of the most vicious variations denounced Lincoln as a despoiler of the free South and included the lines:

> There's blood upon your garments
> There's guilt upon your soul
> For the host of ruthless soldiers
> You let loose without control.

See:

Heaps, Willard, and Porter W. Heaps. *The Singing Sixties: The Spirit of Civil War Days as Drawn from the Music of the Times*. Norman: University of Oklahoma Press, 1960, 89–92.

M. Paul Holsinger

"WEEPING, SAD AND LONELY" (Song). "Weeping, Sad and Lonely" (or as it was sometimes known, "When This Cruel War Is Over") was unquestionably the most popular song during the Civil War to focus on how that conflict separated sweethearts everywhere. With lyrics by one of the most successful of the era's songwriters, Charles Carroll Sawyer, and a sentimentally mournful tune composed by Henry Tucker, it was, according to one contemporary Northern newspaper, "the greatest success ever known in this country" (Silber, 117). With slightly modified words, it was equally popular in the South.

A woman who has sent her lover off perhaps to fall "amid the din of battle" does not doubt that what he is doing is righteous and just:

> Nobly strike for God and liberty
> Let all nations see
> How we love our starry banner
> Emblem of the free.

At the same time, she laments the gulf that separates them:

> Weeping, sad and lonely
> Hopes and fears how vain!
> When this cruel war is over
> Praying that we meet again.

A number of anonymously written variations of "Weeping, Sad and Lonely" served to make the song acceptable throughout the Confederacy. After calling on angels to guide those "Southern boys" who were fighting, one of the more popular added:

> When you strike for God and freedom
> Let all nations see
> How you love our Southern banner
> Emblem of the free.

Melodic responses to the lyrics were soon heard on both sides of the battle lines. In the South, there was "Wait Till the War, Love, Is Over," as well as John H. Hewitt's "When upon the Field of Glory: An Answer to When This Cruel War Is Over." Northern contributions included "Yes, I Would the War Were Over" by the popular songwriter Septimus Winter (using the pseudonym Alice Hawthorne), "When the War Is Over, Mary," and "Mother, When the War Is Over."

See:

Silber, Irwin. *Songs of the Civil War.* New York: Columbia University Press, 1960, 117–118, 124–127.

Randal W. Allred

"WHEN DEY 'LISTED COLORED SOLDIERS" (Poetry). Unquestionably, the most popular African-American poet in white America at the end of the nineteenth century was Ohio-born Paul Laurence Dunbar. This son of former slaves published his first book of poetry in 1893 and followed it up with a number of other volumes, including the best-selling *Lyrics of Lowly Life* (1896), which was praised by the American novelist William Dean Howells. During his short publishing career, Dunbar frequently used "Negro" dialect to emphasize the gulf that existed between white society and the economically deprived African-Americans.

A number of Dunbar's best poems center on the years of slavery or the heady days when the U.S. government began to recruit African-American soldiers for the Union Army. "The Colored Soldiers," for instance, seeks to

[S]ing a song heroic
Of those noble sons of Ham
Of the gallant colored soldiers
Who fought for Uncle Sam!

"The Unsung Heroes" also looks closely at the almost 10 percent of the Union Army that was black, many of whom "feared the master's whip but did not fear the fight," and who often died to protect their newborn freedom.

It is Dunbar's dialect poem "When Dey 'Listed Colored Soldiers" that is perhaps his most famous tribute to the men of color who fought and died for freedom and the Union. Told by a young slave whose "loved un" volunteered for the Union Army and went to war, it contrasts the white masters in their gray suits and her 'Lias, "in his coat o' sojer blue." Her pride at first knows no end. God, she feels, has called him to war, but, inexorably, both master and slave die, 'Lias "way down souf . . . wid de flag that he had fit for shinin' daih acrost his breas.' "

Dunbar wondered if such deaths were worth the sacrifice. As he watched legal segregation settle over the nation, he questioned whether colored soldiers who in 1865 "were comrades then and brothers" were any "less today." In "Robert Gould Shaw," a poem dedicated to the white commander of the famed Fifty-fourth Massachusetts Colored Regiment, he was even more pessimistic. There, a telling line laments both Shaw and "those who with thee died for right . . . but in vain!"

See:

Best, Felton O. *Crossing the Color Line: A Biography of Paul Laurence Dunbar, 1872–1906.* Dubuque, IA: Kendall-Hunt, 1996.

                                                                    M. Paul Holsinger

"WHEN JOHNNY COMES MARCHING HOME" (Song). One of America's most famous band directors in the days immediately before, during, and certainly after the Civil War was Patrick Sarsfield Gilmore. In 1861, he and his entire band enlisted in the Union Army, and the music they provided was an important boost to soldiers throughout the war years. Gilmore's greatest contribution to the war, however, was "When Johnny Comes Marching Home," which was written in summer 1863 while he was serving as the army's bandmaster in New Orleans. Though it was originally published under the pseudonym "Louis Lambert," its popularity led Gilmore to claim authorship even before the war ended.

Musicologists debate the origin of "Johnny's" melody. Some maintain that it is an old Irish tune; others believe that Gilmore, who was born and raised in Ireland, may have taken bits and pieces of Irish folk music and built an entirely new song. In either case, it provided martial music for both sides during the war. New lyrics were frequently added to fit a particular situation. For example, a version for badly wounded veterans included the thought, "And if they lost a leg, the girls won't run / For half a man is better than none."

When "Johnny Comes Marching Home" continued to be heard frequently in every subsequent war. It was sung and played so often during the Spanish-American War of 1898 that it probably became the single most popular song of that conflict. It also was one of the favorite patriotic pieces of World War I and was often sung during World War II as well.

See:

Olson, Kenneth E. *Music and Musket: Ballads and Bandsmen of the American Civil War.* Westport, CT: Greenwood Press, 1981.

                                                                 M. Paul Holsinger

WHITMAN, WALT (Poet). Noted American poet and journalist (not to mention carpenter, schoolmaster, nurse, and government clerk) Walt Whitman wrote more extensively about the Civil War than any other poet. *Drum-Taps*, a collection of twenty-eight poems that look closely at the human cost of war, is the most famous of Whitman's war-related works. Initially printed in 1865, it was later incorporated as a part of Whitman's ever-evolving masterwork *Leaves of Grass* and expanded a number of times with each edition. Probably the most anthologized poem from the collection, "Cavalry Crossing a Ford," is noted for its imagery and excellent versification. In the volume, Whitman ranges widely from first-person narratives of the march to requiems for the fallen dead. His attitudes toward the war cover a wide spectrum of emotions, from blind patriotism ("First Songs for a Prelude"), to the urgency of recruiting ("Beat! Beat! Drums!"), the despair at the many early Union losses ("Year that Trembled and Reel'd Beneath Me"), and even grief ("Come Up from the Fields, Father").

Whitman's best-known Civil War poems are those dedicated to Abraham Lincoln: "When Lilacs Last in the Dooryard Bloom'd" and "O Captain! My Captain!" both of which were written in spring 1865 and initially published in a twenty-four page "Sequel" to *Drum-Taps*. The former, which is often praised as Whitman's best poem, notes the irony of Lincoln's death occurring in springtime, when the ending of the war seemed to present so much promise of renewal. Though obviously, the "battle-corpses . . . and white skeletons of young men" who perished in the war were beyond further suffering, how, Whitman wondered, can the living continue in the face of such loss? A similar theme is struck in "O Captain! My Captain!" As the captain of a victorious ship enters its harbor amid the cheers of the crowd, the dying leader falls stricken to the deck, just as Lincoln had done at the very moment of national jubilation.

The remainder of Whitman's Civil War–related writing can be found in his *Memoranda during the War Days* (1875) and the essays in *Specimen Days* (1882). Nearly all his Civil War poetry and prose is permeated with notes of deep despair, in contrast to the more optimistic, democratic vision that is seen in *Leaves of Grass*. If some poets applauded the North's victory as a means to heal the country's sectional bitterness, Whitman considered it a permanent wound, which had not only divided brother from brother in the past but was destined to continue to do so in years to come.

See:

Reynolds, David S. *Walt Whitman's America: A Cultural Biography.* New York: Knopf, 1996.

Randal W. Allred

7

Indian Wars West of the Mississippi, 1862–1890

Once the United States Army completed the task of driving most of the various Native American tribes west of the Mississippi River (in the years before 1840), its contacts with the Indians were few. With the exception of the ongoing Seminole Wars in southern Florida, which continued into the 1850s, there was little need for the U.S. government to be concerned about the many tribes in the Far West, whether they were Sioux, Comanche, Cheyenne, or even some of the Mandan peoples that Lewis and Clark encountered during their trek to the Pacific Ocean in 1803–1805. Not until the opening of the famous Oregon and Santa Fe Trails in the early 1840s did more than a handful of white men and Indians come in direct contact with one another. The Mexican War and the subsequent California Gold Rush in 1849, however, exacerbated racial tensions. As settlers passed through, or began to claim, Indian lands, the issue became, as Thomas Jefferson had described slavery years earlier, "a fire bell in the night."

The first major confrontation between the United States Army and the Native American tribes of the West took place on the Minnesota frontier when the Sioux of that region went on the warpath in summer 1862. Bloodily crushed, with their captured leaders executed in one of the largest mass hangings in American history, the remaining Sioux were forced farther west. As they moved away from their homes, their bitterness festered; soon, the frontier, from the northern Great Plains to southern Texas, was aflame. Wagon trains of settlers were waylaid, and homesteaders throughout the West were killed. The white military retaliated. At the infamous Sand Creek Massacre, in fall 1864, Colorado Volunteers overran a peaceful Arapahoe community in the southeastern portion of that territory and slaughtered hundreds of tribesmen and -women, who had hoisted an American flag in deference to their pledge of peace.

The end of the Civil War brought tens of thousands of new settlers into the West. The Homestead Act (passed by Congress in 1862) allowed for white settlement and the development of lands throughout the western territories, with no consideration of whether those lands might be in any way Indian. With the discovery of gold and silver in California, Colorado, Nevada, and then, during the Civil War, places such as Idaho and Montana, the threat of bloodshed became even more pronounced. In 1866, Sioux warriors under Red Cloud trapped more than eighty army troopers stationed in eastern Wyoming at Fort Phil Kearny and, led by a young warrior named Crazy Horse, killed them all, in the so-called Fetterman Massacre. Two years later, however, the brashly confident Lieutenant Colonel George Armstrong Custer and troops under his command attacked a Southern Cheyenne camp on the Washita River in present-day Oklahoma and massacred hundreds of the "enemy." For the next twenty-two years, though there were occasions of relative peace between the Indians and the white settlers—the United States repeatedly forced the different tribes to sign treaties that required them to settle down peacefully on specially set-aside reservations—the underlying tensions between the two races continued unabated.

Hundreds of books have been written analyzing, in minute detail, the many campaigns and the individual battles between the various native peoples and the forces of the United States. Four particular series of events stand out. In 1874, Custer and his men confirmed the discovery gold in the Black Hills of present-day South Dakota. Though that area was a religious sanctuary for the Sioux, the moment word leaked out, the white men's rush to discover the "mother lode" began. When the Indians went on the warpath once again to protect their sacred lands from destruction at the hands of greedy miners, the army believed it had no choice but to attempt to drive them back to their reservations. The running series of confrontations during the next year culminated in the infamous Battle of the Little Big Horn in eastern Montana on June 25, 1876. There, more than 5,000 Sioux, Cheyenne, and Arapahoe warriors met and slaughtered a force of less than 300 United States Seventh Cavalrymen under Custer. It was the high watermark of the Indian quest for self-control. Over the next months, however, the army systematically tracked down the Indian foes on the northern Great Plains. Sitting Bull, a Sioux medicine man, managed to escape across the borders into the Dominion of Canada, accompanied by a handful of his followers. The war chief Crazy Horse was not as fortunate, however. Defeated and physically exhausted, he and his fellow Sioux surrendered to the army at western Nebraska's Fort Robinson. Less than a week later, he was dead, having been killed after he refused to consent to imprisonment.

That same year (1877), a second Indian war began between eastern Oregon's Nez Perce and the United States Army, which was attempting to protect white miners searching for gold in the region. The Nez Perce refused to be sent away and, when it became clear they had no choice, they began an impossible, 1,600-mile trek to the freedom of Canada, where they hoped to began anew. Fighting repeated battles with troops trying to stop them, they came within miles of the border. In early October 1877, however, their leader, Joseph, was forced to capitulate. His statement of surrender, "From where the sun now stands, I will fight no more forever," has become one of the honored quotes in American history.

Far to the south, in the deserts and mountains of southern Arizona, the United States found itself facing some of its more formidable foes: the Chiricahua Apaches, led first by the formidable Cochise and then, later, by the even fiercer Geronimo. For nearly twenty years, the Chiricahuas rejected attempts to corral them on reservations. The Apache Wars of the early 1870s were among the nation's most gory. Finally, through brute strength and a large dose of deceit, General Nelson Miles was able to bring about Geronimo's surrender in 1886 with the promise that he and his warring people would be allowed to live in peace on their own lands. It was, of course, a lie, and the majority of the Apaches were soon forcibly relocated more than a thousand miles away. Geronimo died years later, not in his native Southwest, but on a small farm in Oklahoma.

The last major gasp for the Native American peoples came in 1890. The army and others from the U.S. government had been systematically slaughtering the buffalo on the Great Plains for years in the hope that, once the great herds no longer roamed freely, the various native tribes would have to settle down. When, after dancing the so-called Ghost Dance, which they hoped would bring back the buffalo, many of the Sioux in South Dakota broke out of their reservation, the army moved to crush them once and for all. There is still much debate about who deserves the blame for the infamous Wounded Knee Massacre, but in any case, when it was over, more than 300 native men, women, and even small children had been slaughtered.

There have been few events in American history that have interested the public more than the Indian Wars west of the Mississippi River during the last decades of the nineteenth century. Fictional and historic books, poems, films, magnificent artwork, sculpture, television series, and more have continually reminded us of that vital part of our past. In the latter days of the nineteenth century, for instance, the many fictional works of Captain Charles King that focused on the West were always best-sellers, with their descriptions of how the cavalry rode and, eventually, bested the marauding native peoples. Today, ironically, those same "villains" have, in many cases, become heroes. It is the Indian peoples rather than the soldiers who defeated them that the majority of Americans now hold up as models of bravery and courage against overwhelming odds. We remain fascinated by General George Custer, but we build a gigantic memorial to Crazy Horse, his opponent at the Little Big Horn. Patriotic, flag-waving pot-boilers such as Hollywood's 1942 paean to Custer, *They Died with Their Boots On*, have now been replaced in popularity by such pro-Indian films as the Academy Award–winning *Dances with Wolves*. The times, as the renowned rock writer-singer Bob Dylan noted in the 1960s, clearly are "a-changin'."

See:

Dunn, J. P. *Massacre of the Mountains: A History of the Indian Wars of the ar West, 1815–1875*. New York: Archer House, 1965.

Potomac Corral of the Westerners. *Great Western Indian Fights*. Lincoln: University of Nebraska Press, 1970.

Utley, Robert M. *Frontier Regulars: The United States Army and the Indian, 1866–1891* Lincoln: University of Nebraska Press, 1984.

THE BATTLE AT ELDERBUSH GULCH **(Silent Film)**. D. W. Griffith, one of America's renowned movie directors, will always be intimately connected with the most influential silent motion picture during the early years of the twentieth century, *The Birth of a Nation*. Two years earlier, however, he had also directed *The Battle at Elderbush Gulch* (Biograph, 1913), one of Hollywood's earliest attempts at accurately depicting warfare between Indians and white men in the Far West. Opening in the United States on March 28, 1914, the two-reeler was an immediate popular success, just as it had been in Great Britain when Griffith premiered it in late 1913.

Filmed in California's San Fernando Valley, with the beautiful Lillian Gish and Mae Marsh as its two stars, when seen in the harsh light of hundreds of subsequent western cinematic productions, the picture appears trite and unimaginative. It recounts how, when the son of a local Indian chief is accidentally killed by a white settler, the tribesmen, in their fury, attack the tiny village of Elderbush Gulch and graphically massacre many of the community's men, women, and children. In the ensuing melee, a young mother (Gish) and her small toddler are separated. She is hysterical, but another woman, played by Marsh, risks her own life to rescue the child. Alerted by a settler who manages to get to the nearby army post, the cavalry arrives dramatically and saves the day, and the film ends on as happy a note as possible.

Critics in 1914 thought *The Battle at Elderbush Gulch* ''one of the finest battle pictures ever made'' (Niver, back cover). In retrospect, at the end of his long, distinguished career, Griffith also ranked it among his best work. Like most silent films today, however, it is rarely seen and, sadly, even less appreciated.

See:

Niver, Kemp R. *D. W. Griffith's The Battle at Elderbush Gulch*. Los Angeles: Locare, 1972.

M. Paul Holsinger

BLACK ELK SPEAKS **(Autobiography-Drama)**. In fall 1930, John G. Neihardt, a narrative poet then in the midst of his long work, *The Song of the Indian Wars*, came to South Dakota's Pine Ridge Reservation hoping to interview some of the older Sioux men who remembered the days of the Ghost Dance and the massacre at Wounded Knee forty years earlier. He was directed to Black Elk, one of the great medicine men of the Oglala Sioux. Though Black

Elk had long refused to talk to most white men, he accepted Neihardt and, from early 1931 onward, allowed the poet to record his account of Sioux history and culture. *Black Elk Speaks, Being the Life Story of a Holy Man of the Oglala Sioux*, was published in 1932 and became, not only the primary authoritative study of the Sioux religious heritage, but also one of the few Indian accounts of warfare on the northern Great Plains.

At thirteen, Black Elk took part in the Battle of the Little Big Horn, along with his second cousin, Crazy Horse. He was at Nebraska's Fort Robinson the following year when Crazy Horse was killed, and in the winter of 1890, he was injured at Wounded Knee as he and some of the younger men attempted to fight back against the overwhelming might of the cavalry. His brief, almost poetic description of that later fight and the slaughter by U.S. troops of unarmed old men, women, and children is one of the most poignant in print.

A one-act play, *Black Elk Speaks* (1995), was adapted by Christopher Sergel from the pages of Neihardt's book.

See:

Steltenkamp, Michael F. *Black Elk: Holy Man of the Oglala.* Norman: University of Oklahoma Press, 1993.

M. Paul Holsinger

BROKEN ARROW (Novel–Film–Television Series). *Blood Brother*, a fine historical novel by Elliott Arnold about the real-life friendship between the famed Chiricahua Apache chieftain Cochise and the white Army scout Tom Jeffords, was published in 1947. Panoramic in its scope, *Blood Brother* covers, often in great detail, the conflict between the United States Army and the Apaches from 1858 to Cochise's death in 1874.

Three years later, Hollywood director Delmar Daves used Arnold's novel to make *Broken Arrow* (20th Century–Fox, 1950). Longtime actor Jimmy Stewart played Jeffords, and Jeff Chandler played Cochise. Tensions build, though Jeffords tries to help create harmony between the two sides. In an attempt to appeal to feminine viewers, Stewart finds "true love" with a young Indian girl, played by Debra Paget. The screenplay received an Academy Award nomination, as did Chandler, for best supporting actor. Neither won, but Chandler became so intimately connected in viewer's minds with Cochise that he reprised that casting in two later films: *Battle at Apache Pass* (1952) and *Taza, Son of Cochise* (1954).

Audiences nearly fifty years ago packed theaters to see *Broken Arrow*, and most critics liked it. Seen today, however, the production is disappointing. Historical facts are muddled or purposefully altered, and, though the cinematography offers beautiful scenery and some good action sequences, there is little else to recommend it. Certainly the choice of two white performers to play the most important Native American roles, though typical of Hollywood at the time, is particularly offensive.

In 1956, the film version was developed into a regular weekly television series on ABC. This show, which starred John Lupton as Jeffords and Michael Ansara as Cochise (Chandler had died suddenly in 1954), ran for two years, with reruns shown in spring and summer 1960 as well.

See:

Manchel, Frank. "Cultural Confusion: *Broken Arrow* (1950)." In *Hollywood's Indian. The Portrayal of the Native American in Film*, ed. Peter C. Rollins and John E. O'Connor. Lexington: The University Press of Kentucky, 1998, 91–106.

M. Paul Holsinger

BUGLES IN THE AFTERNOON (Novel-Film). Long before he died in 1950, devotees of western Americana recognized Ernest Haycox as one of that genre's most distinguished novelists and short story writers. The popularity of such exciting works as *The Wild Bunch* (1943) continues to keep Haycox accepted as one of a select handful of "great" authors in the field. Of his many works, however, none has been so well received as the carefully researched *Bugles in the Afternoon* (1944), a fictional account of the Seventh Cavalry in the days immediately before and during its defeat at the Battle of the Little Big Horn. Originally published as a serial in the *Saturday Evening Post* at the height of World War II, it remains one of the strongest fictional interpretations of the army's Sioux Campaign of 1876 available in print.

Bugles in the Afternoon tells the story of former Union Army Lieutenant Kern Shafter, who, being sick of civilian life, reenlists in the Seventh Cavalry as a private in fall 1875. Though Haycox focuses on the young man's readjustment to the military at Dakota Territory's Fort Abraham Lincoln, the best sections of the book are those that deal directly with the cavalry itself in the months immediately before the Great Sioux War. There is a thoughtful picture of army life on the frontier as officers and enlisted men alike prepare for the inevitable battles they know are coming. Haycox's Custer (unlike Hollywood's more recent version, the Errol Flynn–recreated "Boy General" in 1942's *They Died with Their Boots On*) is arrogant and, ultimately, willing to lead his men to a senseless death rather than tarnish his own image. Now a sergeant, Shafter, of course, does not die in the battle. Assigned to Reno's command, he is badly wounded but lives to be recommissioned once again.

Eight years after its appearance as a novel, *Bugles in the Afternoon* (Warner Brothers, 1952) was transformed into a mediocre motion picture starring Ray Milland as Kern. The screenplay, by Geoffrey Homes and Harry Brown, tries to follow the novel closely but the film is disappointing and offers little except an appropriately bloody re-creation of Reno's fight at the Little Big Horn.

See:

Tanner, Stephen. *Ernest Haycox*. New York: Twayne, 1996.

M. Paul Holsinger

BURY MY HEART AT WOUNDED KNEE (Oral History–Drama). Dee (Alexander) Brown wrote seventeen nonfictional studies and eight novels during his long career. Though most focused primarily on Indian-white relations in the years after the Civil War, only one, *Bury My Heart at Wounded Knee. An Indian History of the American West*, was a blockbuster hit. First published in January 1971, it had gone through thirteen different printings by October of that year. The Book-of-the-Month Club, the Playboy Book Club, and even the Popular Science Book Club issued separate editions, while the Des Moines, Iowa, *Register-Tribune* syndicated it nationally. Critics were ecstatic, using such terms as "first rate," "noble," and "powerful" to describe it. Long before it appeared in paperback, Brown's history had become the number one best-seller in the United States. More than a million hardcover copies of the book were sold, along with several million more paperbacks

Bury My Heart tells the story of the far western expansion of white Americans after 1860 from a Native American point of view. Brown employs both written and oral records and, whenever possible, uses the actual words of the Indians themselves. "This is not a cheerful book," he writes in his introduction, "but history has a way of intruding upon the present, and perhaps those who read it will have a clearer understanding of what the American Indian is, by knowing what he was."

Though critical praise for *Bury My Heart* was at first universal, some conservatives later found the book flawed. Calling it "revisionist history," they denounced Brown's seeming refusal to interpret any of the disputes except from the Indians' side of the issue. Others objected that there was nothing new in the book, since all the material was readily available previously. Such charges did little to diminish the volume's enormous popular support. No other work did more after the early 1970s to awaken Americans' interest in Native American life and culture than *Bury My Heart at Wounded Knee*.

In 1973, parts of *Bury My Heart* were arranged dramatically for theater production by the Indian playwright Man-Who-Stands-Looking-Back. It is still occasionally staged today.

See:

Hagan, Lyman B. *Dee Brown*. Boise, ID: Boise State University Press, 1990.

M. Paul Holsinger

CHEYENNE AUTUMN (Nonfiction-Film). After the Civil War, the United States Army attempted to force the Indian tribes of the Far West to settle peacefully on reservations, which were often far from their ancestral lands. Such was the case of the Northern Cheyennes, who were given a small plot in the Indian Territory of present-day Oklahoma, more than 1,500 miles from their home along the Yellowstone River. In September 1878, 278 sick and half-starved Cheyennes, under the dual leadership of chiefs Little Wolf and Dull Knife, left their arid reservation and headed back to Wyoming. Many died along the way, but before those who were still alive surrendered, more than 10,000 United States Army troops were called to the Great Plains in an attempt to stop them.

The story of these brave men, women, and children, as well as that of their conquerors, was eloquently told by Mari Sandoz in the excellent nonfiction study, *Cheyenne Autumn* (1953). One of the finest chroniclers of the life of the great Sioux warrior Crazy Horse, Sandoz writes with great compassion, understanding, and respect for the Cheyennes. Unfortunately, the same cannot be said for director John Ford and the screenwriters who supposedly used Sandoz's book as the basis for a big-budget Hollywood film, *Cheyenne Autumn* (Warner Brothers, 1964). Ford had depicted Indians in such earlier films such as **Drums along the Mohawk** (1939), **Fort Apache** (1948), and **She Wore a Yellow Ribbon** (1949) as vile and brutal savages. Though some critics noted a softening of attitude in the director's view toward the Cheyennes, they still appear as little more than stick figures. Ford so grossly manipulates the facts that he makes a mockery of the bravery of the peoples he supposedly means to honor.

Entirely filmed in Monument Valley, Arizona (hundreds of miles from the actual scene of the Indians' journey north), *Cheyenne Autumn* is sterile, with little or nothing to recommend it. Its stars, Richard Widmark and Carroll Baker, portraying a cavalry officer and a Quaker missionary to the Cheyennes, respectively, are wooden and just barely believable. Heavy coloring makes the skin of Gilbert Roland and Ricardo Montalban, neither of whom is Native American, look dark enough that they can try to portray the two leaders of the escaping Indian peoples, though neither is convincing. The film does include a few sympathetic scenes of the Indians' hardship, but just as much time is spent on a long and inappropriate slapstick segment apparently designed to allow Ford to showcase a number of big-name stars such as Jimmy Stewart in the role of Wyatt Earp and Arthur Kennedy as Doc Holliday.

Cheyenne Autumn's Academy Award-nominated cinematography by William H. Clothier is well worth studying. In the main, however, it is a movie best forgotten.

See:

Place, J. A. "Cheyenne Autumn." Chapter 16 in *The Western Films of John Ford*. Secaucus, NJ: Citadel Press, 1974, 228–246.

M. Paul Holsinger

CRAZY HORSE MONUMENT. When it is completed, perhaps by the year 2050, the largest equestrian statue in the world will honor Crazy Horse, the great war chief of the Oglala Sioux who conquered George Armstrong Custer at the Battle of the Little Big Horn. Located in the Black Hills of South Dakota, seventeen miles south of Gutzon Borglum's presidential carvings on Mount Rushmore, the Crazy Horse Monument was the dream of sculptor Korczak Ziolkowski. Ziolkowski won first prize at the New York World's Fair in 1939, and the award brought him to the attention of several Sioux chiefs, including Henry

Standing Bear, who asked him to carve a monument to Crazy Horse. The sculptor agreed and, after working for a short while with Borglum at Mount Rushmore to get a feel for carving on such a grand scale, he determined to turn an entire mountain into his statue.

Because of the advent of World War II, Ziolkowski was unable to begin fulfilling his dream until 1948, but for the rest of his life, he devoted himself tirelessly to the gigantic project. Since his death in 1982, his wife, Ruth, and his ten children have continued the work. The monument, when completed, will be 141 feet long and 563 feet high. It will show Crazy Horse sitting proudly on his horse with his arm outstretched and his finger pointing to the lands of the Sioux nation being stolen by white men. More than 8.3 million tons of rock have been removed from the mountain so far, and as of summer 1997, the nine-story-high profile of the great Indian chieftain was slowly becoming clear. In June 1998, fifty years after the first blast, the face of Crazy Horse was dedicated.

More than a million visitors annually have, for years, made the site a major tourist attraction. The money raised from admission fees has helped fund this private monument as well as provided thousands of dollars in scholarships for young Indian students in the area.

See:

Dewal, Robb, ed. *Korczak: Storyteller in Stone.* Crazy Horse, SD: Korczak's Heritage, 1994.

                                                    M. Paul Holsinger

DANCES WITH WOLVES (Film). In 1988, screenwriter Michael Blake wrote *Dances with Wolves*, a first novel about the last free days of the Comanche Indians on the plains of Texas. Published originally in paperback, the book initially received little critical attention, but, two years later, it was transformed into one of the era's most popular films. Starring actor-director Kevin Costner, *Dances with Wolves* (Tig/Majestic, 1990), not only won the Academy Award for best motion picture but also became the year's top-grossing movie, taking-in more than $184 million. Costner, working from a script written by Blake, gained a second Oscar for best director.

Centered on the life of Lieutenant John W. Dunbar, a wounded Civil War veteran (played convincingly by Costner), the film is set at an isolated outpost in South Dakota (the locale was purposely moved hundreds of miles north of the novel's original location so that the movie makers could incorporate the nation's largest bison herd as an integral part of the picture). Dunbar, who comes to love the wilderness, gradually integrates himself into a nearby tribe of Lakota Sioux; in the end he fights with them against a murderous troop of fellow white soldiers sent to crush out the Sioux and corral them on a reservation. Through his portrayal of Dunbar, Costner laudably seeks to rewrite Hollywood's overwhelmingly negative treatment of all Native Americans. So pleased were the Sioux with the result that they made him an honorary member of their tribe.

The overall critical reaction to *Dances with Wolves*, in spite of its obvious good intentions, remains ambivalent and, in some cases, quite hostile. Though most reviewers were willing to grant Costner at least qualified praise for creating a film that is uncharacteristically sympathetic to the Native American perspective, they frequently took him to task for over-sentimentalizing the lifestyles of the Lakota. They also pointed out the numerous historical inaccuracies as well as the actor-director's simplistic, melodramatic approach to an extremely complex subject. As valid as these objections are, however, they cannot diminish the movie's real emotive power.

Dances with Wolves's willingness to take a new look at the historical past inspired, almost single-handedly, a new cycle of "revisionist" westerns, most notably Clint Eastwood's 1992 Oscar-winning *Unforgiven*. Such pictures instantly evoke, yet simultaneously subvert, nearly all the genre conventions of earlier American frontier films.

See:

Castillo, Edward D. "Dances with Wolves." *Film Quarterly* 44.4 (Summer 1991): 14–23.
Costner, Kevin, Michael Blake, and Jim Wilson. *Dances with Wolves: The Illustrated Story of the Epic Film.* New York: Newmarket, 1990.
Ostwalt, Conrad. "*Dances with Wolves*: An American *Heart of Darkness.*" *Literature Film Quarterly* 24 (1996): 209–216.

Philip L. Simpson

A DISTANT TRUMPET (Novel-Film). Paul Horgan's exceptionally well-crafted fictional and nonfictional works gained him two Guggenheim Fellowships and two Pulitzer Prizes for history, but it was his often powerful novel about military life in Arizona during the 1880s that first brought him to the attention of the mass of American readers. Based heavily on events during the fifteen-year running war between the United States and the Apaches, *A Distant Trumpet* (1960) is centered around young Matthew Carlton Hazard, a recent West Point graduate (and Horgan's fictional representation of the United States Army's heroic Lieutenant Charles B. Gatewood). Assigned to "Fort Delivery" in the southern part of the territory, Hazard must learn, not only to accept the strictures of military life in an entirely new and desolate environment, but also how to deal with an enemy unlike any found in the many books of soldiering he had studied. These tensions underlie all the plots and subplots of *A Distant Trumpet*.

When the tale opens, Hazard has just refused to accept the Medal of Honor and has resigned from the army. Readers are drawn into an account of heroism that sees the war with the Apaches, not so much in terms of absolute good versus evil, but rather in shades of ambiguous gray. Many of Hazard's superiors prove to be duplicitous; indeed, a number of the Apache enemies are far more honorable than their white counterparts. Showing himself sympathetic to the Native American peoples (especially the loyal Apache scout White Horn, whose arrest precipitates Hazard's decisions), Horgan avoids stereotyping any of the combatants, offering instead a fair and balanced picture of a bloody time in the nation's past.

Critics were mixed in their reviews, with some praising the novel as one of the finest ever written about the American Southwest and others seeing it as overly long and "tedious." Readers, however, quickly made it a best-seller, with more than 600,000 hardcover copies and six different paperback editions in circulation by the end of the decade.

A big-screen adaptation, *A Distant Trumpet* (Warner Brothers, 1964), starring Troy Donohue, Suzanne Pleshette, and Diane McBain, was a dismal failure when it tried, unsuccessfully, to appeal to a wider female audience by amplifying a romantic triangle to which the novel's author had paid short shrift. It bears little resemblance to Horgan's far-superior work of quality fiction.

See:

Dippie, Brian W. "Jack Crabb and the Sole Survivors of Custer's Last Stand." *Western American Literature* 4 (1969): 189–202.
Gish, Robert. *Paul Horgan*. Boston: Twayne, 1983.

M. Paul Holsinger

***FORT APACHE* (Film).** *Fort Apache* (Argosy/RKO, 1948) is the first film in director John Ford's famous horse soldier trilogy, which recounts crucial moments in the careers of officers (portrayed in each movie by John Wayne) serving on the trans-Mississippi frontier with the United States Army Seventh Cavalry. It was followed in succeeding years by *She Wore a Yellow Ribbon* (1949) and *Rio Grande* (1950).

Starring Henry Fonda and John Wayne and featuring Victor McLaglen, Ward Bond, Shirley Temple, and John Agar, *Fort Apache* (based on "Massacre," a story by James Warner Bellah), recounts an ill-fated attack on an Apache war party by the stiff-necked, self-aggrandizing Colonel Owen Thursday (played very successfully, against type, by Fonda). Embittered at being assigned a frontier command instead of a politically advantageous posting in Washington, D.C., Thursday does not hide his contempt for the seedy, battle-hardened cavalry-men serving under him. He ignores the prudent advice of Captain Kirby Yorke (Wayne) and leads his regiment into an Apache ambush, where he proves himself as brave as he is wrong-headed. After the massacre, which costs Thursday his life, Yorke takes temporary command and defends the honor of the regiment by encouraging newspaper correspondents to memorialize Thursday as a hero rather than the stubborn incompetent that he really was.

To Ford, myths of national heroism, even if they were at odds with the facts of history, were essential to preserving America's social unity and cultural identity. *Fort Apache* strongly reflects that belief. Equally important, perhaps, is the portrait of Yorke, who represents one of those myths. In *Stagecoach* (1939), Ford cast John Wayne as the classic western hero, the self-sufficient loner who embodies a nineteenth-century version of American individualism. In the horse soldier films, the resolutely independent frontier hero gives way to the loyal military professional who places the good of his organization above personal concerns. It was this latter role that was instrumental in transforming Wayne's screen persona into that of the archetypal American hero.

See:

Place, J. A. "Fort Apache." Chapter 6 in *The Western Films of John Ford.* Secaucus, NJ: Citadel Press, 1974, 74–91.

Philip J. Landon

FROM WHERE THE SUN NOW STANDS **(Novel).** Will Henry once said that he was willing to have his reputation "stand or fall" on *From Where the Sun Now Stands* (1960), his brilliant account of the Nez Perce War of 1877. Awarded the Golden Spur Award of the Western Writers of America as the year's best western novel, it is one of the most poignant fictional studies of the life and times of any Native American people ever written. Immensely popular with the general public, it has attracted high praise from many serious literary scholars as well.

The story of Chief Joseph and his tribes' running battle, in summer and fall 1877, to escape the United States Army's attempt to take them forcibly to a reservation far from their eastern Oregon homeland is one of the most famous in U.S. history, just as is the chief's famous soliloquy at the end of the journey, which said, in part: "Hear me, my chiefs, my heart is sick and sad. From where the sun now stands, I will fight no more forever" (Beal, 229). Unlike most westerns, however, *From Where the Sun Now Stands* is told, not from a white point of view, but through the eyes of the now-aged Heyets (Mountain Sheep), Joseph's nephew. A young teenaged pony-herder at the outset of the novel, the boy is quickly forced to become an adult during the tribe's 113-day, nearly 1,600-mile retreat. Henry makes Heyets one of the most engaging and, eventually, sympathetic heroes in western American fiction. The young brave's accounts of the tribe's many trials and tribulations, the brutal and senseless death of the young girl he loves, and the sorrow of being forced away from his beautiful mountain home are related with great feeling.

More than 15 million copies of the author's fifty-three novels have been sold through the years, but few are as strong as *From Where the Sun Now Stands.* No one has done a better job of making the events of the Nez Perce War come alive than Will Henry. Henry—the pen name used by former Hollywood screenwriter Henry Wilson Allen—has been called the most critically acclaimed western writer of this or any other time. This exciting and well-told story certainly merits such an accolade.

See:

Beal, Merrill D. *"I Will Fight No More Forever":* Chief Joseph and the Nez Perce War. Seattle: University of Washington Press, 1963, 229.

Gale, Robert L. *Will Henry/Clay Fisher (Henry W. Allen)*. Boston: Twayne, 1984.

M. Paul Holsinger

F TROOP (Television Series). ABC-TV showcased a number of war-related shows in the mid-1960s. Some, like the long-running **Combat**, focused realistically on the trials and tribulations of a rifle company of GIs in Europe during World War II. Others, like the even more popular **McHale's Navy**, sought to squeeze laughs out of that same conflict. During fall 1965, those two shows were followed sequentially on Tuesday evenings by a newly created situation comedy, *F Troop*. Set at the fictitious frontier Fort Courage (a United States Cavalry post somewhere in Kansas) shortly after the end of the Civil War, the half-hour show chronicled the misadventures of a group of misfits led by Sergeant Morgan O'Rourke (longtime character actor Forrest Tucker) and his larcenous sidekick, Corporal Randolph Agarn (Larry Storch). The fort's commander, Captain Wilton Parmenter (Ken Berry), was an incapable fool, but the Hekawi Indians (as in where the "heck-are-we"?) never posed a problem with which he had to deal seriously. Even when wandering tribes sought to coax them to attack the fort, the Hekawis opted for indolence. The troopers were little better. As inept and bumbling as their supposed adversaries, they spent more time drinking, sleeping, and gambling than anything else. Wrangler Jane (a Calamity Jane–like character), played by the beautiful Melody Patterson, was added to give the show an occasional burst of romantic tension.

  F Troop was a total farce, with a heavy emphasis on physical, slapstick humor. Though always filled with dozens of funny one-liners in every segment, it was such images as a repeatedly destroyed lookout tower shown in every episode and the cannon that never fired until kicked by Corporal Agarn that kept viewers laughing and returning for more. Filmed in black-and-white in its first year, *F Troop* was renewed for a second year, now shot entirely in color. Though it never made it into the top twenty-five most popular shows, it continued steadily to attract regular viewers until finally canceled in August 1967. Almost immediately syndicated, the series' sixty-five episodes were still occasionally seen on some television stations in the late 1990s.

See:

Yoggy, Gary. "Spoofing the Television Western, or, How the 'F Troop' Found 'Pistols and Petticoats' on 'Dusty's Trail.' " Chapter 11 in *Riding the Video Range: The Rise and Fall of the Western on Television*. Jefferson, NC: McFarland, 1995, 425–440.

M. Paul Holsinger

"GARRY OWEN" (Song). General George Armstrong Custer's favorite march, "Garry Owen," will always be inextricably connected with the United States Seventh Cavalry and the Battle of the Little Big Horn. On June 16, 1876, as Custer and his men broke camp on the Powder River, the regimental band, high on a bluff overlooking the troops heading west, played the song in honor of the men who, unknowingly, were going to their deaths nine days later, in eastern Montana.

From the moment that Custer took command of the newly formed Seventh Regiment, shortly after the Civil War, "Garry Owen" became its official marching song. It was always played before, and sometimes during, campaigns against the Indians of the Plains. In November 1868, Custer brought his band with him and, even in the freezing, snowy weather, had it play the air before he launched the infamous Battle of the Washita. Four days later, parading before General Philip Sheridan, the band once again struck up the march in triumph.

It is not clear whether the selection of "Garry Owen" was made at the suggestion of Custer or his subordinate, Captain Miles Keogh. Like many of the troopers in the Seventh Cavalry, Keogh was an immigrant from Ireland and may very well have heard regiments using the tune as their own long before he came to America to fight and die. In any case, the choice of the melody, which was an old Irish quickstep dating back at least to the Napoleonic Wars, guaranteed stirring times in camp. Indeed, when "Garry Owen" is played with bagpipes and full brass accompaniment, the effect is often dramatic.

The five stanzas of the song, though rarely sung, are strangely appropriate to the dashing Custer and his men. They laud a stereotyped image of virile masculinity—hardened men boozing, brawling, rioting in the streets, and terrorizing legal authority. "We are the boys no man dares dun / if he regards his whole skin," goes one partial verse. However, Crazy Horse and his Sioux warriors were obviously unimpressed.

See:

Barnett, Louise. *Touched by Fire: The Life, Death, and Mythic Afterlife of George Armstrong Custer.* New York: Holt, 1996, 153, 326, 387–388.

M. Paul Holsinger

***GERONIMO: AN AMERICAN LEGEND* (Film).** The great Chiricahua Apache chief Geronimo and the war he fought against the white settlers of Arizona Territory and the United States Army troops sent to protect them have long fascinated Americans. Though his autobiography, *Geronimo's Story of His Life* (1906), attempted to give his point of view on the so-called Apache Wars, most books, films, and other material written about him through the years was usually extremely negative. In the 1970s, however, a more balanced reevaluation of the chief began, which has continued to the present day.

Two full-length motion pictures about the chief's life and times offer testimony to that altered approach. *Geronimo* (Turner Pictures, 1993), which was especially made to be shown on Ted Turner's Atlanta cable television stations, attempts to cover the Apache chieftain's entire adult career, and it does so in a thoughtful and fair manner. Director-producer Walter Hill's *Geronimo: An American Legend* (Columbia, 1993), though restricted only to the last year of the Apache War, is even more attuned to the Indian perspective. Covering much of the same historical material that Paul Horgan used in his excellent 1960 novel, *A Distant Trumpet*, the story and screenplay, by John Milius and Larry Gross, blend truth and legend flawlessly to capture the last free days of the Chiricahua Apaches. Geronimo, who is powerfully played by Wes Studi, is matched against the Sixth Cavalry. General George Crook (Gene Hackman), who sincerely feels that the army is the Apaches' best friend, tries to deal honestly with the hostile warriors, but his efforts fail to conquer Geronimo. General Nelson Miles (Kevin Tighe), who is sent to replace Crook, finally crushes the Indians through brute strength, cruelty, and outright dishonesty. After being promised justice if he will surrender, Geronimo and all the other Chiricahuas (including even those who, as army scouts, had helped capture him) are jailed and sent to Florida or Oklahoma in chains. It is a sorry story that is movingly told.

Geronimo: An American Legend also stars Robert Duvall as Indian scout Al Sieber and Jason Patric as Lieutenant Charles Gatewood, the man responsible for Geronimo's final capitulation. Young Lieutenant Britton Davis (Matt Damon), the narrator, however, has the most telling lines in the film. Resigning his commission after realizing what the army intends to do to the great Apache warrior, he tells Miles: "I thought the United States Army kept its word. I thought maybe we were the only ones left who did. . . . I'm ashamed." Most viewers will agree.

Like many contemporary motion pictures, *Geronimo: An American Legend* was fictionalized by Robert J. Coney into an original full-length paperback novel in January 1994.

See:

"Geronimo: The Last Renegade." In *A & E Biography*, dir. Bill Harris, prod. Michael Cascio. Arts and Entertainment Network, 1996.

M. Paul Holsinger

THE GIRL I LEFT BEHIND ME (Drama). In the early 1890s, public interest in the fate of the country's Native Americans was at an all-time high. The Indian defeat of General George Custer and the men of the United States Seventh Cavalry was still fresh in many people's minds, as was the still-recent Wounded Knee massacre. When asked by theatrical impresario Charles Frohman to write a play that could be used to open a new Broadway theater, playwright David Belasco, working in collaboration with Franklin Fyles, the drama critic of the New York *Sun*, saw the advantage of capitalizing on the public's fascination with the Army-Indian struggles in the West. The result was the extremely popular *The Girl I Left behind Me*.

When the melodramatic play was first staged at the Empire Theater on January 25, 1893 (after a one-week trial run in Washington, D.C.), it was an instant hit. Though critics pointed out that there was little in the plot that was new or unique, everyone agreed that Belasco's interwoven tales of romance, bravery, cowardice, cruel Indian attacks, and a culminating army victory did a masterful job of holding the audience's attention. The initial production ran for 208 consecutive performances—a significant number at the time—though the original cast left Broadway in late March to bring the play to Chicago and the World's Fair, which was then in full swing. *The Girl I Left behind Me* never waned in popularity during the decade. It was revived in late 1893, 1894, 1896, 1897, and, twice, in 1899, always to enthusiastic audiences.

The drama is set in summer 1890 at an isolated United States Cavalry post in the heart of Montana. The often-defeated Sioux, led by their embittered chief Scar-Brow (or, as he is also known, John Ladru) want to hold a "Sun Dance." When General Kennion, the post's commander, refuses to allow it, the angry tribe attacks the fort and, for a while, seems certain to kill all its defenders and rape their wives and daughters. The general has his pistol cocked and ready to kill his only child, the beautiful heroine Kate Kinnion, to save her from "a fate worse than death" when Edgar Hawksworth, the young officer she loves, arrives at the last second with the bulk of the cavalry. The Indians are defeated, the fort is saved, and the young lovers are united as the curtain falls.

See:

Hughes, George, and George Savage. "Introduction: *The Girl I Left Behind Me*." In *America's Lost Plays*, ed. Barnett Clark. 1940. Reprint. Bloomington: Indiana University Press, 1965, 18: 10–14.

Jones, Eugene H. *Native Americans as Shown on the Stage, 1753–1916*. Metuchen, NJ: Scarecrow, 1988, 123–126.

M. Paul Holsinger

I WILL FIGHT NO MORE FOREVER (Film). Novelists have been far more successful than moviemakers at capturing the plight of the many Native Americans who, in the late nineteenth century, fought—and lost—their battle to control their tribal lands in the Far West. This is particularly so in regard to the Nez Percé and their great war leader, Joseph. In 1877, faced with the prospect of being exiled thousands of miles from their homes in the Wallowa Mountains of eastern Oregon, the Nez Percé chose, instead, an impossible 1,600-mile retreat into Canada. Though they lost, they provided one of the most famous legends of bravery in adversity ever written.

Perhaps because of the sweeping panorama of the Nez Percé's story, few motion pictures have been willing to attempt to re-create its drama. In April 1975, however, the Xerox Corporation sponsored, and ABC-TV aired, a Richard Heffron–directed, two-hour, made-for-television production about the plight of the Nez Percé, *I Will Fight No More Forever*. Though advertised as the "true story" of the Nez Percé's struggle for freedom, Theodore Strauss and Jeb Rosebrook's screenplay alters the historical facts on far too many occasions for the sake of a more sympathetic accounting. General O. O. Howard (James Whitmore), for instance, is seen in the movie as sympathizing with the Indians and their plight, but in reality, he did neither. Dates are changed, and the Nez Percé far too often look blameless for much of what befell them when frequently they were not. Even Joseph, who is played with dignity by the non-Indian actor Ned Romero, was not as sainted as he appears.

In 1977, the American Film Festival awarded *I Will Fight No More Forever* its Blue Ribbon as the year's best feature length film dealing with U.S. history and culture. Despite its flaws, the honor was not undeserved. The battle scenes are always believable, the story is appealing, and the Native American viewpoint is fairly considered. Time and place also are thoughtfully captured. Beautifully photographed (ironically for a piece of U.S. history, in Mexico), the film, which is still often seen today on videotape, deserves to be studied and appreciated, not as pure history but as dramatic entertainment.

See:

Yoggy, Gary. "Meanwhile Back on the Reservation: 'Good' and 'Bad' Indians in Television Westerns." Chapter 9 in *Riding the Video Range: The Rise and Fall of the Western on Television*. Jefferson, NC: McFarland, 1995, 373–376.

M. Paul Holsinger

KING, CHARLES (Author). At the end of the nineteenth century, Captain (later, General) Charles King was America's most popular writer of war-related fiction. Appointed to West Point by Abraham Lincoln in 1861, King participated in the Civil War, the occupation of the Southern states during Reconstruction, the Indian Wars, the Philippine Insurrection (where he commanded troops in battle), and World War I. Shortly before his death in 1933, he was recognized by the U.S. War Department for seventy years of active service, the only man in American history ever to be so honored.

Shortly after he was badly wounded in 1874 by the Apaches while serving as a lieutenant in the United States Cavalry, King began to write, and he never stopped. Though many of his nonfictional studies were popular, and his *Campaigning with Crook* (1880), an account of his experiences as a young officer during the Sioux Wars, quickly became a classic, it was his nearly sixty novels and literally hundreds of short stories about the United States Army that made him best known by the general public. Critics could carp about what they considered King's trite, formulaic writing, but for more than thirty years, his books never failed to sell. Based on personal experiences, each novel resonated with the sights and sounds of the "old army," whether fighting in the Civil War, crushing Moro tribesmen in the Philippines, or even patrolling the Chicago rail yards during the notorious Pullman Strike.

Unquestionably, however, King's most popular works were those dealing with America's Indian Wars in the trans-Mississippi West. *Warrior Gap: A Story of the Sioux Outbreak of '68* (1897), for example, recounts the early fighting on the Great Plains. *Sunset Pass, or Running the Gauntlet through Apache Land* (1890) carefully looks at the Apache Wars. The Nez Percé War of 1877 is featured in *Captain Blake* (1891), and *A Soldier's Secret: A Story of the Sioux*

War of 1890 (1893) is centered in the events surrounding the Ghost Dance and the Wounded Knee massacre; there were dozens more. It is not too much to say that thousands of contemporary readers of each King frontier tale came away from it vicariously feeling that they, too, had been in the saddle helping to put down another Indian uprising somewhere in the western territories.

See:

Russell, Don. *Campaigning with King: Charles King, Chronicler of the Old Army.* Lincoln: University of Nebraska Press, 1991.

M. Paul Holsinger

THE LAST INDIAN BATTLES (**Silent Film**). Thousands of silent films have disappeared since they were first shown in the early decades of the twentieth century, but few are more important than Buffalo Bill Cody's *The Last Indian Battles, or From the Warpath to the Peace Pipe* (also known by such titles as *The Indian Wars Refought, The Wars for Civilization in America, Buffalo Bill's Indian Wars*, and *The Adventures of Buffalo Bill*). In September 1913, Fred Bonfils and Harry Tammen, owners of the *Denver Post*, in tandem with Chicago's Essanay Company, founded a new production firm to make a film that would chronicle the Indian wars in the trans-Mississippi frontier after the Civil War. The elder Cody, who was less than four years from his death, was supposedly paid $50,000 to star in the picture. Thanks to his participation, the army sent three troops of U.S. cavalry, uniforms, and matériel to South Dakota's Pine Ridge Reservation to recreate various events, including the battles of Summit Springs (1869), Warbonnet Creek (1876), and Wounded Knee (1890). According to many Sioux residents of the reservation who appeared in the picture, the screenplay, by General **Charles King**, was well-researched and the depiction of the battles between white and Native Americans were reasonably accurate. Lieutenant General Nelson Miles, who served as technical adviser, insisted on shooting the action on the actual battlefields. Consequently, the reenactment of Wounded Knee took place exactly where, twenty-three years earlier, he and the U.S. Army had massacred hundreds of Sioux men, women, and children.

When *The Last Indian Battles* (Cody Historical Pictures, 1914) was first screened, it received much critical acclaim, but after several more showings in New York and Denver, it was rarely seen again. Though there is much controversy surrounding the picture, it seems clear that the U.S. government consciously suppressed it, since its view of the army is, quite inadvertently, less than flattering. According to legend, the last copies decomposed in the 1920s while in the possession of the U.S. Bureau of Indian Affairs. Though part of one reel was discovered in Chicago in the early 1970s, no complete print appears to exist today. That has not deterred film historians from diligently continuing to search. The discovery of this important work by Cody would be one of the most significant events in American popular cultural history.

See:

Brownlow, Kevin. *The War, the West and the Wilderness.* New York: Knopf, 1979, 224–
    235.

M. Paul Holsinger

LITTLE BIG MAN (**Novel-Film**). Thomas Berger published his third novel,
Little Big Man, in 1964. Though a number of critics were disappointed with its
tale of 121-year-old Jack Crabb (supposedly the only white man to survive the
Battle of the Little Big Horn), general opinion now ranks it as one of the very
best American works of fiction written during the 1960s. Indeed, a *New York
Times* reviewer called it "the best novel ever written about the American West."
Captured by the Indians who attacked his family's wagon train, Crabb is, co-
incidentally, present at dozens of major events in the opening of the far western
frontier before 1890. Drifting back and forth between the white and Indian
worlds, he is, at times, a buffalo hunter, muleskinner, storekeeper, patent medicine peddler, and friend of Wild Bill Hickok. As the novel's narrator, Crabb
offers readers an Indian view, not only of the massacre of General Custer and
his men, but also of the Sand Creek Massacre, twelve years earlier.

Working from screenwriter Calder Willingham's script, director Arthur Penn
turned *Little Big Man* (National General, 1970) into a panoramic, 2½ hour
motion picture. Starring Dustin Hoffman as Jack, it featured a host of other
character actors, including Richard Mulligan as General Custer. Throughout the
many episodes, neither Custer nor the United States cavalry come off well. The
general is depicted as an obnoxious and vainglorious fool; the cavalry is deceitful, vicious, and bloodthirsty, attacking peaceful villages and killing women
and children. Critics were divided in their evaluation. Some thought the film
"interminable" and "boring"; others called it "superb." Native American actor
Chief Dan George, who plays Crabb's mentor, did receive an Academy Award
nomination as the year's best supporting actor and won a similar honor from
the New York Film Critics Circle.

Both the original novel and the screen adaptation of *Little Big Man* combine
humor and tragedy to create, at times, a rich tapestry of a significant part of the
American past. Unfortunately, the motion picture has overshadowed Berger's
novel, which deserves better.

See:

Oliva, Leo E. "Thomas Berger's *Little Big Man* as History." *Western American Liter-
    ature* 8 (1973): 33–54.
Wylder, Delbert E. "Thomas Berger's *Little Big Man* as Literature." *Western American
    Literature* 3 (1969): 273–284.

Jack Colldeweih

MY CAPTIVITY AMONG THE SIOUX INDIANS (**Captivity Narrative**).
Fanny Kelly was a nineteen-year-old bride traveling with her husband and other

Idaho-bound emigrants from their homes in Kansas when their wagon train was attacked on July 12, 1864, and five of the men killed. Taken prisoner, she remained in the hands of the Indians until she was ransomed five months later, at Fort Sully in Dakota Territory. In 1872, homeless and financially burdened, Kelly published an account of her experiences titled, *My Captivity among the Sioux Indians*. For more than two hundred years, many captivity narratives circulated throughout the United States; this is one of the most distinguished.

Unlike so many similar tales, Kelly's work, which is filled with affidavits from army officers and Indian chiefs alike to prove its authenticity, pays careful attention to the facts. Where the great majority of other such studies fictionalized and, at times, overglamorized the "noble savages" of the frontier, Kelly is a careful student who never allows herself to embellish on the truth. She frequently includes passages that focus on the cruelty or treachery of the Sioux, but at the same time, she freely cites instances, such as during the Sand Creek Massacre, where the United States Army is just as cruel, if not more so, than the so-called savages of the Great Plains.

Fanny Kelly's story is that of a brave and intelligent woman. A popular bestseller in the 1870s, it continues to be exciting and often moving more than 125 years later.

See:

Zenger, Jules. "Introduction." In *My Captivity among the Indians*, by Fanny Kelly. 1872.
    Reprint. New York: Corinth, 1962, v–viii.

M. Paul Holsinger

NO SURVIVORS (Novel). Will Henry's *No Survivors* (1950) is one of the most unique books, fictional or non-fictional, to deal with the infamous Battle of the Little Big Horn. This first novel (of more than fifty) to be published by the author tells the imaginative story of the last ten years in the life of a former Confederate Army cavalry officer, Colonel John Buell Clayton. Having come west after the war, Clayton is nearly killed while scouting for the United States at the time of the Fetterman Massacre in 1866. Captured by the victorious Sioux and adopted by Crazy Horse because of his unusual bravery, Clayton consciously opts to remain with his captors. For the next ten years, Walking Hawk, as he now is known, lives with an Indian wife and fights bravely beside the Sioux against their foes. Only when the United States Army comes to the plains in full force, during summer 1876, is he forced to make a choice: fight with his adopted brothers against other whites or attempt to warn General George Armstrong Custer (the officer to whom Clayton surrendered at Appomattox Court House in 1865) of the Seventh Cavalry's impending doom. He chooses, rather inexplicably, the latter course, and even though the general refuses to believe him, he joins "Yellow Hair," Captain Marcus Reno, Captain Frederick Benteen, and others in the forthcoming battle. Clayton/Walking Hawk—rescued a second time by Crazy Horse—is the only non-Indian to survive the massacre. That respite does not last long, however. His wife dies in childbirth (though their son becomes the hero of a later Henry novel, the 1956 *North Star*), and within a year, the doomed Clayton freezes to death during a blizzard in far northern Canada. Only his journal, on which the novel is supposedly based, remains to tell this strange, but often-fascinating, story.

Henry's narrative is undeniably slanted against the United States Cavalry and Custer. Crazy Horse and Sitting Bull, on the other hand, are seen as almost-mythic characters, worthy of praise, if not adulation. Will Henry, one of the several pen names used by M-G-M scriptwriter Henry W. Allen during his long and illustrious career, has, through nearly fifty years, sold more than 15 million copies of his many books; *No Survivors* remains one of the most intriguing and clearly one of the best.

See:

Dippie, Brian W. "Jack Crabb and the Sole Survivors of Custer's Last Stand." *Western American Literature* 4 (1969): 189–202.

M. Paul Holsinger

THE PLAINSMEN (Novels). No contemporary American writer of fiction has done more to revive interest in the Indian Wars in the trans-Mississippi West than Terry C. Johnston, the author of a number of highly regarded novels, including the well-received, ongoing *Son of the Plains* series. In 1990, Johnston and his publisher, St. Martin's Press, introduced *The Plainsmen*, an even more ambitious series featuring vivid accounts of the major United States Army campaigns against the Native American tribes of the West. The twelve volumes that, as of late 1997, comprise the series have earned such adjectives as "unforgettable," "compelling," and "masterful" from reviewers. Set between 1866 and 1877 and researched with the closest attention to historic detail, each centers on the life and times of a former Union Army cavalry sergeant, Irish-born soldier of fortune Seamus Donegan. Seeking adventure and profit, Donegan finds himself in the midst of some of the bloodiest battles in American military history, and it is to Johnston's credit that none of the situations seem contrived nor the hero anything but brave.

The Plainsmen's story begins chronologically in 1866 with *Sioux Dawn* (1990), an account of the famous Fetterman Massacre in Wyoming. It is followed in rapid order with other volumes that focus on the Indian wars on the northern Great Plains in 1867 (*Red Cloud's Revenge*, 1990), the 1868 Battle of Beecher Island (*The Stalkers*, 1990), and the 1869 Battle of Summit Springs (*Black Sun*, 1991). California's Modoc War of 1872–1873 is examined in *Devil's Backbone* (1991), and then, in rapid order, come novels dealing with the 1873 Southern Plains Uprising (*Shadow Riders*, 1991) and the 1874 Battles of Adobe Wells and Palo Duro Canyon (*Dying Thunder*, 1992). *Blood Song* (1993), *Reap the Whirlwind* (1994), *Trumpet on the Land* (1995), and *A Cold Day in Hell* (1996) are all set during the Sioux War of 1876. *Wolf Mountain Moon* (1997) deals with Crazy Horse's last engagement with the army, the 1877 Battle of the Butte.

More than 1 million copies of *The Plainsmen* series are in circulation. Johnston, a former history teacher, seemingly gains new devotees every year. His
work has won a number of awards from the Western Writers of America
(WWA), including two nominations for the WWA's Golden Spur Award, emblematic of the year's best work of western fiction.

See:

"Terry C(onrad) Johnston." In *Contemporary Authors*, ed. Hal May. Vol. 113. Detroit,
    MI: Gale, 1985, 244.

M. Paul Holsinger

REMINGTON, FREDERIC (Painter-Sculptor). Most people associate Frederic Remington with fine western art, but much of his skill was developed as a
field artist during the Indian wars of the American frontier. His first published
drawing, made during the army's search for Geronimo, appeared on the cover
of **Harper's Weekly** in 1886. Over the next few years, he also accompanied
General Nelson Miles through Wyoming, the Dakotas, and Montana and rode
with the Tenth Cavalry's "Buffalo Soldiers" as a free-lance illustrator. "Vagabonding with the Tenth Horse," which appeared in *Cosmopolitan* in 1897 and
featured several of his illustrations, described his experiences with the renowned
black troopers.

   Remington was attracted to war. In the years before the conflict with Spain,
he often said he longed to go to war so he could "see men do the greatest thing
which men are called to do" (Dippie, 22). The army's constant conflict with
the Indians of the trans-Mississippi West gave him repeated opportunities to
fulfill his dreams. He quickly became a popular illustrator, and, although he
preferred *Harper's*, his illustrations soon appeared in a number of magazines
and books. Many became famous; his painting, "General Forsyth's Fight on the
Republican River, the Sioux Campaign of 1868–1869," for instance, still has
many admirers. His interpretation of the Battle of the Little Big Horn continues
to be used today in works dealing with the Sioux War.

   His popularity reached its peak in 1897 shortly before the Spanish-American
War, when Remington's reputation prompted William Hearst to hire him to
provide artwork for a book by **Richard Harding Davis** about the troubles in
Cuba. He continued to draw throughout the subsequent war, but his illustrations
were not as popular as those made in the West. He found modern warfare
inhuman and demoralizing, and, feeling disillusioned about the valor and romance of war that he had earlier found so appealing, he turned his attention
back to the frontier and to the art that was to make him world-renowned.

See:

Dippie, Brian W. "Frederic Remington's Wild West." *American Heritage* 26 (April
    1975): 6–23, 76–79.
Van Steemwyk, Elizabeth. *Frederic Remington: Artist of the American West*. New York:
    F. Watts, 1994.

Michael Brown

RIO GRANDE (Film). *Rio Grande* (Republic/Argosy, 1950), the last film in John Ford's famous horse soldier trilogy was based on "Mission with No Name," a short story by James Warner Bellah which first appeared in the September 27, 1947, *Saturday Evening Post.* Depicting the life of officers (all played by John Wayne) serving on the frontier with the Seventh Cavalry Regiment, the films (*Fort Apache* (1948), *She Wore a Yellow Ribbon* (1949), and *Rio Grande*) focus far less on the battles between the army and Native Americans than on the ways in which a military man must deal with conflicts between his private life and his professional commitment.

In *Rio Grande*, Lieutenant Colonel Kirby Yorke (Wayne) is joined on the frontier by his estranged son Jeff (Claude Jarman, Jr.). A dropout from West Point, the boy has enlisted in the army as a private, hoping to prove to his father that he can stand on his own without the help or influence of either parent. Separated years earlier from his son after the boy's mother (Maureen O'Hara), refusing to endure the hardships of frontier cavalry posts any longer, took him back East, Yorke now warns the boy that the life of a military professional is one of "suffering and hardship, an uncompromising devotion to your oath and your duty." It is a devotion that Yorke knows only too well, since it estranged him from his family and denied him personal happiness with a woman whom he still loves.

When Mrs. Yorke arrives at the fort determined to buy back her son's enlistment, she and the captain are reunited. In the dramatic conclusion, Jeff proves himself a worthy soldier against hostile Indians, and it is clear that he is willing to carry on the family's tradition of military service in the years ahead.

See:

Place, J. A. "Rio Grande." Chapter 10 in *The Western Films of John Ford*. Secaucus, NJ: Citadel Press, 1974, 146–159.

Philip J. Landon

RUSSELL, CHARLES (Painter-Sculptor). Charles Russell was born in St. Louis, Missouri, but, at sixteen, he went west to Montana and never returned. Unlike many other transplants, whose lives became intimately connected with the "Wild West" as soldiers or illustrators, for years Russell was a cowboy; only later did he become one of the frontier's most evocative artists. In 1888 he lived with the Bloods, a tribe of Blackfeet Indians, in Canada. He learned their language, hunted with them, and listened to their tales of war. When he began to paint, much of his work featured Indians to whom he was invariably sympathetic. He once said, "man for man, an Injun's as good as a white man any day" (Hassrick, 70).

Though most of his art (unlike that of his contemporaries, **Frederic Remington** and **Charles Schreyvogel**), had little to do with the Indian wars in the West, Russell did, on a number of occasions, capture scenes of bloody confrontation between some of the various Indian tribes as well as a few that featured fights between white soldiers and their Native American enemies. After being told a story by Chief Medicine Whip that described the act of striking an enemy at close range to claim his scalp, for instance, Russell prepared *Counting Coup*, one of his most popular and critically acclaimed paintings. *Indians Attacking* (1895) shows a skirmish between two Indian tribes. His pencil sketch of the 1866 Fetterman Massacre in Wyoming titled, *The Last of the Fetterman Command*, depicts the triumphant Indians leaving the dead troopers behind them. Like Remington, Russell also became a sculptor of some note, and several of his best works in that field feature Indian war parties or young braves preparing for combat.

Russell was always a friend of the West's Native American tribesmen, and the great majority of his works, especially those that include pictures featuring encounters between Indians and white men, place the Indians prominently in the foreground. In doing so, however, he always understood the poignancy that underlay such scenes. Typical is *Indians on a Bluff Surveying General Miles' Troops*, in which a handful of tribesmen gaze wistfully at the overwhelming lines of white soldiers that have invaded their former lands. They know, as do the viewers, that their days as a free people are clearly numbered.

See:

Dippie, Brian W. "Charlie Russell's Lost West." *American Heritage* 24 (April 1973): 4–21, 89.

Hassrick, Peter H. *Charles M. Russell.* New York: Harry N. Abrams, 1989.

Taliaferro, John. *Charles M. Russell: The Life and Legend of America's Cowboy Artist.* Boston: Little, Brown, 1996.

Michael Brown

SCHREYVOGEL, CHARLES (Painter). No American artist better pictured the post–Civil War army in its many battles with Indian tribesmen than Charles Schreyvogel. Though during his lifetime he painted everything from portraits of rich men and women to miniatures on ivory, the subjects that he loved the best, and those for which he is best known, were the far western frontier and the military men sent to tame it.

Schreyvogel grew up in Hoboken, New Jersey. In 1893, being ill, he went West with the hope of regaining his health. Fascinated by the men in the United States Army cavalry forts that he visited during his yearlong stay, he determined to bring their story to life on canvas. Once back home, he began to paint vivid action scenes of the frontier-based cavalry in battle against the Indians. Not until 1900, however, did the first of his army pictures gain wide recognition. When *My Bunkie*, an oil painting of a mounted cavalryman pulling a friend up behind him as the two anxiously hurry to escape a band of unseen Indians, won first prize in a show sponsored by the prestigious National Academy, Schreyvogel was "discovered." *The Silenced War Whoop*, *Attack at Dawn*, *Defending the Stockade*, and *A Sharp Encounter*—to mention only a few of his many, superb paintings—followed in the next few years.

172   WAR AND AMERICAN POPULAR CULTURE

Schreyvogel soon had many devotees. One of Buffalo Bill Cody's favorite works, for example, was *The Summit Springs Rescue—1869* (in which the former scout was prominently featured). Theodore Roosevelt, who was also a fan, not only invited the artist to discuss his work in depth at the White House but also gave him a special presidential permit to visit any army post or Indian reservation in the United States in order to advance his frontier art.

Schreyvogel once told a reporter, "[S]ome of the finest men I know are stationed on the frontier" (McCracken, 202). His usually mammoth canvases, which were always filled with carefully researched details, repeatedly reflect this feeling.

See:

Horan, James D. *The Life and Art of Charles Schreyvogel, Painter-Historian of the Indian-Fighting Army of the American West.* New York: Crown, 1969.
McCracken, Harold. *Great Painters and Illustrators of the Old West.* New York: Dover, 1988.

M. Paul Holsinger

SERGEANT RUTLEDGE **(Film-Novel).** In 1866, the army created two new cavalry regiments, the Ninth and the Tenth, composed exclusively of African-American troops (the "Buffalo Soldiers") and sent them throughout the trans-Mississippi West to help subdue the many warring Indian tribes of the region. Over the next fifty years, members of the two units earned several Medals of Honor and untold other decorations for their bravery under fire.

Surprisingly, American popular culture before the mid-1970s paid little attention to the Buffalo Soldiers. One exception was the film *Sergeant Rutledge* (Warner Brothers, 1960). Directed, somewhat reluctantly, by the famed John Ford and set in Arizona Territory in 1881, the motion picture tells the story of the court-martial of Master Sergeant Braxton Rutledge (Woody Strode), a former slave accused of the rape and murder of the white daughter of his commanding officer. In a series of flashback testimonies, most elicited by the questions of defense attorney Lieutenant Tom Cantrell (Jeffrey Hunter), it soon becomes clear that Rutledge is only guilty of being an extremely brave soldier who loves his regiment above even his own life. This "ain't the white man's war," he tells a wounded soldier after a pitched battle with rampaging Apaches. "We're fighting to make us proud." In the end, the real rapist-murderer (the post's resident white trader) is uncovered in a melodramatic (and rather unbelievably staged) denouement, and Rutledge proudly becomes the Ninth Cavalry's "top soldier" once again.

The memory of the Buffalo Soldiers deserves better. Though the historical background of *Sergeant Rutledge* is important, the movie version of the story is one of Ford's lesser works. Strode's performance in the title role is strong, and the Monument Valley setting in Arizona (which Ford used for nearly all his western productions) photographs beautifully in technicolor, but there is little else about the film which justifies watching it today.

In 1960, James Warner Bellah, one of the film's two screenwriters, fictionalized *Sergeant Rutledge* into a better-than-average, full-length novel. As it was issued only in an original paperback edition, there is little reason to search for it today.

See:

Leckie, William H. *The Buffalo Soldiers: A Narrative of the Negro Cavalry in the West.* Norman, University of Oklahoma Press, 1967.

Place, J. A. "Sergeant Rutledge." Chapter 13 in *The Western Films of John Ford.* Secaucus, NJ: Citadel Press, 1974, 186–197.

M. Paul Holsinger

SHE WORE A YELLOW RIBBON **(Film).** *She Wore a Yellow Ribbon* (Argosy/RKO, 1949), the second of the famous horse soldier trilogy directed by John Ford, begins where the first film, *Fort Apache* (1948), ends—Custer's defeat at Little Big Horn. Ford often drew on the excellent short stories of James Warner Bellah for his western films, and *She Wore a Yellow Ribbon* is adapted from Bellah's "The Big Hunt," a *Saturday Evening Post* story originally published on December 6, 1947.

With the Indians once again on the attack, the aging Captain Nathan Brittles (John Wayne in one of his finest performances) is assigned to escort two women (Joanne Dru and Mildred Natwick) from a cavalry outpost to a town where the stagecoach can take them to safety. Attacked and cut off by a band of warring "savages," Brittles, who has just six days left to serve, faces the prospect of ending his career in defeat, but at the last minute, he stops the attack by stampeding the Indian horses, saving both his charges and most of his men.

Typical of this trilogy, which also includes *Rio Grande* (1950), the hero's battlefield exploits are less important than the tribulations he experiences as a professional cavalry officer. Having sacrificed both his family and private life to his duties on the frontier, Brittle's home has been the Seventh Cavalry. Retirement promises only a lonely old age. In the final scene, having been appointed chief of scouts, he is able to defer his retirement indefinitely. Despite such an upbeat ending, however, Ford's meditation on the inevitable losses that come with passing time creates a mood of nostalgic melancholy that pervades the film.

See:

Place, J. A. "She Wore a Yellow Ribbon." Chapter 8 in *The Western Films of John Ford.* Secaucus, NJ: Citadel Press, 1974, 108–127.

Philip J. Landon

SOLDIER BLUE **(Film).** During the war in Vietnam, filmmakers who stood in opposition to the American presence in Southeast Asia frequently attempted to find ways to criticize the role of the United States, and especially the army, in attacking "innocent" peoples. Ralph Nelson's *Soldier Blue* (AVCO Embassy,

1970), a movie ostensibly based on the infamous 1864 Sand Creek Massacre in Colorado, is such a film. Though the Indians he pictures kill white settlers from time to time, it soon becomes clear that they are fighting to protect their ancestral lands from the rapacious acts of white invaders. The real "savages" are the multitude of army troopers, all of whom generally seem to take pleasure in killing as many native men, women, and children as possible.

The plot of *Soldier Blue* is based loosely on Theodore V. Olsen's novel *Arrow in the Sun* (1969), though in that work, the cavalry troops are heroes rather than villains. Here, on the other hand, the white soldiers mercilessly slaughter at will. Women are raped; babies are impaled on swords or lances; and there are innumerable decapitated bodies and severed limbs. Publicity for the film promised that viewers could expect lots of bloody gore and stated: "Now, more than ever, [it] is the time for the truth" (Sarf, 186).

Soldier Blue, however, is far from accurate. Heavy-handed and dishonest, it seeks to convince audiences that everyone of the thousands of American soldiers in the West at the end of the nineteenth century was violent, brutish, and unfeeling. Though such an assertion allows Nelson and his two leading stars, Peter Strauss and Candice Bergen, to make a clumsy parallel between Sand Creek and the My Lai massacre in Vietnam, it does so without the benefit of historical fact. Most critics severely panned the film in 1970, and it is just as easily forgotten today.

See:

Sarf, Wayne M. *God Bless You, Buffalo Bill: A Layman's Guide to History and the Western Film*. Rutherford, NJ: Fairleigh Dickinson University Press, 1983, 184–191.

M. Paul Holsinger

THE SONG OF THE INDIAN WARS* (Poetry).** John G. Neihardt is best known for his close association with Black Elk, one of the greatest Oglala Sioux medicine men, and the publication of that warrior's memoirs, ***Black Elk Speaks. Yet Neihardt, who grew up in a sod house on the Kansas prairie, was also a brilliant, poetic chronicler of the trans-Mississippi West. His epic poems, especially those dealing with the men and women who tamed the frontier in the nineteenth century, earned him a reputation that often paralleled his more famous contemporary, Stephen Vincent Benét.

Neihardt's most famous poetic work was the monumental *Cycle of the West* (1949), a collection of five separate, book-length poems written between 1915 and 1941. Part 4, *The Song of the Indian Wars* (1925), focuses most directly on America's wars in the West. The fourteen separate sections of the 179-page epic cover, sequentially, the days immediately after the end of the Civil War through the fall of 1877. All the great leaders and major events of the Indian Wars are included: Red Cloud, Sitting Bull, Crazy Horse, Dull Knife, Spotted Tail, the Fetterman Massacre, the Wagon Box Incident, the Battle of the Little

Big Horn. Neihardt's focus is undeniably pro–Indian. The white army officers who move though the pages of *The Song of the Indian Wars* are boastful, pig-headed, and often hypocritical; the Indian leaders, on the other hand, are always honest, brave, and clearly doomed.

The Song of the Indian Wars is thoughtful and carefully crafted. Meticulously researched, it movingly captures, not only the truth, but also the heartbreak of the Indians of the West in their last "free" days.

See:

DeLoria, Vine. *A Sender of Words. Essays in Memory of John G. Neihardt.* Salt Lake City, UT: Howe, 1984.
Whitney, Blair. *John G. Neihardt.* Boston: G. K. Hall, 1976.

M. Paul Holsinger

SON OF THE MORNING STAR (Biography-Film). The life and, more significantly, the death of General George Armstrong Custer and the men of the Seventh Cavalry under his command have fascinated Americans in all walks of life since their massacre at the June 1876 Battle of the Little Big Horn. Hundreds of books have been written about the battle and the enigmatic Custer, but few have been as well received as Evan S. Connell's carefully researched and beautifully written biography, *Son of the Morning Star* (1984). Universally praised when it first appeared, it has become (in the words of one expert reviewer) "by far the most accurate version [of the Custer Massacre] ever filmed" (Paul Andrew Hurron quoted in Yoggy, 391).

It was inevitable that *Son of the Morning Star*, like so many other popular books in recent years, would be adapted into an extended (two-part), made-for-television movie. Starring Gary Cole as Custer; Rosanna Arquette as his wife, Libby; and Rodney Grant as Crazy Horse; the four-hour motion picture premiered on ABC on February 3–4, 1991. Written by the Academy Award–winning Melissa Mathison, who closely based her script on Connell's text "and other historical accounts," the new production was quickly acclaimed as the most accurate screen version of the events surrounding the Battle of the Little Big Horn.

Director Mike Robe's picture has not one, but two, narrators: Libby Custer, who tearfully presents the story from her viewpoint as the wife of the slain general, and Kate Bighead, a Northern Cheyenne woman, whose words are read by actress-singer Buffy Saint Marie. Though the first two-hour segment is often confusing as it tries to encapsulate all of Custer's early career and the background to the Sioux War of 1876 into a handful of easy-to-understand settings, the second half is exceptionally well done. Kees Van Oostrum's cinematography hauntingly captures the beauty of the Great Plains, and his shots of the restaged Sioux victory, which was shot in Montana less than forty miles from the original site, are excitingly realistic and always believable.

Though the filmed version of *Son of the Morning Star* is inevitably Custer's story, it ends with a revealing "postscript" composed of a brief scene of Crazy Horse's assassination (following his surrender in 1877) at the hands of his captors. The scene is particularly appropriate. Because of their slaughter of "Yellow Hair" and his 265 men, the Sioux and their allies were crushed within the following year by the overwhelming military might of the United States Army. Recognizing this outcome, Kate Bighead says regretfully at the end of the film: "They called it Custer's last stand, but it was not his—it was ours."

See:

Yoggy, Gary. "Meanwhile Back on the Reservation: 'Good' and 'Bad' Indians in Television Westerns." In *Riding the Video Range: The Rise and Fall of the Western on Television.* Jefferson, NC: McFarland, 1995, 386–393.

M. Paul Holsinger

THEY DIED WITH THEIR BOOTS ON (Film). In the days after the Japanese attack on Pearl Harbor and the many subsequent American losses to the Imperial Army and Navy throughout the Pacific, the United States desperately needed military heroes. Director Raoul Walsh used George Armstrong Custer for this purpose in *They Died with Their Boots On* (Warner Brothers, 1942), a film supposedly based on the general's life and the massacre at the Little Big Horn in June 1876.

Featuring the popular Australian actor Errol Flynn, the production tries to follow Custer from the moment he arrives at West Point until his death, many years later. Along the way, Walsh and screenwriters Aeneas MacKenzie and Wally Kline torture historical fact almost to the breaking point by portraying Custer as a caring leader who believed that the Indians had a right to keep their land, which in fact could not have been less true. After his last battle, army leaders in the movie even promise Custer's wife, played by a demure Olivia de Havilland, that her husband's dream will soon be a reality, which also never occurred. Walsh reinforces the image of a heroic Custer fighting to the end: he is the last American trooper to die on the battlefield. Having emptied his guns, he stands dramatically, saber in hand, to meet, single-handedly, the charge of thousands of enraged Sioux warriors. With little change, he could just as easily have been one of the American defenders of Wake Island or Bataan, and the rampaging Sioux, Japanese soldiers on the attack.

They Died With Their Boots On is a fairy tale, which distorts history and repeatedly turns truth into fiction. However, this did not bother Walsh, the producers, or the critics, one of whom noted that, even if the film was not true to the facts of the past, it was history "as it should have been[:] . . . all honor and glory" (Sarf, 172). Almost everyone at the time agreed.

See:

Hutton, Paul Andrew. " 'Correct in Every Detail': General Custer in Hollywood." In *The Custer Reader*, ed. Paul Andrew Hutton. Lincoln: University of Nebraska Press, 1992, 488–524.

Sarf, William Michael. "Never a Last Stand, or Custer Died for Your Cash." Chapter
    6 in *God Bless You, Buffalo Bill. A Layman's Guide to History and the Western
    Film*. Rutherford, NJ: Fairleigh Dickinson University Press, 1983, 156–192.

M. Paul Holsinger

ULZANA'S RAID **(Film).** Few Hollywood motion pictures have done a better
job of dealing with the army's struggle to control the Native American tribes
of the Far West than Robert Aldrich's *Ulzana's Raid* (Universal, 1972). Set in
Arizona, the picture chronicles one extremely bloody week during the Apache
Wars as a troop of U.S. cavalrymen systematically attempt to capture or kill the
small band of Chiricahuas who have left their reservation in order to "burn,
maim, torture, and murder." Ulzana (Joaquin Martinez) and his men ultimately
die, but not before terrorizing everyone in their path. They slaughter their foes
without mercy. One settler is horribly tortured before being burned to death;
another is cruelly raped and left a raving lunatic; a trooper assigned to escort a
mother and her son to the nearest fort puts a bullet into her head and then blows
out his own brains after being surrounded by the rampaging Indians. Alan
Sharp's screenplay, however, is bluntly honest in its portrayals of both warring
factions. If the Apaches are cruel and murderous, so, too, at times are the men
of the cavalry. The troop's young commanding officer (Bruce Davison) believes
initially in love and Christian brotherhood but quickly realizes, to his dismay,
that beneath the surface of every man is the capacity for brutal savagery.

Starring Burt Lancaster as Macintosh, the aging, and ultimately doomed, Indian scout responsible for finding the renegades, *Ulzana's Raid* offers an honest
depiction of the hundreds of mini-campaigns that comprised the U.S.-Indian
wars in the Southwest. The closer that the troopers get to Ulzana, the more the
bloodshed escalates. Day in and day out, the two warring groups play a deadly
cat-and-mouse game that, before the last Apache is finally killed, results in
dozens of deaths on both sides.

Like many of Aldrich's other films, *Ulzana's Raid* has long been overlooked
by most students of cinematic history. It deserves far more attention.

See:

Arnold, Edwin T., and Eugene L. Miller. *The Films and Career of Robert Aldrich*.
    Knoxville: University of Tennessee Press, 1986, 165–174.
Milne, Tom. "Robert Aldrich (1962–1978)." In *Robert Aldrich*, ed. Richard Combs.
    London: British Film Institute, 1978, 23–36.

M. Paul Holsinger

8

The Spanish-American War and the Philippine Insurrection

Long before 1898, many Americans contemplated the annexation of Cuba. As early as the mid-1850s, plans were made by a number of pro-slavery U.S. diplomats in Europe to add Cuba to the nation's territorial possessions with the thought of being able to expand the "peculiar institution" of slavery into another congenial climate. That power grab failed, but in the 1860s and again in the 1870s, others were on the verge of advocating an attack on the Spanish-held colony and taking it by brute force. Even though, once again, nothing came of such plans, thousands of Americans began to show increasing interest in Cuba, Puerto Rico, and other Caribbean possessions of the Kingdom of Spain.

In 1868, a bloody war for Cuban independence broke out. It took the Spanish ten years to crush the revolt, and over the next few years, the oppression of the Cuban peoples grew steadily. When another revolution, which looked toward the ultimate independence of the island, erupted in 1895, the people of the United States were, in many cases, overwhelmingly supportive of the underdog Cubans and, conversely, antagonistic to anything Spanish. That attitude was encouraged continually by a number of U.S. newspapers, especially two large New York competitors, William Randolph Hearst's *Journal* and Joseph Pulitzer's *World*. These two men, often called the fathers of **yellow journalism**, frequently filled their pages with lurid stories of real and supposed Spanish horrors. By early 1898, both the *Journal* and the *World* had their readers worked up to a fever pitch of hatred against the Spanish Army.

With the United States just beginning to come out of a four-year-long national economic depression, many readers found excitement and welcome diversion in the power struggle in Cuba. At the very moment when the American press became its most jingoistic, in February 1898, President William McKinley made the fateful decision to send the battleship *Maine* to Havana. When, on the evening of February 15, an explosion onboard the ship sank it, with the resulting deaths of more than 250 American seamen, the majority of citizens was ready to agree instantly with Hearst's *Journal*, which emblazoned the slogan "**Remember the *Maine!* To Hell with Spain!**" on its front page. Though the Spanish tried everything they could (short of giving Cuba its immediate independence) to be conciliatory, the United States was primed for war. On April 11, with the nation's press demanding war, McKinley finally asked Congress for power to intervene militarily in Cuba. Eight days later, both the U.S. House of Representatives and the Senate passed a resolution declaring that Cuba was a free and independent nation-state and demanding that Spain withdraw all its troops immediately. Spain refused, broke off diplomatic relations with the United States, and prepared to fight if necessary. On April 25, an angry U.S. Congress declared war.

It was future Secretary of State John Hay who coined the term a "splendid little war" to describe the ensuing conflict between the two nations. Looked at with the hindsight of nearly a hundred years, it seems evident that what history has labeled the Spanish-American War was one of this nation's most lopsided military adventures. Though the Spanish Army and Navy fought as hard and as bravely as possible, by the time hostilities ended in Cuba, on July 17, and in the Philippines, on August 13, the United States was victorious on all fronts.

The great majority of the American people were ecstatic, and heroes were created overnight. The war had hardly begun before Admiral George Dewey, leading the six-ship Asiatic Fleet, steamed into Manila harbor and systematically destroyed the Spanish opposition in less than seven hours. The Battle of Manila Bay caused thousands of American men, young and old, to rush to the colors for the first time since the end of the Civil War. One such volunteer was Assistant Secretary of the Navy Theodore Roosevelt (TR). Resigning his post, he recruited his own private cavalry troop, composed not only of polo-playing sons of Eastern socialites, but also of cattlemen and other rough-edged westerners. The flamboyant Rough Riders (see *The Rough Riders*) quickly became the darlings of the American press. When they and others manfully captured the Spanish fortifications on top of San Juan Hill, just outside the city of Santiago, and thus opened the door to that vitally important port, the public turned both the men and Roosevelt into public icons. For a people seeking heroes to honor, TR and his Rough Riders became among the most renowned.

The utter destruction of the Spanish fleet under Admiral Pascual Cervera just outside the harbor of Santiago, Cuba, on July 4, 1898—a victory in which only one American seaman was killed—was also widely applauded. The date of the victory, "a Fourth of July present," as Admiral William Sampson called it in his telegraph to Washington, was lost on no one. Only 385 American men were dead as a result of battle by the time Spain sued for peace in August and, at least for those who gloried in absolute triumphs, it was hard not to be enthusiastic. Though technically the war dragged on until February 1899, when the U.S. Congress ratified the Treaty of Paris and ended the conflict, Hay's definition seemed apt. In less than five months, the nation had fought a common foe (whether justifiably or not), overwhelmingly defeated it, freed Cuba, and acquired as possessions the islands of Puerto Rico, Guam, and the Philippines.

It was the latter acquisition that immediately caused the United States untold problems. Insurgent Filipinos had helped the United States defeat the Spanish. Like their Cuban counterparts, they had dreamed for many years of complete independence, but to their surprise, it soon became clear that the conquering American army had no intention of granting it to them. Emilio Aguinaldo, the rebel leader, and his supporters openly went to war against their supposed benefactors. Just as the Spanish-American War was ending, the Philippine Insurrection began.

The far more powerful U.S. forces easily won the first major face-to-face confrontations, but by the summer of 1899, the war had become a bloodbath. This was the first (but certainly not the last) war where American forces were fighting "gooks" and burning villages in retribution for dead, and usually badly mutilated, comrades who had been captured earlier. American soldiers found it easy to sing lustily a new marching chorus sung to the tune of an old Civil War anthem: "**Tramp! Tramp! Tramp!**" became "Damn, Damn, Damn, the Filipinos."

American victories were frequent, but never total. Though General Arthur MacArthur, father of the future General Douglas MacArthur, could report, in November 1899, that the insurrection had been crushed, the fighting continued for nearly another three years. Aguinaldo was finally captured in March 1901, and, shortly afterwards, he called on his followers to lay down their arms. Even as their battlefield losses approached 20,000, however, many Filipinos continued the fight. Not until July 4, 1902, did now-President Theodore Roosevelt officially declare the United States the victor. More than 4,200 American soldiers lost their lives during the Philippine Insurrection, ten times the number who died trying to subdue the Spanish in 1898. Moreover, this American victory was not complete. No sooner was one revolt crushed than, on other islands, like Samar, the native Moro peoples went to war against their new American overlords. For more than another decade, the United States Army found itself fighting an often-invisible foe. Both sides slaughtered each other whenever possible. It was 1913 before the last battle had been fought and won.

The Spanish-American War and Philippine Insurrection made the United States a major player on the world scene. Even if the armed forces of the nation remained untested against the troops of any of the world's great powers, it was clear that the majority of Americans took pride in what the nation had accomplished. For every isolationist who wanted to return to the past, there were dozens of Americans who believed that Presidents McKinley and Roosevelt were correct in leading the nation into war.

See:

Freidel, Frank. *The Splendid Little War.* New York: Branhall House, 1958.

Tebbel, John W. *America's Great War with Spain: Mixed Motives, Lies, and Racism in*

Cuba and the Philippines, 1898–1915. Manchester Center, VT: Marshall Jones, 1996.

Trask, David. *The War with Spain in 1898*. New York: Macmillan, 1991.

"BREAK THE NEWS TO MOTHER" (Song). The most popular sentimental war-related ballad during the Spanish-American War was Charles Harris's "Break the News to Mother" (1897). Inspired by the dying request of a young Confederate drummer boy in William Gillette's Civil War melodrama *Secret Service* to "break the news to Mother," Harris, one of the nation's most-published songwriters, that same evening quickly composed the words and music to this latest song.

At first, it got little attention. Harris's friends told him that Americans simply no longer cared about the Civil War, and, indeed, sales of the new number's sheet music seemed to bear out the truth of their assertions. The following spring, however, when the nation went to war with Spain, everything changed dramatically. Suddenly the possibility of death in battle seemed a certainty, and "Break the News to Mother" became an overnight, smash success. During summer 1898, it was sung by the troops in Cuba and the Philippines and by the citizens at home alike.

See:

Ewen, David. *Panorama of American Popular Music*. Englewood Cliffs, NJ: Prentice-Hall, 1957, 26–27.

M. Paul Holsinger

CHRISTY, HOWARD CHANDLER (Painter). Howard Chandler Christy was an unknown novice until *Scribner's* and *Frank Leslie's Illustrated Weekly* gave him the opportunity to practice his craft, sketching Spanish-American War battle scenes with both the Second Infantry Regiment and the soon-to-be-famous Rough Riders (see *The Rough Riders*), Christy primarily illustrated articles written by the renowned war correspondent **Richard Harding Davis**. At times he also accompanied **Frederic Remington**, whom he attempted to emulate. The large number of sketches he made are honest portraits lacking in sensationalism and are considered one of the best pictorial records of the war.

Once he returned to New York, Christy produced more substantial works of art. *The Battle of Santiago, Cuba*, for instance, was created from a number of his sketches and is considered one of the finest depiction's of the offensive launched against San Juan Hill. Another image, the *Soldier's Dream* (seen first in *Scribner's*), shows a beautiful young woman appearing in the dreams of a lonely soldier. This was a model of what would become his trademark, the "Christy Girl," who took the form of an idealized young woman of the early twentieth century

During World War I, Christy also provided a number of patriotic magazine illustrations and War Bonds posters. Rather than showing troops in battle, they featured the Christy Girl in a variety of roles supporting the war effort. Several of his recruitment posters for the United States Marine Corps and Navy remain classics. They have been reprinted by the National Archives and remain for sale by that branch of the government even today.

See:

Hodgson, Pat. "Howard Chandler Christy." *The War Illustrators.* New York: Macmillan, 1977, 181–182.
Miley, Mimi C. *Howard Chandler Christy: Artist/Illustrator of Style.* Allentown, PA: Allentown Art Museum, 1977, 6–14.

Michael Brown

DAVIS, RICHARD HARDING (War Correspondent–Newspaperman). The popular correspondent Richard Harding Davis became the managing editor of the famed *Harper's Weekly* in 1890, but it was not until seven years later that he found his true calling. In that year, the *New York Herald* sent him to cover the Greco-Turkish War, and soon he was reporting on wars all over the world.

In 1897, Davis went to Cuba at the insistence of William Randolph Hearst to help roil up war with Spain, and once the conflict began, he returned to that island with the American troops. Later in that year he was in South Africa reporting on the Boer War between the English and Dutch. Davis also covered the Russo-Japanese War of 1904–1905 and, in 1914, the Mexican Civil War and the U.S. military occupation of Vera Cruz. During the first years of World War I, he was assigned to British and French forces fighting in central Europe. After being captured by the Germans, he came close to being executed as a British spy.

During the last years of his life, Davis authored several extremely popular novels as well as a series of books recounting some of his experiences on the battlefronts. Two of his best works, *A Year from a Reporter's Notebook* (1903) and *Notes of a War Correspondent* (1912), are still worth reading today. *Notes* contains much of the story of Davis's Spanish-American War adventures. His last book, *With the French* (1916), features an eloquent plea for the United States to enter the "Great War" on the side of the French; it was completed the very day that Davis died, suddenly, of a massive heart attack.

See:

Lubow, Arthur. *The Reporter Who Would Be King: A Biography of Richard Harding Davis.* New York: Charles Scribner's Sons, 1992.

M. Paul Holsinger

FIGHTING WITH OUR BOYS IN CUBA (Film). Americans were at a fever pitch after the U.S. declaration of war against Spain in spring 1898. Any account about Cuba, the Philippines, or the supposed evils of the Spanish government was sure to draw millions of interested observers, and it soon became obvious that a company that could produce filmed footage of the war would be guaranteed instant monetary rewards. The Vitagraph Company, the cinematic brainchild of entertainers Albert E. Smith and J. Stuart Blackton, was one of the first to capitalize on the public's patriotic fervor.

Vitagraph and the far larger (Thomas) Edison Company had been in competition for some months before the outbreak of the war. Now both vied to become the first in the United States, if, indeed, not in the entire world, to capture live military events in motion pictures. It is impossible today to know which came first. Edison's firm certainly made pictures of volunteers embarking for Cuba and of troops landing on that island. Smith and Blackton, however, came closest to the battle lines. In one memorable film spanning a number of minutes, they even recorded the so-called Rough Riders' somewhat torturous advance up San Juan Hill (see *The Rough Riders*). This segment, edited together with other documentary footage taken by the two men, was released that summer under the title, *Fighting with Our Boys in Cuba* (Vitagraph, 1898). Though the majority of the scenes were unspectacularly pedestrian, American theatergoers were overwhelmingly enthusiastic and made the movie one of the most popular successes of the year.

Some historians, who are aware of the fact that Smith and Blackton had developed a reputation in their early years for manufacturing fraudulent documentary motion pictures for profit, maintain that all the action shots in *Fighting with Our Boys in Cuba* were also faked. Most, however, accept Smith's claim that he was the first wartime newsreel photographer.

See:

Fielding, Raymond. *The American Newsreel, 1911–1967*. Norman: University of Oklahoma Press, 1972, 29–45.
Musser, Charles. "American Vitagraph: 1897–1901." *Cinema Journal* 22.3 (1983): 16.

M. Paul Holsinger

GLACKENS, WILLIAM (Artist). William James Glackens served as a field artist for *McClure's* magazine during the Spanish-American War. Trained as an impressionist, he illustrated for a number of newspapers before *McClure's* exclusively hired him to cover the campaigns of U.S. troops in Cuba. One of the most talented artists to cover the war, Glackens's views of the military landing at Daiquiri as well as those of soldiers in battle at both Bloody Brook and San Juan Hill, are among the small handful of excellent visual scenes to come out of the conflict.

Because *McClure's* did not have an established organization in Cuba to provide support, Glackens ate the regular mess food served to the troops and lived with them in often-primitive conditions. As a result, after his return to the United States, he became sick with malaria. To make matters worse, much of his artistic work from the battlefields was never seen. The war ended abruptly before many of his drawings arrived at *McClure's*, and that magazine chose to pay him only for those it actually used. Disillusioned because a great deal of his work had gone unrewarded and unpublished, Glackens never again served as a field artist.

For several years after the war, Glackens continued to produce a steady stream of popular work for a variety of magazines and books. He gradually quit illustrating early in the twentieth century to become a successful artist and, ultimately, one of the most important members of the "Ashcan School" of American realism.

See:

Gerdts, William H. *William Glackens.* New York: Abbeville Press, 1996.

Michael Brown

"HE'S COMING TO US DEAD" (Song). One of the all-time great standards of country-and-western music, "He's Coming to Us Dead," was written by the renowned African-American composer Gussie Davis in 1899, the year after the conclusion of the Spanish-American War. It tells the sad tale of an elderly father who has just arrived at a city express station to pick up the body of his dead son. The manager wonders if there has been a mistake—the train depot is on the other side of town—but in maudlin terms the old man tells him that his boy is not coming home a passenger; rather, "he's coming to us dead." He reminisces "with trembling lips" about his "darling Jack," and then, as the casket is lowered from the train, concludes, "Thank God he died a hero's death while with the boys in blue."

"He's Coming to Us Dead" gained instant popularity among many "hillbilly" musicians and was resurrected during every war in which the United States was involved over the next fifty-plus years. During World War I, for instance, country singers frequently performed it, and as early as 1929, the renowned country musician Stuart Hamblen recorded it under the title, "Boys in Blue." Texas Ruby, one of the first significant female country stars, sang it as a standard on her radio broadcasts during the Great Depression, and in the middle of World War II, a number of performers recorded the song, including the popular Molly O'Day, a young Kentuckian whose regular shows from Renfro Valley in that state were heard regularly on Armed Forces Radio throughout both major theaters of war. In 1947, O'Day rerecorded "He's Coming to Us Dead" under the new title, "A Hero's Death," for Columbia, and as recently as the war in Korea, it was still being widely played.

See:

"Mollie O'Day and the Cumberland Mountain Folks [Booklet]." In *Mollie O'Day and the Cumberland Mountain Folks.* Bear Family Records, 1992.

M. Paul Holsinger

***THE HIKER* (Memorial).** The success of U.S. forces during the Spanish-American War and the subsequent Philippine Insurrection produced a new image of the American infantryman, which sculptors and other artists soon exploited. After U.S. troops rescued the beseiged western delegations in Peking during the 1900 Boxer Rebellion in China, the representation of a young soldier with a large, broad-brimmed, soft hat; an open-necked shirt with the sleeves rolled up; and a gun held at the ready gained even wider national acceptance.

The first statue in the United States honoring these young soldiers is a larger-than-life–sized (eight-foot, five-inch high) bronze known as *The Hiker*, created by Theo Alice Ruggles in 1906 for the University of Minnesota's campus in Minneapolis. It was so immediately popular that she eventually made more than fifty fascimilies which, over the next few years, were placed in city parks in such diverse places as Oshkosh, Wisconsin; Savannah, Georgia; Providence, Rhode Island; New Orleans, Louisiana; and Portland, Maine. A replica can also be found in Arlington National Cemetery. As late as the 1940s, other *Hiker* sculptures were still being dedicated to honor veterans from America's earlier wars. Two of the most famous of these stand on the lawn of the state capitol in Lansing, Michigan, and in Penn Valley Park near Memorial Drive in Kansas City, Missouri. A slightly different variation of the same theme was sculpted by Allen G. Newman in 1916.

The Hiker is a reflection of the nation's warring spirit at the time and symbolizes the young soldier at the end of the nineteenth century in the same way that Daniel Chester French's even more famous *The Minute Man* became, after its unveiling in 1875, the representation of all colonial volunteers during the American Revolution.

See:

Reynolds, Donald Martin. *Masters of American Sculpture: The Figurative Tradition from the American Renaissance to the Millennium.* New York: Abbeville, 1993, 154.

M. Paul Holsinger

A MESSAGE TO GARCIA (Essay-Film). In the days immediately before the United States went to war with Spain, in April 1898, Andrew Summers Rowan, a young army lieutenant attached to military intelligence, was smuggled into Cuba to find the local insurgent leader, General Calixto Garcia Iniquez, and obtain information about Spanish troop deployments. Though Rowan had to fight through jungles and across several mountain ranges, he succeeded in his mission, and the story of his quest became legendary, especially after the American victory in the Spanish-American War.

In March 1899, magazine editor Elbert Hubbard popularized Rowan's story in his journal the *Philistine* under the title, "A Message to Garcia." Hubbard made the account into a strong moral lesson in loyalty and responsibility by emphasizing the importance of never flagging from one's responsibility regardless of the difficulty.

Hubbard estimated that at least 40 million copies of "A Message to Garcia" were sold over the next decade. It has never gone out of print in the almost one hundred years since it was first penned. Indeed, so much a part of American life has it become that its title is now an accepted way to emphasize a person's perseverance in the face of adversity.

Director George Marshall very loosely attempted to tell Rowan's story in *A Message to Garcia* (20th Century–Fox, 1936). Starring Wallace Beery, Barbara Stanwyck, and John Boles (who, the previous year, had been cast as Shirley Temple's father in the Civil War musical *The Littlest Rebel*) as Rowan, the film strains the actual facts almost to the breaking point. Though often entertaining, it was also, the *New York Times* noted, "as undocumented a piece of historical claptrap as [Hollywood] has [ever] produced" (April 10, 1936, 27: 1). It is memorable today only because it remains one of the very few attempts by the motion picture industry to focus on the war with Spain.

See:

Champney, Freeman. *Art and Glory: The Story of Elbert Hubbard*. Kent, OH: Kent State University Press, 1983.
Dirlam, H. Kenneth. *The Story of "A Message to Garcia."* Mansfield, OH: [The Author], 1960.

                                                                        M. Paul Holsinger

MR. DOOLEY IN PEACE AND IN WAR (Newspaper Columns). In 1893, Finley Peter Dunne, a political reporter for the *Chicago Evening Post*, created "Mr. Dooley," a local shanty Irish saloonkeeper, as an alter ego through whom he could regularly comment (in dialect) about contemporary events. He soon became the voice of the common man, and, for the next thirty-three years, Dooley's always humorous views kept Americans laughing both at, and with, him and his friend, Hennessy.

When the United States declared war on Spain, in spring 1898, Dooley's essays, which were now, for the first time, being read nationwide, looked at everything from reasons for the conflict to battlefield victories by American troops in Cuba and the Philippines. In November, Dunne's first book, *Mr. Dooley in Peace and in War*, pulled together the best of these writings, including perhaps his most famous war-related piece, "On the Destruction of Cervera's Fleet." It was an instant success. More than 10,000 copies of the book sold monthly, propelling it onto the best-seller list for more than a year. Mr. Dooley was quoted in Congress, and his thoughts were read aloud in President McKinley's cabinet meetings. Politicians began to ask, in all seriousness, "What would Mr. Dooley say?" when considering how to vote on an issue, and the public looked forward to even more of the fictional Irishman's often-perceptive thoughts.

"Mr. Dooley" continued to discuss war until the end of his journalistic career, in the mid-1920s. Nearly fifty different pieces dealt with, not only the Spanish-American War and its aftermath, but also the Boer War, the Russo-Japanese War, and World War I. As Dunne aged, his already jaundiced views about war became even more pessimistic. In one of his last essays, he expressed doubt that "there'll iver be peace in this fractious wurruld" (Eckley, 101). Finley Peter Dunne's death three years before the outbreak of World War II spared him from seeing just how correct "Mr. Dooley" had been.

See:

Eckley, Grace. *Finley Peter Dunne*. Boston: Twayne, 1981.

M. Paul Holsinger

THE REAL GLORY (Film). *The Real Glory* (Samuel Goldwyn, 1939) is set in the early years of the United States Army's occupation of the Philippines. Based on Charles L. Clifford's 1937 novel of the same name and directed by Henry Hathaway, it is one of the few Hollywood-made films to examine the Moro insurrection in the Philippines immediately after the beginning of the twentieth century. Many of Hollywood's top stars, including Gary Cooper, David Niven, and Broderick Crawford, appear as stalwart army leaders.

As U.S. forces withdraw from their fortifications in Mindanao, a small contingent of Christian native troops is left behind under the command of two American line officers: an army physician, and a sergeant. It is the Moros, depicted in the movie as nothing more than vicious Muslim pirates bent on terrorizing and plundering the peaceful Filipinos, who are the stereotypical villains. Unlike Aguinaldo and other real-life Philippine nationalists, whose goal was freedom and justice for their people, the Moros, according to Jo Swerling and Robert Presnell's screenplay, have no political ambitions other than their bandit chief's selfish desire to consolidate his power over the entire island. Forced to take charge when the commander of the contingent falls ill, the physician (convincingly played by the popular Cooper), uses his training in medicine and psychology to defeat the Moros and, in the end, to help justice and American imperialism triumph.

The Real Glory is dedicated to the "members of the Philippine Constabulary" who "struggled valiantly to wrest their independence from those that sought to enslave them." With Japan already dominating much of China and Mongolia, *The Real Glory* served as ironic, but prescient, propaganda in preparation for the events that were soon to follow.

See:

Walsh, John E. *The Philippine Insurrection, 1899–1902: America's Only Try for an Overseas Empire*. New York: F. Watts, 1973.

Jack Colldeweih

"REMEMBER THE *MAINE*" (Slogan-Songs). On February 15, 1898, the United States battleship *Maine* blew up in the harbor of Havana, Cuba, killing 266 seamen. Though it was another two months before war was declared on Spain, the majority of Americans had long been primed for Congress to act. Popularized by the *New York Journal*, the sentiment "Remember the *Maine*, To Hell with Spain," was pervasive across the nation in the late winter of 1898. There were candies, matchboxes, paperweights, cutlery, and dozens of other items emblazoned with the slogan.

One of the reasons for such feeling was the appearance of no less than forty different songs lamenting the fate of the *Maine* and her crew. Written between February 15 and April 25 (when war was declared), they had such titles as "Disaster of the Good Ship *Maine*," "My Sweetheart went down with the *Maine*," and "He Sleeps upon Havana's Shore in a Suit of Navy Blue." There were also "Our Nation's Battle Cry, 'Remember the *Maine*' " and " 'Remember the *Maine*' Is Our Battle Cry."

Echoing the popular slogan, at least ten different songs were called "Remember the *Maine*." Most called for retribution against Spain. One, which was written by N. A. Jennings and W. A. Phillips and printed on the front page of the *New York World* came quickly to the point:

> From North and South and East and West
> From city, farm, and plain
> Loud comes a cry will never rest
> For vengeance unto Spain.

William Broderick's "Captain of the *Maine*" made it clear what Spain's fate would be: "With our navy to the front / we'll make the Spanish grunt," the song opined. The great majority of Americans wanted to do just that.

See:

McNeil, W. K. " 'We'll Make the Spanish Grunt': Popular Songs about the Sinking of the *Maine*." *Journal of Popular Culture* 2 (1978): 537–551.

M. Paul Holsinger

THE ROUGH RIDERS (Memoir-Painting-Films). After Assistant Secretary of the Navy Theodore Roosevelt organized the often-flamboyant First United States Volunteer Cavalry, or the "Rough Riders" (as they became known colloquially everywhere across the nation in summer 1898), the unit gained instant fame. When the men, fighting alongside troopers from the Ninth (Colored) United States Cavalry, charged up the steep slopes of San Juan Hill outside Santiago, Cuba, the public was captivated. No single event during the war became more enshrined in American popular culture. On his return home, the already prolific Roosevelt wrote *The Rough Riders* (1899), a personal memoir of the campaign. Some critics, such as the irreverent "Mr. Dooley" (see *Mr. Dooley in Peace and in War*) thought that the book should have been called "Alone in Cuba," but it became a popular best-seller nonetheless.

Though the Rough Riders' story seemingly was a "natural" for screen adaptation, it was not until the late 1920s that producer B. P. Schulberg and director Victor Fleming announced plans to film, "on a lavish and impressive scale," a fictional tale about the men. Charles Farrell, Mary Astor, and Noah Beery (all top Hollywood stars) were selected for major roles. Shot in San Antonio, Texas (where Roosevelt had recruited "his boys"), and California, *The Rough Riders* (Paramount Famous Players–Lasky, 1927), literally had "a cast of thousands" portraying either U.S. troops or their Spanish or Cuban enemies. Though there was a good amount of humor in the early part of the script (by screenwriters Robert N. Lee and Keene Thompson), the best segments were those that focused closely on Roosevelt (played by a look-alike from Los Angeles named Frank Hopper) and his men in battle. Audiences apparently agreed with one critic who called the film "100 percent pure unadulterated American entertainment" (*Movie Picture News*, March 25, 1927) and made it a box-office success. Sadly, however, like so many other early Hollywood motion pictures, no prints have survived.

In summer 1997, the highly successful screenwriter-director John Milius developed another version based on the Rough Riders' adventures named simply *Rough Riders* (Turner Pictures, 1997). Starring Tom Berenger as Theodore Roosevelt, the four-hour miniseries (called by Atlanta's TNT cable channel "a saga of guts and glory") stretches many of the facts almost to the breaking point. Historical inaccuracies abound, but the drama remains constantly interesting and, occasionally, even exciting.

See:

Jones, Virgil C. *Roosevelt's Rough Riders*. Garden City, NY: Doubleday, 1971.
Thompson, Frank. "Rough Riders." Chapter 18 in *Lost Films: Important Movies That Disappeared*. New York: Citadel Press, 1996, 166–175.

M. Paul Holsinger

STRATEMEYER, EDWARD (Author). Although he published no less than twenty-five magazine stories and seventy-seven volumes under his own name, Edward Stratemeyer also used eighty-three pseudonyms in writing and supervising approximately 900 dime novels and series books for children. The Rover Boys, the Hardy Boys, the Motor Boys, Tom Swift, Nancy Drew, Bomba the Jungle Boy, the Bobbsey Twins, and dozens of other characters were all the creation of this one writer and entrepreneur, who applied the principles of mass production to children's literature.

Stratemeyer was working as a tobacco-store clerk when he sold his first children's story, in 1889. In 1893, he became editor of a boys' story paper but gradually shifted his attention to children's series (i.e., inexpensive, formulaic novels featuring a set of clean-living juvenile protagonists who reappear for new adventures in each subsequent volume). Unable to do all the writing himself, Stratemeyer formed the Stratemeyer Syndicate around 1905, establishing an assembly-line system in which he outlined new episodes for his cast of characters before assigning others in his fiction factory to fill in the rest.

Many of Stratemeyer's novels have war-related themes, including six about the Spanish-American War in the Old Glory Series (1898–1901), four set in the Pacific in the Soldiers of Fortune Series (1900–1906), three in the Mexican War Series (1909), and six dealing with World War I in the Air Service Boys Series (1918–1920). *Under Dewey in Manila, or the War Fortunes of a Castaway* (1898), his first war-related volume, is typical of all the rest. It tells the story of an orphan, Larry Russell, who runs away from his cruel guardian and goes to sea. After being shipwrecked, he is picked up by Admiral Dewey's fleet as it steams towards Manila Bay, and he is thus able to take part in the American Navy's famous victory over Spain. Stratemeyer devotes an inordinate amount of the novel to giving his readers details about the Spanish-American War or a military overview about the U.S. victory in the battle itself. Larry almost disappears from the story during these sections of the book, but he is brought back to celebrate at the end.

After Stratemeyer's death in 1930, his eldest daughter, Harriet Stratemeyer Adams, continued the syndicate, which was sold to Simon and Schuster in 1982, following her death. During the last one hundred years, it is estimated that well over 200 million copies of Stratemeyer series books have been sold worldwide.

See:

Johnson, Deidre. *Edward Stratemeyer and the Stratemeyer Syndicate*. New York: Twayne, 1993.

James Deutsch

TEARING DOWN THE SPANISH FLAG (Film). In 1897, less than a year after Thomas Edison perfected the Vitascope, his device for projecting pictures onto a screen, a young English immigrant named J. Stuart Blackton and his friend, Albert E. Smith, bought a projector from Edison and went into business. Taking their camera to the roof of a downtown Manhattan building, they began to make movies, usually in the form of short, one-reelers with such forgettable, but obvious, titles as *The Burglar on the Roof.*

Nothing suggested in these early days that the nascent filmmakers would ever do anything noteworthy, but in April 1898, just a few days after the United States declared war on Spain, the duo went to their roof and made *Tearing down the Spanish Flag* (Vitagraph, 1898). It was the world's first commercial war movie. Shot by Smith and simple in the extreme, it was an enormous success, even though it consists of nothing more than a close-up of Blackton's hands reaching up to pull down a flag of Spain and then running up the American standard in its place. Audiences flocked to nickelodeon theaters to see it, and Blackton and Smith quickly made other pictures with Spanish-American War themes. Most, like their first hit, were remarkably simplistic and not a little dishonest. In *The Battle of Manila Bay* (Vitagraph, 1898), for instance, they recreated Admiral George Dewey's famous victory in the Blackton family bathtub; Smith took close-ups of cutouts of battleships that Blackton moved around in the water, while Mrs. Blackton puffed cigarette smoke at the lens to give the effect of gunfire from the ship's cannons.

Seen today, most of Blackton's and Smith's earliest work seems unbelievably amateurish, but in 1898, the war craze provided the men with the foundation for careers that eventually made them two of the industry's most renowned filmmakers. Before 1925, when it was sold to Warner Brothers, their firm, Vitagraph Studios, became one of America's foremost production companies and certainly its most famous maker of war-related films.

See:

Fielding, Raymond. *The American Newsreel, 1911–1967.* Norman: University of
    Oklahoma Press, 1972, 29–45.

M. Paul Holsinger

"THERE'LL BE A HOT TIME IN THE OLD TOWN TONIGHT" (Song).
The most popular song of American troops fighting in Cuba during the Spanish-
American War, "There'll Be a Hot Time in the Old Town Tonight," originally
had nothing to do with that, or any other, war. Theodore Metz, its author and,
for a time, bandleader of the McIntyre and Heath Minstrels, claimed that he was
inspired to jot down the melody after watching a group of black children put
out a fire in Old Town, Louisiana, in 1886. Such may be the case, though there
is even more evidence that he appropriated the tune after hearing it played in a
St. Louis brothel. A singer in Metz's group, Joe Hayden, penned the lyrics.
    Regardless of its heritage, "There'll Be a Hot Time in the Old Town To-
night" was the minstrel show's lead-in for more than ten years before it was
finally published in 1896. It was soon featured on vaudeville stages across the
country. When the war with Spain broke out, the soldiers took it with them and
sang it in anticipation of their return home from the battlefields. Teddy Roosevelt's Rough Riders (see *The Rough Riders*) even made it their unit's theme
song. According to one French newspaper report, the survivors of the Battle of
San Juan Hill enthusiastically sang "There'll Be a Hot Time" the evening after
their sensational victory. Indeed, so often did military bands play the tune that
some foreign observers concluded that it must be the American national anthem.
    When he ran for governor of New York in 1899, Theodore Roosevelt initially
used the song in his campaign but quickly tired of it. Though Republican groups
continued to play it as late as his presidential campaign of 1904, Roosevelt by
that time had come to resent the fact that it was so intimately connected with
his past glories. Today, if it is sung at all, most people erroneously think it was
written because of Chicago's famous fire of 1871.

See:

Ewen, David. *All the Years of American Popular Music.* Englewood Cliffs, NJ: Prentice-
    Hall, 1977, 145–146.

M. Paul Holsinger

WAR IS KIND **(Poetry–Choral Music).** When *War Is Kind*, Stephen Crane's
second book of poetry, was published in 1899, most Americans were still euphoric over the nation's victory in the Spanish-American War the previous year.
If they thought they were buying a volume glorifying that "splendid little war,"
however, they were sadly mistaken. Though Crane was in Cuba during the
fighting, the great majority of his poems have little or nothing to do with the
volume's ironic title. Indeed, even the featured work, which first appeared in

February 1896, stands out in the canon of war literature only for its facetious commentary on the waste and brutality of military conflict.

"War Is Kind," one of only two poems in the book actually to deal with war, approaches its subject with ironic hyperbole and understatement. "Do not weep, maiden, for war is kind," Crane says, but it is soon clear that just the opposite is true. There is no glory in war, with its bloodshed and death. Words and phrases—some oxymoronic, such as "drill and die," "yellow trenches," "the virtue of slaughter," "splendid shroud," and "a field where a thousand corpses lie"—all emphasize the horrors of the battlefield. A young maiden who has lost her lover, a child who will grow up fatherless, and a mother whose son will return in a funeral shroud are all shown suffering because of the war.

Crane's verse is not as well known as his fiction, but "War Is Kind" remains an unforgettable commentary on the brutality and senselessness of armed struggle. During the nation's bicentennial in 1976, John Carter set it to music as a choral piece with baritone solo and piano accompaniment, and it is frequently sung today by high school ensembles across the nation.

See:

Hoffman, Daniel. *The Poetry of Stephen Crane*. New York: Columbia University Press, 1957.

Catherine Calloway

YELLOW JOURNALISM (Prowar Reporting). In early 1896, William Randolph Hearst of the New York *Journal* and Joseph Pulitzer of the New York *World* began a circulation war. To win subscribers, the two men began to print, as a part of a Sunday colored comics section, the most famous cartoon of the day, Richard F. Outcault's *The Yellow Kid*. Outcault originally drew the cartoon for the *World* but then, along with nearly all that newspaper's staff, deserted to Hearst's higher-paying *Journal*. Critics of the two papers saw *The Yellow Kid* as symbolic of the kind of journalism that put more stock in selling papers than anything else. It was Ervin Wardman of the rival *New York Press* who first coined "yellow press" to describe his competitors, and others quickly picked up the phrase. "Yellow journalism" appearing in a "yellow press" eventually became the accepted term for sensationalism in print.

Neither Pulitzer nor Hearst did anything to discourage such slurs. On the contrary, within a few months both newspapermen were working overtime to foment a war in Cuba between the United States and Spain, as much to sell more papers as to report the news. Each sent reporters to the island in hopes that the ongoing war of independence between Spain and its Cuban colonists might spread. According to one of the most famous legends in American publishing history, **Frederic Remington**, who was sent by Hearst to Cuba to sketch scenes of the fighting, told him "there will be no war," to which the publisher reportedly replied, "You furnish the pictures and I'll furnish the war" (McCullough, 29), Though Hearst later denied making such a remark, the *Journal* became one of the most jingoistic newspapers in the United States. When the USS *Maine* exploded in Havana harbor in February 1898, the *Journal* automatically proclaimed that it was the work of an enemy and called on everyone to encourage the president and elected representatives to go to war as soon as possible (see **"Remember the *Maine*"**).

"Yellow journalism" stressed the sensational side of the news, and even manufactured it when necessary for bigger headlines, but it did occasionally produce some exceptional reporting after the war began. On several occasions, even Hearst showed up on the front lines, once writing a story for the *Journal* while under fire from entrenched Spanish positions.

See:

Brown, Charles H. *The Correspondents' War: Journalists in the Spanish-American War.* New York: Charles Scribner's Sons, 1967.

McCullough, David. "Remington the Man." In *Frederic Remington: The Masterworks*, ed. Michael Edward Shapiro and Peter H. Hassrick. St. Louis, MO: The St. Louis Art Museum, 1988.

Milton, Joyce. *The Yellow Kids: Foreign Correspondents in the Heyday of Yellow Journalism.* New York: Harper, 1989.

M. Paul Holsinger

9

World War I and the 1920s

On April 6, 1917, a divided U.S. Congress accepted President Woodrow Wilson's call for a declaration of war against the "Central Powers," Germany, Austria, and Hungary. Ever since the first "guns of August" opened fire in 1914, a majority of American citizens clamored to stay far removed from the European bloodletting. Though there were some young men, like poet **Alan Seeger**, who immediately joined the French Foreign Legion to fight for that nation against its totalitarian foe, in the United States most persons sang, with conviction, **"I Didn't Raise My Boy to Be a Soldier."** That song, which was one of the most popular of early 1915, came far closer to touching the spirit of most citizens than those with a martial lilt. When Wilson ran for reelection the following year, it seemed appropriate to many of his supporters to note proudly, "He Kept Us Out of War." Now, however, for both idealistic and very practical economic considerations, the nation at last had become a part of the fray.

With characteristic fervor, the nation devoted itself to winning quickly and totally. "I Want You," a tough-looking **Uncle Sam** declared from James Montgomery Flagg posters, and millions responded. Volunteers crowded recruitment centers to sign up for the army, navy, or Marine Corps. When it was determined that even more were necessary, Congress quickly passed the Selective Service Act to "draft" men for the war. Though not everyone was pleased at the thought of fighting an overseas conflict, by June 1917, nearly 10 million men were registered for the draft. A month later, on July 20, 1917, Secretary of War Newton Baker drew the first draft lottery numbers, and long before the summer was over, training camps throughout the United States were filling up with men ready to fight the Kaiser and his hoards of German "Huns."

The American Expeditionary Force (AEF), though often not fully trained, was rushed hundreds of thousands strong, to Europe. As early as July 4, 1917, members of the Sixteenth Infantry marched through the streets of Paris. "Lafayette, We Are Here," they trumpeted, and they chafed at not immediately being sent into battle. Even when they did arrive at the seemingly endless trenches that spanned the Western Front, most of their fighting consisted of isolated sorties into "No Man's Land." Though often bloody, these skirmishes offered little opportunity for the increasing numbers who were arriving each month to push for the inevitable victory that nearly all Americans felt sure would come once they were fully involved.

In March 1918, the last, great German offensive began, and at last, U.S. troops had the chance that so many had been longing for. In April, General John "Black Jack" Pershing led his men into battle for the first time. The freshness of the American troops, if not their bravery and courage under fire, soon began to make a difference. On May 28, at Cantigny, they scored their first significant victory, and it was not the last. Later that month and into the next, at Chateau Thierry on the Marne, American boys blunted the German advance that had flowed virtually unchecked for many weeks. On June 6, twenty-six years to the day before another generation of American troops landed on the beaches at Normandy as part of the greatest amphibious invasion in history, the Marines went on the offensive at Belleau Wood. For nearly a month, the battle continued. When it ended, the American "Devil Dogs," as the German Army nicknamed the Marines, had won the day.

There were times when American battle losses were terrible, but after mid-July, the Germans were pushed back along the entire front. By the end of that month, more than 1.2 million American military men were in France, and that number was climbing every day. One of the nation's greatest victories came during the St. Mihiel offense early in September, when the German opposition collapsed under the onslaught of the American "doughboys." The Meuse-Argonne offensive began on September 26, and, within two weeks, the Americans drove the enemy out of the entire sector. It was during this campaign that the most renowned U.S. hero, Sergeant Alvin York (see *Sergeant York*), single-handedly captured 132 Germans and killed another 25. Amazing as the feat was (it earned the sergeant a Medal of Honor and the praise of General John J. Pershing), to many, it seemed symbolic of the entire AEF's prowess under fire.

The last weeks of the war saw the Americans and the Allies breaking through all along the Western Front. To General Pershing, now, more than ever, seemed like a good time to demand unconditional surrender, but the equally weary Allies were as ready to stop fighting as were the Germans. On November 11, 1918, Armistice was declared, and the guns on the Western Front finally fell silent for the first time in more than four years.

World War I, like the American Revolution and the Civil War, was a singing war. New York City's "Tin Pan Alley" cranked out more than seven thousand songs to cheer on the nation's military men as they supposedly were marching directly on Berlin and conquering the German Kaiser himself. At home, wives and sweethearts promised to **"Keep the Home Fires Burning,"** and to "Smile,

Smile, Smile.'' Flag-waving, patriotic silent films kindled a war-like spirit in their viewers. It was hard not to want to rush off to fight after viewing scenes of the beautiful Mary Pickford, ''America's sweetheart,'' being brutalized by vicious enemy officers or seeing through the eyes of the ''Little Tramp,'' Charlie Chaplin, how remarkably easy, and even funny, war could be.

In comparison with the massive destruction of men and matériel that other Allied nations experienced during World War I, American losses in the country's less than one year of combat (slightly more than 53,000 deaths and ''only'' 200,000 wounded) were relatively light. Sadly, however, such sacrifices produced little of significance. In January 1918, President Wilson had enunciated his famous ''Fourteen Points'' to help the American public understand why they were in the war. Freedom of the seas, no entangling alliances, home rule for all peoples, and an end to war all seemed worth fighting and, if necessary, dying for. Now, with the war at an end, it was clear that none of these lofty dreams had been achieved. The seas remained in the hands of the great powers. Though Germany was stripped of all its colonies, colonialism continued unabated. Europe's entangling alliances were becoming even more confused. When the Allies created the League of Nations, the Republican-controlled U.S. Senate, as much to spite Wilson as anything else, refused to allow the nation to become a member.

The frustration felt by many was dulled by large doses of alcoholic beverages with no apparent thought about their illegality (after the passage of the Eighteenth ''Prohibition'' Amendment to the Constitution). Others, including a significant number of veterans, found their answer in expatriation. Ernest Hemingway, William Faulkner, and dozens of similar young writers, poets, and others fled the United States for the cities and towns of Great Britain, France, or Spain. Everyone wondered whether the war had been worth its deaths and destruction. Certainly, the world was not ''made safe for democracy.'' New wars, especially in Russia and the old Hapsburg Empire, broke out immediately after Armistice Day and continued for years to come. Americans had gone **''Over There''** brimming with confidence, but now, as the ''Roaring Twenties'' were about to begin, it was clear to nearly everyone that they had returned with neither a real peace nor the guarantee of having made any lasting difference at all.

In the 1920s, far from retreating from military encounters around the world, however, the United States found itself sending young men to fight, and often die, in places thousands of miles from home. Though the nation took a leading role in trying to reduce the number of warships that the major powers possessed and Secretary of State Frank Kellogg won a Nobel Peace Prize for his efforts in negotiating a supposed end to all ''offensive war'' through the implementa tion of the so-called Kellogg-Briand Peace Pact in 1928, the U.S. Marines fought a long and bloody war in Nicaragua at the end of the decade that carried over into the years of the Great Depression. The navy and the Marines also played an important role in the internal affairs of the Chinese Republic during its many bloody civil wars after 1911. Long before American airmen found themselves in China fighting the Japanese during World War II, thousands of other young men fought and died to further the diplomatic and economic policies of the U.S. government. By the time the country was finally plunged into another full-scale war, in December 1941, many of its men had been fighting for years.

See:

Freidel Frank. *Over There: The Story of America's First Great Overseas Crusade*. Rev. ed. New York: McGraw-Hill, 1990.

Harris, Meirion, and Susie Harris. *The Last Days of Innocence: America at War, 1917–1918*. New York: Random House, 1997.

Kennedy, David M. *Over Here: The First World War and American Society*. New York: Oxford University Press, 1980.

Talley, Kemp. *Yangtze Patrol: The United States Navy in China*. Annapolis, MD: Naval Institute Press, 1985.

Tessendorff, K. C. *Uncle Sam in Nicaragua: A History*. New York: Atheneum, 1987.

THE BATTLE CRY OF PEACE (Silent Film). J. Stuart Blackton, a pioneer in the filming of re-created and actual war-related events during the Spanish-American War, had, by 1915, become the first of many motion picture million-aires. An ardent patriot, he had a home next to Theodore Roosevelt in Oyster Bay, New York, and, like the ex-president, he was appalled at the U.S. position of neutrality toward the rapidly escalating war in Europe.

Blackton determined to "wake up America" cinematically. The result was *The Battle Cry for Peace, A Call to Arms against War* (Vitagraph, 1915). Dedicated to America's mothers, his adaptation of Hudson Maxim's semifictional *Defenseless America* (1914) premiered in New York City on September 14, 1915. It sets out to warn viewers what would happen to the United States if it were unprepared to repel aggressors. Actors in quasi-Germanic uniforms attack New York City, occupy its major buildings, and then engage in an orgy of drunkeness and rape. John Harrison, the hero, favors preparedness, while his fiancée, Virginia Vandergriff, is for peace at any price. In the end, both die— John, bayoneted to death by German soldiers as he tries to protect his fiancée; Virginia and her sister, shot by their mother to save them from "a fate worse than death."

Blackton readily admitted to a group of students in 1929 that his picture was deliberate propaganda to embroil the United States in the war. It clearly worked. Theodore Roosevelt told one reporter; "[*The Battle Cry of Peace*] has done more for the Allied cause than twenty battalions of soldiers." The film was extremely popular both in the United States and in Great Britain, where it was called *An American's Home*. Between 50 and 75 million people saw one version or another, and in an era of low-priced admissions, it grossed more than $1 million.

A sequel, *Womanhood, the Glory of a Nation* (Vitagraph, 1917), directed by Blackton, appeared immediately after the entrance of the United States into the war. Although not as popular as its predecessor, it also drew large crowds wherever it was shown.

See:

Brownlow, Kevin. *The War, the West, and the Wilderness.* New York: Knopf, 1979, 30–
     38.

                                                                M. Paul Holsinger

THE BIG PARADE (Silent Film). *The Big Parade* (Metro-Goldwyn-Mayer, 1925) is one of the greatest war movies ever made. Presented from the viewpoint, not of officers and heroes, but of ordinary American soldiers in World War I, it does not take sides but rather shows convincingly how soldiers try to survive in a situation not of their own making. Written by Laurence Stallings, an ex-Marine who lost a leg at Belleau Wood and the coauthor of the then extremely popular Broadway drama (and subsequent motion picture) **What Price Glory?**, *The Big Parade* finds no honor in war, but only death, misery, and despair. If men go off to battle filled with glowing patriotism, they all too frequently return—if they return at all—maimed for life.

Surprisingly, despite the movie's clearly enunciated antiwar sentiments, director King Vidor received the cooperation of the United States Army and Air Service in the making of his film, which shows repeatedly in some of the many camera shots of both the men and the machinery of war. Veterans who attended showings were uniform in their praise. Enormously popular throughout the United States, *The Big Parade*, with more than $15 million in box office receipts, became one of the highest-grossing pictures of the silent era.

The screenplay is unpretentious. Three men—the rich socialite Jim Apperson (played brilliantly by John Gilbert); Michael "Bull" O'Hara (Tom O'Brien), a bartender; and Slim Jensen (Karl Dane), a welder—caught up in the midst of their city's excitement over the declaration of war, enlist in the army, are sent to France, and eventually engage in battle. Slim is fatally wounded while attempting to destroy a German gun emplacement. Bull dies, and Jim is badly hurt (and eventually loses a leg) trying to rescue their friend. There is no glory as he returns home a cripple. In the days before going into battle, however, he met and fell in love with Melisande (Renee Adoree), a vivacious Frenchwoman. That love (and, perhaps, that of his pacifist mother) keeps him going and eventually brings him back to France and to the arms of his sweetheart as the concluding titles roll.

Although the melodramatic and dated acting style takes away from the power of the film for modern viewers, the battle sequences of soldiers marching to their death, stepping over bodies, falling into shell holes, and being confused by the smoke and flame rank as some of the finest war sequences ever shot.

See:

Isenberg, Michael T. "The Great War Viewed Through the Twenties: *The Big Parade*
     (1925)." In *Hollywood's World War I: Motion Picture Images*, ed. Peter C. Rol-

lins and John E. O'Connor. Bowling Green, OH: Bowling Green State University
    Popular Press, 1998, 39–58.
Soderbergh, Peter. " 'Aux Armes': The Rise of the Hollywood War Film, 1916–1930."
    South Atlantic Quarterly 65 (Autumn 1966): 509–522.

Sally E. Parry

THE BOY ALLIES (Young Adult Novels). Between 1915 and 1919, American publishers of juvenile literature produced well over 200 different books detailing the fictional adventures of earnest young boys who raced around Europe and somehow supposedly participated in every major battle in the rapidly spreading "Great War." None were more popular than Clair Wallace Hayes's twenty-three Boy Allies books. Divided into two separate miniseries, the first thirteen dealing with two sixteen-year old high school graduates fighting with the various Allied armies and the other ten (authored by "Robert L. Drake," one of Hayes's many pen names) with two slightly older fellows serving in the Allied navies, the Boy Allies books were filled with almost nonstop adventure.

Hal Paine and Chester Crawford (the land-based Boy Allies) join the Belgian Army at Liège. Later, they are in the trenches at the Marne; before their half of the series is completed, they fight with the Russians, the British, the Italians, and, eventually, with the forces of the United States. By the end of the war, both boys, now age twenty, are United States Army colonels. Jack Templeton and Frank Chadwick (the two at sea) volunteer to fight with the British in the North Sea and also see service in the Adriatic, the Mediterranean, the Baltic, and elsewhere. By the conflict's end, Frank has become a naval lieutenant and Jack, a captain.

There is nothing about the Boy Allies to distinguish them in any way, but a generation of young boys loved them and their exploits nonetheless. They were emulated by dozens of other series throughout the war and, a generation later, when World War II began, it seemed natural to everyone that all new series of juvenile war stories for boys must be judged on how well they either succeeded or failed to match Hayes's popular successes during the earlier war.

See:

Prager, Arthur. "Beating the Boche." Chapter 6 in *Rascals at Large, or, The Clue in
    the Old Nostalgia*. Garden City, NY: Doubleday, 1971, 167–213.

M. Paul Holsinger

THE DAWN PATROL (Film). John Monk Saunders, author of the screenplay for the first Academy Award–winning motion picture *Wings*, also furnished the stories for a number of other movies about air combat during World War I. One of the best was *The Dawn Patrol* (First National, 1930), which was based on a Saunders short story, "The Flight Commander." Directed by Howard Hawks and starring Douglas Fairbanks, Jr., and Richard Barthelmess, the picture focuses on a squadron of American fliers in the Royal Air Force (RAF) of Great Britain. The men hate their commanding officer (Neil Hamilton), who they feel is heartless and uncaring as he sends them out every day, often to their deaths. Before the film ends, Barthelmess and Fairbanks, who were both early critics of the commander, discover the terrible truth that in war, the men in command often have no choice but to send others to die. Though Hollywood had never chosen to deal with such a theme so strongly before, it revived it again in the years after World War II with the excellent *Command Decision* (1948) and *Twelve O'Clock High* (1949).

Director Edmund Goulding remade *Dawn Patrol* (Warner Brothers, 1938) with Errol Flynn, David Niven, and Basil Rathbone in the starring roles. Utilizing much of the aerial combat footage from the original 1930 production, the new version received even more plaudits than did its predecessor. Rathbone gives a strong performance as the stern commander, and viewers found the close relationship between Flynn and Niven as flying comrades particularly appealing. Where the original picture was heavily colored by a sense of doom, the Flynn-Niven remake focuses more on the pressures of battlefront aerial combat and the psychological tensions that war can exact. It is also unquestionably far more prowar in its emphasis.

To differentiate between the two films, Hawks's 1930 version is sometimes shown on television as *Flight Commander*. Both, however, are well worth searching for and watching.

See:

Isenberg, Michael. *War on Film: The American Cinema and World War I, 1914–1941*. Rutherford, NJ: Fairleigh Dickinson University Press, 1981, 125–126.

Pisano, Dominick A. "*The Dawn Patrol* (1930) and the World War I Air Combat Film Genre: An Exploration of American Values." In *Hollywood's World War I: Motion Picture Images*, ed. Peter C. Rollins and John E. O'Connor. Bowling Green, OH: Bowling Green State University Popular Press, 1998, 59–78.

David J. Tietge

DERE MABLE—LOVE LETTERS OF A ROOKIE (Military Humor). In the first few months of America's participation in World War I, First Lieutenant Edward Streeter of the twenty-seventh (New York) Division, wrote *Dere Mable—Love Letters of a Rookie*, a work that today many consider to be the prototype of all contemporary soldier humor. Published initially in *Gas Attack* (a base magazine published at Camp Wadsworth in Spartansburg, South Carolina, where he was stationed), before getting nationwide circulation, it was an instant success. Readers laughed repeatedly at Private Bill Smith's antics as Streeter recounted them in Bill's purposely illiterate letters home to his girl, Mable Gimp of Philopolis, New York. The small book sold more than a half-million copies after it was first published in April 1918.

Streeter has Bill complain, tongue-in-cheek, about all those things that have bothered young men in the armed forces since the beginning of time: bad food, uncomfortable housing, uncaring officers, heat, cold, marching, and excessive guard duty. Though the illustrations by Bill Breck could have been drawn by any American grade-schooler and nearly all the humor is forced, the American public, anxious to laugh with, rather than worry about, their "doughboy" sons and lovers, apparently found the many accounts of a "typical" soldier and his comrades' lives in training camp hilariously funny. Indeed, so popular was *Dere Mable* that in 1919, the book's publisher also issued a response by Florence E. Summers entitled, *Dere Bill: Mable's Love Letters to Her Rookie*.

Two more collaborative efforts of Streeter and Breck were published in the postwar years: *That's Me All Over, Mable* (1919) and *As You Were, Bill!* (1920). Neither approached the original book in popularity, though the former did sell more than 225,000 copies.

See:

"Edward Streeter, 1891–1976." In *Contemporary Authors*, ed. Ann Evory. Vol. 113. Detroit: Gale, 1981, 614–615.

M. Paul Holsinger

DUNN, HARVEY (Artist). Renowned magazine illustrator Harvey Dunn joined the United States Army's War Art Program on March 7, 1918, with a captain's commission and, after a brief training period, was sent to the battle lines in France. Carrying a specially designed sketch box that allowed him to scroll one drawing after another, he went through virtually every major engagement fought by American troops and on several occasions even hired an observation balloon to get a better view of the action. Seeking to show "the shock and loss and bitterness and blood" of the war (Karolevitz, 6), he would finish one set of sketches, return to a Paris studio, and there turn his crude drawings into permanent records of the men and fighting. Some, like *The Machine Gunner* are among the most realistic depictions to come out of the war.

Dunn returned from Europe in February 1919, planning to spend at least another two years at the National War College completing his artistic legacy of the war, but the army discharged him two months later. Forced to change his focus, he now turned his attention back to the scenes of his childhood in the Dakotas. Some of these latter works are among his most famous. Together, they mark perhaps his single greatest accomplishment as an artist.

His dream of turning his World War I sketches into paintings was, however, also realized. After seeing the artist's original works, William MacLean, an assistant art editor for the *American Legion Monthly*, asked him if he would create a number of World War I–related scenes for the magazine's covers. Dunn enthusiastically agreed, and from January 1928 through August 1938, he produced dozens of new paintings, all of which added to the artistic chronicle he had created while serving on the Western Front more than twenty years earlier.

See:

Karolevitz, Robert F. *Where Your Heart Is: The Story of Harvey Dunn, Artist*. Aberdeen, SD: North Plains Press, 1970.

M. Paul Holsinger

A FAREWELL TO ARMS **(Novel-Films).** Ernest Hemingway wrote *A Farewell to Arms* (1929), a novel about the futility and horror of war, after serving as an ambulance driver in World War I. The story focuses on Lieutenant Frederic Henry, a young American attached to an Italian ambulance unit on the Italian front, who brings back the wounded to field hospitals behind the lines. After his legs are seriously injured at the front, he is cared for at a British hospital in Milan, where he falls in love with a British nurse named Catherine Barkley. They spend several romantic months together before he returns to the war, knowing that she is pregnant with his child. He is at the front when the Germans reinforce the Austrians and force the Italians into a retreat at Caporetto that turns into a rout. Henry tries to keep his ambulance going with hospital supplies; when it gets stuck in the mud, he shoots a sergeant who is running away rather than helping. German snipers kill one of Henry's group, and others are caught by the Italian military, which is executing retreating officers. Having become disgusted by the needless loss of life, Henry deserts and escapes with Catherine to Switzerland. Their baby is born dead, and Catherine dies shortly afterwards of a hemorrhage. Henry's farewell to war becomes inextricably tied to his farewell to his beloved.

A *Farewell to Arms* has been filmed twice (Paramount, 1932; 20th Century–Fox, 1957). The earlier movie, starring Gary Cooper and Helen Hayes, is far superior, and received Academy Award nominations for best picture, art direction, and cinematography. In the second version, David O. Selznick was so anxious to produce a blockbuster at the box office that he even alienated the original director, John Huston, who quit in the middle of filming. The final result, starring Rock Hudson and Jennifer Jones, is less than satisfactory.

See:

Magill, Frank N. *Cinema: The Novel into Film.* Pasadena, CA: Salem, 1980, 155–162.
Reynolds, Michael S. *Hemingway's First War: The Making of A Farewell to Arms.* University Park: Pennsylvania State University Press, 1979.

Sally E. Parry

THE FIGHTING 69th **(Film).** With American involvement in a second world war clearly on the horizon, motion pictures about America's role in World War I became popular once again. One of the better of these was director William Keighley's tribute to the 165th New York Infantry's "Irish" Regiment, *The Fighting 69th* (Warner Brothers, 1940). Tracing the formation of the predominantly Irish Catholic regiment—one that included in its ranks the doomed poet Joyce Kilmer—from its background on the streets of New York City to the "no man's land" in France, the film starred James Cagney and Pat O'Brien (at the time, two of Hollywood's biggest box office attractions). Also featuring a host of major character actors, including Dennis Morgan, Alan Hale, and Frank McHugh, *The Fighting 69th* is a mix of comedy and serious drama. The very realistic battle scenes, which are filled with depictions of frightened, wounded, and sometimes dying American doughboys, are carefully staged and always sobering.

O'Brien plays Father Francis P. Duffy, the regiment's chaplain, and Cagney, a young Irish tough (one of the dozens of stereotyped troublemakers that he made a career portraying). Rejected because of his arrogant, boastful attitude and apparent cowardice, he saves the day (and Father Duffy as well), by throwing himself on a German grenade in the dramatic climax.

The Fighting 69th is an overwhelmingly flag-waving and overtly patriotic movie. With its stress on such time-honored concepts as honor, duty, and love of country, it consciously helped prepare its many viewers for yet another war in the year ahead.

See:

Leab, Daniel J. "An Ambiguous Isolationism: *The Fighting 69th* (1940)." In *Hollywood's World War I: Motion Picture Images*, ed. Peter C. Rollins and John E. O'Connor. Bowling Green, OH: Bowling Green State University Popular Press, 1998, 101–120.

———. "Viewing the War with the Brothers Warner." In *Film and the First World War*, ed. Karel Dibbets and Bert Hogenkamp. Amsterdam: Amsterdam University Press, 1995, 223–233.

M. Paul Holsinger

FLAGG, JAMES MONTGOMERY (Artist). "I Want You," James Montgomery Flagg's renowned World War I recruiting poster, is unquestionably the single most recognized piece of art in American history. Millions who know nothing of the artist's long and storied career can instantly describe it: a stern and uniquely original **Uncle Sam** and the words "I Want You for U.S. Army." Probably adapted from a well-known 1915 British picture of that country's army chief of staff, Lord Kitchener, Flagg's drawing originally appeared without words as a cover of *Leslie's Weekly* (see **Frank Leslie's Illustrated Newspaper**), a popular magazine of the day. After the army subsequently selected the illustration, more than 4 million reproductions were printed by the government and distributed throughout the country.

Too old to enlist in World War I, Flagg threw himself into drawing some of the most colorful (and most successful) posters in the nation's history. Besides "I Want You," there were posters for the navy (one saying "Don't Read about American History—Make It!"), the U.S. Shipping Board, the American Red Cross, War Relief, the U.S. Department of the Treasury, **War Savings Stamps, Victory gardens**, and dozens of other war-related causes. The Marine Corps was the beneficiary of three of the more persuasive illustrated slogans ("Tell That to the Marines!"; "Travel? Adventure? Join the Marines!"; and "First in the Fight, Always Faithful, be a U.S. Marine!"). All his work was bright, heavily patriotic, and immensely effective, with clear, sharp, telling images.

When the United States entered World War II, 2 million copies of "I Want You" were reprinted and circulated. Flagg, who by that time was probably the most famous magazine illustrator in the United States, once again used his creative talents to benefit the war effort. He did several dramatic new posters for the Marines, one for the United States Army Air Corps, and a much-reprinted one for the Red Cross. Perhaps his most famous work during this period was a 1945 poster for the United States Army, in which a determined-looking Uncle Sam, sleeves rolled up and menacingly holding a huge wrench in his hand, says: "Jap . . . You're Next! We'll Finish the Job!"

Flagg's posters during World Wars I and II make up only a tiny portion of his artistic output. More than any other work, however, they continue to make him known and respected around the world.

See:

Meyer, Susan E. *James Montgomery Flagg*. New York: Watson-Guptill, 1974.

M. Paul Holsinger

FLIGHT (**Film**). The civil war in Nicaragua offers mute testimony to how contentious the United States could be when dealing with a tiny, neighboring state. As early as 1912, U.S. Marines actively supported the Nicaraguan government in crushing protesters, and even after the revolt was squashed, a Marine guard remained in the capital of Managua. In the mid-1920s, when rebels led by the popular Ernesto Sandino took up arms against the corrupt government, it was the Marines who were called on to intervene in that country's internal affairs. From 1927 until 1933, they fought a series of bloody battles on the ground and in the air against the so-called Sandinistas, finally defeating them and, once again, propping up a dictatorship that, it was felt, best served U.S. national interests.

Flight (Columbia, 1929), one of the first films directed by the soon-to-be renowned Hollywood director Frank Capra, gave theatergoers a fictional, though extremely reactionary, look at that latter, undeclared war. Though the Sandinistas were praised by a few American reporters, such as Carleton Beals (whose articles in the *Nation* attacked U.S. imperialism and the Marines' role in expanding it), to most Americans they were little more than bandits terrorizing the Nicaraguan people. *Flight*, which was produced in both silent and "talkie" versions, adopts that latter position, with the evil "Lobo" and his men pillaging and looting at will. With a script by Capra based on a story by Ralph Graves, *Flight* starred Jack Holt and Graves as Marine Corps aviators Panama Williams and Lefty Phelps. In scenes based on the Marines' slaughter of several hundred Nicaraguan rebels at the Battle of Ocotal in July 1927, the two heroes, who are rivals for the hand of a vivacious nurse (Lila Lee), repeatedly attack the "gooks" in support of their comrades on the ground. Eventually, they help destroy the Sandinistas—though not before Lefty crashes in the jungle and is saved by Panama right under the noses of the enemy soldiers.

Flight's battle scenes in the air are often exciting. In making the movie, Capra had the Marines' full support and used their San Diego base for authenticity, as well as a nine-plane squadron of their newest Curtis fighter-bombers piloted by some of their best pilots. (Two of them, Lieutenants Jerry Jerome and Bill Williams, both later became generals). Filmed entirely in southern California, with Digger Indians from nearby reservations playing the majority of the "Nicaraguans," the extremely popular *Flight* packed audiences into motion picture houses across the United States. Whether it changed anyone's view of the conflict in Central America is questionable, however.

See:

McBride, Joseph. *Frank Capra: The Catastrophe of Success.* New York: Simon 1992.

M. Paul Holsinger

GIBBONS, FLOYD (War Correspondent–Newspaperman). Floyd Gibbons, a war correspondent for the *Chicago Tribune*, was covering the advance of a group of American Marines near Belleau Wood in June 1918 when he was wounded three times by German rifle fire. Two bullets hit him in his left arm; one came up through his left eye and forehead. Although he survived, he was forced to wear an eye patch for the remainder of his life, making him immediately recognizable.

When he was released from the hospital, Gibbons wrote *And "They Thought We Wouldn't Fight,"* his observations of American ground experiences during World War I up to the time he was wounded. It was extremely popular, partly because his willingness to engage in close action with the troops allowed him to provide detailed descriptions of American involvement on the Western Front. Indeed, Gibbons has often been favorably compared with his better-known World War II counterpart, **Ernie Pyle**, as someone who reported on the events of the war with both accuracy and nerve.

In the mid-1920s, Gibbons also wrote *The Red Knight*, the first English-language account of the exploits of the famous German air ace Baron Manfred von Richtofen. Searching for information, Gibbons visited museums in Berlin and even interviewed the dead pilot's mother, who showed him her son's trophy room. Appearing first serially in the then-popular *Liberty Magazine*, the story was so popular that it ran consecutively for twenty-three issues. It finally was published in book form in 1927.

See:

Crozier, Emmet. *American Reporters on the Western Front, 1914–1918.* New York: Oxford University Press, 1959.
Gibbons, Edward. *Floyd Gibbons, Your Headline Hunter.* New York: Exposition Press, 1953.

David K. Vaughan

***HEARTS OF THE WORLD* (Silent Film).** *Hearts of the World* (Griffith/Artcraft, 1918) is one of World War I's most influential motion pictures. Personally anxious to encourage the United States to enter the war on the side of the Allies, the famed film director D. W. Griffith worked closely with the government of Great Britain to make one of the classic propaganda movies of all time. Filmed throughout 1917 and early 1918 and filled with scenes of good, decent men and women being terrorized by evil, rapacious Germans, *Hearts*, had a huge impact on its viewers. After it opened in New York City (where it played for seven straight months), thousands of young men rushed to volunteer for the American armed forces, even though Griffith had toned down some of the film's initial brutality at the personal request of President and Mrs. Woodrow Wilson, who had attended an early preview. So popular was the picture that, when Griffith redid some of the titles to reflect the Allied victory after the Armistice, the "new" version continued to pack persons into the theaters.

Starring the beautiful Lillian Gish (the heroine of Griffith's earlier *Birth of a Nation*), her sister Dorothy, and Robert Harron, *Hearts of the World* tells the story of a young American expatriate girl (Gish) and her fiancé (Harron), who is also an American living in France at the beginning of the Great War. When hostilities break out, "The Boy" (Herron), though technically neutral, volunteers to fight with the French and goes to war, leaving "The Girl" (Gish) and their respective families in the hands of God. While he is gone, the Germans attack, wreak havoc on the young couple's village, and kill their parents. Gish almost goes mad, especially when she finds Harron lying badly wounded and near death. The Germans make the villagers into slaves and mistreat them all horribly. There is sort of a happy ending, however. Harron escapes, becomes a spy, and, finally returning to the village, helps his love to reach Allied lines. Yet nothing could blot out the earlier images of German atrocities. *Hearts of the World* reinforced most of the worst stereotypes of the "Huns" that Americans and the other Allies believed to be true, and the Germans suffered as a result.

Griffith made three versions of the movie: one British, one French, and one American. Each was enormously popular, breaking box office records wherever it was shown.

See:

Welsh, Jim. "The Great War and the War Film as Genre: *Hearts of the World* (1918) and *What Price Glory* (1926)." In *Hollywood's World War I: Motion Picture Images*, ed. Peter C. Rollins and John E. O'Connor. Bowling Green, OH: Bowling Green State University Popular Press, 1998, 27–38.

M. Paul Holsinger

HELL'S ANGELS (Film). Producer-director Howard Hughes assembled the largest air fleet Hollywood had ever seen for *Hell's Angels* (Caddo, 1930). Set in England and Germany just prior to and during World War I, it follows the adventures of the Rutledge brothers, Roy (Ben Lyon), who is patriotic and sincere, and Monte (James Hall), who is shallow and lazy. After studying in Germany, when the war starts they leave for England and join the Royal Flying Corps—Roy out of patriotic duty and Monte because he is shamed into it. Helen

(Jean Harlow), the woman they both love, admires Roy, has an affair with Monte, and then leaves them both for another soldier. In drunken despair, they fly a captured German plane on a suicidal mission and are shot down by Baron Von Richthofen. In prison, Roy shoots Monte so that he will not reveal military information to the Germans. Roy then is executed by a firing squad.

Hell's Angels is considered by many critics to be one of the greatest aerial movies ever made. Hughes spent over half of the $4 million budget on the air battles. Four pilots died during filming that included a spectacular bombing attempt on London by a zeppelin (with the brothers' school friend Karl as the bombardier), various dogfights, and the climactic air battle. Though it was originally conceived as a silent picture, Hughes added dialogue scenes staged by James Whale, some color scenes, and some wide screen shots so that he could visually capture on film the 20,000 extras.

Hell's Angels remains memorable for its aerial spectacles and for launching Jean Harlow as a star. American theatergoers more than a decade removed from World War I, having already shown with their support of such huge hits as *Wings* that they would gladly pay for combat-oriented entertainment, did so once again.

See:

Baird, Robert. "*Hell's Angels* above the Western Front: Hollywood's First War Dialectic of Romance and Realism." In *Hollywood's World War I: Motion Picture Images*, eds. Peter C. Rollins and John E. O'Connor. Bowling Green, OH: Bowling Green State University Popular Press, 1998, 79–100.

Quirk, Lawrence J. "Hell's Angels." Chapter 11 in *The Great War Films from The Birth of a Nation to Today*. New York: Citadel, 1994, 54–56.

Sally E. Parry

"HOW YA GONNA KEEP 'EM DOWN ON THE FARM?" (Song). Walter Donaldson, one of the most prominent songwriters of the early years of the twentieth century, authored such still-famous standards as, "Yes Sir, That's My Baby," "Carolina in the Morning," "My Blue Heaven," and the Al Jolson classic, "My Mammy." During World War I, Donaldson frequently entertained troops at Camp Upton, New York, and while there, often picked up fresh material for new songs. After he heard that the supposedly naive American fighting men would never be the same once they had been to the more sophisticated capitals of Europe, "How Ya Gonna Keep 'Em Down on the Farm, after They've Seen Paree?" was born.

Written in conjunction with Sam M. Lewis and Joe Young and introduced to vaudeville by the famous Sophie Tucker, the novelty number was an instant success. Later, Eddie Cantor, one of the Ziegfield Follies' biggest stars, made it "his," and the sheet music and his recording both sold in large numbers. Though intended to be funny, the song, which appeared in 1919, only a few months after the conclusion of the war in Europe, ironically zeroed in on a very real problem facing the United States as it rushed hurriedly toward the so-called

Roaring Twenties. American innocence was, in the aftermath of World War I, unquestionably gone, and the nation's youth, whether because they had seen "Paree" or not, were no longer content to stay "down on the farm." They demanded more, and the country was never the same again.

See:

Ewen, David. *All the Years of American Popular Music.* Englewood Cliffs, NJ: Prentice-Hall, 1977, 225.

M. Paul Holsinger

"I DIDN'T RAISE MY BOY TO BE A SOLDIER" (Song). In the years after the beginning of World War I in Europe, many Americans were fearful that the United States might be forced into the conflict. Pacifism ran high, and songwriters from New York's so-called Tin Pan Alley capitalized on that anxiety. Among the many antiwar musical numbers were such forgettable ones as, "Uncle Sam Won't Go to War," and "We Stand for Peace While Others War." Certainly the best-known of all was, "I Didn't Raise My Boy to Be a Soldier." Published in 1915, it was sung widely over the next several years in the hope of discouraging President Woodrow Wilson and other politicians from involving the nation in war.

Written by two professional songwriters, Al Piantadosi and Alfred Bryan, "I Didn't Raise My Boy to Be a Soldier" was introduced on the vaudeville stage by Ed Morton. Soon it became a part of the repertory of the famed performer Nora Bayes, and sales soared. The sheet music melodramatically pictured an old, gray-haired mother protecting her son from the exploding shells of the battlefield as the lyrics proclaim:

> I didn't raise my boy to be a soldier
> I brought him up to be my pride and joy
> Who dares to place a musket on his shoulder
> To shoot some other mother's darling boy?

Later, as public sentiment began to shift in favor of the war, parodies such as, "I Didn't Raise My Boy to Be a Coward" and "I'd Be Proud to Be the Mother of a Soldier" were sung as lustily as the original number had been in 1915 and 1916.

During the Vietnam War, antiwar automobile bumper stickers resurrected the song title with a minor change, declaring, "I Didn't Raise My Son to Be a Soldier."

See:

Vogel, Frederick. *World War I Songs: A History and Dictionary of Popular American Patriotic Music.* Jefferson, NC: McFarland, 1995, 20–22.

M. Paul Holsinger

JOHNNY GOT HIS GUN (**Novel-Film**). One of the most powerful antiwar novels of the twentieth century, Dalton Trumbo's *Johnny Got His Gun* (1939), is told from the point of view of Joe Bonham, a human vegetable, and former World War I soldier, whose arms and legs have been amputated and whose face has been shot off. His mind, however, is still quite active. He wonders first where he is and then curses the fates that left him alive but unable to see, speak, or hear. In the first half of the book, "The Dead," we learn about Joe's past life, his girlfriend, his family, his jobs, and the death and decay he saw on the battlefield. Like many other young men, he served during the war, not out of a sense of patriotism, but because the government said he must. In the second half of the story, "The Living," Joe decides that he must try to connect with the rest of the world. He begins to estimate time by counting between the nurses' visits and feeling the sun rise, and he then has a major breakthrough when a young nurse writes "Merry Christmas" on his chest. He bangs his head up and down on the pillow in a grotesque form of Morse Code until, after several months, someone signals back, "What do you want?" Joe has much to communicate but can only plead for an end to war.

This winner of the National Book Award in 1939 was turned into a movie at the height of the Vietnam War. Directed by Trumbo and starring Timothy Bottoms, *Johnny Got His Gun* (Cinemation, 1971) is only occasionally successful in capturing the claustrophobic world of the soldier-narrator. Most critics found it "talky" or "preachy," but it was nominated as one of the best films of the year at the Cannes Film Festival.

See:

Cook, Bruce. *Dalton Trumbo*. New York: Scribner's, 1977.
Norden, Martin F. "*Johnny Got His Gun* (1971): Evolution of an Antiwar Statement from Fiction to Film." In *Hollywood's World War I: Motion Picture Images*, ed. Peter C. Rollins and John E. O'Connor. Bowling Green, OH: Bowling Green State University Popular Press, 1998, 161–176.

Sally E. Parry

"KEEP THE HOME FIRES BURNING" (**Song**). There were few, if any, songs during World War I that were more popular than "Keep the Home Fires Burning." Written in the fall of 1914 by British actor-musician (and later, playwright-director) Ivor Novello, with (most of) the lyrics composed by Lena Guilbert Ford, an expatriate American living in Great Britain, after its first public performance the number became an overnight success. It was recorded by early 1915, and soon the English were purchasing tens of thousands of copies of sheet music. Throughout the war, "Keep the Home Fires Burning" (or, as it was officially titled, " 'Til the Boys Come Home") was also a best-seller in the United States, Canada, Australia, and New Zealand. A generation later, during World War II, it continued to provide hope and comfort.

The *New York Tribune* formally introduced the song to Americans when it published words and music on August 22, 1915. Newspapers across the country soon followed suit, and, though the United States remained neutral for more than a year and a half, "Home Fires" quickly became one of the most important symbols of the Allied cause in its battle against the Kaiser and German imperialism. By 1916, it was being played regularly in American motion picture theaters during newsreels about the war on the Western Front. In fact, some historians of the era have speculated that "Keep the Home Fires Burning" was largely responsible for the wave of pro-Allied feeling that swept America at the time.

When the United States declared war on the Central Powers in April 1917, the well-known Irish tenor John McCormack recorded "Home Fires" for Victor, and these recordings sold so rapidly that, by the end of the first year, McCormack alone had earned more than $100,000 in royalties. Fellow opera singer Rosa Ponselle, backed by the "Stellar Quartet," recorded another version for Columbia that was almost as well received.

It was hard not to like "Home Fires." Easily adapted to American realities after 1917, and certainly one of the loveliest of all World War I songs, the expressions in its chorus that "There's a silver lining / Through the dark cloud shining" and its call to "Turn the dark cloud inside out / 'Til the boys come home" were inspirational.

Ivor Novello lived for many years, to become one of both Europe's and America's most famous directors of both stage and screen. Sadly, Lena Ford never realized the huge popularity of her song in her native United States. She was killed during one of the many 1918 German bombing raids on London.

See:

Bowman, Kent. "Echoes of Shot and Shell: Songs of the Great War." *Studies in Popular Culture* 10.1 (1987): 27–41.

M. Paul Holsinger

THE LITTLE AMERICAN (Silent Film). The soon-to-be famous director Cecil B. DeMille had already made a number of pro-Allied propaganda films before the United States entered World War I. Few of those pictures, however, did a better job of serving the cause than did *The Little American* (Paramount, 1917), which was shot almost immediately after this country's declaration of war.

Starring "America's sweetheart," Mary Pickford (a symbol already to millions of viewers of the nation's purest and best), and the leading male actor, Jack Holt, the movie focuses on Angela Moore (Pickford), a young American born on the Fourth of July, and her German-American boyfriend, Karl von Austreim (Holt). The movie is patriotic, chauvinistic, dramatic, and, at times, spectacular. Jeanie Macpherson's screenplay is complicated but manages to weave in many of the facts leading up to the U.S. entry into the war. In 1914, with the outbreak of war, Karl returns to Europe to enlist; Angela soon follows. In the middle of the Atlantic, her ship, like the doomed *Lusitania*, is torpedoed without warning by a U-boat and hundreds are apparently killed. The young girl survives, but once in France, she has the opportunity to witness even more horrors inflicted on the defenseless. Women are sexually molested by drunken German soldiers—the local commandant tells a pleading Angela that his men need "relaxation"—and old men and young boys are shot down in cold blood. The "Huns" rip priceless paintings from a chateau's walls and destroy antique furniture at will. The little American can stand no more. Renouncing her neutrality, Angela becomes a spy for the French. Soon captured by the Germans and condemned to be shot, she is miraculously saved at the last minute when a French counterattack forces the enemy to retreat. Begging a pardon for the wounded Karl (who had also come close to being executed after renouncing the Kaiser and the evil policies of his country), Angela and her young lover are allowed to return to the freedom of the United States. A last, brief shot of the Statue of Liberty gives promise that the couple will soon find many happy days ahead.

See:

Whitford, Eileen. "The Little American." Chapter 7 in *Pickford: The Woman Who Made Hollywood*. Lexington: University of Kentucky Press, 1997, 174–181.

M. Paul Holsinger

MY FOUR YEARS IN GERMANY (Autobiography–Silent Film). James W. Gerard, a former justice of the New York State Supreme Court, served as the U.S. ambassador to Imperial Germany from 1913 to 1917. Returning home several months before the outbreak of war between the United States and Germany, Gerard published his memoirs from Berlin in summer 1917 under the title, *My Four Years in Germany*. The ambassador's accounts of German concentration camps and his allegations of witnessing numerous German atrocities gave the volume instant notoriety. A reading public anxious for information about America's new foe kept it popular throughout the war. During 1918, it was the number one nonfiction best-seller.

Inevitably, Gerard's story was made into a motion picture. Director William Nigh mixed re-created scenes and factual newsreels—or so the producers claimed when the picture was released—to make *My Four Years in Germany* (First National, 1918). Footage supposedly taken inside some of the most notorious German concentration camps was, in fact, shot on location in New Jersey using American actors and actresses, but the ruse worked. Though the movie was little more than simple-minded, almost primitive, propaganda, the purportedly shocking scenes packed audiences into theaters across the country. The public was ecstatic, even at a scene where an American "doughboy" happily rams his bayonet into one German soldier after another.

Gerard was so buoyed by the reception of his book and its screen adaptation that he seriously considered a run for the Democratic nomination for president in 1920. When he attempted a sequel to *My Four Years in Germany*, however, it failed dismally.

See:

Gerard, James W. *My First Eighty-Three Years in America: The Memoirs of James W. Gerard.* Garden City, NY: Doubleday, 1951.

                                                M. Paul Holsinger

"OH, HOW I HATE TO GET UP IN THE MORNING" (Song). Irving Berlin was already one of America's most famous songwriters, with dozens of best-selling songs to his credit, when he joined the army in 1918. In an attempt to raise money for a much-needed service center at Camp Upton, New York (a temporary station for European-bound troops), Berlin wrote, produced, and then acted in an all-soldiers' show, which he called *Yip, Yip, Yaphank.* It opened at the Century Theatre in New York on July 26, 1918, and brought in more than $158,000 for the camp fund. Of all the original songs in the show, none was more lasting than Berlin's famous lament after staggering from his cot at reveille, "Oh, How I Hate to Get Up in the Morning."

With the reinstallation of the draft in 1940, the song was resurrected and became just as popular as it had been a generation earlier. Like their fathers had before them, millions of young American men fantasized about murdering the bugler and spending the rest of their lives in bed. Berlin wrote and directed a new Army review, *This Is the Army*, in 1942, and he sang his now-classic song, while dressed in his old army private's uniform, to audiences around the globe. When the review was transformed into a popular Hollywood picture of the same name, one of the hits of the film was Berlin's rendition of "Oh, How I Hate to Get Up in the Morning."

See:

Bergreen, Laurence. *As Thousands Cheer: The Life of Irving Berlin.* New York: Viking, 1990.

                                                M. Paul Holsinger

"OVER THERE" (Song). On April 7, 1917, the great Broadway producer-songwriter George M. Cohan read in the morning papers that the United States had declared war on Germany. Already renowned for such patriotic songs as the longtime favorite, "You're a Grand Old Flag" (1905), and his trademark, "I'm a Yankee Doodle Dandy," he immediately set out to compose something appropriate for the situation. In less than two hours, "Over There," which was soon to be one of the most popular American war songs of all times, was written and scored.

At first, surprisingly, the new piece was poorly received. Troops at Fort Myers, Virginia, in fall 1917, for instance, were, at best, cool in their response after hearing Cohan sing his new song for them. That response changed quickly, however. When the popular Charles King performed it during a Red Cross benefit, "Over There" became a great success. Cohan later auditioned the piece for the famed female vaudevillian Nora Bayes, whose rendition of it in a musical nearly caused a stampede in the theater. Once she recorded the number, its popularity was assured.

By war's end, more than 2 million copies of the sheet music and 1 million records had been sold. Dozens of the nation's top performers, including even the Metropolitan Opera's Enrico Caruso, recorded "Over There." President Woodrow Wilson called it "a genuine inspiration to all American manhood." In 1941, with the United States poised to enter another world war, Cohan (whose career, ironically, had gone downhill shortly after the success of his most famous song), was personally awarded a special Medal of Honor by President Franklin Delano Roosevelt, largely in belated recognition for his 1917 hit.

See:

Scheele, Carl H. "Over There." Liner notes. In *Praise the Lord and Pass the Ammunition: Songs of World War I and II*. LP New World, 1977.

M. Paul Holsinger

PATHS OF GLORY (Novel-Drama-Film). In 1935, Humphrey Cobb wrote *Paths of Glory*. A forceful novel about World War I, it was based on a true incident, in which three French soldiers, who were picked arbitrarily from the ranks after a disastrous attempt to take a German stronghold, were court-martialed for cowardice and executed as an example and a warning to the other soldiers. Sidney Howard adapted the work into a play the same year, but its most telling depiction came almost a generation later, when Stanley Kubrick turned Cobb's story into one of the most powerful antiwar films of all time. With a screenplay written by Kubrick, Jim Thompson, and Calder Willingham, *Paths of Glory* (United Artists, 1957) is an attack on war and its conduct, whereby politicians and generals often make unwise decisions that may mean the unnecessary deaths of hundreds, or even thousands, of men.

One focus of the movie is on the machinations of General Broulard (Adolphe Menjou), a wily man who never takes blame, and General Mireau (George Macready), who is so hungry for promotion that he is always willing to sacrifice his men to impress his superior officer. A second focus looks at the soldiers in the trenches, who must carry out the often-misguided orders. After his men have failed to overrun a heavily armed enemy position, Mireau randomly chooses Corporal Paris (Ralph Meeker), Private Ferol (Timothy Carey), and Private Arnaud (Joseph Turkel) to be court-martialed and executed. Despite the brilliant legal defense of their line commander, Colonel Dax (Kirk Douglas), all three men are convicted. Moreover, one of the condemned must be tied to a stake to be killed because he is already dying. Mireau becomes a scapegoat for the outraged public and is demoted, but the system remains the same.

Paths of Glory was ignored by voters for Hollywood's 1957 Academy Awards, but in Great Britain, it received nominations, not only for best picture, but also for best director. Banned in France because of its obvious denunciation of French military procedure, the film was also forbidden to be shown on U.S.

military bases for many years. During the late 1960s, it received renewed interest in the United States when critics of the war in Vietnam drew parallels between the story and what seemingly was occurring in Southeast Asia.

See:

Kelly, Andrew. "The Brutality of Military Incompetence: *Paths of Glory* (1957)." In *Hollywood's World War I: Motion Picture Images*, ed. Peter C. Rollins and John E. O'Connor. Bowling Green, OH: Bowling Green State University Popular Press, 1998, 143–160.

Miller, Gabriel. "Murder in the First Degree: *Paths of Glory.*" *Screening the Novel: Rediscovered American Fiction in Film*. New York: Frederick Ungar, 1980, 116–142.

Sally E. Parry

THE SAND PEBBLES (Novel-Film). From the summer of 1900, when the U.S. Marines played a major role in lifting the so-called Boxer siege of the various international legations in Peking, through the many civil wars that raged in nearly all parts of China after 1911, American military men played an important role in that nation's internal affairs. The U.S. troops stayed long after any threat was past, especially in Peking, Canton, and Shanghai. The Marine Corps had a semipermanent post within China, and nearly all members expected at some time in their career to spend at least one tour of duty in that section of the world. The United States Navy also remained indefinitely, often operating out of gunboats stationed along the Yangtze and Huang Ho Rivers. In the 1920s, naval personnel frequently found themselves involved in any number of often-bloody skirmishes between one side or another.

The Sand Pebbles (1962), a thoughtful first novel by Richard McKenna, who was a longtime navy engineer with many years on the "China Station," focuses on one of those internecine wars. Set in 1925, the novel tells the interrelated story of three Americans: Jake Holman, a common seaman serving on the antiquated gunboat, USS *San Pablo* ("The Sand Pebbles," as the men call the ship, not always lovingly); Lieutenant William Collins, the ship's captain; and Shirley Eckert, an American missionary serving at a backcountry station on the Yangtze River. Collins represents all that was wrong with the "peacetime" navy in the Orient before World War II. His insistence on getting involved between the two warring sides results in the death of hundreds, including Jake (the novel's central figure), who dies trying to save his shipmates. Chosen as the $10,000 Harper Prize Novel, *The Sand Pebbles* remains a carefully written, thoughtful account of a long-forgotten series of events between the two world wars.

With Robert Wise directing, *The Sand Pebbles* (Argyle/Solar/20th Century–Fox, 1966) became a major Hollywood film four years after its novelization. Steve McQueen, who gained an Academy Award nomination as the year's best actor, was given the role of Jake; Candice Bergen became Shirley; and Richard Crenna portrayed the ship's obsessive captain. Reasonably faithful to the novel, the movie is both lush and long—more than three hours in length. It, too, received an Oscar nomination as one of the year's best pictures.

See:

"Richard (Milton) McKenna." In *Contemporary Authors*, ed. Linda Metzger. Vol. 13. New rev. ser. Detroit: Gale, 1984, 359–360.

M. Paul Holsinger

SEEGER, ALAN (Poet). Alan Seeger was living in Paris when France declared war on Imperial Germany in August 1914. Although he was an American, he quickly volunteered to fight. It was a decision that he never regretted. In summer 1915, he wrote his mother from the front lines: "I would be nowhere else in the world than where I am."

The twenty-six-year-old Seeger had been attempting to gain recognition as a poet for some years before he entered the military, but his best work came only after he joined the French Foreign Legion. "Ode in Memory of the American Volunteers Fallen in France," for instance, was critically acclaimed both in Europe and in Seeger's native United States. However, as the months passed and he watched thousands being slaughtered, he became obsessed with dying. Though he had earlier written home: "Death is nothing terrible at all. It may mean something even more wonderful than life" (Seeger, xxxv), his best-known poem (and unquestionably the most renowned war-related poetic composition by any American), "I Have a Rendezvous with Death," effectively captures the fatalistic outlook of most soldiers after the first heady days of the war. "I have a rendezvous with death,' " Seeger wrote, "at midnight in some flaming town . . . / And I to my pledged word am true; / I shall not fail that rendezvous." He was prophetic. On July 4, 1916, he and most of his fellow legionnaires were killed by German machine gunners in a battle near the town of Belloy-en-Santerre.

Poems by Alan Seeger (1916), and *Letters and Diary of Alan Seeger* (1917) were published posthumously. Once the United States entered the war, *Poems* gained instant popularity, with six editions being printed in less than a year.

See:

Seeger, Alan. *Poems of Alan Seeger*, ed. William Archer. New York: Charles Scribner's Sons, 1918.
Werstein, Irving. *Sound No Trumpet: The Life and Death of Alan Seeger*. New York: Crowell, 1967.

David K. Vaughan

SERGEANT YORK (Film). General John Pershing called Alvin C. York of the Eighty-Second Division "the greatest civilian soldier" in the American Expeditionary Forces during World War I. France's Marshal Foch thought that York's capture of more than 130 Germans and killing of 25 others in the Argonne on October 8, 1918 was "the greatest thing accomplished by any private soldier of all the armies of Europe'' (Brandt, 57). Nations flocked to award him medals; not only did he receive the French Croix de Guerre and the Italian War Cross but also, in March 1919, the Congressional Medal of Honor. Considering the fact that he originally tried, unsuccessfully, to register as a religious conscientious objector, the thirty-one-year-old sergeant's feat was even more noteworthy.

Director Howard Hawks brought a highly imaginative version of York's story to the motion picture screen in his film, *Sergeant York* (Warner Brothers, 1941). Though the script by John Huston, Abem Finkel, Howard Koch, and Harry Chandlee occasionally gives hints that war might be horrible, its tone is far more patriotic and prointerventionist than historical. The semiliterate, Tennessee-born York, who was played in the movie by the popular box office attraction Gary Cooper, is transformed into an individual who, after he ''gets religion,'' can do little wrong. His actions always mirror truth, justice, and the American Way.

Both the viewing public and professional critics found *Sergeant York* worthy of adulation. Though it won neither an Academy Award nor a New York Film Critics Circle award as best picture, it was the top-grossing motion picture for 1941. Cooper, who was clearly too old in real life to play the intrepid sergeant, received both an Oscar and the Critics Circle award as the year's best actor. Walter Brennan, a longtime star in character roles, also received an Academy Award as the year's best supporting actor for his portrayal of the York family's minister back home in the Tennessee hills. Eleven others, including the screenwriters, the cinematographer, and the director, were also nominated.

See:

Birdwell, Michael. '' 'The Devil's Tool': Alvin York and the Movie *Sergeant York* (1941).'' In *Hollywood's World War I: Motion Picture Images*, ed. Peter C. Rollins and John E. O'Connor. Bowling Green, OH: Bowling Green State University Popular Press, 1998, 121–142.
Brandt, Nat. ''Sergeant York.'' *American Heritage* 32.5 (August/September 1981): 57–64.
Toplin, Robert B. ''Sergeant York: 'If That Is Propaganda, We Plead Guilty.' '' Chapter 3 in *History by Hollywood: The Use and Abuse of the American Past*. Urbana: University of Illinois Press, 1996, 81–101.

M. Paul Holsinger

***SHOULDER ARMS* (Silent Film).** Most motion picture comedies about World War I—and there were many—were instantly forgettable. One that was not, however, was Charlie Chaplin's three-reeler, *Shoulder Arms* (First National, 1918), a film that, to many silent picture scholars, is the only war-era film worthy of unqualified praise.

Sporting the famous small mustache of his most-renowned character, ''The Little Tramp,'' Chaplin parodies warfare on the Western Front. Though there was little that was humorous about life in the bleak, endless trenches, the comedian causes his audiences to laugh with him when, as usual, he bumbles his way to hero status, on one occasion disguised as a tree so that he can sneak behind enemy lines and disrupt the enemy. Chaplin also has his milquetoast American doughboy dream of single-handedly capturing the Kaiser and the German Crown Prince, taking them back to his lines, and, just before surrendering them, planting a well-aimed kick in the pants of his royal captive.

Concerned that humor about war topics was ill-advised, Chaplin's close friend, the famous director D. W. Griffith, had cautioned him to wait until the conflict was over before making *Shoulder Arms*, but Chaplin wisely ignored the advice. Box office records were broken in almost every city where the movie was shown, and in some theaters, the crowds became so unruly in their eagerness to see the film that they trampled police detachments sent to keep order.

See:

Maland, Charles J. *Chaplin and American Culture: The Evolution of a Star Image.* Princeton, NJ: Princeton University Press, 1989.

M. Paul Holsinger

"THE SOLDIER'S SWEETHEART" (Song). Searching for new "hillbilly" recording stars, Ralph Peer of the Victor Talking Machine Company came to Bristol, Tennessee, in fall 1927. Among those trying out was a young Mississippi railroader, Jimmie Rodgers, a singer who is recognized today by virtually everyone as the "Father of Country Music." On August 4, Rodgers recorded two songs, one of which was an original composition called "The Soldier's Sweetheart," which he had written in 1918 shortly after the death of a close boyhood friend in the Argonne Forest.

Using the music of an old Irish ballad, "Where the River Shannon Flows," Rodgers created a lush, but mournfully sentimental, lament for the deaths of the many innocent young American boys in "this awful German war." The lyrics tell of a prewar courtship, the fiancé's decision to go fight the Germans, his correspondence from "no man's land," and finally, the letter from the soldier's captain telling of his death in battle. Rodgers's recording, which was backed by an even older yodeling lullaby, "Sleep Baby Sleep," sold well—he claimed, probably with great exaggeration, sales of more than 2 million recordings within the first year—and Victor signed him to a long-term contract.

By 1929, "The Singing Brakeman," as he became known, was the company's best-selling artist, but unfortunately, Rodgers's career was short-lived. Infected with tuberculosis, he died suddenly in May 1933, just a day after his final recording session.

See:

Porterfield, Nolan. *Jimmie Rodgers: The Life and Times of America's Blue Yodeler.* Urbana: University of Illinois Press, 1979.

M. Paul Holsinger

STARS AND STRIPES (Newspaper). During World War I, General John Pershing, head of the American Expeditionary Force in Europe, authorized the publication of an official newspaper for the United States Army, to be known as *Stars and Stripes*. From February 8, 1918, to June 13, 1919, seventy-one weekly issues of straitlaced reportage and "good" literature appeared from the paper's headquarters in Paris. Distinguished writers, editors, and critics, such as Alexander Wolcott, Franklin P. Adams, Harold Ross, and Grantland Rice, were among the correspondents. The paper's humor was, on the other hand, little more than collegiate.

Stars and Stripes was resurrected during World War II, but with an irreverent spirit far more representative of the "average" GI than its predecessor. Begun in Belfast on April 18, 1942, it was moved shortly thereafter to London, where it became an eight-page daily. Eventually, there were thirty-nine editions (thirty-two in Europe, seven in the Pacific). Some professional newsmen did serve as editors and reporters, but there were also neophytes, like Andy Rooney, who were just learning the trade. Leading cartoonists included newcomers such as **Bill Mauldin** and Syd Hoff, and many future columnists and television commentators learned their craft as roving field reporters.

Priority was always given to war news and comic strips before domestic news bureau releases. Like its counterpart *Yank*, the various editions included soldiers' letters and poems, human interest features, and interviews with ordinary GIs. Scatological humor abounded, like variations on the obscene ditty, "Dirty Gertie from Bizerte."

Stars and Stripes has continued publication without interruption since World War II, with both a European and a Pacific edition. After 1951, though the staff was reasonably free to make its own editorial policies, officers heavily suppressed sexual content, and even canceled cartoonist Mort Walker's *Beetle Bailey* for "disrespect." Except for a stress on military affairs and some superior GI cartoonists during the 1950s (especially Shel Silverstein), since the Cold War and after, *Stars and Stripes* has been indistinguishable from other newspapers.

See:

Cornebise, Alfred E. *The Stars and Stripes: Doughboy Journalism in World War I.* Westport, CT: Greenwood Press, 1984.

Hutton, Oram C., and Andrew A. Rooney. *The Story of Stars and Stripes.* New York: Holt, Rinehart, and Winston, 1946.

Zumwalt, Ken. *The Stars and Stripes: World War II and the Early Years.* Austin, TX: Eakin Press, 1989.

Kalman Goldstein

THROUGH THE WHEAT (Novel). One of the most powerful novels to focus on American troops during World War I, *Through the Wheat* by Thomas Boyd, was first published in 1923. Boyd, an Ohioan, left high school to join the Marine Corps and eventually saw action at Verdun, Belleau Wood, Soissons, and St. Mihiel. Gassed at Blanc Mont and awarded the Croix de Guerre by the French government, he used his firsthand knowledge of the battlefield to fill his semiautobiographical work with realistic scenes of war as it was experienced by American forces.

William Hicks, a young farm boy from Ohio, has been in France for more than nine months when the action in *Through the Wheat* begins. Suddenly, he and the other soldiers are thrown into battle. For weeks on end, they endure constant shelling and gassing from the German lines, which at times are only hundreds of feet away. One by one, the men perish horribly. Hicks, though burned during a particularly bad gas attack and repeatedly wounded, is one of the few "veterans" left in the line. He survives, but in many ways he is a beaten man, having been left shell-shocked and heartsick at the carnage he has seen.

Though Boyd spares no one's sensibilities in telling his story, his honesty impressed readers and critics alike, and *Through the Wheat* brought him an instant crush of praise. Novelist F. Scott Fitzgerald, for instance, thought it the best American book about war to have been written since ***The Red Badge of Courage***. The literary scholar Edmund Wilson went even further. Boyd, he stated emphatically, had penned the most authentic war novel ever produced by an American writer.

The following year, Boyd wrote *The Dark Cloud*, a second novel with a war setting, and in 1925, he produced *Points of Honor*, a collection of war stories. *In Time of Peace*, which continues Hicks's story after the Armistice, was published just before Boyd's death at age thirty-six from a heart attack.

See:

Vecchi, Linda. "Thomas Boyd." In *American Novelists, 1910–1945. Part 1: Louis Adamic–Vardis Fisher*, ed. James J. Martine. Dictionary of Literary Biography. Vol. 9. Detroit: Gale, 1981, 81–83.

M. Paul Holsinger

***TOMB OF THE UNKNOWNS* (Memorial).** Arlington National Cemetery has become one of the nation's most popular tourist attractions, in part because it includes America's Tomb of the Unknown Soldier, or, as it has now been re-christened, the Tomb of the Unknowns. Imposing, stark, and yet unusually beautiful, the marble monument originally was dedicated on Armistice Day 1932, eleven years after the remains of one of the many unknown dead American "doughboys" from World War I had been buried at the specially selected site. On Memorial Day 1958, the bodies of unknowns from World War II and Korea were added. The body of a soldier from the Vietnam War, buried on Memorial Day 1984, was identified fourteen years later and returned to his family in July 1998. No other unknown from that war has been buried in the tomb.

The Tomb of the Unknowns is guarded year-round by soldiers from the army's Old Guard, the Third United States Infantry, which is stationed at Fort Myers, Virginia. Tourists come both to pay their respects and to observe the impressive changing of the guard ceremony, which is performed each half-hour or hour, depending on the weather.

See:

Hinkel, John V. "The Unknown Soldier." Chapter 20 in *Arlington: Monument to Heroes.* Englewood Cliffs, NJ: Prentice-Hall, 1970, 144–151.
Kegel, James. "Lest We Forget: A Tribute to the Unknown Soldier." *American History Illustrated* 16.7 (November 1981): 16–22.

Leslie Kennedy Adams

VETERANS' DAY (National Holiday). In the months after the end of World War I, many different people throughout the United States clamored for November 11, the day on which the Armistice was signed, to be set aside as an official national holiday in recognition of the sacrifice of the more than 50,000 young Americans who had died on the Western Front. The following year, President Woodrow Wilson partly acquiesced and officially proclaimed Armistice Day; however, though he readily eulogized the fallen troops, he made no attempt to do more. As pressure mounted from such groups as the newly formed American Legion, however, Congress, in 1926, finally passed a resolution recognizing the end of the war, and, on November 11, 1928, Armistice Day became a national holiday.

Shortly after the end of the Korean War, it was decided that honoring only the dead from World War I on November 11 was too limiting. In 1953, Congressman Edward Rees of Kansas introduced a resolution to create a true Veterans' Day to recognize all those young men and women, living or dead, who had served their country through the years, as part of its armed services. The resolution passed without opposition. Fifteen years later, however, Congress began tinkering with the day once again. In order to provide longer three-day holidays for American workers, the Uniform Monday Holiday Law was passed. It proclaimed that, beginning in 1971, four of the nation's national holidays (George Washington's Birthday, **Memorial Day**, Colombus Day, and Veterans' Day) would always be celebrated on the Monday nearest their official anniversary dates. Though Veterans' Day still falls occasionally on November 11, it just as often is now celebrated on dates ranging anywhere from the eighth through the fourteenth of the month.

See:

Myers, Robert J. "Veterans' Day." Chapter 39 in *Celebrations: The Complete Book of American Holidays.* Garden City, NY: Doubleday, 1972, 265–270.

M. Paul Holsinger

***WHAT PRICE GLORY?* (Drama-Films).** The comedy-drama *What Price Glory?* by Maxwell Anderson and Laurence Stallings, about a pair of brawling soldiers during World War I, is not so much a protest against war as an exposé of its absurdity. Stallings, an ex-Marine who was seriously wounded in the war, and Anderson, a pacifist, created a play in which Acts 1 and 3 feature two memorable career soldiers, First Sergeant Quirt and Captain Flagg, who fight over a woman, alcohol, their respective ranks, and anything else they can think of. The middle act is much more serious in tone and takes place in a cellar at the front where the wounded and dying are a reality, and where a shell-shocked soldier asks: "What price glory now? Why in God's name can't we all go home?" The final act reverts to a comic mode, with Flagg and Quirt fighting because they are so glad to see each other, showing their awareness that the comradeship of the military is the only thing they can count on. "What a lot of God damn fools it takes to make a war," Quirt exclaims as the old soldiers return to the front at the end, aware of their duty, but not the righteousness of their cause. The play, with William Boyd as Quirt and Louis Wolheim as Captain Flagg, opened on Broadway in 1924 to great reviews.

There have been two film adaptations of *What Price Glory?* (Fox, 1926, 20th Century–Fox, 1952). Raoul Walsh directed the earlier silent movie. At times very funny, the picture was also sometimes overbearingly horrific as the men are caught in the midst of massive bombardments from the enemy lines. Starring Edmund Lowe as Quirt, Victor McLaglen as Flagg, and Dolores Del Rio as Charmaine de la Cognac, the woman over whom they fight, it was a popular box office success. John Ford directed a less interesting version featuring James Cagney as Flagg and Dan Dailey as Quirt, which strangely, and very unconvincingly, includes musical numbers sung by the two men.

See:

Brittain, Joan. *Laurence Stallings*. Boston: Twayne, 1975.
Brownlow, Kevin. *The War, the West, and the Wilderness*. New York: Knopf, 1979, 194–198.
Welsh, Jim. "The Great War and the War Film as Genre: *Hearts of the World* (1918) and *What Price Glory?* (1926)." In *Hollywood's World War I: Motion Picture Images*, ed. Peter C. Rollins and John E. O'Connor. Bowling Green, OH: Bowling Green State University Popular Press, 1998, 27–38.

Sally E. Parry

WINGS (Silent Film). John Monk Saunders, a former American airman during World War I, suggested the idea that became the nucleus of *Wings* (Paramount, 1927), one of the most distinguished Hollywood films about World War I. Paramount's president, Jesse Lasky, who was anxious to make a picture that would rival Metro Goldwyn Meyer's great success of 1925, **The Big Parade**, liked the plot about young American boys in training and combat and agreed to make it into a movie if the United States government would cooperate. When the studio eventually gained the use of hundreds of planes and their pilots, thousands of soldiers, and the entire air force school at San Antonio's Kelly and Brooks Fields for its location work, filming began.

Named as director was the still relatively untried William Wellman. A much-decorated airman in France's Lafayette Escadrille, he knew air combat and proved to be an excellent choice. The male leads, Jack Powell and David Armstrong, went, respectively, to Charles "Buddy" Rogers and Richard Arlen, two of the screen's most famous male stars. Clara Bow portrayed Mary Preston, the "girl back home," and a young Gary Cooper had a tiny dramatic part as a doomed American flyer.

Wings, the last great silent movie, took a year to produce, and before its filming was complete, Paramount had invested more than $2 million in it. With that money, however, Wellman was able to shoot some of the most dramatic scenes of aerial combat ever put on film. Though the melodramatic screenplay by Hope Loring and Louis Lighton includes Jack accidentally shooting down and killing David, *Wings* was a huge success when it premiered in New York on August 12, 1927

For the next year and a half, the movie ran only in selected theaters. Then, in January 1929, with new sound effects added, it was released for showing across the United States; it easily recouped Paramount's investment many times over. Almost as a reaffirmation, members of the newly formed Academy of Motion Pictures Arts in May voted it the first Academy Award in film history as the year's best picture.

See:

Brownlow, Kevin. *The War, the West, and the Wilderness*. New York: Knopf, 1979, 205–211.

Suid, Lawrence H. *Guts and Glory: Great American War Movies*. Reading, MA: Addison-Wesley, 1978, 25–33.

M. Paul Holsinger

Emanuel Leutze, *Washington Crossing the Delaware* (1850). One of America's best-loved historical paintings, Emanuel Leutze's artistic recreation of George Washington and his men, won awards wherever it was shown in the mid-19th century. In 1976, the commemorative sheet of five 24-cent-stamps featuring the painting (above) was issued by the U.S. Postal Service in honor of the bicentennial of the American Revolution.

"The Constitution and the Guerriere." On August 19, 1812, the USS *Constitution*— "Old Ironsides"—won the most famous victory of her illustrious naval career when she destroyed the stronger British frigate, HMS *Guerriere*, in an all-day encounter. The contemporary painting of that victory (above), as well as songs, poems, and other works, honored the famed ship and her crew throughout the nineteenth century.

Nathaniel Currier, *The Battle of Cerro Gordo*. Nathaniel Currier helped to pioneer the lithographic process in the United States and, long before the outbreak of the Civil War, his fame (and that of his later partner, James Merrit Ives) spread rapidly. Between 1846 and 1848, dozens of Currier's prints, featuring such scenes from the War with Mexico as *The Battle of Cerro Gordo* (above), gained him immense popularity.

Gone with the Wind. Margaret Mitchell's Civil War novel, *Gone with the Wind* (1936), sold millions of copies and critically acclaimed, won the Pulitzer Prize for fiction the following year. Two years later, David O. Selznick transformed Mitchell's tale into one of the most popular motion pictures in history. In 1990, the U.S. Postal Service issued a commemorative stamp (above) in the film's honor.

Civil War Battlefield Reenactments. During the past forty years, thousands of men and women, North and South, have sought to reenact the major events of the Civil War. The photograph above, typical of literally hundreds of battlefield engagements, shows a battalion of Pennsylvanians preparing to attack Confederate lines, during the 1997 reenactment of the western Maryland battle of Antietam. (Courtesy of Michael Higgs.)

Frederic Remington, *Surrender of Chief Joseph* (1896). The famous Frederic Remington's *Surrender of Chief Joseph*, which appeared originally in the *Reminiscences of General Nelson Miles* (1896), helped not only to elevate the mythic image of brave Joseph in many Americans' eyes but also solidified its painter-sculptor's reputation as perhaps the most outstanding interpreter of the U.S. Army's wars in the West.

29 USA
Buffalo Soldiers

Buffalo Soldiers on the Trans-Mississippi Western Frontier. After the Civil War, the U.S. Army's two new mounted regiments manned exclusively with African-American volunteers, the "buffalo soldiers," as their Indian opponents called them, soon proved themselves in battle. Later, during the Spanish-American War, they also fought bravely at the Battle of San Juan Hill and elsewhere. Not until 1994, however, did the U.S. Postal Service produce a stamp (above) in honor of these fine black troopers.

W. G. Read, *The Rough Riders at San Juan Hill* (1898). Though completely inaccurate, W. G. Read's painting of the Rough Riders gallantly charging up San Juan Hill during the Spanish-American War played an important role in creating the heroic image of Colonel Theodore Roosevelt that, less than a year after the war, helped elect the forty-one-year-old soldier as governor of New York.

Howard Chandler Christy, "Gee!! I Wish I Were a Man" (1918). Howard Christy first gained fame as a war artist during the Spanish-American War illustrating articles about the U.S. Army for both *Scribner's Magazine* and *Frank Leslie's Illustrated Weekly*. Twenty years later, during World War I, many of his pictures of idealized young women, including the famous poster (above), successfully recruited men for the nation's armed forces.

Harvey Dunn, "Over the Top." In 1918, the renowned magazine illustrator and now U.S. Army captain, Harvey Dunn, produced hundreds of sketches of American soldiers during World War I. Ten years later, beginning with its January 1928 issue (above), *The American Legion Monthly* published the first of more than fifty Dunn covers with themes based on his World War I efforts. Those paintings remain among the best art to come from any of the nation's many wars. (Courtesy of *The American Legion Monthly*.)

"Willie and Joe" keep spirits high, 1943

Bill Mauldin, ''Willie and Joe Keep Spirits High.'' Sergeant Bill Mauldin, winner of the 1944 Pulitzer Prize, was World War II's most famous American front-line cartoonist. His prototypical ''dogfaces,'' Willie and Joe, became not only instantly popular but also the personification of the American GI in the European theater. When the U.S. Postal Service honored the 50th anniversary of the war, it issued the commemorative stamp featured above in recognition of Mauldin's influence during those years.

War Savings Stamps (1942–1945). To finance the war effort after Pearl Harbor, the Department of Treasury sold War Savings Stamps such as the one pictured above. Stamps were collected and put into a book which, when filled, allowed the owner to purchase a $25.00 War Bond. Millions of young children and adults purchased the red ten-cent stamps featuring Daniel Chester French's famous *The Minute Man* sculpture honoring the many Revolutionary War heroes who left their homes to stand and fight at the Battles of Lexington and Concord.

Raising the Flag on Iwo Jima (1945). Associated Press photographer Joe Rosenthal's February 23, 1945, photograph of U.S. Marines raising a flag on the heights of Iwo Jima's Mount Suribachi won him that year's Pulitzer Prize for news photography. Even before the end of the war, the picture had been adapted for use on a postage stamp (above) as well as becoming the centerpiece of the Seventh (and last) War Bond drive. The United States Marine Corps War Memorial, dedicated in 1954, is also based directly on the famous Rosenthal shot.

Bombers over Europe. No single group of Americans so dramatically doomed the Axis Powers as those men who almost daily after the summer of 1942 flew B-17s and other bombers out of British airbases to attack occupied Europe. Their stories have been told repeatedly in many different forms of American popular culture: novels, plays and films such as *Command Decision* (1948) or *Twelve O'Clock High* (1949), documentaries like *Memphis Belle* or *Pistol Packin' Mama*, or poetry by men such as Randall Jarrell. Fifty years after the high point of those raids in 1944, the United States Postal Service issued the stamp above in honor of both the brave United States airmen of World War II and their planes.

Henry C. Casselli, Jr., "Corpsman" (1968). The youngest Marine Corps combat artist when he was sent to Vietnam in 1968, Henry Casselli, Jr. produced nearly 700 war-related drawings during the next two years. "Corpsman," his 1968 pencil on watercolor paper drawing (above) is one of the most intensely poignant. (U.S. Marine Corps Art Collection.)

The Vietnam Veterans' Memorial ("The Wall"). The Vietnam Veterans' Memorial, listing the engraved names of nearly 60,000 dead American servicemen and women, has become, since its dedication in 1982, perhaps the most visited of all American war monuments. Thousands of daily visitors leave flowers, letters, and other items in moving tribute to dead friends or loved ones. (Dane Penland, The Smithsonian Institution, photo no. 82-13670/20.)

10

World War II

Most Americans were disillusioned over the results of World War I; few wanted to risk going to war again as a result of Europe's problems, no matter how evil the aggressor might be. In the midst of the Great Depression of the 1930s, therefore, the United States officially became a neutral power, trying as diligently as possible to avoid all entangling foreign entanglements. It was not possible for long, however. Civil war broke out in Spain in summer 1936, and both Adolf Hitler's Nazi Germany and the Fascist government of Benito Mussolini in Italy quickly sent troops and matériel to that beleaguered nation to aid the military coup of General Francisco Franco, which was attempting to suppress the democratically elected, but partially Communist, Popular Front government.

Though the United States and all the other Allies in Europe officially refused to become involved in the conflict, more than 5,000 Americans, having seen the rise of totalitarianism in Europe, volunteered to fight against the advancing fascist tide. Organizing themselves into such groups as the so-called George Washington or Abraham Lincoln Battalions, they went to Spain on their own, snuck into the country in contravention of the U.S. role as a neutral power, and, for more than two years, fought "the good fight." Even though more than half of them died and, when the end came in March 1939, the survivors were forced to admit defeat, their battle against such overwhelming odds marked an important turning point in American history. In fighting fascism in Spain, the American volunteers (as well as the thousands of British, French, Scandinavians, and others who joined them in support of the Popular Front) fired the first shots for the defeat of Adolf Hitler and his ilk. It was to be another six years before they saw the successful completion of that fight.

At 7:55 A.M. on the morning of Sunday, December 7, 1941, Japanese planes began attacking army and navy installations on the Hawaiian island of Oahu.

Two hours later, eight battleships, comprising the heart of the American Pacific Fleet, were sunk or lay smoldering in Pearl Harbor. More than 2,400 people were dead, almost half of whom had been onboard the now-destroyed USS *Arizona*. The next day, proclaiming December 7 a "date that will live in infamy," President Franklin Roosevelt asked a joint session of Congress to declare war on Japan. There was only one dissenter. Three days later, after Germany and Italy joined their Axis partner in war against the United States, the nation found itself facing a two-ocean war and the prospects of endless months of combat to defeat its collective foe.

The "dastardly" Japanese attack on Hawaii came as a surprise to most Americans, but the prospect of war did not. Though officially neutral because of congressional acts passed in the years after 1935, the United States was inexorably moving toward war almost from the moment the Japanese attacked mainland China in July 1937. President Roosevelt (FDR) and Secretary of State Cordell Hull repeatedly expressed righteous indignation over the aggression of Japan, Italy, and Germany. Even before the September 1, 1939 German attack on Poland began the European side of World War II, FDR was working diligently to show the American public how important it was to "quarantine" one, or all, of the totalitarian nations.

After the German blitzkrieg in spring 1940 destroyed all the opposing armies in Europe except for a battered British force, Congress reluctantly approved the first peacetime "draft" of men in September. Soon, millions of Americans between the ages of twenty-one and forty-five found themselves in army training camps. As German bombs fell on London and other British cities, young men at dozens of sites began learning the skills of war. At sea, the navy occupied Greenland and later Iceland to keep those Danish possessions out of the hands of Nazi Germany. American destroyers were also sent to protect the many convoys taking tons of U.S.-manufactured goods and raw materials to the beleaguered British. America rejoiced at every English victory, no matter how small, and in May 1941, when the Royal Navy trapped and sank the huge German battleship *Bismarck*, there was an almost audible sigh of relief. With American merchant seamen and U.S. naval personnel dying as a result of Nazi U-boat attacks, the nation became primed for war. The torpedoing of the USS *Reuben James* and the deaths of more than 100 of its crew seemed like the proverbial last straw. Armament factories went into the twenty-four-hour-a-day production of goods. A nation that, only a year before, was ill-prepared to fight now looked forward almost eagerly to the fray. There was the conviction that the United States had been victorious in World War I and would be equally so once again.

The song "Goodbye Mama, I'm Off to Yokohama (for the Red, White, and Blue, My Country and You)" reflected the enthusiasm of thousands of American boys in December 1941. In the months after Pearl Harbor, however, the Japanese rode roughshod over Allied troops in the Pacific. The American-held island of Guam fell, and then Wake Island (but only after a valiant effort by the Marines and other personnel responsible for that base). Hong Kong was captured from the British, followed in the next several months by Malaysia and Singapore. In April 1942, almost 80,000 Americans surrendered to their Japanese foes when the United States finally admitted defeat in Luzon's Bataan Peninsula—the worst military defeat in the nation's history. A month later, the capitulation of the American-occupied "Rock" of Corregidor in Manila Bay resulted in an additional 15,000 Americans becoming prisoners of war.

At sea, the situation was just as bleak. In February, in the Battle of the Java Sea, a small combined fleet of British, Dutch, and U.S. cruisers and destroyers was annihilated by the Japanese on their way to attack and occupy the islands of the Netherlands East Indies. Even when the Battle of the Coral Sea, in May, forced the Japanese to turn back from the threatened invasion of Australia, the USS *Lexington*, one of the navy's few aircraft carriers, was sunk, and there was little reason to rejoice. Only the famous April "Doolittle Raid" on Tokyo, where U.S. B-25 bombers flew from the aircraft carrier *Hornet* to bomb the Japanese mainland, was unquestionably a victory. Though little long-range damage was done to any of the four cities hit by American bombs, the "Thirty Seconds over Tokyo" (see *Thirty Seconds over Tokyo*) that the courageous airmen spent went a huge way toward renewing national pride and the belief that, ultimately, America would win the war.

The tide began to turn in June 1942 at the Battle of Midway. A large Japanese task force headed by four aircraft carriers escorting thousands of troops destined to occupy that strategic Pacific base was met by an outmanned and outgunned American armada and badly mauled. Navy torpedo planes sank all four Japanese carriers, and the enemy was forced to retreat. It was the high watermark of the war in the Pacific. Though a smaller Japanese force did attack the American-held Aleutian Islands off the coast of Alaska and capture two of them as a part of the larger Midway operation, it was little compensation for that nation's failure to drive its enemy from the central Pacific.

Two months later, the United States went on the offensive for the first time. In early August 1942, members of the First Marine Division began landing on Guadalcanal in the Solomon Islands. Though it took more than five months and some of the bloodiest fighting of the entire war to drive the Japanese out of that important port, the success of the Guadalcanal invasion marked the beginning of the steady destruction of the Axis Powers around the world. In November, "Operation Torch" saw American troops under General Dwight Eisenhower successfully attack the German, Italian, and Vichy French allies of the Nazis in North Africa. In summer 1943, the British, Canadian, and American armies crossed the Mediterranean to attack Sicily in July, and then Italy itself in September. The Marines captured the strategically vital, Japanese-held Tarawa atoll, in the Pacific in what were some of the bloodiest few days in Marine Corps history, but also among the proudest.

After more than two years of planning, D-Day, the invasion of the continent of Europe, occurred on June 6, 1944. The fighting throughout western France was fierce and effective. By July, Paris fell, and by autumn, American forces were pushing steadily toward the German border. In the Pacific, General Douglas MacArthur effectively blocked the Japanese in New Guinea. As promised, he then returned to the Philippines (from where he had been evacuated in March 1942) with hundreds of thousands of American soldiers, landing at Leyte and then, at the beginning of 1945, on the main island, Luzon. Off the coast of Leyte in October, the Japanese Navy threw the full weight of its armaments against the United States Navy, only to suffer a calamitous defeat. If Pearl Harbor had marked the nadir of American naval strength, the Battle of Leyte Gulf was its apex.

The last year of the war was filled with a series of Allied victories. The Germans attempted one last great push in the Ardennes Forest in December 1944, but though they created a huge bulge in the American lines, they were unable to break through completely. Not more than two months later, U.S. troops were pushing the Germans back all along the line and had reached the German homeland. On Valentine's Day 1945, American and British planes firebombed the ancient German city of Dresden. The death toll will probably never be known (the city was packed with refuges escaping the Russian armies invading from the east), but even the lower estimates suggest no less than 100,000. In March, the Rhine was crossed over the captured Remagen Bridge, and the end was in sight to the war in Europe.

In the Pacific, on February 18, 1945, Marines landed on the tiny island of Iwo Jima. It was there that Associated Press photographer Joe Rosenthal snapped what instantly became the most famous image to come from the entire war years: the raising of the American flag on the summit of Iwo's Mount Suribachi. Less than two months later, other Marine and army forces invaded Okinawa, setting the stage for the eventual invasion of the Japanese home islands. Meanwhile, in the sky, U.S. B-29 bombers were repeatedly blasting every major Japanese city almost at will. On March 9–10, the first deliberate firebombings took place and the heart of Tokyo was gutted. The might of the United States, fueled by the greatest industrial buildup ever seen in recorded history, seemed endless.

By April 1945, the war in Europe was "won" in everything but name. On April 30, Adolf Hitler and his new wife, Eva Braun, committed suicide; Berlin fell two days later. On May 7, the new head of Germany, Admiral Karl Doenitz, sued for peace, and the following day, the world celebrated V-E day. In retrospect, the Germans were lucky. Teams of American and other Allied scientists had been working since 1942 on a nuclear bomb that would be more powerful than any weapon known up to that time. In July, they managed to perfect and test their prototype. Harry S. Truman, who had served as president since the sudden death of FDR in April, gave the go-ahead for the new weapon to be used against the Japanese, and the Atomic Era began at Hiroshima on August 6. More than 125,000 men, women, and children died, and tens of thousands of others suffered permanent poisoning of their systems. Three days later, a second bomb was dropped on the smaller city of Nagasaki. On August 14, the Japanese, led by Emperor Hirohito, surrendered, and World War II was over.

Of the nation's many wars, only the Civil War was won with more sacrifice of American lives than World War II. More than 16 million men and women served in either the U.S. Army, Navy, Marine Corps, and Coast Guard during the period between 1941 and 1945. More than 400 thousand died, while nearly 700 thousand were wounded. At the same time, however, World War II was also, in the words of Chicago radio personality Studs Terkel, our only "good war." Though there were a few pro-German or pro-Japanese traitors on the American home front during the war, the vast majority of citizens not only gave their loved ones to the conflict, they gave themselves as well. Millions of dollars of war stamps and war bonds were sold, as Americans pooled their resources to aid the war effort. When the federal government announced the beginning of a comprehensive rationing program for everything from gas and oil to food-stuffs, citizens complained a little but patriotically accepted the need and re-solved to do the best they could until the war brought the boys home once again. Housewives became like "**Rosie the Riveter**" as they traded their brooms for rivet guns or other industrial tools. Children collected newspapers, tin cans, and even milkweed pods for **Uncle Sam**.

The war years brought unprecedented turmoil to many Americans. In the Pacific Coast states of California, Oregon, and Washington, more than 110,000 Japanese-Americans were rounded up by order of the army and forced to leave their homes and businesses. Sent under military guard to euphemistically named "war relocation centers" in some of the most desolate areas of the American landscape, many remained in what were little more than concentration camps for the next four years. That most of these persons were also U.S. citizens who had been deported from the three Pacific Coast states solely because of their racial heritage seemed not to bother most white Americans.

Though Dorrie Miller, an African-American steward in the navy, was cheered as a hero for manning a gun and shooting down a Japanese plane during the attack on Pearl Harbor, the majority of persons of African descent were at first denied the chance to stand as equals with their white counterparts. When "Ne-groes" moved to the northern cities in large numbers to take jobs in some of the nation's many defense plants, they were all too frequently shunned. In some places, such as Detroit, Michigan, race riots erupted, and bitterness continued to spill over long after the war ended. Only the unparalleled success of groups like the much-honored "Tuskegee Airmen" helped slowly to create a more positive view.

World War II has continued to fascinate Americans. Popular culture reflects only too clearly this obsession with remembering the nation's last totally vic-torious war. In addition to thousands of books, stories, songs, artworks, and other representations of the conflict that were created while the war was in progress, an even greater number of similar items have appeared since 1945. "Real men" had won the war, and authors, filmmakers, and others set out in the postwar years to capture that "macho" image. Norman Mailer's *The Naked and the Dead*, Leon Uris's *Battle Cry*, and James Jones's *The Thin Red Line* vividly portrayed some of these masculine "real Americans," as, too, did Hollywood's directors. Seeing John Wayne, for instance, portraying a Marine Corps sergeant in *The Sands of Iwo Jima*, a Marine aviator in *Flying Leathernecks*, or even a forceful navy admiral in *Operation Pacific* seemed like perfect casting to many viewers. The same was true for Lee Marvin playing the part of a Marine in one film (*Hell in the Pacific*), a tough, grizzled army sergeant in Europe in another (*The Big Red One*), and the leader of a secret team of paroled convicts wreaking havoc behind German lines in yet a third (*The Dirty Dozen*). It had obviously taken tough men to win the war, and popular culture glorified them now.

In the late 1990s, new books about the war find a ready audience, and television stations continue to attract viewers by scheduling stories about World War II. For instance, when Herman Wouk's popular novel *War and Remembrance* was transformed into a seemingly endless (twelve-episode, thirty-hour-long) television miniseries, it was one of that medium's most watched shows. Films such as *A Midnight Clear* and *The Memphis Belle* remain popular, ardent collectors rush to purchase dozens of types of war memorabilia, and the list could go on and on.

World War II mirrored what was best in America as well as what was worst. It defined who Americans were as a people, and their victory over the evil forces of Nazi Germany, Italy, and Japan gave them all a reason to be proud.

See:

Ambrose, Stephen. *The American Heritage New History of World War II*. New York: Viking, 1997.
Kennett, Lee. *G.I.: The American Soldier in World War II*. New York: Scribner's, 1987.
Weatherford, Doris. *American Women and World War II*. New York: Facts on File, 1990.

ACTION IN THE NORTH ATLANTIC (**Film**). Directed by Lloyd Bacon with a screenplay by John Howard Lawson, *Action in the North Atlantic* (Warner Brothers, 1943) was Hollywood's paean to the United States Merchant Marine during World War II. Starring Humphrey Bogart, Raymond Massey, Alan Hale, and a host of other character actors, the production is a melodramatic account of the perils faced by the convoys taking supplies to Europe.

Shortly after the start of the film, a Liberty ship commanded by Massey is torpedoed by a German U-boat; the survivors' lifeboat is then rammed by the submarine. The few who are rescued join another ship that becomes part of a huge international convoy sailing out of Halifax, Nova Scotia, for the Russian port of Murmansk. Once again, the crew is attacked, this time by both a submarine and a German bomber. Battered but not beaten, the ship eventually lands in the Soviet Union, to the cheers and gratitude of the Russians. In one of the most dramatic scenes, involving the burial at sea of a teenaged sailor, Bogart makes sure that the movie's message is clear. "A lot of people are going to die before [the war] is over," he says in eulogy, but everyone has to "make sure they didn't die for nothing."

Though some critics found the battle scenes stagy and the dialogue often unconvincing, audiences packed the theaters, and the U.S. Merchant Marine used the picture as a part of its training program. At the New York premier in May 1943, a group of seventeen torpedoed seamen, three hundred sailors, and members of the Merchant Marine band marched into the theater to present Jack Warner, the picture's producer, with that service's victory flag, the first time any member of the Hollywood community was so honored.

See:

Quirk, Lawrence J. "Action in the North Atlantic." Chapter 21 in *The Great War Films from The Birth of a Nation to Today.* New York: Citadel, 1994, 79–82.

Suid, Lawrence. *Sailing on the Silver Screen: Hollywood and the U.S Navy.* Annapolis, MD: Naval Institute Press, 1996, 60.

M. Paul Holsinger

AIR FORCE (Film). More than 300 motion pictures about military life were produced in Hollywood during World War II in an attempt to introduce the American public to various aspects of military life as well as to encourage popular support for the war effort. The combination of historical events, prowar propaganda, and Hollywood heroics evolved into a genre that has shaped American war films for over a half-century. *Air Force* (Warner Brothers, 1943), directed by Howard Hawks, is a classic example.

Dudley Nichols's screenplay, which focuses on the crew of a B-17 Flying Fortress, the *Mary Ann*, invokes the major events of the Pacific theater during the first six months of World War II. It opens in early December 1941 as the aircrew, most of its members fresh from flight school, prepares to fly to the Philippines. They arrive at Pearl Harbor on December 7, leave Clark Field for the Philippines, make a stop at Wake Island just as it is being overrun by the Japanese, retreat to Australia for repairs and retraining, and take part in the Battle of the Coral Sea in May 1942.

The crew, which is played by such fine young actors as Arthur Kennedy, John Garfield, Gig Young, and Harry Carey, exemplifies the genre's practice of presenting the military unit as a cross-section of American life. It includes urban ethnics and rural southerners, members of the working and middle classes, college-educated professionals, and factory hands. In combat, they learn to transcend both social differences and personal disappointments in order to achieve the teamwork necessary to defeat a totalitarian enemy. Although nearly all Hollywood war films of the 1940s delivered this message, very few of them are as convincing as *Air Force.* Hawks's success lies, not in greater historical accuracy, but in his ability to transform the characters into a group of skilled and dedicated professionals similar to those who inhabit the world of his other pictures from **The Dawn Patrol** (1931) to *Rio Bravo* (1959).

Air Force was nominated for a number of Academy Awards, especially in the areas of cinematography and film editing. It also received a best picture nomination from the New York Film Critics Circle.

See:

Paris, Michael. "Democracy Goes to War: *Air Force* (1943)." *Film and History: An Interdisciplinary Journal of Film and Television* 27 (1997): 48–53.
Suid, Lawrence H. *Guts and Glory: Great American War Movies*. Reading, MA: Addison-Wesley, 1978, 40–44.

Philip J. Landon

"ANCHORS AWEIGH" (Song). "Anchors Aweigh," which has long been renowned as the official song of the United States Navy, was penned originally as a march for the 1906 Army-Navy football game by Alfred H. Miles, a member of the United States Naval Academy's class of 1907, and the academy's bandmaster, Charles A. Zimmerman. Members of the corps of midshipmen sang the song, first known simply as the "March of the Class of 1907," on the field for the first time just before the game began. Though George D. Lottman made several revisions to the first several stanzas after it was published in 1907, for the next twenty years it was connected with little more than the academy's football season.

In 1926, Royal Lovell, another midshipman, added new lyrics, which were published commercially that year, and "Anchors Aweigh" gradually began to take on broader significance. By the time the United States entered World War II, it had become synonymous with the navy as a whole. Sheet music could be found in music stores everywhere in America, and there were dozens of recordings. Nearly every American, young and old, knew the words to the piece and sang it patriotically along with the other service anthems: **"The Marines' Hymn," "The Army Air Corps Song,"** and **"The Caissons Go Rolling Along."**

See:

Ewen, David. *All the Years of American Popular Music*. Englewood Cliffs, NJ: Prentice-Hall, 1977, 146.

M. Paul Holsinger

THE ANDREWS SISTERS (Entertainers). The Andrews Sisters (Patti, Maxene, and LaVerne) were the most popular singing group in America during the era of World War II and perhaps the most successful and popular female group of all time. Their many recording hits, including "Boogie Woogie Bugle Boy of Company B"—a song that, when reprised by Bette Midler in 1973, rose to number one on the popular charts—and **"Don't Sit under the Apple Tree"** kept the group among the top two or three ensembles in the United States for almost fifteen years.

During the war years, the Andrews Sisters toured frequently overseas with the **United Services Organization (USO)** as well as appearing in both the **Stage Door and Hollywood Canteens**. They participated in war bond drives and often visited military hospitals to perform for wounded GIs. Though they made the

Hit Parade with their version of "Remember Pearl Harbor" in December 1941, most of their successful numbers were not "war songs" but rather happy tunes or novelty pieces designed to take the public's mind off the death and destruction overseas and, as Maxene remembered years later, "to help America smile."

By 1945, *Time* magazine was calling the three young women, with their syncopated, jitterbugging rhythms, the "queens of the juke box." During their career, the Andrews Sisters appeared in twenty-two motion pictures and sold more than 60 million records. Patti tried, fairly successfully, to launch a career in the 1950s as a soloist, but the three sisters also sang together until Laverne's death in 1967. Maxene and Patti brought many of their famous routines to Broadway in the musical *Over Here* (1974) and performed them for more than a year. Though she and Patti became estranged in later life and never sang together again after 1975, Maxene continued to sing numbers from the war years as a part of *Swingtime Canteen*, a popular off-Broadway show, until just a few weeks before her 1995 death from a heart attack.

In 1987, Maxene received the Department of Defense's Medal for Distinguished Public Service, the Pentagon's highest civilian honor. Today, Patti occasionally tours with the latest edition of the famous Glenn Miller Orchestra, singing many of the songs that made the Andrew Sisters so popular.

See:

Andrews, Maxene. *Over Here, Over There: The Andrews Sisters and the USO Stars in World War II*. New York: Kensington, 1993.

M. Paul Holsinger

"THE ARMY AIR CORPS SONG" (Song). Millions of Americans during World War II knew by heart the lyrics of "The Army Air Corps Song." A former voice teacher at Princeton University's School of Music, Army Captain Robert M. Crawford, composed the piece in 1939 as an entry in *Liberty Magazine*'s search for a new publishable song. Thousands responded in hopes of winning the magazine's $1,000 top prize money, but it was Crawford's "Off We Go" (as "The Army Air Corps Song" was originally titled) that was selected.

Adopted almost immediately by the Army Air Corps as its official anthem, "The Army Air Corps Song," though still relatively new, was already well known and extremely popular before the United States entered World War II. It gained even greater popularity when **Winged Victory**, Moss Hart's Broadway play and subsequent Hollywood movie, used both its words and melody as background music. When the air corps became a separate branch of service in 1948, the song's title was formally changed to "The U.S. Air Force."

During World War II, Crawford became a major in the Air Transport Command and also wrote that unit's official ballad, "Born to the Sky." Less well-known, but certainly far more explicitly honest, a third piece by Crawford which he called simply, "Kill the Bastards," expresses clearly the author's feelings toward the Axis Powers.

See:

Ewen, David. *All the Years of American Popular Music.* Englewood Cliffs, NJ: Prentice-Hall, 1977, 147.

M. Paul Holsinger

ATTACK (**Film**). On October 12, 1954, playwright Norman A. Brooks's *The Fragile Fox*, a drama about an ineptly run United States National Guard rifle company during the Battle of the Bulge, opened on Broadway. Starring Andrew Duggan as Captain Erskine Cooney and Dane Clark as First Lieutenant Joseph Costa, it was a financial failure and closed after only fifty-five performances.

Two years later, director Robert Aldrich adapted the play into *Attack* (Associates, 1956), one of the strongest combat movies about World War II yet made. Set in western France in December 1944, it focuses on a single unit commanded by the cowardly Captain Cooney (Eddie Albert). Charged with attacking a heavily fortified German position, Cooney orders Costa (Jack Palance) to lead the assault. Costa reluctantly obeys, fearing that Cooney, who has already revealed his timidity in the face of enemy fire and has kept his command only because of his father's influence over the battalion commander (Lee Marvin), will not risk himself to help the platoon if it encounters stiff resistance. As Costa suspected, Cooney abandons the platoon and the Germans decimate it. Horribly wounded, the lieutenant makes his way back to headquarters intent on killing Cooney, but he dies before he can do so. When the frightened captain attempts to surrender to the advancing Germans, however, he is shot and killed by another of his young lieutenants. Two enlisted men, witnesses to the murder, also shoot into the captain's body, clearly believing that justice has, at last, been done.

Attack, which won the Critics Prize at the Venice Film Festival, has never received the attention it deserves in the United States. It is an excellent example of the manner in which Aldrich transformed familiar Hollywood genre films. The savagely brutal (and realistic) combat sequences, the exploration of the military's capacity for mendacity and cowardice, and the bitterly ironic conclusion all serve to subvert the heroic ideals that characterized the war film during the decade following World War II. *Attack* deserves comparison with Stanley Kubrick's more famous **Paths of Glory** (1957) and, like that motion picture, reflects the antimilitary sentiments that began to appear in Hollywood productions during the later 1950s.

See:

Arnold, Edwin T., and Eugene L. Miller. *The Films and Career of Robert Aldrich.* Knoxville: University of Tennessee Press, 1986, 60–75.
Krueger, Eric. "Robert Aldrich's *Attack!*" *Journal of Popular Film* 2 (Spring 1973): 262–276.

Philip J. Landon

AXIS SALLY (Historical Figure). Mildred Gillars was known to her World War II Radio Germany listeners as "Axis Sally." In regular broadcasts to Allied soldiers, she attempted to heighten their feelings of isolation and weariness and to indicate the futility of continuing to fight. Whether her propaganda efforts were even minimally effective remains debatable. Most GIs largely ignored the German propaganda and listened only for the latest American music, which was always liberally sprinkled throughout her programs.

Gillars, born Mildred Elizabeth Sisk in Portland, Maine, went to Germany in 1934. Eventually hired to broadcast in English over Radio Germany, she was, at best, a minor performer until 1941. When the United States entered the war, however, Gillars, as one of the few American voices on which the Nazis could call for propaganda purposes, became instantaneously successful. After being featured on *Smiling Through*, a radio show broadcast first to American troops in North Africa and later throughout the European theater of operations, she became a star.

On being found guilty of treason in 1949, Gillars was sentenced from ten to thirty years' imprisonment and fined $10,000. By the time she was released on parole in 1961, most Americans had forgotten her infamous past. In 1973, she completed a bachelor's degree in speech begun many years before at Ohio Wesleyan University; she then spent the last sixteen years of her life teaching in a parochial school in Columbus, Ohio.

See:

Edwards, John C. *Berlin Calling: Americans Broadcasting in Service to the Third Reich.* New York: Praeger, 1991.
Harper, Dale P. "American-born Axis Sally Made Propaganda Broadcasts for Radio Berlin in Hitler's Germany." *World War II* 10.4 (November 1995): 8, 10, 81–82.

Philip J. Harwood

"THE BALLAD OF RODGER YOUNG" (Song). Private Rodger Young, a twenty-five-year-old member of the army's Thirty-Seventh Infantry Division, was killed on the island of New Georgia in the Solomons when he single-handedly attacked a hidden Japanese machine gun emplacement to give the other trapped members of his platoon the chance to retreat to safety. He was post-humously awarded the Congressional Medal of Honor early in 1944. When the infantry later asked composer Frank Loesser, author of several popular war songs including **"Praise the Lord and Pass the Ammunition,"** to write a musical number glorifying that branch of the service, he selected Young's heroism (based on a newspaper account) as the perfect focal point.

"The Ballad of Rodger Young" was first heard on the coast-to-coast radio program of band leader Meredith Willson in early 1945. Sung simply by Earl Wrightson with only a guitar accompaniment, it quickly became one of the most requested songs of the war years. The return of Young's body to his native Ohio for burial accelerated interest in the ballad, and best-selling recordings of it were made by Burl Ives, Nelson Eddy, and a host of other male singers before the end of the war later that year.

See:

Frankel, Stanley A. "Heroic Rodger Young Lives on in Song and in the Memories of
    His Comrades in Arms." *World War II* 8.4 (November 1993): 66, 68, 70, 72.
Loesser, Susan. *A Most Remarkable Fella: Frank Loesser and the Guys and Dolls in
    His Life.* New York: D. I. Fine, 1993.

                                                            M. Paul Holsinger

BATAAN (Film). *Bataan* (Metro-Goldwyn-Mayer, 1943) is among the most
emotionally powerful films about World War II. Robert D. Andrews's screenplay, as directed by Tay Garnett, focuses on a group of mismatched servicemen
who are separated from their units in the early days of the attack on the Philippines. They volunteer to delay the Japanese at a ravine in order to give the
main American forces time to retreat down the Bataan peninsula. The thirteen
men represent a cross-section of national, regional, and ethnic types—Philippine
and American, urban and rural, WASP, Hispanic, Jewish, and black—and of
the service branches; they are, in microcosm, the American forces in the Philippines and the stand they made against hopeless odds. The men manage some
victories: they blow up the bridge the Japanese construct; a wounded air force
lieutenant (George Murphy) spectacularly crashes his plane into the rebuilt
bridge; they drive back a full assault of the Japanese with hand-to-hand combat.
One by one, the men are killed until, in a striking image, only their leader,
Sergeant Bill Dane (Robert Taylor), remains, awaiting the final attack in the
grave he has dug for himself.

   The movie's visceral force has two sources. The Japanese are particularly
despicable here; at the beginning they bomb and strafe retreating U.S. forces,
including ambulances, and at the end they slither snakelike through the ground
fog toward the outnumbered Dane. The Allies are particularly noble, doing their
duty with no hope of relief or possibility of retreat, and thus sacrificing themselves to give the rest of the army, and by extension, the audience, the time and
opportunity to win.

See:

Basinger, Jeanine. *The World War II Combat Film: Anatomy of a Genre.* New York:
    Columbia, University Press, 1986, 50–62.
Kane, Kathryn. *Visions of War: Hollywood Combat Films of World War II.* Ann Arbor,
    MI: UMI, 1982, 61–67.

                                                            Robert L. McLaughlin

BATTLE CRY (Novel-Film). Leon Uris was a radio operator with the Second
Marine Division in the Pacific during World War II. Like many returning veterans after the conflict ended, he drew on his personal experiences to create a
true picture of what the war was like to the average American fighting man.
Battle Cry (1953), Uris's first published work of fiction, was the best-known
novel about the United States Marine Corps to come out of the war. Describing
the progress of a group of young Marines from their training until they are

bloodied in combat in late 1942 at Guadalcanal and, a year later, on Tarawa, *Battle Cry* offers its readers a firsthand look at the horrors of war, based on Uris's own experiences in battle. Though the book spares little in its depictions of death and violence, there are enough romantic interludes, during training camp in California and while the men were in New Zealand, to make it a best-seller for many months.

Two years later, Hollywood director Raoul Walsh, using a screenplay written by Uris, adapted *Battle Cry* (Warner Brothers, 1955) into an equally popular, two-and-a-half-hour technicolor movie starring Van Heflin, Aldo Ray, James Whitmore, and Tab Hunter. Though he spent far more time exploring at length the interpersonal relationships of the picture's characters than re-creating scenes of combat, *Battle Cry* became the year's top-grossing film. Critics were less enchanted; only Max Steiner's dramatic martial score received an Academy Award nomination.

See:

Quirk, Lawrence J. "Battle Cry." Chapter 40 in *The Great War Films from The Birth of a Nation to Today.* New York: Citadel, 1994, 132–136.

David K. Vaughan

BATTLEGROUND (**Film**). *Battleground* (Metro-Goldwyn-Mayer, 1949), directed by William Wellman, was the first Hollywood movie to commemorate the famed Battle of the Bulge. It opens as a platoon of the 101st Airborne Division on the outskirts of Bastogne, Belgium, is unexpectedly ordered to the front. Shrouded in snow and fog and cut off from the rest of the division, they find themselves under attack by two enemies: the white-clad members of a German armored division and the bitter winter cold. Their position becomes increasingly desperate as supplies dwindle. Though the men feel abandoned by the high command in London, they continue to resist until a break in the weather allows Allied air operations to resume. The last German offensive of the war is then broken, and the platoon's tattered survivors march to the rear past columns of their untested replacements.

A critical and box office success, *Battleground* has been credited with reviving the popularity of Hollywood war films, a genre that had little appeal in postwar America. It was nominated for six Academy Awards, including best picture and best director. The screenplay, by Robert Pirosh, who fought in the Battle of the Bulge and who later conceived the popular television series **Combat**, was praised for its realism. Today it seems less an exercise in cinematic realism than a classic example of the war genre in which a unit of citizen soldiers representing a regional, social, and ethnic cross-section of America and under the leadership of a seasoned professional (James Whitmore) prevails in the struggle against a totalitarian enemy.

Until well into the 1960s, the narrative and thematic conventions established in *Battleground*, **The Sands of Iwo Jima** (1949), and *Twelve O'Clock High* (1949) defined the Hollywood war film.

See:

Broderick, Suzanne. "Tough Ombres and *Battleground*: The Reel War and the Real War." *Film and History: An Interdisciplinary Journal of Film and Television* 27 (1997): 62–67.
Rubin, Stephen Jay. "The Lion Returns to War: *Battleground* (1949)." Chapter 2 in *Combat Films: American Realism: 1945–1970.* Jefferson, NC: McFarland, 1981, 24–42.

Philip J. Landon

***THE BATTLE OF MIDWAY* (Documentary).** Director John Ford served as the commander of a U.S. naval photographic unit during World War II, and in this capacity, he wrote and photographed a seventeen-minute documentary that detailed the first American victory in the Pacific War. Though subject to wartime censorship and somewhat misleading in its focus on a relatively minor portion of the immense naval confrontation, *The Battle of Midway* (1942), with dramatic combat footage shot by Ford himself during the preliminary Japanese bombing raid on Midway Island, had an authenticity that was heretofore lacking in documentaries.

After returning to the States, Ford commissioned a script, musical score, and voice-over dialogue by Henry Fonda, Donald Crisp, and Academy Award–winning actress Jane Darwell. The end product was a piece of unashamedly sentimental and patriotic propaganda depicting courageously dutiful midwestern boys flying their planes into the Japanese inferno waiting for them at Midway, juxtaposed with poignant images of their anxious mothers and sweethearts back home. Ford was careful to show all the service branches, accompanied by their signature musical themes on the soundtrack, equally participating in the battle and contributing to the final victory—4 Japanese aircraft carriers, 28 warships, and 300 aircraft were destroyed, the end titles enthusiastically informed the audience.

Released theatrically three months after the battle by 20th Century–Fox, the production was an instant success and went on to win the 1942 Academy Award for best documentary. A relatively new genre, which had been held in disrepute by mainstream filmmakers before America's involvement in World War II, the documentary now achieved commercial respectability throughout the United States. *The Battle of Midway*'s value as wartime propaganda was also immediately apparent to individuals in Washington, D.C. With government cooperation, other famous directors, such as Frank Capra and John Huston, soon began to produce similar wartime films. In doing so, they helped to change every American's view of how war should be recorded.

Hollywood attempted to make a big budget, full-color, epic study of the battle in *Midway* (Universal, 1976). Filled with dozens of important male stars, including Charlton Heston, Henry Fonda, Robert Mitchum, Glenn Ford, and Hal Holbrook, it is a dismal soap opera with little to recommend it. Only some of the re-created battle scenes that make up a good portion of the second part of the two-hour-plus movie offer reason for anyone to watch.

See:

Barsam, Richard M. *Nonfiction Film: A Critical History.* Rev. and enlarged ed. Bloomington: Indiana University Press, 1992, 230–231.
Gallez, Douglas W. "Patterns in Wartime Documentaries." *Quarterly of Film, Radio, and Television* 10.2 (1955): 125–135.

Philip L. Simpson

BEACH RED (Novel-Film). Undeniably the most unique American combat novel to come out of World War II, *Beach Red* was published by Random House in 1945. Written in free verse by Peter Bowman, a staff reporter for *Air Force* (the official service journal of the army air forces), it tells the story of an amphibious landing by American troops on an unnamed Pacific island. Perceptive, analytical, and overwhelmingly antiwar—Bowman uses such terms as "ugliness" and "stinking horror" to describe the war he knew—*Beach Red* was a critical success when it first appeared. Though fellow authors like John P. Marquand were overwhelmingly impressed with Bowman's achievement and the Book-of-the-Month Club made the volume one of its main selections in December 1945, the reading public found the strange verse, with its many allusions, hard to fathom. Although in many ways it was quite brilliant, *Beach Red* soon faded into undeserved obscurity.

Twenty-two years later, actor-producer-director Cornel Wilde made *Beach Red* (United Artists, 1967) into a motion picture. Working from a screenplay by Jefferson Pascal and Donald A. Peters and using a cast of young, relatively unknown actors, Wilde created what one critic has rightly called "a neglected masterpiece." Graphic in its visual effect, the film at times almost resembles a horror movie, as severed limbs float casually up on the beach and men die needlessly, and even stupidly. Combat, even when American forces are ultimately victorious, is seen as evil and demoralizing. Wilde, who plays the unit's commanding officer, makes no attempt to glamorize anything about the landing and the men's subsequent destruction of their Japanese enemies. Unlike most Hollywood war movies, there are no clichés about such things as American bravery, Mom, or apple pie. The men have a job to do so that they can go home to their loved ones a little sooner. Some live; but many die.

Shot in color in the Philippines, *Beach Red* was not a popular success when it first appeared. Probably too strong for the late 1960s, even with the war in Vietnam becoming more bloody every day, the movie, like the book on which it is based, soon disappeared from public view. Only recently have copies begun to make the rounds of late-night television. To many, it has become something of a cult classic, a film to be watched and finally appreciated.

See:

Atkinson, Michael. "Naked Prey. The Cinema of Cornel Wilde." *Film Comment* 32 (November/December 1996): 70–75.
Quirk, Lawrence J. "Beach Red." Chapter 57 in *The Great War Films from The Birth of a Nation to Today*. New York: Citadel, 1994, 196–198.

M. Paul Holsinger

A BELL FOR ADANO (Novel-Drama-Film). *A Bell for Adano* (1944) by John Hersey recounts the efforts of U.S. Major Victor Joppolo to bring order and justice to a Sicilian town that has been in fascist hands for many years. Although the immediate needs of Adano are practical ones—necessities such as water, fish, and pasta to fill the stomach—spiritually there is also a need: for a new bell for the clock tower to fill the hearts of the population. Joppolo, who is an Italian-American, tries to meet all these needs while wrestling with the bureaucracy created by the former officials of the town and the even more dense bureaucracy of the American military. That he does so, despite the enmity of the townspeople toward each other and the bitterness caused by the often-thoughtless behavior of the American soldiers toward both the women of the town and the property of the Italians, is commendable. That he does so in such a way that the citizens of Adano recognize him as representative of wisdom and justice is a miracle. The Allied command, on the other hand, does not appreciate him, since he countermands military orders for the good of the town. He is relieved of command, just as the new bell of the town starts to ring.

Even before the novel won the 1945 Pulitzer Prize for fiction, it had been transformed into a reasonably successful play, written by Paul Osborn and produced for the stage by Leland Heyward. Starring Fredric March as Victor Joppolo, the play ran for 304 performances before closing in October 1945. That same year *A Bell for Adano* (20th Century–Fox, 1945) became a very popular motion picture, this time featuring John Hodiak (as Joppolo), Gene Tierney, and William Bendix. Directed by Henry King from a script by Lamar Trotti and Norman Reilly Raine, it is a perceptive and often entertaining adaptation.

See:

Sanders, David. "John Hersey: War Correspondent into Novelist." In *New Voices in American Studies*, ed. Ray B. Browne. Lafayette, IN: Purdue University Press, 1966, 49–58.

Sally E. Parry

THE BEST YEARS OF OUR LIVES (Film). One of Hollywood's greatest films, *The Best Years of Our Lives* (RKO/Goldwyn, 1946) focuses on the problems faced by servicemen returning home after World War II. Produced by Samuel Goldwyn, directed by William Wyler, and scripted by Robert E. Sherwood from MacKinlay Kantor's critically failed novel *Glory for Me* (1945), the movie follows three men as they adjust to postwar life. Banker Al Stephenson (Fredric March), an army sergeant, finds that financially sound decisions about loans for veterans are at odds with his knowledge of the men. Captain Fred Derry (Dana Andrews), a decorated bombardier, cannot find a job that matches his ambitions and discovers that he and the woman (Virginia Mayo) he married just before he went overseas now have little in common. Seaman Homer Parrish (Harold Russell), whose hands have been replaced by hooks, struggles to be accepted without pity by his family and to believe that his fiancée (Cathy O'Donnell) can still love him. There is a happy ending: at Homer's wedding, Fred, who has found a job and divorced his wife, declares his love for Al's daughter (Teresa Wright).

The Best Years of Our Lives offers no pat answers to the issues it raises and disturbingly leaves unresolved: the difficulty of functioning in a society that does not understand the serviceman's experiences; the hostility of the economic status quo to perceived intruders; the changes undergone by families and servicemen during the war; and psychological terrors that do not end even after returning home. There are, however, some striking scenes. Al declaring war on his bank's loan policies at a dinner in his honor, Homer fighting a stranger who tells him he lost his hands for nothing, and Fred sitting in one of the hundreds of no longer needed B-17s (the only place he has ever been important), are among the most memorable cinematic moments in film history.

The Best Years of Our Lives is one of Hollywood's most honored motion pictures. Nominated for eight Academy Awards, it won seven, including best picture, best actor (March), best supporting actor (Russell), best direction, and best screenplay. Russell won a second Oscar for showing what a paraplegic could accomplish. The movie also won best picture honors from the New York Film Critics Circle, the British Academy, and the voters of the Golden Globe Award.

Returning Home, a slightly different version of *The Best Years of Our Lives*, was filmed as a made-for-television movie and shown on ABC in April 1975. Dabney Coleman, Tom Selleck, and James Miller (who, like Harold Russell, was an amputee as a result of war wounds) played the returning veterans. There is little, however, to recommend this newer adaptation.

See:

Jackson, Martin A. "The Uncertain Peace: *The Best Years of Our Lives* (1946)." In *American History/American Film*, ed. John E. O'Connor and Martin A. Jackson. New York: Ungar, 1979, 147–165.

Robert L. McLaughlin

THE BIG RED ONE (Film). Samuel Fuller, a longtime director of Hollywood war and action movies, was a member of the First Infantry Division—the "Big Red One"—during World War II. For more than thirty-five years, he dreamed about making a movie that would recapture some of those experiences as well as tell, episodically, the history of that proud unit during the war. Years after completing films such as the Korean War–centered **The Steel Helmet** (1950) and *Fixed Bayonets* (1951) and the World War II-focused *Merrill's Marauders* (1962), Fuller finally got the opportunity to make "his" picture. *The Big Red One* (Lorimar, 1980), which he both wrote and directed, is the result.

Rather than restaging a host of full-scale battle scenes, Fuller turns his attention to the lives of four young riflemen-recruits. Viewers follow them and their sergeant, a tough, gnarled World War I veteran (played almost perfectly by an aging Lee Marvin), from their preinvasion fears, immediately before landing in North Africa in November 1942, until the very last days of the war in Europe, in May 1945. Though others die or are wounded in battle, Fuller's five central figures survive and, in doing so, are victorious. Fuller's message is clear: there is no glory in war. Simply to live one more day is the essence of combat.

The picture, which was shot on location in Israel in full color, was nominated for honors at the Cannes Film Festival. *The Big Red One* is a truthful, honest, realistic production, and certainly one of the best pictures about the American army in World War II yet made.

See:

Basinger, Jeanine. *The World War II Combat Film: Anatomy of a Genre.* New York: Columbia University Press, 1986, 216–219.
Wood, Denis. "The Bodies We Keep Tripping Over: Critical Commentary on Sam Fuller's *The Big Red One.*" *Journal of Popular Film and Television* 9.1 (1981): 2–12.

                                                              M. Paul Holsinger

BILOXI BLUES (Drama-Film). Winner of the prestigious Antoinette Perry ("Tony") Award of the American Theater Wing as the best play of 1984–1985, *Biloxi Blues* is distinguished playwright Neil Simon's semiautobiographical account of life at an army training base in Bixoli, Mississippi, during summer 1943. Eugene Morris Jerome, the teen featured in Simon's earlier *Brighton Beach Memoirs*, is now old enough to be drafted and head off to service. In an aside to the audience early in the play, he says that he has three goals in mind during the war: "become a writer, not get killed, and lose my virginity." He manages all three in this thoughtful, but sprightly, comedy, which focuses on topics as significant as anti-Semitism in the army and as trivial as Eugene's quest to accomplish the last of his goals with a prostitute from the nearby city of Gulfport.

Bixoli Blues, starring Matthew Broderick as Eugene, opened on Broadway on March 28, 1985, and ran for 524 performances before it closed. Three years later, veteran director Mike Nichols turned it into a Hollywood film with Broderick and many of the original Broadway cast. Though most critics liked the new version, *Biloxi Blues* (Rostar/Universal, 1988), far too often violates the spirit of original play. In its run on Broadway, for instance, the comedy-drama was filled with tension from a number of angles, not the least of which was the fact that in 1943, the young men all know that the successful completion of their training might lead directly to their deaths in combat. On the screen, however, the chronology was inexplicably changed to summer 1945, causing much of Simon's dramatic bite to be removed. The men finish their training but, with the development of the atomic bomb, they are never placed in harm's way.

See:

Simon, Neil. *Rewrites: A Memoir.* New York: Simon and Schuster, 1996.

M. Paul Holsinger

BOURKE-WHITE, MARGARET (Photojournalist). Few photographers in American history are more famous than Margaret Bourke-White. One of the world's most distinguished industrial and architectural photographers, she gained even more fame when she joined the staff of the new *Life* magazine in 1936. That magazine's first issue featured a photojournalist essay centered around her work, as did numerous issues over the next several years. When *Life* decided to send a journalist to the Soviet Union in spring 1941 to cover the possible attack of that nation by Nazi Germany, it was Bourke-White whom they chose. Thus she was in Russia on June 22, 1941, when German troops launched their offensive against the Soviet Union, and though she had to battle much red tape to gain permission to take pictures of the fighting, she was the first Western journalist to send accurate photographs out of the country. These include a number of uniquely beautiful shots of the German bombing of Moscow. In 1942, *Shooting the Russian War*, a collection of the best of her pictures during that period, became a popular success.

As a woman, Bourke-White frequently encountered reluctance from military leaders when requesting permission to film scenes of combat, but she never relented in her demands. While she was in North Africa on January 22, 1943, for instance, she became the first woman to fly on a combat mission with an American bomber crew. She managed to see, and record, more frontline combat than any other war correspondent. Filled with dozens of her photographs, her 1944 book *They Called It "Purple Heart Valley,"* an account of the American army's battle to take Rome during the Italian campaign, was highly praised by many reviewers.

Bourke-White was one of the first photographers to get pictures of the Nazi death camps, with their heaps of dead bodies and starving, emaciated survivors. She remained in Germany after V-E day, and many of the pictures she took then became part of a third World War II–related volume, *"Dear Fatherland, Rest Quietly": A Report on the Collapse of Hitler's "Thousand Years"* (1946).

It is virtually impossible to study World War II or examine pictures from that war without seeing one or more of Bourke-White's memorable photographs. A laudatory made-for-television biographical movie, *Margaret Bourke-White*, starring Farrah Fawcett and Frederic Forrest, aired April 24, 1989, on the TNT cable television network.

See:

Goldberg, Vicki. *Margaret Bourke-White: A Biography.* New York: Harper and Row, 1986.

M. *Paul Holsinger*

***BUCK PRIVATES/IN THE NAVY* (Films).** In the months before Pearl Harbor, Hollywood tried to make the best of the new selective service draft, which was bringing hundreds of thousands of young men into the armed forces. Most of the films dealing with the training camps scattered across the United States were comedies, such as *Caught in the Draft* (1941), featuring Bob Hope and Eddie Bracken. Funny men Bud Abbott and Lou Costello starred in two others: *Buck Privates* (Universal, 1941) and *In the Navy* (Universal, 1941).

In *Buck Privates*, the comedians' first featured release, the duo takes shelter from a pursuing policeman in what they believe to be a movie theater line, only to discover, too late, that they are at a local draft board. Before they realize what they are doing, both have enlisted. Many of their vaudeville routines are funny, and the training camp location also lets them come into contact with the singing **Andrews Sisters**, who perform several songs, including their popular "Boogie Woogie Bugle Boy." Several months later, *In the Navy* again brought together the five stars, along with leading actor Dick Powell. Lou inadvertently comes close to destroying the entire American fleet, and the sisters get to harmonize on more of their hit songs.

Following up their wartime successes, Abbott and Costello made one of their funniest movies, *Buck Privates Come Home* (Universal-International, 1947). Having survived the war unscathed, the new veterans work diligently to smuggle an orphan they discovered in Europe into the country. They finally succeed, but not before providing their audience with innumerable opportunities to laugh at their antics.

See:

Cox, Stephen, and John Lofflin. *The Abbott and Costello Story: Sixty Years of "Who's on First?"* Nashville, TN: Cumberland, 1997.
Thomas, Bob. *Bud and Lou: The Abbott and Costello Story.* Philadelphia: Lippincott, 1977.

M. *Paul Holsinger*

***THE CAINE MUTINY* (Novel-Drama-Films).** The setting of Edward Dmytryk's *The Caine Mutiny* (Columbia, 1954) may be the Pacific theater during World War II, but the cultural contexts are rooted in the domestic front of the Cold War. The movie, which was adapted by Stanley Roberts from Herman Wouk's Pulitzer Prize–winning novel of 1952 and his Broadway hit, *The Caine Mutiny Court-Martial* (1953), focuses, not on the threat of the Japanese (the enemy without), but on the cowardice and disloyalty of Lieutenant Tom Keefer (the enemy within). When the command of the minesweeper *Caine* is given to the neurotic, vindictive Captain Philip Queeg (Humphrey Bogart), his junior officers, encouraged by Keefer, conclude (with considerable justification) that he is mentally unbalanced and unfit for command. During a typhoon, Queeg's obsessions nearly cause the *Caine* to founder. His executive officer, Lt. Steve Maryk (Van Johnson), relieves him of command and is subsequently court-martialed for insubordination.

Marine Lt. Barney Greenwald (José Ferrer) reluctantly defends Maryk and his fellow officers. Under pressure, Keefer (unctuously played by Fred Mac-Murray) betrays Maryk on the witness stand. After Grunwald wins an acquittal by revealing Queeg's mental weakness to the entire court, he turns on his clients (especially Keefer) and blames them for not supporting Queeg, who had served his country when the rest of them were comfortable civilians.

The film's moral, which is driven home to the ship's newly commissioned ensign, Willie Keith (Robert Francis), is the importance of institutional loyalty, the obligation to support flawed superiors, and the danger of out-of-place intellectuals. Ironically, *The Caine Mutiny*'s effective dramatization of ideological positions that were dominant in Cold War America was the work of a director who, a few years before, had been denounced as a communist sympathizer and had cleared his name only by testifying against many of the notorious "Hollywood Ten."

Buoyed, perhaps, by the number of leading stars who appeared in it, *The Caine Mutiny* was one of the most popular motion pictures and the year's top-grossing production. The critics were also impressed, and the film was nominated for a handful of awards, including best picture, best actor (Bogart), and best screenplay. In 1988 Robert Altman directed a well-crafted television version of Wouk's original play entitled, *The Caine Mutiny Court-Martial*, and starring Brad Davis in the role of Captain Queeg. Shown for the first time as a CBS Sunday Movie that May, it, too, received positive reviews from the critics.

See:

Mazzeno, Laurence W. *Herman Wouk*. New York: Twayne, 1994.
Suid, Lawrence H. *Guts and Glory: Great American War Movies*. Reading, MA: Addison-Wesley, 1978, 129–139.

Philip J. Landon

"THE CAISSONS GO ROLLING ALONG" (Song). The official march of the American field artillery, "The Caissons Go Rolling Along," was, for many years, credited to the "march king," John Philip Sousa. He and his band performed a personal arrangement of the tune at a Liberty Loan Drive in New York in 1918, and when it was published, Sousa took credit for its composition. In 1921, the number was also copywritten by Philip Egner and Frederick C. Mayer, both of whom had been responsible for preparing several spirited pieces of their own at West Point. However, not until after Sousa's death in 1932 did research reveal that the music was actually the work of none of the claimants.

The real composer of "The Caissons Go Rolling Along" was Edmund L. Gruber, who, while stationed in the Philippines as a lieutenant in the Fifth Artillery, wrote the song in 1908 to celebrate the joining together of two units of his regiment. Moreover, it had been played by army bands for some time before Sousa made it nationally famous. Though it took much legal maneuvering, the copyright was finally assigned to Gruber in 1936, and the official sheet music of "Caissons," with new lyrics written by Robert Danford and William Bryden, began at last to list him as the songwriter. Even more changes were made by W. H. Arberg just before the United States entered World War II. Now called "The Army Goes Rolling Along," it became the army's official march.
See:

Ewen, David. *All the Years of American Popular Music*. Englewood Cliffs, NJ: Prentice-Hall, 1977, 144–145.

M. Paul Holsinger

CANIFF, MILTON (Cartoonist). For over fifty years, Milton Caniff was one of America's most respected and popular adventure comic-strip artists. A master of drawing and cinematic staging as well as witty dialogue, he embroiled vivid characters in complex, but realistic, plots that set sophisticated standards for the genre. His heroes were vulnerable and believable, his villains picturesque, his women beautiful and intelligent. A staunch anticommunist, Caniff set his strips against a background of contemporary political struggle, especially the wars in China (from 1937 to 1945), Korea, and Vietnam. Until the early 1970s, he strongly reflected public sentiment, though by the end of his life, he was out of step with many of the newer generation of readers.

Caniff's first major position as a professional cartoonist came in 1933, when fellow Ohio State alumnus Joseph Patterson of the Tribune-Times Syndicate hired him to do a strip titled *Dickie Dare*. A year later, *Terry and the Pirates*, for which Patterson suggested the title and initial plot line, debuted. It began with soldier of fortune Pat Ryan and his youthful companion, Terry Lee, searching for a gold mine in China while battling river pirates. Within a few years, Terry grew up and took center stage, flying missions for the Chinese against their Japanese invaders. After Pearl Harbor, he joined the army air corps and, with a new set of friends, he continued fighting "Japs" for the rest of the war. Caniff dedicated *Terry* to rallying the nation with such skillful passion that one Sunday strip (October 17, 1943), which cited duty, tradition, and respect for collective effort, was entered into the *Congressional Record*.

During the war years, *Terry and the Pirates* also appeared in comic books, young adult novels, several of the popular Better Little Books (published by Whitman), and a children's radio serial. At the same time, Caniff illustrated training manuals, pocket guides, and civil defense and bond drive posters, he also designed over 70 unit insignia. He continued *Terry* until the end of 1946, when he left over a contractual dispute and began to create *Steve Canyon*.

Caniff was never afraid to defy the sexual conventions of the day. One of his characters in *Terry* was a lesbian and another, a nymphomaniac. A third, "Burma," was based on the 1930s movie sirens. His fascinating "Dragon Lady" used both her body and mind for mercenary espionage. In *Male Call*, "Miss Lace," a provocatively semiclad (but chaste) young woman, flattered and flirted with GIs and quickly joined the ranks of the favorite pinups in military camps around the world. This strip was distributed free of charge to over 3,000 military papers from January 1943 to March 1946. It has been reprinted three times since.

See:

Adams, John Paul. *Milton Caniff: Rembrandt of the Comic Strip*. Endicott, NY: Flying
     Buttress, 1981.

Kalman Goldstein

CAPA, ROBERT (Photojournalist). In 1936, after little success as a freelance photographer, a twenty-three-year-old Hungarian émigré in Paris started selling his pictures as the works of a fictitious, but supposedly brilliant, American named Robert Capa. The ruse worked, and by the time the hoax was discovered, Capa's pictures were becoming too famous to ignore. Seeing no other choice, Andre Friedmann became Capa for the rest of his life. Later that summer, he found his niche while photographing the still-new Spanish Civil War. His September 1936 shot, *Falling Soldier*, which captures a Spanish Republican soldier at the moment of his death in combat, is probably the single most famous battle photo of all time. When it was republished in *Life* on July 12, 1937, it made Capa world-renowned. After filming the early battles in Japan's war against China in 1937–1938 and having his pictures again featured prominently on the pages of *Life*, Capa was universally acclaimed as "the greatest war photographer in the world."

At the beginning of World War II, Capa (who was still technically a Hungarian citizen) was at first listed as an enemy alien by the Allies. Though able to take pictures of the London Blitz and other home-front scenes, it was not until March 1943 that he pulled enough strings to get to North Africa to photograph some of the last days of the fabled Afrika Korps for *Collier's* magazine. Later, working for *Life*, Capa participated in the American invasion of Sicily, in July 1943. He was also one of the first war photographers to land with the troops on D-Day. Always operating on the belief that "if your pictures aren't good enough, you aren't close enough" (*Robert Capa*, 76), Capa took some of the most memorable action pictures of Americans in battle during World War II.

He died as he had lived—in the front lines. Capa was killed during one of the last battles between French foreign legionnaires and the Communist Viet Minh in Vietnam.

See:

Robert Capa, ed. Anna Farova. New York: Groseman, 1969.
Whelan, Richard. *Robert Capa: A Biography*. New York: Knopf, 1985.

M. Paul Holsinger

CAPTAIN AMERICA (**Multimedia Character**). In late 1940, almost a year before the United States entry into World War II, the team of Joe Simon and Jack Kirby created Captain America as a featured comic book hero for Timely Comics. Steve Rogers was a ninety-seven-pound "4-F" weakling, a reject from the draft, when a government scientist injected him with a serum that transformed him into a muscular military super-agent assigned to ferret out Nazi fifth columnists in the armed forces. Clad in a red, white, and blue costume and carrying a patriotic shield, the new Captain America was the first major comic book hero to take a political stand against fascism. The captain and his young teen sidekick, Bucky, became instant successes at fighting and besting such villains as Fang, the Archfiend of the Orient, and the Red Skull, a quintessential Nazi butcher. Captain America was so popular that soon hundreds of junior Sentinels of Liberty clubs, all ostensibly headed by Captain America, were formed across the United States to oppose the Axis powers.

At the conclusion of World War II, Rogers continued to battle any number of world-class criminals but they were not the same as Hitler and his henchmen, and four years after the end of World War II, the series was canceled in 1949. A decade and a half later, in 1964, Kirby and editor-writer Stan Lee, fresh from their successful creation of several new comic book superheroes such as the Fantastic Four and the Incredible Hulk, re-invented Captain America as a regular feature for Marvel Comics. According to that storyline, Rogers had been frozen in an iceberg (and Bucky killed) in 1944, after his plane crashed in the Arctic. For no clear reason, staunchly opposed to the Soviet Union and overwhelmingly anti-communist, the revitalized Captain America quickly became one of Marvel's top best-sellers.

During the past two generations, Captain America, besides being featured in comic books, has also appeared in a 15-episode movie serial (1944), a syndicated television cartoon series (1966), and three full-length motion pictures, *Captain America* (1979), *Captain America II* (1979), and *Captain America* (1990). Today, more than fifty years after the end of World War II, he remains one of the most popular and enduring of comic book heroes.

See:

Daniels, Les. *Marvel: Five Decades of the World's Greatest Comics*. New York: Harry
     N. Abrams, 1991, 100–107, 170.
Simon, Joe. "Captain America—America's Answer to Hitler." In *The Comic Book Mak-*
     ers, ed. Joe Simon and Jim Simon. New York: Crestwood, 1990, 49–55, 70–71.
Wyman, Ray, Jr. *The Art of Jack Kirby*. Orange, CA: Blue Rose Press, 1992, 38–42,
     138–158.

M. Paul Holsinger

CAPTAIN MIDNIGHT AND HIS SECRET SQUADRON (**Multimedia Characters**). *Captain Midnight*, an adventure serial that began in 1939 as a regional production of WGN, Chicago, and then moved to the Mutual Broadcasting System and a national audience on September 30, 1940, quickly attracted an impressive number of enthusiastic and loyal young listeners. In his unrelenting campaign against evil, Captain Midnight led a Secret Squadron that consisted of youthful Chuck Ramsey and Patsy Donovan (later replaced by Joyce Ryan), as well as Ichabod (''Ikky'') Mudd, who served as the squadron's mechanic. Ivan Shark and his daughter, Fury, assisted by Gardo and an assemblage of other criminals, personified evil in many of the programs.

During World War II, the squadron often confronted Axis enemies, but from time to time, the heroes also continued to battle Shark and his diabolic followers. Sponsored by Ovaltine, the fifteen-minute, early-evening program was presented five days a week. Consumers eagerly sent in bottle seals and dimes to become members of one of the Secret Squadrons located around the country or to obtain enticing premiums such as metal badges or ''Code-O-Graphs,'' which allowed each youngster to unravel secret messages that the captain broadcast each week.

Captain Midnight made a successful transition to comic books, novels for young adults, and Whitman's popular Better Little Books after 1941. A regular newspaper strip, written by the prolific Russ Winterbotham and drawn by Erwin Hess, began in 1942 in the *Chicago Sun*. Soon syndicated nationally, it ran throughout the war, ending in spring 1945. There was a fifteen-chapter movie serial as well.

The radio version of Captain Midnight ended on December 15, 1949—all of the Secret Squadron's missions presumably having been successfully concluded—but in 1954, the captain moved to television where, for the next four years, he continued to fight worldwide evil.

See:

Dunning, John. *Tune in Yesterday: The Ultimate Encyclopedia of Old-Time Radio, 1925–1976*. Englewood Cliffs, NJ: Prentice-Hall, 1976.
Grossman, Gary H. *Saturday Morning TV*. New York: Dell, 1981, 153–158.

Philip J. Harwood

CASABLANCA (**Film**). A critical success and the winner of Academy Awards in 1943 for best picture, director, and screenplay, *Casablanca* (Warner Brothers, 1942) ranks among Hollywood's most popular films. Screenwriters Philip and Julius Epstein and Howard Koch adapted Murray Burnett and Joan Alison's unproduced play *Everybody Comes to Rick's* into a combination of romance, intrigue, political idealism, and arch wit. Just before Pearl Harbor, resistance leader Viktor Laszlo (Paul Henreid) and his wife, Ilsa Lund (Ingrid Bergman), arrive in Casablanca seeking to escape to the United States. Gestapo Major Strasser (Conrad Veidt) and the apolitical Vichy French Police Captain Louis Renaud (Claude Rains) plan to trap them. They all join the European refugees who gather nightly to drink, gamble, and plot at Rick Blaine's Cafe Americain.

A former freedom fighter and expatriate American, Rick (Humphrey Bogart) has sunk into cynicism and apathy. His philosophy is, "I stick my neck out for nobody"; this attitude resulted from the unhappy termination of an affair with Ilsa in Paris. Feeling bitter, Rick refuses to give Laszlo and Ilsa two stolen exit visas in his possession. Ilsa, operating from an ambiguous motivation, visits Rick's room, pleading, threatening, and, finally, making love to him. Rick convinces the authorities that he intends to betray Laszlo and leave Casablanca with Ilsa, but instead he eludes the police, kills Strasser, and sends Laszlo and Ilsa off with the exit visas. In turn, he plans to head south to join the Free French forces under Charles DeGaulle, where he can make a small difference in helping to defeat the spread of fascism. *Casablanca* presents Rick's movement from selfishness to commitment as an argument against American isolationism: like Rick, Americans loved justice and hated bullies too much to stand by while the Nazis terrorized the weak.

Skillfully directed by Michael Curtiz, *Casablanca* is, in many ways, one of the screen's most memorable motion pictures. One of the World War II's more thoughtful propaganda pieces, it is equally strong as an action film, an effective drama, and one of Hollywood's greatest romances. Filmed by Arthur Edeson, the picture is filled with many of the screen's greatest scenes. Though unconventional (Rick's and Ilsa's relationship does not, for instance, have a happy ending), the movie's muted, but triumphant, conclusion is still one of the most inspiring ever put on film. *Casablanca* is a movie to be seen, and savored, repeatedly.

See:

Francisco, Charles. *You Must Remember This: The Filming of Casablanca.* Englewood Cliffs, NJ: Prentice-Hall, 1980.

Robert L. McLaughlin

CATCH-22 (**Novel-Film**). A groundbreaking experiment in form and characterization and an antiwar manifesto that was revered in the Vietnam era, Joseph Heller's *Catch-22* (1961) has become a contemporary classic. Set on the fictional Mediterranean island of Pianosa during World War II, it centers on the experiences of an eccentric bombardier, Yossarian, who has "decided to live forever or die in the attempt." Each time he comes close to reaching the number of missions needed for rotation home, his squadron commander raises the number. Yossarian then retreats to the hospital, to Rome on leave, and to increasingly crazy adventures with his increasingly crazy comrades.

Catch-22 is concerned with both the inefficiency and self-perpetuation of bureaucracies and the cold greed at the heart of capitalism. The tendency of the military to objectify friend and foe is another problem. All three are symbolized by the ultimate meaning of Catch-22: "they have a right to do anything we can't stop them from doing." The novel is structured in a fragmented, loop-the-loop manner, in which chronology is discarded and some episodes reappear with differences while others are echoed by strikingly similar, new ones. Thus, the reader, who laughs at the black humor of the early chapters, is later implicated in the abuses of power revealed to have been beneath the humor. Rather than be a part of this cycle of victims and victimizers, Yossarian deserts, seeking to escape the system completely.

Nearly a decade after its original publication, director Mike Nichols attempted to adapt Heller's book based on a screenplay prepared by Buck Henry. With Alan Arkin as Yossarian and an all-star cast, he was able to capture the humor and horror of some of the novel's scenes in *Catch-22* (Paramount, 1970), but he found it impossible to transfer to the screen the complex narrative structure.

In 1994, Heller published a disappointing sequel, *Closing Time*, in which Yossarian and his friends, now old men, remember the war and their youth.

See:

Eller, Jonathan R. "Catching a Market: The Publishing History of *Catch-22*." *Prospects: An Annual Journal of American Cultural Studies* 17 (1992): 475–525.
Miller, Wayne Charles. "Joseph Heller's *Catch-22*: Satire Sums Up a Tradition." Chapter 7 in *An Armed America: A History of the American Military Novel*. New York: New York University Press, 1970, 205–243.

Robert L. McLaughlin

CHERRY AMES NURSE STORIES (**Young Adult Novels**). Cherry Ames, created by Helen Wells, was the most popular fictional nursing heroine during World War II. Wells saw the government's need for nurses as an impetus for writing about a student nurse who enlists in the military. The success of the stories far outlasted the war, but its initial popularity was due to Cherry's wartime adventures. Three books focus on the war: *Cherry Ames, Army Nurse* (1944), *Cherry Ames, Chief Nurse* (1944), and *Cherry Ames, Flight Nurse* (1945). In volume one, Cherry joins the army nurse corps, goes through basic training, and serves first at a military hospital in Panama and then in the Pacific. In *Flight Nurse*, she helps transport wounded soldiers from European battlefields to England, suffers combat fatigue, and receives the United States Air Medal for courage under fire. Back in the United States, she nurses invalided soldiers in *Veterans' Nurse* (1946) and then returns to civilian life. The series continued until 1978.

Cherry serves in the military with a group of friends from Spencer Nursing School, including Bertha Larsen, Mai Lee, Vivian Warren, and Gwen Jones, who share later nonmilitary adventures with her. Also a part of her war experiences are her twin brother, Charlie, a flier with the Army Air Force; boyfriend Dr. Lex Upham; and Captain Wade Cooper, an army air force officer who is briefly her fiancé.

There were a number of other nursing series written for juvenile readers during World War II, such as those featuring Elizabeth Lansing's Nancy Naylor and Ann Bartlett, Dorothy Deming's Penny Marsh and Ginger Lee, William

Starret's Nurse Blake, and Louise Logan's Susan Merton. All showed patriotic young women how nurses could help the war effort in a productive way.

See:

Parry, Sally E. " 'You Are Needed, Desperately Needed': Cherry Ames in World War II." In *Nancy Drew and Company: Culture, Gender, and Girls' Series*, ed. Sherrie A. Innes. Bowling Green, OH: Bowling Green State University Popular Press, 1997, 129–144.

Sally E. Parry

COMBAT **(Television Series).** Between October 2, 1962 and March 14, 1967, millions of Americans set aside the 7:30–8:30 hour on Tuesday nights to watch the ABC-TV World War II drama, *Combat*. The long-running series was developed by Robert Pirosh, a master sergeant during the Battle of the Bulge and the author of both the story and the screenplay for the 1949 Hollywood movie **Battleground**. Robert Altman, later one of Hollywood's most famous directors, was in charge of ten of the 152 episodes. Films of the hour-long show (which still, more than thirty years later, appear regularly on several pay-for-view television channels), make excellent and often-exciting viewing. *Combat*, as one astute observer noted some years ago, was "among the finest series that television has ever produced" (Rovin, 83).

Featuring a carefully selected cast of actors, including Rick Jason as Lieutenant Gil Hanley and Vic Morrow as squad leader Sergeant Chip Saunders, the show followed the triumphs and tragedies of a GI infantry unit in Europe during the last year of the war. A wide spectrum of guest stars frequently appeared in realistic stories, which ranged from straight combat episodes to an occasional show filled with humor (especially the first year when comedian Shecky Greene was a member of the permanent cast).

Ironically, after the show was canceled, in summer 1967, it was replaced by another World War II–based drama, *Garrison's Gorillas*, a takeoff on the hit motion picture, **The Dirty Dozen**. One of the most inept shows dealing with the war to appear on nationwide television, it was canceled within the year.

See:

Rovin, Jeff. *The Great Television Series*. South Brunswick, NJ: A. S. Barnes, 1977, 83–84.

M. Paul Holsinger

"COMIN' IN ON A WING AND A PRAYER" (Song). Of the many militant popular songs of the World War II era, "Comin' in on a Wing and a Prayer" was one of the best. Written by Harold Adamson and Jimmy McHugh, it was inspired by a letter McHugh received from the former football star Sonny Bragg, now a pilot, who said that he remembered landing after a mission to North Africa "on one engine and a prayer."

The new song was introduced by Hollywood star Eddie Cantor at an air force base to great applause and soon became a standard throughout the United States. A recording by the Song Spinners was number one on the hit parade, and several other versions also reached the top twenty. In addition, more than 1 million copies of the sheet music were sold. "Comin' in on a Wing and a Prayer" may not have been great music, but it was overwhelmingly popular when it first appeared in 1943, and it continued to be played and sung enthusiastically throughout the rest of World War II. *Yank* (the army weekly), for instance, cited it as the most popular song of 1945 among servicemen. In recent times, *Variety* has listed it on its fifty-year hit parade as one of the top musical numbers during the past two generations.

See:

Ewen, David. *All the Years of American Popular Music*. Englewood Cliffs, NJ: Prentice-Hall, 1977, 433.

M. Paul Holsinger

COMMAND DECISION **(Novel-Drama-Film).** On V-E day, William Wister Haines, a lieutenant colonel in the army air corps, began to write *Command Decision*, a play about the pressure of leadership that so many of the officers in the vaunted Eighth Air Force faced everyday as they sent men to their deaths on bombing runs over occupied Europe. A prospective publisher, however, suggested that the story first appear as a novel, with the play held until the book achieved recognition. Wister did just that; a fictional *Command Decision* appeared to positive critical reviews early in 1947. When the original drama finally opened on Broadway, on October 1, 1947, it, too, was a success, running for 408 performances before it closed.

With a screenplay by William R. Laidlaw and George Froeschel, *Command Decision* (Metro-Goldwyn-Mayer, 1948) became a blockbuster motion picture. Directed by Sam Wood and starring Clark Gable, Walter Pidgeon, Van Johnson, Brian Donlevy, and Charles Bickford, the film (like the play) dramatizes the dilemma of Army Air Force General K. C. "Casey" Dennis (Gable). In command of several bomber squadrons flying missions against heavily defended German targets, he must face the mounting loss of men and aircraft, which has placed in doubt the future of strategic-bombing operations. The general is under pressure from his press-conscious superiors to discontinue the costly raids, while at the same time, he must confront increasing resistance from his aircrews, who consider their missions suicidal. A dedicated professional who refuses to bow to political pressure or allow sympathy for his men to stand in the way of his job, Dennis proves himself by conducting a series of raids that cripple a crucial German weapons factory.

Until 1945, war films tended to describe the transformation of a socially, culturally, and ethnically diverse collection of freedom-loving civilians into a fighting force capable of defending democracy from totalitarian predators. *Command Decision*, however, placed its emphasis on the military professional and the problems of command that he faced. In doing so, it opened the way for the shift in the conventions that is evident in many of the motion pictures that followed it, including two 1949 Hollywood classics: *The Sands of Iwo Jima* and *Twelve O'Clock High*. Its success dramatically renewed Hollywood's interest in movies about World War II combat and helped to define the themes and narrative conventions of a genre that flourished for nearly the next two decades.

See:

Quirk, Lawrence J. "Command Decision." Chapter 31 in *The Great War Films from The Birth of a Nation to Today*. New York: Citadel, 1994, 107–110.

Philip J. Landon

THE CORPS (Novels). W.E.B. Griffin, one of several pen names of the prolific William Edward Butterworth III, has been termed "the poet laureate of the American military" (*Los Angeles News*), and "the best chronicler of the United States military ever to put pen to paper" (Phoenix *Gazette*). A veteran of the United States Army (including two years as a combat correspondent during the Korean War), Griffin almost seems incapable of writing an unpopular novel. At one stretch in the early 1990s, he had sixteen consecutive books on the *New York Times* best-seller lists. Of his more than one hundred fictional works, perhaps the most renowned and most popular comprise *The Corps*, an ongoing series focusing on the United States Marine Corps during the years of World War II. After seven volumes (through 1996), Griffin's narrative chronology had only reached early 1943, but his millions of readers offer no complaint, eagerly awaiting the next installment and the chance to purchase yet another of his exciting novels.

The Corps begins in 1986 with the publication of *Semper Fi*, which introduces many of the continuing characters and historically takes them from China to the first days of the Japanese attack on the Philippines. *Call to Arms* (1987) tells of the earliest days of the Marine Raiders and follows a group through their training and on to their successful attacks of both Makin and Kwajalein Islands in the Pacific. *Counterattack* (1990) sets the stage for the first American offensive of the war by the Marines at Guadalcanal; *Battleground* (1991) sends them into that bloody maelstrom of constant action. *Line of Fire* (1992) continues the fighting in the Solomon Islands, while *Close Combat* (1993) deals with recruitment and explores the question of what constitutes heroism. *Behind the Lines* (1995) traces what happened in early 1942 to many of the men who went into the Philippine bush to fight the Japanese on their own terms rather than surrender.

Griffin seemingly has a magic touch for writing novels that appeal to a mass audience. Each includes plenty of excitement, a significant amount of blood and gore, and always a good dash of sex. Best of all, each is carefully researched. Griffin knows his historical facts and uses them well.

See:

"W(illiam) E(dward III) Butterworth." In *Contemporary Authors*, ed. Susan Trosky. New rev. ed. Vol. 40. Detroit, MI: Gale, 1993, 52–54.

M. Paul Holsinger

CRY HAVOC (**Film**). *Cry Havoc* (Metro-Goldwyn-Mayer, 1943), like Paramount's *So Proudly We Hail* (1943), saluted the army nurses at Bataan. Based on Allen Kennard's play *Proof Thro' the Night*, which ran briefly on Broadway in 1943 and featured Ann Shoemaker and Carol Channing, the film starred Margaret Sullivan, Ann Sothern, Joan Blondell, and Fay Bainter. Richard Thorpe directed the adaptation from Paul Osburn's screenplay.

Like many other World War II narratives, both the film and the play focus on a group of people from different regional and economic backgrounds, including a Southern belle, an ex-burlesque queen, and a character who believes that the war is a religious experience. Some of the women are civilian volunteers, while others are professional nurses. All are living in a converted gun emplacement while helping to nurse the troops at a mobile hospital. They face a number of crises, including one woman being buried alive in a foxhole for four days, another feeling confused about her sexuality, and the realization that one of their number is a Japanese spy. As the Japanese advance and no relief appears, they must also come to terms with the fact that the bunker is their tomb. There is no happy ending.

Some critics praised *Cry Havoc*'s realism in showing American nurses sweating and dying in the Philippine jungle. Many others, however (including the head of the army nurses in the Philippines, Florence MacDonald), criticized it severely for its emphasis on sex and melodrama rather than the true bravery and endurance shown by the nurses at Bataan.

See:

Basinger, Jeanine. *The World War II Combat Film: Anatomy of a Genre*. New York: Columbia University Press, 1986, 235–240.

Sally E. Parry

"DEAR JOHN" (**Idiom**). During the years of World War II, American GIs coined the term "Dear John letter" in reference to mail received from one's wife or sweetheart to announce the breakup of a couple's relationship. Though for some women, absence may have made the heart grow fonder, during the war, thousands of young men were still forced to read the dreaded words, "I have found someone else . . ." After a number of studies showed that men receiving such mail were far more likely to act rashly in combat, the armed forces frequently halted all deliveries prior to an upcoming battle.

So pervasive were "Dear John letters," however, that a majority of the public since World War II has come to believe—thanks to Hollywood war movies, which almost always include a scene in which one of the characters receives a letter of rejection from his beloved on the home front—that they were almost automatic. The TV series *M*A*S*H* added to such a view with an episode that featured the various cast members stationed in Korea also receiving their share of such mail.

The term quickly carried over into peacetime life. Getting a "Dear John letter" meant being left by one's girlfriend, whether the man was a sergeant or an accountant. In 1953, country-and-western star Ferlin Husky's recording of the 1947 Billy Barton song entitled "Dear John" became a major hit, despite its almost tearfully sentimental lyrics, and Pat Boone rerecorded it in 1960. From 1988 to 1992, there was also a popular television series, *Dear John*, recounting the forlorn experiences of a milquetoast high school teacher whose wife has run off with his best friend.

"Dear John letters" refer exclusively to physical mail between one party and another, but it will be interesting, as the computer age progresses, to see if the term falls out of usage or whether E-mail or other forms of Internet communication will preserve it.

See:

Horstman, Dorothy. *Sing Your Heart Out, Country Boy.* New York: Dutton, 1975, 237.

Christine DeLea

DICKEY, JAMES (Poet). James Dickey served as a radar operator in a P-61 night fighter in the Pacific theater during World War II. After March 1945, he was involved in many of the U.S. bombing raids on the home islands of Japan, which devastated that nation's cities and towns. "The Firebombing," Dickey's best-known poem about the war, describes his (mostly unsuccessful) attempt to imagine what the results of one of those raids over Japanese territory must have been like for someone caught on the ground in the firestorm. Published originally in 1965 as part of his National Book Award–winning book of poetry, *Buckdancer's Choice*, "The Firebombing" recalls Dickey's night flight, its many hazards, and his return to base in Okinawa.

Literally and figuratively removed from the horrors on the ground, the poet-narrator, now an American suburban home owner twenty years after the bombings, admits to being aware, but at the same time absolved, of all guilt for his actions. Such honesty bothered some critics, who attacked both the poem and the poet for not being more expressively antiwar. In response, however, Dickey noted that having seen friends die in action, he no longer had the ability to feel guilty. Poets, he added, often found it easy to lament others' actions in war; he did not. Though that answer did not satisfy everyone, "The Firebombing," with its recognition of man's lost, or misplaced, humanity in committing such horrendous acts, remains one of the poet's landmark works.

The great bulk of Dickey's work, including his popular novel *Deliverance* (1970), has no relation to his war experiences, but many other poems (some written early in his career) clearly do. Among the best are "The Performance,"

"The Enclosure," "The War Wound," "The Driver," and "Drinking from a Helmet." The latter, which was written in 1963 and is clearly one of the best, features a first person narrator's attempt to identify himself with the dead soldier whose helmet he has appropriated. Filled with sexual imagery, the poem emphasizes the impersonality of war and also the ways in which, at times, it can force social awareness.

See:

Baughman, Ronald. *Understanding James Dickey*. Columbia: University of South Carolina Press, 1985.

David K. Vaughan

THE DIRTY DOZEN (**Novel-Film–Television Series**). Though the United States Army has never formally utilized convicted criminals in combat, *The Dirty Dozen* (1965) by E. M. Nathanson, which is based on just that premise, became one of the best-selling novels ever written about World War II. Office of Strategic Services Captain John Reisman, a tough veteran of covert operations, is put in charge of molding a group of twelve murderers, thieves, and rapists into an effective fighting unit. Parachuted into occupied France immediately before the D-Day invasion with orders to kill a number of Nazi generals (in return for pardons for all their crimes if they survive), the men have limited success. Most are killed; only one returns, wounded, to England. Filled with tense action, loads of violence, and more than its share of primal savagery, the novel was widely praised. Published originally by Random House, it soon became a top selection of both the Book-of-the-Month Club and the Literary Guild. A Dell paperback version sold millions of additional copies.

Two years later, *The Dirty Dozen* (Metro-Goldwyn-Mayer, 1967) was adapted by director Robert Aldrich into a big-budget Hollywood motion picture. Starring Lee Marvin, Ernest Borgnine, Donald Sutherland, and Robert Ryan, the film was well received by critics and the viewing public alike. It was followed nearly twenty years later by three vastly inferior made-for-television movies on NBC: *The Dirty Dozen: The Next Mission* (1985), *The Dirty Dozen: The Deadly Mission* (1987), and *The Dirty Dozen: The Fatal Mission* (1988). In spring 1988, the then-new Fox television network also developed an hour-long weekly series based on *The Dirty Dozen*, beginning with a two-hour, made-for-television movie, *Dirty Dozen: The Series: Danko's Dozen* (1988). Thirteen episodes were cheaply filmed in Yugoslavia with a cast of relatively unknown actors in lead roles, but only seven were ever shown in the three months for which the series lasted.

In 1987, Nathanson published a sequel to his earlier novel entitled *A Dirty Distant War*. In it, Reisman is sent to the China-Burma-Indo-China theater with another paramilitary team and parachuted behind enemy lines. He soon is forced to deal with both Chaing Kai-shek and Ho Chi Minh as well as a bevy of ruthless Asian tribesmen and drug dealers. Some critics praised this new volume, but it was not a popular success.

See:

Arnold, Edwin T., and Eugene L. Miller. *The Films and Career of Robert Aldrich.*
    Knoxville: University of Tennessee Press, 1986, 123–132.
Parish, James Robert. *The Great Combat Pictures: Twentieth-Century Warfare on the
    Screen.* Metuchen, NJ: Scarecrow, 1990, 133–138.

Devon Westmoreland

**"DON'T SIT UNDER THE APPLE TREE WITH ANYONE ELSE BUT
ME" (Song).** Sam H. Stept wrote the music and Lew Brown and Charles Tobias
the lyrics for "Don't Sit under the Apple Tree," one of the most popular songs
from World War II as well as one of only a handful on *Variety*'s fifty-year
musical hit parade. The tune was originally used for "Anywhere the Bluebird
Goes," but was introduced with its present title in the 1939 Broadway musical
Yokel Boy. After Pearl Harbor, Brown and Tobias changed the last line of their
original lyric, and it quickly became one of the most successful numbers of the
early war years.

In the refrain, a young soldier, who is anxious to guarantee the loyalty of the
girl that he is leaving behind as he goes to war, pleads (as the title says), "Don't
Sit under the Apple Tree with Anyone Else But Me" until his return. Sung by
the famous **Andrews Sisters** in their 1942 film *Private Buckaroo* and then
recorded by them on the Decca Record label, it became a great success. When
Glenn Miller and His Orchestra recorded it with vocals by Tex Beneke, Marion
Hutton, and the Modernaires; it reached number two on the charts. Kay Kyser's
band also had a popular version. This was one of the few times in history that
three different recordings of the same song reached the radio's Hit Parade simultaneously.

It was inevitable, given the song's unusual popularity, that a retort from the
distaff side would appear, and soon, thanks to a new, unoriginal number, young
females could musically promise their boyfriends, "I Won't Sit under the Apple
Tree with Anyone Else But You."

See:

Ewen, David. *All the Years of American Popular Music.* Englewood Cliffs, NJ: Prentice-
    Hall, 1977, 431.

M. Paul Holsinger

"DOUBLE V" (Symbol). "Should I sacrifice my life to live half an American?" one reader wrote to the Pittsburgh *Courier,* the nation's most prominent
Negro newspaper, in late 1941. There was no easy answer. Though editors of
the African-American press were quick to agree after Pearl Harbor that the
totalitarian policies of Nazi Germany and the Empire of Japan must be defeated,
most, like George S. Schuyler (one of the *Courier*'s renowned editorial writers),
felt uneasy about encouraging young black men to fight the Axis Powers if, at

the same time, they did not also work to overthrow the overt policies of "Jim Crow," which had been pervasive in America for too long.

The "Double V" campaign was created in response to that dilemma. On February 7, 1942, the *Courier*'s front page prominently featured an emblem with two large "V"s and a banner bearing the words, "Double Victory." No explanation was given at the time, but several days later, an editorial urged readers to fight, not one enemy, but two: "The first V [stands] for victory over our enemies from without"; the second V [is] for victory over our enemies from within." The Chicago *Defender*, the New York *Amsterdam News*, and most other members of the black press quickly joined the campaign, and "Double V" symbols soon began appearing, not only in the pages of those newspapers, but also on posters, sheet music, and many other items in every predominantly African-American community.

That anyone would dare criticize long-established policies, no matter how racist, during wartime seemed to many white leaders almost treasonous. When the *Courier* and its sister newspapers refused to relent in their attacks on racism throughout the United States, Federal Bureau of Investigation director J. Edgar Hoover ordered his agents to harass men like Schuyler and even contemplated prosecuting them for sedition. On a number of military bases, papers like the *Courier* and the *Defender* were banned for fear that their frequent reports of the mistreatment of black draftees would cause problems. Government officials also gave serious consideration to removing copies of the papers from the mails.

In the end, the "Double V" campaign was a qualified success. If little changed during the war, the wheels were nonetheless set in motion for considerable change in the decade and a half afterwards. Young black men and women returned from the war determined to attack institutionalized racism at home in such areas as segregated housing, public accommodations, and schools, and by the late 1950s, they were well on their way.

See:

Washburn, Patrick S. *A Question of Sedition.* New York: Oxford University Press, 1986.

M. Paul Holsinger

FAREWELL TO MANZANAR (Autobiography-Film). During the years of World War II, the United States physically removed more than 100,000 persons of Japanese ancestry from California, Oregon, and Washington and placed them, eventually, in ten separate "relocation centers" scattered throughout the West. One of the largest of these centers—all of which have been more appropriately called by historian Roger Daniels, America's "concentration camps" (*Concentration Camps USA*)—was located in the California desert at Manzanar. At its peak, during summer 1942, it was the largest city between Reno, Nevada, and Los Angeles. One of the many Japanese-Americans to be held in that desert city from 1942 until late 1945 was Jeanne Wakatsuki [Houston]. *Farewell to Manzanar* is her attempt to tell readers what it was like to be a prisoner in one's own homeland.

At the time of its publication in 1973, Jeanne's autobiographical account (written in conjunction with her husband, author James D. Houston, primarily for young adults) was one of the first about the relocation of the West Coast Japanese to be authored by a Japanese-American citizen. Reviewers were uniform in their praise. An instant popular success as well, the book has never gone out of print. Soon, others who had suffered in Manzanar or the camps in Utah, Wyoming, Colorado, and elsewhere also began to relate their stories for the first time, but it is Houston's study, told without bitterness, that remains the standard by which every other work must be judged.

Designed primarily for students in the upper elementary and junior high school grades (the same age that Jeanne was when she was forced to leave her home in Inglewood, California), *Farewell to Manzanar* provides an honest picture of the Wakatsuki family's life before, during, and after relocation. In 1944, one U.S. Supreme Court justice called the government's actions a part of "the ugly abyss of racism" (*Korematsu v. U.S.*, 323 US 233 [1944]); it is this racism that Jeanne attempts to dissect in her brilliant account. Today, nearly thirty years since its publication, hers is the one book given to most schoolage children who seek to discover what it was like to be the "wrong" race and color in the United States during World War II. It is hard to imagine a better choice.

In March 1976, Houston's memoirs were turned into an excellent made-for-television movie. First shown on NBC, *Farewell to Manzanar*, which follows the book's account very closely, was highly praised. Houston; her husband, James; and John Korty, the film's producer and director; all received Emmy nominations for their teleplay, as did Hiro Narita for his cinematography. Readily available on VHS, the tape makes a fine companion to the original book.

See:

Armor, John, and Peter Wright. *Manzanar*. New York: Viking, 1988.
Daniels, Roger. *Concentration Camps USA*. New York: Holt, Rinehart and Winston, 1971.
Tateishi, John. *And Justice for All: An Oral History of the Japanese American Detention Camps*. New York: Random House, 1984.

M. Paul Holsinger

FIBBER McGEE AND MOLLY (**Radio Show**). Real-life husband-and-wife team Jim and Marian Jordan were an enormously popular radio duo whose durable network comedy program, *Fibber McGee and Molly*, spanned twenty-two years (1935–1957). Throughout much of the 1940s, it was also America's top-rated show. The program owed much of its success, not only to its two central characters, but also to the creativity of its gifted writer, Don Quinn, who, each week, placed the McGees in situations with which the average American family could identify. Fibber exuded a self-confidence and boastfulness that often simply did not square with his abilities; more often than not, it was Molly who exerted control and ultimately extricated Fibber from his bumbling predicaments.

During World War II, patriotic wartime themes were very much in evidence in many of the programs. One such show, for example, featured the pair singing the National Anthem at its conclusion; in 1942, Fibber made famous the phrase, "Buy a bond and slap a Jap across the pond." For a number of years, too, the McGees rented a spare room to a female boarder who was employed at one of the local defense plants. Their programs regularly addressed such wartime issues and concerns as gas and rubber rationing, air raid wardens, women factory workers, knitting clothing for soldiers, buying meat on the black market, and war bond rallies. Fibber also encouraged local citizens to write letters to members of the armed forces.

It is difficult to overestimate the importance of such comedy programs in promoting wartime patriotism and morale. There was little, if any, government propaganda of the time that contained the entertainment value or manipulative potential of *Fibber McGee and Molly*.

See:

Stumpf, Charles. *Heavenly Days! The Story of Fibber McGee and Molly*. Waynesville, NC: World of Yesterday, 1987.

Philip J. Harwood

THE FIGHTING LADY (Documentary). *The Fighting Lady* (20th Century–Fox, 1945), William Wyler's feature-length documentary depicting life aboard a modern aircraft carrier deployed in the Pacific, won the Academy Award for best documentary of 1944. Produced by Louis de Rochemont, whose successful *March of Time* newsreel series led him to believe that there were commercial possibilities for feature-length documentary films, and narrated by Robert Taylor, the movie uses the naval photography of an Edward Steichen–directed group of war cameramen for most of its documentary footage of carriers in action. Alfred Newman wrote a dramatic musical score for the picture.

The focus of the narrative is a group of young pilots during their first year aboard the USS *Intrepid*, one of the many Essex-class carriers that made up the fast carrier fleet of Admiral Chester Nimitz's famous Task Force 58. The newly commissioned fliers are introduced to carrier life; undergo rigorous training; get their first taste of combat, in the Gilbert Islands; and, in the finale, help devastate the Japanese carrier force during the battle of the Marianna Islands.

Although the aim of this documentary is to show audiences the operations of the navy's new queen of battle, its narrative structure is very similar to the generic conventions of the fictional war film. The creation of an effective fighting unit out of a group of regionally, ethnically, and socially diverse young civilians who represent America in microcosm is the meta-narrative shared by most war films released between 1941 and 1945. In utilizing this form, *The Fighting Lady* carries with it a powerful propaganda message concerning the ability of a democracy to unite in the face of a totalitarian enemy. As a result, the picture, which should not be confused with Hollywood's Korean War epic,

Men of the Fighting Lady (1954), offers many insights into the ways in which the boundary between fiction and nonfiction tends to blur when documentaries and genre films share common cultural myths and ideological positions.

See:

Barsam, Richard M. *Nonfiction Film: A Critical History*. Rev. and enlarged ed. Bloomington: Indiana University Press, 1992, 233–234.
Basinger, Jeanine. *The World War II Combat Film: Anatomy of a Genre*. New York: Columbia University Press, 1986, 127.

Philip J. Landon

THE FIGHTING SULLIVANS (Film). *The Fighting Sullivans* (20th Century–Fox, 1944), or, as it was first known, simply *The Sullivans*, was based on the true story of the five doomed Sullivan brothers, George, Francis, Joseph, Madison, and Albert, of Waterloo, Iowa. After a friend was killed at Pearl Harbor, all five enlisted in the navy. Granted the unusual right to serve together on the same ship, they died together when that ship, the *Juneau*, was sunk by a Japanese torpedo off Guadalcanal, on November 12, 1942. Directed by Lloyd Bacon from a screenplay by Mary C. McCall, Jr., and a story by Edward Doherty and Jules Schermer, the movie focuses more on the years leading up to the brothers' enlistment than it does on their short naval careers.

As children, the boys are rambunctious, frequently fighting each other and other children and constantly causing trouble, but never enough to make their loving and understanding parents (Thomas Mitchell and Selena Royle) angry for long. Their adventures prefigure their adult relationships and foreshadow later events—for instance, the boys, launch a dilapidated boat that sinks, leaving them to help each other swim to shore. As adults, the brothers continue to get each other into and out of trouble. These mundane, but typical, experiences teach them love for family, aggressive self-defense, and fierce loyalty, qualities that lead to their sacrifices: four of the brothers refuse to abandon ship without trying to rescue the fifth, who is below in sick bay. The film demonstrates the necessity of sacrifice of oneself for others and of one's sons for the good of the country. In the final scene, the navy christens a ship *The Sullivan Brothers*, suggesting that the spirit of the boys fights on.

In April 1997, a new destroyer, the USS *The Sullivans*, was commissioned and named in the men's honor, thus keeping their heritage alive for other generations of sailors.

See:

Morella, Joe, Edward Z. Epstein, and John Griggs. *The Films of World War II*. Secaucus, NJ: Citadel Press, 1973, 171–173.
Suid, Lawrence. *Sailing on the Silver Screen: Hollywood and the U.S. Navy*. Annapolis, MD: Naval Institute Press, 1996, 71–72.

Robert L. McLaughlin

FOR WHOM THE BELL TOLLS (**Novel-Film**). More than 5,000 Americans went to Spain between 1936 and 1939 in the hope of stopping the fascist take-over of that country. Nearly half of those volunteers, including Robert Jordan, the fictional hero of Ernest Hemingway's Pulitzer Prize–winning 1940 novel, *For Whom the Bell Tolls*, died in the process. Though the United States officially refused to get involved in the Spanish Civil War, those citizens who did had few doubts that it was of the greatest import and the forerunner of what appeared to be a coming World War II.

Hemingway, who spent many happy years in Spain before the outbreak of the war and returned to that nation to cover its civil war as a reporter for the North American Newspaper Alliance in 1937, focuses his story on the attempt of a band of Republican guerillas to destroy an isolated mountain bridge. Though historically, many supporters of the Republican cause, including a significant number of the American volunteers, were members of the Communist Party, Jordan, a Spanish instructor at the University of Montana, is not. A believer in "liberty and equality," he dies manning a machine gun, even though he knows that his death will only temporarily halt the advancing fascist troops.

Working from a Dudley Nichols screenplay, director Sam Wood turned Hemingway's novel into a memorable motion picture three years later. Starring the popular Gary Cooper as Jordan, *For Whom the Bell Tolls* (Paramount, 1943) won plaudits from film critics and theatergoers alike. Though it received only one Academy Award—an Oscar for Katina Paxinou as best supporting actress—it was nominated for nine others, including best picture, best actor (Cooper), best actress (Ingrid Bergman), and best art direction.

See:

Josephs, Allen. "Reality and Invention in *For Whom the Bell Tolls*; Or Reflections on the Nature of the Historical Novel." In *Hemingway Repossessed*, ed. Kenneth Rosen. Westport, CT: Greenwood Press, 1994, 87–95.

Sanderson, Rena. *Blowing the Bridge: Essays on Hemingway and For Whom the Bell Tolls*. Westport, CT: Greenwood Press, 1992.

M. Paul Holsinger

FOUR FREEDOMS (**Paintings-Symphony**). In his January 6, 1941, State of the Union message to Congress, President Franklin Roosevelt called on Americans to become leaders in a new world focusing on four essential human freedoms: freedom of speech, freedom of worship, freedom from want, and freedom from fear. Seven months later, he reaffirmed America's determination to work toward these vital goals in the momentous Atlantic Charter, which he and British Prime Minister Winston Churchill signed on August 14.

It was Norman Rockwell, one of America's most popular artists, who best made Roosevelt's abstractions real to the average American. For many months after Pearl Harbor, Rockwell tried to find a way to put the Four Freedoms in terms everybody could understand. Then, one evening in July 1942, he decided that if he could paint everyday Americans enjoying those freedoms, the effect would be dramatic. He immediately began to put his ideas on canvas. The *Saturday Evening Post*, which had earlier published dozens of his paintings and illustrations, enthusiastically hired him to create four covers, one for each of the four freedoms.

Using many of his Vermont neighbors as his models, Rockwell completed the four canvases in the fall of 1942. "Freedom of Speech" showed a man expressing his views at a New England town meeting; "Freedom of Worship" featured different Americans at prayer; "Freedom from Want" depicted a large family gathered around a Thanksgiving table; and "Freedom from Fear" portrayed parents peacefully tucking their two sons in bed at night. The *Post* began to run the covers consecutively on February 20, 1943, along with feature essays by Booth Tarkington, Will Durant, Stephen Vincent Benét, and a number of others.

The United States government quickly saw how effective the paintings could be, and with the *Post*'s permission, the U.S. Office of War Information printed more than 4 million copies to help sell **War Savings Stamps** and bonds. The originals were sent on tour to highlight so-called "Four Freedoms Shows" in most of the nation's largest cities. By mid-1944, more than 1 million people had seen the shows; almost $133 million in war bonds were sold. Today, the paintings are in Stockbridge, Massachusetts, part of the new Norman Rockwell museum in that city. Few, if any, graphic images are as well known.

Rockwell's most famous works also inspired a symphony, *The Four Freedoms*, by Robert Russell Bennett. Performed for the first time at Radio City Music Hall in September 1943, the music, according to the composer, "tried to follow the pictures as a motion picture score follows the idea of the film" (Murray and McCabe, 88).

In 1994, the U.S. Postal Services memorialized the four famous Rockwell paintings by issuing a block of commemorative stamps featuring representations of each one.

See:

Marling Karal Ann. *Norman Rockwell*. New York: Harry N. Abrams, 1997.
Murray, Stuart, and James McCabe. *Norman Rockwell's Four Freedoms: Images That Inspire a Nation*. Stockbridge, MA: Berkshire House, 1993.

M. Paul Holsinger

***FROM HERE TO ETERNITY* (Novel–Film–Television Series).** The story of men and women in Hawaii in the months just prior to Pearl Harbor, *From Here to Eternity* (1951) is a powerful novel about the courage, brutality, and comradeship of the regular army. The author, James Jones, served in the army at Schofield Barracks on the island of Oahu, where the story takes place, and was there during the Japanese attack. He received the Purple Heart at Guadalcanal and wrote about his wartime experiences in a number of novels including *The Thin Red Line* (1962), *Go to the Widow-Maker* (1967), and the posthumously published *Whistle* (1978).

Considered Jones's best work for its unflinching portrayal of army life, *From Here to Eternity* focuses on Private First Class Robert E. Lee Prewitt, a non-conformist who has been both a champion boxer and a fine bugler. On being transferred to another company, he refuses to fight any longer, despite intense pressure by his new commander. His intransigence and his love affair with Lorene, a prostitute, doom him. Prewitt's story, and that of the young Italian-American who befriends him, Angelo Maggio, is interwoven with that of First Sergeant Milton Warden, who runs the company and has an affair with Karen Holmes, his commander's wife. The conflicts that arise as his comrades torment Prewitt end after the Japanese strafe Schofield Barracks and he is shot by military police during a curfew.

A toned-down version of *From Here to Eternity* (Columbia, 1953) won eight Academy Awards, including best picture, best director (Fred Zinnemann), best screenplay (Daniel Taradash), best cinematography (Burnett Guffey), and best supporting actress and actor (Donna Reed as Lorene and Frank Sinatra as Maggio). Burt Lancaster as Warden, Montgomery Clift as Prewitt, and Deborah Kerr as Karen were also nominated.

From Here to Eternity was made into a six-hour miniseries in February 1979. Perhaps more faithful to Jones's novel than the 1953 film, it was a popular success and convinced NBC-TV to develop a weekly television series, which inexplicably was set immediately after the Japanese attack on Pearl Harbor, which had concluded the original novel. Though there were a number of top-billed stars in the series, including William Devane, Natalie Wood, Don Johnson, and Kim Basinger, it was canceled within the first month. The unshown programs were eventually aired as specials during spring and summer 1980.

See:

Suid, Lawrence H. *Guts and Glory: Great American War Movies.* Reading, MA: Addison-Wesley, 1978, 117–29.

Uffen, Ellen S. "James Jones' Trilogy, or Is War Really Hell?" *Midamerica. The Yearbook of the Society for the Study of Midwestern Literature* 10 (1983): 139–151.

Sally E. Parry

GI BILL (Congressional Action). The GI Bill of Rights, which was signed into law in 1944, is one of the most important pieces of American wartime legislation. Though some veterans' benefits had been adopted following World War I, they did little to protect the returning soldiers. The new bill set out to correct those oversights. It provided special benefits to millions of World War II veterans and, as a result, had a sweeping impact on American postwar society. Originally presented to Congress by President Franklin Roosevelt in October 1943, the bill included such benefits as educational supplements, life insurance, medical care, and pension and reemployment rights. In January 1944, the American Legion proposed, and ultimately received, an expansion of the legislation to include both a provision for a centralized Veterans' Administration and one guaranteeing federal loans for homes and farms.

By 1955, some 4 million veterans had used the home loan benefits, over 5 million had received the readjustment allowance, and 7 million had taken advantage of the education and training opportunities, including 25 thousand African-Americans who were given the chance to attend college for the first time. The bill also provided millions of working-class Americans with opportunities for education, home and business ownership, and other advantages that would not have been available otherwise.

One major reason for the development of the bill was the interest in "readjustment," a concerted emphasis on the reacclimation of veterans from a combat to a civilian way of life. Part of this concern was economical: the need for returning veterans to become part of the workforce again necessitated, it was believed, continued education and financial incentives for those coming home from the war.

In the late 1940s, fascinated by the implications of the GI Bill, Hollywood screenwriters created a number of motion pictures that featured young veterans making the transition from war to peacetime thanks to the bill's provisions. One of the most enjoyable was *Apartment for Peggy* (20th Century–Fox, 1948), which was based on a story by Faith Baldwin and starred William Holden, Jeanne Crain, and Edmund Gwynn. In the story, a newly married couple faces challenges as the husband (Holden) uses his veterans' benefits to enroll in college.

See:

Greenberg, Milton. *The G.I. Bill: The Law That Changed America.* New York: Lickle, 1997.
"The G.I. Bill: The Law That Changed America." Narr. Cliff Robertson, Dir. Karen Thomas. PBS. Broadcast by WILL, Urbana-Champaign, Illinois, 22 October 1997.

David J. Tietge

"G.I. JOE"/"PRIVATE BREGER" (Cartoons). Professional cartoonist Dave Breger was thirty-two years old when he was drafted into the army in 1940. Though trained as an auto mechanic, by mid-1942 he was drawing two weekly panels: "Private Breger" for the *Saturday Evening Post* and "G.I. Joe" (same character, fewer freckles) for **Yank**. Usually given credit for creating the latter term to represent every draftee during the war years, Breger looked critically at the army with its hidebound rules and found it, and them, wanting. Even after he become a lieutenant, he never lost his resentment of the military's pomposity and caste.

In both series, Breger's undersized, apple-cheeked, myopic hero chafed at pointless regulations and rank-pulling brass. Although at times maladroit, adolescent, and egotistic, "Private Breger/G.I. Joe" entertained through comic resistance—sitting in dentists' offices to watch abusive officers squirm, throwing garbage in their trenches, fleecing them in crap games. Maintaining an exaggerated individuality, he kept a personal morale chart and even held up a troop landing to tie his shoelaces. His sergeant repeatedly ordered him to ''wipe his opinions off his face,'' but he rarely did. From military prison, for instance, he could not help noting sarcastically that his ''fight for the Four Freedoms [had] been temporarily suspended.'' When he appeared in a series of cartoons illustrating violations of the Articles of War and General Orders, ''Joe'' subtly underlined their frequent absurdity.

Three cartoon collections of Dave Breger's work were published during the war—*Private Breger* (1942), *Private Breger's War* (1944), and *G.I. Joe* (1945). Unlike many war-related fictional characters, who quickly vanished once the conflict was over, however, the now-civilian ''G.I. Joe''/''Private Breger'' made a relatively smooth, if somewhat acidulous, transition to suburban life when, as ''Mr. Breger,'' the once-suffering private became the central feature of a regular Hearst newspaper cartoon until 1970.

See:

Nunn, Roy. ''G.I. Joe's Dad: Dave Breger.'' *Hobbies* 89 (January 1985): 60–65.

Kalman Goldstein

''GOD BLESS AMERICA'' (Song). Irving Berlin was already America's most famous songwriter when, on November 10, 1938, the renowned **Kate Smith** sang his ''God Bless America'' for the first time on her popular, nationwide radio program. Originally written twenty years earlier as the grand finale for Berlin's World War I army revue, *Yip, Yip, Yaphank*, it was shelved at the last moment, tucked away, and forgotten until Smith asked for a patriotic number that she could introduce on the air. Disturbed by the spread of Nazism across Europe, Berlin added some new lyrics to his old piece, and the result was greeted with much enthusiasm.

It was not until August 1940 that Smith recorded ''God Bless America,'' but when she did, it sold more than 1 million copies and quickly became her trademark, which was requested almost everywhere she performed. Indeed, on many occasions, events were not over until Smith sang her version of ''God Bless America'' for the audience. During the 1940 presidential election, both political parties prominently played it at their nominating conventions, and by the time the United States entered World War II, it was already, according to one national poll, the country's most popular patriotic song.

During the war years, ''God Bless America'' was performed countless times and sung by everyone. Though she rarely appeared in motion pictures, Smith agreed to sing ''her'' song as a part of *This Is the Army* (1943); her rendition is one of the most moving parts of the star-studded film. Royalties brought in more than a half-million dollars; Berlin, refusing to capitalize on his patriotism, assigned all its earnings to the Boy Scouts and Girl Scouts of America.

After the war, a number of influential persons sought to have Congress make ''God Bless America'' the country's national anthem. That did not occur, but there remain many Americans today who reverently believe that the song is far superior to **"The Star-Spangled Banner,"** Key's famous War of 1812 classic. In 1955, President Dwight Eisenhower presented a congressional gold medal to Berlin in recognition for all his work through the years, and especially for the writing of "God Bless America."

See:

Bergreen, Laurence. *As Thousands Cheer: The Life of Irving Berlin.* New York: Viking, 1990.
Ewen, David. *All the Years of American Popular Music.* Englewood Cliffs, NJ: Prentice-Hall, 1977, 422–423.

M. *Paul Holsinger*

GOD IS MY CO-PILOT (**Autobiography-Film**). *God Is My Co-Pilot* is an autobiographical account of the military career of Robert Lee Scott, who flew P-40s during 1942 with General Claire Chennault's famed American Volunteer Group—the "Flying Tigers." After returning to the United States in 1943 and being sent on a publicity and fund-raising tour, he dictated his story on seventy-five recording cylinders over a three-day period. When the book appeared in 1943, it was an immediate best-seller, largely because it dealt with one of the few Allied successes early in the war. Its harsh, strident, anti-Japanese tone would be deemed politically incorrect today, but at the time, it served as a propagandistic rallying cry for most Americans. Shortly after the book's popular acceptance, a song, "God Is My Co-Pilot" appeared, dedicated ostensibly to "the U.S. Air Forces."

Hollywood also attempted to transform *God Is My Co-Pilot* (Warner Brothers, 1945) into a blockbuster motion picture. Starring Dennis Morgan, Raymond Massey, Alan Hale, and a host of veteran character actors, it was only partially successful. Scott's autobiography took its title from his belief that someone was physically watching over him and helping him achieve success in the air, often against overwhelming odds. The movie, however, introduced the role of a chaplain and put great emphasis on religious piety above all else. Most reviewers found the film "slapped together" and overly sentimentalized. Like the book, however, it was a popular success.

In 1944, Scott wrote a collection of stories that focused, not only on the men of the Flying Tigers, but also on other pilots fighting in the Philippines, the Aleutians, and North Africa. The result, *Damned to Glory*, was praised by critics as "a good collection of breath-taking yarns," but it never gained the success of *God Is My Co-Pilot* and soon disappeared from general sight.

See:

Cockfield, Jack H. "Robert Scott—God Was His Co-Pilot." *World War II* 10.5 (January 1996): 26–32, 78–79.
Scott, Robert Lee, Jr. *The Day I Owned the Sky.* New York: Bantam, 1988.

David K. Vaughan

***THE GOOD FIGHT* (Documentary).** In 1984, directors Mary Dore, Noel
Buckner, and Sam Sells put together an exceptional historical documentary film
about the 3,200 American members of the so-called Abraham Lincoln Battalion
who, from 1936 to 1939, fought fascism, Hitler, and Mussolini during the Spanish Civil War. More than half of them died; another 700-plus were wounded.
In the end, they also failed to stop the forces of General Francisco Franco, but
in putting themselves in harm's way, they offered mute testimony of their commitment to justice. The battalion was the first truly integrated American fighting
force, and though most were "leftists," and therefore suspect to many fellow
citizens, their sacrifices marked the first small step in the defeat of Nazi tyranny
in Europe.

Funded with a grant of $225,000 from the National Endowment for the Hu-
manities, *The Good Fight* offers, not only much excellent film footage from the
era, but also the often-fascinating recorded testimonies of eleven veterans of the
original battalion—soldiers such as Ed Balchowsky, Bill Bailey, Dave Thompson, and Steve Nelson; nurses like Ruth Davidow and Salaria Kea O'Reilly; and
even ambulance driver Evelyn Hutchins. It is narrated throughout by Chicago
author-radio personality Studs Terkel; Colleen Dewhurst reads the words of one
of the great Spanish women leaders as the remaining battalion members are
boarding ships to head home at the end of the fighting.

The Good Fight is documentary filmmaking at its best. Though there were a
handful of conservative critics who could not bring themselves to find anything
good to say about the often procommunist sympathizers whose testimonies appear in the picture, Dore and her colleagues have captured a vital part of American military history on the screen.

See:

Aufderheide, Pat. "The Good Fight." In *New Challenges for the Documentary*, ed. Alan
    Rosenthal. Berkeley: University of California Press, 1988, 488–494.
Katz, William L., and Marc Crawford. *The Lincoln Brigade: A Picture History*. New
    York: Atheneum, 1989.

M. Paul Holsinger

***GRAVITY'S RAINBOW* (Novel).** One of the landmark novels of the century,
Thomas Pynchon's *Gravity's Rainbow* (1973), combines history, science, philosophy, popular culture, bizarre characters, and unconventional storytelling in
a sprawling encyclopedic narrative. Set in London and on the European continent at the end of, and just after, World War II, the novel focuses on the V-2
rocket—its development and use by the Germans as a terrorist weapon and the
postwar pursuit of rocket parts and scientists by the Allies.

The plot begins when the British Special Operations executive discovers that
a map kept by American Lieutenant Tyrone Slothrop of the dates and places of
his many sexual encounters matches exactly the map of V-2 rocket strikes on
London, except that the sexual encounters preceded the rocket strikes. At the

same time as military officials and scientists are scrambling to discover the connection, Slothrop travels across the occupied zone that was Germany in search of the secret of his identity. Instead, he finds a Red Army colonel seeking to destroy his African half-brother, who is the commander of black rocket troops who are trying to put together a working V-2 so that they can re-create a launch by a mad Nazi captain. This rocket sacrifice becomes emblematic of Western culture's march toward death in the twentieth century. The V-2—and, by implication, the atomic bomb, which will be paired with the rocket in world-threatening intercontinental ballistic missiles—represents the attempt by a shadowy, threatening elite to manipulate and use nature in an ideology of control.

Gravity's Rainbow brilliantly uses its wartime setting to critique and encourage reform of our contemporary world. Critics agreed; the novel won the National Book Award for fiction shortly after it was published.

See:

McLaughlin, Robert L. "I. G. Farben's *Synthetic War Crimes* and Thomas Pynchon's *Gravity's Rainbow.*" In *Visions of War: World War II in Popular Literature and Culture,* ed. M. Paul Holsinger and Mary Anne Schofield. Bowling Green, OH: Bowling Green State University Popular Press, 1992, 85–95.

Robert L. McLaughlin

GUADALCANAL DIARY (Personal Account–Film). Based on war correspondent Richard Tregaskis's extremely popular 1943 nonfictional best-seller, *Guadalcanal Diary* (20th Century–Fox, 1943) was directed by Lewis Seiler from Lamar Trotti and Jerry Cady's screenplay. The movie follows an ethnically and regionally diverse group of Marines day-by-day, over a several-month period, from the monotony of their troop transport to their August 7, 1942, landing on Guadalcanal, and then through several battles and the final routing of the Japanese. Filmed on location at the Marine base at Camp Pendleton, California, with a cast of character actors that included such well-known faces as William Bendix and Lloyd Nolan, *Guadalcanal Diary* was Hollywood's first attempt to depict an American victory during World War II.

The film is concerned, however, less with historical accuracy—indeed, here the navy wins, rather than loses, the sea battle off Savo Island on the night of August 8, and the Marines literally drive the Japanese into the sea—than in using the campaign as a symbol for winning the larger war in the Pacific. The Japanese are shown as tricky, but capable of being beaten. In an honest fight, the Marines win easily, their casualties and defeats result from failing to recognize Japanese treachery. The Marines earn their victory by growing from boys to men. Beginning with unearned bravado, they learn to win through their battlefield experiences and witnessing spilled blood.

Reviewers noted that this generalizing of the story resulted in an episodic plot that failed to capture the tension and desperation of the Marines on Guadalcanal. The propaganda elements in the movie are also more heavy-handed and clumsily managed than in the best World War II motion pictures. Nonetheless, the flag-waving patriotism that is exuded throughout the production pleased most audiences and resulted in box office success comparable to other combat films of the era such as *Wake Island* (1942) and *Bataan* (1943).

See:

Kane, Kathryn. *Visions of War: Hollywood Combat Films of World War II*. Ann Arbor, MI: UMI, 1982, 104–111.

Robert L. McLaughlin

GUARD OF HONOR (Novel). *Guard of Honor*, James Gould Cozzens's Pulitzer Prize–winning 1948 novel, focuses on the difficulties African-American aviators experienced in their efforts to achieve flying status during World War II. Though trained at Tuskegee Institute, they were, at first, largely restricted from the war fronts, but eventually, through the assistance of First Lady Eleanor Roosevelt, they were able to fly in combat with distinction.

However, no African-American aviators were allowed to see combat as pilots or other crewmen on the large B-26 bombers. In *Guard of Honor*, Cozzens describes an actual September 1943 incident at an air base in Florida in which black flight officers training to fly those planes confronted the restrictive attitudes of a white-oriented military society. Arguing that bomber training and maintenance requirements were too difficult for African-Americans to handle, white officials created an atmosphere where failure was often inevitable. In doing so, they handled minority representation in the air corps with a "separate, but not equal," approach.

Cozzens, a well-established white writer who served as a staff officer in Washington, D.C., during the war, had written seven other novels previous to *Guard of Honor*. Published the year before President Harry Truman ordered the complete integration of the armed forces, his book educated many Americans about the difficulties that black aviators faced daily. Although it seems somewhat dated today, it still remains a powerful indictment of the world "that was."

See:

Bruccoli, Matthew J. *James Gould Cozzens: A Life Apart*. San Diego, CA: Harcourt, 1984.
Jones, Peter G. *War and the Novelist: Appraising the War Novel*. Columbia: University of Missouri Press, 1976, 79–85.

David K. Vaughan

HAIL THE CONQUERING HERO (Film). Released the day after D-Day, *Hail the Conquering Hero* (Paramount, 1944), a movie set on the home front, anticipates the postwar world. Writer-director Preston Sturges tells the story of Woodrow Lafayette Pershing Truesmith (Eddie Bracken), the son of a Marine hero of World War I. Washed out of the Marines because of chronic hay fever and working in a shipyard, he wrote his mother (Georgia Caine) and fiancée (Ella Raines) that he was overseas. When he tells his story to six Marines on leave, they decide to take him home, say that he has been discharged after heroic service, and reunite him with his loved ones.

Things quickly get out of hand. Woodrow's hometown treats him like a returning hero—greeting him with bands, burning his mother's mortgage, proposing to build a statue in his honor, and even nominating him for mayor. As the deception steamrolls, the Marines tell wilder and wilder lies about Woodrow's heroism. When Woodrow finally confesses the truth, the Marine sergeant (William Demarest, in perhaps his best performance) convinces the townspeople to reconsider their notions of heroism. Woodrow is welcomed back, regains his fiancée, and presumably will be the town's new mayor.

Critics loved the picture's farcical humor and praised its slapstick comedy. The New York Film Critics Circle nominated it as one of the year's best films, and Sturges received an Academy Award for the picture's original screenplay. However, *Hail the Conquering Hero* explores several serious issues that go far deeper than its surface humor: the inability of stateside Americans to understand the military experience; the returning soldiers' potential to disrupt the social and political status quo; the greed and selfishness rampant under the pull-together-and-sacrifice rhetoric of the war effort. In many ways, the movie subverts the messages of the typical World War II war film. It also looks ahead to postwar problems caused by the reintegration of the serviceman into society, which were explored in later motion pictures like *The Best Years of Our Lives* (1946).

See:

Koppes, Clayton R., and Gregory D. Black. *Hollywood Goes to War: How Politics, Profits, and Propaganda Shaped World War II Movies.* New York: Free Press, 1987, 170–175.

                                                          Robert L. McLaughlin

***HOGAN'S HEROES* (Television Series).** Combining nostalgia for World War II with the popularity of James Bond–type spy fare, CBS-TV's *Hogan's Heroes* was a situation comedy in which espionage agents worked from under the cover of a German prisoner of war (POW) camp, Stalag 13. Commanded by Colonel Robert Hogan (Bob Crane), the prisoners communicated top secret information (via an antenna secreted in the camp flagpole), smuggled downed fliers and fugitives from Germany to England (thanks to a network of tunnels, a costume shop, and expert identification forgers), and sabotaged Nazi weapons and supplies (with their own store of armaments). All the while, Hogan and his "heroes" continually outsmarted the incompetent camp commandant, Colonel Klink (Werner Klemperer), and his inept top sergeant, Schultz (John Banner).

The series, which ran weekly from September 1965 to July 1971 for 168 episodes, drew on the conventions of POW films like *Stalag 17* (1953) and *The Great Escape* (1963) at the very moment that it parodied them. Though there was undeniably a cross-sectional representation of national and ethnic types, a transformation of the villainous Nazi into a comic one, and the belief that prisoners could contribute to the war effort, so, too, were these ideas stretched almost to the breaking point. The prisoners, for instance, leave and enter the camp at will; their underground complex offers the technology of a military headquarters and the luxury of a hotel. Through psychological manipulation of the Germans, the prisoners actually run the camp. Indeed, the incongruity of Stalag 13 and real POW camps was the basis for the humor. Interestingly, at the same time Americans were concerned about United States POWs in Vietnam, they enjoyed a comedy about how much fun POW life as a prisoner could be.

See:

Andrews, Bart, and Brad Dunning. *The Worst TV Shows Ever.* New York: E. P. Dutton, 1980, 53–58.

McCall, Michael. *The Best of 60s TV.* New York: Mallard Press, 1992, 94–95.

Robert L. McLaughlin

HOME OF THE BRAVE (Drama-Film). Arthur Laurents served in the United States Army from 1940 until the end of the war, devoting most of his efforts to writing radio scripts, one of which, *Assignment Home* (1945), won a number of awards. *Home of the Brave*, the first of many Broadway plays and Hollywood films that he authored or coauthored, opened on Broadway on December 27, 1945. A graduate of Cornell University, Private Peter Coen, the play's Jewish protagonist, is paralyzed by guilt. During a scouting mission on a Japanese-held island, he failed to prevent the death of a fellow squad member, and though doctors now can find nothing physically wrong with him, Coen's legs will not move. *Home of the Brave*, one of the earliest dramas to focus on the psychosomatic traumas caused by war, looks closely, not only at the young private's mental breakdown, but also at the pervasive anti-Semitism that ran through the army during the war years. Before he can be helped by his psychiatrist, Coen must be made to see that being a Jew makes him no less worthy of forgiveness than anyone else in the unit. This is accomplished, but not without a great deal of pain and anguish.

Home of the Brave was selected as one of the year's best plays by New York drama critics. Ironically, when it was made into an excellent motion picture by producer Stanley Kramer, the Coen character was transformed into a black GI named Moss and the theme of anti-Semitism became one of racial prejudice instead. Laurents, who coauthored the screenplay with Carl Foreman, apparently acquiesced in the switch. *Home of the Brave* (United Artists, 1949) was no less powerful. It was nominated as the best film of 1949 by both the New York Film Critics Circle and the National Board of Review of Motion Pictures.

See:

Leab, Daniel J. *From Sambo to Superspade: The Black Experience in Motion Pictures.* Boston: Houghton Mifflin, 1976, 146–150.

Pines, Jim. *Blacks in Films. A Survey of Racial Themes and Images in the American Film.* London: Studio Vista, 1975, 63–66.

M. Paul Holsinger

HOPE, BOB (Entertainer). No performer has been more intimately connected with entertaining U.S. troops throughout the world than Leslie Townes "Bob" Hope. For more than fifty years, from 1941 and the dark days of World War II, through Korea, Vietnam, and various smaller conflicts, American GIs looked forward to seeing a "Bob Hope Show" headlined by the comedian, who told his (seemingly always funny) one-line jokes about military life and was accompanied by beautiful starlets and top-name musicians. Hope's last show was in 1990 for troops taking part in Operation Desert Storm.

The star of *The Pepsodent Show*, one of radio's most popular broadcasts prior to the outbreak of World War II, Hope began taking his program to American troops on May 6, 1941, when he broadcast live from March Field near Riverside, California. Soon he was entertaining across the country and, later, around the world. After the Japanese attack on Pearl Harbor, Hope, along with a USO troupe that included many of his radio program's regulars, toured "the foxhole circuit" (Sicily, Great Britain, North Africa, and numerous outposts in the South Pacific). In September 1943, *Time* magazine featured him on its cover with a caption pointing out that he was "first in the hearts of the servicemen." He also became a mainstay on the Armed Forces Radio Service, which broadcast, to a network of stations in both the European and Pacific theaters of war, such specialty shows as *Command Performance, GI Journal*, and *Mail Call*. These shows, too, brought together performers such as the **Andrews Sisters** and even the new sensation of the day, Frank Sinatra.

In July 1944, Hope published *I Never Left Home*, an account of entertaining the troops at the front. It quickly rose to number one on the best-seller charts and remained there almost steadily for the next four and a half months. Even though it was available for less than six months altogether, it outsold every other work of nonfiction published that year. Twenty-two years later, in 1966, *Five Women I Loved: Bob Hope's Vietnam Story* recounted his activities in Southeast Asia.

In 1987, Hope was selected "Citizen of the Century" during a Hollywood celebration honoring the **USO**. In recent years, too, both the navy and the air force have also officially recognized Hope's efforts on their behalf. In 1996, the navy christened a 950-foot support vessel, the USNS *Bob Hope*. The following year, the air force dedicated one of its huge C-17 Globemaster cargo planes, *The Spirit of Bob Hope*. Though Hope never served in any war, Congress also, by specially enacted legislation, made him an honorary veteran in 1997, the only American ever given that honor.

See:

Faith, William Robert. *Bob Hope: A Life in Comedy.* New York: Putnam, 1982.

M. Paul Holsinger

THE HUMAN COMEDY (Novel-Film). Adapted from a story by William Saroyan, *The Human Comedy* (Metro-Goldwyn-Mayer, 1943), one of the war years' most bittersweet films, was directed by Clarence Brown from Howard Eastabrook's screenplay. The episodic story focuses on the Macauleys of Ithaca, California. Their recently dead patriarch (Ray Collins) narrates while observing his wife Kate (Fay Bainter), daughter Bess (Donna Reed), and sons Homer (Mickey Rooney) and Ulysses (Jack Jenkins). Another son Marcus (Van Johnson) has just joined the army when the story begins. Homer, who is simultaneously dealing with the experiences of adolescence—high school, sports, the pangs of first love—and adapting to the role of family provider, takes a job as a telegram delivery boy. Eventually, he must take home the telegram announcing his older brother's death, but when he arrives, he finds Tobey, an orphan whom Marcus befriended, outside the house, as if he has come, symbolically, to replace the dead son. As the youngsters enter the house, the father and Marcus materialize on the porch, demonstrating that they are not really gone.

Saroyan, who was angered at not being allowed to direct the movie, published his screenplay as a novel before the production was released, but that only served to make the picture more popular. *The Human Comedy* was, other than the overwhelmingly successful *Casablanca*, 1943's most honored film. It received Oscar nominations for best picture, best director, best actor (Rooney), and best cinematography; Saroyan won an Academy Award for best original story.

Reviewers who criticized the overly sentimental screen depiction of life and its preachy dialogue missed the point: the idealized picture of life here is like the idea of home conjured by Marcus, which he and Tobey shared. It is the thing for which they are fighting, and it gives their mission and sacrifice meaning and purpose.

See:

Anderegg, Michael. ''Home Front America and the Denial of Death in MGM's *The Human Comedy.*'' *Cinema Journal* 34.1 (1994): 3–17.

Floan, Howard R. *William Saroyan.* New York: Twayne, 1966.

Robert L. McLaughlin

"I'LL WALK ALONE" (Song). Sammy Cahn and Jule Styne, authors of hundreds of best-selling hits in the 1940s and early 1950s, wrote "I'll Walk Alone" in 1944 at the height of America's war effort for the all-star Hollywood film, *Follow the Boys*. Introduced by Dinah Shore and later recorded by both Shore and Frank Sinatra, the song quickly became one the most popular ballads in the country. Playing on all the emotions of the millions of men in service and the women they had left at home, it promised listeners that their loved one would be faithful only to them.

Though "I'll Walk Alone" quickly went out of favor with the war's end, it was resurrected in 1952 during the war in Korea. A recording by the popular male singer, Don Cornell, became another best-seller.

See:

Ewen, David. *All the Years of American Popular Music.* Englewood Cliffs, NJ: Prentice-
	Hall, 1977, 431.

								M. Paul Holsinger

JARRELL, RANDALL (Poet). Randall Jarrell was already a well-published
poet when he joined the army air corps in 1942. Unable to pass pilot training,
he became an enlisted man and served on the celestial navigation training staff
at Davis-Monthan Army Air Field in Tucson, Arizona, for the remainder of the
war. Even though he never saw combat, Jarrell wrote some of the best poems
about the war and its effects on both the men who flew and those who faced
their bombs on the ground. "Eighth Air Force," "Losses," "The Wingman,"
"Burning the Letters," and "Siegfried" are among his strongest works. Most
of Jarrell's World War II–related poetry was initially published in *Selected Poems* (1955).

	The shortest of Jarrell's poems (at only five lines), "Death of the Ball Turret
Gunner," is perhaps the most powerful. American B-17 and B-24 bombers were
equipped with ball turrets on the underside of their fuselages. In combat, the
turrets projected into the windstream and pivoted 360 degrees, allowing a gunner, crammed in a curled-up fetal position, to fire between his legs, in order to
offer protection from attacking fighters. The chance that any member of a
bomber crew would complete twenty-five missions was slim—and the possibility that a ball turret gunner, completely exposed to enemy cannon fire, would
be that fortunate was infinitesimal. In "Death of the Ball Turret Gunner," which
is narrated by one of the many dead gunners, Jarrell uses this physical setting
to suggest that a gunner's life is so brief that he literally passes from the womb
of his mother into the (womb-like) environment of the ball turret, and at the
end, his umbilical cord is transformed into a hose used to clean out his blood
inside the turret after his death.

See:

Pritchard, William H. *Randall Jarrell: A Literary Life.* New York: Farrar, Straus and
	Giroux, 1990.

								David K. Vaughan

JEEP (Artifact). As early as 1936, E. C. Segar, the creator of "Popeye," introduced to the public a strange little character known as "Eugene the Jeep."
He was capable of going anywhere, doing anything, and existing seemingly
forever on nothing more than a diet of orchids. When the Willys Overland
Company developed a tough little all-terrain vehicle for the United States Army
in early 1941, the choice of the name "jeep" for it was natural. That manufacturer's public relations firm officially told reporters during World War II that it
believed the nickname of the popular vehicle was selected by American GIs
who took the name from Segar's cartoon character.

There are, however, two other possible explanations for the "jeep" designation. One claims that, once Willys Overland turned its vehicle over to the
army, it was officially designated as that service's "General Purpose Car" or,
more popularly, its "GP." It was an easy jump from such letters to the term
"jeep." Yet another possibility, according to some scholars, is the fact that what
became the "jeep" was originally designed by Ford Motor Company engineers
specifically as that firm's Model G-P, and, again, the resulting nickname was
obvious.

Whatever the correct explanation, there is no doubt that by the middle of the
war, the term was well-established throughout the United States. When Hollywood made a popular musical film, *Four Jills in a Jeep* (20th Century–Fox,
1944), no one had to interpret the reference to any of the many viewers.

See:

Brown, Arch. *Jeep: The Unstoppable Legend.* Lincolnwood, IL: Publications Interna-
    tional, 1994.
Conley, Manuel A. "World War II's Mechanical Marvel: The Legendary Jeep." *Amer-
    ican History Illustrated* 16.3 (June 1981): 18–28.

M. Paul Holsinger

"KILROY WAS HERE" (Slogan). During World War II, wherever American
GIs were, so, too, was "Kilroy." It did not matter whether it was in Europe or
the Pacific, the ubiquitous sign "Kilroy Was Here" seemed to sprout everywhere—on walls, fences, doorsills, mess hall walls or even trucks and trains.
Though it was understood long before 1945 that Kilroy represented every American soldier, reporters never stopped trying to discover who the "real," or at
least original, Kilroy might be.

There were dozens of claims, all conflicting. Immediately after the conclusion
of the war, *Newsweek* awarded the honor to Sergeant Frank J. Kilroy, Jr., of the
army air corps. According to that magazine's story, the first notice, announcing
that Kilroy would be there the following week, appeared in 1943 on a Florida
air base bulletin board written by Kilroy's friend, Sergeant James Maloney. Even
after Maloney was transferred, his messages continued until others, liking the
sound and brevity of the note, also began to use it wherever they went.

In 1962, the Associated Press offered a different explanation. According to
its reporters, James J. Kilroy, an inspector at the Bethlehem Steel Company's
Fore River Shipyard in Quincy, Massachusetts during the war, began to scrawl
"Kilroy Was Here" in yellow crayon on ship sections that he and his men
inspected. When the USS *Lexington* was launched in 1942, Kilroy claimed that
he scrawled his name on its hull and continued doing so on others throughout
the entire war. As those ships made their way around the world, so, too, did the
slogan.

"Kilroy Was Here" was the most popular single piece of graffiti during the
war years. Some writers also added a small, bald-headed face with large, ex-

pressive eyes to their signs, and most GI's soon came to expect to see the two together whenever they arrived in a new location. One thing was almost a surety: Kilroy always seemed to get to any landing site long before the men who had to fight arrived.

See:

Dickson, Paul. "Kilroy: He Was There, But Who Was He?" In *War Slang: American Fighting Words and Phrases from the Civil War to the Gulf War*, ed. Paul Dickson. New York: Pocket Books, 1994, 181–182.

M. Paul Holsinger

KIRKPATRICK, HELEN (War Correspondent–Newspaperwoman). No female journalist during World War II was more in the national spotlight than Helen Kirkpatrick. Even before the outbreak of the war, while serving as a stringer for a number of British and American papers, including the *New York Herald Tribune*, she warned of the impending conflict. The author of two books in the 1930s examining Adolf Hitler and his threat to world peace, Kirkpatrick's accurate analysis of the events leading up to the German attack on Poland proved exceptionally accurate. In 1939, Frank Knox, the owner of the *Chicago Daily News*, hired her as that paper's European correspondent.

Though some men were reluctant to work with Kirkpatrick, she scooped them all in spring 1940 by reporting that Hitler and the German Army were about to invade the Low Countries. Some of the best reporting to appear in the press about the bravery of the British public during the London Blitz came from her typewriter. Indeed, so strong were her reports that **Edward R. Murrow** tried to hire her as one of CBS radio's regular war correspondents. As the war progressed, even the most ardent male chauvinists had to admit that Kirkpatrick was more than their equal. The *Daily News* was so pleased with her regular war columns that it soon began to advertise "Our Helen" throughout Chicago as a focal selling point for the newspaper. After D-Day, Kirkpatrick was assigned to cover the French Army's part in the liberation of France, and she was with DeGaulle when he and his comrades entered Paris later that summer.

After the war, she resigned from the newspaper and served for a number of years as an adviser in Europe to the U.S. Department of State. Few war correspondents, male or female, were better at obtaining important, firsthand stories than Kirkpatrick in the years before her retirement.

See:

Voss, Frederick S. *Reporting the War: The Journalistic Coverage of World War II.* Washington, DC: Smithsonian Institution Press, 1994, 88–93.
Wagner, Lilya. "Helen Kirkpartrick." Chapter 8 in *Women War Correspondents of World War II*. Westport, CT: Greenwood Press, 1989, 75–80.

M. Paul Holsinger

LEA, TOM (Painter). Of all the many combat artists who created a permanent record of the American effort in World War II, none is more famous than Tom

Lea. After studying painting at the Art Institute of Chicago, he spent most of the 1930s working either as a commercial artist or a muralist for the Public Works Administration. In 1941, he was hired by *Life* as one of that magazine's first full-time war artists. Over the next four years, Lea sketched the U.S. armed forces preparing for war or in combat on every continent and sea, but it was on the Japanese-held island of Peleliu, in the southwest Pacific, that his reputation as a great combat artist was permanently cemented.

Tom Lea was with the first wave of young American Marines to land on the beaches of Peleliu, in September 1944. Almost immediately, he watched dozens of young men die, and those experiences became the basis for some of the greatest war-related art ever put on canvas. For instance, his most expressive work from the invasion, *The Price*, shows an enlisted man, whose face has been half blown away by an exploding mortar shell and with blood running down his mangled arm, staggering back to the beach, with his legs buckling beneath him and only a few moments separating him and death. Seen in the bright greens and reds that Lea used to capture the scene, the oil painting, which is one of the most-often reprinted of all World War II art, is unforgettable. Almost as powerful is *The 2,000 Yard Stare*, a portrait of a Marine obviously suffering from shell-shock, his mind totally blank, staring helplessly into space. Other depictions catch, with similar precision, scenes of devastation and despair. The original sketches and the oil paintings that Lea made from them brilliantly evoke the horror of the first hours on the beach and the hundreds on both sides who died. So careful, and yet so unnerving, were these works, however, that it was not until June 11, 1945 (nine months after the invasion), that *Life* finally published eleven of them.

See:

Antone, Evan Haywood. *Tom Lea: His Life and Works*. El Paso: Texas Western Press, 1988.
West, John O. *Tom Lea: Artist in Two Mediums*. Southwest Writers Ser. 5. Austin, TX: Steck-Vaughn, 1987.

M. Paul Holsinger

***LET THERE BE LIGHT* (Documentary).** Mental breakdowns during wartime have been known variously as soldier's heart (Civil War), shell-shock (World War I), psychoneurosis (World War II), and posttraumatic stress disorder (Vietnam). During World War II, there were roughly 320,000 veterans who received premature discharges from the armed forces due to psychoneurosis, and countless others who returned home "nervous from the service." Hoping to eliminate the stigma attached to this condition, in June 1945 the War Department assigned John Huston (then a major with the army signal corps), who had already made two controversial combat documentaries, to produce a new one about the "Returning Soldier—Nervously Wounded."

On location for ten weeks at the Mason General Hospital in Brentwood, Long

Island, Huston shot seventy hours of film as he followed a small group of psychoneurotic soldiers from their admission to their eventual cure and discharge from the hospital. By February 1946, the footage, now entitled *Let There Be Light*, was edited into a sixty-minute documentary of men overcoming amnesia, paralysis, speech loss, and other emotional wounds of war with the help of hypnosis, sodium amytol, and psychotherapy provided by a sympathetic team of military doctors. A few weeks later, however, the army suddenly decided that the film was ''unsuitable'' for public release, officially claiming that the privacy of four patients (who supposedly did not sign releases) must be respected. A more likely explanation is that the military was too disturbed by Huston's unsparing look at the horrors of war.

The documentary remained out of circulation, except for a few bootleg screenings, until the army lifted its ban in December 1980. Seen more than fifty years after it was made, it remains unforgettably powerful.

See:

Barsam, Richard M. *Nonfiction Film: A Critical History*. Rev. and enlarged ed. Bloomington: Indiana University Press, 1992, 233–234.
Edgerton, Gary. ''Revisiting the Recordings of Wars Past: Remembering the Documentary Trilogy of John Huston.'' *Journal of Popular Film and Television* 15.1 (1987): 27–41.

                                                                James Deutsch

LIFEBOAT (**Film**). Directed by Alfred Hitchcock from a screenplay by Jo Swerling (based on an unpublished story by John Steinbeck), *Lifeboat* (20th Century–Fox, 1944) is among the most disturbing films of World War II. The action is confined to a lifeboat inhabited by the survivors of a U-boat attack on a merchant marine ship. They represent a cross-section of nationalities and classes and include the captain of the U-boat, which has also been sunk (Walter Slezak). As they face a series of crises—a suicide, no navigation equipment, the amputation of Gus's leg, a storm, the loss of water and food—the German gradually takes over the boat, changing from their prisoner to their captor. The survivors submit until the German's treacherous killing of Gus (William Bendix) and his hoarding of both water and energy pills are exposed. Then, in a horrifying scene, they fall on him, brutally beat him, and throw him overboard. Without the German, they drift aimlessly. As they are about to be picked up by a German supply ship, however, an Allied battleship attacks, destroys the German ship, and rescues them.

Lifeboat seems to subvert many of the most typical World War II films' messages about the war. The German may be evil, but he is also the only character who has the ability to function as a leader. When the Allies do pull together to fight the enemy, they become little more than a mob. One character's religious faith is mocked; another character bemoans every sacrifice. The survivors' adherence to democratic and Christian principles is not only superficial, but also provides the means for the German to take control. Having promoted the war effort in *Foreign Correspondent* (1940) and *Saboteur* (1942), Hitchcock here asks questions about the war: Why are we fighting it? How are we fighting it? Can we beat our enemies without becoming like them?

Some critics were dissatisfied by Hitchcock's lack of answers to such disturbing questions, but no one denied the movie's high quality. It received four Academy Awards nominations, including best director. At the same time, the New York Film Critics Circle named Tallulah Bankhead, one of the picture's stars, the year's best actress.

See:

Spoto, Donald. *The Dark Side of Genius: The Life of Alfred Hitchcock.* Boston: Little, Brown, 1983, 265–270.

Robert L. McLaughlin

THE LONGEST DAY (History-Film). In filming the best-selling popular history of D-Day, *The Longest Day* (1959) by Cornelius Ryan, producer Darryl F. Zanuck himself became something like General Dwight Eisenhower in coordinating "forty-two international stars," three directors (Ken Annakin, Andrew Martin, and Bernard Wicki), tons of World War II-vintage equipment, and the military forces of four nations and the North Atlantic Treaty Organization (NATO). By the time it was released, *The Longest Day* (20th Century–Fox, 1962) was the costliest black-and-white motion picture ever made, but it soon also became the highest-grossing film of its kind in history. Ryan's screenplay (with uncredited assistance from several other writers, including novelist James Jones) dramatizes the events of June 5–6, 1944, in a bottom-up manner, employing the multiple points of view of a variety of individuals from the different nations involved. We see the small twists of fate that doomed the German defensive plans, the factors in Eisenhower's agonized decision to invade, the behind-the-lines contributions of the Resistance, the preparatory infiltrations of parachute and glider troops, and the spectacularly recreated landings. Even more emphasized are such pivotal events as the eighty-second Airborne's costly capture of the strategically vital town of Ste.-Mère-Eglise, the British sixth Airborne glider infantry's capture of the Orne River bridge and its rescue of their fellow commandos after their landing at Sword Beach, the army rangers' assault on the (nonexistent) big guns at Pointe du Hoc, and the climactic breakthrough at Omaha Beach.

A computer-generated, color version of *The Longest Day* has been made in recent years, but it should be avoided whenever possible. The original black-and-white cinematography by Jean Bourgoin and Walter Wottitz (which won an Academy Award) creates a documentary-like quality that is made stronger by allowing the participants to speak in their native French and German (with subtitles in English at the bottom of the screen). The film's epic style was copied with less success for *Tora! Tora! Tora!* (1970) and *Midway* (1976).

See:

Suid, Lawrence. "The Making of *The Longest Day.*" *Journal of Popular Film* 3.4
    (1976): 211–252.

Robert L. McLaughlin

LOONEY TUNES (Animated Cartoons). Warner Brothers was one of Hollywood's earliest and most committed anti-Axis studios. After 1939, its directors and contract players unsparingly attacked the enemy nations and their leaders. Films such as **Casablanca**, although topical, became classics and were shown repeatedly long after their immediacy passed, and so, too, was the case with the studio's wartime Looney Tunes cartoons. If, in nearly every case, they were violent and racist and their characters were grating, the triumphant aggressiveness that they championed seemed to most viewers a worthy American trait.

Producer Leon Schlesinger and directors Robert Clampett, Isidor Freleng, Chuck Jones, and Frank Tashlin created for the moment. Some Looney Tunes so denigrated the Germans and Japanese (*Bugs Nips the Nips, Tokio Jokio, Daffy the Commando*) and are so embarrassingly politically incorrect that they are virtually unwatchable today. In most cases, however, audiences then found them screamingly funny and constantly demanded more.

Before the war, Bugs and Daffy were simply "loony," with Bugs acting anarchic and Daffy, truly insane. The war cartoons gave their characters dimension and motivation. The chase scenes (minus Nazis or Japanese) became inspirations for younger animators, and their use of music—Looney Tunes were always filled with the finest swing jazz—helped shape the seven-minute cartoon for almost the next twenty years.

Such films as *Herr Meets Hare, Super Rabbit, Falling Hare*, and *Little Red Riding Rabbit* represent the efforts of some of the finest cartoonists in Hollywood's illustrious history. More than museum pieces, they reappear periodically on television in the late 1990s to the delight of a new generations of viewers.

See:

Beck, Jerry, and Will Friedwald. *Looney Tunes and Merrie Melodies. A Complete Illustrated Guide to the Warner Bros. Cartoons.* New York: Henry Holt, 1989.
Schneider, Steve. *That's All Folks! The Art of Warner Bros. Animation.* New York: Holt, 1988.

Kalman Goldstein

"THE MARINES' HYMN" (Song). "The Marines' Hymn," sometimes known simply as "From the Halls of Montezuma," first appeared in print when the *National Police Gazette* published its four stanzas on June 16, 1917. Two years later, the Marine Corps officially copyrighted the song. Though the melody comes from the obscure operetta *Genevieve de Brabant* by French composer Jacques Offenbach, there is considerable doubt about who the lyricist was or when the words were first written. Originally, the Marine Corps claimed that the words were penned by a battalion officer during the Mexican War in 1847. In 1926, however, *The Book of Navy Songs* credited the lyrics to Colonel Henry C. Davis (who does appear to have at least worked on revising the third and fourth verses). Yet another Marine copyright names L. Z. Phillips as the author, and an official Marine Corps publication out of Quantico, Virginia, ascribes them to General Charles Doyen.

"The Marines' Hymn" became recognized as that branch of service's official anthem in 1929, but, as with the songs from the other armed forces, it was World War II and the hymn's repeated performances that assured its permanent popularity with an American singing public. The Marines' anthem leaves no doubt that they, above all others, are the most favored. According to the last verse, even God, who realizes their prowess under pressure, exclusively uses Marines to protect the streets of heaven from interlopers.

See:

Albertson, J. K. "Offenbach, Sousa, and the Marines' Hymn." *The Sonneck Society for American Music Bulletin* II (Fall 1985): 68.
Ewen, David. *All the Years of American Popular Music.* Englewood Cliffs, NJ: Prentice-Hall, 1977, 146–147.

M. Paul Holsinger

MAULDIN, BILL (Cartoonist). With a Purple Heart for wounds received in Italy, Bill Mauldin was World War II's foremost front-line cartoonist and, the winner of the Pulitzer Prize in 1944. His work, most of which appeared in the *45th Division News*, and, beginning in 1944, in **Stars and Stripes** as well, focused on the average infantry foot soldier. Four collections were published prior to the spring of 1945 for use within the service: *Star Spangled Banter* (1941), *Sicily Sketch Book* (1943), *Mud, Mules and Mountains* (1943), and *This Damned Tree Leaks* (1945). *Up Front*, his fifth book and the first published for civilians, was issued just as the war in Europe was ending. It was an instant success. When the Book-of-the-Month Club made it one of its main selections, in July 1945, millions of Americans also came to appreciate Mauldin's work.

His early cartoons in the army, most dealing with basic training and camp life, were clean, clever, and always genial. By the Sicilian campaign, his work began to take on a gritty, harder edge, but it was not until 1944, when he was finally assigned to detached service as a journalist, that Mauldin began to portray the grim, but often humorous, side of existence on the front lines. Two archetypal combat infantrymen, "Willie" and "Joe," evolved. Drawn to heroic proportions and broadly crayoned and shaded, they were anything but classical heroes. Hunkering in foxholes, reluctant to initiate fire and thus reveal their positions; dealing with blisters, exhaustion, and their own malaise; and improvising creature comforts while yearning to become drunk; their main concern was little more than sheer survival. It was clear that Mauldin's war lacked glory—the victors were as bedraggled as the vanquished—but his prose commentary offered reassurance: America's combat soldiers were loyally and stolidly prepared to suffer. Willie, Joe, and Mauldin's other GIs introduced American readers to war in a powerful, and often sardonic, way. A definitive collection of his World War II cartoons and commentary, *Bill Mauldin's Army*, appeared in 1951; it is still in print.

After the war, Mauldin published *Back Home* (1947), a close look at problems faced by many veterans returning to the United States. Though that volume was critically praised, most readers showed little interest. The same was true of two attempts to translate the artist's cartoons to the screen. *Up Front* (Universal, 1951), starring David Wayne and Tom Ewell, returned Willie and Joe to the foxholes of Europe with only occasional humor. The following year, *Back at the Front* (Universal, 1952) put the two GIs in postwar Tokyo. Neither film was particularly successful.

In 1958, Mauldin began a second distinguished career as an editorial cartoonist, first in St. Louis, and then later for the *Chicago Daily News*. In doing so, he won another Pulitzer Prize and helped reinvigorate the profession.

See:

Mauldin, Bill. *The Brass Ring*. New York: W. W. Norton, 1971.

Kalman Goldstein

McHALE'S NAVY (Television Series–Film). After finishing last in popularity during the 1961–1962 season, ABC-TV added a number of new shows the following year. One of the most popular was the World War II–based situation comedy *McHale's Navy*. The half-hour show, which was set in the Pacific theater of war, centered around Lieutenant Commander Quinton McHale (portrayed by Oscar-winning actor Ernest Borgnine), a con man with his own island base who did everything in his power to avoid fighting so that he and his PT boat crew could enjoy the war out of harm's way.

Tim Conway and Joe Flynn played McHale's bumbling second-in-command, Ensign Parker and commanding officer, respectively. Overall, the show's scripts were pathetically weak and the slapstick comedy often ludicrous, but the public loved them, and *McHale's Navy* ran for four full years. During the height of its popularity, it also spawned two Hollywood motion pictures, *McHale's Navy* (Universal, 1964) and *McHale's Navy Joins the Air Force* (Universal, 1965).

Bryan Spicer directed an update of *McHale's Navy* (Universal, 1997). Starring comedian Tom Arnold as a now-retired naval officer living in the Caribbean and skippering an equally hapless crew, the movie was even more inept than its predecessors.

See:

Castleman, Harry, and Walter J. Podrazck. *Watching TV: Four Decades of American Television*. New York: McGraw-Hill, 1982, 158–159.
McCall, Michael. *The Best of 60s TV*. New York: Mallard Press, 1992, 77.

M. Paul Holsinger

THE MEMPHIS BELLE (Documentary-Films). William Wyler's *The Memphis Belle* (1943), which won an Academy Award for best feature-length documentary, was one of many patriotic and educational projects sponsored by the U.S. Office of War Information during World War II. In filming the inspirational account of the last mission of the *Memphis Belle*, the first B-17 Flying Fortress to complete twenty-five missions against German targets in Europe, Wyler encouraged audiences to support the war effort while introducing them to the Eighth Air Force's strategic-bombing operations in Europe.

The film opens with the aircrews and ground support units preparing their squadron for a raid on submarines docked at Wilhelmshafen, Germany. Later, the ten-man crew of the *Memphis Belle* is introduced individually and then, despite heavy antiaircraft fire and enemy fighter attack, the men bomb their targets and return home safely. After being greeted by members of the British royal family and awarded medals, the crew is speedily sent home to be featured at war bond rallies.

The Memphis Belle has been described as less a newsreel than a form of prose poetry. Wyler's choice of narrative structure and the *Belle*'s particular aircrew tend to blur the distinction between fact and fiction, myth and history. His use of a socially and ethnically diverse military unit as a symbol of America and of a single encounter with the enemy to represent the larger war were familiar conventions of fictional war movies. At the same time, Wyler's ability to transform newsreel footage into an emotionally charged narrative makes *The Memphis Belle* particularly appealing.

Memphis Belle (Enigma, 1990) is a far less successful fictionalized version of the story. Coproduced by Wyler's daughter and directed by Michael Caton-Jones, it also recounts the final bombing mission of the B-17 in 1943. Braving heavy antiaircraft fire and swarming Luftwaffe fighters, the *Belle*'s crew, led by the all-American captain, Dennis Dearborn (Matthew Modine), manages to bomb their target and nurse their damaged plane back to England. *Memphis Belle* presents the patriotic heroism of the *Belle*'s youthful crew and the necessity of strategic bombing without the slightest irony. Evoking the innocence and idealism of an earlier generation, the film seems oddly old-fashioned, as though it emerged from a culture not yet skeptical enough about military institutions to produce a *Dr. Strangelove* (1964) or a **Catch-22** (1970).

See:

Duerksen, Menno. *The Memphis Belle: Now the Real Story of World War II's Most Famous Warplane.* Memphis, TN: Castle, 1987.

Gallez, Douglas W. "Patterns in Wartime Documentaries." *Quarterly of Film, Radio and Television* 10.2 (1955): 125–135.

Philip J. Landon

THE MEN (Film). Thanks to new antibiotics and improved surgical techniques developed during World War II, roughly 2,500 veterans with paraplegia (i.e., paralysis of the lower body caused by an injury to the spinal cord) were able to survive their wounds. *The Men* (United Artists, 1950) was not only was the first Hollywood motion picture to focus on the rehabilitation problems of the paraplegic veteran but also the screen debut of the talented actor Marlon Brando. One of the leading proponents of Method acting, Brando spent a month in a hospital among real paraplegics to immerse himself in the role. Stanley Kramer, who is noted for his social message films, served as producer; Carl Foreman, who was later a victim of the 1950s blacklist, wrote the screenplay (which received the picture's lone Academy Award nomination); and Fred Zinnemann directed.

In the film's opening minutes, Brando's character, Lieutenant Ken "Bud" Wilozek, is shot in the back while on a combat mission and sent to a Veterans Administration hospital for treatment. While many of the paraplegic veterans there have learned to accept their disabilities, Wilozek is bitter and sullen. When asked if he wants to die, he replies, "It'd sure save the taxpayers a lot of money." By the end of the movie, however, after being helped by a dedicated doctor (Everett Sloan), his fiancée from before the war (Teresa Wright), and his fellow patients, Wilozek starts on the road toward rehabilitation.

Subsequent productions about paraplegic veterans, including *Coming Home* (1978) and *Born on the Fourth of July* (1989), have largely followed the model established by *The Men*.

See:

Manso, Peter. *Brando: The Biography.* New York: Hyperion, 1994, 275–288.
Spoto, Donald. "Brando Wheels Himself into Movies—*The Men*, 1950." *Stanley Kramer: Film Maker.* New York: Putnam's, 1978, 54–64.

James Deutsch

A MIDNIGHT CLEAR (Novel-Film). Set during Christmas Week 1944 while the Battle of the Bulge rages nearby, *A Midnight Clear*, a 1982 novel by William Wharton, is a story of six American GIs on surveillance patrol in the Ardennes Forest. Occupying a deserted French chateau, they find themselves in the midst of a small but playful band of Germans who build snowmen, decorate Christmas trees, and sing carols like "Silent Night." Fortunately for the Germans, these Americans are not belligerent; they all have IQ scores above 150 and were initially placed in the Army Specialized Training Program Reserve to continue their college education until that program was dissolved and they were reassigned to the infantry. They write poetry, read *All Quiet on the Western Front* and *A Farewell to Arms*, and sketch drawings on old K ration boxes. They agree to fake a skirmish and take the Germans prisoner without anyone getting hurt. Unfortunately, one of the Americans is a borderline psychotic who mistakes the fake skirmish for the real thing, starts firing, and tragically destroys the separate peace that had been arranged.

Many critics disliked the novel, calling it dull and boring reading; nonetheless, nearly a decade after its original publication, Keith Gordon wrote, directed, and filmed a version of *A Midnight Clear* (Interstar, 1992). Starring several young actors who subsequently achieved greater renown (including Ethan Hawke, Gary Sinise, Peter Berg, and Frank Whaley), the movie was generally well received with some reviewers using such terms as ''eloquent'' and ''first-rate'' to describe it. Others, however, found it far less praiseworthy, and much of the public seemed to agree; it grossed barely $1.5 million.

Wharton, the pseudonym for an American painter living in Paris since the 1960s, earlier wrote *Birdy* (1979), a first novel that dealt with the horrors of World War II and the psychosomatic problems that combat can bring.

See:

Ebert, Roger. Review of *A Midnight Clear*. *Cinemania 97*. CD-ROM. Redmond, WA: Microsoft, 1997.
O'Brien, Tom. Review of *A Midnight Clear*. *Commonweal*, 11 March 1983, 155–157.

James Deutsch

MISTER ROBERTS **(Novel-Drama-Film–Television Series).** Thomas Heggen served in the United States Navy throughout World War II. In 1946, while working as an editor at *Reader's Digest*, he published *Mister Roberts*, his only novel. Based on some of his experiences as a lieutenant in the Pacific during the war, it received almost universal popular and critical acclaim. Set in spring 1945, *Mister Roberts* describes the efforts of Doug Roberts, a lieutenant on board the supply ship *AK 601* (or, as its men sardonically call it, the USS *Reluctant*), to be reassigned to a ship of the line closer to action against the Japanese. In the process, he has to deal with the ship's tyrannical captain, John Morton, a retread from the merchant marine, as well as a handful of misfits including Ensign Frank Pulver, a bright, fun-loving troublemaker whose sour relationship with his slightly unbalanced captain threatens to destroy his career. Roberts, who is loved by nearly everyone, ultimately prevails, only to be killed some weeks later during a kamikaze raid on his destroyer at Okinawa. The book, which interlaces humor with pathos and drama, provides a good picture of the daily activities onboard a navy ship and illustrates how the peculiarities of the man in charge can cause undue difficulties for those who work under him.

In conjunction with Heggen, Josuha Logan transformed the novel into a humorous drama for the Broadway stage in February 1948. Starring Henry Fonda as Roberts and David Wayne as Pulver, it ran for 1,157 performances before closing in early 1951—making it one of the most popular shows to appear on Broadway up to that time. Logan and Heggen also collaborated on the screenplay for an equally successful film version of *Mister Roberts* (Warner Brothers, 1955). Fonda reprised his role as Roberts, James Cagney played Morton, and Jack Lemmon became Ensign Pulver. Audiences loved it, and it became the top-grossing American motion picture of the year.

In September 1965, NBC attempted to use the basic story line to develop a television situation comedy. Filled with a cast of relative unknowns and airing late on Friday evenings, it had little chance of success and was canceled at the end of its first year after only 30 episodes.

See:

Leggett, John. *Ross and Tom: Two American Tragedies.* New York: Simon and Schuster, 1974, 207–432.
Magill, Frank N. *Cinema: The Novel into Film.* Pasadena, CA: Salem, 1980, 311–317.

David K. Vaughan

MURROW, EDWARD R. (War Correspondent–Broadcast Journalist). Throughout his career, Edward R. Murrow elevated broadcast journalism to new levels of prestige and professionalism. In February 1937, he became the Columbia Broadcasting System's representative in Europe. In summer 1939, after successfully persuading CBS to employ its own correspondents to cover news events in Europe, Murrow began hiring a number of individuals, including H. V. Kaltenborn and Eric Sevareid, who soon became some of the most renowned reporters of World War II. Also that summer, Murrow used for the first time in his on-the-air broadcasts the phrase, *"This . . . is London,"* a greeting that later came to symbolize the fortitude of that city's inhabitants as they were subjected to incessant German air raids during the blitz after September 1940. It was his daily programs from London that supplied American listeners with their best sense of the British war experience of the time.

On the evening of December 2, 1943, Murrow went along on an air strike against Berlin. His vivid reporting of that raid later became known as "Orchestrated Hell." One of his most famous wartime broadcasts occurred in April 1945, when he described the Buchenwald concentration camp after its liberation by the Allies. His vivid portrait of the horrors of that camp is no less chilling and compelling today than it was when first aired over fifty years ago. In the years after the war, Murrow moved into the new medium of television. During the Korean War, he visited the GIs on the front lines, and his show back home let viewers see up close some of that "forgotten war." Beginning in the early 1950s, he distinguished himself even further with such award-winning programs on CBS-TV as *See It Now* (1952–1955), *Person to Person* (1953–1959), and *Small World* (1958–1960); before his death he also won a number of Emmys as the country's best news reporter.

See:

Cloud, Stanley. *The Murrow Boys: Pioneers on the Front Lines of Broadcast Journalism.* Boston: Houghton Mifflin, 1996.
Persico, Joseph. *Edward R. Murrow: An American Original.* New York: McGraw-Hill, 1988.
Smith, R. Franklin. *Edward R. Murrow: The War Years.* Kalamazoo, MI: New Issues Press, 1978.

Philip J. Harwood

THE NAKED AND THE DEAD (**Novel-Film**). Norman Mailer uses the American invasion of a Japanese-held island, the fictional Anopopei, to discuss ideas of power, control, knowledge, and identity in his first novel, *The Naked and the Dead* (1948). The book alternately focuses on the commander of the invasion force, General Cummings (who argues his fascistic social philosophy with his vaguely liberal protégé, Lieutenant Hearn) and a reconnaissance platoon commanded by the sadistic Sergeant Croft. To punish Hearn and break his resistance, Cummings sends him to lead the platoon on a mission around the island in order to assess the enemy strength from the rear. As the mission progresses, Mailer takes readers inside the mind of each of the several characters who make up the platoon. Their inability to articulate their experiences and feelings creates constant misunderstandings. As each constructs a private, self-serving version of common experiences, the walls between the men become insurmountable, and the possibility for real communication, sympathy, and knowledge, impossible. Eventually, when Hearn and Croft disagree on procedure—Croft wants to go forward and climb Mount Anaka, while Hearn wants to go back—Croft allows the lieutenant to lead the platoon into an ambush and the young officer is killed.

Raoul Walsh directed a mediocre film version of *The Naked and the Dead* (RKO, 1958) from a screenplay by Denis Sanders and Terry Sanders. Though longtime character actors Raymond Massey and Aldo Ray are reasonably convincing as Cummings and Croft, respectively, the selection of Cliff Robertson as Hearn was ill conceived. As the storyline unwinds, the picture becomes a simplistic ''good guy–bad guy'' story with, inexplicably, Hearn living to see Cummings's career destroyed. Mailer found the movie completely unrepresentative of his book, but there was little he could do to change the end result.

See:

Parish, James Robert. *The Great Combat Pictures: Twentieth-Century Warfare on the Screen.* Metuchen, NJ: Scarecrow, 1990, 289–291.

Walsh, Jeffrey. *American War Literature, 1914 to Vietnam.* New York: St. Martin's, 1982, 112–120.

Robert L. McLaughlin

THE NEGRO SOLDIER (**Documentary**). Academy Award–winning director Frank Capra volunteered for the United States Army during World War II and, as an officer in the signal corps from 1942 to 1945, produced some of the most renowned documentaries in motion picture history. One of the most important was *The Negro Soldier* (1944), a production that played a major role in the ultimately successful campaign to desegregate the armed forces in the years shortly after the conclusion of the war.

Capra originally scheduled William Wyler as director, but when Wyler left to shoot ***The Memphis Belle*** in England, the job was turned over to Stuart Heisler. The script was largely written by Carleton Moss, a young black author who had worked on a number of Capra projects, though both Ben Hecht and

Jo Swerling contributed to the final draft. Because the military wanted to use the picture, in part, as a recruiting device and therefore was concerned that it not look discriminatory, Moss's script ignored as best it could "what's wrong with the Army" and concentrated on "what's right with my people."

Screened for the first time in October 1943 before General George Marshall and other army officials at the Pentagon, *The Negro Soldier* was later shown to more than 200 black journalists and an equally large number of African-American leaders in Harlem before its official public release in April 1944. Though always popular in the nation's black communities, the forty-three-minute documentary at first did poorly at the box office when placed in competition with the many combat-oriented films of the day. Later, however, after being cut to twenty minutes, it proved a success and went a long way toward convincing white theatergoers that young black men could, and should, serve their country in both peace and war.

See:

Cripps, Thomas, and David Culbert. "The Negro Soldier (1944): Film Propaganda in Black and White." In *Hollywood as Historian. American Film in a Cultural Context*, ed. Peter C. Rollins. Lexington: University of Kentucky Press, 1983, 109–133.
Garrett, Greg. "It's Everybody's War: Racism and the World War Two Documentary." *Journal of Popular Film and Television* 22 (Summer 1994): 70–78.

M. Paul Holsinger

ON THE TOWN (**Musical-Film**). In April 1944, the twenty-five-year-old assistant conductor of the New York Philharmonic Orchestra, Leonard Bernstein, staged his composition *Fancy Free* to great acclaim. Choreographed by Jerome Robbins, the modern ballet is about three young sailors, fresh from sea duty, who are "on the prowl for girls" during their first leave in New York City. They find, fight over, and then lose two young women; as their twenty-four-hour pass ends, they are madly chasing a third. Impressed by the ballet's obvious popularity, Oliver Smith, its designer, convinced Bernstein and others to reconfigure it into a full-length Broadway musical, to be called *On the Town*. Bernstein recruited two of his friends, Betty Comden and Adolph Green, as the musical's lyricists. When George Abbott, the most renowned musical-comedy director of the day, agreed, in summer 1944, to stage it, the new show quickly began to take shape into the story of three sailors, Gabey, Ozzie, and Chip, and their quest for sexual enjoyment in the midst of war.

Shortly after *On the Town* opened on December 28, 1944, to almost unanimous rave reviews, Comden told a New York Times reporter that we "wanted to . . . at least touch on the frantic search for gaiety and love and the terrific pressure of time that war brings" (quoted in Burton, 130). But in doing so, she and Green consciously shifted the focus to the three women—Ivy, Hildy, and Claire—that the guys meet and on the many ways that they and most other women's roles were constantly changing in wartime America. The public loved the happy music, including the still-famous "New York, New York," and the production ran for 463 performances before closing on February 2, 1946.

On the Town was groundbreaking in a number of ways. At the very moment that more than 100,000 Japanese-Americans were being held in "relocation centers" scattered throughout the West, one of the stars of the production was the beautiful Sono Osaka, a young Nisei (second-generation) actress-dancer. The musical was also the first in Broadway history to feature white and black dancers together on the stage even, in some numbers, holding hands as equals. Two revivals were produced in 1959 and in 1971, neither of which was particularly successful. A third, which was staged at the Delacorte Theater in New York's Central Park during the summer of 1997, however, was a huge success.

Four years after the conclusion of World War II, the musical was transformed to the Hollywood screen starring singer-dancer Gene Kelly, the popular Frank Sinatra, and comedienne Nancy Walker. Six new songs were written, and though privately, Bernstein was appalled, theatergoers made the movie a financial success. Updating the story to the postwar years, however, inadvertently took away all its tension and bite. Though still enjoyable, *On the Town* (Metro-Goldwyn-Mayer, 1949) offers little for contemporary viewers.

See:

Burton, Humphrey. "On the Town." Chapter 14 in *Leonard Bernstein*. New York: Doubleday, 1994, 129–137.

James, Robert, and Michael R. Pitts. *The Great Hollywood Musical Pictures*. Metuchen, NJ: Scarecrow, 1992, 486–489.

                                                                M. Paul Holsinger

OUR ARMY AT WAR (Comic Books). Though there were dozens of comic books published during World War II that featured American GIs fighting the nation's enemies in Europe and throughout the Pacific, one of the most important series to focus on that conflict did not begin until August 1952, when DC Comics issued the first volume of *Our Army at War*. At first, there were stories in each issue that used the ongoing Korean War as a setting, but it was World War II that engendered the majority of strips. Indeed, in 1959 writer-editor Frank Kanigher created *Our Army at War*, featuring the most important of all World War II American military heroes to appear in a comic, Sergeant Frank Rock of the United States Army's Easy Company.

Rock was the epitome of all the war's platoon leaders as he and his men (including Jackie Johnson, the first black character in comic book history to be created with respect) fought battle after battle to defeat the country's foes. Rock's principal artist was Joe Kubert, one of the industry's most famous; Kubert's visualization of Kanigher's stories soon made Frank Rock overwhelmingly popular with a huge audience of comic book readers.

During the 1960s, most war-related comic book series came to an end, but *Our Army at War* continued unchecked. Even when DC Comics finally ended that series in 1977, twenty-five years after it began, it created a new series, *Sgt. Rock*, exclusively featuring the sergeant and his men. That group of books continued for another eleven years until DC finally canceled it in 1988.

See:

Daniels, Les. *DC Comics: Sixty Years of the World's Finest Comic Book Heroes*. Boston: Little, Brown, 1995, 104–105.

Jones, Gerard. "Sgt. Rock." In *The Encyclopedia of American Comics from 1897 to the Present*, ed. Ron Goulart. New York: Facts on File, 1990, 328.

M. Paul Holsinger

PATTON (Film). Only a handful of American army generals have been more simultaneously loved and hated than George Smith Patton. Best known as the commander of the United States Third Army, which helped to liberate France in 1944 and broke the back of Nazi opposition in Germany the following year, "Old Blood and Guts" Patton seemingly cried out for a Hollywood screen biography. Director Franklin J. Schaffner's enormously popular *Patton* (20th Century–Fox, 1970) was not only the top-grossing film of the year but also one of the most acclaimed. It won seven Academy Awards, including best picture, best director, best screenplay, and best actor.

Few movies have undergone such a remarkable evolution during development as *Patton*. Beginning in 1951, producer Frank McCarthy struggled for years against the objections of both the United States Army and Patton's family to bring the general's controversial World War II career to the screen. Ironically, as originally conceived, *Patton* was to have been a fairly standard celebration of the general's individual heroics and triumphs in battle. By the time it was made, however, the increasing social debate generated by American involvement in Vietnam compelled screenwriters Francis Ford Coppola and Edmund H. North (out of concern for alienating an increasingly antiwar audience) to craft a much more ambiguous portrait than they might have otherwise. Taking material from both General Omar Bradley's *A Soldier's Story* (1951) and Ladislas Farago's best-selling *Patton, Ordeal and Triumph* (1963), the two created an imperial Patton who, as brilliantly portrayed by George C. Scott, is at once vainglorious and noble, cruel and compassionate, profane and refined—a man representing the best and worst of the American character in its relationship to war. Though Scott later refused to accept his well-deserved Academy Award as best actor, his portrayal of Patton remains one of the most remembered in film history.

See:

Suid, Lawrence H. "Patton: The Nineteen Year Struggle." In *Guts and Glory: Great American War Movies*. Reading, MA: Addison-Wesley, 1978, 244–265.

Toplin, Robert B. "Patton: 'Deliberately Planned as a Rorschach Test.' " Chapter 6 in *History By Hollywood: The Use and Abuse of the American Past*. Urbana: University of Illinois Press, 1996, 155–178.

Philip L. Simpson

PINUP GIRLS (Pictures). Young men have probably always taken likenesses of the opposite sex with them to war, but, during World War II, tens of thousands of American GIs expanded on the idea, substituting sexually alluring depictions of so-called pinup girls in their lockers, over their bunks or hammocks, or even on the nose cones of their Boeing bombers in place of "the girl back home." It was the army weekly, *Yank*, that first used the term *pinup* in its April 20, 1943, issue, but long before that, pictures of Hollywood stars (such as Lana Turner, Hedy Lamar, Veronica Lake, and Ann Sheridan), often in provocative poses, adorned thousands of barracks walls. Unquestionably the two favorite pinup girls were Betty Grable and Rita Hayworth. Grable, a singer-dancer-actress renowned for her long legs and curvaceous body, posed for the single most popular pinup shot of the war years in a one-piece bathing suit looking wistfully over her shoulder with an irresistible "let's have fun together" look. Hayworth, one of the most beautiful women ever to appear on the screen, was voted by GIs who read *Yank* as their most admired physical beauty in each of the last three years of the war. A photograph of her kneeling on a bed in a lacy black and white satin nightgown was second only to Grable's famous shot in popularity.

For those young men who wanted even more sexually titillating pictures, however, each month after 1942 *Esquire* magazine included a centerfold featuring a buxom young woman in a sheer bathing suit, a sarong, a hula skirt, or a tight-fitting sweater. Though none of the models (almost all of whom were painted by the artist Alberto Vargas in full color) were ever naked, they came as close as the law would allow and left little to the imagination of the young men who purchased them for display. So in demand were the *Esquire* pinups that soon there were also Varga Girl calendars and Varga Girl playing cards, all guaranteed to appeal to the millions of sexually starved young men away in service. Indeed, so sensual or seductive did these become that the nation's postmaster general, the puritanical Frank Walker, banned the magazine from the mails after 1944 for "obscenity reasons." GIs everywhere were furious. "Who the hell got the bright idea of banning [your] pictures," wrote one frustrated GI to the magazine's editors. "You won't find one barracks overseas that hasn't got an *Esquire* Pin Up Girl [in it]" (*This Fabulous Century*, 122). He was unquestionably correct.

See:

Martignette, Charles G., and Louis K. Meisel. *The Great American Pinup*. New York: Taschen, 1996.

Robotham, Tom. *Varga*. New York: Mallard Press, 1991.

This Fabulous Century, ed. Editor of Time-Life. Vol. 5 (1940–1950). New York: Time-Life, 1969.

                                                                                    M. Paul Holsinger

***PISTOL PACKIN' MAMA: THE MISSIONS OF A B-17* (Documentary).**
Since the end of World War II, American filmmakers have produced numerous

documentaries focusing on one or more aspects of that war. One of the very best is *Pistol Packin' Mama: The Missions of a B-17* (Kenwood Productions, 1990). Directed by Tom Jenz from a script by Jenz and Bill Semans, it tells the story of the crew of one of the thousands of American B-17 bombers that flew out of Great Britain during the last three years of the war. Before May 1945, the 390th Bomb Group flew more than 300 missions and dropped 19,000 tons of bombs on Germany and other parts of Nazi-occupied Europe. Though the *Betty Boop* or, as she was better known, *Pistol Packin' Mama*, exploded over Berlin in March 1944, killing all on board, five of its original crew—pilot James Geary, copilot Richard Perry, navigator Gus Mencow, high turret gunner Shir Hoffman, and ball turret gunner Cliff Puckett—survived. That Jenz and his colleagues were able to craft such an emotionally moving film from these five men's memories more than forty years after the conclusion of the war is a tribute to their especially talented movie making.

Pistol Packin' Mama first went into service in June 1943 with a rookie crew that trained together for only a few months. Their baptism of fire came quickly, and, though several of the crew were soon killed, the plane flew on to become one of the most highly praised in the group. However, even after its magical twenty-fifth flight in February 1944—a milestone that allowed a plane's crew a temporary respite from active combat duty—little changed. Puckett flew an additional thirty-seven missions; Mencow became head navigator of a bomber wing; Geary continued as a lead pilot in other aircraft until he was finally shot down over Berlin and made a prisoner of war; Perry and Hoffman also flew until the end of the fighting over Europe.

It is hard not to be deeply touched by the testimonies of these five undeniable heroes. In going into harm's way again and again, they, and the more than 80,000 others who failed to return, gave the world a lasting heritage of bravery that may never be eclipsed.

See:

Jablonski, Edward. *Flying Fortress: The Illustrated Biography of the B-17s and the Men Who Flew Them.* Garden City, NY: Doubleday, 1965.
Van Pelt, Charles. "An Airplane You Could Trust." *American History Illustrated* 4.6 (October 1969): 22–31.

                                                                    M. Paul Holsinger

"PRAISE THE LORD AND PASS THE AMMUNITION" (Song). Frank Loesser became one of Hollywood's top lyricists as well as the author and composer of two of Broadway's biggest musicals, *Where's Charley?* and *Guys and Dolls.* During World War II, he also wrote the most popular song dealing with an actual event during the conflict. "Praise the Lord and Pass the Ammunition" was based on the words reputedly uttered by Navy Chaplain William Maguire during the Japanese attack on Pearl Harbor as he helped man an antiaircraft gun. (Maguire later claimed that the famous line was not his, though on

November 2, 1942, *Life* magazine did attribute it to him. The real spokesman appears to have been Lieutenant Howell Forgy, a Presbyterian chaplain from New Orleans.)

The number became a smash success after it was first recorded by the popular singing quartet, the Merry Macs, and then later by the Kay Kyser orchestra. More than 1 million copies of the sheet music and 2.5 million recordings were sold. "Praise the Lord" was played so often on radio stations across America that the U.S. Office of War Information finally suggested that stations broadcast it no more than once every four hours to avoid having listeners grow weary of the sentiment that only by working together and passing the ammunition would the nation ever become truly free. *Variety* lists "Praise the Lord and Pass the Ammunition" on its fifty-year hit parade of songs.

See:

Scheele, Carl H. "Praise the Lord and Pass the Ammunition." Liner Notes. In *Praise the Lord and Pass the Ammunition: Songs of World War I and II.* LP New World, 1977, 5–6.

M. Paul Holsinger

***PRIDE OF THE MARINES* (Film).** On August 21, 1942, Sergeant Albert "Al" Schmid and others from Company H, second Battalion of the first Marines, came under heavy Japanese fire in the battle of Tenaru River on Guadalcanal. When the gunner was killed and his squad leader badly wounded, Schmid, who was a loader, took over the unit's machine gun, alternately loading and firing until an enemy grenade blinded him and put the gun out of action. The next day, the victorious Marines found more than 200 dead Japanese in front of Schmid's position. He was awarded the Navy Cross, that branch of the armed forces' second highest medal of valor, and idolized as one of the country's most popular war heroes.

In 1944, Roger P. Butterfield told the young Marine's story in a moving biography entitled simply *Al Schmid—Marine.* The following year, the book was turned into an almost documentary-like motion picture, *Pride of the Marines* (Warner Brothers, 1945), or *Forever in Love,* as it was called in the United Kingdom. Scripted by Albert Maltz (who was on Hollywood's blacklist during the 1950s) and starring John Garfield as Al and Eleanor Parker as Ruth (Al's future wife), the film was one of the first attempts by the movie industry to focus on problems that many handicapped servicemen faced after returning from the war. Director Delmer Daves's war scenes are among the very best put on the screen up to that time. Garfield's Schmid, a Philadelphian from a poor, working-class family, comes across as very real, especially in his anger and self-pity at being blinded. Critics liked the thought-provoking and believable production, and audiences packed theaters to cheer the cinematic hero, just as they earlier had applauded the real-life Marine after Guadalcanal. There is a "happy," and true, ending when Al accepts his handicap and determines to live a productive, useful life in the days ahead.

Al Schmid lived until 1982. He was buried with honors in Arlington National Cemetery.

See:

Morella, Joe, Edward Z. Epstein, and John Griggs. *The Films of World War II*. Secaucus, NJ: Citadel, 1973, 226–228.

Parish, James Robert. *The Great Combat Pictures: Twentieth-Century Warfare on the Screen*. Metuchen, NJ: Scarecrow, 1990, 323–324.

M. Paul Holsinger

***PT 109* (History-Film).** In 1961, Robert J. Donovan, a feature writer for the New York Herald Tribune published *PT 109: John F. Kennedy in World War II*, a nonfictional account of the newly elected president's war experiences in the Solomon Islands. Many Americans already knew how the supposedly intrepid Kennedy (JFK), as a young naval officer in August 1943, singlehandedly rescued his crew after their torpedo boat was cut in two by a Japanese destroyer. Stories of his heroism abounded during all of his political campaigns after the war; tie clips featuring the boat were worn by many Kennedy supporters during his victorious 1960 presidential race. A life-sized replica, manned by many of the original crew members, was even towed down Pennsylvania Avenue as a part of the inaugural parade.

Donovan's carefully researched retelling of the legendary events, praised by the president as "highly accurate," quickly became a popular best-seller. Several different hardcover and paperback editions, including one edited especially for young adults, were printed. The book was transformed into a nearly 2½ hour long motion picture directed by Leslie Martinson. Though moviegoers obviously appreciated the factually embellished action sequences and perhaps even some of the unnatural patriotic speeches, most reviewers labeled *PT 109* (Warner Brothers, 1963) tedious, or worse. All the actors, including Cliff Robertson, whom the president had hand-picked to portray him, seemed to sleepwalk through their roles. Though JFK's tragic assassination late in the year kept the book, now rereleased in conjunction with the film, and the movie itself in the public eye, both soon faded from sight.

See:

Reeves, Richard. "PT 109." In *Past Imperfect: History According to the Movies*, ed. Mark C. Carnes. New York: Holt, 1995, 232–235.

Suid, Lawrence. *Sailing on the Silver Screen: Hollywood and the U.S. Navy*. Annapolis, MD: Naval Institute Press, 1996, 152–156.

M. Paul Holsinger

***THE PURPLE HEART* (Film).** *The Purple Heart* (20th Century–Fox, 1944), directed by Lewis Milestone and starring Dana Andrews, Richard Conte, and Farley Granger, recounts the fate of two B-25 bomber crews who are captured by the Japanese after taking part in Lieutenant Colonel Jimmy Doolittle's famed

1942 air raid against Tokyo. The eight airmen are imprisoned in Japan and tried as war criminals who deliberately dropped their bombs on hospitals and other civilian targets. The charges are false, and, under the leadership of Captain Harvey Ross (Andrews), none of the Americans can be compelled into making a false confession. Each is taken individually from the cell and tortured while the others listen to his screams. Their tormentor, the sadistic General Mitsubi (Richard Loo), is more interested in learning where the raid was launched from than in securing confessions. Despite being informed of the fall of Corregidor, the fliers remain undaunted and go to their deaths with their secret safe. Humiliated at his failure, Mitsubi commits suicide. His fate, the story implies, foreshadows the eventual defeat of his country.

The Purple Heart is typical of the war films produced by Hollywood during World War II. The bomber crews, with their diverse ethnic, regional, and class backgrounds, become a microcosm of America itself. The movie also presents the enemy in crude racial stereotypes that exemplify the picture of the Japanese drawn by American propagandists. The dramatic playing and singing of "**The Army Air Corps Song**," with its emphasis that "nothing can stop the Army Air Corps" as the prisoners march to their deaths, was a great morale booster for millions of American theatergoers.

See:

Millichap, Joseph R. *Lewis Milestone*. Boston: Twayne, 1981, 124–128.

Philip J. Landon

PYLE, ERNIE (War Correspondent–Newspaperman). Ernie Pyle was the most famous war correspondent of World War II. Articles written for the Scripps-Howard chain of newspapers from London during late 1940 and early 1941 gave him his start as a war reporter. After Pearl Harbor, he joined American GIs training for battle and went ashore with the army in North Africa in November 1942. His frontline stories soon made him renowned throughout the United States. A regular column appeared six days a week in more than 300 newspapers and was read by a circulation of 12.5 million Americans. *Here Is Your War* (1943), Pyle's first best-selling book, combined many of his most outstanding reports and stories from the fighting in North Africa, including his much-discussed description of the American defeat at the Kasserine Pass by Erwin Rommel's Afrika Korps.

Few persons were surprised when Pyle was awarded the Pulitzer Prize for "distinguished war correspondence" in 1943. *Brave Men* (1944), the second compilation of his columns from the front, including his most republished piece, "The Death of Captain Waskow," starts with the invasion of Sicily, jumps to the five months he spent with the GIs in Italy, and concludes with material written in France during September 1944. That volume had an advance sale of more than a quarter-million copies and was number one on the *New York Times* best-seller list for thirty-four weeks.

All of Pyle's war stories condemned the war while praising those young GIs who fought in it. No other World War II reporter so consistently presented so realistic a description of soldier life. On April 18, 1945, Ernie Pyle was killed by Japanese machine gun fire while reporting the Marine landing on Ie Shima. His death, just a week after that of President Franklin Roosevelt, seemed to some Americans almost more traumatic.

See:

Tobin, James. *Ernie Pyle's War: America's Eyewitness to World War II.* New York: Free Press, 1997.

M. Paul Holsinger

"RATION BLUES" (Song). In April 1941, the U.S. Office of Price Administration (OPA) was created—though with little power—to prevent "price-spiraling, rising costs of living, profiteering and inflation." Once the war began, its authority was expanded. Soon the OPA controlled almost every aspect of the nation's economy. One of its first moves was to ration virtually all disposable consumer items except fruit and vegetables. Ration boards were set up in every county throughout the United States. Each American man, woman, and child was issued a series of ration books, which contained coupons that were required to purchase everything from sugar to meat and from shoes to fuel oil. Gasoline was limited, with most citizens entitled to no more than four gallons a week; rubber products such as tires became almost impossible to find. Children especially missed treats like chocolate or chewing gum.

Though most persons unhappily adjusted to the new restrictions, nearly everyone complained. A number of songwriters soon mirrored that frustration. One of the best examples was "Ration Blues" by Louis Jordan, Antonio Casey, and Collenane Clark. Recorded in December 1943 by the popular Jordan (father of the "jump blues" and one of the earliest inductees into the Rock and Roll Hall of Fame) and his band, the Tympany Five, the song deplores, not only the loss of sugar, but also the government's new decision to cut back on the availability of most meats. Rubber was rapidly disappearing, the song concludes, and now, with little gas for the average person, even romance would have to be put on the back burner.

Millions apparently could sympathize with Jordan's mournful lament; by February 12, 1944, "Ration Blues" had risen to the top of both the country and rhythm-and-blues charts as well as to number eleven on the pop music chart.

See:

Chilton, John. *Let the Good Times Roll: A Biography of Louis Jordan.* London: Quartet Books, 1992.

M. Paul Holsinger

RHYMES OF A PFC (Poetry). Lincoln Kirstein enlisted in the United States Army during World War II and served in a staff support role for American forces in France and Germany. He apparently never rose above the rank of private first class and, in fact, he removed all indication of rank from his uniforms. Being Harvard-educated and from a distinguished Boston family, Kirstein's act of self-effacement was intentional. While in the service, he began to write poetry about military life. With the conclusion of hostilities, other war-related poems appeared, and, in 1964, they were all collected in *Rhymes of a Pfc*. A second, revised version, *Rhymes and More Rhymes of a Pfc.*, was published in 1966; a definitive edition was issued in 1981.

While Kirstein's gay orientation is sometimes evident, nearly all the *Rhymes* describe typical experiences of army enlisted men in training and in areas near the front lines in France and Germany. The ninety-five poems that make up the final version are witty, insightful, accurate, and artistically of the highest order. The critic Paul Fussell suggested that Kirstein may very well be the "greatest poet of the Second World War." Certainly, his collected work is among the best war poetry to emerge from the conflict.

See:

Vaughan, David K. "Snapshots in the Book of War: Lincoln Kerstein's *Rhymes of a Pfc*." In *Visions of War: World War II in Popular Literature and Culture*, ed. M. Paul Holsinger and Mary Anne Schofield. Bowling Green, OH: Bowling Green State University Popular Press, 1992, 8–17.

David K. Vaughan

ROLFE, EDWIN (Poet). One of America's most distinguished left-wing poets in the late 1920s and early 1930s, Edwin Rolfe went to Spain in June 1937 to join the thousands of volunteers from the United States and Europe fighting with the Republican Army in that nation's bloody civil war. A dedicated Marxist, he was at first assigned to propaganda work (authoring dozens of news items for the *Daily Worker*, broadcasting via short wave to the United States, and editing the International Brigades' official journal, *The Volunteer for Liberty*). Eventually he was allowed to fight in the front lines. Before he and the other Americans left Spain in December 1938, he had months of combat experience.

During the time he served in Spain, Rolfe also continued to produce some of his best poetry, much of it dealing directly with those young Americans who came to Spain to fight against General Francisco Franco and his fascist allies. Three of his best poems, "Entry" (an account of his and his friends' clandestine journey across the Pyrenees into Spain), "Epitaph," and "Elegy for the Dead" are powerful poetic studies of commitment and sacrifice far from home.

After returning to the United States, Rolfe authored the first, and one of the best, first-person accounts of the Spanish Civil War from an American viewpoint. *The Lincoln Battalion: The Story of the Americans Who Fought in Spain in the International Brigade* was not published, however, until November 1939, two months after the German invasion of Poland. Few copies sold, as readers turned their attention to new and even bloodier battles on other fronts.

In his long "City of Anguish," written after one of the frequent bomb attacks on Madrid in late summer 1937, Rolfe poetically concluded that it was impossible to understand the full impact of war unless one had run panicking for shelter as bombs were falling or hugged the ground helplessly trying to avoid strafing by enemy aircraft. Few poets, before or since, have captured the immediacy of war any better.

See:

Nelson, Cary. *Edwin Rolfe: A Biographical Essay and Guide to the Rolfe Papers at the University of Illinois at Urbana-Champaign.* Urbana: University of Illinois Press, 1990.

M. Paul Holsinger

ROSIE THE RIVETER (Symbol-Movie-Song). Millions of American women left the security of their homes during the years of World War II to support the war effort. Some joined the armed forces, and many others volunteered as Red Cross workers or **USO** hostesses. It was those women who went directly into the workplace, especially into America's factories, however, who garnered the most attention. Though only a few ever ran a rivet machine or assembled an airplane, tank, or ship, it was these women who symbolized to most Americans all feminine activity during the war.

Quickly named "Rosie the Riveter," the quintessential female factory worker took on all forms and shapes in the popular culture of the day. Norman Rockwell drew perhaps the most famous visual of Rosie for the May 29, 1943 cover of the *Saturday Evening Post.* Appearing muscular in her jeans and denim blouse and cradling her large rivet machine in her lap, Rockwell's depiction of the "new woman" shows her contentedly munching on a sandwich during her lunch break. Many women were appalled at what they considered such an unfeminine sight, and most other artists' work soon softened Rosie's masculine appearance.

"Rosie" also appeared in other media. "Rosie, The Riveter," Redd Evans and John Jacob Loeb's 1942 song, was one of the most popular throughout the war years. With its bouncy tune and lyrics recorded by the Four Vagabonds, it quickly became a radio Hit Parade number at the same time that it helped to solidify the idea of the hard-working, sacrificing woman "on the assembly line." There was also a grade B film, *Rosie the Riveter* (Republic, 1944), featuring an attractive young female working in an airplane factory.

That image of dedication because of patriotic fervor on the part of America's women has been modified in recent years. In 1980, for instance, five females, who were long accustomed, even before the war, to working at low-paying, dead-end jobs, were profiled in documentary filmmaker Connie Field's prize-winning *The Life and Times of Rosie the Riveter.* The mixed (black-and-white and color) motion picture was an instant popular success and one of the best documentary accounts of the American home front during World War II. More than 1 million persons saw it during its first year of showing—a remarkably high figure for any noncommercial production. Universally praised throughout the United States, it was dubbed into six languages and shown throughout Europe, where it won several major prizes in film festivals.

Actress-producer Goldie Hawn presented yet another view of the many "Rosies" in *Swing Shift* (Warner Brothers, 1984). The several featured actresses (including Christine Lahti, who received an Academy Award nomination as best supporting actress) are shown struggling to adjust to sometimes unpleasant working conditions. While separated from their husbands or boy friends, they face, and sometimes succumb to, temptations to cheat on loved ones who are overseas (the married Hawn, for instance, has an affair with her immediate supervisor in the plant where she works). When the men come home, most of the female workers find that they are no longer needed (or wanted) in the workforce. *Swing Shift* spends perhaps too much time highlighting Hawn's extramarital relationship, but its view of the thousands of America's factory women is both straightforward and fair.

See:

Kessler-Harris, Alice. "The Life and Times of Rosie the Riveter (U.S., 1980): The Experience and Legacy of Wartime Women Wage Earners." In *World War II: Film and History*, ed. John W. Chambers II and David Culbert. New York: Oxford University Press, 1996, 107–122.

White, Mimi. "Rehearsing Feminism: Women/History in *The Life and Times of Rosie the Riveter* and *Swing Shift*." *Wide Angle: A Film Quarterly of Theory, Criticism, and Practice* 7.3 (1985): 34–43.

M. Paul Holsinger

SAD SACK (Cartoon-Book–Film Character). George Baker, creator of the famous World War II cartoon character "Sad Sack," was born in Lowell, Massachusetts, but grew up in Chicago. After a month at art school, he went to work for Disney Studios from 1937 until shortly before he was drafted into the army, in 1941. When Baker won a **USO** contest with cartoons about his little antihero, "Sad Sack" became the first permanent feature in the weekly **Yank** on June 15, 1942. By 1944, regular "Sad Sack" cartoons were also being carried in **Stars and Stripes**.

Sack (a euphemism for "sad sack of shit") was a classic scapegrace: gangly, with huge feet and an oversized, almost rectangular nose. Baker balanced his character's docile incompetence with satire; through passive aggression, Sack defeated attempts to make him into a spit-and-polish soldier, and occasionally he even got revenge on his tormentors. GIs responded viscerally, wrote fan mail, and put Sack's face on their fatigues, field packs, and raincoats. When he was victimized by military inequities, they empathized with him, writing letters of protest to *Yank* or *Stars and Stripes*.

Simon and Schuster published two collections of the cartoons, *The Sad Sack* (1944) and *New Sad Sack* (1946), and Baker marketed the little GI on ashtrays and drinking glasses as well. After the war came to an end, Consolidated News

Features continued to syndicate a strip featuring Sad Sack (from 1946 to 1958). CBS radio broadcast a regular "Sad Sack" serial during the summer of 1946. Jerry Lewis also made a movie, *The Sad Sack* (Paramount, 1957), that (very loosely) featured the now classic character. By the time that Baker died, of cancer, in 1975, "Sad Sack" was firmly established as one of America's most illustrious cartoon creations.

See:

Baker, George. "The Real Sad Sack." *New York Times Magazine*, 9 July, 1944, 16–17.
Kluger, Steve. "Roll Call: George Baker." In *Yank: The Army Weekly: World War II from the Guys Who Brought You Victory*. New York: St. Martin's, 1991, 352.

Kalman Goldstein

SAHARA (Films). Less than six months after the war in North Africa, the Zoltan Korda–directed *Sahara* (Colombia, 1943) premiered. Adapted by screenwriter John Howard Lawson from a Philip MacDonald story (which, in turn, was inspired by an incident in a Soviet picture), it tells the tale of a group of British, American, and other international soldiers cut off from their fellow troops, desperate for life-sustaining water, and facing imminent attack by a vastly superior German force. Starring Humphrey Bogart as United States Army sergeant Joe Gunn, *Sahara* became one of the greatest propaganda films of World War II. Retreating from Tobruk after its collapse to the victorious Germans, the commander of a small M-3 tank named *Lulubelle*, and his two-man crew manage to collect an odd assortment of men including several British soldiers, a Free Frenchman, a South African, and a Sudanese bringing in tow an Italian prisoner, who also claims to hate the Nazis. The nine men are able to find a small oasis with the only fresh water for miles. Under attack by more than 500 Germans, the disparate group is able to defend the well and, working together, win an improbable victory. Though most die in the process, Gunn and his tank survive to reach Allied lines just in time to hear of the German defeat at El Alamein.

Critics praised the production and its small cast, which also included Lloyd Bridges, Dan Duryea, and Kurt Krueger. Its realistic settings (the desolation of the desert near Camp Young, California, provided a good substitute for the Sahara), its vicious and deceitful Nazis, and its decent, dedicated Allied soldiers guaranteed appreciative audiences. Moviegoers ignored the obvious fact that there were no American tanks fighting alongside the British at the time the action supposedly took place and made it one of the most popular American films of the war.

In 1996, *Sahara*, starring James Belushi as Sergeant Gunn, was remade for the Showtime cable television network. Though the actors try manfully, it suffers in every way when compared with the original.

See:

Quirk, Lawrence J. "Sahara." Chapter 24 in *The Great War Films from The Birth of a Nation to Today*. New York: Citadel, 1994, 88–90.

Suid, Lawrence H. *Guts and Glory: Great American War Movies*. Reading, MA: Addison-Wesley, 1978, 47–51.

David K. Vaughan

THE SANDS OF IWO JIMA (Film). *The Sands of Iwo Jima* (Republic, 1949), directed by Alan Dwan and starring John Wayne, is perhaps the best known and most influential World War II combat film. Written originally for the screen by Harry Brown, author of the earlier successful World War II drama, *A Walk in the Sun* (1946), it opens with a squad of young Marines being trained for battle by the imposing Sergeant Stryker (Wayne) and follows them through the battle of Tarawa to the invasion of Iwo Jima. On the way, they learn that their squad leader is a dedicated professional whose sometimes ruthless tactics have prepared them to survive on the modern battlefield. In the final sequence, after Stryker has been killed by a Japanese sniper just below Mount Suribachi, a corporal who was once his most severe critic (John Agar) is won over to Stryker's view of command and replaces him as squad leader. The American public loved the movie; it was the top-grossing motion picture of the year.

The battle scenes, which combine reenactment and documentary footage, are among the best to be found in Hollywood war films. His performance not only won Wayne an Academy Award nomination for best actor, but it also (together with his role in Howard Hawks's *Red River*, released the same year) revived his faltering acting career and established him as the archetypal American military hero. Over the next two decades he would appear in the uniforms of the army, the navy and the air force, as well as the Marines, but always in the same basic role, that of the tough organization man who never sacrifices his sense of personal integrity.

Ironically, it was Kirk Douglas, not Wayne, who was the first choice for the role of Stryker. With Wayne as the leading character, however, *The Sands of Iwo Jima* became so popular that it was used to recruit Marines during the Korean War, and its image of tough, battle-hardened Marines, as defined by Wayne, continued to attract young men to the corps during the war in Vietnam.

See:

Basinger, Jeanine. *The World War II Combat Film: Anatomy of a Genre*. New York: Columbia University Press, 1986, 163–170.
Parish, James Robert. *The Great Combat Pictures: Twentieth-Century Warfare on the Screen*. Metuchen, NJ: Scarecrow, 1990, 345–349.

Philip J. Landon

SEE HERE, PRIVATE HARGROVE (Military Humor–Films). Marion Hargrove, Jr., was only twenty-two and recently drafted when he submitted humorous essays about army life to his home town *Charlotte* (N.C.) *News*. These evolved into a collection, *See Here, Private Hargrove*, which sold over 2 million copies during World War II. In 1942, it headed the best-seller lists as the number one work of nonfiction, and, even in 1943, its sales were still strong enough to finish in tenth place.

Discovered by playwright Maxwell Anderson at Fort Bragg while researching material, the young Hargrove was included in Anderson's *The Eve of St. Mark* (1943), and his own written work was then accepted by Henry Holt for publication. Prepared largely before Pearl Harbor, *See Here, Private Hargrove* treated basic training as analogous to hazing, reassuring soldiers' families that the service was neither grim nor brutalizing. It was loosely autobiographical, recounting innocuous adventures reminiscent of summer camp. Hargrove scrubbed garbage cans and clumsily handled military equipment, innocently asked embarrassing questions, and bedeviled patient sergeants with his earnest ineptitude. He never seemed truly irritated by army rules, but rather ambled genially toward maturity, self-reliance, and pride. His book was, in many ways, a humorous coming of age story; Private Hargrove was, according to his creator, a "basic good-natured Southern country boy," like the gangly kid next door.

The first book during World War II to introduce civilians to military lingo, *See Here* was immediately popular. Hargrove's ear for sophomoric hyperbole, deadpan humor, and ironic conclusions also made it fun to read. Two movies based on the book were soon produced: *See Here, Private Hargrove* (Metro-Goldwyn-Mayer, 1944) and *What Next, Corporal Hargrove?* (Metro-Goldwyn-Mayer, 1945). Both starred Robert Walker. Hargrove himself became feature editor of **Yank** and was eventually promoted to sergeant. During the war, the *New York Times Magazine* and other periodicals printed articles by Hargrove that commented on soldier morale, behavior, and everyday problems.

See:

Morella, Joe, Edward Z. Epstein, and John Griggs. *The Films of World War II*. Secaucus, NJ: Citadel, 1973, 180–181.

Kalman Goldstein

SINCE YOU WENT AWAY (Film). The American home front during World War II received almost as much attention from Hollywood as did the combat zones. Most pictures sought to inspire and motivate viewers to work harder for the war effort, whether by contributing to War Bond drives, collecting scrap materials, or even taking jobs outside the home, all while keeping a "stiff upper lip" as America's men and boys went off to battle. No single film set on the home front was as all-inclusive of such themes as *Since You Went Away* (Selznick, 1944). Directed by John Cromwell, it starred Claudette Colbert, Jennifer Jones, Shirley Temple, and Joseph Cotton. Based on the published letters of Margaret Buell Wilder to her husband, which had been collected into a book the previous year, the nearly three-hour-long movie was a paean of praise to civilian life on the American home front.

With her husband (who is only seen in a photograph) off at war, Anne Hilton (Colbert) and her two teenaged daughters, Jane (Jones) and Bridget (Temple), aided by their faithful black maid, Fidelia (Hattie McDaniel), attempt to cope with life without a man around. To make ends meet, they take in a boarder, played by the famous character actor Monte Wooley. Jane then falls in love with his grandson (Robert Walker), a young enlistee on the verge of being sent off to the Italian front. With their fabulous house and their country club lifestyle, the Hiltons are clearly no one's "typical" American family, but everyone pitches in to help win the war, nonetheless. Though Jane's boyfriend dies in battle and Commander Hilton is temporarily reported missing in action, the soaring, if melodramatic, conclusion on Christmas Eve has a modestly happy ending after Hilton is rescued at sea and a telegram informs Anne that he will soon be returning home.

Since You Went Away was, in many ways, pure "schmaltz," but even movie critics admitted to shedding tears as they watched it. Even if it won none of the twelve Academy Awards (including best picture, best actress, best supporting actor and actress, and best cinematography) for which it was nominated, audiences loved it, and it took in more than $4 million to become the top-grossing picture of 1944.

See:

Morella, Joe, Edward Z. Epstein, and John Griggs. *The Films of World War II*. Secaucus, NJ: Citadel, 1973, 198–199.
Rogers, Donald I. *Since You Went Away*. New Rochelle, NY: Arlington House, 1973.

M. Paul Holsinger

"THE SINKING OF THE *REUBEN JAMES*" (Folksong). Famed folk singer Woody Guthrie, the musical chronicler of the Dust Bowl in the 1930s, opposed U.S. entry into the spreading world war before June 1941. Once the USSR (whose Communist Party he supported) was threatened, however, his topical music began to reflect the need for preparedness and involvement. When the USS *Reuben James*, an American destroyer patrolling the waters off Iceland, was torpedoed on October 31, 1941, and sunk by a German U-boat, Guthrie quickly penned five stanzas and set them to the tune of the old folk melody, "Wildwood Flower." "The Sinking of the *Reuben James*" attempts to personalize the deaths of the more than 150 who were killed—what were their names, he wonders; did you know any of them? Though the last verse laments that sometimes the worst men fight while far better men die, the lyrics leave no doubt that Nazi Germany, the nation responsible for sinking the *Reuben James*, must be punished.

When war was declared, Guthrie did not shirk from the fight. Though abstaining from military service, he and his close friend and fellow singer, Cisco Houston, joined the U.S. Merchant Marine and throughout the war convoyed important military supplies to men fighting in Africa, Sicily, and the European mainland. Like the men of the now almost mythical *Reuben James*, Guthrie was also torpedoed—twice.

"The Sinking of the *Reuben James*" was often sung during the war years; Houston remembers Woody leading a torpedoed crew in singing it as they awaited rescue. In the late 1950s and beyond, the number also became a staple of the folk music revival. Both Pete Seeger and Houston frequently recorded it, and there are numerous versions still readily available today.

See:

Klein, Joe. *Woody Guthrie: A Life*. New York: Knopf, 1980.
Yates, Janelle. *Woody Guthrie: American Balladeer*. Staten Island, NY: Ward Hill Press, 1995.

M. Paul Holsinger

SLAUGHTERHOUSE-FIVE (Novel-Film). A complex and brilliant novel, *Slaughterhouse-Five* (1969), by Kurt Vonnegut, Jr., draws on its author's experiences as a prisoner of war in Dresden, Germany, where he survived the Allies' notorious firebombing of February 13, 1945. Billy Pilgrim, the story's protagonist, "has come unstuck in time," and the narrator follows him as he leaps randomly from one moment of his life to another. We see Billy's experiences as a prisoner, the firebombing, his postwar marriage and career in optometry, his survival of a plane crash, his meeting with the obscure science fiction novelist Kilgore Trout, and his kidnapping by beings from the planet Tralfamadore.

It is there that Pilgrim learns the philosophy that allows him to cope with his Dresden experience and the mass destruction of life in the twentieth century. Time is not linear and sequential, the Tralfamadorians teach, but already completed, unchanging and unchangeable. Past, present, and future exist simultaneously; death is not something to be mourned as an end because the dead person is still alive elsewhere in time. It is fruitless to try to alter the future because the future has already happened. The narrator adopts this philosophy as he comments on every mention of death with an indifferent, "So it goes." However, in a complex layering, another narrative voice, identified with the author, intervenes, to advocate compassion while celebrating life, and hating death. Thus the Tralfamadorian philosophy becomes associated with worldviews that would objectify humans and cause human destruction.

Slaughterhouse-Five (Universal/Vanadas, 1972) a big-budget film version starring Michael Sacks as Billy and directed by George Roy Hill from a screenplay by Stephen Geller, captures some of the novel's humor but misses its ideas, especially the horror of the Dresden firebombing.

See:

Klinkowitz, Jerome. *Slaughterhouse-five: Reforming the Novel and the World*. Boston: Twayne, 1990.
Schatt, Stanley. "Vonnegut's Dresden Novel: *Slaughterhouse-five*." Chapter 4 in *Kurt Vonnegut, Jr*. Boston: Twayne, 1976, 81–96.

Robert L. McLaughlin

SMITH, KATE (Entertainer). To many Americans in the 1930s, 1940s, and 1950s, no one symbolized what was good about this country better than the famous singer and radio personality Kathryn Elizabeth "Kate" Smith. Indeed, when Franklin Delano Roosevelt presented her to King George VI of England in 1939, he said simply: "This is Kate Smith. This is America." Smith, always known for her oversized body—baseball great Yogi Berra's famous quip, "It's not over 'til the Fat Lady sings," had her in mind—made her radio debut on May 1, 1931. Immensely popular, she soon became the number one attraction on the air.

In November 1938, Smith introduced Irving Berlin's "**God Bless America**" on her show, obtaining from him the exclusive rights to sing it. Even before Pearl Harbor, she turned it into the unofficial national anthem of the country. With the outbreak of war, she entertained troops in the United States and Canada at **United Services Organization (USO)** shows, but her most important role was raising money for war bonds. In four years, she traveled more than 520,000 miles and sold more than $600 million in bonds, far more than any other person. On one radio marathon alone, she was responsible for raising $105,392,700, the most money collected during the war in any single event.

During the 1950s, Kate began to appear on television as well as radio. Though her popularity waned in the mid-1950s, her simple style, her beautiful contralto voice, and her intimate connection with "God Bless America," always made her one of the nation's most famous performers. Just before her death in 1986, President Ronald Reagan, who starred with her in *This Is the Army* (1943), awarded Smith a special medal of honor in commemoration of her service to the country. She was, he said, "a patriot in every sense of the word."

See:

Pitts, Michael. *Kate Smith: A Bio-Bibliography*. Westport, CT: Greenwood Press, 1988.
Smith, Kate. *Upon My Lips a Song*. New York: Funk and Wagnalls, 1960.

M. Paul Holsinger

SNAFU **(Comedy).** Until their rerelease for home video (Bosko, 1990–1992), only military personnel had seen the twenty-eight *Snafu* animated cartoons, which were produced from June 1943 through October 1945. At their height, however, millions in uniform sat expectantly through each *Army-Navy Screen Magazine* newsreel to laugh uproariously at "Snafu" (the acronym for "situation normal, all fucked up") or watch the collections repeatedly.

Late in 1942, Frank Capra suggested creating three- to four-minute cartoons that would improve troop morale and socialize men to military discipline. When Walt Disney's terms were rejected, Warner Brothers received the contract and did all but two. Chuck Jones, "Friz" Freleng, Frank Tashlin, and Robert Clampett directed them; Mel Blanc supplied the voices. Theodore Geisel ("Dr. Seuss") wrote at least nine rhymed scripts.

Though uncredited, episodes of *Snafu* bore the unmistakable stamp of Warner

Brothers cartoons: wild visual and verbal puns; sudden, frantic slapstick; popular song parodies or classical music used for commentary in films without dialogue; caricatures and tag lines of popular radio comedians. Unlike cartoons for the general public, however, these were risqué for the time. "Snafu" was droopy, with jug ears, sleepy eyes, and a bulbous nose; he looked like Elmer Fudd and, thanks to Blanc, sounded like a stammerless Porky Pig.

Snafu presented a series of "Bad Examples" to avoid. Earlier episodes dealt with self-control, military bearing and pride, weapons maintenance, and the need to appreciate home-front sacrifices. Others justified censorship or urged anti-malarial precautions. Most of the later cartoons were more relaxed. Two that were done at war's end went unreleased; another, "Going Home," was pulled because, at the very moment that the Manhattan Project was accelerating, it made references to a "Superbomb."

See:

Culbert, David H. "Private Snafu: The Use of Humor in World War II Army Film." *Prospects. An Annual Journal of American Cultural Studies* 1 (1975): 81–96.
Friedwald, Will, and Jerry Beck. "Private Snafu (1942–1945)." Appendix in *The Warner Brothers Cartoons*. Metuchen, NJ: Scarecrow, 1981, 257–259.

Kalman Goldstein

A SOLDIER'S PLAY **(Drama-Film).** *A Soldier's Play* by Charles Fuller won both the Pulitzer Prize for drama and the New York Drama Critics Circle Prize as best American play of the 1981–1982 season. Staged by the Negro Ensemble Company (NEC), it opened in New York on November 20, 1981, and went through 468 performances. Set entirely at Fort Neal, Louisiana, during 1944, it tells a brutal story of racism between a company of African-American troops and their white officers and the subsequent murder of the top black noncommissioned officer (NCO) in the unit, Technical Sergeant Vernon Walters.

A young black law school graduate from Howard University, Captain Richard Davenport, is sent by the Army to find the killer. Before he can do so, he, too, must deal with the prejudice that continually surfaces because of his color. In the end, after careful detective work, Davenport is able to catch the murderers, who turn out to be not the obvious white segregationists everyone initially suspected but fellow members of Walters's own unit. The young officer earns the grudging admiration of the base commander, who is forced to admit that he was wrong and that he will have to get used to having "Negroes" in command. In the last, and perhaps most quoted, line in the play, Davenport replies: "Oh, you'll get used to it—you can bet your ass on that." There are, however, no "winners" in *A Soldier's Play*. In an ironic coda, Fuller has Davenport note that the entire company, officers and enlisted men, were killed during a battle in the Ruhr.

Director Norman Jewison turned the play into a film, *A Soldier's Story* (Caldix, 1984). Fuller was brought to Hollywood to write the screenplay. Jewison used most of the original NEC cast, including Adolf Caesar as Walters and the then relatively unknown Denzel Washington as Melvin Peterson, Walters's murderer. Grossing more than $22 million at the box office, the movie was highly praised by critics. It received Academy Award nominations for best picture, best supporting actor (Caesar), and best adapted screenplay (Fuller).

See:

DeMaster, William W. "Charles Fuller and 'A Soldier's Play': Attacking Prejudice, Challenging Form." In *Black Literature Criticism*, ed. James P. Draper. Vol. 2. Detroit: Gale, 1992, 43–56.
Storhoff, Cary. "Reflections of Identity in *A Soldier's Story.*" *Literature/Film Quarterly* 19 (1991): 21–26.

M. Paul Holsinger

SO PROUDLY WE HAIL (Film). *So Proudly We Hail* (Paramount, 1943) is the best American film to portray the heroic behavior of the many United States Army nurses on Bataan and Corregidor following the Japanese attack in late 1941. The Mark Sandrich–directed motion picture starred Claudette Colbert and Paulette Goddard. Although the screenplay by Allan Scott is at times melodramatic, it convincingly focuses on the hardships the nurses underwent as they retreated with the Allied forces under the Japanese onslaught. The movie makes clear the harrowing conditions these women worked under while caring for the wounded and dying.

Most of the film is a flashback, as Lieutenant Janet Davidson (Colbert) suffers from posttraumatic stress syndrome and her companions discuss how they can help her recovery. They recall how their unit came to be assigned to the Far East, the difficulty of nursing in the caves at Corregidor, and the evacuation at the beaches. Several episodes in particular contribute to Janet's condition, including a serious burn while trying to rescue a surgeon, her one-night honeymoon with Lieutenant John Summers (George Reeves) before he is sent into battle, and the death of fellow nurse Lieutenant Olivia D'arcy (Veronica Lake), who becomes a human bomb and blows herself up to provide a distraction so that the rest of the nurses can escape from the Japanese.

The production was one of Paramount's biggest hits of the year and was shown with a trailer promoting the need for volunteers for the army nurse corps. It is notable for being one of the few American releases to show women in combat conditions.

See:

Basinger, Jeanine. *The World War II Combat Film: Anatomy of a Genre.* New York: Columbia University Press, 1986, 226–235.
Parish, James Robert. *The Great Combat Pictures: Twentieth-Century Warfare on the Screen.* Metuchen, NJ: Scarecrow, 1990, 365–369.

Sally E. Parry

SPY SMASHER (Comic Book Hero). During World War II, dozens of American comic book heroes became hugely popular as they bested Nazis and other totalitarian enemies of democracy. One of the most important of the many men (and a few women) was Fawcett Comics' incredibly patriotic Spy Smasher. Appearing early in 1940 in the first issue of *Whiz Comics*, Spy Smasher, or, as he was better known out of disguise, Alan Armstrong, fought spies and enemy saboteurs including the Mask, one of Germany's most notorious and diabolical villains. So well liked was the Armstrong character that, in 1941, Fawcett assigned some of its better artists, including C. C. Beck and Emil Gershwin, to create an entire comic book series around the hero. Not until the war was over and no more military enemies remained for Armstrong to fight, did the series finally come to an end. In 1942, Republic Pictures also cast Kane Richmond as the brave Spy Smasher battling the Mask's evil plots week after week in a cliff-hanging serial.

Every month, *Spy Smasher Comics* featured one or more stories of its famed hero fighting Nazi totalitarianism. Privy to all sorts of "inside" information because of his engagement to the daughter of the head of America's naval intelligence program, Armstrong went to Europe in 1942. There, in his green World War I flying ace–like costume, featuring a large red diamond insignia, he constantly fought evil close to its source. On one occasion, for instance, he infiltrated Germany and killed a Hitler look-alike. In another, he stopped in its tracks a proposed Nazi invasion of the United States.

With war's end, Fawcett attempted unsuccessfully until 1953 to transform Spy Smasher into an everyday American crime fighter, replacing his aviator's garb with a Dick Tracy trench coat. After DC Comics acquired the firm, Spy Smasher was reintroduced in 1972 in a *Justice League of America* book. As late as 1996, the character was revived once again in yet another different volume.

See:

Goulart, Ron. "Spy Smasher." In *The Encyclopedia of American Comics from 1897 to the Present*, ed. Ron Goulart. New York: Facts on File, 1990, 344.

Eric D. Sweetwood

STAGE DOOR AND HOLLYWOOD CANTEENS (Entertainment-Radio-Films). Even before the United States entered World War II, a number of prominent Broadway personalities created the roots for what was to become the famous Stage Door Canteen. In January 1940, Antoinette Perry (for whom Broadway's Tony Award is named), Gertrude Lawrence, and others founded the American Theatre Wing of the British War Relief Society to raise money for that nation's refugees and orphaned children. After Pearl Harbor, it was easy to transform the organization, now greatly expanded with the addition of dozens of female and male performers, into the American Theatre Wing War Service.

Though the group continued raising money for war services, by far its most famous role was the establishment of a canteen on New York's Forty-fourth Street between Broadway and Eighth Avenue. Servicemen could dance with many beautiful or famous actresses or be served food by the same stars they saw on the stage or in the movies. Ironically, service women were not allowed in the Stage Door Canteen because its founders were determined not to encourage any "romance" in their club. So popular was the original Stage Door Canteen that, by the end of the war, others were established in Boston, Philadelphia, Cleveland, Newark, San Francisco, and Washington, D.C.

A similar place to entertain the American military personnel on the West Coast was the Hollywood Canteen. Academy Award–winning actress Bette Davis and Hollywood stars such as John Garfield founded this newer version of the canteen in 1942 for those about to be shipped to or just back from the Pacific. Movie stars appeared in the evenings with regularity to dance or just talk with young, and often lonely, GIs. As Maxene Andrews remembered years later: "No one simply performed at the canteens. You sang or danced or . . . whatever your specialty was but you also waited on tables, danced with the guys or gals, and provided a friendly or sympathetic ear whenever the occasion arose in the conversation, which was often" (Andrews, 84).

Inevitably, both radio and the motion picture industry sought to capitalize on the success of the canteens. On July 30, 1942, CBS went on the air with a regular Thursday evening variety show entitled *Stagedoor Canteen*. A full-ranging variety show, which was often broadcast from the New York canteen itself, the show remained on the air throughout the war years as one of the nation's most popular. Several songs also kept the canteens in the public spotlight. Irving Berlin included "I Left My Heart at the Stage-Door Canteen" in his review, ***This Is the Army***. There was also another piece called "Hollywood Canteen." Not to be outdone, the movie industry made star-ladden pictures ostensibly dealing with both venues: *Stage Door Canteen* (United Artists, 1943) and *Hollywood Canteen* (Warner Brothers, 1944). The first, which was based on a screenplay by Delmar Daves, is a pleasant account of the supposed romance of a shy GI with one of the canteen's hostesses. Its two-hour-plus length allowed for almost seventy cameo appearances by actors, actresses, and musical performers. The *Hollywood Canteen* is little different, but the large number of stars, including the Canteen's founders, Davis and Garfield, along with top-name singers such as the **Andrews Sisters** and Eddie Cantor, pleased the viewers, who packed theaters across the nation.

See:

Andrews, Maxene, and Bill Gilbert. *Over Here, Over There: The Andrews Sisters and the USO Stars in World War II*. New York: Zebra Books, 1993.
Woll, Allan L. *The Hollywood Musical Goes to War*. Chicago: Nelson-Hall, 1983.

M. Paul Holsinger

***STALAG 17* (Drama-Film).** The World War II prisoner of war experience is perhaps nowhere better explored than in Donald Joseph Bevan and Edmund

Trzcinski's successful Broadway drama, *Stalag 17*. Staged by José Ferrer, the play, by two former prisoners of war (POWs), is claustrophobically set in a single barrack of a large German POW camp during a Christmas season. Starring John Ericson, Robert Strauss, and Harvey Lembeck, *Stalag 17* opened on May 8, 1951, and ran for 472 performances before closing in June 1952.

The popularity of the play led directly to its being transformed into an even more popular movie, *Stalag 17* (Paramount, 1953). Directed by Billy Wilder, who also coscripted the screenplay with Edwin Blum, the film depicts the antics the prisoners engaged in to fight boredom and the tension caused by the certainty that the Germans have planted a spy among them. Suspicion falls on Sefton (William Holden), a cynical operator who manages to profit by capitalizing on the other prisoners' desires. He despises the others for their weaknesses but revels in power he has never had before. A crisis comes when the Germans capture a downed American flier (Don Taylor) who, while a prisoner, sabotaged a munitions train; the POWs must help him escape before the German plant can discover him. Beaten and ostracized, Sefton discovers the real spy, Price (Peter Graves). As the POWs create a diversion after dark by shoving Price into the camp yard where he is shot down by the guards, Sefton and the flier escape through a tunnel.

Stalag 17's power is marred by heavy-handed attempts at comedy—the lame-brained schemes of Animal and Harry (Strauss and Lembeck)—and pathos—with the POWs caring for a brain-damaged soldier (Robinson Stone). It was, however, praised by critics. William Holden won the 1953 Academy Award as best actor, nominations went to Wilder as best director and Strauss as best supporting actor. Many aspects of the film were adopted and exaggerated between 1965 and 1971 by the TV comedy series ***Hogan's Heroes***, most notably the vainglorious Commandant (Otto Preminger) and the dim-witted Sergeant Schulz (Sig Ruman).

See:

Foy, David A. *For You the War Is Over. American Prisoners of War in Nazi Germany.* New York: Stein and Roy, 1984.
Parish, James Robert. *The Great Combat Pictures: Twentieth-Century Warfare on the Screen.* Metuchen, NJ: Scarecrow, 1990, 370–372.

Robert L. McLaughlin

***THE STORY OF G.I. JOE* (Film).** *The Story of G.I. Joe* (United Artists, 1945), a movie about the early war experiences of famed war correspondent **Ernie Pyle**, was being shot when he left for the Pacific for the last time. Filmed by longtime director William Wellman almost as if it were a documentary and filled with many clips of actual army combat footage for authenticity, the production is an honest tribute to the common footsoldiers about whom Pyle so often wrote. Wellman makes no effort to glorify war; if the picture has one central theme, it is that the common soldier lived, and died, miserably.

Popular character actor Burgess Meredith gives one of his strongest performances in the role of Pyle. A young Robert Mitchum plays Lieutenant Henry
Waskow, the hero of Pyle's most praised and reprinted column from Italy
(though, sadly, his character is renamed Walker so it will sound less Jewish).
When the film premiered in late October 1945, audiences packed theaters, and
it was uniformly praised. Critics applauded; General Dwight Eisenhower called
it "the greatest war picture I have ever seen."

The Story of G.I. Joe received a host of Academy Awards and New York
Film Critics Circle nominations, including one for best supporting actor (Mitchum). Rarely seen today, it was almost certainly the least glamorous war movie
made during World War II—gritty, realistic, and often very moving.

See:

Suid, Lawrence H. *Guts and Glory: Great American War Movies.* Reading, MA:
    Addison-Wesley, 1978, 62–69.

M. Paul Holsinger

SUMMER OF MY GERMAN SOLDIER (Young Adult Novel–Film). *Summer
of My German Soldier* (1973), by Bette Greene, recounts the story of a troubled
adolescent Jewish girl living in a small Arkansas town during World War II.
Narrated in the voice of twelve-year-old Patty Bergen, the novel takes place
during a hot summer when patriotic feelings are running high. Patty, whose only
friend is the family's African-American housekeeper, Ruth, is a lonely and mis-
understood girl, who is inclined to make up stories, abused by her father, and
alternately insulted and ignored by her mother. She meets a German prisoner,
Anton Reiker, at her father's store; he speaks nicely to her, and, after he escapes
from a local prisoner of war camp, she hides him in the family garage, supplying
him with food and clothing. He introduces her to new ideas and authors, and
she blossoms under his friendship. The idyll does not last, however. After Anton
leaves, law enforcement authorities learn of Patty's role in his escape and tell
her that he was killed in New York as an escaped prisoner. Patty's parents are
forced to give up their store because of the publicity about their daughter, and
Patty is sent to a reformatory as a result of her treasonous actions. Despite her
punishment, she has, at least briefly, transcended barriers of religious, national,
and racial identity.

Named one of the American Library Association's Notable Books of the Year,
Summer of My German Soldier was also a finalist for the National Book Award
the year it was published. It was made into an NBC television movie in October
1978 from a screenplay by Jane-Howard Hammerstein. Directed by Michael
Tuchner, the fine, though at times overly sentimental, adaptation starred Kristy
McNichol as Patty and Bruce Davison as Anton. Esther Rolle was awarded an
Emmy as the outstanding supporting actress in a limited series or special for
her portrayal of Ruth.

That same year, 1978, Greene wrote a sequel to Patty's tale. *Morning Is a*

Long Time Coming follows her to young womanhood and a break with her abusive parents.

See:

Alvine, Lynne. "Bette Greene." In *Writers for Young Adults*, ed. Ted Hipple. Vol. 2. New York: Scribner's, 1997, 59–68.

Sally E. Parry

TALES OF THE SOUTH PACIFIC (**Novel-Musical-Film**). James A. Michener, a naval officer during World War II, was posted to the South Pacific in the spring of 1944. For the next year and a half, he toured dozens of American bases inspecting aircraft. From those trips came *Tales of the South Pacific*, a collection of nineteen casually interrelated stories which won the 1948 Pulitzer Prize for Literature.

Set during the crucial months of 1942–1943, the yarns center on events leading up to the U.S. attack on the fictitious island of Kuralei. Emerging from the pages is a picture of the real war in the Pacific, a war of hurry up and wait. There are dozens of "typical" American men and women whose lives repeatedly intersect. No one is a central figure throughout, but navy lieutenant Tony Fry (eventually killed during the attack on Kuralei), nurse Nellie Forbush, the native entrepreneur Bloody Mary, and the womanizing French planter Emile De Becque all are memorable.

Though sales of the book were at first slim, Broadway producer Leland Hayward and director Joshua Logan decided that at least some of the material could be turned into a musical. Richard Rodgers and Oscar Hammerstein II, the most successful theatrical writing team of the decade, agreed to create a show centering on the story of Nellie Forbush's romance with, and ultimate commitment to, Emile De Beque. *South Pacific* opened on Broadway to rave reviews on April 7, 1949. Starring Mary Martin, one of Broadway's most famous musical stars, as Nellie and operatic performer Ezio Pinza as Emile, it was called by one critic "a show of rare entertainment . . . a musical play to be cherished" (*New York Herald Tribune*, April 8, 1949). It won the Pulitzer Prize for drama in 1950 (the first time that any play based on a Pulitzer Prize–winning novel had won a similar prize), eight Tony Awards, and the New York Drama Critics award for the season's best musical play. When it closed on January 16, 1954, the show's Broadway run was a near-record (for the time) 1,925 performances. The original cast phonograph album soon reached "gold" status with sales of more than $1 million. There have been repeated revivals of *South Pacific* since 1954 throughout the United States, Great Britain, Australia, South Africa, Sweden, and Japan.

Joshua Logan also attempted to translate his stage success onto the Hollywood screen. Film critics were lukewarm, but *South Pacific* (20th Century–Fox, 1958), which was loaded with a number of young photogenic stars including Mitzi Gaynor as Nellie, was overwhelmingly popular in both the United States and

Europe. *Tales of the South Pacific*, in all its incarnations, remains one of the most famous, if not truly great, literary works to come from the Pacific theater of war.

See:

Beidler, Philip D. "South Pacific and American Remembering, or, 'Josh, We're Going to Buy This Son of a Bitch!' " *Journal of American Studies* 27 (1993): 207–222.
Mordden, Ethan. "South Pacific." Chapter 5 in *Rodgers and Hammerstein*. New York: Harry N. Abrams, 1992, 106–125.

M. Paul Holsinger

"THERE'S A STAR-SPANGLED BANNER WAVING SOMEWHERE" (Song).

During World War II, dozens of country-and-western songs focused on the American effort. Among the many were such forgettable pieces as "I Spoke to Jefferson on Guadalcanal" and "I'll Take Good Care of Mommy While You're Gone," but none was more popular than "There's A Star-Spangled Banner Waving Somewhere." Written in 1942 by Paul Roberts and Shelby Darnell (though some students of country music believe the publisher Bob Miller was the actual author), it was recorded initially by all-star performer Elton Britt. The maudlin lyrics tell the story of a youth with a crippled leg who desperately wants to fight for his country and do something heroic. He pleads with the military recruiter to find a place for him so that when he dies he will go to that special place in heaven where the American flag flies proudly everyday.

By the end of the year, "There's a Star-Spangled Banner Waving Somewhere" was the top-selling hit in the country field, as well as one of the first songs to cross over unto the popular charts, where it stayed in the top twenty for many weeks. Eventually, more than 4 million copies of Britt's recording were sold, and it became the first country number to win gold record recognition. President Franklin Roosevelt even asked Britt to perform the song at the White House. Overwhelmingly popular throughout the war, it later was recognized by *Variety* as one of the top hits of the first fifty years of the twentieth century.

In 1960, another "cowboy" singer, Red River Dave, re-recorded "There's A Star-Spangled Banner Waving Somewhere" and put it together with "The Ballad of Francis Powers," a paean to the American U-2 pilot who had recently been shot down by the Russians while spying over that country.

See:

Chinn, Jennie A. "There's a Star-Spangled Banner Waving Somewhere: Country-Western Songs of World War II." John Edwards Memorial Foundation Quarterly 16 (1980): 74–80.

M. Paul Holsinger

THEY WERE EXPENDABLE (Nonfiction-Film).

They Were Expendable (Metro-Goldwyn-Mayer, 1945), John Ford's elegiac tribute to the PT boat crews engaged in a doomed rear-guard action during the Japanese invasion of the

Philippines, is one of the two or three best combat films made by a Hollywood studio during World War II. It begins in the days immediately before Pearl Harbor as naval Lieutenant John Brickley (Robert Montgomery) and his executive officer, Lieutenant Rusty Ryan (John Wayne), try to prove the value of the newly developed PT boat to their skeptical superiors. When the Japanese strike, the PT crews are assigned housekeeping duties that rarely allow them to engage the enemy. As loyal professionals, however, Brickley and Ryan must accept the fact that following orders comes before heroics. Eventually, the squadron is given the job of carrying General Douglas MacArthur, his family, and his staff out of Bataan to the planes waiting to fly them to Australia, but it then returns to the embattled peninsula to fight until the end. Each mission takes its toll of boats and crews until the squadron ceases to exist as a fighting unit. The surviving men are dispatched to the army, where defeat and captivity await them; Brickley and Ryan are assigned to Washington, D.C., to plan for the day when the Americans will return.

Based on William L. White's 1942 nonfictional account of the PT boat squadrons in the Philippines before the fall of those islands (also called *They Were Expendable*), the production marked an interesting point of transition in the Hollywood war film as a genre, in the heroes of Ford's movies, and in the screen persona of John Wayne. War pictures made before 1945 were often referred to as ''westerns in uniform'' because of the single-handed exploits of their heroes. In the years following World War II, their protagonists were portrayed less as individualists than as dedicated professionals noted for their institutional loyalty. Wayne, who had played rugged and sometimes self-destructive individualists before and during World War II, became associated with the professional military man ready to sacrifice his private dreams in order to serve his country. After *They Were Expendable*, he created many versions of this new heroic role in such war-related epics as **The Sands of Iwo Jima** (1949) and **The Green Berets** (1968).

See:

Kane, Kathryn. *Visions of War: Hollywood Combat Films of World War II*. Ann Arbor, MI: UMI, 1982, 135–144.
Parish, James Robert. *The Great Combat Pictures: Twentieth-Century Warfare on the Screen*. Metuchen, NJ: Scarecrow, 1990, 390–395.

Philip J. Landon

THE THIN RED LINE (Novel-Film). When James Jones's *The Thin Red Line* (1962) was published in a book-length format (it originally appeared in that year's August, September, and October *Playboy* magazine), reviewers almost universally praised it as one of the best novels to come out of World War II. A clearly fictional account of the victorious United States attack on the Japanese-held island of Guadalcanal, this middle work in Jones's trilogy dealing with the American military during the era of World War II (1951's **From Here to Eter-**

nity and 1978's posthumous *Whistle*, are numbers one and three, respectively) follows a company of young Marines from its initial landing in August 1942 to the campaign's conclusion, more than five months later. In attempting to show the reality of war, Jones convincingly demonstrates how tenuous is the thin line between life and death, normal and abnormal behavior, or success and failure.

Jones's view of war in this creative and important work is always fatalistic; the only "successful" fighting men, he maintains, are those who understand that their names are "written down in the rolls of the already dead." Only when that happens does a man's individual ego vanish to be replaced by a hardened ability to kill without thought. Some of "Charlie Company's" men learn this lesson and live, though only to prepare for the invasion of yet another enemy island; those who do not, die ugly, bloody deaths.

Two years after its publication, *The Thin Red Line* (Allied Artists, 1964) was transformed by director Andrew Marton into a weak and generally failed Hollywood motion picture. Bernard Gordon's unsatisfactory screenplay concentrates the bulk of its attention on the relationship between Corporal Gregory Fife (Keir Dullea) and First Sergeant Edward "Mad" Welsh (Jack Warden)—only a small part of the novel. The combat-centered film is always bloody but misses most of the "message" that Jones set out to convey. Long out of print and unavailable, even on VHS, this first screen version will be replaced in 1998 by a new one, featuring an all-star cast headed by Sean Penn and directed by famous writer-director Terrence Malick.

See:

Quirk, Lawrence. "The Thin Red Line." Chapter 54 in *The Great War Films from The Birth of a Nation to Today.* New York: Citadel, 1994, 186–188.
Uffen, Ellen S. "James Jones' Trilogy, or Is War Really Hell?" *Midamerica. The Yearbook of the Society for the Study of Midwestern Literature* 10 (1983): 139–151.

David K. Vaughan

THIRTY SECONDS OVER TOKYO (Autobiography-Film). *Thirty Seconds over Tokyo* (1944), by Air Force Captain Ted W. Lawson and journalist Robert Considine, recounts Lawson's experiences in the Doolittle Raid on the mainland of Japan. As the military fought a defensive war after Pearl Harbor, President Roosevelt sought to strike directly at the enemy. Lawson was one of sixteen pilots chosen by then–Lieutenant Colonel James "Jimmy" Doolittle to participate in a daring plan to launch fully loaded B-25s from an aircraft carrier, bomb six Japanese cities, and then fly on to China for refueling and escape.

Lawson describes the secret training in Florida, where the pilots learned to take off on a shortened runway, and the tense voyage toward Japan on the *Hornet.* When Japanese ships spotted the carrier, the planes had to take off 400 miles farther away from Japan than planned. As a result, although the bombers hit their targets around noon on April 18, 1942 (scoring a victory for American morale and embarrassing the Japanese military), they lacked the fuel to reach the Chinese airfields. All but one B-25 crashed; Lawson and his crew were seriously injured when they landed on a Japanese-occupied island off the Chinese coast. Hundreds of Chinese cared for the raiders and helped them escape, but Lawson's left leg had to be amputated. He explores the anxieties of the returning wounded soldier, successfully resolving them when his wife and the paternalistic Doolittle welcome him home.

A film version of the best-selling book, directed by Mervyn Leroy from a screenplay by Dalton Trumbo, starred Van Johnson as Lawson and Spencer Tracy as Doolittle. Praised for its documentary-like quality, *Thirty Seconds over Tokyo* (Metro-Goldwyn-Mayer, 1944) emphasized the events leading up to the raid and the raid itself rather than the escape so as to introduce the themes of teamwork and interservice cooperation.

See:

Oxford, Edward. "Against All Odds." *American History Illustrated* 27.1 (March/April 1992): 28–43, 60–65, 67.

Suid, Lawrence. *Sailing on the Silver Screen: Hollywood and the U.S. Navy.* Annapolis, MD: Naval Institute Press, 1996, 77–79.

Robert L. McLaughlin

THIS IS THE ARMY (Musicial-Film). Of the many all-service shows staged during the war years, none was more famous than Irving Berlin's *This Is the Army*. In 1942, at the request of the army, Berlin, who was a veteran of World War I, made a return visit to Camp Upton, New York, where he had been stationed during that earlier conflict. In 1918, he wrote the popular military revue *Yip, Yip, Yaphank* while there; now, after talking with many of the new draftees about their experiences, he completed a second all-army show, which premiered in New York on July 4, 1942. Following a twelve-week run on Broadway, the show, with its host of original songs including the very popular "I Left My Heart at the Stage Door Canteen," toured the United States. Over $10 million was raised and assigned to the United States Army Emergency Relief; another $.35 million was given to British relief agencies after the show's London run. More than 2.5 million men and women in uniform saw the revue before its last performance, on October 22, 1945. For his efforts, Berlin received the Medal of Merit from General George C. Marshall.

Director Michael Curtiz transformed *This Is the Army* (Warner Brothers, 1943) into a major Hollywood musical using many of the original Army performers and a host of major actors and actresses, including then-Lieutenant Ronald Reagan in a starring role. Critics praised the film effusively, though, seen today, it seems overly saccharine. During the war, however, its overt flag-waving patriotism unquestionably was a morale booster for all Americans.

See:

Cabaniss, Dan. "*This Is the Army*: The Show Musical Goes to War." *Film and History: An Interdisciplinary Journal of Film and Television Studies* 27 (1997): 54–61.

M. Paul Holsinger

TO HELL AND BACK (**Autobiography-Film**). Audie Murphy was the most highly decorated soldier in American history. While serving with the Third Infantry Division in Italy, France, and Germany during World War II, he was credited with killing approximately 240 Germans and wounding or capturing dozens more. As a result of such heroics, Murphy won thirty-seven medals, including the Silver Star, the Distinguished Service Cross, and nation's highest award, the Medal of Honor.

Murphy's boyish good looks made him a natural for Hollywood, and in 1948, he began starring in one adventure film after another as a young erstwhile hero fighting evil wherever he found it. The following year, he published his World War II memoirs under the title, *To Hell and Back*. The frequently exciting account caught an appreciative public's imagination. With his acting career placing him repeatedly in the popular spotlight (he won plaudits in 1951, for instance, as the lead in John Huston's version of *The Red Badge of Courage*), plans were made to turn the book account of the young actor's former heroics into a full-length motion picture.

Four years later, those plans became reality when director Jesse Hibbs, working from Gil Doud's screenplay, filmed *To Hell and Back* (Universal International, 1955). At first, Murphy was apprehensive about making the picture. He wanted to highlight not his exploits but those of all infantrymen in the Army. "I love the damned Army," he wrote. "It was father, mother, brother to me for years. It made me somebody, gave me self-respect" (Graham 241). However, the final production, featuring Murphy (portraying himself), David Janssen, and Marshall Thompson, was far more a paean of praise to one man than to many. Theatergoers, however, loved it. A critical and commercial success, it became the firm's all-time box office champion. Murphy (named by several influential polls one of the year's best actors) now became an authentic folk hero, "truly the Sergeant York of World War II conquering everything in sight" (Graham 249).

In the years after *To Hell and Back*, Murphy continued acting, but almost always in stereotypical roles that offered little room for growth. Sadly, by the time of his death in a plane crash in 1971, most Americans no longer remembered his famous exploits, but both his book and movie biography remain as testimony to those heroic years.

See:

Graham, Don. *No Name on the Bullet: A Biography of Audie Murphy*. New York: Viking, 1989.

David K. Vaughan

TOKYO ROSE (**Historical Figure**). During World War II, many American fighting men in the South Pacific found a pleasant, if brief, diversion from the rigors of conflict by listening regularly to a Japanese Broadcasting Corporation propaganda program featuring the latest recorded music from the United States and hosted by a sultry-voiced woman they called "Tokyo Rose." Far from its intent of promoting homesickness, diluting listeners' patriotism, and weakening morale, listeners found the program harmless and even entertaining, and they generally liked it. When word spread that the young broadcaster was an American traitor to her country, her fame grew.

At war's end, a search to find the real Tokyo Rose began. Even though the weight of postwar evidence supported the conclusion that the name "Tokyo Rose" was simply a collective label applied to as many as twenty-seven different women who broadcast for the Japanese during the war, a second-generation Japanese-American, Iva Ikuko Toguri d'Aquino, foolishly identified herself to U.S. officials as the person for whom they were searching. A native of Los Angeles and a 1941 graduate of the University of California in her hometown, Toguri was visiting an ailing aunt in Japan when war broke out with the United States, and she was forced to remain in that country for the duration. She began broadcasting on Radio Tokyo's Zero Hour program in November 1943, calling herself "Your favorite enemy, Ann" or, alternatively, "Orphan Ann," but never, according to available evidence, "Tokyo Rose." After marrying Felippe d'Aquino (a Portuguese citizen who worked for the Domei News Agency) in 1944, she continued broadcasting for Radio Tokyo until August 1945.

Long before her treason conviction, Toguri d'Aquino was tried in the court of a largely vindictive press and an unforgiving public anxious to punish anyone even remotely connected to the Japanese attack on Pearl Harbor in December 1941. National Commander of the American Legion James F. O'Neill, newspaper columnist and radio commentator Walter Winchell, and FBI director J. Edgar Hoover were among those prominent leaders who sought Toguri d'Aquino's prosecution for treason. Eventually, she was charged with eight counts of treason. Found guilty on one count, she was sentenced to ten years' imprisonment and fined $10,000; she served six of those years before being paroled. In January 1977, President Gerald Ford issued her a full and unconditional pardon.

See:

Hunt, Russell W. *The Hunt for Tokyo Rose.* Lanham, MD: Madison, 1990.

Philip J. Harwood

THE TRUE GLORY (Documentary). Produced by Garson Kanin and jointly directed by Kanin and Carol Reed, *The True Glory* (1945) is an Anglo-American documentary compiled from the work of the nearly 1,400 cameramen who recorded the war in Europe from the invasion at Normandy to the final defeat of Germany. The winner of the Academy Award for the best feature-length documentary of 1945, it begins somberly with footage of the Battle of the Atlantic as the German submarine fleet threatens to cut off the supply of men and weapons from the United States, making an invasion impossible. Next come scenes of the allies gathering in Great Britain, where senior officers plan, and their troops train, for the invasion. After covering D-Day in detail, the film follows the Allies across Europe to Germany. It ends as the Russian and American armies meet and Berlin falls. The narration—delivered in an elevated, Shake-spearean style—lends an epic grandeur to the events it describes.

The title is borrowed from Sir Francis Drake who, at the height of the Spanish Armada, wrote a colleague: "There must be a beginning of any great matter but the continuing unto the end until it be thoroughly finished, yields the true glory" (Letter, 134). Speaking to European campaign veterans on their way to take part in the anticipated invasion of Japan, General Dwight Eisenhower makes the significance of this allusion very clear.

Although *The True Glory*, released just after the end of World War II, has never received the attention devoted to more famous World War II documentary films such as **The Memphis Belle** (1943), *Desert Victory* (1943), or *The Battle of San Pietro* (1944), it deserves a place among the very best of World War II documentaries.

See:

Barsam, Richard M. *Nonfiction Film: A Critical History*. Rev. and enlarged ed. Bloo-mington: Indiana University Press, 1992, 235–236.
Letter, Francis Drake to Sir Francis Walsingham, May 17, 1587, quoted in *Navy Records Society* 11 (1898): 134.

Philip J. Landon

TWELVE O'CLOCK HIGH (Novel-Film–Television Series). Many novels suf-fer when screenwriters attempt to translate an author's words to film. *Twelve O'Clock High* (1948) by Beirne Lay and Sy Bartlett is one of the few exceptions. The book, a thoughtful, but flawed, story of the pressure of command, was repeatedly marred by a series of weak, romantic interludes. When the authors adapted it to the screen, minus all hints of romance, however, it became one of the finest, most intelligent World War II motion pictures.

Henry King's *Twelve O'Clock High* (20th Century–Fox, 1949) was one of three war movies made that year (**The Sands of Iwo Jima** and **Battleground** were the other two) whose box office success encouraged Hollywood producers to revive a genre abandoned at the end of World War II. Like **Command De-cision** (1948), *Twelve O'Clock High* dramatizes the pressures endured by Eighth Air Force commanders during 1943 as their long-range bomber squadrons were suffering staggering losses over Europe. When the 918th Bomber Group's for-mer executive officer (Dean Jagger, who won an Academy Award as best sup-porting actor in the role) travels to postwar England, he recalls those dark days.

As the narrative begins, the group's commanding officer (Gary Merrill) is relieved of command because he seems more concerned for the safety of his men than for the success of the air war. His replacement, General Frank Savage (Gregory Peck), is never in danger of overidentification with his men. Indeed, his attempts to improve the group's combat efficiency and morale are resisted by all his junior officers led by a winner of the Congressional Medal of Honor (Robert Patten). Despite the pressure, Savage refuses to ease up on the crews. His policies prove successful: the raids become more effective; the casualties decline; and the rebellious officers rally to his defense. The stress, however, is too much for the general, who suffers a nervous breakdown in the final sequence.

Throughout the 1950s and 1960s, the influence of *Twelve O'Clock High* can be seen in films about air warfare. It even became a successful television series on ABC between 1964 and 1967 (though executive producer Quinn Martin and his writers killed General Savage off at the end of the first season and replaced him with a younger, more dynamic colonel). Perhaps even more significant, the original motion picture was regarded as an inspiring model of corporate professionalism and was screened at seminars designed to improve the leadership skills of business leaders and educational administrators.

See:

Landon, Philip J. "New Heroes: Post-War Hollywood's Image of World War II." In *Visions of War: World War II in Popular Literature and Culture*, ed. M. Paul Holsinger and Mary Anne Schofield. Bowling Green, OH: Bowling Green State University Popular Press, 1992, 18–26.

Rubin, Stephen Jay. "A Change of Emphasis: *Twelve O'Clock High* (1949)." Chapter 5 in *Combat Films. American Realism: 1945–1970*. Jefferson, NC: McFarland, 1981, 121–142.

Philip J. Landon

UNITED SERVICES ORGANIZATION (USO) (Entertainment). The United Services Organization (USO) predates the entrance of the United States into World War II by eight months. Founded in April 1941 by six major national organizations—the Young Mens and Young Womens Christian Organizations (YMCA and YWCA), the Salvation Army, the National Catholic Community Service, the National Jewish Welfare Board, and the National Travelers Aid Association—it was privately funded from the beginning. Though the U.S. government did agree to build up to 300 buildings around the country as USO facilities, to take charge of directing the programs, and to keep track of the organization's budget, it was men like Broadway impresario Billy Rose who guaranteed the success of the venture. Within the first week, Rose announced that he would put on "draftee shows" in army camps across the United States and, before the end of the summer, more than 3.2 million GIs had attended a performance.

Between 1941 and 1945, USO Camp Shows presented 293,738 performances in 208,178 separate visits to military personnel. Estimates were that more than 161 million servicemen and women, both in this country and abroad, were entertained. The USO also took shows into military hospitals; by late 1945, more than 3 million wounded soldiers and sailors in 192 different hospitals had been entertained. In all, there were 702 different USO troupes that toured the world during the war, some spending as much as six months at a time on the road. Twenty-eight performers died in the course of their service, some in plane crashes and others from illnesses and disease contracted while on tour.

By the end of the war, the USO had become the most successful theatrical producer in the history of show business. *For the Boys* (20th Century–Fox, 1991) attempts to tell the story of two USO performers. Starring Bette Midler and James Caan, the movie chronologically spans fifty years of USO shows from the early 1940s through Operation Desert Storm.

See:

Andrews, Maxene, and Bill Gilbert. *Over Here, Over There: The Andrews Sisters and the USO Stars in World War II.* New York: Zebra, 1993.

M. Paul Holsinger

UNITED STATES MARINE CORPS WAR MEMORIAL. On February 23, 1945, after three days of fighting, the United States Marine Corps captured Mount Suribachi, the highest point on the desolate, Japanese-held island of Iwo Jima. Because the small victory flag could not be seen clearly from naval ships off the coast, however, it was taken down and, late that morning, replaced by a newer staff already flying a larger Old Glory. At the moment that five young Marines and a navy corpsman were getting the pole upright in the rocky soil, Associated Press photographer Joe Rosenthal took the most famous American photograph of the entire war. Two days later, newspapers across the United States featured the shot on their front pages, and it became the symbol of the entire war effort.

Rosenthal won the Pulitzer Prize for news photography for ''Raising the Flag on Iwo Jima,'' and his picture was soon being used as the centerpiece for the government's last, and biggest, war bond drive. Millions of posters, outdoor signs, and car cards replicated Rosenthal's work. A maudlin new song, ''Stars and Stripes on Iwo Jima,'' became an enormous popular hit. Late in the year, the U.S. Post Office featured a likeness on a new commemorative stamp. By February 1946, Felix de Weldon, a sculptor assigned to the Navy's artists corps, completed a life-sized statue based on the photograph. It was temporarily erected on Washington, D.C.'s Constitution Avenue.

The Marine Corps, however, wanted more. After much debate, it was decided to have De Weldon recreate his original memorial on a colossal scale and place it on a twenty-seven acre site immediately to the west of Arlington National Cemetery and within easy view of the Pentagon. The corps came up with the bulk of the $850,000 required to complete the project, and on November 10, 1954, the Marine Corps War Memorial, with its six gigantic bronze servicemen, was dedicated before a crowd of thousands. The names of other great Marine victories adorn the base of the monument, but it is the flag raising on Iwo Jima that has become the major symbol of almost everything connected with the corps. Today, the memorial has become one of the National Capitol Area's most visited tourist sites and is seen by millions very year.

See:

Marling, Karal, and John Wetenhall. *Iwo Jima: Monuments, and the American Hero.*
    Cambridge, MA: Harvard University Press, 1991.

M. Paul Holsinger

"V FOR VICTORY" (Slogan). No slogan was more pervasive in the United
States during World War II than the ubiquitous "V for Victory." Americans
lived in "V-Homes," wore hundreds of variations of "V-Pins," wrote "V-
Mail" to their husbands and sweethearts in service, and, if young, even played
"V for Victory" games. There were Victory comic books, Victory chewing
gum, Victory paper dolls, and, of course, millions of **Victory gardens**. There
was a "V for Victory" song as well as others with such titles as "V to Victory,"
"V Calls for Victory," "Victory Cavalcade," and "Victory Polka." Even in
the bleakest days after Pearl Harbor, no one doubted that the United States and
its Allies would ultimately win the war. The only question in everyone's mind
was "when."

   The term "V for Victory," however, predated America's entry into the war
by almost a year. In January 1941, Victor de Laveleye, a Belgian refugee broadcasting for the British Broadcasting Corporation (BBC), urged his fellow countrymen to chalk a large letter "V" in every public place as a sign of their
confidence in final victory over the Nazis. In June of the same year, BBC an-
nouncer Douglas Ritchie went much further. Emphasizing the Morse Code symbols for the letter "V"—three dots and a dash—he suggested that everyone
start using them as a universal signal of their belief in freedom from tyranny.
When it was realized that the first notes of Beethoven's Fifth Symphony echoed
the same signal, that piece was played incessantly, and millions began to hum
the music. After Great Britain's Prime Minister Winston Churchill flashed an
ebullient two-finger "V for Victory" sign, people also began making V-signals
with their fingers, sat with their legs stretched out in V-shapes, and contorted
their bodies in any number of other ways to stress their belief in the coming
victory over Axis aggression. By fall 1941, the use of the letter "V" was
commonplace in every Allied nation.

   When the United States entered World War II, it was inevitable that Americans from coast to coast would also adopt the "V for Victory" campaign.
Obsessed with "V for Victory" wax paper or "V for Victory" men's suits,
citizens longed for war's end. It was no accident that, when the Axis powers
finally surrendered, the two dates were quickly designated "V-E" (Victory in
Europe) and "V-J" (Victory over Japan) day respectively.

See:

"Fighting Words: A Guide to America's Wartime Lingo." *Life* 8 (Spring/Summer 1985):
    19–21, 24.
Taylor, A. Marjorie. *The Language of World War II.* Rev. ed. New York: H. W. Wilson,
    1948.

M. Paul Holsinger

VICTORY AT SEA (**Documentary Series–Musical Score**). Beginning on October 26, 1952, and continuing at 3:00 Eastern Standard Time on every subsequent Sunday afternoon for the next twenty-six weeks, NBC-TV showed one of the most famous documentary series ever produced exclusively for television. Written by Henry Salomon and Richard Hanser and utilizing more than 60 million feet of film from ten different countries, *Victory at Sea* chronicled the worldwide role of naval power during the years of World War II. Acclaimed as the best public affairs programming of the year (for which it received an Emmy), and then later shortened into an 108-minute-long abbreviated version for theatrical viewing, the series was enhanced by a musical score written by Richard Rodgers, the composer of such masterpieces of the Broadway stage as *Oklahoma* and *South Pacific*.

Variety thought Rodger's music, arranged by Robert Russell Bennett, one of the most original works ever written by an American. Rodgers later adapted the melody of one of the nine movements of his orchestral suite "Beneath the Southern Cross" into the hit song, "No Other Love" in his musical *Me and Juliet*. So well-known did the music of the *Victory at Sea* series become that, shortly after it aired for the first time, the navy awarded Rodgers its Distinguished Public Service Medal in recognition of his efforts for that branch of the armed forces. An RCA Victor album of the series' main musical numbers received a gold record the same year when it had sales of more than $1 million.

The *Victory at Sea* series is still occasionally seen on television stations throughout the United States. With its advent in 1996, the pay-for-view History Channel has made the shows regular programming fare on a weekly basis.

See:

Rollins, Peter C. *"Victory at Sea*: Cold War Epic." *Journal of American Culture* 6 (1972): 463–482.

M. Paul Holsinger

VICTORY GARDENS (**Home-Front Involvement**). The U.S. government worked overtime during World War II to encourage everyone, from the youngest child on a midwestern farm to the eldest resident in a New York City apartment complex, to further the war effort by planting "Victory gardens." Any available space, whether city rooftops, vacant lots, public parks, or unused farmland, was to be utilized. Posters, radio programming, magazine articles, and books reiterated the message. There was even a song entitled, "Get Out and Dig, Dig, Dig," which was featured regularly on the National Farm and Home hour-long radio show and which, that program officially proclaimed, was "the Victory Garden Theme." The American people responded and pitched in as never before.

According to a Gallup Poll taken in March 1943, more than 21 million families either had, or planned to grow, victory gardens. Later that year, a survey showed that more than 7 million acres were under cultivation across the nation, an area ten times the size of the state of Rhode Island. The Victory Gardens Committee of the U.S. Department of Agriculture announced that nearly 8 million tons of vegetables were grown that year, two-thirds the amount grown by the nation's farmers.

Not only was the planting of a garden encouraged, but so, too, was the canning or preservation of crops that were grown. With food shortages across the country, home canning, then generally unknown in most homes, was taught. Millions of women, their daughters, and often husbands and sons as well, pitched in. Urban residents, who never before gave much thought to where the food they ate came from or how it was prepared, now became "experts."

Victory gardens were, for the most part, a wartime phenomena. Though many persons who grew their first crop in 1942 or 1943, continued to plant and harvest after the war was over, most did not. Still, there have been few more dramatic instances of national unity.

See:

Cole, Garold. "Gardening for Victory: Victory Gardens in *American Periodicals* during World War II." *NDQ: North Dakota Quarterly* 61 (Summer 1993): 163–176.

M. Paul Holsinger

VIP (Cartoons). During the 1940s and 1950s, Virgil Franklin Partch II ("VIP") was one of America's most distinctive cartoonists, producing what *Newsweek* once called "maniacal humor for a maniacal world" (June 14, 1943). A Disney Studios' animator and a frequent cartoon contributor in *Collier's*, he continued to draw after he was drafted into the army in 1942. His first two books, *It's Hot in Here* (1944) and *Water on the Brain* (1945), dealt largely with military life as he experienced it. His *Here We Go Again* (1951), which was published at the beginning of the Korean War, was a sarcastic guide to basic training.

VIP's cartoons were male oriented. Set in bars, desert islands, camp, or combat, both characters and circumstances were grotesque. Big-headed figures on squat torsos lacked foreheads and had gigantic, sharply angled noses; their faces and bodies were contorted, responding to absurdity with either non sequitur or understatement. Partch excelled at visual surrealism: desert soldiers inflate a rubber camel, another navigates in a gym-rowing machine, a bathing Marine is totally submerged in his helmet. Other cartoons provided biting comments on war: stumbling upon naked men in a pond, soldiers inquire: "Er—is it 'hello' or 'heil'?"

VIP's nutty style was related to other cartoonists such as Basil Wolverton, Leonard Sansone, or Dick Wingert who drew gross figures of soldiers. Mirroring the fears and tensions during the war, Partch always found a wide and appreciative audience.

See:

"Call Him VIP." *Newsweek*, 14 June 1943, 99.

Larier, Lawrence. "Virgil Partch." In *Best Cartoons of the Year 1943*, ed. Lawrence Lariar. New York: Crown, 1943, 111.

Kalman Goldstein

WAKE ISLAND (Film). On the morning of December 8, 1941, Japanese bombers attacked Wake Island, about 2,000 miles west of Hawaii. The attack came just hours after a different Japanese task force plunged the United States into World War II by attacking Pearl Harbor. Wake's defenses were manned by about 525 Marines, a handful of army communications specialists, some sailors, and some of the approximately 1,100 civilian construction workers on the island. As other American outposts in the Pacific buckled under repeated Japanese assaults, Wake Island remained unbowed. The island was eventually overrun, and resistance collapsed on December 23, but not before its defenders killed more than 800 Japanese attackers and sank two enemy destroyers, the first Japanese warships to be lost in World War II.

A Hollywood studio quickly recognized the potential of a motion picture based on the defense of Wake and announced plans for such a production even before the Japanese captured the island. Adhering carefully to the U.S. Office of War Information guidelines, *Wake Island* (Paramount, 1942) was the first war movie to be made and released after America's entry into the war. Starring Brian Donlevy, Macdonald Carey, Robert Preston, and William Bendix, it called up almost every cultural and racial stereotype imaginable. Even though the screenplay took generous liberties with the facts of the battle (the Americans in the movie, for example, grimly continue to fight to the last man when, in fact, most survived the battle to become prisoners of war), theatergoing audiences and critics alike loved the heroic portrayals of the island's defenders. Almost sixty years later, the film still appears with regularity on late-night television.

See:

Basinger, Jeanine. *The World War II Combat Film: Anatomy of a Genre.* New York: Columbia University Press, 1986, 28–34.
Parish, James Robert. *The Great Combat Pictures: Twentieth Century Warfare on the Screen.* Metuchen, NJ: Scarecrow, 1990, 430–433.

                                                                    James M. McCaffrey

A WALK IN THE SUN (Novel-Film). Together with John Ford's *They Were Expendable* (1945) and William Wellman's *The Story of G.I. Joe* (1945), Lewis Milestone's *A Walk in the Sun* (20th Century–Fox, 1945) has often been described as one of the best and most realistic war motion pictures produced in Hollywood during World War II. The narrative structure is typical of the war film genre. An American fighting unit (in this case an infantry platoon) composed of a cross-section of Americans (a Hispanic from the Southwest, an Italian from Jersey City, a midwestern farmer, a Jew from New York City, among others), is tested in battle and emerges victorious. As this platoon lands at Salerno, Italy, the commanding officer is killed, leaving the platoon in the command of a sergeant who must lead the survivors to their objective, an enemy-held farmhouse a short distance inland. The pressures of command drive the sergeant to a nervous collapse, but, when another sergeant named simply Tyne (Dana Andrews) takes over, the platoon accomplishes its mission before the end of the day.

The illusion of reality created in *A Walk in the Sun* depends less on its fidelity to actual battlefield experiences than to the way it subverts generic conventions and relies on documentary-style camera work. Instead of individual heroics, the audience sees soldiers enduring pain and exhaustion; leadership is presented as an unwanted responsibility; and true heroism is identified with doggedly pursuing what may be an impossible goal. Screenwriter Robert Rossen's script, which was based on the very popular 1944 novel of the same name by Harry Brown, was widely praised by critics. Its supposed honesty appealed to everyone, and audiences made it a box office success when it was first shown early in 1946.

See:

Rubin, Stephen Jay. "Bullets or Ballads: *A Walk in the Sun* (1945)." Chapter 1 in *Combat Films. American Realism: 1945–1970*. Jefferson, NC: McFarland, 1981, 4–23.

Philip J. Landon

WALT DISNEY CARTOONS. After Pearl Harbor, every Hollywood film company "went to war," but few were more active in the war effort than the Walt Disney Studio. Even before the U.S. entry into the war, Disney was doing war bond work for the National Film Board of Canada. Now, over 200 instructional films, such as *The Thrifty Pig, The Seven Wise Dwarfs, Donald's Decision, All Together Now*, and *Stop that Tank*, were created, combining earlier animation excerpts with cartoon scenes of combat or industry to present technical information with light humor. The studio also contributed directly to war propaganda. The maps and diagrams for Frank Capra's **Why We Fight** series came from Disney, so, too, did animations of Nazi irrationality (*Reason and Emotion, Education for Death, Chicken Little*) which combined exposé with lampoon. The most noted efforts, however, starred Donald Duck, whose feistiness suited their tone and purpose. *The New Spirit of 1942* plumped for willing payment of income taxes, while *The Spirit of '43* abetted a bond sales campaign. A small children's book, *The Victory March*, was prepared at the behest of the Treasury Department to encourage its readers to buy **War Savings Stamps**, which could be turned into bonds. The most popular propaganda piece was *Der Fuerher's Face* (1943), a cartoon with a sarcastic razzing title song set in "Nutziland," an industrial nation of jackboots and swastikas. So successful was the Disney staff in all these endeavors that, by mid-war, the U.S. government was commissioning 94 percent of its footage.

The studio's work for various government agencies can be seen in many different areas. It designed, for instance, more than 1,100 insignia for units of the army, navy, and Marine Corps. Early in 1942, at the request of the navy, it also produced WEFT (for "Wings, Engine, Fuselage, Tail"), a series on aircraft and ship identification. These were poorly done (wags called WEFT "wrong every fucking time"), but access to bases, props, and personnel soon enabled the studio to crank out accurate, minimally animated shorts for the navy, air force, and Signal Corps. When the Council on Inter-American Affairs sought Hispanic customers to replace disrupted European and Asian markets, Disney produced two feature-length films, *Saludos Amigos* (1943) and *The Three Caballeros* (1945). At the same time, over two dozen home defense cartoons, many featuring Mickey and Minnie Mouse, came from Disney-employed artists. Films that featured infant care, sanitation, or nutrition were shown to an estimated 4 million people a month until the war's end.

See:

Finch, Christopher. *The Art of Walt Disney: From Mickey Mouse to the Magic Kingdoms.* New York: Abrams, 1995.
Shale, Richard Allen. "Donald Duck Joins Up: The Walt Disney Studio during World War II." Ph.D. dissertation, University of Michigan, 1976.

Kalman Goldstein

THE WAR ADVENTURE SERIES (Young Adult Novels). Robert Sidney Bowen published the first of the fifteen books that make up the War Adventure Series in May 1941. Also known as the "Dave Dawson" series, after their young, American, erstwhile hero, they were unquestionably the most popular juvenile novels written about World War II during the war years.

In *Dave Dawson at Dunkirk*, seventeen-year-old Dave witnesses German planes shooting unarmed civilians and determines to "trim the pants off the Nazis." For the next five years, first in the RAF and then, after Pearl Harbor, with the United States Air Force, he and his English friend, Freddy Farmer, adventurously fight Germans, Italians, and, eventually, the Japanese. The stories, designed to emulate the World War I **Boy Allies** adventures, appalled critics, who condemned them as exceedingly bloody—Dave and Freddy kill at least 2,500 enemies before V-J day—but that was what young boys found so attractive. They voraciously read each book and begged for more.

The result was a second Bowen-authored eight volumes featuring two other teenagers, Red Randall and Jimmy Joyce, who exclusively fight the Japanese in the Pacific. Together with Dave Dawson's many adventures, these new novels helped make Bowen's name a household word for popular boys' stories.

See:

Holsinger, M. Paul. "For Freedom and the American Way: Robert Sidney Bowen's World War II Heroes: Dave Dawson and Red Randall." *The Horatio Alger Newsboy* 32 (1994): 9–16.

M. Paul Holsinger

WAR AND REMEMBRANCE **(Novel–Television Miniseries).** *War and Remembrance* (1978), a historical romance by Herman Wouk, is a fictionalized account of World War II from America's entry into the war in the wake of Pearl Harbor to the final weeks of the war in the summer of 1945. The novel is a sequel to Wouk's *The Winds of War* (1971), which covered the events leading to the war during the late 1930s and the war itself from the German invasion of Poland to Pearl Harbor.

War and Remembrance, like its predecessor, is an old-fashioned narrative both in theme and in form. In the tradition of the historical novel, a fictional protagonist, naval Captain Victor "Pug" Henry, is present at many of the war's crucial moments and meets the leaders, civilian and military, who determine their outcome. The war impacts the lives of the entire Henry family. One son dies at Midway; another seeks his Jewish wife, who is caught up in the Holocaust; a daughter becomes part of the entertainment industry; his wife has an affair with one of the scientists working on the atomic bomb. Not to be outdone, Captain Henry himself serves as an informal aide to President Franklin Roosevelt.

Herman Wouk's remembrance of World War II is very different from the ironic, anti-heroic treatments of the war made popular by Joseph Heller in **Catch-22** (1962) and Kurt Vonnegut in **Slaughterhouse-Five** (1969). For Wouk, it was the professional competence and the restrained but dedicated patriotism of men like his hero who saved America from a predatory totalitarianism.

In the late 1980s, Dan Curtis directed a twelve-episode, thirty-hour television miniseries adapted from Wouk's novel. Airing on ABC over seven days in November 1988 and another five in May 1989, it was the most expensive television program ever made at an estimated cost of $110 million. Starring Robert Mitchum as Henry, the series was also a sequel. Six years earlier, Curtis had directed most of the same cast in another miniseries adapted from *The Winds of War*. Like the novel, the filmed version of *War and Remembrance* has a nostalgic quality as it looks back to a period when the country was united in an epic struggle against evil. Extremely popular, it was awarded an Emmy as the year's most outstanding miniseries.

See:

Mazzeno, Laurence W. *Herman Wouk*. New York: Twayne, 1994.

Philip J. Landon

WAR SAVINGS STAMPS (Home Front Involvement). Millions of American children saved their pennies between 1942 and 1945 so that, at least once a week in their classrooms or in local stores, they could purchase War Savings Stamps and "buy a piece of the war." Though there were four different War Savings Stamps denominations: 10¢, 25¢, 50¢, and $1—a fifth, $5, was issued only in 1945 as the war was ending—it was the bright, rose-red 10¢ stamps that were the most popular. Prominently featuring Daniel Chester French's famous **The Minute Man** statue in their center, the stamps could be used to purchase a $25.00 war bond once $18.75 worth had been collected and pasted into a small book.

Everyone was encouraged to buy as many stamps as possible, but small children were especially targeted. At the request of the U.S. Treasury Department, for instance, Walt Disney Studios developed a picture book featuring many of its cartoon characters purchasing and collecting War Savings Stamps. Donald Duck and Mickey Mouse were hard to resist as patriotic salesmen, but, in case the message still missed its mark, every copy came with one stamp inside a "treasure chest" to get even the youngest boy or girl started. For those slightly older youth, *War Victory Comics*, the first government-sponsored comic book, was created. Also produced by the Treasury Department, the various issues were filled with the work of a number of top cartoonists, all promoting War Bonds and War Savings Stamps.

The idea of War Savings Stamps started during World War 1. As early as 1917, the U.S. government sold stamps that could be used to purchase Liberty Bonds. The 25¢ and $5 stamps (the only two denominations) were, however, prohibitively expensive for most youngsters, and relatively few were sold in comparison to the tens of millions that were purchased during World War II.

See:

Cohen, Stan. *V for Victory: America's Home Front during World War II.* Missoula, MT: Pictorial Histories, 1991, 60–77.

M. Paul Holsinger

"WE DID IT BEFORE (AND WE CAN DO IT AGAIN)" (Song). In the aftermath of the Japanese bombing of Pearl Harbor (and even before President Franklin Roosevelt asked Congress, on Monday, December 8, to declare war on Japan), Charles Tobias and Cliff Friend composed "We Did It Before (and We Can Do It Again)." Flag-waving and jingoistic, the lyrics leave no doubt that, since it was the American armed forces who won World War I, it would also be a group of American boys that would now put an end to Axis aggression.

Two days later, Eddie Cantor, Tobias's brother-in-law, put the song into *Banjo Eyes*, the Broadway show in which he was then starring, and it nearly brought down the house. Quickly recorded by Barry Wood and the Wood Nymphs, "We Did It Before" zoomed up the popularity charts. On March 2, Warner Brothers used the tune of "We Did It Before" for the first time as background music for one of its **Looney Tunes** animated cartoons, *Daffy's Southern Exposure*. For the rest of the war, the company featured the piece again and again, adding to the number's continued popularity. It was also part of a Hollywood tribute to the Navy, *Sweetheart of the Fleet* (1942). Soon nearly everyone was humming the tune or singing its bombastic lyrics.

See:

Scheele, Carl H. "We Did It Before and We Can Do It Again." Liner Notes. In *Praise the Lord and Pass the Ammunition: Songs of World War I and II*. LP New World, 1977, 4–5.

M. Paul Holsinger

WHY WE FIGHT (**Propaganda Films**). Between 1942 and 1945, the Special Services Division of the United States Army made perhaps the greatest propaganda films in the history of American cinema. Produced under the leadership of Academy Award-winning Hollywood director Frank Capra, the *Why We Fight* series—*The Nazis Strike* (1942), *Prelude to War* (1942), *The Battle of Britain* (1943), *The Battle of Russia* (1943), *Divide and Conquer* (1943), *The Battle of China* (1944), and *War Comes to America* (1945)—was initially designed as indoctrination for the millions of newly drafted American troops, more than 35 percent of whom had less than a high school education. Capra and the dozens of professionals he was able to recruit from the major Hollywood studios quickly threw themselves into creating pictures that would explain, clearly but forcefully, why it was necessary for the United States to stop totalitarianism throughout the world. Material from dozens of older movies, including even footage from silent films such as D. W. Griffith's *America*, was incorporated into the new pictures. Actors such as Walter Huston and Lloyd Nolan provided narration; Dimitri Tiomkin, Meredith Wilson, and Alfred Newman, three of the premier musical composers for the big screen, wrote original music.

At a total cost of only $400,000, the seven *Why We Fight* pictures were a bargain. Though flag-waving, patriotic, and always heavy with conservative rhetoric, in keeping with Capra's personal beliefs, each systematically told its story in easy-to-understand pictures and words. After viewing several of the earliest ones British Prime Minister Winston Churchill said: ''I have never seen nor read any more powerful statement of our cause or of our rightful case against Nazi tyranny than these films portray'' (McBride, 453). Other U.S. officials agreed, and, soon after their completion, *Prelude to War* and *The Battle of Russia* were released for theatrical showings around the United States.

The success of the *Why We Fight* series encouraged the armed forces to have Capra produce more than sixty other short features during the war years, several of which were shown commercially. *The Negro Soldier* (1944) and *Here Is Germany* (1945), for instance, both earned high praise from critics after their screenings. Two others, *Hitler Lives?* (1945) and *Seeds of Destiny* (1946), won Academy Awards for best documentary short subject.

See:

Culbert, David. ''*Why We Fight*: Social Engineering for a Democratic Society at War.'' In *Film and Radio Propaganda in World War II*, ed. K.R.M. Short. Knoxville University of Tennessee Press, 983, 173–191.
McBride, Joseph. *Frank Capra: The Catastrophe of Success*. New York: Simon and Schuster, 1992.
Rollins, Peter C. ''Frank Capra's *Why We Fight* Film Series and Our American Dream.'' *Journal of American Culture* 19.4 (1997): 81–86.

M. Paul Holsinger

WINGED VICTORY (**Drama-Film**). In spring 1943, Moss Hart, the renowned Broadway playwright, was asked by the army air corps to write a play that could be used to raise much-needed money for the Army Emergency Relief fund. After weeks of flying to training bases across the United States, Hart created *Winged Victory: The Army Air Forces Play* in three weeks and, with the army's direct support, staged it first in Boston with only seventeen days' rehearsal.

Flag-waving and intensely patriotic, the two-act drama follows the lives of three young men and the women they love from the small town of Mapleton, Ohio, into the air force, through training, and finally off to war. With the exception of nine professional female actresses, the cast was composed entirely of army personnel or their real wives. From its first performance, the play was an instant success, packing every theater in which it played. It opened on Broadway on November 20, 1943, and closed after 212 performances, on May 20, 1944. During that time more than $10 million was raised for the relief fund.

After touring Chicago, San Francisco, and Los Angeles, some of the cast (which included such budding Hollywood stars as Red Buttons, Lee J. Cobb, Karl Malden, and Edmond O'Brien) appeared in Darryl Zanuck's screen version. *Winged Victory* (20th Century–Fox, 1944) premiered in December, with Hart's Broadway script, and was directed by George Cukor. Several young female stars, including Jeanne Crain and Judy Holliday, were added to the cast in the hope of attracting a larger audience. Critics were somewhat ambivalent about the film, but audiences across the country made it a popular moneymaker. The repeated use of Robert Crawford's **"The Army Air Corps Song"** as background helped to make that piece a huge hit.

See:

Morella, Joe, Edward Z. Epstein, and John Griggs. *The Films of World War II*. Secaucus, NJ: Citadel, 1973, 214–216.

M. Paul Holsinger

WINGS COMICS. *Wings Comics*, an aviation-oriented, adventure comic book, was published by Fiction House from 1940 through the Korean War. During 1940–1941, it glorified Britain's air war against the Axis and advocated American preparation for war. In the March 1941 issue, American intelligence agent F-4 frustrates an anonymous "Oriental Power" making "war-like plans" to attack Hawaii. Once the United States entered World War II, the magazine quickly became dominated by American army or navy pilots such as Captain Wings. Slapstick comedy was provided by Greasemonkey Griffin, a bumbling, yet always triumphant, army airplane mechanic. In addition to fiction, *Wings* often had features about real air aces and actual Allied and enemy planes. It invited readers to join the Wings of America Club, buy war bonds, and send in ideas for new airplanes and weapons.

Like other Fiction House publications, *Wings* featured heroic women characters, often drawn in a "cheesecake" style, which was daring for the mid-1940s. Jane Martin was one such woman; this war nurse-turned Allied intelligence agent was the only female title character in *Wings*. In many cases, however, women played the more traditional comic book female role—that of a "plucky" victim who is rescued by the male lead.

After World War II, *Wings* favored stories about freelance fliers fighting escaped Nazi or Japanese villains, ordinary criminals, and—by the late 1940s—thinly disguised Russian agents. Jane Martin became an airplane saleswoman and then a newspaper reporter. During the Korean War, armed forces pilots gained prominence again. Heroic women like Jane Martin disappeared, as ferocious anticommunist combat took over the pages of *Wings*.

See:

Benton, Mike. "Fiction House (1938–1954)." In *The Comic Book in America: An Illustrated History*, ed. Mike Benton. New ed. Dallas, TX: Taylor, 1993, 119–120.

Karl G. Larew

WONDER WOMAN (Multimedia Character). Psychologist William Moulton Marston created the comic book heroine Wonder Woman in 1941 as an alternative to what he termed the "bloodcurdling masculinity" of most comics of the age. In the original story, a plane piloted by Captain Steve Trevor of United States Army Intelligence crashes on uncharted Paradise Island, the home of a group of Amazons who rescue him. The tribe's princess, who is "as lovely as Aphrodite, as wise as Athena, [as speedy as] . . . Mercury and [as strong as] Hercules," brings him back to the United States. Once in America, she takes the name Diana Prince and, since she can conveniently deflect bullets fired point-blank at her with the magical bracelets that she wears on both wrists, is soon dubbed "Wonder Woman" by the press.

Almost immediately, Diana finds herself helping the United States fight "the forces of hate and oppression" in the world. By the end of the war, whether dressed in a red, white, and blue costume with a symbolic eagle emblazoned across her bosum or serving as a member of the women's army corps, she has bested (at times single-handedly) Nazis, Japanese, and other Axis saboteurs. Thousands of young girl readers soon came to see that women could be just as brave and loyal as men in the service of their country. Though there were many other female heroines created for juvenile readers during the years of World War II, none was so dynamic, nor as long-lasting as Wonder Woman.

In March 1974, a made-for-television movie starring Cathy Lee Crosby pitted Wonder Woman against a group of evil Nazi spies. Though there is little about the film to distinguish it, it did result in an irregular series which ran for the next three years on ABC with Lynda Carter in the title role. After the 1975–1976 season, however, the writers changed the setting from World War II to the present day, and the show became little more than another rather unconvincing minidrama of "super-heroine" versus modern American crime.

See:

Chesler, Phyllis, and Gloria Steinem. *Wonder Woman*. New York: Bonanza, 1972.
Daniels, Les. *DC Comics: Sixty Years of the World's Finest Comic Book Heroes*. Boston: Little, Brown, 1995, 60–63, 170–171.

M. Paul Holsinger

YANK **(Newspaper).** *Yank*, the Army weekly, was, according to its commanding officer during World War II, "the most unique publication in the annals of publishing history" (Forsberg, v). Produced entirely by enlisted men, it accepted literature and art from ordinary servicemen and promised GIs relatively free expression about army life in letters to the editor. After its first issue on June 17, 1942, *Yank* became a compendium of colloquial speech. Available only to service personnel, it was full of shop talk, vulgar acronyms, and soldiers' argot.

Yank was a twenty-four-page weekly, which was eventually published in twenty-one editions at seventeen different locations. A separate navy one had its own staff, as did Anglo-American magazines for Southeast Asia theaters (*SEAC* and *CBI Roundup*). Four to six pages in each issue were allocated to locally contributed items; the remainder were compiled in *Yank's* New York headquarters, and thus spread a fairly uniform GI culture throughout the army. Letters commented on enlisted-officer relations, food, the **United Services Organization (USO)** and Red Cross, and home-front news. GI poetry, playlets, short stories, and feature essays ranged from parody, to evocations of exhaustion and fear in battle. Cartoons by George Baker, Leonard Sansone, and Dave Breger appeared regularly, but the back pages featured aspiring professionals like Bil Keane and Phil Interlandi as well as ordinary GIs. *Yank* also disseminated home-front popular culture: sports news, selected features, and comic strips from civilian publications—and, of course, photos and **pinup girls**.

Yank ceased publication on December 28, 1945. Two anthologies were published for civilians shortly after the war, *The Best From Yank* (1945) and *Yank—The Story of the War* (1947). A compilation of the best writing from the paper's pages, *Yank*, appeared in 1991.

See:

Cornebise, Alfred E. *Ranks and Columns: Armed Forces Newspapers in American Wars.* Westport, CT: Greenwood Press, 1993.
Forsberg, Franklin A. *Yank: The Story of World War II as Written By the Soldiers.* 1984. Reprint. Washington, D.C.: Brasseys (US), 1991.
Kluger, Steve. *Yank: The Army Weekly. World War II from the Guys Who Brought You Victory.* New York: St. Martin's, 1991, xi–xii.

Kalman Goldstein

THE YEAR IN PERIL **(Paintings).** Thomas Hart Benton was one of the most original, and certainly one of the most famous of modern American artists. Renowned for his many, often gigantic, studies of the American Midwest, Benton turned to his attention to the battle against fascism in the days immediately after Pearl Harbor when he prepared a series of eight paintings known collectively as *The Year in Peril*. Powerful in their conception, they offer no room for doubt as to who the enemy of the American people was. *The Sower*, for instance, shows a Nazi soldier planting the earth with human skulls. *Starry Night* features a helpless sailor sinking beneath the water as his unarmed freighter, torpedoed by a U-boat, lists in the background. Even more graphic, *Again* depicts German, Italian, and Japanese soldiers spearing a crucified Christ while a

Nazi fighter plane sprays machine-gun bullets into the wounded body on the cross.

Abbott Laboratories, a large Chicago pharmaceutical firm, purchased the pictures and quickly utilized reproductions in advertisements. More than 160,000 pamphlets featuring facsimiles were also printed by the company. Later in 1942, it offered the paintings to the United States for possible propaganda use. During the war years, the government distributed more than 26 million copies of the eight works throughout the country. When the originals were put on display in New York City, more than 75,000 persons stood in line to see them. They were also featured in a Paramount newsreel that was shown more than 22 million times.

The Year in Peril was almost certainly the most famous American anti-fascist propaganda tool produced during World War II. Though the pictures fell out of national favor shortly after the war, they still possess an overwhelming power. Today, the originals are in Columbia, Missouri, a gift from Abbott Laboratories to the Missouri Historical Society.

See:

Adams, Henry. *Thomas Hart Benton: An American Original.* New York: Knopf, 1989, 314–316.

M. Paul Holsinger

THE YOUNG LIONS (Novel-Film). Some critics have called Edward Dmytryk's *The Young Lions* (20th Century–Fox, 1958) one of Hollywood's best treatments of World War II. Others see it as little more than a bloated, overproduced adaptation of the 1948 novel of the same name by Irwin Shaw. Unlike the classic war films of the 1940s, which focused on the creation, training, and battlefield experience of a small combat unit (namely, a bomber crew or an infantry platoon), *The Young Lions* has epic ambitions. In parallel plots, it recounts the fate of three protagonists, shows how the war transforms their lives, and brings them face to face as the movie draws to a close.

An idealistic German, Christian Diestl (Marlon Brando) is attracted to the heroic possibilities offered by the Nazis only to become bitterly disillusioned with their crimes and cruelties. Two Americans, Noah Ackerman (Montgomery Clift), who is from a modest Jewish background, and wealthy playboy Michael Whiteacre (Dean Martin), meet as draftees and undergo training together. They become part of the final offensive against Germany and, outside a Nazi death camp, they confront and kill Diestl. Before reaching its climax, *The Young Lions* offers a panorama of historical and fictional events, including the Nazi occupation of Paris, the North African campaign, American anti-Semitism, London under attack by V-2 rockets, and the romantic entanglements of the three main characters.

The Young Lions reflects two interesting developments in Hollywood's treatment of World War II during the 1950s. The first was the attempt to create epic effects by recreating historical events on a grand scale while, at the same time, fitting them to generic conventions. This tendency culminated in Darryl Zanuck's all-star production of *The Longest Day* (1962). The second was to present the enemy more sympathetically by distancing him from his totalitarian superiors and portraying him as a reluctant or disillusioned warrior. The two German sea captains, played, respectively, by John Wayne and Kurt Juergens, in *The Sea Chase* (1955) and *The Enemy Below* (1957), offer excellent examples to parallel Diestl in *The Young Lions*.

See:

Giles, James Richard. *Irwin Shaw*. Boston: Twayne, 1983.

Philip J. Landon

The Korean War

Two days after the United States dropped the first of two atomic bombs on cities in Japan, the USSR, in fulfillment of an agreement between President Franklin Delano Roosevelt and Joseph Stalin at the Yalta Conference in January 1945, launched a full-scale attack on Japanese-held Manchuria. Before the Japanese could sue for peace (on August 14), the Red Army was deep into Korea, routing its defeated enemy as it stormed ahead. Such moves had an ulterior motive. Seizing huge caches of arms and supplies, the Soviet forces were able to turn them over to their communist allies, especially in the northern provinces of Korea. Later in the year, when an arbitrary dividing line was drawn at the thirty-eighth parallel, creating two separate nations, the People's Republic of North Korea was firmly entrenched as a puppet of the USSR.

For almost the next five years, constant tensions flared between North Korea and the newly established Republic of Korea (ROK), a nation strongly supported by the United States during the escalating Cold War between East and West. A small contingent of regular American troops continued to occupy parts of the South, while its officers helped to train a new Korean standing army. By June 1950, things were slowly beginning to take shape; the ROK forces had 95,000 men, and, with direct U.S. aid, the government of President Syngman Rhee appeared to be gaining the ability to be truly independent. Then, on June 25, tens of thousands of seasoned troops of the North Korean People's Army crossed the thirty-eighth parallel and began what many came to call, quite logically, the Korean War.

Though the United Nations quickly condemned the invasion and declared war on them when the North Koreans refused to withdraw, the American and South Korean troops on the scene were, at first, badly mauled and almost driven into the sea as they retreated, lost, then retreated some more. In early September, with only a few international contingents in South Korea, everything seemed lost. But United Nations (UN) Supreme Commander Douglas MacArthur was far from defeated. Developing an audacious plan that called for an amphibious attack at Inchon, hundreds of miles behind enemy lines, MacArthur was able to convince his superiors in Washington to allow him to attempt it, and, on September 15, 1950, the plan worked perfectly. The dominant First Marine Division carried the day at Inchon, and, within a few days, other allied troops in the south broke out of their tiny foothold in South Korea to go on the offensive as well. Within weeks, the predominantly American forces recaptured the South Korean capital of Seoul and began driving the People's Army back to and then across the thirty-eighth parallel.

In October, a major change in policy occurred. Despite a number of muted threats from the new Communist Chinese government in Peking that any advances by allied troops north of the border would result in its army becoming involved in the fighting, MacArthur, who hated all things communist, was able to convince the administration of President Harry Truman and the Joint Chiefs of Staff to allow him to launch a major attack on the North Koreans. Less than two months later, the First Marines and other American divisions reached the Yalu River, which divided North Korea from China's province of Manchuria. True to its threats, the People's Liberation Army of Communist China, first in small numbers, then, increasingly, by the tens of thousands, began appearing in opposition to the seemingly victorious UN forces. In November, more than 300,000 Red Chinese attacked the allied troops all along the Yalu, and, in the second reversal of the short war, the Marines and their comrades were overwhelmingly driven back. Though most escaped to fight another day, it was a devastating defeat. In Washington, President Truman was forced to declare a national emergency on December 15, 1950, and begin to call up many World War II reservists and rush them into battle.

By January 1951, the front lines were established roughly along the thirty-eighth parallel, and, though both sides constantly jockeyed for control during the next two years, a bloody stalemate soon set in. Appalled by his forces' losses along the Yalu and throughout the north, General MacArthur now began to talk openly about using nuclear weapons on both North Korea and China. There was, he maintained, "no substitute for victory." Though his superiors tried to detract him from such threats, he persisted, and, in April, President Truman relieved the popular general of his command.

Peace talks between representatives of the United States, South Korea, their many allies, and representatives of North Korea and Communist China began in November 1951 at the small town of Panmunjom, close by the thirty-eighth parallel. Even as they talked, the two sides continued military operations against each other throughout 1951 and into 1952. With U.S. jets controlling the skies and the navy dominating the sea, it seemed obvious to most impartial observers that, even without nuclear warfare, the United States would ultimately win the war. The communists, however, refused to admit defeat, and the massive bloodletting continued unabated. Only the successful development of U.S. mobile surgical hospitals up and down the line and the use of helicopters to move the wounded rapidly from one station to another, kept the death toll dramatically lower than it might otherwise have been.

In the election of 1952, the Republican Party nominated General Dwight Eisenhower as its presidential candidate. To a worshipful American public, he seemed the perfect man to solve the stalemate in Korea, and in November, he easily defeated his opponent, Adlai Stevenson of Illinois. The next month, even before assuming the office of president, Eisenhower went to Korea, and though his visit effected no immediate results, public support for the nation's newest leader seemed boundless. Certainly the concluding days of the war were no less brutal and the fighting no less fierce, but, on July 27, 1953, an armistice was finally reached between the two sides. The war, after more than 1,100 days of combat, had officially come to an end.

In the three years of the war in Korea, more than 2 million Americans were sent to the front lines; 33,651 of them died in action. If it was any consolation, China and North Korea collectively lost at least 1 million and possibly as many as twice that number. However, though the United States could claim at least a limited victory, there were also a number of ominous consequences. Once again, or so it seemed, an army composed of mostly white Americans had bested a group of ''yellow men.'' For many, there appeared to be a clear and unequivocal truth in such a result. Movies championed that notion of invincibility; comic books confirmed it; and a generation of citizens gained a false sense of over-confidence. To many persons' shock, on the other hand, the end of the war brought forth the revelation that dozens of American GIs collaborated with the enemy while prisoners of war. Millions of moviegoers remembered vividly **The Purple Heart** during World War II, in which a fictitious crew of downed American fliers from the Doolittle Raid on Tokyo went resolutely to their deaths rather than aid the enemy in any way. Though, at best, based only loosely on facts, the story had defined for Americans the way that soldiers under stress supposedly acted. Now, accusations of ''brainwashing'' seemed a weak excuse less than a decade later for what many considered to be cowardly acts.

Perhaps most disquieting of all was the fact that the Korean War clearly taught the wrong lessons about military involvement in Southeast Asia. Both the Truman and Eisenhower administrations, when analyzing the reasons why the United States became involved in Korea, determined that a similar situation must never happen again. To guarantee that America would not have to sacrifice its boys in another Asian war, the two leaders began to pour increasing moneys into the hands of the French colonial powers in Indochina who were, at the very moment, fighting their own brand of communist revolutionaries. A year after peace came in Korea, Secretary of State John Foster Dulles, as an outcome of the defeat of the French by the Viet Cong, helped to establish a separate ''democratic'' government in South Vietnam, buoyed up with large American military and financial support. The tide was set by the end of the decade for yet another full-scale confrontation in Southeast Asia.

See:

Alexander, Bevin. *Korea: The First War We Lost.* New York: Hippocrene, 1993.
Brady, James. *The Coldest War: A Memoir of Korea.* New York: Pocket Books, 1991.
Giangreco, D. M. *War in Korea, 1950–1953.* Novato, CA: Presidio, 1993.
Halliday, Jon, and Bruce Cummings. *Korea: The Unknown War.* New York, Penguin, 1990.
Stokesbury, James L. *A Short History of the Korean War.* New York: Murrow, 1988.

BAND OF BROTHERS (Novel). Ernest Frankel's terse, unsentimental 1958 novel *Band of Brothers* follows the heroics of a company of young Marines as it fights a rearguard action during the corps' retreat from the Chosin Reservoir in November–December 1950. Frankel, a Marine veteran of World War II action in the South Pacific, not only sketches a vivid picture of the horrific climactic conditions encountered by the American forces in that brutal winter fighting, but also succinctly expresses, through his characters' voices, many of the tensions and frustrations that are found in much of the popular culture of the Korean War. Gruff, hard-bitten Lieutenant Andy Anderson, for example, castigates the American people for their lack of understanding and concern about the mission and plight of the American fighting men in Korea and offers scathing critiques of an American culture that, since World War II, has gone "soft."

Frankel takes the title of his book from Shakespeare's *Henry V*, in which, prior to the Battle of Agincourt, Henry exhorts his outnumbered forces as "we few, we happy few, we band of brothers." Though praised initially by most reviewers for its realism, the novel came under attack by some who found the overabundance of obscene language in the dialogue of its Marines offensive.

See:

Hammel, Eric M. *Chosin: Heroic Ordeal of the Korean War.* Novato, CA: Presidio, 1981.
Jones, Peter G. *War and the Novelist: Appraising the American War Novel.* Columbia: University of Missouri Press, 1976, 182–185.

Dan Cabaniss

BATTLE HYMN (Autobiography-Film). The most sought-after personal story of the Korean War was that of Colonel Dean Hess ("The Flying Parson"), who founded an orphanage in South Korea during the war and saved over 1,000 children from starvation and death. His autobiography, *Battle Hymn* (1956), became a best-seller and was quickly turned into a dramatic film as well. Introduced by Hess's commander in Korea as "the actual experiences of this pilot," *Battle Hymn* (Universal, 1957) had everything the studios and the military could have wanted: jet acrobatics, dogfights, a love interest, orphans, and refugees.

Starring the popular Rock Hudson as Hess, it was a well-received box office success.

Like many other Korean War movies, this "bio-pic" begins in World War II, where "Killer" Hess accidentally bombs a German orphanage, killing forty-seven children. He returns home and becomes a minister to find peace and "make amends." Unable to forget the children he killed and over the strident objections of his wife and the deacon of his church, Hess volunteers for Korea, not as a combat minister, but to train ROK pilots. The plight of the Korean orphans greatly disturbs him. With the help of the beautiful En Soon Yang, a young half-Korean, half-Indian woman, Hess rescues the orphans through "Operation Kiddy Car" and removes them to the safety of Cheju Island, outside the war zone.

See:

Parish, James Robert. *The Great Combat Pictures: Twentieth-Century Warfare on the Screen.* Metuchen, NJ: Scarecrow, 1990, 38–39.
Quirk, Lawrence. "Battle Hymn." Chapter 44 in *The Great War Films from The Birth of a Nation to Today.* New York: Citadel, 1994, 148–151.

D. Melissa Hilbish

THE BRIDGES AT TOKO-RI (Novel-Film). In a May 10, 1952, *Saturday Evening Post* article, "Forgotten Heroes of Korea," James Michener confronted public apathy towards the Korean War by offering a "special salute" to a group of "brave" naval pilots and the "crusty officers" serving with the United States Task Force off the coast of Korea. Michener, clearly enamored with the courageous flyers, wrote in great technical detail of the capabilities of the jet aircraft as they took off and landed on the pitching deck of the aircraft carriers. This article was followed by *The Bridges at Toko-Ri* (1953), a novella featuring naval pilots risking life and limb to bomb a formidable set of bridges.

The Bridges at Toko-Ri (Paramount, 1954) and 1954's *Men of the Fighting Lady*, two of the most powerful and exciting films about U.S. involvement in the Korean War, were based on James Michener's earlier writings about the war in Korea. *Bridges*, in particular, has become a classic of the Korean War period for its clear and unambiguous statement on why we fight, coupled with exciting aerial footage. Lieutenant Harry Brubaker (William Holden), a lawyer, has been called up again. He complains bitterly about his misfortune. He is symptomatic of a new kind of hero: flawed, frightened, and cynical. His admiral (Fredric March), while critical of the conduct of the Korean War, considers it necessary to stem communist expansion. He calls the war a "tragedy" and a "dirty job," but maintains that the United States cannot, as Brubaker suggests, simply pull out: "Now that's rubbish son. If we did they'd take Japan, Indo-China, and the Philippines. Where would you have us make our stand? The Mississippi?" For the admiral (and Michener), every war is the wrong war when forced upon the country and the men who have to fight it. Though Brubaker overcomes his fear and ably serves his country, *Bridges* concludes on a somber note when he crashes behind enemy lines and dies in a shoot out with the North Koreans.

The special effects in the movie, especially the scenes of aerial combat, won an Academy Award. *Bridges*, which also starred Grace Kelly, was enormously popular with critics and "average" theatergoers alike. Rereleased in the mid-1960s, it received equally strong reviews.

See:

Quirk, Lawrence. "The Bridges at Toko-Ri." Chapter 41 in *The Great War Films from The Birth of a Nation to Today*. New York: Citadel, 1994, 136–139.
Suid, Lawrence. "The Navy and Korea." Chapter 6 in *Sailing on the Silver Screen: Hollywood and the U.S. Navy*. Annapolis, MD: Naval Institute Press, 1996, 94–112.

D. Melissa Hilbish

DUNCAN, DAVID DOUGLAS (Photojournalist). Some of the most memorable pictures from three of America's most bloody wars—World War II, Korea, and Vietnam—were shot by David Douglas Duncan, one of the twentieth century's most renowned photographers. Though a multitalented artist whose portraits hang in many museums around the world, it was his work in Korea that first brought him to the attention of most Americans.

Duncan had already proved himself in combat between 1943 and 1946 as a Marine Corps officer who photographed fighting throughout the Pacific. When the Korean War began, on June 25, 1950, he was in Tokyo. Going immediately to South Korea, his pictures of the war for *Life* magazine were some of the first to be seen by Americans on the home front. He landed with the Marines at Inchon and was with them at the Chosin Reservoir on the Yalu when the Communist Chinese broke through. In 1951, many Duncan photos, accompanied by extensive commentary from the photographer, appeared in one of the best American volumes of combat photography ever published, *This Is War!* Though it includes many exceptional panoramic views of the fighting, the most moving pictures are the numerous close-ups of exhausted, wounded, frightened GIs before, during, and after battle. "I wanted to show what war does to a man," Duncan wrote; "I wanted to show the comradeship that binds men together when they are fighting a common peril.... I wanted to show the agony, the suffering, the terrible confusion, the heroism [of] those men who actually pull the triggers of rifles aimed at other men" (6). He does so brilliantly.

Sixteen years later, Duncan returned to battle in Vietnam, filming for both *Life* and ABC News. Accompanying the First Marines in 1967 and 1968 on three separate actions (including the siege at Khe Sanh in 1968), he took hundreds of pictures that mirror what the war was like for a new generation of young Americans far from home. The best were put into two exceptional photographic studies: *I Protest: Khe Sanh, Vietnam* (1968) and *War without Heroes* (1970).

See:

Pomeroy, Ralph. "David Douglas Duncan." In *Contemporary Photographers*, ed. Colin
    Naylor. 2nd ed. Chicago: St. James, 1988, 263.

M. *Paul Holsinger*

***FIXED BAYONETS* (Film).** Directed and scripted by Samuel Fuller, *Fixed
Bayonets* (20th Century–Fox, 1951), is based loosely on John Brophy's 1942
World War II novel, *Immortal Sergeant*, and the subsequent motion picture
adaptation (20th Century–Fox, 1943), which starred Henry Fonda. It offers a
story of responsibility as 48 men are left behind in a rear guard operation that
will supposedly save 15,000 lives. The squad is commanded by "Rock," an
old World War II retread who, like Fuller himself, has fought the good fight
"from Tunisia to Czechoslovakia." The sergeant, played by Gene Evans, is a
seasoned, professional soldier who acts as a father figure to his men, teaching
them the lessons of war. Rock adopts a cowardly corporal (Richard Basehart)
who is running away from leadership responsibilities and cannot bring himself
to shoot another human being. The coward partly redeems himself by risking
his own life to bring back a wounded comrade, but it is only when he is able
to kill that he is accepted as a part of the group and as a leader.

Fuller's combat films offer a collision between the rules governing civilized
society and the chaos of the combat zone. You can only be normal in combat
if you are willing to kill, and *Fixed Bayonets* focuses on this basic paradox.
The squad has been slowly decimated by enemy snipers, and, when Rock is
killed, the young corporal has to lead. The men panic and want to pull out, but
he forces them to stand and finally kill the enemy. As the rear guard wades out
of the river to safety, Rock's voice narrates on duty and responsibility: "Ain't
nobody goes out looking for responsibility. Sometimes you get it whether you're
looking for it or not."

See:

Basinger, Jeanine. *The World War II Combat Film: Anatomy of a Genre*. New York:
    Columbia University Press, 1986, 182–185.
Server, Lee. *Sam Fuller, Film Is a Battleground: A Critical Study*. Jefferson, NC:
    McFarland, 1994.

D. *Melissa Hilbish*

***THE GLORY BRIGADE* (Film).** *The Glory Brigade* (20th Century–Fox, 1953)
and, to a lesser extent, *Target Zero* (Warner Brothers, 1955) are the only Korean
War films to treat the war as a United Nations action. American combat engineers and Greek guerilla fighters are sent off together on a mission. The Americans (who include such actors as Victor Mature, Richard Egan, and a very
young Lee Marvin) resent having to serve with and under "foreigners," while
the Greeks acknowledge the U.S. position in the post–World War II world ("Today the world speaks your language"). Misunderstandings ensue, with the

Americans believing the Greeks are cowards and ineffective and the Greeks becoming increasingly irritated with the American know-it-all attitude. Each group wants to abandon the other at some point during the mission, but respect grows and they join together in a final fight against the enemy.

The Glory Brigade is significant for its acknowledgement of a distinctive visual iconography. Filmed in Fort Leonard, Missouri, which reviewers thought resembled Korea's woods and hills, the movie was one of the first to feature helicopter rescue teams in action.

See:

Dolan, Edward F. *Hollywood Goes to War.* New York: Gallery, 1985, 107.

D. Melissa Hilbish

HIGGINS, MARGUERITE (War Correspondent–Newspaperwoman). Few war correspondents were more controversial or more successful than Marguerite Higgins. She covered three major conflicts—World War II, Korea, and Vietnam—and, in 1951, was the first woman to win the Pulitzer Prize for overseas reporting.

Higgins, one of the first full-time women reporters to be hired by the New York *Herald Tribune*, was sent to Europe in fall 1944 and managed to get onto the front lines in March 1945. Almost immediately, she began to scoop most of her male colleagues, many of whom resented her. She was with the first troops that liberated Dachau concentration camp. Her story was published around the world and earned her a campaign ribbon for outstanding service and the New York Newspaper Women's Club award as the nation's best foreign correspondent.

Five years later, Higgins was one of the first journalists to reach Korea after the North Korean army crossed the thirty-eighth parallel. Constantly under attack and forced to deal with attempts to expel her from the country, she continued reporting at the risk of her own life from "somewhere in Korea." Wheeling and dealing, she was the only woman to land with the Marine Corps at Inchon in fall 1950. At the time, one male correspondent noted that Higgins was "either brave as hell or stupid. Her energy and recklessness make it tough on all the [the rest of us]" (May, 180). *War in Korea: The Report of a Woman Combat Correspondent* (1951), an excellent book, recounts in more detail the fighting she witnessed.

Higgins remained in Korea until the end of the war and then went to Vietnam to witness the fall of the French and the beginning of American involvement in that small nation-state. Unlike many foreign correspondents, whose view of Vietnam came from a seat in a plush hotel in Saigon, Higgins insisted on accompanying the troops into battle on the front lines. She did not like what she found, and her reports from that country, spanning the next ten years, were often critical of what she believed to be ultimately a losing battle. In 1965, she expressed her thoughts succinctly in a best-selling book, *Our Vietnam Nightmare*.

Marguerite Higgins spent more than twenty years of her life risking death to write about America's fighting men. When she died of a rare tropical disease she contracted in Vietnam, burial in Arlington National Cemetery so that she could be with "her boys," seemed to everyone involved more than justified.
See:

May, Antoinette. *Witness to War: A Biography of Marguerite Higgins.* New York: Penguin, 1985.

M. Paul Holsinger

HOLD BACK THE NIGHT (Novel-Film). One of the first novels to come out of the Korean War, Pat Frank's *Hold Back the Night*, was published in 1952 as the war continued. Frank's subject matter is the extraordinary United States Marine Corps retreat from the Chosin Reservoir in November–December 1950, during which a force of some 20,000 Marines successfully withdrew in the face of massive attacks by a Chinese force of over 100,000. (This action was the source of the now-legendary assertion by Marine General Oliver P. Smith that the American forces were not retreating, but rather "advancing in a different direction.")

Frank (the pen name used by Harry Hart), a longtime war correspondent and successful novelist, builds his novel around the struggles of Dog Company as it battles harsh winter conditions and Chinese harassment to protect the large American withdrawal. Before the men reach the safety of Hungnam and the opportunity to be evacuated, a force of 126 has been reduced to only 14. Combat situations are realistically rendered, and the various characters' backgrounds are explored in flashbacks.

There is little to recommend the screen adaptation, *Hold Back the Night* (Allied Artists, 1956), starring John Payne, Mona Freeman, Peter Graves, and Chuck Connors. Director Allan Dwan chooses to center his attention on the unopened bottle of liquor that Payne, the company's tough commander, carries at all times rather than on the Marines' truly heroic retreat from the Manchurian border. The reasons for his seemingly strange behavior are gradually told, mostly in flashbacks to the days of World War II, but, with few scenes of combat, this minor plot is not enough to save the film.
See:

Aichinger, Peter. "Korea." Chapter 11 in *The American Soldier in Fiction, 1880–1963: A History of Attitudes toward Warfare and the Military Establishment.* Ames: Iowa State University Press, 1975, 66–69.
"Pat Frank (Harry Hart)." In *Contemporary Authors*, ed. Barbara Harte and Carolyn Riley. Rev. ed. Vol. 5–8. Detroit: Gale, 1969, 400–401.

Dan Cabaniss

THE HUNTERS (Novel-Film). James Salter, one of the most respected writers in the United States, has earned critical acclaim over the past forty years for his short stories, essays, and novels. He was still a pilot in the United States Air Force and a combat veteran of the Korean War when his first book, *The Hunters* (1956), was published. Though praised today as "a great American novel" and "arguably the single most distinguished work of fiction . . . to come out of the Korean War" (Cheuse, 9), the reading public in the mid-1950s showed little interest and it soon went out of print. When it was resurrected in a slightly revised format forty years later, it became a smash success. *The Hunters* (1997) now gained a new generation of appreciative readers.

Salter's story line is simple. Captain Cleve Saville (or, as he is inexplicably renamed in the 1997 revision, Cleve Connell), an experienced jet pilot, is assigned to a fighter wing near the front lines in Korea. He and his men regularly patrol the skies over the Yalu River, but in winter 1951–1952, the enemy is rarely seen and even less frequently shot down. Such a situation is unacceptable to Saville's superiors, whose only concern appears to be keeping score of "kills." If pilots are unable to rack up impressive numbers of enemy dead, they are rated failures and put under tremendous pressure to achieve victories. Things get even worse when Pell, a hotshot pilot, joins the group. Though he frequently endangers others by leaving his position in formation to go alone after the enemy, he gets "results." Within weeks, he has become an official air ace with five kills and the darling of the base commander. Tensions inevitably build between Cleve and Pell (as well among others under Saville's command), and they never cease until the very last scene.

Salter's personal knowledge of the war air in Korea shows on every page of *The Hunters*. The pilots' anxiety to get into combat, their often-long waits between flights, the pressure for "kills," and even "rest and recreation" time in Tokyo all ring true. *The Hunters* is certainly not the best novel about Americans at war in the air, but Salter is a careful wordsmith, and his first book offers an intriguing view of an important part of military life during the Korean War.

A Hollywood version was made of *The Hunters* (20th Century–Fox, 1958), directed and produced by Dick Powell and starring Robert Mitchum as Saville, Robert Wagner as Pell, and Richard Egan as their commanding officer. Adapted to the screen by Wendell Mayes, it is a melodramatic disaster—though all three lead actors acquit themselves with some skill. Mayes throws in a romantic triangle involving Saville and the wife of one of the men serving under him, and then adds a conclusion in which Saville and Pell work together to save a colleague who has been shot down by the North Koreans. Shot in CinemaScope and color, *The Hunters* features some spectacular aerial scenes but little else.

See:

Cheuse, Alan. "Soaring." *Chicago Tribune*, July 27, 1997, 14: 9.

Parish, James Robert. *The Great Combat Pictures: Twentieth-Century Warfare on the Screen*. Metuchen, NJ: Scarecrow, 1990, 222–223.

Salter, James. *Burning the Days: Recollection*. New York: Random House, 1997.

M. Paul Holsinger

KOREAN WAR VETERANS' MEMORIAL. After more than thirty years of apathy toward remembering publicly the men and women who served in the United States armed forces during the Korean War, Congress finally, on October 28, 1986, approved plans to build a memorial in their honor. Nearly two years later, on September 16, 1988, a site adjacent to the Lincoln Memorial and close by the **Vietnam Veterans' Memorial** ("The Wall") was selected.

In a national competition the following spring, the winning design was developed by a group of architects from State College, Pennsylvania. It featured nineteen full-sized, battle-clad foot soldiers hiking through a rice paddy in front of, and alongside, an etched granite mural and a pool of remembrance. Frank Gaylord of Barre, Vermont, sculpted the nineteen stainless steel figures, and Louis Nelson Associates, of New York City, created the more than 2,500 different faces that appear on the mural. The completed memorial was dedicated in July 1995. Inscribed at the base of the flag flying over the memorial are the following words: "Our nation honors her sons and daughters who answered the call to defend a country they never knew and a people they never met."

See:

Highsmith, Carol M. *"Forgotten No More": The Korean War Veterans Memorial Story.* Washington, DC: Chelsea, 1995.

M. Paul Holsinger

"LAST NIGHT I HAD THE STRANGEST DREAM" (Song). Folk singer Ed McCurdy wrote and first sang "Last Night I Had the Strangest Dream" in spring 1950. A sincere cry for peace—the songwriter dreams about men throwing away their weapons and agreeing to sign a treaty that would abolish all future wars—McCurdy's lyrics could not have appeared at a worse time. With the Cold War expanding, Senator Joseph McCarthy and others in Congress creating another "Red Scare," and, after June 1950, a very hot war spreading rapidly throughout Korea, the sentiments sounded far too similar to those being voiced daily by Soviet Russia and its allies to be acceptable to the mostly chauvinistic Americans.

After World War II, there were few persons in the United States who agreed with the idea that wars against the enemies of this country could be anything but good and righteous. To suggest otherwise, as did McCurdy, seemed almost blasphemous. Though left-wing authors, such as the editors of the new folk music journal *Sing Out*, championed the piece, and other folk singers such as Joan Baez recorded poignant versions of it in the early 1960s, its greatest popularity came during the folk music revival of the mid-1960s, when the Chad Mitchell Trio made it one of their biggest hits. Since that time, however, though still a standard reprinted in many anthologies, it is rarely heard and McCurdy's "dream" remains unfulfilled.

See:

Rodnitzky, Jerome. "They All Sang Songs of Peace: Pacifism and Folk Music in the 1960s." In *Give Peace a Chance: Music and the Struggle for Peace*, ed. Marianne Philbin. Chicago: Chicago Review, 1993, 77–86.

M. Paul Holsinger

MACARTHUR (Film). General Douglas MacArthur is one of the more colorful wartime characters in American history. His service spanned three wars: World War I, World War II, and Korea. During the last conflict, however, his ego and recalcitrant behavior resulted in President Harry Truman's 1951 decision to withdraw him from command in Korea for insubordination. MacArthur returned to the United States, not in disgrace, but to a hero's welcome, and many condemned Truman's decision as a victory for the communists.

MacArthur (Universal, 1977), with Gregory Peck in the lead role, is a complex bio-pic presenting General Douglas MacArthur's wartime biography from the fall of Corregidor in 1942 during World War II to his recall early in the Korean War. The story begins as MacArthur lectures the West Point cadets on "duty, honor, country" and portrays his hasty retreat from the Philippines, his return as the commander of Allied Forces in the Pacific, his tenure as supreme allied commander of Japan before service in Korea, and the pivotal Inchon landing of 1950. There is an attempt to balance the brilliant tactician and loyal family man with the "dangerous demagogue" and media hound who refused direct orders from the commander-in-chief and who professed intense dislike for the concept of limited war. The film lacks the dramatic impact of *Patton* and fails to explore MacArthur as a military man out of place in a rapidly changing world, but it was generally well received by critics and theatergoers alike.

A second motion picture, *Inchon* (1981) starring Sir Lawrence Olivier, also attempted to highlight MacArthur's famous attack on the North Koreans in fall 1950. Partly funded by the Reverend Sun Myung Moon, it is extremely weak. Of the two productions, only *MacArthur* bears watching.

See:

Parish, James Robert. *The Great Combat Pictures: Twentieth-Century Warfare on the Screen.* Metuchen, NJ: Scarecrow, 1990, 263–266.

D. Melissa Hilbish

THE MANCHURIAN CANDIDATE (Novel-Film). Based on a 1959 novel by Richard Condon, *The Manchurian Candidate* (United Artists, 1962) presents a complicated plot of political intrigue, which unites North Koreans, Chinese, Soviets, and internal domestic spies in an elaborate conspiracy to gain control over the U.S. government. In retrospect, it seems contrived and predictable, but with its release during a period of heightened international tensions, the film stands as a cultural marker of the Cold War period and the real fear of communist conspiracy and subversion.

The story begins with Sergeant Raymond Shaw's return from the Korean War to a hero's welcome. He is awarded the Congressional Medal of Honor for saving his men, and his mother and stepfather, Senator Johnny Iselin, use his heroic exploits to great political advantage. The other members of the squad suffer disturbing nightmares, leading Marco (Frank Sinatra) to launch an investigation. It soon becomes clear that Pavlovian techniques of brainwashing and thought control, engineered by the Chinese and orchestrated by the Soviets, have turned Shaw (Laurence Harvey) into a programmed killer and planted in the minds of the men the incident of his heroism. Shaw's "Mother," a highly manipulative and intelligent spy played by Angela Lansbury (nominated for an Academy Award as best supporting actress), will use anybody, including her own son, to further communist goals. Wreaking havoc in Shaw's personal life and cutting him off from any real friendships, she prepares him for his major role: the assassination of the future president of the United States. In a stunning conclusion set in Madison Square Garden at the Republican National Convention, Shaw turns his rifle, not on the presidential nominee, but on "Mother" and Johnny.

Directed by John Frankenheimer, *The Manchurian Candidate* foreshadows the assassinations of the 1960s. In its presentation of Johnny's rapid rise to power, it predicts the emergence of a vast and powerful media culture. The movie also reinforces the negative stereotype of the Korean War POWs and gives support to the public's acceptance of "brainwashing" as a possible danger to American democracy.

See:

Gardner, Jared. "Bringing the Cold War Home: Reprogramming American Culture in *The Manchurian Candidate*." In *Proceedings of the Conference on Film and American Culture*, ed. Joel Schwartz. Williamsburg, VA: College of William and Mary, 1994, 23–29.

D. Melissa Hilbish

M*A*S*H **(Novel-Film–Television Series).** The mobile army surgical hospital (MASH) was new during the Korean War, but, coupled with helicopters, it still provides that conflict's most enduring iconography. Indeed, for many Americans, the war in Korea centers solely around the mythical 4077th MASH, with its surgeons, nurses, and other enlisted personnel, which was first made famous in Richard Hooker's 1968 novel, *M*A*S*H*. Hooker, a pseudonym for physician Richard Hornberger, worked in just such a hospital in 1952. Through a series of interconnected vignettes, he highlights the supposed antics of the 4077th staff from November 1951 until April 1953. While practicing "meatball surgery," "Hawkeye Pierce" and "Trapper John McIntyre" engage in sexual horseplay, thumbing their noses at "regular army clowns." Rejected sixteen times before publication, Hooker's novel fueled many Americans' ambivalence over the escalating war in Vietnam and soon became a popular best-seller.

Director Robert Altman transformed Hooker's book into a major Hollywood film, also titled *M*A*S*H* (20th Century–Fox/Aspen, 1970). Starring Elliot Gould as "Trapper John," Donald Sutherland as "Hawkeye," Sally Kellerman as Major Margaret "Hot Lips" Houlihan, and Robert Duvall in the role of the inept Major Frank Burns, the movie, based on Ring Lardner, Jr.'s, Academy Award–winning screenplay, followed a format of individual escapades connected by twelve-hour surgical shifts, poker games, and the pursuit of the perfect martini. The theatergoing public loved *M*A*S*H*. It shot to the top of the popularity charts and, by year's end, had become the top-grossing motion picture. Critics were also impressed; the Academy of Motion Picture Sciences, the British Academy, and the Cannes Film Festival all nominated it as best film and Altman as best director.

A television adaptation with Alan Alda as "Hawkeye," Wayne Rogers as "Trapper John," Loretta Swit as Major Houlihan, and Larry Linville as Frank Burns debuted in fall 1972. After a slow start, *M*A*S*H* won an Emmy as outstanding comedy series at the end of the 1973–1974 season and was rarely out of the top ten for the next decade. Like Altman's film, the CBS version took advantage of the intensification of antiwar protest against Vietnam to provide a satiric look at America's overseas wars, but most viewers tuned in to laugh or cry with the characters rather than worry about the show's political ramifications. The 2½ hour last original episode (February 28, 1983) was seen by the largest audience ever to watch a single television program, a record that still stands. Reruns and syndication have kept shows available for easy viewing.

Shortly after the conclusion of the television show, an exhibit at the Smithsonian Institution attempted to merge the Korean War with its popular culture. "M*A*S*H: Binding Up the Wounds" opened in July 1983; few thought it strange that the exhibit included Hawkeye and Trapper John's tent ("The Swamp"), a re-creation of the operating tent, or other television memorabilia. Millions of Americans, when hearing M*A*S*H's theme song, "Suicide Is Painless," still instantly visualize helicopters sweeping low over the hills of Korea bringing wounded soldiers to the 4077th.

In summer 1997, the last mobile army surgical hospital permanently closed. It seemed only fitting that members of the television cast that made "M*A*S*H" a household word should be a part of the official ceremonies.

See:

McGilligan, Patrick. "M*A*S*H." Chapter 23 in *Robert Altman: Jumping Off the Cliff.* New York: St. Martin's, 1989, 295–324.

Plecke, Gerald. "M*A*S*H." Chapter 2 in *Robert Altman*. Boston: Twayne, 1985, 10–21.

Reiss, David S. *M*A*S*H: The Exclusive, Inside Story of TV's Most Popular Show.* Indianapolis, IN: Bobbs-Merrill, 1983.

                                                        D. Melissa Hilbish

MEN IN WAR **(Film).** Directed by Anthony Mann, *Men in War* (United Artists, 1957) is set in September 1950 during a major retreat of the U.S. and South Korean forces before the battle for Inchon. Based on a fine novel about World War II by Van van Praag, *Day without End* (1949), the production offers a powerful antiwar perspective on the Korean War by praising the heroism of the soldier while confronting the numbing psychological effects of war.

Except for the traditional dedication and historical marker, the film literally cuts the men, and the audience, off from the conduct of the war. In the aftermath of a retreat, soldiers are ordered to rejoin their battalion at yet another hill, and the camera follows their journey past snipers and through minefields. The men are frightened and burned out on war. The squad, led by a by-the-book lieutenant played by Robert Ryan, encounters a shell-shocked colonel escorted by his sergeant (Aldo Ray). When ordered to give up his jeep, the sergeant pulls a gun on the lieutenant and then a knife. The soldier has removed himself, and his colonel, from the war. This is a new kind of soldier. He can "smell" the enemy, senses when someone is watching the squad, and plays by the new rules of war ("Shoot first or die first").

Despite the ambivalence, the movie concludes with a valiant fight to retake the hill. Victory is achieved, at least for the moment, though only Ryan and Ray survive. With reinforcements on the way, the question is clear: Were the lives worth the price of the hill? It depends on each viewer's perspective.

See:

Basinger, Jeanine. *Anthony Mann.* Boston: Twayne, 1979.

D. Melissa Hilbish

MEN OF THE FIGHTING LADY **(Film).** Directed by Andrew Marton, *Men of the Fighting Lady* (Metro-Goldwyn-Mayer, 1954), was based on two separate *Saturday Evening Post* stories, "The Forgotten Heroes of Korea," by James Michener (May 10, 1952), and "The Case of the Blind Pilot," by Commander Harry A. Burns, USN (November 29, 1952). Though at times questioning aspects of the war, the motion picture is unwavering in its intense support of the courageous navy pilots doing a difficult job far from home for an apathetic public. There were heroes in Korea, it stresses strongly, and the nation owes them a debt of gratitude.

The movie begins with author James Michener (played by Louis Calhern) boarding an aircraft carrier during the war to chronicle the "Christmas Story." The basic themes include a hard squad leader who pushes his men and himself to the limits of endurance, a World War II retread who objects to the waste of life for questionable objectives, exciting semidocumentary aerial footage of the jets, and helicopters rescuing downed pilots from the sea. Assigned to bomb railroad tracks at Won Song, the pilots on the aircraft carrier *The Fighting Lady*, off the Korean coast, question their orders because the tracks can be rebuilt overnight. This war is different, they say: "This isn't a war. It's a police action and nobody back home wants to read about it.'' Why risk lives for questionable goals? Even the commander of the ship categorizes Korea as a ''dirty little war,'' but the film does present heroic acts, particularly in the story of a blinded pilot (Dewey Martin) who, flying ''by the seat of his pants'' and aided by a fellow pilot (Van Johnson), makes it back safely to the ship.

See:

Suid, Lawrence. ''The Navy and Korea.'' Chapter 6 in *Sailing on the Silver Screen: Hollywood and the U.S. Navy.* Annapolis, MD: Naval Institute Press, 1996, 94–112.

D. Melissa Hilbish

PORK CHOP HILL (Film). *Pork Chop Hill* (United Artists, 1959) is based on ''a true story'' by the renowned military historian, United States Army Brigadier General S.L.A. Marshall. ''Pork Chop'' was one of the ''outposted hills'' along the eastern edge of the Korean War's Iron Triangle, an area that witnessed some of the most intense fighting of the war as both sides tried to gain military and political advantage before resumption of the stalled peace talks in spring 1953. By the end of the decade, as many Americans wondered about the value of having fought in Korea, the story of the taking of that one particular hill by American forces provided a good medium through which to explore the conduct and conclusion of the war.

Released on Memorial Day weekend, 1959, *Pork Chop Hill* chronicles the capture and defense of ''Hill 255'' on the eve of the armistice. Though director Lewis Milestone had supported the United States position during World War II as both necessary and honorable, the majority of his motion pictures, including the Academy Award–winning *All Quiet on the Western Front* (1930), strongly stress war's waste of life and innocence. In *Pork Chop Hill*, the soldiers are victims caught up in a military and political poker game in which the strategic importance of the hill shifts with each day of ongoing negotiations. By moving back and forth between the calm of peace talks and the chaos of the battle where the men await word of a longed-for cease fire, Milestone captures the agonizing political aspects of the war. No one wants to die on what might be the last day of fighting, and the soldiers have to be encouraged, threatened, physically tackled, and forced to fight.

Although the film, which starred Gregory Peck as the intrepid commander of the troops, concludes with a heroic and successful fight for the hill, it criticizes the military and the government for becoming so mired down in political negotiations that they have no real understanding or empathy for the conduct of the war in the field.

See:

Marshall, S.L.A. *Pork Chop Hill: The American Fighting Man in Action: Korea, Spring 1953.* New York: Morrow, 1956.

Parish, James Robert. "Pork Chop Hill." In *The Great Combat Pictures: Twentieth-Century Warfare on the Screen*. Metuchen, NJ: Scarecrow, 1990, 320–323.

D. Melissa Hilbish

***RETREAT, HELL!* (Film).** *Retreat, Hell!* (United States/Warner Brothers, 1952), an early Korean combat film, issued a wake-up call to Americans by recreating the defeat of the U.S. forces near the Chosin Reservoir in December 1950. It follows men of the First Marine Battalion in training camp at Camp Pendleton, California, at the victorious amphibious landing at Inchon; and then into battle near the Manchurian border. Though it incorporates many of the attitudes found in World War II productions—honor, duty, bravery, perseverance—it couples them with a number of unique themes and an emerging visual iconography found only in Korean War representations.

The troops include Jimmy McDermid (Russ Tamblyn), a freckle-faced boy from a Marine family, and Captain Hansen (Richard Carlson), a World War II retread, now unsure of his ability to lead. After pushing inland against the North Koreans and the Chinese, the group is ordered to withdraw. When a soldier wonders if they are not simply retreating, the crusty commanding officer (CO) (Frank Lovejoy), mimicking the real-life Major General Oliver P. Smith, gives an inspirational speech explaining the action. ("Retreat? Hell! We're just attacking from another direction.")

Marching to **"The Marine's Hymn,"** dodging sniper attacks, suffering from frostbite and the cold, many of the men are killed as they make a sixty-five-mile trek to the sea, but the majority survive to fight another day. Interspersing combat footage with a number of carefully staged Hollywood action scenes, the movie presents the retreat as a victory of spirit and determination with the soldiers escaping their pursuers and coming out of the encounter with dignity and purpose.

See:

Hammel, Eric M. *Chosin: Heroic Ordeal of the Korean War*. Novato, CA: Presidio, 1981.

Schoell, William. "Retreat, Hell!" In *The Great War Films from The Birth of a Nation to Today*, ed. Lawrence Quirk. New York: Citadel, 1994, 122–125.

D. Melissa Hilbish

***THE STEEL HELMET* (Film).** The Korean War took the motion picture industry by surprise, but Director Samuel Fuller, a decorated veteran of World War II, acted quickly and made *The Steel Helmet* (Lippert, 1951) in only twelve days in the fall of 1950. Released in January 1951, this low-budget production—it cost only $165,000—was the first feature film to focus on the war.

The Steel Helmet displays a heavy dose of skepticism towards the conduct of the war in Korea, though Fuller is careful to present an honest, almost gritty, portrait of this nation's fighting men. A small squad of soldiers cut off from command is fighting for survival against a superior force of North Koreans. The leader, a naive and ineffective lieutenant (Steve Brodie), is challenged by a retread sergeant (Gene Evans). "Zack" operates outside the normal chain of command and is interested only in his own welfare and personal survival. In Fuller's war, soldiers are stressed, frightened, and prone to irrational acts. He captures the confusing tactics of the war, as the patrol wanders in circles. The enemies of World War II have been replaced by the communists, or "reds," who refuse to play by the standard rules of warfare. They kill innocent civilians and booby trap dead American soldiers. When they charge the Buddhist temple where the Americans have taken refuge, they kill most of the squad, but they, too, are slaughtered by the men, led in the end by Zack.

The picture lost technical support from the Defense Department because Fuller insisted on including a scene in which the "hero" assassinates an unarmed Chinese POW, but *The Steel Helmet* set the standard for the Korean War films to follow. With its low-budget style, unknown cast, and stark, cynical view of war, it has become a cult favorite.

See:

Basinger, Jeanine. *The World War II Combat Film: Anatomy of a Genre.* New York: Columbia University Press, 1986, 179–182.
Fuller, Sam. "War That's Fit to Shoot." *American Film* 2 (1976): 58–62.

D. Melissa Hilbish

TIME LIMIT (Film). *Time Limit* (United Artists, 1957) is one of several major films that deal with the issue of prisoner of war collaboration during the Korean War. Like Rod Serling's *The Rack* (Metro-Goldwyn-Mayer, 1956) and many similar motion pictures, it uses a court-martial setting to examine the issue of heroism in an effective and thoughtful way. The focus is on the court martial case of Major Harry Cargill (Richard Basehart) and his abrupt transformation from camp leader and active resister to enemy collaborator and Communist "teacher." An investigator (Richard Widmark) tries to defend Cargill, who admits to collaboration and offers nothing in his own defense. A general whose son died in the same camp pushes the investigation. As is typical of these productions, the investigation yields some surprises. In a dramatic confrontation with the General, Cargill finally reveals a long-held secret; the general's son was killed by the other men after he informed on an escape plan. Cargill also asserts that his own cooperation was given in return for the lives of his men.

Adapted from Henry Denker and Ralph Berkey's 1956 three-act Broadway play of the same name and directed by Karl Malden, *Time Limit* questions a military code that demands absolute loyalty at any price. The General blames his son for less than courageous behavior and maintains that you should "give your life for the code." Cargill, however, defends the young man, questioning the very definition of bravery and loyalty: "Well you can't ask a man to be a hero forever. There ought to be a time limit." While sympathetic to his motives, the movie condemns Cargill's actions and suggests that, while the goal of saving his men was laudatory, he should have led them in defiance of the enemy.

See:

Hyams, Jay. *War Movies.* New York: Gallery, 1984, 122.

D. Melissa Hilbish

TWO-FISTED TALES (Comic Books). *Two-Fisted Tales,* one of the first comic books to explore the Korean War, was originally published in December 1950 by William Gaines's EC comics. Several months later, the company also began publication of *Frontline Combat* (1951–1954). Harvey Kurtzman, a veteran of World War II and several years later the creator of the irreverant *Mad Magazine,* edited and drew both publications. Though the first issue contained a number of bloody adventure stories, most were not war-related; once the war heated up, stories of combat were added and often dominated the bimonthly issues.

The editorial policy of *Two-Fisted Tales* differed considerably from other comic books of the period. Artists and editors were identified to readers through individual profiles. *Frontline Combat,* which was totally concerned with the depiction of the wars, and the more broadly based *Two-Fisted Tales* continually interchanged ideas and stories. Readers often suggested story lines for one comic only to see them appear in a later issue of the other.

Kurtzman approached his work with both comics seriously, emphasizing "authenticity" and careful attention to history, historical dates, and places. All the stories involved meticulous research. The January–February 1951 issue was the first to focus almost exclusively on the war in Korea. Those stories, and most that followed, had a dark, violent, pessimistic tone. Though heroism was clearly in evidence and the need to fight was repeatedly stressed, the drawing in each issue was always stark and acknowledged the waste, futility, and loss of innocence that war inevitably brought. "All of our stories," Kurtzman once wrote, "really protested war. . . . The whole mood of our stories was that war wasn't a good thing. . . . You got killed suddenly for no reason" (Kurtzman, 53).

Though the Korean War dominated most issues of *Two-Fisted Tales,* it was not the only target of interest. Two issues were devoted to the Civil War, and there were also stories on the Revolutionary War, World War I, and World War II before the comic ceased publication in 1954.

See:

Cochran, Russ, ed. *The Complete Two-Fisted Tales.* Vols. 1–4. West Plains, MO: Cochran, 1980.

Kurtzman, Harvey. *My Life as a Cartoonist.* New York: Pocket Books, 1988.

D. Melissa Hilbish

WAR HUNT (Film). *War Hunt* (United Artists, 1962) is a complex story of two soldiers, one good and one a killer, in a struggle for the soul of a South Korean boy orphaned after his parents were killed by American napalm. Scripted by Stanford Whitmore from a newspaper account called "The Candy-Bar Kid," and set near Panmunjom and the ongoing peace negotiations, the film questions the conduct of the Korean War: "We've got a funny kind of war here. A war we really can't win," says one of the characters. Both sides wage a psychological battle for control; Communist loud-speakers, for instance, blare propaganda messages constantly. The same types of "mind games" are fought between the newly arrived Private Loomis (Robert Redford in his first motion picture) and Private Endore (John Saxon), a seasoned soldier who has slipped over the edge to become a "pure," psychotic killer. It is this particular story which provides an examination of the dark side of war.

Endore slips out almost every night to engage in freelance killing of the enemy and encourages Charlie, the Korean boy, to follow in his footsteps. Endore is obviously insane, but his actions are silently condoned by a captain grateful for the information garnered through Endore's nocturnal outings. Loomis tries to interest Charlie in more American-like interests (playing ball), but as the armistice is signed and Endore realizes he cannot return home, he takes the boy and escapes into the wilderness to continue "his" war. Loomis and the captain follow, and the captain eventually shoots his creation rather than risk breaking the truce. As Endore dies, the boy escapes into the demilitarized zone to remain, sadly, a child of the night.

See:

Hyams, Jay. *War Movies*. New York: Gallery, 1984, 168–170.

D. Melissa Hilbish

***WHY KOREA?* (Propaganda Film).** Assembled from newsreel footage in the style of Frank Capra's award-winning *Why We Fight* documentary films of World War II, *Why Korea?* (Movietone, 1951) attempts to explain why the United States should be at the forefront of the war in Korea. The script by Joseph Kenas and Ulric Bell, the hawkish former overseas representative of the U.S. Office of War Information during World War II, creates a sweeping historical logic for intervention in Korea. Citing a range of events including the 1931 Japanese invasion of Manchuria, the Italian attack on Ethiopia, Soviet aggression in Finland, the ascendancy of German fascism prior to and during World War II, and postwar Communist aggression in Poland and Czechoslovakia, the picture argues that in each case it was the failure of the world to step in and stop aggressive actions early on that eventually resulted in larger, more destructive conflicts.

A burst of controversy followed the production's release when P. J. Wood, the secretary of the Independent Theater Owners of Ohio, wrote a scathing letter to John R. Steelman, an adviser to President Harry Truman. With the endorsement of the president, Steelman had asked theater owners to show *Why Korea?* but Wood, asserting that "millions" of Americans opposed U.S. involvement in Korea, argued that no one should be forced to endure such pro–Korean War propaganda. He challenged the administration to show the other side of the controversy by authorizing the making of a film titled *Why We Should Get Out of Korea.*

The controversy was short-lived. Most reviewers and other critics applauded the Kenas-Bell script, and, later in the year, *Why Korea?* won the 1950 Academy Award for best short documentary.

See:

Wald, Marvin. "1950's Best Short Documentaries." *Films in Review* 2.6 (1951): 11–14.

Dan Cabaniss

12

The War in Vietnam

On September 2, 1945, Ho Chi Minh, the most important Communist leader in the French colony of Indochina, announced the creation of the Democratic Republic of Vietnam. He hoped that the United States would support his desire to free his people from colonial rule—whether imposed by the just-defeated Japanese or the French, who eagerly awaited the chance to return to their Southeast Asian possessions. American military officials were invited as honored guests, and, at independence celebrations later that day, Ho ordered **"The Star-Spangled Banner"** played in their honor. The euphoria did not last long. Several weeks later, more than 220,000 British and Nationalist Chinese troops arrived in the area around Saigon determined to deny freedom to the Vietnamese. Instead of uniting the country, Ho and his Vietminh guerillas found themselves forced to continue their fight. Less than a month later, the first American, A. Peter Dewey, the head of the U.S. Office of Special Services (OSS) mission, was dead. Before the war in Vietnam ended thirty years later, more than 58,000 other Americans, mostly young draftees fighting a war they rarely understood, were offered as similar sacrifices.

The First Indochina War, which was fought between the communist-backed Vietminh and the French, ran officially from December 1946 to July 20, 1954. Though the United States was not a participant in that conflict, American funds were continually funneled into Vietnam. Two days after the North Korean Army crossed the thirty-eighth parallel line to begin the Korean War (June 25, 1950), then-President Harry S. Truman announced that the nation would significantly expand its military assistance to make sure that Ho Chi Minh and the communists did not win in that country as they had only the year before in neighboring China.

Over the next few years, American military men grew more determined than ever to make Vietnam the place in Asia where communism was halted in its tracks. In March 1954, when insurgents attacked and surrounded the French at Dienbienphu in northern Vietnam, Admiral Arthur Radford was but one of many military leaders who were willing, if necessary, to provoke a third world war by using atomic weapons in support of the beleaguered French. Though former general of the army and now President Dwight Eisenhower decided not to provide such aid (thus effectively dooming the last French foothold in Indochina), he did note that, unless Vietnam was saved, all other free Asian nations would collapse like falling dominoes. That analogy, which was used repeatedly over the next two decades, helped to explain how America could so easily prop up, and then support militarily, a local South Vietnamese puppet leader or refuse to allow free elections irrespective of the wishes of a huge number of the citizens of that nation.

The American presence in Vietnam grew slowly but steadily after 1954. There were 760 United States military personnel there by 1959, 900 the following year, and 3,200 by the end of 1961. In November 1961, General Maxwell Taylor, claiming that 8,000 additional troops would result in the communists' defeat, called on President John Kennedy to send them as soon as possible. Such a small number, he argued, would win the victory without getting the United States trapped in the quagmire that Vietnam soon became. Kennedy complied with the request, and the numbers of Americans "in country" climbed dramatically; 11,500 "advisers" and other military personnel were stationed in Vietnam by the end of 1962, 16,300 in 1963, and 23,300 in 1964. There seemed no end in sight.

The constantly increasing numbers, however, failed to stem the tide. It did not seem to matter where in the country American personnel were placed. Communist Viet Cong sympathizers were ever present to contest the area and to challenge Army of the Republic of Vietnam (ARVN) forces for control. Though the United States continually revamped its military leadership in Southeast Asia—hoping in the process to find a winning team that would destroy the communist presence—it became clear that, unless something were done, and done quickly, the nation was at risk of losing its first war.

Many persons, including a minority of military leaders, argued for pulling out of Vietnam before it was too late. President Lyndon Baines Johnson, who assumed office in late November 1963 after the assassination of John Kennedy, had no intention of giving up, however. Determined not to be the first American president in office when the United States lost a war, Johnson, in early August 1964, was given the opportunity to expand the war when two destroyers, the *Maddox* and the *Turner Joy*, were attacked by patrol boats in the Gulf of Tonkin. Scholars have long disputed the "innocence" of either vessel, but the president's announcement of the attacks had the desired effect. Five days later, Congress overwhelmingly passed the so-called Gulf of Tonkin resolution, giving the chief executive the power to send troops into Vietnam to protect threatened American boys from communist aggression. It was virtually an open invitation to full-scale war, but it was a war that the nation's military leaders were sure they would win.

On October 1, 1964, the army's Fifth Special Forces Group (the "Green Berets") arrived in Vietnam. Five months later, in early March, the first official combat troops, the Third Marines, landed at DaNang, and the rapid deployment of large numbers of military personnel into the war began. By the end of the year, more than 184,000 men and women were stationed in Vietnam, a 700 percent increase over the previous year and an almost 1,100 percent rise since the death of John Kennedy. Such a buildup, however, did not stop the communist forces any more than did the seemingly endless bombing of North Vietnam, which began in March 1965. When the South Vietnamese–based Viet Cong and their North Vietnamese Army allies met American forces head on in such bloody confrontations as those in the Ia Drang Valley during November 1965, it quickly became evident that the expected victory was not going to be easy.

Even as more American troops were poured into Vietnam (385,300 by the end of 1966; 485,600 by December 1967), little seemed to change. Army commander General William Westmoreland and his subordinates continually implemented a number of major operations, but the enemy, though terribly battered, continued the war without any sign of surrender. On January 21, 1968, in one of the most important enemy offensives of the war, the communists laid siege to the American base at Khe Sanh. Less than two weeks later, the so-called Tet Offensive began, and American troops reeled under the onslaught of Viet Cong and North Vietnamese Army attacks. Though bloodied United States forces were able to drive the communists back, victory was, at best, ephemeral. Professing to see the proverbial "light at the end of the tunnel," however, General Westmoreland called for another 206,000 troops in February 1968.

Opposition to the war at home—which was at first almost nonexistent—was, by summer 1968, mounting every day. In the midst of protests, antiwar marches, draft card burnings, and the like, President Johnson, under pressure from all sides, announced his decision not to run for reelection. The Democratic Party convention in Chicago revealed to the world a terribly divided nation unable to decide on what policy to pursue. Though the number of American troops climbed once again in 1968 (to 536,000), it was obvious by the time Richard Nixon became president in January 1969 that "more of the same" was a failed response to the war in Vietnam. By October 15, when hundreds of thousands participated in a National Moratorium Day and called for an immediate end to the war, antagonism toward the "unjust" and "immoral" war was spreading rapidly. It grew even worse the following month, when the March 1968 massacre by army troops of more than 500 defenseless Vietnamese men, women, and children in the small hamlet of My Lai was made public. If support for the war was increasingly angry before the announcement, it now became even more embittered.

The Nixon administration continued to bomb North Vietnam and sent American troops into Cambodia to cut supply lines into South Vietnam from the north—an act that caused riots on hundreds of American college and university campuses and, indirectly, the deaths of four students at Ohio's Kent State University—but it also began slowly, but systematically, to withdraw troops from the war. As early as June 1969, the first 25,000 Americans returned home, and those numbers continued to escalate in 1970–1972. American troop strength in Vietnam was down to only 35,000 by the 1972 presidential election, when the Republicans and Richard Nixon won a stunning political victory at the polls over his even more openly antiwar opponent, Senator George McGovern of South Dakota.

On January 27, 1973, the Paris Peace Accord was signed by the major combatant nations. Negotiated by Henry Kissinger from the United States and Le Duc Tho of North Vietnam (both of whom were awarded the Nobel Peace Prize the following year for their efforts), it allowed the first American prisoners of war—mostly bomber pilots and their crews shot down while flying missions over North Vietnam—to be released, much to the relief of millions of Americans who saw their vile treatment in such places as the ill-named "Hanoi Hilton" as but another sign of this nation's impotence. By August, all direct American military operations ceased, as conduct of the war was placed in the hands of the ARVN and their South Vietnamese mentors. At the end of the year, there were only 50 United States military personnel left in Vietnam, the lowest total in more than twenty years.

The Watergate scandal forced Richard Nixon from office in August 1974, and his vice president, Gerald Ford, replaced him. At the same moment, North Vietnamese forces were rapidly solidifying control over huge chunks of South Vietnam, action that the ARVN troops could not (or would not) prevent. In April, as the North Vietnamese closed in on Saigon, American embassy staff and the handful of remaining military guards and other advisers were quickly evacuated, many from the rooftop of the embassy itself. Finally, as the north proclaimed a united Socialist Republic of Vietnam, the thirty-year war came to an end.

The war in Vietnam, unlike the many earlier wars that the United States had clearly won, continued to bedevil Americans long after the last shots were fired. More than 58,000 young men and women died during the conflict, with 46,163 killed in action. Millions of citizens wondered if anything could possibly justify such staggering losses. Returning veterans were often shunned. Wounded, disabled, addicted to drugs, or facing other ailments, many found readjustment to civilian life almost impossible to make. Having never lost a war before, it now was hard for most Americans to know how to respond. When a monument in honor of the thousands who died was proposed for the Mall in Washington, D.C., many vehemently opposed it because they felt that listing the names of the dead—its most prominent feature—was an admission of shame destined to remind Americans endlessly of our failure in Asia

Though Hollywood at first released a number of motion pictures that examined our lost national innocence, it was not long before other movies such as the ''Rambo'' series with Sylvester Stallone (see **Rambo: First Blood, Part II**) and three ''Braddock'' pictures featuring karate champion Chuck Norris as an American colonel during and immediately after the war were produced to appease the hurt psyches of a large part of the Amerian public. In these six films, both men single-handedly destroy hundreds of enemy troops while freeing American POWs in the jungles of Vietnam from the clutches of evil foes. Enormously popular, they served as cheap therapy for a nation smarting under the pain of rejection and loss.

Not until 1991, sixteen years after the last deaths of American troops in Vietnam, did the majority of Americans openly come to terms with the nation's loss in one of the—if not the—most unpopular wars in American history. Ironically, it was victory in another military engagement—Operation Desert Storm—that finally brought about the change.

See:

Baritz, Loren. *Backfire: A History of How American Culture Led Us into Vietnam and Made Us Fight the Way We Did.* New York: Morrow, 1985.
Levy, Guenter. *America in Vietnam.* New York: Oxford University Press, 1978.
Olson, James S., and Randy Roberts. *Where the Domino Fell: America and Vietnam, 1945–1975.* 2nd ed. New York: St. Martin's, 1996.
Stanton, Shelby L. *The Rise and Fall of an American Army: U.S. Ground Forces in Vietnam, 1965–1973.* Novato, CA: Presidio, 1995.

ALI, MUHAMMAD (Antiwar Activist). Born Cassius Marcellus Clay in Louisville, Kentucky, Muhammad Ali was the heavyweight boxing ''Champion of the World'' when his opposition to the war in Vietnam made him a major symbol of protest. His announcement that he had joined the Black Muslim religion (the Nation of Islam), made shortly after he became champion in February 1964, polarized America along racial lines. Many whites, who thought of the Black Muslims only in violently anti-white terms, castigated the young boxer; African-Americans, on the other hand, thought of him far more positively.

The controversy surrounding Ali grew in 1967 when, on religious grounds, he refused induction into the U.S. armed forces. Though former black champions such as Joe Louis and Sugar Ray Robinson encouraged him to serve, Ali, claiming to be a Muslim minister, adamantly refused. Indicted and tried for draft evasion, he was convicted by an all-white jury in twenty-one minutes and sentenced in federal court to serve the maximum sentence of five years in prison. Claiming ''I ain't got no quarrel with them Viet Cong,'' Ali now became an icon of rebellion and opposition to the war on campuses across the United States. While many persons reviled him as a traitor, to others he represented ''pride, self-respect, and defiance.''

Because of his refusal to serve in the army, Ali's championship was taken from him. He remained free on bond while, for the next three years, his lawyers appealed the verdict against him. In 1971, the U.S. Supreme Court unanimously reversed the lower court's judgement. Resuming his career, Ali rewon his championship in 1974, lost it and then rewon it again in 1978, the only man in professional boxing history to hold the heavyweight championship on three different occasions.

Muhammad Ali has become an American legend since the war in Vietnam. By the summer of 1996, with old controversies dead, the now long-retired prizefighter was given the honor of lighting the Olympic torch in Atlanta. Suffering from the ravages of Parkinson's disease, he was cheered by virtually everyone.

See:

Gorn, Elliot J. *Muhammad Ali: The People's Champ.* Urbana: University of Illinois Press, 1995.

Anthony O. Edmonds

"ALICE'S RESTAURANT" (Song-Film). In 1967, Arlo Guthrie, the twenty-year-old son of legendary folk songster Woody Guthrie, wrote, and sang at the Newport Folk Festival, his ironic and autobiographical, "Alice's Restaurant." In the eighteen-minute-long song, he tells how, having been arrested and convicted for littering in Stockbridge, Massachusetts, he was refused induction into the United States Army. As the young Guthrie satirically notes, somehow in the army's mind his conviction made him immoral and thus no longer capable of representing the country as it killed thousands of women and children in Vietnam. To him, this was something to be savored.

Released commercially in September 1967, the song made Guthrie an overnight success. So popular did "Alice's Restaurant" become that Dave Marsh, one of the most knowledgeable of rock music's critics, some years later placed it number 1 on his list of "Anti-war Top 40" musical numbers. A shortened version, "Alice's Rock and Roll Restaurant," was also recorded for sales.

Using Guthrie's lyrics as the nub of his story, director Arthur Penn filmed *Alice's Restaurant* (United Artists, 1969). Starring Guthrie, James Broderick, and Pat Quinn, the movie offers trenchant social commentary about American society and the war in Vietnam, blending it neatly with satire and a melodramatic touch. Guthrie does a good job on the screen, especially in a very funny, brief scene when he is temporarily inducted into the army. Though he failed to win either award, Penn received an Oscar nomination as the year's best director as well as a New York Film Critics Circle nomination as best screenwriter for his work on the film.

See:

Storey, John. "Rockin' Hegemony: West Coast Rock and Amerika's War in Vietnam." In *Tell Me Lies about Vietnam: Cultural Battles for the Meaning of the War,* ed. Alf Louvre and Jeffrey Walsh. Philadelphia: Open University Press, 1988, 181–198.

M. Paul Holsinger

AND BABIES (Antiwar Poster). The Vietnam War produced thousands of shocking photographs of death and destruction, but few scenes were more disturbing than the horrific color picture of dozens of dead South Vietnamese women and children taken by combat photographer Ronald Haeberle immediately after the infamous My Lai Massacre in March 1968. The bloody, unarmed civilians, some of the more than 580 killed by a unit of United States Army troops under the command of Lieutenant William Calley, lay grotesquely on the rural path where they fell. When the photo was first seen in late 1969, after having been kept secret for more than a year, its effect on viewers was electric. No single work went further to convince many Americans that the United States had no reason to be an active participant in a war where even the smallest children were the "enemy."

Haeberle's photograph gained even greater visibility in 1970 when the Art Worker's Coalition (AWC), a group of artists staunchly opposed to the war, used it to create a soon-to-be-famous poster, *And Babies*. AWC members Irving Petlin, Jon Hedricks, and Fraser Dougherty overlaid two telling phrases in blood-red lettering: "Q. And babies?" at the top of the picture; "A. And babies" at the bottom. They did not need to say more. Though the directors of the Museum of Modern Art reversed themselves at the last minute and voted not to finance the distribution of the disturbing two-by-three-foot artistic representation, the city's lithographers' union printed 50,000 posters and circulated them worldwide. Many newspapers published copies of the AWC work, and, when it was made into posters and other visual representations, it got even more attention.

And Babies was easily the most successful poster to vent the outrage that so many felt against the conflict in Southeast Asia. Copies are still frequently seen in retrospectives dealing with the popular culture of the Vietnam War era or in collections of art from the period.

See:

Lippard, Lucy R. *A Different War: Vietnam in Art.* Seattle, WA: Real Comet Press, 1990, 27–28.

M. Paul Holsinger

THE ANDERSON PLATOON (Documentary). *The Anderson Platoon* (Home Vision Cinema, 1966), directed by Pierre Schoendorffer, is one of the better documentaries on the Vietnam War. Shot in Vietnam, this black-and-white film won the 1967 Academy Award for best documentary. Schoendorffer, a French veteran of the Indochina War, spent six weeks with a United States Army platoon in order to rediscover the Vietnam he had left years before. Instead, he finds Americans and things American.

The production is similar to Tim O'Brien's novel *The Things They Carried* (1990) in focusing on a specific American platoon named after its leader, who is a West Point graduate. Like O'Brien, Schoendorffer introduces various members of the platoon at the start of the piece, providing each soldier's name, place of origin, and (in some cases) tells the audience whether that soldier was wounded or killed later in the fighting.

The Anderson Platoon includes the types of footage or scenes that viewers and readers have come to expect from Vietnam narratives: men on patrol, men under fire, men being transported from place to place and wounded men and villagers being transported out of danger via Ruey and Chinook helicopters, and men on rest and relaxation (R&R) in Saigon. It offers something unique as well, however: beautiful, sweeping views of the Vietnamese countryside; the forbidding, fog-enshrouded Annamese range; and tropical sunsets.

Though American actor Stuart Whitman occasionally provides voiceover narration and Schoendorffer uses music, such as Nancy Sinatra's "These Boots Were Made for Walking" as commentary, the majority of the picture stands alone. This strategy allows the viewer to experience the eerie silence of the jungle when the men are on patrol as well as the terrifying sounds of artillery and being under fire.

See:

James, David E. "Documenting the Vietnam War." In *From Hanoi to Hollywood: The Vietnam War in American Film*, ed. Linda Dittmar and Gene Michaud. New Brunswick, NJ: Rutgers University Press, 1990, 239–254.

Leslie Kennedy Adams

APOCALYPSE NOW **(Film).** Director Francis Ford Coppola's *Apocalypse Now* (United Artists, 1979) is one of only a handful of significant American-made efforts to capture the Vietnam experience on film. In John Milius' script, based loosely on Joseph Conrad's classic novel *Heart of Darkness* (1895), Captain Willard (Martin Sheen), an executioner for army intelligence, is given the mission of tracking down renegade Green Beret Colonel Willard Kurtz (Marlon Brando). Holed up somewhere in Cambodia with a private army of native tribesmen who idolize him, Kurtz is said to be waging his own war on the communists using methods that, though effective, are "totally outside the pale of acceptable human conduct." Consequently, Willard's job is to find and kill him quickly.

Willard's journey up the Nung River into Cambodia takes up more than two-thirds of the movie. The experiences that he has along the way are meant to demonstrate both the absurdity of the war and the futility of the way that the U.S. military is fighting it. In one of the most memorable sequences, the captain meets an airmobile commander named Kilgore (Robert Duvall, in an Oscar-nominated performance) who cheerfully wipes out a communist-controlled village because the adjacent beach offers good surfing. When Willard reaches Kurtz, it quickly becomes clear that the colonel is, indeed, mad but no more so than U.S. commanders who think they can win a guerilla war with bombers. By the time the young "executioner" finally does his assigned job by killing Kurtz with a machete, he is convinced that the colonel wants to die, "to take the pain away." There is evidence that he is right.

Apocalypse Now, which was shot completely on location in the Philippines, went massively over budget, helped greatly by Coppola's rental of the entire Philippine air force. *Heart of Darkness: A Filmmaker's Apocalypse*, a short documentary film shown for the first time on the Showtime cable network on October 12, 1991, showcases some of the endless problems and setbacks encountered. Awarded an Emmy as the outstanding individual achievement in informational programming, that film, which was based on notes and video footage taken by Coppola's wife, Eleanor, helps to show even more clearly what an achievement the original motion picture really is.

Apocalypse Now should not be viewed as an attempt to render accurately the history of the Vietnam conflict, but it does manage to deliver something of the feel of the war—its surrealism, absurdity, and, frequently, futility. Reviewers generally agreed. Nominated for eight different Academy Awards, including best picture, it won two (best cinematography for Vittorio Storaro and best sound for Walter Murch). Robert Duvall also received the 1979 best supporting actor award from the British Academy. Criticized as it has been, the film remains ''must'' viewing for anyone anxious to know how Americans remembered ''their'' latest Asian war.

See:

Tomasulo, Frank P. ''The Politics of Ambivalence: *Apocalypse Now* as Prowar and Antiwar Film.'' In *From Hanoi to Hollywood: The Vietnam War in American Film*, ed. Linda Dittmar and Gene Michaud. New Brunswick, NJ: Rutgers University Press, 1990, 145–158.

J. Justin Gustainis

''THE BALLAD OF THE GREEN BERETS'' (Song). In 1966, Sergeant Barry Sadler wrote ''The Ballad of the Green Berets'' in honor of the members of the army's elite special forces teams. The American public, for the most part still strongly supportive of the U.S. intervention in Southeast Asia, made it a tremendous hit. Climbing quickly on the best-seller charts to number one, it remained there for five weeks, and by December, it had become the year's top-selling record.

Sadler, at the time a Green Beret himself, also recorded an entire album about his comrades, including such numbers as ''Letter from Vietnam'' and ''Badge of Courage.'' Though they never approached the popularity of his best known work, RCA Victor claimed on the album's dust jacket that ''many years from now these songs . . . will be recalled as a true expression of the Vietnam combat soldier's feelings during the time of that fierce encounter.'' Not everyone agreed, however. For example, music critic Dave Marsh called *Ballads of the Green Berets* the worst popular album of the last forty years.

''The Ballad of the Green Berets'' soon fueled a wave of special forces–related items for sale to American consumers. There was a Green Beret comic book, Green Beret bubble gum (with five trading cards in each package), Green

Beret hats, toy guns (including an eighteen-inch submarine gun, an M-16 rifle, and a .45 caliber pistol that shot plastic bullets), and several Green Beret games. Thousands of American boys, properly outfitted, now gleefully pretended to kill Viet Cong guerillas just as their fathers had killed multitudes of German or Japanese soldiers a generation earlier.

As opinions about Vietnam soured after early 1968, the glorification of the Green Berets faded rapidly. On the other hand, "The Ballad of the Green Berets," with its almost jaunty tune, remained popular throughout the war. John Wayne used it as the theme music for *The Green Berets* (Batjac, 1968), his cinematic attempt to rationalize U.S. participation in Vietnam, and others who believed that the American cause in Southeast Asia was both just and winnable made it almost an anthem of praise.

See:

Denisoff, R. Serge. "Fighting Prophecy with Napalm: 'The Ballad of The Green Berets.'" *Journal of American Culture* 13.1 (1990): 81–93.

M. Paul Holsinger

"THE BATTLE HYMN OF LT. CALLEY" (Song). On March 16, 1968, the troops of Charlie Company (First Battalion, Twentieth Infantry), led by young Lieutenant William Calley on a routine search-and-destroy mission against communist guerillas, calmly murdered more than 500 civilians at the small, central South Vietnamese hamlet called My Lai 4. It was one of the most inexcusable military acts by Americans during the twentieth century. Though the army tried to cover up the massacre, word leaked out and Calley and many of his men were put on trial. After prolonged hearings, the lieutenant was convicted and sentenced to life imprisonment at hard labor.

Opponents of the war applauded the verdict, but there were many others who somehow believed that a bona fide American hero had suffered a grave miscarriage of justice. James Smith and Justin Wilson's "The Battle Hymn of Lt. Calley," a song of praise written shortly after the conclusion of the courtmartial, expressed the thoughts of many of this latter group. Recorded by a pickup band of Alabamans calling themselves "C Company," with lead vocals by Terry Nelson, the song debuted within two weeks of Calley's guilty verdict. It was an instant success. Demands for copies of the record (an LP, *Wake Up America*, which included the new song, also soon appeared) were staggering, especially in the Deep South. More than 200,000 copies sold within the first three days, and it became, according to *Billboard* magazine, "the nation's hottest single property." Though some radio stations in the United States refused to put the "hymn" on the air, Armed Forces radio in Saigon played it regularly. By early May, it had reached number thirty-seven on *Billboard*'s top one hundred popular singles chart and began rapidly climbing on the country chart as well.

The popularity of "The Battle Hymn of Lt. Calley" waned almost as rapidly as it had risen. By mid-June, C Company's version vanished from the charts. Other recordings failed to gain public acceptance; one by Tex Ritter was canceled even before its release. The popular support that Lieutenant Calley received, however, clearly did not hurt the army's decision to be more lenient in its punishment of him. After the intervention of President Richard Nixon, the lieutenant was allowed the freedom of his base while he awaited the appeal of his conviction. Though a court of military review finally refused to commute the sentence, Calley was paroled by the secretary of the army in 1974, having spent only a few weeks behind bars.

See:

Belton, Michael, and Kevin Sim. *Four Hours in My Lai.* New York: Viking, 1992, 339–342.

M. Paul Holsinger

BLOODS: AN ORAL HISTORY OF THE VIETNAM WAR BY BLACK VETERANS **(Oral History–Documentary).** The 1980s, a decade that collectively produced the most important body of film and literature yet about the Vietnam War, had no individual work more significant than Wallace Terry's *Bloods: An Oral History of the Vietnam War by Black Veterans* (1984). Part of its importance lies in the fact that, despite a high degree of participation by African-Americans in the war, they have been badly underrepresented (not to mention misrepresented and stereotyped) in white-authored literature and films. However, another part lies in the general paucity of works by and about black veterans: a total of only six memoirs, three novels, and three poetry collections, plus the films *The Walking Dead* (1994) and *Dead Presidents* (1995), both of which came much later. As a result, for most Americans, black and white, the African-American experience in Vietnam will be derived, directly or indirectly, from *Bloods.*

Terry, a correspondent for *Time,* covered the war from 1967 to 1969, writing extensively about black soldiers and Marines. When he later interviewed the twenty veterans whose stories appear in *Bloods,* the trust established by his own experiences in Vietnam resulted in a candor otherwise inconceivable. A couple of the narrators—both former POWs—are fairly well known; most are relatively anonymous, yet their stories have a psychological and cultural resonance so right that readers can instinctively perceive them as collectively representative of the thinking of all black participants.

Especially telling are the repeated observations about the inherent racism that the war revealed. No matter what the particular circumstances of the narrators—some were support troops; many others, grunts—they ultimately cite the perception of racial difference as integral to their individual experiences in Vietnam. This is a dimension lacking in other oral histories of the war.

In 1986, Terry directed a documentary, *The Bloods of 'Nam,* for showing on the Public Broadcasting System. The fifty-eight-minute film offers a thoughtful

look at the African-American military experience during the Vietnam War era and features many of the same men Terry initially interviewed for *Bloods*.
See:

Williams, John A. "*Bloods* Revisited." *Vietnam Generation* 1.2 (1989): 125–130.

Jeff Loeb

BORN ON THE FOURTH OF JULY (Autobiography-Film). *Born on the Fourth of July*, Ron Kovic's searing autobiographical indictment of the U.S. government's involvement in Vietnam, was published in 1976, shortly after the war officially ended. However, the scars caused by the war were still fresh in the minds of the American public who made this controversial book a best-seller. Kovic's story is like that of many other young, patriotic men who grew up on the war movies of John Wayne and were glad to fight for their country. He enlists in the Marines, goes through degrading boot camp experiences, and then serves two tours in Vietnam. During the second tour, he is severely wounded and paralyzed from the chest down.

On his return home, the outward show of support for veterans contrasted with the poor conditions in the Veterans Administration (VA) hospitals appalls Kovic. He speaks honestly about his disabilities, identifying strongly with the protagonist of *Johnny Got His Gun*, Dalton Trumbo's often-horrifying 1939 antiwar novel. Kovic documents his conversion from a patriot convinced that war is right to a patriot convinced that war is wrong by alternating between stories of his naive, military self and his cynical, experienced self. He attends antiwar rallies in a wheelchair, is arrested by the police, and has his medals torn off his jacket. The high point of his protest is gaining access to the Republican National Convention in 1972, being interviewed by Roger Mudd, and interrupting President Nixon's acceptance speech with shouts of "stop the war."

Kovic and Oliver Stone wrote a highly successful film treatment of *Born on the Fourth of July* (Universal, 1989). Tom Cruise, in what many consider his best role, starred. Stone won an Oscar for his direction that is often moving, honest, and powerful. There were some who disliked the picture intensely, just as many of them had earlier found all antiwar demonstrators reprehensible, but, in the main, reviews mirrored the public's overwhelming support. Most critics certainly were high in their praise. Besides Stone's Oscar, *Born on the Fourth of July* received seven other nominations including best picture, best actor (Cruise), best screenplay, best music, and best cinematography.
See:

Devine, Jeremy M. "Born Again, 1988–1989." In *Vietnam at 24 Frames a Second: A Critical and Thematic Analysis of over 400 Films about the Vietnam War*. Jefferson, NC: McFarland, 1995, 304–315.
Doherty, Thomas. "Witness to War: Oliver Stone, Ron Kovic, and *Born on the Fourth of July*." In *Inventing Vietnam: The War in Film and Television*, ed. Michael Anderegg. Philadelphia: Temple University Press, 1991, 251–268.

Sally E. Parry

THE BOYS IN COMPANY C (**Film**). *The Boys in Company C* (Golden Harvest, 1978) was one of the first motion pictures to examine, even superficially, the military side of America's losing war in Vietnam. Not since John Wayne's disappointing *The Green Berets* (1968) had Hollywood tried to highlight for the American public the war in Southeast Asia. Directed by Sidney J. Furie from an original story written by Furie and Rick Nathan and starring a number of promising, but relatively unknown, actors, it is simplistic in its examination of the war and little more than a rehashed World War II film, with young draftees who are transplanted to Asian rice paddies instead of the beaches or hedgerows of France. Focusing on five different, but crudely stereotypical, United States Marine Corps recruits—a young African-American from the streets of Brooklyn, a good-looking athletic hero from the Deep South, a hippie pacifist who has been drafted and forced into service, a loud-talking and sex-starved big city boy, and a shy, aspiring writer who hopes to get into combat so he will be able to write about his experiences—the movie asks viewers to empathize with their trials and tribulations as they train for, then fight in, Vietnam. It is hard to do so, however.

The chronology of *Boys* covers only five months—from late August 1967, when they first arrive for basic training in San Diego, until January 1968, when they land in Vietnam and quickly move "in-country," fight, and, in some cases, die. The five and their fellow "grunts" become a smooth, well-oiled fighting machine thanks to the efforts of their cruel, but efficient, drill instructors. The same cannot be said for their officers, who are generally portrayed as stupid, cowardly, or, in some instances, simply corrupt. Though it is never explicitly stated, it seems clear that Furie believes the United States lost in Asia not because of poor, weak-willed troops in the field but rather due to the selfish, ineffective leaders the country sent to Vietnam. That is certainly an arguable contention, but *Boys* oversimplifies it and will convince few viewers.

See:

Devine, Jeremy M. *Vietnam at 24 Frames a Second: A Critical and Thematic Analysis of over 400 Films about the Vietnam War.* Jefferson, NC: McFarland, 1995, 134–140.

M. Paul Holsinger

CARRYING THE DARKNESS (**Poetry**). *Carrying the Darkness: American Indochina—The Poetry of the Vietnam War* (1985), edited by W. D. Ehrhart, is described on its cover as "The Best Work by the Best Poets of the Vietnam Generation." Indeed, with the notable absence of Michael Casey, the anthology is that, at least for poetry then published. In fact, *Carrying the Darkness*, which takes its title from a poem by Horace Coleman, is one of the indispensable literary works of the Vietnam War in that, far more than any single prose work, it brings together the emotions and attitudes of an entire cross-section of the war's American survivors, veteran and nonparticipant, white and black, men and women (although the latter are still conspicuously underrepresented).

Diversity aside, the volume is also notable for the quality of its offerings. It is, for instance, one of the few places where the impressive work of Basil Paquet, who has not published since 1972, can be found. Similarly, the book contains most of the important early work of John Balaban, perhaps the war's preeminent poet. The anthology also features substantial offerings from Bruce Weigl, Yusef Komanyakaa, and Gerald McCarthy, all of whom won important prizes in the years after its publication. In addition, it has a generous smattering of the poetry of Ehrhart himself, one of the most prolific of all Vietnam writers. Ehrhart's work is singular for its ethical dimension, as is he for his tireless work—as memoirist, editor, and lecturer—in bringing to light the war's poetry.

Impressive poetry of the Vietnam War has been published since *Carrying the Darkness*—much of it by American women veterans and Vietnamese in translation—but as yet, no other single anthology is so complete or so powerful.

See:

Gotera, Vince. *Radical Visions: Poetry by Vietnam Veterans*. Athens: University of Georgia Press, 1994.

Jeff Loeb

CASSELLI, HENRY, JR. (Artist). During the war in Vietnam, the United States Armed Forces employed dozens of combat artists who turned out thousands of works of art depicting all facets of the conflict. Perhaps the most skillful, though by far the youngest and the least experienced, was Henry C. Casselli, Jr. Barely out of art school when sent to Vietnam, the twenty-one-year-old created a vivid portfolio of war as it was fought. His work, most sketched or painted in 1968 and 1969 while the artist, then a corporal in the Marine Corps, wandered from one battle to the next, remains one of the most accurate views of the Vietnam experience.

By the time of his discharge in 1970, he had produced 680 drawings and paintings telling the story of individual Marines in the conflict. His pencil sketches made during and immediately after the battle for Hue during the Tet Offensive in early 1968 are among the most poignant pictures to come from the war. They, like all of his works, have an eyewitness quality to them that draws observers into the scenes, whether they are views of exhausted young Marines, fresh from days of battle, or, as in a 1969 acrylic, the heartrending portrait of two men crying over the death of a friend. "I had no idea of the horror that existed there," Casselli said recently, "[but] it became very, very real. I sketched everything but the gung ho men's magazine stuff. I showed the emotion that existed between guys. I learned how to cry out there, how to hurt[,] . . . how to express feelings" (Kemp, 51–52).

In 1968, with the war still in full swing, the first of Casselli's drawings were published in *Vietnam Combat Art*, a collection of images done by Marine artists. Since leaving the Marines, he has made his home in New Orleans, Louisiana, where in 1987, he won the Gold Medal of the American Watercolor Society, which is awarded the nation's best artist in that medium.

See:

Kemp, John H. "Henry Casselli." *American Artist*, August 1987, 48.

M. Paul Holsinger

CASUALTIES OF WAR (**Film**). Brian De Palma's *Casualties of War* (Columbia, 1989) focuses on the kidnap, rape, and murder of a Vietnamese girl by a five-man squad of American soldiers from the Twenty-third Americal Division during the Vietnam War. David Rabe, the author of such excellent Vietnam-era dramas as *Sticks and Bones* (1969) and *Streamers* (1976), based his screenplay on a true incident that took place in 1966. The film shows war's effect on the soldiers' humanity, exploring such subjects as the loss of innocence, evil, guilt, moral obligations, Vietnam, and the military.

The squad leader, Sergeant Meserve (Sean Penn), represents evil, and Private Eriksson (Michael J. Fox), the one member of the squad who abstains from the atrocity and who reports his fellow soldiers' war crime, represents innocence. De Palma uses the moral and ethical confusion that confronted Eriksson in an amoral war to demonstrate that "casualties of war" refer to more than the physically wounded and dead. Both Eriksson and his bestial squad members are victims of the war's ability to transform neophyte warriors into monsters.

The inclusion of such well-known actors as Penn and Fox and the shooting of some scenes in a Southeast Asian location (Thailand) guaranteed the production a profitable box office; it grossed more than $18 million during its initial run. It was not overly popular, however, with most critics, who generally viewed it as unrealistic and stereotyped. Only its skillful depiction of tracer rounds, a special effect normally difficult to capture on film, received universal praise.

See:

McMahon, Kathryn. "*Casualties of War*: History, Realism, and the Limits of Exclusion." *Journal of Popular Film and Television* 22.1 (Spring 1994): 12–21.

Catherine Calloway

CHAPELLE, DICKEY (Photojournalist). Georgette "Dickey" Chapelle was one of the few female war photojournalists whose record on the frontlines not only far exceeded most of her male counterparts but also made her an unquestioned "superstar" in her profession. "I think gunfire turned her on," one of her friends wrote after her death. "You couldn't go to a war where she didn't show up," said another (Ostroff, 302, 377). Neither a great photographer nor a brilliant journalist, Chapelle was always an exceptional eyewitness. Her photoessays from the last days of World War II to the war in Vietnam made millions of readers feel that they, too, were experiencing the immediacy of battle.

Active throughout all of World War II, Chapelle's first opportunity to see the war up close came in early 1945, when she became the first woman photographer accredited to operate in the Pacific theater. She immediately set out for the front and soon produced some of the best work of her career. One photograph,

"*Dying Marine*," which she shot on a hospital ship lying off Iwo Jima, remains emotionally draining more than fifty years later. Though she developed a close and long-lasting relationship with the Marine Corps after 1945, she was denied access to cover the war in Korea. Undeterred, she reported on such events as the Hungarian revolt, the Algerian Civil War, and Fidel Castro's insurrection in Cuba. When President Dwight Eisenhower sent U.S. Marines into Lebanon in 1958, Chapelle was there, and seven years later, she watched Marines land in the Dominican Republic to support the American-backed ruling junta.

Chapelle's most famous war work, however, came during the first years of the U.S. involvement in Vietnam. She arrived there in May 1961 and began creating photographic stories about the American fight against the forces of communism in Vietnam, Cambodia, and Laos. Her prize-winning "Helicopter War in South Viet Nam," which appeared in the November 1962 issue of *National Geographic*, provided one of the first in-depth photographic looks that most Americans had of the escalating conflict. (A follow-up, "Water War in Viet Nam," appeared posthumously in that same magazine in February 1966). Over the next four years, she returned to the frontlines repeatedly, but, on November 4, 1965, while traveling with a Marine "search and destroy" team, she was killed instantly when a Viet Cong land mine exploded next to where she was standing. She was the only female press corps member to die during the war.

Chapelle published a partial autobiography, *What's a Woman Doing Here? A Reporter's Report on Herself*, in 1962.

See:

Ostroff, Roberta. *Fire in the Wind: The Life of Dickey Chapelle*. New York: Ballantine, 1992.

M. Paul Holsinger

THE CHILDREN OF AN LAC (Film). In October 1980, *The Children of An Lac*, a made-for-television movie, debuted on CBS. Based on the true story of the heroic, heartwarming effort of Americans Betty Tisdale (Shirley Jones) and Ina Balin (played by herself) to evacuate 219 orphans before the fall of Saigon in April 1975, it captures the fear and tension of those last days before the communist takeover of the entire country. Blanche Hanalis's screenplay for *The Children of An Lac* is often touching. Though the picture is essentially a "woman's film," it offers an important historical footnote to America's failed adventure in Southeast Asia.

Balin, a former Hollywood star, first became interested in the war orphans of Saigon while on a **United Services Organization (USO)** tour of South Vietnam in 1970. Some months later, working closely with Tisdale and a number of dedicated Vietnam men and women, she helped establish the city's An Lac ("Happy Place") orphanage. Gradually she devoted more and more time to its growth and caring environment. When it became clear that the United States would do nothing more to prevent South Vietnam's fall, Tisdale and Balin (who also acted as story consultant and associate producer) began trying to find a way to get themselves and their charges to the United States. With nearly all of Saigon panicked by the imminent arrival of the supposedly vindictive North Vietnamese army, they ran into innumerable roadblocks, but, at the last minute, the two women talked an American embassy official into allowing them the use of a large C-130 cargo plane. In a moving, happy ending, they were able to bring at least their young children ''home.'' Sadly, tens of thousands of others were not as fortunate.

The Children of An Lac focused national attention on the plight of the more than 40,000 deserted Amerasian children. During the next few years, several other motion pictures, most notably *Don't Cry, It's Only Thunder* (1982), also based on a true story, featured similar dramatic accounts of the care and rescue of Vietnamese orphans.

See:

Devine, Jeremy M. *Vietnam at 24 Frames a Second: A Critical and Thematic Analysis of over 400 Films about the Vietnam War.* Jefferson, NC: McFarland, 1995, 205–206.

M. Paul Holsinger

CHINA BEACH (**Television Series**). Like so many projected television series, *China Beach* originated as a two-hour made-for-television movie. Set in 1967 at an evacuation hospital and an adjoining rest and recuperation resort in Vietnam near the big U.S. base at DaNang, the film, which was shown for the first time on ABC in early 1988, introduced a cast of nurses, doctors, and support personnel. The focus of the show, as opposed to *M*A*S*H* (which was ostensibly set in the Korean War), was on women instead of men. The lead character, Colleen McMurphy (Dana Delaney), is an idealistic but competent nursing volunteer for Vietnam service. Other main characters are also female, including the unit commander (Concetta Tomei), McMurphy's best friend (a sometime prostitute played by Marg Hellgenberger), and a Red Cross aide. A cast of other women and a number of men as doctors, mechanics, soldiers, and civilians ably support them. Produced and scripted by John Sacret Young (who also wrote the 1977 *A Rumor of War*), hour-long episodes began in late April 1988. The last original telecast came on July 22, 1991.

The war occasionally intrudes directly in enemy attacks on the base, but usually, only indirectly, in the form of casualties to be treated. Though the series does not shy away from graphically portraying the horrors of war—Beckett, a young soldier who runs the morgue, for instance, is frequently concerned over the increasing number of bodies—it is relationships, rather than combat, that are highlighted. It is those relationships among staff and patients that keep McMurphy there even after her initial enlistment is up. This provides the opportunity to explore women's roles and contributions on the warfront much more deeply than did, say, *So Proudly We Hail* (1943) in World War II.

During the last year, the series also follows McMurphy for some time after she leaves Vietnam and struggles with readjustment to civilian life and to the wrenching loss of the intimate relationships that had sustained her. Consequently, many political and social issues are examined, and the audience is shown a participant's view from both the combat and home front. At times, it is almost as if *A Walk in the Sun* (1945) and *The Best Years of Our Lives* (1946) were rolled into one.

See:

Vartanian, Carolyn Reed. "Women Next Door to War: China Beach." In *Inventing Vietnam: The War in Film and Television*, ed. Michael Anderegg. Philadelphia: Temple University Press, 1991, 190–203.

Jack Colldeweih

COBB, RON (Cartoonist). During the social disruptions of the 1960s and early 1970s over such issues as social repression, institutionalized racism, and the war in Vietnam, one of the primary means of communication among the "new left" and other dissenting groups was the underground press. This constantly evolving group of (usually) tabloid weekly newspapers not only informed their own individual readers about events, activities, opinions, and styles but also were connected, via the Underground Press Syndicate, so as to exchange material in somewhat the same manner as the Associated Press (AP). One of the first items usually traded was the weekly editorial cartoon by the young artist Ron Cobb, drawing for the *Los Angeles Free Press*.

A painter, photographer, and film animator as well as a cartoonist, Cobb was on military duty in Saigon in the fall of 1963 when President Ngo Dinh Diem was overthrown, and many of the anti–Vietnam War attitudes apparent in his cartoons reflected his experiences there. The nature of combat was psychically and socially integrating for him and affected his subsequent approach to cartooning. He believed that crisis stripped away the social facade and put man in touch with his real nature. "I do a caricature of reality to bring about a model crisis and place it before the eyes of another human being so that he can experience the . . . integrating effect," he once wrote (*"Mah Fellow Americans,"* 6). One of his favorite methods of doing this was by paradox, especially by using popular middle-class slogans in unexpected and contrasting situations, so as to make his readers reevaluate their thinking and policies. For example, a cartoon titled "Pacification" showed several marines sitting around a shell hole rolling and smoking marijuana. Another depicted B-52s bombing a Vietnamese city while a peasant led his haloed Madonna-like wife and child away on a donkey. On the home front, he pictured a couple proudly wheeling a carriage with a flag-draped coffin down an idyllic, picket-fenced, American street.

Cobb rarely drew cartoons related to specific events, preferring to deal with general ideas and actions. This, along with his great skill, enabled his work to be understood and applied broadly, making him the most widely published of all the new left cartoonists during the period.

See:

Colldeweih, Jack. "Ron Cobb: A Voice from the Underground." *Prospects. An Annual Journal of American Cultural Studies* 2 (1976): 68–91.
"Excerpts from an Interview with Ron Cobb." In *"Mah Fellow Americans": Editorial Cartoons by Ron Cobb from the Underground Press Syndicate.* Los Angeles: Sawyer, 1968, 5–7.

Jack Colldeweih

COMING HOME (Film). *Coming Home* (United Artists, 1978), directed by Hal Ashby, is the story of Sally Hyde (**Jane Fonda**); her husband, Marine Captain Bob Hyde (Bruce Dern); and ex-Marine Luke Martin (Jon Voight), a paraplegic wounded in Vietnam. When Bob is sent to Vietnam, Sally, the loyal wife, remains in California near the Marine base, where she volunteers in the local VA hospital. There she meets the embittered Luke, who is about to be released.

Though patriotic at first, Sally gradually changes her attitudes as a result of the severe neglect at the VA hospital and the government's indifference to the plight of its disabled patients. An affair ensues between her and Luke. After a patient's suicide, Luke chains himself to the gates of the base to protest the war. This act results in surveillance by government agents, who tape his and Sally's liaisons and then promptly inform Bob, who has just been shipped home with a minor wound. In the dramatic climax, Bob's deep self-conflicts, over both Sally and his experiences in Vietnam, impel him to suicide, while, in a parallel scene, Luke lectures high school seniors on how his country duped him into volunteering for a meaningless war.

Coming Home met with controversy from the moment of its release. Fonda's presence alone was enough to distress the war's apologists, still angry over President Carter's pardon of draft evaders the year before. At the same time, its sympathetic portrayal of veterans as victims alienated the left, who preferred the then-current cinematic image of crazed killers. Members of the film community were far more appreciative of Ashby's work. Though the movie failed to win the best picture honors for which it was nominated, Fonda was voted an Academy Award as the year's best actress, Voight was selected best actor, and the screen-writing team of Waldo Scott, Robert C. Jones, and Nancy Dowd won a best screenplay Oscar. Dern was also nominated as best supporting actor and Ashby, as best director. *Coming Home* presents a balanced and human account of the country's dilemma, and the sound track, a who's who of late-1960s rock and soul artists, evokes the period well.

See:

Katzman, Jason. "From Outcast to Cliché: How Film Shaped, Warped and Developed the Image of the Vietnam Veteran, 1967–1990." *Journal of American Culture* 19 (1995): 7–24.

Jeff Loeb

COMING HOME (Novel). *Coming Home* (1971), George Davis's fictional account of three fighter pilots flying missions over Vietnam from Thailand, is often viewed simply as dealing with racial conflicts during the war. Such readings essentially ignore its other dimensions, which include complex examinations of gender and caste exploitation. Davis himself is one of only three black veterans to have written novels about Vietnam—John Carn and A. R. Flowers are the other two—and his subtle perceptions and savage vision of the effects of prejudice lend the book a unique texture.

Told in a series of first-person interior monologues by a variety of characters, *Coming Home* essentially concentrates on the thoughts of the three pilots and the wife of one. Ben, who is Harvard-educated and of patrician background, has "forgotten how to be black," but at the same time, he feels an intense, though totally intellectualized, hatred for whites. Childress, a true predator, has more contempt for Ben than he does for whites like Stacy, to whom he feels superior. Stacy, who is deeply racist without realizing it, cannot understand Ben's innate hostility for him. Rose, Ben's wife, deeply resents the conformist pressures he put her under and strives to hurt him emotionally.

Rose eventually sleeps with Childress out of revenge when he returns to the States. He, after turning in his Thai girlfriend as a communist rather than seeing her become Ben's mistress, is arrested for killing a white policeman. Stacy, with thoughts of racial and sexual hatred in his mind, is shot down over Vietnam, and Ben, sick of killing in a white man's war, deserts.

Neglected in recent years, *Coming Home* is one of the fine novels of the war, revealing many of the paradigms for the black experience in Vietnam.

See:

Mitchell, Verner D. "I, Too, Sing America: Vietnam in Metaphor in *Coming Home*." *Vietnam Generation* 1.2 (1989): 118–124.

Jeff Loeb

DEAR AMERICA: LETTERS HOME FROM VIETNAM (Documentary). *Dear America: Letters Home from Vietnam* (1987), directed by Bill Couturie, is a highly effective documentary blend of footage of events in both Vietnam and the United States; personal photographs; compelling music (such as the Rolling Stones' "Gimme Shelter," Bob Dylan's "A Hard Rain's Gonna Fall," and Tim Buckley's "Once I Was"); and dramatic readings of actual letters by actors including Mark Harmon, Kathleen Turner and Howard Rollins, Jr. Based on a 1985 book of the same title edited by Bernard Edelman, it was originally produced by HBO for television screening then later released for theatrical showing.

Loosely composed as history (superimposed legends keep us informed about when certain events took place, with total casualty counts at those points), the production is actually about people, large and small. The large are the country's leaders—Lyndon B. Johnson (LBJ), General William Westmoreland, Richard

Nixon, even Bob Hope, all represented in footage from NBC's vaults—and the small, the grunts who fought the war. Ultimately, an intense drama grows out of the represented conflict between the two, the foolish, and even pernicious, leaders on the one hand, and the suffering, and often unwilling, ground troops on the other.

The film's heart and soul, however, are the dramatic letters that are emotionally read over scenes of intense trauma or photographs of the original frequently dead writers. The climax comes with footage of My Lai on the screen, the moving "Signed D. C." in the background, and Robert De Niro's voice reading: "I just can't accept the fact of the human damage. I feel like I'm at the bottom of a great sewer." This is followed by Sean Penn reading (apparently in a response to the grieving mother of a dead comrade): "I'm hollow; I'm a shell, and when I'm scared, I rattle. I can't tell you about your son. I'm sorry." Although this technique can occasionally become maudlin, more often it is effective and highly moving. *Dear America: Letters Home from Vietnam* won an Emmy as the year's outstanding informational special.

See:

Dornfield, Barry. "*Dear America*: Transparency, Authority and Interpretation in a Vietnam War Documentary." In *From Hanoi to Hollywood: The Vietnam War in American Film*, ed. Linda Dittmar and Gene Michaud. New Brunswick, NJ: Rutgers University Press, 1990, 283–297.

Jeff Loeb

THE DEER HUNTER (Film). Michael Cimino's *The Deer Hunter* (EMI, 1978) was one of the first Hollywood motion pictures about the war in Vietnam since *The Green Berets* a decade earlier. Production companies assumed that American audiences were not interested in movies about a war that divided the country and ended in disaster until Cimino's film and *Coming Home* (1978) proved otherwise. *The Deer Hunter*'s five Academy Awards (including best picture and best director) and success at the box office helped pave the way for other views of the war in Vietnam.

The Deer Hunter focuses its attention on three young, Vietnam-bound, naively patriotic Pennsylvania steelworkers, Nick (Christopher Walken, who won an Oscar as the year's best supporting actor), Steven (John Savage), and Michael (Robert De Niro, nominated for best actor). It unfolds in three segments. In the first, Nick and Michael attend Steven's wedding—a celebration of the solidarity of their working-class, Ukrainian community—then the three friends embark on one last deer hunt. The middle section of the film is set in Vietnam, where they are taken prisoner and forced to play a murderous game of Russian roulette. Even though Michael, identified earlier as the trio's natural leader and a modern embodiment of James Fenimore Cooper's Natty Bumppo, engineers their escape, Steven is badly wounded, and Nick is left mentally unbalanced. The final sequence focuses upon Michael's return home and his unsuccessful attempts to reunite the veterans with their family and friends. Steven is crippled, Nick is dead, and Michael has lost the will to hunt. When Nick's funeral finally brings the survivors together, it is clear that, in addition to shattering bodies and minds, the war has shattered a community's faith in the cultural myths which defined their American identity.

See:

Quart, Leonard. "*The Deer Hunter*: The Superman in Vietnam." In *From Hanoi to Hollywood: The Vietnam War in American Film*, ed. Linda Dittmar and Gene Michaud. New Brunswick, NJ: Rutgers University Press, 1990, 159–168.

Philip J. Landon

DIEN CAI DAU (Poetry). *Dien Cai Dau* (1988), by Yusef Komanyakaa, winner of the 1993 Pulitzer Prize, is one of the three or four most important collections of poetry about Vietnam from a war that produced reams of veteran poetry. Loosely translated, the title means crazy (often pidginized by American soldiers to "dinky dow," frequently the only Vietnamese they knew). For Komanyakaa, the phrase seems to sum up the war and its effects, which still haunt his poetic characters across the years. These include both Americans and Vietnamese—indeed, one of the collection's strengths is its sensitivity to the suffering of the Vietnamese. In one, an American serviceman agonizes over the probable fate of an Amerasian child he left behind several years before; in another, a mother "sits before the TV" with an uncashed U.S. government death benefit check in her Bible, waiting for her son to come home after fourteen years—"That closed casket was weighed down with stones," she says.

The importance of Komanyakaa's *Dien Cai Dau* also lies in the fact that it is one of the very few collections about the war by an African American veteran, and racial division, a subject frequently straddled by white authors, is one of his major subjects. In "Tu Do Street," his black speaker strays into a white, country-and-western bar and ironically is refused service by a Vietnamese bargirl schooled in the racist customs of America. In "Report from the Skull's Diorama," he observes Viet Cong propaganda leaflets left for black soldiers at a remote firebase: "VC didn't kill / Dr. Martin Luther King." And in "Facing It," the collection's best-known poem, his speaker's "black face fades, / hiding inside the black granite" of the **Vietnam Veterans' Memorial**, while all around white survivors lament their losses.

See:

Gotera, Vicente F. "Depending on the Light: Yusef Komanyakaa's *Dien Cai Dau*." In *America Rediscovered: Critical Essays on Literature and Film of the Vietnam War*, ed. Owen W. Gilman, Jr., and Lorrie Smith. New York: Garland, 1990, 282–300.

Jeff Loeb

DISPATCHES (Personal Accounts). Michael Herr, a war correspondent for *Esquire* magazine, went to Vietnam in 1967 and spent years roaming the war-ravaged countryside. He wrote about a nightmare war where almost everything that happens is confusing, horrifying, and ultimately senseless. He shaped his writings and recollections into *Dispatches*, published in 1977.

The book is divided into six sections: "Breathing In," "Hell Sucks," "Khe Sanh," "Illumination Rounds," "Colleagues," and "Breathing Out." Written in a purposely fragmented style, *Dispatches* presents grunts, medics, Lurps (reconnaissance patrols), special forces, survivors, marines, gooks, Viet Cong (VCs), NVAs, correspondents, and politicians in their own words. The war often seems to be viewed, both by Herr and fellow correspondent Sean Flynn, son of actor Errol Flynn, through an alcohol and drug-induced haze. Theirs is a generation influenced by World War II movies, but there are no John Waynes or Errol Flynns in the bush, only young, scared, profane, shell-shocked, filthy, messed-up men. It is unclear to them when the war started or why they are even there. The people they are bombing and the people they are feeding look (and possibly are) the same. Most of the men only count the days before they can leave. They have no fear of punishment, since the worst thing they can imagine is being sent to Vietnam. Bombings and body bags, ambushes and artillery, drinking and drugs, and, only very occasionally, a hero are part of this war.

Herr later collaborated on two films about Vietnam, as writer of the narration for *Apocalypse Now* (1979) and as the associate producer and coauthor of the screenplay for 1987's *Full Metal Jacket*, for which he received an Academy Award nomination.

See:

Myers, Thomas. "The Writer as Alchemist." Chapter 4 in *Walking Point: American Narratives of Vietnam*. New York: Oxford University Press, 1988, 146–171.

Sally E. Parry

DOONESBURY (Comic Strip). Few, if any, comic strips have so trenchantly examined this nation's history and social mores as Garry Trudeau's long-running *Doonesbury*. Created during 1968 as a *Yale Daily News* feature spoofing the foibles of everyone from the university's president to its football team quarterback, the cartoon went into national syndication on October 26, 1970. Always controversial, *Doonesbury* (named after one of its major continuing characters, former Yale undergraduate Mike Doonesbury) has commented on nearly every social, cultural, or political issue over the last thirty years. In doing so, Trudeau's sarcastic, tongue-in-cheek comics have influenced popular opinion for more than a generation.

From late 1970 until well past the day in April 1975 when the last troops were airlifted off the roof of the American embassy in Saigon, Trudeau explored every aspect of the U.S. role in Vietnam, including the notorious "body counts" of dead enemies, the socalled domino theory, the "light at the end of the tunnel," Jane Fonda's visit to North Vietnam, a Bob Hope visit, the My Lai Massacre, POWs and MIAs, and drug usage by many American GIs. One of the longest-running storylines involved "B.D.," a Yale football "jock" and Mike's roommate, who initially volunteered for the army to avoid completing a term paper. A "gung ho" soldier, he was quickly sent in-country where, from February to May 1972, he tried to fight with the same degree of blind stupidity that had earlier characterized his football days at Yale. Captured by a Viet Cong guerilla named Phred within the first week, B. D. soon developed a lasting love-hate relationship with the small terrorist. (In 1996, a far older, but not much wiser, B. D. returned to peacetime Vietnam where he discovered that Phred had become a leading commissar, raking in money on everything from the black market to planned tours of the battlefields for returning GIs such as his old friend.)

In the spring of 1975, Trudeau became the first newspaper comic strip artist to win the Pulitzer Prize for editorial cartooning, much to the chagrin of more traditional editorial artists around the United States. Though Trudeau's *Doonesbury* musings about the war in Vietnam made up only a small part of the huge body of material with which he has dealt over the past thirty years, they were, unquestionably, among the most important in the strip's long and illustrious history. In late 1990 and 1991, *Doonesbury* turned its focus back to yet another war, this time in Kuwait. Trudeau's thoughts on the so-called Desert Storm campaign were no less acerbic than they had been fifteen years earlier in Vietnam.

See:

Trudeau, G. B. *Flashbacks: Twenty-Five Years of Doonesbury.* Kansas City, MO: Andrews and McMeel, 1995.

M. Paul Holsinger

DRAFT CARD BURNING (Antiwar Protests). There is no record of when the first draft card, which all men between the ages of eighteen and thirty-five were required to carry after registering for the military draft, was burned publicly in protest to the war in Vietnam, but on July 29, 1965, a *Life* photographer in New York City took probably the first picture of such an event. After its appearance in that magazine, hundreds of other draft-age men also symbolically ignited their cards to demonstrate against the war.

There were few acts that so infuriated those persons who supported the administration's position in Southeast Asia. On August 10, the House of Representatives passed, 392–1, a bill that made it a federal crime to destroy willfully one's card. A $10,000 fine and up to five years in jail were set as penalties. The Senate approved the bill by a voice vote, and President Johnson signed it into law. It did little to stop the symbolic protests. One reporter in the liberal *Catholic Worker* wrote pointedly: "draft cards are for burning." Two months later, marchers in New York, carrying signs that read "Would Christ Carry a Draft Card?" and "Burn Draft Cards Not Children," publicly burned their draft cards at the U.S. Court House (Ferber and Lynd, 21–27, 72–76, 136–137). By 1967, college campuses across the country were the sites for numerous burnings;

students at Cornell University went so far as to issue a public "Call to Burn Draft Cards" and sent it nationwide. Later that year, a meeting on the Boston Common resulted in sixty-seven cards being burnt and hundreds more being turned in to the rally's organizers.

In October, at the massive antiwar protests conducted mainly by students, church groups, and a number of peace activists—an event memorialized by Norman Mailer in his 1968 non-fictional study, *Armies of the Night*—the largest mass draft card burning in the history of protest against the Vietnam War took place in front of the Pentagon. Whenever cards were burned publicly, it was not uncommon for conservative Americans to suggest that those igniting their cards were "Commie scum" who ought to be burned instead of their cards, but the burnings continued unabated throughout the war.

See:

DeBenedetti, Charles, and Charles Chatfield. *An American Ordeal: The Antiwar Movement of the Vietnam Era*. Syracuse, NY: Syracuse University Press, 1990, 128–130, 195–196.
Ferber, Michael, and Staughton Lynd. *The Resistance*. Boston: Beacon Press, 1971.
Wells, Tom. *The War Within: America's Battle over Vietnam*. Berkeley: University of California Press, 1994, 124–134.

M. Paul Holsinger

"DRAFT RESISTER" (Song). Unlike other American wars when opponents of military service were often jailed for speaking out in opposition to the government's policy, it was always possible during the war in Vietnam to record lyrics of protest, have them purchased by the millions, and hear them played on the nation's radio stations. The heavy metal band Steppenwolf's 1969 song "Draft Resister" offers an excellent example.

"We must save this country because it is the best one in the world," Steppenwolf's founder and lead singer, German-born John Kay (Joachim Krauledat), once wrote, but he and the others in the band refused to support American foreign and military policies automatically. The heroes in "Draft Resister" are those young men who choose jail over serving in the military. At a time when the United States was systematically betraying the innocent peoples of Vietnam, the song adds, only the draft resisters stand for sanity in an insane world.

Though "Draft Resister" never became as popular a smash hit as the band's most famous recording, "Born to be Wild," it was one of the band's biggest sellers. It is hard to know, however, whether Steppenwolf's millions of young fans made it so because of its strong political messages or simply because they liked the group's powerful combination of blues and rock.

See:

Storey, John. "Bringing It All Back Home: American Popular Song and the War in Vietnam." In *The Vietnam Era: Media and Popular Culture in the U.S. and Vietnam*, ed. Michael Kline. London: Pluto Press, 1990, 82–106.

M. Paul Holsinger

84 CHARLIE MOPIC **(Film).** *84 Charlie Mopic* (Charlie Mopic, 1989), written and directed by Vietnam veteran Patrick Duncan and considered to be one of the best low-budget films to emerge from the Vietnam War, focuses on a seven-man reconnaissance patrol from the 173rd Airborne Brigade. During the ground patrol, a combat soldier, an "84c," or motion picture specialist (Mopic), uses a single camera lens to film the reconnaissance mission, thus providing a direct view of guerilla warfare. Despite its low budget, the presence of an unknown cast of actors, and some occasional inaccuracies in types of equipment and uniforms, *84 Charlie Mopic* is considered one of the most realistic depictions of a patrol's actions in Vietnam.

In the production, the North Vietnamese military is respected by the American soldiers, who acknowledge, "It's Charlie's war." Such a thought, openly expressed, is unique for most pictures that deal with the Vietnam War. *84 Charlie Mopic*'s accurate portrayals of artillery, the soldiers' language, camaraderie, and radio communications help account for its realism and popularity.

See:

Whillock, David Everett. "The Fictive American Vietnam War Film: A Filmography." In *America Rediscovered: Critical Essays on Literature and Film of the Vietnam War*, ed. Owen W. Gilman, Jr., and Lorrie Smith. New York: Garland, 1990, 303–312.

Catherine Calloway

FIELDS OF FIRE **(Novel).** *Fields of Fire* (1978), a novel of the war in Vietnam by James Webb, is notable mainly because its author, a former Marine officer who served in that war, later became the secretary of the navy in the Reagan administration. Immensely popular in the years following its publication, it essentially ratifies a whole series of racial and cultural stereotypes. Never apologizing for American involvement, it basically states that the war effort was undermined by poor leadership and the treachery of the antiwar movement.

The action consists chiefly of stock battle scenes that strain credulity. The Americans are bested, not because of any lack of personal courage, but rather through failures of leadership. The clichéd characters come out of the World War II literary "melting pot" tradition, one that reflects America's bright post-war image of itself. There is, for instance, a ghetto kid who is, inexplicably, white and, naturally, the most proficient killer. A "good" officer who, like a doomed Faulknerian hero, prizes honor above the war, also appears, as does a college boy named Goodrich, who, despite his poor instincts (he is against the war), is nevertheless finally able to measure up. There is a single African-American, who is carefully apolitical though radicalized by racism he encounters in the rear, and the obligatory Hispanic, occupying his space on the page but denied full subjectivity.

Most are killed, of course, but the climax, key to the novel's political message, comes after Goodrich is flown back to the States and agrees to speak at an antiwar rally at Harvard, his alma mater. At the dais on crutches, he is outraged at the sight of what he regards as privileged and coddled youth, and he ends up publicly condemning them for cowardice. Goodrich emerges from the ensuing confrontation the clear moral winner.

See:

Palm, Edward F. "James Webb's *Fields of Fire*: The Melting-Pot Platoon Revisited." *Critique* 24.2 (1983): 105–118.

Jeff Loeb

FONDA, JANE (Antiwar Activist). Jane Fonda, winner of two Academy Awards as best actress (1971 and 1978) and a nominee on four other occasions (1969, 1977, 1981, and 1986) as either best actress or best supporting actress, was the Vietnam War era's most controversial film personality. Though her current marriage to billionaire television executive Ted Turner, the founder of the **Cable News Network (CNN)**, makes her seem a model of upper-class respectability to anyone who does not remember the war, many veterans of the conflict will always think of her simply as "Hanoi Jane," a traitor to the United States.

Ironically, Fonda began her political activities in 1962 strongly supporting the U.S. military. Draped in red, white, and blue ribbon as that year's "Miss Army Recruiting," she gave an emotional acceptance speech encouraging support for the army in its fight against communist aggression. She soon changed, however. As the war in Vietnam began to heat up, Fonda spoke out frequently against it and, in 1972, helped produce the controversial *F.T.A.* (politely rendered as "Free the Army"), a traveling alternative **USO** show that she and other Hollywood performers took around the country to entertain embittered draftees. When she flew illegally to North Vietnam later that year, she became even more notorious. Photographed aiming an anti-aircraft gun skyward, Fonda also broadcast a series of propaganda messages for Radio Hanoi denouncing the American military as "war criminals." Though she met with American POWs, many claimed later that they were tortured when they refused to adopt her position or broadcast for their captors as she had done. When Fonda returned to the United States, she faced congressional attempts to have her tried for sedition and bitter denunciations from the many supporters of the nation's war efforts. Though little came of the protests, there are still many Americans who believe that her actions should be punished. As late as 1988, for instance, the Veterans of Foreign Wars, not only asked Congress to investigate the actress's "many treasonous activities" but also called on citizens across the United States to boycott her films and other business ventures.

See:

Andersen, Christopher. *Citizen Jane: The Turbulent Life of Jane Fonda*. New York: Holt, 1990.

M. Paul Holsinger

FORREST GUMP (Novel-Film). *Forrest Gump*, a 1986 novel written by Vietnam War veteran Winston Groom, is a tall tale that features, as its title character, an idiot savant who experiences a number of fantastic adventures including a tour of duty in Vietnam. Though it received mixed reviews, it sold a very respectable 40,000 copies in hardback and hundreds of thousands of paperback copies as well.

Groom's book was transformed into a wildly successful movie. In its Vietnam War segment, *Forrest Gump* (Paramount, 1994) combines realistic combat scenes with the improbable rescue (thanks to Forrest's almost superhuman speed) of most of his embattled platoon. Personally awarded (through the use of special effects) a Medal of Honor from President Lyndon Baines Johnson, the naïve Gump later also becomes involved with a number of less-than-credible stereotypical members of the antiwar movement, including several violent and profane peace demonstrators as well as a group of angry black militants. Theatergoers and critics alike loved the film. It grossed more than $300 million during its first-run engagement and won six Academy Awards (of the ten for which it was nominated) including best film, best director (Robert Zemeckis), and best actor (Tom Hanks in the title role).

There is great disagreement about *Forrest Gump*'s "message." Conservatives such as Newt Gingrich have praised it as a positive portrayal of American goodness and family values. Supporters of the left, on the other hand, see it as little more than a series of silly images that trivialize a very serious attempt to change America for the better. Which side is correct depends on the viewer.

See:

Chumo, Peter N., II. " 'You've Got to Put the Past behind You Before You Can Move On': *Forrest Gump* and National Reconciliation." *Journal of Popular Film and Television* 23.1 (1995): 2–7.

Anthony O. Edmonds

"FORTUNATE SON" (Song-Autobiography). Few rock bands were more successful in the late 1960s and early 1970s than Creedence Clearwater Revival (CCR) with its lead singer-composer John Fogarty. Before the group disbanded in 1972, eight of its singles reached "gold" status. One of the best was CCR's October 1969 recording of "Fortunate Son" and "Down on the Corner." Though neither song reached number one on the charts—"Down on the Corner" rose to number three and "Fortunate Son" to number fourteen—both were great popular successes. In the latter, Fogarty screams in frustration at the hypocrisy of flag-waving, conservative, upper-class Americans who willingly seek exemptions from military service for their sons while patriotically sending other young men off to die. These same people with their "star-spangled eyes," he wails bitterly, insist on constant sacrifice for the country but are unwilling to risk their children's futures for its survival.

Long after the war in Vietnam was over, Lewis B. Puller, Jr., son of the most decorated man in United States Marine Corps history, used the title of Fogarty's popular song to write his Pulitzer Prize–winning *Fortunate Son: The Autobiography of Lewis B. Puller, Jr.* (1991). Filled with the need to serve his country, Puller joined the Marines shortly after graduating from college. In October 1968, just three months after being sent to Vietnam, the twenty-three-year old stepped on a booby-trapped howitzer round. Both legs were blown off, as was most of his left hand and several fingers on his right. Famous enough to be immediately flown home, he survived but was never able to create a "normal" life for himself, his wife, and baby.

Bitter at the United States for sending him and so many others to be slaughtered in an unnecessary war, Puller became an alcoholic. Though his autobiography (an honest account of his battle to overcome both his infirmities and his alcoholism) won sweeping praise, Puller's life continued to deteriorate. Acutely depressed, he committed suicide in 1995. *Fortunate Son* offers little in the way of battlefield memoirs, but it, like the song of the same name, is a work of unique importance.

See:

Loeb, Jeff. "Childhood's End: Self-Recovery in the Autobiography of the Vietnam War." *American Studies* 37.1 (1996):95–116.

Storey, John. "Bringing It All Back Home: American Popular Song and the War in Vietnam." In *The Vietnam Era: Media and Popular Culture in the U.S. and Vietnam*, ed. Michael Klein. London: Pluto Press, 1990, 82–106.

M. Paul Holsinger

FRIENDLY FIRE (Biography-Film). When Peg and Gene Mullen's son Michael was killed in Vietnam on February 17, 1970, the Iowa farming couple wanted details. The army responded indifferently to the Mullens' requests, though it knew that he had been inadvertently killed by "friendly fire" rather than by the enemy. On April 12, 1970, the frustrated Mullens placed a half-page "silent message to fathers and mothers in Iowa" in the state's largest newspaper, the *Des Moines Register*, asking "how many more lives do you wish to sacrifice because of your silence." Novelist C.D.B. Bryan was intrigued by the Mullens' story, and, after extensively interviewing them and the others involved (including Michael's battalion commander, Lieutenant Colonel Norman Schwarzkopf, whom the Mullens for many months blamed erroneously for their son's death), he wrote an article in the *New Yorker* about the family's search for the truth. *Friendly Fire*, his 1976 full-length book, continues to be one of the best personal accounts of the war from the perspective of the American home front.

Three years later, on April 22, 1979, a three-hour made-for-television movie based on Bryan's book was shown for the first time on ABC. Starring Carol Burnett as Peg, Ned Beatty as Gene, and Sam Watterston as Bryan, the film won an Emmy Award as the year's most outstanding drama. Emmies also went to David Greene (best director), Leonard Rosenman (best music score), and

William H. Wistorm (outstanding film sound editing). Burnett and Beatty were nominated for their roles, as was teleplay writer Fay Kanin. The production, now available on VHS videotape, has become a classic of its kind.

See:

Beidler, Philip D. *American Literature and the Experience of Vietnam.* Athens: University of Georgia Press, 1982, 150–153.

M. Paul Holsinger

***F.T.A.* (Documentary).** In 1972, Francine Parker directed *F.T.A.*, a semidocumentary film recording one of the many shows that the Free Theater Associates—antiwar actors and actresses such as Donald Sutherland and **Jane Fonda**, and singers like Holly Near, Rita Martinson, and Len Chandler—put on near United States Army bases the previous year. The initialed title stands, ostensibly at least, for the name of the performing troupe or perhaps for "Free the Army," the gist of the film's message, but neither states the obscenity that is repeatedly used throughout the ninety-six-minute show.

There is no subtlety in *F.T.A.* Working from a screenplay written in part by Fonda and Sutherland (who also produced the picture), Near, and antiwar author Dalton Trumbo, *F.T.A.* intended to offer an alternative to regular **United Services Organization (USO)** shows featuring performers such as **Bob Hope**. The stars repeatedly lambaste the army for its supposed insensitivity. There are close-up interviews with many of the soldiers in the audience, some of whom hate the war specifically and others who find the military that has drafted them repugnant. Fonda talks about the "prison" the men are in, often to much applause. There is considerable singing in the movie as well, the best done by Near and Martinson. It received an "R" rating because of the vulgar, gutter language used to appeal to the military men in its audience.

See:

Devine, Jeremy M. *Vietnam at 24 Frames a Second: A Critical and Thematic Analysis of over 400 Films about the Vietnam War.* Jefferson, NC: McFarland, 1995, 90–91.

M. Paul Holsinger

***FULL METAL JACKET* (Film).** *Full Metal Jacket* (Warner Brothers, 1987), Stanley Kubrick's screen adaptation of Gustav Hasford's 1979 novel about the Marines in Vietnam, *The Short Timers*, is, at the same time, both highly structured and oddly fragmented. Kubrick's, Hasford's, and Michael Herr's screenplay is sharply divided into two narrative sequences. The first half follows a group of recruits through their training at Parris Island, where they are driven and humiliated by their drill instructor, Sergeant Hartman (Lee Emery), until they either crack or become the efficient killing machines he is trying to create. One of the group, Joker (Matthew Modine), manages to preserve a degree of ironic detachment, but another, the overweight and hopelessly incompetent Pyle

(Vincent Phillip D'Onofrio), is driven into a murderous rage, which explodes into violence. He kills the sergeant and then commits suicide. The second half of the film depicts the now-trained Marines in Vietnam, culminating in the battle of Hue during 1968's bloody Tet Offensive.

Once *Full Metal Jacket* gets to Vietnam, its narrative becomes a series of loosely connected and rather uneven episodes. A well-staged firefight in Hue is an impressive display of meaningless violence and suffering, but the scene in a Marine pressroom, with the Joker and others discussing propaganda, seems oddly flat. Despite the brilliant cinematography of Douglas Milsome and the film's overarching theme of dehumanization begetting violence (both familiar aspects of the director's work), *Full Metal Jacket* does not measure up to Kubrick's strongest movies. Finding a narrative structure appropriate to the American experience in Vietnam has confounded many of the best directors in Hollywood. In the end, Kubrick, like most, also fails.

See:

Doherty, Thomas. "Full Metal Genre: Stanley Kubrick's Vietnam Combat Movie." *Film Quarterly* 42.2 (Winter 1988–1989): 24–30.
Reaves, Gerri. "From Hasford's *The Short Timers* to Kubrick's *Full Metal Jacket*: The Fracturing of Identification." *Literature/Film Quarterly* 16 (1988): 232–243.

Philip J. Landon

***GARDENS OF STONE* (Novel-Film).** Nicholas Proffitt, *Newsweek*'s former Saigon bureau chief, wrote *Gardens of Stone* in 1984. This home-front novel about the war in Vietnam focuses on a handful of soldiers of the third Army— the "Old Guard"—who, between 1968 and 1970, manned Arlington National Cemetery's burial details.

Gardens of Stone looks intimately at the close relationship that develops between Sergeant Clell Hazard, a veteran of World War II, Korea, and Vietnam, and Jack Willow, the son of one of Hazard's friends from Korea, who has also been assigned to Arlington. Willow, a naive, gung-ho enlistee, cannot wait to get into battle in Vietnam. When he does, he returns not as a hero but as one of the seemingly endless bodies destined for the cemetery's "gardens of stone." Proffitt paints a bleak picture, concluding with his antihero Hazard seeking to return to Vietnam for a third time, not to lead men to victory but to save them from dying.

Though most reviewers disliked the novel, complaining about its vulgarity or gratuitous sex scenes, Francis Coppola decided to bring *Gardens of Stone* (Tri-Star, 1987) to the screen. In doing so, screenwriter Ronald Bass cut almost all the foreboding Vietnam action experienced by Willow in the months before his death. To play on the heartstrings of hoped-for female viewers, Willow (D. B. Sweeney), who is unmarried in the original story, weds his childhood sweetheart. It is she who is featured in the pivotal opening and closing shots taken, melodramatically, during the young officer's funeral. James Caan (who plays

Hazard), James Earl Jones and Anjelica Huston all provide capable, workman-like acting, but the film, far more superficial than Proffitt's novel, fails to allow its audience to understand fully any of the characters or the reasoning behind their beliefs. With gross receipts of only slightly more than $5 million, it was one of the few major movies about the Vietnam War to be a commercial, and critical, failure.

See:

Kinney, Judy Lee. "*Gardens of Stone, Platoon*, and *Hamburger Hill*: Ritual of Remembrance." In *Inventing Vietnam: The War in Film and Television*, ed. Michael Anderegg. Philadelphia: Temple University Press, 1991, 153–165.

M. Paul Holsinger

G.I. JOE ACTION FIGURE (Toy). As the war in Vietnam was heating up in 1964, "G.I. Joe," a new toy soldier designed by Don Levine, was marketed for the first time. It quickly became the most popular such toy ever produced for boys. The original 11-inch tall figure, jointed at the neck, shoulders, arms, waist, and legs and thus capable of being posed in virtually any position imaginable, had a face ostensibly composed from that of twenty-three Congressional Medal of Honor winners. There were four different versions of G.I. Joe: Action Soldier, Action Sailor, Action Marine, and Air Force Action Pilot. Each sold initially for $3.88 and had a realistically designed uniform and equipment that could be purchased separately. The following year, a Black Action Soldier was introduced, as was a Green Beret, complete with an accurate uniform, an M-16 rifle, a radio set, a .45 caliber pistol, a bazooka, and hand grenades. In 1967, the company even produced an Army nurse "Joe," the only female version of the toy until the late 1990s.

G.I. Joe mania quickly spread across the nation, and other manufacturers soon added coloring books, lunch boxes, rub-on tattoos, and face masks. A G.I. Joe fan club was started. To offer their young boy buyers options, Hasbro, the toy's manufacturer, now also made a German Storm Trooper Joe, a Japanese Imperial Soldier Joe, and a Russian Infantryman Joe.

As the war in Asia turned into a bloody stalemate, the toy's popularity quickly waned. To counter the malaise, Hasbro created a talking Joe who, when his dog tags were pulled, could give eight different commands. "Life-like hair" was added in 1970; when that still failed to attract significant numbers of new purchasers, Joe was transformed into a fighter against worldwide evil instead of an American soldier. Full-sized action figures were taken off the market in 1978 and, four years later, replaced by 3½ inch toys.

In the mid-1990s, with the war in Vietnam long forgotten, nostalgia "buffs" made the original G.I. Joe figures treasured collectors' items, many selling for thousands of dollars apiece. Capitalizing on that interest, Hasbro not only brought back a slightly redesigned large doll but also a number of new figures representing everything from the contemporary space program to two female Eighty-second Airborne helicopter pilots, one white, and one African American.

In 1997 and 1998, the firm introduced a historical "Classic Collection" of figures. Now selling for $24.99 and packaged in boxes replete with factual information about a particular era or the specific person being honored, at least seven of the new "Joes" have a World War II orientation: a General Dwight Eisenhower, a General George S. Patton, two different Tuskegee Airmen, a figure honoring the United States First Army—the "Big Red One"—at D-Day, a Japanese-American nisei soldier from the famous 442nd Regiment, and even a doll that honors Francis S. Currey, a Medal of Honor winner from the Battle of the Bulge. There are two Civil War soldiers—one in a Union uniform, the other in Rebel gray—a Revolutionary War officer, and, in a bent toward modernity, a General Colin Powell doll.

See:

Santelmo, Vincent. *The Complete Encyclopedia to GI Joe.* 2nd ed. Iola, WI: Krause, 1997.

M. Paul Holsinger

"GIVE PEACE A CHANCE" (Song). "Give Peace a Chance," by ex-Beetle John Lennon, is one of the most poignant calls for non-violence written during the war in Vietnam. Believing that peace had to "be sold to the man in the street" and anxious "to make peace big business for everybody," Lennon wrote the song in Montreal during July 1969 while spending four highly publicized days in bed with his wife, Yoko Ono. The message in the title is repeated over and over in the original Apple recording by the Plastic Ono Band, and pile-drives the message home. By October, when the Hot Chocolate Band also recorded it, it had become a favorite with nearly all antiwar youth throughout the United States.

On Moratorium Day (November 15, 1969), more than 30,000 antiwar marchers chanted the lyrics of "Give Peace a Chance" in front of the White House. Later that same day, folksingers Pete Seeger, Peter, Paul, and Mary, and even the popular band leader Mitch Miller led more than 300,000 demonstrators at the Washington Monument in the song. Eventually more than 900,000 copies of one or more recordings of the number were sold in the United States; another 400,000 were sold internationally. For the rest of the war, "Give Peace a Chance" was perhaps the most frequently heard of all songs at antiwar rallies, and John Lennon, already famous, became a cultural hero of almost mythic proportions.

See:

Wiener, Jon. " 'Give Peace a Chance': An Anthem for the Antiwar Movement." In *Give Peace a Chance: Music and the Struggle for Peace*, ed. Marianne Philbin. Chicago: Chicago Review Press, 1983, 11–17.

M. Paul Holsinger

***GOING AFTER CACCIATO* (Novel).** Tim O'Brien's astonishing novel, *Going after Cacciato*, elicited a flood of praise following its publication in 1978 and has remained a standard for both academic and popular assessments of imaginative writing about the American war in Vietnam. The winner of the National Book Award for fiction in 1979, it features a complex structure in which three distinct narratives are mixed among forty-six chapters. Seventeen chapters report the horrific day-to-day experiences of Pfc. Paul Berlin and his Alpha Company cohorts during Berlin's year-long tour of duty in Vietnam; these sections are characterized by a harsh realism and feature meaningless death, aimless killing, a hostile climate, and debilitating illness. A second story line, told in nineteen chapters, chronicles Alpha Company's fantastic pursuit of the deserter Cacciato as he sets out with the notion of walking from Vietnam to Paris. It is a picaresque and often comic journey that leads from the jungles of Vietnam to Burma, India, Iran, Greece, and finally to Paris, as Cacciato stays one step ahead of his pursuers. Ten chapters, all entitled "The Observation Post," record the musings of Paul Berlin as he stands watch one night atop a tower on the Vietnam coast overlooking the South China Sea.

Using this triple-narrative structure, O'Brien is able not only to represent the on-the-ground experiences of many American combatants in Vietnam, but also to explore the various and myriad ways in which human imagination interacts with reality in the face of fear, confusion, and despair. In the end, O'Brien's book is not so much about escaping Vietnam as it is about having the courage to face it.

See:

Calloway, Catherine. "Pluralities of Vision: *Going after Cacciato* and Tim O'Brien's Short Fiction." In *America Rediscovered: Critical Essays on Literature and Film of the Vietnam War*, ed. Owen W. Gilman, Jr., and Lorrie Smith. New York: Garland, 1990, 213–224.

Griffith, James. "A Walk through History: Tim O'Brien's *Going after Cacciato.*" *War Literature and the Arts* 3.1 (1991): 1–34.

Dan Cabaniss

GOOD MORNING, VIETNAM (Film). *Good Morning, Vietnam* (Touchstone, 1987), directed by Barry Levinson, was the most popular comedy film to emerge from the Vietnam War. Robin Williams (nominated for an Academy Award as best actor) portrays Adrian Cronauer, a comic Armed Forces Radio disk jockey who broadcasts to the troops in Vietnam in 1965. While the movie has been faulted for its weak plot and stereotypical characters, there was considerable praise for its depiction of the dilemma confronted by the Vietnamese people, who had to play dual roles in the war: one for the Americans and one for the North Vietnamese Army.

Williams' character becomes friends with a group of supposedly friendly Southeast Asians, especially a Vietnamese youth, who turns out to be a North Vietnamese terrorist wanted in connection with a number of bombings. Ironically, the boy saves Cronauer's life twice, once when an army superior who dislikes Cronauer jeopardizes his life by placing him in an extremely dangerous position and again before an explosion at Jimmy Wah's Bar. The picture demonstrates the American frustration of not knowing the exact identity of the enemy as well as the plight of the Vietnamese people, for whom war has become a way of life. Although set in the city of Saigon, *Good Morning, Vietnam* still manages to portray the dangers inherent in a war zone.

See:

Gilman, Owen W., Jr. "Vietnam, Chaos, and the Dark Art of Improvisation." In *Inventing Vietnam: The War in Film and Television*, ed. Michael Anderegg. Philadelphia: Temple University Press, 1991, 231–250.

Catherine Calloway

A GOOD SCENT FROM A STRANGE MOUNTAIN (Novel). Robert Olen Butler, a Vietnam veteran and former army linguist fluent in Vietnamese, received a number of awards including the 1993 Pulitzer Prize for Fiction for his seventh book, *A Good Scent from a Strange Mountain* (1992). Like most of his other writing, especially his first novel, *The Alleys of Eden* (1981), *A Good Scent from a Strange Mountain* deals with the legacy of the Vietnam War. Unlike his earlier works, however, which were populated with Vietnam veterans, the main characters here are the Vietnamese people themselves. As refugees, they have immigrated to the United States from Vietnam and settled in the Louisiana Gulf Coast bayou area, where they are in the process of assimilating into American life and culture.

The fourteen short stories and one novella cover a wide range of topics: folklore and superstition, love, Vietnamese traditions, fairy tales, hopes and dreams, friendship, Ho Chi Minh, the influence of American culture, and a mock battle between two veterans, one American and one American-Vietnamese. *A Good Scent from a Strange Mountain*'s popularity comes in part from Butler's ability to dramatize, through first person narrators, the continuing conflict that the refugees undergo in their attempt to embrace two cultures—an old one they had to abandon physically due to the war and the new one, which encroaches on their ties to the past.

Almost half of the stories in the collection were published earlier in such periodicals and journals as the *Sewanee Review, the Virginia Quarterly Review*, and the *New England Review*. They can also be found individually in a number of anthologies such as *New Stories from the South* and *The Best American Short Stories*.

See:

Sartisky, Michael. "Robert Olen Butler: A Pulitzer Profile." In *The Future of Southern Letters*, ed. Jefferson Humphries and John Lowe. New York: Oxford University Press, 1996, 155–169.

Catherine Calloway

GO TELL THE SPARTANS (Film). *Go Tell the Spartans* (Mar Vista, 1978), which was directed by Ted Post, tells the story of a group of American military advisers serving in Vietnam early in 1964. The title is taken from the quote above the entrance to an abandoned French graveyard where much of the action takes place—"Stranger, go tell the Spartans how we lie; loyal to their laws, here we die"—and it serves as an ironic comment to the meaningless deaths awaiting Major Asa Barber (Burt Lancaster) and his men.

Barber, a decorated veteran of World War II and Korea, is obliged to follow orders handed down from superiors whose tactics are based on the theories of "management teams" armed with computers. Disillusioned with the modern military technobureaucracy, Barber does his best to protect his men until they can leave Vietnam. When told to set up camp at Muc Wa, an old French stronghold, he resists, but to no avail. The Viet Cong attack his force, made up of his advisers and a platoon of South Vietnamese militia. Some of his men are evacuated by helicopter, but, before they can return, Barber and all but one of the Americans are killed.

Go Tell the Spartans was overshadowed by **Coming Home** and **The Deer Hunter**, which, between them, collected most of the major Academy Awards for the year. It has never received the attention it deserves. Lancaster gives an impressive performance as an aging officer whose old-fashioned professionalism has earned him the nickname "Old World War II." The film, adapted from Daniel Ford's 1967 novel *Incident at Muc Wa*, captures Ford's ironic treatment of the myths that led America into Vietnam and of the self-seeking and folly of those who managed the misadventure.

See:

Devine, Jeremy M. *Vietnam at 24 Frames a Second: A Critical and Thematic Analysis of over 400 Films about the Vietnam War.* Jefferson, NC: McFarland, 1995, 140–148.

Philip J. Landon

THE GREEN BERETS (Novel-Film). *The Green Berets* (Warner Brothers, 1968), codirected by John Wayne and Ray Kellogg, served as a vehicle for Wayne's hawkish views on the war in Vietnam. James Lee Barrett's screenplay, which was based rather loosely on a 1965 best-selling book of the same name by Robin Moore, opens at a Green Beret base in the United States where a skeptical newsman (David Janssen) criticizes American participation in the war. The Green Beret commander Colonel Mike Kirby (Wayne) invites the reporter to accompany them on a mission to Vietnam, where events quickly convince the writer that the Green Berets play a key role in defending South Vietnam from Viet Cong invaders bent on murder, rape, and pillage. During their stay, the unit repulses the enemy, cares for women and children, and captures a Viet Cong general lured into a trap by a beautiful South Vietnamese spy. In the concluding scene, as the sun sets in the East, Kirby explains to the unit's young Vietnamese mascot, "You're what we're here for."

Wayne is badly miscast as the Berets' combat leader, but, by 1968, his personal popularity almost guaranteed that the film would be a commercial success. Although the title evolved from the popular "**The Ballad of the Green Berets**" (which serves as the movie's musical score), its narrative is borrowed from *Back to Bataan* (1945), a World War II film that also starred John Wayne. Because *The Green Berets* combines (probably indirectly) the American effort in Southeast Asia with the liberation of the Philippines and presents events in Vietnam as a Hollywood version of World War II, it is filled with unintentional (and often comic) ironies. If the tactics that had worked in earlier wars failed in Vietnam, the generic formulas developed to dramatize them failed as well. During the 1970s, both writers and filmmakers were forced to search for narrative structures appropriate to the American experience in Vietnam.

See:

Suid, Lawrence. "The Making of *The Green Berets*." *Journal of Popular Film* 6 (1977): 106–125.

Philip J. Landon

HAMBURGER HILL (**Film**). Between May 8 and June 7, 1969, members of the Third Brigade of the 101st Airborne Division, the Ninth Marine Regiment, and the Third ARVN Regiment took part in "Operation Apache Snow" in the A Shau Valley in western Vietnam, just north of the Laotian border. One of the major objectives in that campaign was Ap Bia Mountain—Hill 937, as it was officially known to the army, or "Hamburger Hill," as the troops soon named it because of the nearly 70 percent casualty rate North Vietnamese regulars inflicted on them. Airborne units attacked the hill again and again over a ten-day period before they were able to capture it. The ferocity of the fighting, which Senator Edward Kennedy later was to call both "senseless" and "irresponsible," raised a storm of protest escalating the already bitter vocal opposition to the war throughout the United States.

Jim Carabatsos, screenwriter for the previous year's *Heartbreak Ridge*, a film about the American invasion of Grenada, wrote and coproduced *Hamburger Hill* (RKO, 1987), which is ostensibly centered on the victorious American campaign of early 1969. The re-created battle scenes directed by John Irvin in the Philippines are excessively gory, filled with horrifically wounded American GI's and the exploding bodies of friend and foe alike. The script is laden with innumerable trite clichés about the hell of war, the importance of interracial understanding during stressful times, and the girl back home who has promised to be true no matter how long her loved one is away. When they are not being systematically killed off one by one, the cast of unknowns seems to take regular breaks from the fighting so they can expound on weighty issues or fill the screen with obligatory scatological references to each other's sexual lives.

An obvious attempt to cash in on the continual interest in the war in Vietnam, *Hamburger Hill* was a critical failure. It offers viewers plenty of death, but little else.

See:

Kinney, Judy Lee. "*Gardens of Stone, Platoon,* and *Hamburger Hill*: Ritual of Remembrance." In *Inventing Vietnam: The War in Film and Television,* ed. Michael Anderegg. Philadelphia: Temple University Press, 1991, 153–165.

Parish, James Robert. "*Hamburger Hill.*" In *The Great Combat Pictures: Twentieth-Century Warfare on the Screen.* Metuchen, NJ: Scarecrow, 1990, 200–203.

M. Paul Holsinger

HEARTS AND MINDS (Documentary). *Hearts and Minds* (Paramount, 1974) won the Academy Award as best feature documentary film of its year. Unlike most American-made documentaries about the Vietnam War that focus on what it did to the United States, *Hearts and Minds* concerns itself with what the war did to the Vietnamese. Director Peter Davis is never ambiguous in his point of view. The United States, he argues, brutally inflicted immense destruction on Vietnam and its peoples. He frequently uses the common documentary technique of juxtaposition—the placing of scenes or images one after another to invite comparison and contrast—to make his point. One such instance shows General William Westmoreland, former commander of U.S. forces in Vietnam, claiming that there are so many people in southeast Asia, that "the Oriental does not put the same value on human life as does the westerner." This is immediately followed by a scene of Vietnamese at a funeral. There, a woman, presumably the widow of the deceased, is beside herself with grief, screaming hysterically. In another parallel series, Richard Nixon is shown at a dinner for released American POWs praising the "Christmas bombing" of 1972, which supposedly resulted in their release. Next comes a shot of the rubble and wasted remains of a hospital in Hanoi destroyed by the raid.

Hearts and Minds spends a considerable time (for an American film) focusing on individual Vietnamese. Davis is not concerned about the generals or politicians but rather the peasants whose families, homes, and lives have been destroyed by the war. Again and again, the camera lingers after a person has finished speaking to show the pain and suffering that must be lived with every day because the Americans came to Vietnam.

The last section of *Hearts and Minds* is probably the least effective. Its logic is dubious, and its prevailing attitude is not so much sympathy for the Vietnamese people as scorn for the United States. After several brief segments intending to "prove" that many Americans fighting in Vietnam were racist killers, Davis implies that the devastation that was visited on Vietnam by the United States was no more than an outgrowth of this nation's supposed culture of violence, a culture that glorifies hatred of one's enemy and borders, all too often, on hysterical bloodlust.

See:

Grosser, David. " 'We Aren't on the Wrong Side, We Are the Wrong Side': Peter Davis Targets (American) *Hearts and Minds.*" In *From Hanoi to Hollywood. The Vi-*

etnam War in American Film, ed; Linda Dittmar and Gene Michaud. New Brunswick, NJ: Rutgers University Press, 1990, 269–282.

J. Justin Gustainis

"HELLO VIETNAM" (**Song**). Though there were dozens of anti–Vietnam War songs, there were only a handful that offered unqualified support for President Lyndon Johnson's decision to send an indeterminate number of ground troops into Southeast Asia after 1964. One of the most popular was "Hello Vietnam," written by former Army veteran Tom T. Hall, but recorded in 1965 by longtime country and western recording artist Johnny Wright.

"Hello Vietnam" was an instant success, moving on to *Country Music*'s top forty chart shortly after being released and staying there for more than five months. Though Wright's "old-fashioned" musical interpretation sung in a nasal twang, was at best, tearfully sentimental, the song eventually reached number one, remaining in that position for three weeks. According to the lyrics, which are sung by a young man to his sweetheart, the United States has heard South Vietnam's cries and has no choice but to help stop communist aggression before it can take root. Advocating the "domino theory" being pushed by the Johnson administration, the narrator makes it clear that, if communism succeeds in southeast Asia, America's freedoms will also soon disappear. As he heads patriotically off to war, he has but two requests—a farewell kiss and the promise from his sweetheart that she will write him while he is gone. After that, there is nothing left to say but goodbye and "Hello Vietnam."

Hall, who later became a country music recording star in his own right, also penned the flag-waving "Mama, Tell Them What We're Fighting For." Ironically, in 1972, he became a supporter of antiwar Democratic presidential candidate George McGovern.

See:

Lund, Jens. "Country Music Goes to War: Songs for the Red-Blooded American." *Popular Music and Society* 1.4 (1972): 210–230.

McCloud, Barry. "Tom T. Hall." In *Definitive Country: The Ultimate Encyclopedia of Country Music and Its Performers*, ed. Barry McCloud. New York: Perigee Books, 1995, 363–364.

M. Paul Holsinger

A HERO'S WELCOME (**Autobiography**). James A. Daly's *A Hero's Welcome: The Conscience of Sgt. James Daly vs. the U.S. Army* (1975) is perhaps the most fascinating memoir to come out of the Vietnam War. As an African-American account, it explores incipient racism, as white narratives do not.

Daly, a Jehovah's Witness who opposed violence, filed for conscientious objector status at eighteen, but his draft board challenged this declaration and a duplicitous recruiter advised him instead to join so that he could possibly avoid Vietnam. Realizing his error once in the army, he vainly requested a discharge from his various commanders. Instead, he was sent to Vietnam. There, he refused to carry a weapon and, later, when forced to do so, to load it. Astound-ingly, he was still sent on patrols, and, on one, was wounded and captured by the Viet Cong.

After being shuttled from place to place for two years, starved, beaten, and generally mistreated, Daly was taken to North Vietnam, where conditions im-proved marginally. As many prisoners eventually did, he joined the so-called "Peace Committee" and cooperated on a limited basis with the North Vietnam-ese. Upon his release and return in 1973, charges of treason were brought against him by two fellow captives, both air force officers, but a military court dismissed them all. Daly was finally able to exit the army with his disability pension intact.

Rather than reflecting bitterness at his treatment, he remains true to his ethical persuasions, criticizing the war and America's part in it but never any of his antagonists. Daly thus closes by positioning himself as morally superior to those who victimized him.

See:

Loeb, Jeff. "MIA: The African American Autobiography of the Vietnam War." *African American Review* 31.1 (1997): 105–123.

Jeff Loeb

"I FEEL LIKE I'M FIXIN' TO DIE RAG" (Song). During the early years of the war in Vietnam, Country Joe McDonald and the Fish was an acid rock band whose antiestablishment, antiwar repertoire gained a large youthful follow-ing. Certainly its most popular song was "I Feel Like I'm Fixin' to Die Rag," which was filled with repeated cynicism and despair. What difference did it make why we were fighting in Vietnam, the nihilistic chorus says, since every-one was going to be sent to Vietnam anyway. Under those circumstances, why give a "damn"? Released in November 1967, the piece pokes fun at Wall Street investors, the military establishment, and even flag waving but naive American parents who are sarcastically encouraged to send their son off to war as quickly as possible so that they can be the first on their block to have him return in a flag-draped government coffin. "Fixin' to Die" quickly became a minor classic and elevated McDonald to almost cult-like status among many college students.

In summer 1968, Country Joe and the Fish entertained the many antiwar protesters and picketers at the Chicago Democratic National Convention. Raw-edged, the group sang their rag to much applause; their "Fish Cheer" ("Gimme an F . . . a U . . . a C . . . a K!") only added to the anger against President John-son and the war. The following year, McDonald and his band led more than 300,000 at the famed Woodstock Festival in a sing-along of "Fixin' to Die," and, when that event was prominently featured in the Acacemy Award–winning documentary *Woodstock* (Warner Brothers, 1970), the song's popularity inten-sified even more among young listeners.

By 1982, however, Country Joe had come full circle, entertaining groups in San Francisco to raise money for the Vietnam Veteran's Project in that city.

Five years later, in conjunction with Daniel Keller, McDonald directed *Vietnam Experience* (Green Mountain Post/Rag Baby Productions, 1987). For the thirty-minute color documentary, he composed a number of new songs (all of which focus on the war as it was fought and its long aftermath) and reprised his old band's famous rag. Still a thoughtful and perceptive lyricist, he leaves no doubt, even after more than twenty years, of his unyielding opposition to the war.

See:

Storey, John. "Rockin' Hegemony: West Coast Rock and Amerika's War in Vietnam." In *Tell Me Lies about Vietnam: Cultural Battles for the Meaning of the War*, ed. Alf Louvre and Jeffrey Walsh. Philadelphia: Open University Press, 1988, 181–198.

M. Paul Holsinger

IF I DIE IN A COMBAT ZONE (Autobiography). Tim O'Brien's 1973 memoir of his year as an infantryman in Vietnam, *If I Die in a Combat Zone*, has been praised by many reviewers as the finest personal narrative to come out of the war in Vietnam. He strives to evaluate his own wartime experience against a background of classical, Christian, literary, and cultural models ranging from Plato to Hemingway's *A Farewell to Arms* (1929) or even to Alan Ladd, in the film *Shane* (1953). Historic events play a small part in the account (though there is a small section that focuses on the infamous My Lai massacre). Establishing a pattern in this, his first book, that would come to distinguish his later career as a novelist, O'Brien seeks to stretch formal boundaries. *If I Die in a Combat Zone*'s condensed dialogue, for instance, has the intensity of fictional language. Each of the several vignettes that are a part of the book's episodic structure has a dramatic coherency of its own.

O'Brien's views of his experiences are both personal and political. Seeking to understand the nature of courage, he also attempts to develop a clearer perspective on the role of the United States in Vietnam. Characteristically self-effacing, he frequently questions the significance of his own work. At the conclusion of Chapter 3, for instance, he muses whether foot soldiers, simply because they were in action, can teach anything important about war. Probably not, he responds, but they do have war stories to tell that are vital to understanding what occurred. His acceptance of such an assertion continues to influence all of his subsequent Vietnam War fiction.

See:

Myers, Thomas. "The Memoir as 'Wise Endurance.' " Chapter 2 in *Walking Point: American Narratives of Vietnam*. New York: Oxford University Press, 1988, 70–104.

Dan Cabaniss

IN COUNTRY (Novel-Film). Bobbie Ann Mason's novel *In Country* (1985) is an anomaly in the literature of Vietnam War in that it is written by a nonparticipant. One of a spate of successful novels on Vietnam to come out of the Eighties, it was also made into a popular, but critically unsuccessful, motion picture, *In Country* (Warner Brothers, 1989) directed by Norman Jewison. Its message suggests a cultural healing of the spirit, one accomplished through a repatriation of the image of veterans similar to that undertaken by films like **Born on the Fourth of July** (1989), *Jackknife* (1989), or **Forrest Gump** (1994).

The protagonist is Samantha Hughes, a seventeen-year-old whose father was killed in Vietnam before she was born. Her mother is remarried and lives in the city, a few hours away, though Sam has chosen to remain in the small Kentucky town of Hopewell to look after her reclusive uncle Emmett, a Vietnam veteran suffering from a number of maladies possibly related to the war. Searching for her own identity, Sam becomes increasingly obsessed with that of her unknown father and undertakes to find out more about him and how he died. She queries everyone who knew him, including Emmett, her mother, her grandparents, and her father's remaining friends.

Unsatisfied with both the paucity of information she receives and its literalness, Sam sets out to commune with her father's spirit by camping out in the woods and imagining herself with him in Vietnam. Emmett finds her there and, in an emotional climax, finally tells her about Vietnam and her father, effecting a catharsis for both of them. The book and its less-satisfying screen version (which starred Emily Lloyd and Bruce Willis) end in a symbolic gesture of healing with the three generations, Sam, Emmett, and her grandmother, traveling to Washington to visit the **Vietnam Veterans' Memorial**.

See:

Durham, Sandra B. "Women and War: Bobbie Ann Mason's *In Country*." *Southern Literary Journal* 22.2 (1990): 45–52.

Jeff Loeb

IN PHARAOH'S ARMY (**Autobiographical Fiction**). In 1975, shortly after his tour of duty in Vietnam was completed, Tobias Wolff published *Ugly Rumors*, a generally well-received novel based on his experiences in the war. Though in the intervening years he has dealt with many nonmilitarily-related themes, Wolff has frequently turned his attention back to Southeast Asia. *The Barrack Thief and Other Stories* (1983), for example, offers a host of short stories centered around the war years.

Most readers of war fiction such as Wolff's recognize its essential elements: induction and training, initiation, battle, the return home. *In Pharaoh's Army. Memories of the Lost War* (1994), one of his most recent and more prestigious books, encompasses these elements, but not necessarily in this order. Some of the thirteen short stories, like "Command Presence" and "A Federal Offense," deal with Wolff's decision to join the army and his experiences at boot camp and ranger training. Others, like "Thanksgiving Special" and "The Lesson" (a story about the Tet offensive), offer brief glimpses into his experiences as a

Green Beret in Vietnam. "Civilian" and "Last Shot" provide insight into his life stateside after the war.

Nominated for the National Book Award, *In Pharaoh's Army* is certain to become a classic of Vietnam War–related fiction. Like Philip Caputo (*A Rumor of War*) and Tim O'Brien (*The Things They Carried*), Wolff chooses the memoir as his form of expression. Although his tone is much lighter than that of either of those writers, he is no less brilliant in capturing what the war in Southeast Asia was really like.

See:

Lyons, Bonnie, and Bill Oliver. "An Interview with Tobias Wolff." *Contemporary Literature* 31.1 (1990): 1–16.

Leslie Kennedy Adams

KENT STATE MASSACRE (Event). During a noon rally at Kent State University in Ohio on Monday, May 4, 1970, a national guard unit opened fire upon a large crowd of students protesting the Guard's presence on campus. Nine students were wounded, and four students—Allison Krause, Jeffrey Miller, Sandra Scheuer, and William Schroeder—were killed. Community and national reaction to the shootings was quickly polarized between those who applauded it as an appropriate response to student "rioters" and those who condemned the soldiers's action (such as writer Peter Davies) as a clear example of conspiracy by the state to suppress antiwar dissent. Those same attitudes exist today.

Because of the controversy, many powerful images and symbols of the confrontation at Kent State quickly entered the popular consciousness. Perhaps none were more haunting than the Pulitzer Prize-winning photograph of an anguished young woman kneeling beside the bloody body of Jeffrey Miller. The slogan "Flowers are better than bullets," reportedly uttered by Allison Krause to a Guardsman prior to the shootings, also became a popular expression of antiwar sentiment, as did the Crosby, Stills, Nash, and Young song "Ohio." The Russian poet Yevtushenko and the popular American Erich Segal both eulogized Krause.

Several documentaries about the May 4 confrontation exist, but there have been few fictionalized treatments. The NBC made-for-television movie *Kent State* (1981), and the Gerald Green novel *Not in Vain* (1984), in which the national guard covers up its culpability in the shootings of students at "Joshua College," are among the best. The film, which was scripted by Green and Richard Kramer and photographed in Alabama, does a thoughtful job of depicting the events, though there are a number of factual errors in it just as there were in the earlier best-selling book about the confrontation: novelist James Michener's *Kent State: What Happened and Why* (1971). Nonetheless, in September 1981, the National Academy of Television Arts and Sciences awarded James Goldstone an Emmy as the year's best director in a limited series or special.

A popular folk song, "The Kent State Massacre," by Jack Warshaw and

Barbara Dane, was also written in 1971 and was widely sung in protest to the government's action.

See:

Heineman, Kenneth J. " 'Look Out Kid, You're Gonna Get Hit!': Kent State and the Vietnam Antiwar Movement." In *Give Peace a Chance: Exploring the Vietnam Antiwar Movement*, ed. Melvin Small and William D. Hoover. Syracuse, NY: Syracuse University Press, 1992, 201–222.
Lewis, Jerry M. "Kent State—The Movie." *Journal of Popular Film and Television* 9.1 (1981): 13–18.

Philip L. Simpson

LOVE AND DUTY (Autobiography). One of the most important prisoner-of-war narratives to emerge from the Vietnam War, Ben and Anne Purcell's *Love and Duty: The Remarkable Story of a Courageous MIA Family and the Victory They Won with Their Faith* (1992) alternately recounts the story of a husband's five-year imprisonment by the North Vietnamese and his wife's stateside efforts to cope with her husband's absence and missing in action (MIA) status. Lieutenant Colonel Ben Purcell, a career army officer who volunteered for duty in Vietnam, was the highest-ranking army officer to become a POW. He was captured after a helicopter crash during the Tet Offensive in January 1968. Ben narrates sixteen chapters of the book, and Anne, his wife and the mother of their five children (then ages two to fourteen), narrates the remaining nine. His chapters reveal the isolation, health problems, and poor living conditions in a POW camp; Anne's, the difficulty of not knowing if she was a wife or a widow and the challenge of raising five children alone.

Even after his initial release, Purcell refused to leave Vietnam until all other known American prisoners were released in March 1973. *Love and Duty* is one of the few Christian-based narratives to emerge from the Vietnam War. Neither author is bitter over the ordeal, instead viewing it as a gift from God, who made them stronger people and better Christians in spite of their hellish experiences. "It wasn't *what* one had to face that was important," writes Anne, "but *how* one faced it that mattered."

See:

Gruner, Elliott. *Prisoners of Culture: Representing the Vietnam POW*. New Brunswick, NJ: Rutgers University Press, 1993.

Catherine Calloway

LOWELL, ROBERT (Poet). Robert Lowell, one of the most critically respected American poets of the twentieth century, is also famous for his stands against this nation's wars. When, for example, he opposed the Allied demand for unconditional surrender in World War II, he was jailed in New York City. He also was an early opponent of the U.S. stance in Vietnam. In summer 1965, following the first American aerial bombardments in that country, Lowell reconsidered a previously accepted invitation to give a poetry reading at a White House Festival of the Arts. He not only refused to attend but also made public his dissatisfaction with President Lyndon Johnson's Vietnam policies in a public letter to the *New York Times*.

Many of Lowell's most overtly political poems, such as "Waking Early Sunday Morning," were written shortly after his snub of President Johnson. He also wrote a number of thoughtful essays against the war in Vietnam that were published in *Notebook 1967–1968*. Among the best are ones about his participation in the antiwar March on the Pentagon during October 1967, his political involvement with presidential candidate Eugene McCarthy, his disillusionment following the violent 1968 Democratic National Convention in Chicago, and his somber reaction to Richard Nixon's election.

See:

Mariani, Paul. *Lost Puritan: A Life of Robert Lowell.* New York: W. W. Norton, 1994.

Philip L. Simpson

MACBIRD! (**Drama**). Speaking at a 1965 antiwar rally at the University of California in Berkeley, Barbara Garson accidentally called President Lyndon Johnson's wife Lady MacBird. Her slip of the tongue caused her to think about Shakespeare's famous tragedy *Macbeth*, and she determined to write a fifteen-minute skit using the format of the original play to parody LBJ. The skit was never completed because, by spring 1966, Garson had created a widely circulated, full-length play.

Friends convinced the young playwright to stage an updated version in New York, and, on February 22, 1967, *MacBird!* debuted, with Hollywood actor Stacey Keach playing the LBJ/MacBird role. It was biting in its satire and frequently cruel in its skewering of the president. Certainly there was no question of the unwavering antiwar sentiment. In one scene, MacBird, sounding completely like Shakespeare's MacBeth, tells "Lord MacNamara," his "valiant chief of war," to destroy the communists in Vietnam using whatever force necessary. MacNamara replies that he will do what he has been commanded and that, even before the setting of the sun, the Viet Cong will be eliminated. In another, a character modeled after Oregon's staunchly antiwar legislator Wayne Morse, one of only three U.S. senators to vote against the Tonkin Gulf resolution in 1964, openly laments to fellow senators the bombings, the "casual slaughters," and the traumatic events that are happening throughout Vietnam but being ignored by virtually everyone in this country.

Though the critics were at best ambivalent in their praise for Garson's often clever juxtaposition of Shakespeare into modern American politics, Keach was awarded both a Drama Desk award and an Obie Award as the year's best actor. Hundreds of thousands of copies of the play were printed and circulated throughout the country by New York's Grove Press. The play closed after 386 performances on January 21, 1968, just a few days before President Johnson announced his decision not to stand for reelection for a second term.

See:

Alter, Nora M. "Playing Imperialism (America's War)." Chapter 1 in *Vietnam Protest Theatre: The Television War on Stage*. Bloomington: Indiana University Press, 1996, 26–46.

M. Paul Holsinger

MEDITATIONS IN GREEN (Novel). Like Michael Herr's *Dispatches* and Tim O'Brien's *Going after Cacciato*, Stephen Wright's novel *Meditations in Green* (1983) demonstrates that received language is inadequate to convey the essential nature of the Vietnam War. Believing that the use of a naturalistic style would only serve to underscore the innumerable lies of the war, Wright fills *Meditations in Green* with a mixture of deep cynicism and a zany exuberance similar to that found in Thomas Pynchon's *Gravity's Rainbow*. The result is, at times, impressionistically exhausting.

The central metaphor of the multilayered *Meditations* is vegetation (hence the title). During the novel, the protagonist and sometime narrator James Griffin is both an intelligence analyst in Vietnam and a deluded and confused veteran of the horrors of the war fought there. "In-country" and perpetually stoned, he pours over deep green aerial photographs searching for potential targets to defoliate. Beset with treacherous commanders and ever at the mercy of a horrific, absurd, and completely unpredictable war, he ultimately is reduced to sociopathic lunacy. After his return to the United States, he remains addicted to heroin and spends his time contemplating real vegetation, the hothouse plants he nurtures. Endeavoring to escape the nightmarish flashbacks that beset him, he locks himself in with his greenery and spends the days trying to understand the meaning of the war that he helped to fight. Finally, completely out of touch with reality, he and a similarly deluded veteran friend undertake the (unsuccessful) assassination of a man they imagine to be a former sergeant of theirs.

Brilliantly styled, *Meditations in Green* is a powerful reminder of the difficulty so many veterans had as they sought to return to "the World." In the final analysis, it provides a grim but effective argument for the proposition that neither love nor psychiatry can cure the self-divisions resulting from personal or cultural trauma.

See:

Myers, Thomas. "Shades of Retrieval." Chapter 5 in *Walking Point: American Narratives of Vietnam*. New York: Oxford University Press, 1988, 197–210.
Ringnalda, Donald. "Chlorophyll Overdose: Stephen Wright's *Meditations in Green*." *Western Humanities Review* 40.2 (1986): 125–140.

Jeff Loeb

MEMPHIS-NAM-SWEDEN (Autobiography). *Memphis-Nam-Sweden: The Autobiography of a Black American Exile* (1971) by Terry Whitmore is one of the very few African-American memoirs of Vietnam and among the finest personal accounts of that war by any participant. Written in an engaging vernacular voice that is both humorous and ironic, it problematizes race as a central component of both the war and American culture.

Whitmore joined the Marines in 1967 in order to get "off the block" in Memphis and away from an oppressive family life. "Free" for the first time, he was all-too-quickly rushed off to the escalating war in Vietnam. There, unable to understand the logic of that conflict, but knowing somehow that it was linked to racial oppression, he grew increasingly disillusioned. Seriously wounded and sent to Japan to recuperate, Whitmore soon came to the conclusion that he was nothing more than a pawn in a military machine that cared little for him or for the many other "niggers" who had joined the fight.

Freedom—the major question in African-American literature since the first slave narratives—thus changes for Whitmore, and an exploration of its elusive nature becomes the point of his story. Ordered back to the combat zone as soon as he was in "A-1 condition," he chose to desert instead. Eventually, with the help of Beheiren, the international peace movement, he reached neutral Sweden. Thirty years later, Whitmore continues to live in his adopted land.

Whitmore's autobiography is not only a Vietnam memoir but also one that represents a significant part of the entire African American experience. It was reissued by the University Press of Mississippi in 1997 as *Memphis-Nam-Sweden: The Story of a Black Deserter.*

See:

Loeb, Jeff. "MIA: The African American Autobiography of the Vietnam War." *African American Review* 13.1 (1997): 105–123.

Jeff Loeb

MISSING IN ACTION (Films). During the 1980s, the fate of servicemen listed as missing in action in Vietnam became the center of a major political controversy in America. Concern that the Vietnamese might still be holding hundreds, if not thousands, of GIs as prisoners of war was a major issue not only in the halls of Congress or Ronald Reagan's White House, but also in many Hollywood studios. From Ted Kotcheff's *Uncommon Valor* (1983) to Eric Weston's *The Iron Triangle* (1989), a number of movies took up the subject. Among them was a trilogy starring martial arts expert Chuck Norris both as a prisoner and as a liberator.

The first, *Missing in Action* (Cannon, 1984), recounts the exploits of Colonel James Braddock (Norris) as he returns to Vietnam and rescues the men left behind when he made his escape from a Viet Cong prison camp. *Missing in Action 2—The Beginning* (Cannon, 1985) is a prequel describing Braddock's capture and escape. In *Braddock: Missing in Action III* (Cannon, 1988), the hero returns to enemy territory to rescue his Amerasian child. All three offer Norris the opportunity to practice his martial arts skills but little else.

Like other POW/MIA films, the Norris trilogy helped to mythologize the POWs, who became a symbol of America in defeat. To imagine them liberated

from an evil enemy was to imagine the defeat avenged and the country redeemed. The same sort of reasoning can be seen in the bitter debates over
whether or not Americans are actually being held in Vietnam that continue today
more than twenty years after the end of the war. While historians and others
analyze the evidence, there remain hundreds of persons who, refusing to accept
the loss of their loved ones, haunt the offices of government officials demanding
their return, fly POW/MIA flags, or wear bracelets engraved with the name of
a supposed American prisoner of war.

See:

Williams, Tony. "*Missing in Action*: The Vietnam Construction of the Movie Star." In
    From Hanoi to Hollywood: The Vietnam War in American Film, ed. Linda Ditt-
    mar and Gene Michaud. New Brunswick, NJ: Rutgers University Press, 1990,
    129–144.

Philip J. Landon

MISS SAIGON **(Musical).** *Miss Saigon*, a two-act musical spectacular by Alain
Boublil and Claude-Michel Schönberg, the award-winning composers of the
smash box-office success *Les Miserables*, is a modern version of Puccini's opera
Madame Butterfly. It is also a provocative and often bitter commentary on the
utter failure of the United States during the Vietnam War.

Originally written in French, the play was adapted into English by Richard
Maltby, Jr. and first produced in London on September 20, 1989, to rave reviews. It opened on Broadway on April 11, 1991, to one of the largest advance
sales in New York theater history. Critically acclaimed, it was nominated for
almost every major Tony Award for which it was eligible, including best musical, best book of a musical, and best score. Jonathan Pryce won a Tony as
best actor in a musical, as did Lea Salonga as best actress. By mid-November
1997, *Miss Saigon* was still on Broadway after 2,750 consecutive performances,
making it one of the most popular major New York plays of all time. In spring
1997, touring companies began taking the musical across the United States,
playing to packed theaters.

Divided into two chronological periods—April 1975 and the spring, summer
and early fall of 1978—*Miss Saigon* tells the story of Chris Scott, a young
Marine stationed at the American embassy, and Kim, the Saigon bar-girl with
whom he falls in love. Separated from her when the last U.S. forces fly dramatically out of the city leaving behind thousands of their South Vietnamese
allies during the war, Chris does not know until three years have passed and he
is married that Kim bore him a son. When he and his new wife, Ellen, journey
to Southeast Asia to find them, Kim, who has devoted her life since 1975 to
raising her son, kills herself so that there will be nothing standing in the way
of his father taking him to America. There are thousands of Amerasian children
like his son, says one of Chris's buddies from his embassy days, each child a
reminder to all Americans of their failure to do good in the ravished country
while they were there.

It may seem that when the fighting ceases so, too, do wars, but nothing could be farther from the truth. All too often, images remain, and they seem to fill our minds and never go away. *Miss Saigon* offers a great many such pictures, all of them disturbing but all wrapped in the words and music of two of the modern day's most expressive song stylists.

See:

Behr, Edward, and Mark Steyn. *The Story of Miss Saigon.* New York: Arcade, 1991.
The Making of Miss Saigon. Dir. and prod. David Wright. HBO Video, 1989.

M. Paul Holsinger

THE 'NAM (Comic Books). Marvel Comics, renowned for such superheroes as Spiderman, the Hulk, or the X-Men, also developed one of the few comic book series to focus on America's lost war in Vietnam. Written initially by Doug Murray, a veteran of "in-country" fighting, *The 'Nam* was first published in December 1986. Intended to have a limited eight-year run, it was terminated in September 1993 after eighty-four issues.

Murray's original plan was doubly admirable. Realizing that there were so many younger readers who could not remember what happened in Vietnam or why, he sought to use *The 'Nam* to teach them about the war. Each new issue highlighted the lives of average "grunts" in one stereotypical army rifle company. Beginning his story with 1966, when the U.S. presence in the war became paramount, he hoped to have his men experience "real time," some finishing their tours of duty and going home unscathed, while others were wounded, captured or killed.

Had Murray been able to carry out his idea fully and had Michael Golden, one of Marvel's more talented illustrators and the comic's first artist, been allowed to draw all the strips, the series might have become even more memorable. Though *The 'Nam* still remains, in its entirety, easily the best comic series to focus on the war in Vietnam, Murray, unfortunately, was dropped as its writer after the second year and replaced by less capable (and less knowledgeable) storytellers. Golden, too, was assigned to other Marvel projects, and the artists who took his place also failed to maintain his high standards. Though the editors, in an attempt to keep interest high, created stories that spanned two, three, and, on one occasion, five different issues, the series soon became little more than a carbon copy of dozens of earlier comics of World War II or Korean War vintage. When Marvel terminated it, few readers were particularly bothered.

See:

Huxley, David. "Naked Aggression: American Comic Books and the Vietnam War." In *Tell Me Lies about Vietnam: Cultural Battles for the Meaning of the War*, ed. Alf Louvre and Jeffrey Walsh. Philadelphia: Open University Press, 1988, 88–110.

M. Paul Holsinger

OCHS, PHIL (Songwriter-Folksinger). No single songwriter more clearly expressed the anger and frustration felt by thousands of college-age youth over the United States' participaton in the war in Vietnam than did Phil Ochs. His name was synonymous with protest, and his 1964 "I Ain't Marchin' Any More" became the rallying cry of millions of students determined not to participate in the war. "Peace," "treason," "love," or "reason"—it made no difference what one's rationale for refusing to fight might be, Ochs sang, as long as, in the end, one could state forcibly: "I Ain't Marchin' Any More." His "Cops of the World," penned two years later, fiercely pilloried the nation's armed forces, and that same year's "Draft Dodger Rag" made clear his position in regard to joining such units. When he went to Washington, D.C., in October 1967 to protest the war at the Pentagon, he sang his own "I Declare the War Is Over" to uproarious applause from a mostly youthful audience of fellow protesters.

Despite his anger at the government's role in Southeast Asia, Ochs had an unbounding faith in the American democratic system. After the assassination of Robert Kennedy and his own arrest at the 1968 Democratic National Convention in Chicago, however, his optimism waned drastically. Though more than 50,000 persons cheered him in May 1975, when he and other folk singers in New York City celebrated the official end of the war in Vietnam, Ochs grew deeply depressed. A year later, he committed suicide at the age of thirty-four. Five long-playing albums of his musical work, much of it nonpolitical and some quite lyrical, remain, but it is as the 1960's and the antiwar movement's quintessential protest singer that Ochs will always be remembered.

See:

Schumacher, Michael. *There But for Fortune: The Life of Phil Ochs.* New York: Hyperion, 1996.

M. Paul Holsinger

"OKIE FROM MUSKOGEE" (Song). Though most folk and rock musicians showed antipathy toward the United States' role in Vietnam, country and western musical stars generally took the opposite position. In 1965, for instance, Johnny Wright had a number one best-seller with "**Hello Vietnam**," and the next year Ernest Tubb recorded "It's for God and Country and You, Mom (That's Why I'm Fighting in Vietnam)." No single performer, however, more epitomized the flag-waving view of country music than did Merle Haggard, and no song was more expressive of that view than his "Okie from Muskogee."

On a 1969 road trip with his band, Haggard passed Muskogee, Oklahoma. Discovering that the town had few major social problems, he began to write a new song. Within twenty minutes, he finished both the music and lyrics, which stress, in part, that decent folks in mid-America—such as those in Muskogee—did not burn their draft cards or refuse service when their nation called. When he played it several days later for a group of Green Berets at Fort Bragg, North Carolina, he was greeted by wild applause. A recording soared up the popularity charts, and, several months later, the Country Music Association voted "Okie from Muskogee" the single of the year. An album featuring the run-away hit eventually sold nearly 1 million copies and stayed on the charts for more than seventy-five weeks.

See:

McCloud, Barry. "Merle Haggard." In *Definitive Country: The Ultimate Encyclopedia of Country Music and Its Performers*, ed. Barry McCloud. New York: Perigee Books, 1995, 357–359.
Storey, John. "Bringing It All Back Home: American Popular Song and the War in Vietnam." In *The Vietnam Era: Media and Popular Culture in the U.S. and Vietnam*, ed. Michael Klein. London: Pluto Press, 1990, 82–106.

M. Paul Holsinger

PACO'S STORY* (Novel).** Larry Heinemann's novel *Paco's Story* (1986), winner of the National Book Award, is ultimately a major study in the effects of wartime trauma. At the same time that books like Philip Caputo's *Indian Country* and films like ***Platoon suggested that personal and societal healing from the wounds of Vietnam was possible, Heinemann's work offered a much darker vision.

Paco, an Army veteran, has been psychologically brutalized by two events in Vietnam: witnessing the vicious rape and murder of a peasant girl by his fellow soldiers and his killing an enemy soldier in hand-to-hand combat. Totally alienated and dependent on medication that keeps the worst of his memories at bay, Paco arrives in a small Texas town, blown there by the vicissitudes of his diminished existence, and gets a job as a dishwasher in a small restaurant. While there, he briefly strikes the fancy of a local woman and makes the acquaintance of a few of the more down-and-out residents. Eventually, however, when the woman's brief infatuation passes without any sort of consummation, sexual or otherwise, and he finds himself unable to relate to any of the others, Paco moves on, to where we can only surmise. The book's final sentence suggests the direction of his life: "He climbs aboard, pays his fare, and the bus departs—coasting down the long incline of the entrance ramp—and is soon gone."

There is no resolution of his situation, and the only certainty is that his tortured memories will not abate and his existence will continue "down the long incline." Heinemann's message is clear: There is no redemption from the trauma of Vietnam, no easy path to self-reunion.

See:

Anisfield, Nancy. "After the Apocalypse: Narrative Movement in Larry Heinemann's *Paco's Story*." In *America Rediscovered: Critical Essays on Literature and Film of the Vietnam War*, ed. Owen W. Gilman, Jr., and Lorrie Smith. New York: Garland, 1990, 275–281.

Jeff Loeb

PEACE SIGN/PEACE SYMBOL. The "peace sign" of the Vietnam War era consisted of holding up the first two fingers of either hand, sometimes accompanied by the spoken word "Peace." It came to be associated with the antiwar movement and then later with the counterculture. By the late 1960s, it was used by anyone (especially the young) who wanted to appear "hip" and could be employed as either a greeting or a goodbye.

Prominent members of the antiwar movement often appeared in news photos and film giving the peace sign—it became a shorthand identification of their purpose as well as a gesture of defiance toward the "establishment." This was especially true when antiwar figures such as Abbie Hoffman, Tom Hayden, and Father Daniel Berrigan were shown being arrested or brought to trial.

Emmett Grogan, a member of the Diggers (a San Francisco counterculture group), claims the accidental invention of the peace sign. Grogan asserts that, on release from a short jail term in 1966, he saw a news photographer snapping pictures. On impulse, he made a vulgar British/Irish gesture with the back of his hand toward the camera and the first two fingers extended (a similar gesture in the United States employs only the middle finger). The next day, the photo appeared in the newspaper, and, before the day was out, friends adopted the gesture, thinking that Grogan, in his support of the counterculture, intended it more in the spirit of the "V for Victory" symbol made so famous by Prime Minister Winston Churchill during World War II than the coarse symbolism he really had in mind.

The "peace symbol" also became an important sign of the times. Consisting of a circle with a line through the vertical diameter along with two shorter lines that make triangles when leaned against that diameter, it was immensely popular during the Vietnam War. Worn as a pendant, ring, belt buckle, or as a pin affixed to clothing or a backpack, it was seen everywhere throughout the country that antiwar feeling was evident. The origins of the peace symbol are murky. The best explanation seems to be that it comes from the international semaphore signals for the letters "C," "N," and "D," the letter designation of a prominent British antinuclear group, the Committee for Nuclear Disarmament, in the 1950s and 1960s. Various reactionary groups in the United States tried to discredit the symbol, claiming that it was Satanic. There were many variations on that theme; there is no creditable evidence for any of them.

See:

DeBenedetti, Charles, and Charles Chatfield. *An American Ordeal: The Antiwar Movement of the Vietnam Era.* Syracuse, NY: Syracuse University Press, 1990, 44.

J. Justin Gustainis

PLATOON **(Film).** *Platoon* (Hemdale, 1986), written and directed by Oliver Stone, is perhaps the most watched and discussed film of the Vietnam War. Audiences and critics chiefly note its verisimilitude and intensity, including representations of the forbidding climate—intense heat, unrelenting rain, mosquitoes and leeches—as well the depiction of the conditions of combat.

The narrator is the newly arrived Chris Taylor (Charlie Sheen), who witnesses the unfolding conflict between the "good" Sergeant Elias (Willem Dafoe) and the "evil" Sergeant Barnes (Tom Berenger). The central conflict occurs when Barnes, brooding over North Vietnamese atrocities against Americans, goes on a murderous rampage and, in an Ahab-like frenzy of revenge, drives the men to murder some innocent villagers while the platoon commander stands by ineffectually. Elias forcibly intervenes, saving most of the villagers' lives but incurring the wrath of Barnes and initiating a blood feud in which Barnes eventually kills him. Chris, a disciple of Elias, is the only witness, and, after an apocalyptic fire fight in which nearly all of the Americans die, he in turn kills Barnes.

Brutal and realistic, *Platoon* took in more than $137 million at the box office, making it the top-grossing production of 1986. Though it won only three Academy Awards, two were the most important: best picture and best director. Critics praised it, and, for most Americans, it soon came to define the Vietnam experience. The timing of its release was also crucial, coming as it did in the midst of the Reagan era repatriation of the image of veterans, done in the service of a massive rearmament to defeat the "evil empire" of Russia. In retrospect, while the battle scenes which so impressed audiences are essentially those familiar to any student of stock World War II movies, many of the subjects explored—the war between recruits and "lifers," the failure of command, the exploration of atrocity, systemic racism—remained unexamined in previous war pictures. Only its dualistic structure of good versus evil appears weak and clichéd.

See:

Jeffords, Susan. "Born of Two Fathers: Gender and Misunderstanding in *Platoon*." In *Search and Clear: Critical Responses to Selected Literature and Films of the Vietnam War*, ed. William J. Searle. Bowling Green, OH: Bowling Green State University Popular Press, 1988, 184–194.

Jeff Loeb

PRISONER OF WAR/MISSING IN ACTION (POW/MIA) BRACELETS (Symbols). During the late 1960s, the plight of the growing number of American prisoners of war in southeast Asia became a source of growing concern on the home front. In an effort to draw attention to their predicament, as well as those whose uncertain status was merely "Missing in Action," the nonprofit Voices in Vital America (VIVA) began offering for sale individual commemorative bracelets. Each of these bracelets bore the name and rank of a man who was either known to be a prisoner of war or was missing in action. The flat strips of copper, stainless steel, or nickel-plated brass also contained the date upon which the man had gone missing.

The $2.50 (nickel-plated and stainless steel) or $3.00 (copper) bracelets were instantly popular. By 1972, VIVA was distributing 5,000 a day; by mid-summer, the number climbed to more than 11,000 daily. Americans at all social and educational levels were soon conspicuously wearing one in support of a missing soldier or airman. By January 1973, when delegates from the United States and North Vietnam met in Paris to discuss the possibility of peace, somewhere between 4 and 10 million persons were wearing one or more POW/MIA bracelets.

Sadly, more than 2,000 of the memorialized men never came home when American involvement in the Vietnam War ended in January 1973. The Vietnamese government has since returned a few hundred sets of remains to the United States, thus clarifying the status of at least some of those men. The United States has officially declared the rest of those missing in action as presumed dead.

Many Americans continue to remember those men who failed to return. Although VIVA has long since closed its doors, other vendors still offer aluminum bracelets to satisfy the considerable demand for these mementos and hundreds are sold every day.

See:

Franklin, H. Bruce. *M.I.A., or Mythmaking in America.* Brooklyn, NY: Lawrence Hill, 1992, 56–57.
Keating, Susan Katz. *Prisoners of Hope: Exploring the POW/MIA Myth in America.* New York: Random House, 1994.

James M. McCaffrey

PURPLE HEARTS (Film). Though some critics have faulted *Purple Hearts* (Ladd, 1984) as little more than standard soap opera material or as even the most ridiculous Vietnam War film ever made, its depiction of the military side of the war is carefully reconstructed and generally very believable. Directed by Sidney J. Furie, who had earlier made the Vietnam-focused *The Boys in Company C* (1978), *Purple Hearts* is dedicated to the 347,309 Americans who received the Purple Heart during the Vietnam War. Centered around the growing love between Dr. Don Jardian (Ken Wahl) and operating room nurse Deborah Solomon (Cheryl Ladd), whom he meets in the naval hospital at Da Nang, the movie looks closely at the frequent failure of American military leadership during the war. While the romance (designed to attract female theatergoers) is unquestionably the central theme of the story, in the end, the picture remains a finely crafted account of the bloody horror of the United States' Vietnam experience.

The first shots of *Purple Hearts* set the tone for most of the film. A group of Viet Cong guerillas hidden in the jungle catches a company of young Marines in the open, and the resulting firefight causes a number of casualties, all of whom are airlifted back to the mobile hospital where the young Jardian, a brilliant, but egotistic, surgeon, is assigned. Later the doctor, perhaps too smart for his own good, is sent by his superiors to Con Thien and the bloody, real-life attack by communist sappers in October 1967 that came close to wiping out the American forces in the region. He then joins a secret team of Special Forces attempting to free allied prisoners deep inside enemy territory. Furie does a fine job staging each of these many separate engagements, just as he does later with the VC rocket attack on the hospital at Da Nang which supposedly kills Solomon. She is, of course, not dead, nor is Jardian, who earlier was also reported killed in action while behind enemy lines. In a perhaps too pat, melodramatic ending, the two lovers are reunited at a Veterans' Administration hospital in the states, but even such a hackneyed conclusion fails to diminish the story's overall impact.

See:

Devine, Jeremy M. *Vietnam at 24 Frames a Second: A Critical and Thematic Analysis of over 400 Films about the Vietnam War.* Jefferson, NC: McFarland, 1995, 222–224.

M. Paul Holsinger

RAMBO: FIRST BLOOD, PART II (Film). The character John Rambo became a prominent part of American popular culture, and ''Rambo,'' a word that can function as a noun, adjective, or verb, became part of the English language at the very moment that director George Cosmatos' *Rambo: First Blood, Part II* (Tri-Star, 1985) was released to great box office acclaim. A quick database search reveals references to everything from Rambo sports cars (high powered and rugged) or Rambo litigators (excessively aggressive lawyers) to Rambo banking methods, Rambo diplomacy, or even Rambo economics. Since many of these articles were written more than a decade after the film's first showings, it is clear that the cultural impact of the Rambo character was anything but a passing fancy.

At the beginning of this hyper-violent ''action'' adventure, Vietnam veteran and former Green Beret John Rambo (Sylvester Stallone) is in jail as a result of the rampage recounted in the earlier *First Blood* (1982). He is soon released into the custody of his former commanding officer (Richard Crenna) to undertake a special mission for the CIA. Infiltrating the Vietnamese jungle, Rambo discovers a number of American POWs still being held captive; when he attempts to rescue them, he is abandoned by the same government officials who left the men in the hands of the Viet Cong in the first place. Captured and tortured by enemy troops, Rambo escapes and slaughters his foes—Vietnamese and Soviet ''advisers'' alike—using automatic weapons, a bow firing explosive arrows, a huge combat knife, his bare hands, and even a captured Soviet gunship. Loading the prisoners into the helicopter, he then flies off to confront his betrayers.

Rambo: First Blood, Part II, the top grossing film of 1985, took in more than $150 million at the box office. It also struck a responsive chord in the post-war American psyche by reinforcing two widely-held myths: there were POWs in Southeast Asia that our government had no interest in finding, and, had it not been restrained by cowardly politicians, the United States could have won the war in Vietnam.

As the movie's popularity mounted, there were soon made-for-television animated feature cartoons, a line of "action figures," and, inevitably, *Rambo III* (1988). A fourth Rambo picture is supposedly in the planning stages.

See:

Studlar, Gaylyn, and Davis Desser. "Never Having to Say You're Sorry: Rambo's Rewriting of the Vietnam War." *Film Quarterly* 42.1 (Fall 1988): 9–16.
Waller, Gregory A. "*Rambo*: Getting to Win This Time." In *From Hanoi to Hollywood: The Vietnam War in American Film*, ed. Linda Dittmar and Gene Michaud. New Brunswick, NJ: Rutgers University Press, 1990, 113–128.

J. Justin Gustainis

A RUMOR OF WAR **(Autobiography-Film).** In 1977, ten years after he left Vietnam as a young Marine Corps officer, Philip Caputo published an autobiographical memoir based on his experiences while serving "in country." Critics praised *A Rumor of War* from the moment it first appeared, and, almost overnight, it became a best-seller.

Caputo arrived in Vietnam in March 1965 with the first American ground combat unit in the escalating war. Initially an idealistic college graduate, proud of his country's goals in Vietnam and his future role in it, the ardent young Marine lieutenant is gradually ground down by the events and process of war and transformed into a defendant charged by military authorities for murdering civilians. *A Rumor of War*, according to the book's dust jacket, is "simply a story of war, the things men do in war, and the things war does to them." That is a remarkably accurate description of Caputo's often moving memories.

A Rumor of War, adapted by John Sacret Young from Caputo's work, was one of the first films about the United States' Vietnam experiences to be made after the war's conclusion. Originally presented on CBS as a two-part, made-for-television drama in September 1980, the 3½ hour-long production was directed by Richard Heffron. It reflects the gradual change of mission for U.S. forces from stationary protection of bases and training and supporting the South Vietnamese troops, to taking over the war entirely. The altering of American attitudes toward the war itself—its purposes, strategy, tactics, and costs—is also clearly seen. In the end, Caputo (thoughtfully played by Brad Davis), having struck a deal with the authorities, flies home with a letter of reprimand, on a plane loaded with coffins. The symbolism is striking.

During the Vietnam War, dramatic television programming essentially left combat alone, choosing to deal with the war instead in news and documentary reports. Now, *A Rumor of War* set the tone for the tide of Vietnam combat motion pictures that began to flood movie and television screens in the late 1980s. The day of the John Wayne *Green Berets*-style of war film, begun in 1968 and filled with the inevitable triumph of American men, matériel, and patriotic ideals, had come to a close.

See:

Cronin, Cornelius A. "From the DMZ to No Man's Land: Philip Caputo's *A Rumor of War* and Its Antecedents." In *Search and Clear: Critical Responses to Selected*

Literature and Films of the Vietnam War, ed. William Searle. Bowling Green, OH: Bowling Green State University Popular Press, 1988, 74–86.

Jack Colldeweih

SEEGER, PETE (Songwriter-Folksinger). Pete Seeger, one of America's greatest folksingers, is also one of its most controversial. Though his musical repertoire is voluminous, it is his frequent antiwar advocacy over nearly sixty years, especially during the war in Vietnam, that will intrigue historians in the future.

Before America's entry in World War II, many of Seeger's songs parroted the Communist Party line. When Congress passed the Selective Service Act, for instance, he recorded a staunchly antiwar album, *Songs for John Doe*, which accused President Franklin Roosevelt of being a warmonger, but as soon as the Germans attacked Russia, he backed full-scale American preparedness. His "Dear Mr. President" (1942) called for universal support of the war effort. With the coming of the Cold War years, Seeger refused to tesify before the House Un-American Activities Committee about his communist background or his possible support for worldwide communist goals, and he was blacklisted by the entertainment industry.

In the early 1960s, as the United States was slowly entering the war in Vietnam, many young people began to listen appreciatively once again to Seeger's antiwar songs. His "Where Have All the Flowers Gone," for example, became a best-selling hit in 1962 when recorded by two different folk singing groups, the Kingston Trio and Peter, Paul, and Mary. His plea to pull all American troops out of Southeast Asia, "If You Love Your Uncle Sam, Bring 'Em Home" (1966), became a rallying cry for millions of antiwar demonstrators. Most famous of all was "(Waist Deep in) The Big Muddy" (1967), an unstated but clear attack on President Lyndon Johnson, who, according to Seeger, was steadily sinking the United States Army into an impossible quagmire by "pushing on" without considering the consequences.

Always controversial (on several occasions in the mid-1960s he was denied the opportunity to sing his antiestablishment songs on national television), Seeger suddenly announced his decision to give up singing in the summer of 1968 to concentrate on his growing family. Though he has, from time to time since then, recorded songs dealing with environmental issues, he has refrained almost totally from politics. In the process, he has become recognized by almost everyone as one of the "grand old men" of American folk music.

See:

Dunaway, David K. *How Can I Keep from Singing: Pete Seeger.* New York: McGraw-Hill, 1982.

M. Paul Holsinger

STICKS AND BONES (Drama). David Rabe, a Vietnam veteran who served as a noncombatant in an army hospital support unit in 1965, wrote *Sticks and*

Bones while a graduate student at Villanova University. First performed in an embryonic state at that university in 1969, the final version of the play was staged off-Broadway beginning in November 1971 by Joseph Papp. Opening at the New York Shakespeare Festival's Public Theater, it moved to Broadway in March 1972, receiving rave reviews from a number of New York drama critics, and running for 366 performances before closing on October 1. The second of Rabe's "Vietnam War trilogy"—the Obie Award–winning *The Basic Training of Pavlo Hummel* (1971) and *Streamers* (1976) are the others—*Sticks and Bones* received not only the 1972 Tony Award as the year's best Broadway play but also a New York Drama Critics Circle citation and the Outer Circle Critics Award.

Rabe paints a disturbing portrait of American life in the late 1960s, one haunted by the presence of American military intervention in Vietnam. David, the protagonist, is physically blind as a result of the war, but he can see far more than his parents Ozzie and Harriet (who parody the too-good-to-be-true Nelson family made famous in television's long-running *The Adventures of Ozzie and Harriet*). The Ozzie and Harriet of *Sticks and Bones* are incapable of understanding their son's violent memories of Vietnam and his ability to love someone of another race, a Vietnamese woman whom he abandoned during the war. Preferring to watch television rather than learn to communicate with their war-torn son, they encourage him to hurt himself and are relieved when he finally commits suicide.

A television adaptation of *Sticks and Bones* was canceled by CBS three days before it was to be broadcast in March 1973. Due to its sensitive subject matter and the fear of an irate reception, the network felt it inappropriate to air such a controversial drama at a time when prisoners of war were returning home after months or years of imprisonment in Vietnam.

Sticks and Bones is an important commentary on the entire Vietnam era, especially the dehumanization and racial prejudice, the artificial domestic tranquility, and the horrific reality of both a brutal war and an eroding American society.

See:

Christie, N. Bradley. "David Rabe's Theater of War and Remembering." In *Search and Clear: Critical Responses to Selected Literature and Films of the Vietnam Era*, ed. William Searle. Bowling Green, OH: Bowling Green State University Popular Press, 1988, 105–115.

Catherine Calloway

STREAMERS (Drama-Film). *Streamers* (1976) is the last of a trilogy of Vietnam plays by David Rabe—*The Basic Training of Pavlo Hummel* (1971) and *Sticks and Bones* (1971) are the other two. Rabe, who served in Vietnam during 1965, focuses on what is essentially another lost generation. The title is a term for jumpers who die because their parachutes will not open. Streamers (and the song that is sung about them) becomes a metaphor for his characters who seek help, friendship, and an escape from loneliness, but instead find humiliation, horror, and death.

Although *Streamers* is set in an army camp in the United States, Vietnam and the fear of going there permeate the play. The random violence that occurs is due to sexual and racial tension, regular army versus the draftees, the unknown called Vietnam, and the dehumanizing effects of military life. A crisis arises when one soldier (Martin) cuts his wrist so he will not have to serve, and another soldier (Richie) admits his homosexuality and seeks male companionship in a liaison which triggers the final violence of the play. Carlyle, an African-American soldier who is afraid of Vietnam, of white officers, and of being alone, kills Billy, a white soldier who he thinks is critical of his attraction to Richie. Carlyle also kills Sergeant Rooney, a veteran of World War II and Korea, who is a drunken reminder of wars past. The play ends in denial and despair, echoing United States involvement in Vietnam.

Rabe wrote the screenplay for a movie version that was directed by Robert Altman and starred Matthew Modine, David Alan Grier, and George Dzunda. Though American audiences paid little attention to *Streamers* (United Artists, 1983), it was nominated as one of the year's best films by the Venice Film Festival.

See:

Kolen, Philip C. *David Rabe: A Stage History and a Primary and Secondary Bibliography.* New York: Garland, 1988.

Sally E. Parry

TEACH-INS (Events). On March 18, 1965, just two days after an elderly Quaker woman protesting the war in Vietnam doused herself in gasoline and set herself afire on a Detroit street corner, University of Michigan faculty members organized the first "teach-in" to focus attention "on this war, its consequences and ways to stop it." Inspired by the Freedom Schools of the still-growing civil rights movement, sociologist William Gamson, mathematician Anatol Rapaport, anthropologist Marshall Sahlins, and economist Kenneth Boulding encouraged faculty and students alike to participate in a "teach-in" which would allow for open, but nonconfrontational, protest toward the official U.S. government policies in Vietnam.

The idea and its acceptance mushroomed. On the evening of March 24–25, more than 3,000 faculty and students gathered in a massive teach-in which drew nationwide attention. Soon other teach-ins were being organized at most of the nation's prestigious universities and colleges. Within a week, there were teach-ins at 35 other campuses and, by the end of the academic year, at more than 120. A national radio hookup was established to link schools and faculty in their opposition to the war.

The mounting protests embarrassed the Johnson administration, which began to send its own teams of civilian and military officials to campuses to defend the government's policies. Many students accepted these latter views and continued to back the war, but an increasing number were swayed to the antiwar stance expounded by their professors. The teach-ins, perhaps more than anything else, legitimatized dissent at the outset of the growing war and focused the public opinion of the nation's leading young persons away from support for America's increasingly volatile Vietnam policy.

See:

DeBenedetti, Charles, and Charles Chatfield. *An American Ordeal: The Antiwar Movement of the Vietnam Era.* Syracuse, NY: Syracuse University Press, 1990, 107–109.

M. Paul Holsinger

THE THINGS THEY CARRIED (Fiction). Winner of the *Chicago Tribune* Heartland Award for fiction, *The Things They Carried* (1990) by Tim O'Brien, like his National Book Award–winning **Going after Cacciato** (1978), quickly established itself as one of the most popular books to emerge from the Vietnam War. Ambiguous in genre, *The Things They Carried* defies easy classification; it is in part a novel, a collection of short stories, a series of sketches or vignettes, an autobiography, and a work of advanced fiction. However, despite the ambiguity of genre, the book's subject is easy to identify. It deals with war and, more importantly perhaps, the significance of storytelling about the violence of combat during that war.

Each of the twenty-two chapters focuses on the soldiers of Alpha Company, a fictional platoon of American foot soldiers that served in Vietnam. Characters who are dead in the beginning are brought back to life in later chapters through the process of storytelling. The reader, who becomes an active participant in the text, must piece together the events that surround the characters' deaths, the platoon's activities, and the soldiers' individual and collective stories.

Many chapters were published as individual stories or sketches in magazines and periodicals such as *Harper's* or *Gentleman's Quarterly* prior to the book's publication. "The Things They Carried," "How to Tell a True War Story," "The Sweetheart of Song Tra Bong," and "The Lives of the Dead," all published in *Esquire* between 1986 and 1989, have gained an individual fame on their own. "The Things They Carried," for instance, received the 1987 National Magazine Award in fiction and was also selected for the 1987 *Best American Short Stories* and the *Best American Short Stories of the 1980s.*

Considered an enduring work of literature, *The Things They Carried* has been favorably compared to such popular works of war literature as Crane's **The Red Badge of Courage** (1895) and Erich Remarque's *All Quiet on the Western Front* (1929).

See:

Calloway, Catherine. " 'How to Tell a True War Story': Metafiction in *The Things They Carried.*" *Critique: Studies in Contemporary Fiction* 36 (1995): 249–257.

Catherine Calloway

***THE 13TH VALLEY* (Novel).** John M. Del Vecchio's novel *The 13th Valley* (1982) was perhaps the big Vietnam novel of the Reagan era—big not only in pages and scope, but also mainly in conservative, if not reactionary, myth making. If Americans could not win the war, it seems to say, at least they could go out in a blaze of glory reminiscent of Disney's **Davy Crockett** swinging his empty musket at hordes of Mexicans on the battlements of the Alamo.

Such fantasies pervade *The 13th Valley*, though couched in a sort of gritty naturalism that recalls James Jones's *From Here to Eternity* (1951) or *The Thin Red Line* (1962). Indeed, Del Vecchio's prose reads like Jones's, a mixture of philosophical conversations and realistic detail (he even includes maps of his mythical battles, as well as a glossary of specialized Vietnam combat terms). The only major concession to the fact that the story is set in the early seventies rather than the forties is that one of the major characters, Lieutenant Brooks, is black. Otherwise, in terms of political and cultural sensibilities, the book might have been written thirty years earlier, with the NVA replacing the Japanese.

The pretext—though not the plot—is fairly simple: U.S. troops in the late stages of the war have become so adept at jungle combat that they now "own the night" as well as the day. The only thing standing between them and final victory is a failure of political will that infects high command and ties the hands of the troops in the field. What ensues is a series of ever-escalating battles that culminates in an apocalyptic encounter in which, outnumbered and outgunned, the principals are wiped out in a heroic last stand.

See:

Myers, Thomas. "Diving through the Wreck: Sense Making in *The 13th Valley*." *Modern Fiction Studies* 30.1 (1984): 119–134.

Jeff Loeb

***THREE SERVICEMEN* (Memorial).** Though technically a part of the **Vietnam Veterans' Memorial** in Washington, D.C., the separate, free-standing *Three Servicemen* monument by sculptor Frederick Hart has become a tourist attraction in its own right. The full-size renderings of three young American combatmen in Vietnam, one Caucasian, one African-American, and one Hispanic, is accompanied by a sixty-foot-high flagpole on which the flag is raised every day. The men's portrayal was, according to Hart, historically accurate. Innocent in youth but loaded down with "the equipment of war," they stand as symbols of the sacrifices made by the almost 60,000 men and women whose names are engraved on "The Wall" nearby.

Dedicated on Veteran's Day, November 11, 1984, the statue, which now attracts millions of viewers every year, was initially clouded in controversy. Though Hart's vision for the larger Vietnam Veterans Memorial had finished a distant third in the international competition held to select the design for the monument, there were many right-wing conservatives such as the rich and influential H. Ross Perot who felt that the chosen selection with its simple black granite replete with the names of American dead did not honor the millions who served in southeast Asia. They insisted that a more traditional statue also be placed at the site. When it became clear that the Reagan administration was listening to the memorial's critics and that it was willing to scrap the entire project if they did not get their way, Hart's originally rejected proposal was added.

Maya Lin, the young award-winner, hated Hart's design, accurately calling it "trite," a "simplification," and a blot on her work. "I can't see how anyone of integrity can go around drawing mustaches on other people's portraits," she stated, but the choice was not hers, and, two years after Lin's evocative "Wall" was dedicated, Hart's new sculpture was also put on display. Today, it has become an accepted and respected part of the Vietnam Veteran's Memorial setting, but the two artists—Hart disliked Lin's wall just as much as she despised his servicemen—have never reconciled.

See:

Reynolds, Donald Martin. *Masters of American Sculpture: The Figurative Tradition from the American Renaissance to the Millennium.* New York: Abbeville Press, 1993, 162–163.
Scruggs, Jan C., and Joel L. Swerdlow. *To Heal a Nation: The Vietnam Veterans Memorial.* New York: Harper's, 1985, 93–108, 115–117.

M. Paul Holsinger

TOUR OF DUTY (Television Series). In 1987, CBS-TV aired *Tour of Duty*, a two-hour pilot for a potential series about the war in Vietnam. Starring a host of young, relatively unknown actors, it concentrated on a single platoon during 1967. Mostly composed of new recruits, the unit was almost too predictably made up of a familiar cross-section of American ethnic, racial, and social types: a WASP; an African-American; a "good old boy" from the South; a hip, urban, wise guy; even an antiwar draftee. A fresh new lieutenant filled the almost obligatory Jewish role. It was experienced sergeant Zeke Anderson, played by Terence Knox, who had the job of keeping the men alive until they were sufficiently competent to handle themselves. What was different from similar situations in movies about other wars, however, was the fact that each of the men was not in Vietnam for the duration but only for a limited tour of duty: a year.

Well-received, the film encouraged the development of an hour-long series on CBS. *Tour of Duty* began a three-year run on September 24, 1987. Though it was repeatedly switched to different days and times almost every year before its cancelation in August 1990, many veterans who watched acclaimed it as both realistic and fair. Episodes often focused upon only a few members of the platoon and their various adventures and problems. Fear of combat, isolation in enemy areas, drug addiction, "fragging," or involvement with civilians were highlighted at one time or another.

During the first year, *Tour of Duty* was often gritty and depressing. Several of the regulars were even killed. When it returned for its second season, the producers added several actresses in such roles as reporter, doctor, or helicopter pilot to attract a wider audience.

Tour of Duty was an important part of national reconciliation in regard to the war that took place in the late 1980s. After the show was canceled, several episodes were combined in 1991 into "new" video movies: *Tour of Duty II: Bravo Company* and *Tour of Duty III: The Hill.*

See:

Miller, Daniel. "Primetime Television's *Tour of Duty.*" In *Inventing Vietnam: The War in Film and Television*, ed. Michael Anderegg. Philadelphia: Temple University Press, 1991, 166–189.

Jack Colldeweih

TRACERS (Drama). John DiFusco's *Tracers* (1980), presents an embittered picture of a war where body counts were far more important than humanity, where men became "maggots" to their officers and killers of innocent women and children to many civilians once they returned home. DiFusco served with United States forces in the Central Highlands of Vietnam from late 1967 to 1968. He carried the idea of the play around in his head for more than a decade before, in March 1980, assembling a team of other actors—Vincent Caristi, Richard Chaves, Eric Emerson, Rick Gallivan, Merlin Marston and Harry Stephens—all Vietnam War veterans like himself. The seven, with professional author Sheldon Lettich, constructed the play over the next six months from what they later called "personal improvisation, rap sessions, psycho-drama, physical work, trust and ensemble work" (DiFusco, *Tracers*, vii). It has two possible endings, both depressing and morbid, one in which the entire squad is killed in a Viet Cong ambush, the second in which the men come home doubting the value of their service, filled with cancer caused by Agent Orange, and, in one case, wheelchair-bound and permanently drug addicted.

Initially improvisational, with the original seven cast members reciting, one by one, their individual emotions and hangups from their year of service in Vietnam, *Tracers* opened in Los Angeles on October 17, 1980. It was acclaimed for its direction and received the Los Angeles Drama Critics award for best ensemble performance. After a run in Chicago, where it won the Joseph Jefferson Award as best ensemble, the Joseph Papp production, now in a "frozen" script format, debuted at the New York Shakespeare Festival's Public Theater on January 21, 1985. Running for a total of 186 performances, it was selected as one of the year's best plays by the American Theater Critics Association.

See:

Fenn, Jeffery. "Vietnam: The Dramatic Response." In *Tell Me Lies about Vietnam: Cultural Battles for the Meaning of the War*, ed. Alf Louvre and Jeffrey Walsh. Philadelphia: Open University Press, 1988, 199–210.

M. Paul Holsinger

THE TRIAL OF THE CATONSVILLE NINE (Drama-Film). On May 17, 1968, Fathers Daniel and Philip Berrigan and seven Roman Catholic laypersons calmly walked into the Selective Service offices in Catonsville, Maryland, took nearly four hundred 1-A draft records from the files, poured napalm on them, and then set them afire. Praying and making no attempt to escape, they waited for their inevitable arrest. In early October, the nine were brought to Baltimore's Federal District Court, tried, convicted, and given jail sentences of from 2 to 3½ years in jail.

In summer 1969, Daniel Berrigan, a much-published poet, dramatically told that story as "factual theater" in *The Trial of the Catonsville Nine*. The creative editing of the more than twelve hundred pages of official court records, it is one of the best plays to emerge from the Vietnam War. First published in April 1970, it was initially performed that fall at Los Angeles' Mark Taber Forum by Ed Flanders (as the author) and the other members of the Center Theater Group. In the winter, completely revised by Saul Levitt (the award-winning author of 1959's *The Andersonville Trial*), it was brought to a unique off-Broadway venue, the sanctuary of the Good Shepherd Faith Church, where, between February 7 and May 30, 1971, it played 130 performances. Three days later, moved to Broadway, it ran for 29 more. Critically acclaimed, it was selected as one of 1970–1971's best plays by the New York Drama Critics. Gordon Davidson, the drama's director, received a Tony Award nomination.

A screen adaptation, *The Trial of the Catonsville Nine* (Cinema 5, 1972), with most of the original cast, was also highly praised. A generation later, it remains powerful and sincere.

See:

Alter, Nora M. "Playing Imperialism (America's War)." Chapter 1 in *Vietnam Protest Theatre: The Television War on Stage*. Bloomington: Indiana University Press, 1996, 26–46.

M. Paul Holsinger

VAN DEVANTER, LYNDA (Author-Poet). Lynda Van Devanter served as an army nurse in Vietnam at the 71st Evacuation Hospital in Pleiku in 1969 and 1970. The publication of her autobiography, *Home before Morning: The True Story of an Army Nurse in Vietnam* (1983), brought national attention to both Van Devanter and other female veterans. Generally considered the first extensive treatment of a woman's experiences in the Vietnam War, it unquestionably inspired numerous other women to step forth and publicly acknowledge their own war experiences.

Home before Morning examines Van Devanter's life before, during, and after her tour in Vietnam, recording the ways in which the war turned her John F. Kennedy–inspired patriotism to disillusionment and cynicism. The book reveals that women were not considered serious military personnel while in the war or real veterans after returning home; that doctors and nurses underwent grueling physical and psychological ordeals in Vietnam, frequently working seventy-two-hour shifts; that posttraumatic stress syndrome can affect both men and women.

Van Devanter, in tandem with Joan A. Furey, also edited *Visions of War, Dreams of Peace: Writings of Women in the Vietnam War* (1991), the most important collection of poetry by female veterans, both American and Vietnamese, now in print. The over one hundred poems, written by ex-military nurses, Red Cross volunteers, antiwar activists, and entertainers, were published with the intention of demonstrating that women have indeed made contributions in war zones. A national spokeswoman for women veterans and an organizer of the Vietnam Veterans of America Women Veterans Project, Lynda Van Devanter has not only opened doors of opportunity for women veterans, but she has also made significant contributions to women's rights in general.

See:

Dunn, Joe P. "Women and the Vietnam War: A Bibliographical Review." *Journal of American Culture* 12.1 (1989): 79–86.
Puhr, Kathleen M. "Women in Vietnam War Novels." In *Search and Clear: Critical Responses to Selected Literature and Film of the Vietnam War*, ed. William J. Searle. Bowling Green, OH: Bowling Green State University Popular Press, 1988, 172–183.

Catherine Calloway

VIETNAM: A TELEVISION HISTORY (Documentary Series). Eight years after the last United States Marines lifted off from the American Embassy in Saigon, the Public Broadcasting System and its Boston affiliate (WGBH) compiled a made-for-television history of the war in Vietnam. Spanning more than thirty years, from 1945 through 1975 and beyond, the series' writers, Richard Ellison, Lawrence Lichty and Stanley Karnow, utilized the archives from eleven countries and viewed more than 200,000 feet of film to create the thirteen-hour production. Narrated by Will Lyman from WGBH and backed by a musical theme written by Mickey Hart and Bill Kreutzmann of the Grateful Dead, *Vietnam: A Television History*, won six Emmy Awards and the almost universal praise of critics everywhere who used such terms as "extraordinary" to describe the various episodes. Watched by millions during its initial run from October 10 to December 20, 1983, *Vietnam: A Television History* became one of the PBS's most watched and most discussed shows. Karnow's 750-page text, *Vietnam: A History* (written to accompany the series) was also a great success.

Just as the U.S. policies in Vietnam were controversial, so, too, was the new series. Leftists attacked the show for its attempts to be objective when, they argued, it was impossible for anyone to feel that way. Conservative groups on the other hand, were so enraged at the liberal bias they claimed to see throughout the series that in 1985 they aired a meticulously detailed, two-hour-long televised rebuttal, *Television's Vietnam*, written and directed by Peter C. Rollins and narrated by Charleton Heston to point out the supposed errors.

Today, *Vietnam: A Television History* is readily available in a VHS format and, in summer 1997, it was reshown in its entirety on Public Broadcasting Stations across the United States. Visually exciting, it remains a valuable, if potentially flawed, source for understanding much about the war that divided so many Americans in the late 1960s and early 1970s.

See:

Lichty, Lawrence W. "Vietnam: A Television History: Media Research and Some Comments." In *New Challenges for the Documentary*, ed. Alan Rosenthal. Berkeley: University of California Press, 1988, 495–505.

Slater, Tomas J. "Teaching Vietnam: The Politics of Documentary." In *Inventing Vietnam: The War in Film and Television*, ed. Michael Anderegg. Philadelphia: Temple University Press, 1991, 269–290.

Springer, Claudia. "*Vietnam: A Television History* and the Equivocal Nature of Objectivity." *Wide Angle: A Film Quarterly of Theory, Criticism, and Practice* 7.4 (1985): 53–60.

M. Paul Holsinger

VIETNAM VETERANS' MEMORIAL. The Vietnam Veterans' Memorial in Washington, D.C., has become one of America's most visited and most honored monuments. Dedicated on Veteran's Day weekend in 1982, "The Wall," as it has commonly become known, was the dream of Vietnam War veteran Jan Scruggs. Between 1979 and 1982, he devoted almost every spare hour from a full-time job to gaining permission to build a monument on the Mall near the Lincoln Memorial for those men and women who fought and died in Southeast Asia. Though many opposed commemorating a "lost" war within the nation's capital (Arlington Cemetery, it was argued, would be a better locale), Scruggs fought for its placement and, ultimately, won.

A national contest to select the best design for the memorial drew 1,441 entries from around the world. The winning entry, a series of polished black marble sections containing the names of each of the nation's Vietnam war dead, was designed by Maya Lin, a twenty-year-old Yale University architectural student. "The Wall" was intended to be different from any previous war memorials. Far from being a "static object" for people to look at, Lin wanted her memorial to blend into the land in such a way that everyone would see it differently and take something personal away from it

It is impossible to assess in words the emotional impact the Vietnam Veterans' Memorial has had on the American psyche. Since it was first opened to the public, tens of millions of persons have made a pilgrimage to stand before it, often in awe at its power to move even the most hardened individual. Thousands take rubbings of one or more of the almost sixty thousand names etched into the marble; and every day, floral wreaths appear, often brought by school children far too young to remember the war or the men who died in it. To date, more than 54,000 different personal mementos have been left at the Wall, such as love letters from sweethearts, medals from friends in honor of a buddy lost, or even six packs of beer or fine cigars in remembrance of times past. No other

American war memorial has ever produced a more visible outpouring of emotions.

To Heal a Nation, a thoughtful, made-for-television movie about Jan Scruggs and his associates' drive to build "The Wall" was shown on NBC on May 29, 1988. Based on Scruggs and Joel L. Swerdlow's 1985 book of the same name, Lionel Chetwynd's screenplay almost seamlessly combines historical re-creations and newsreel film to tell the often-moving story of how the Vietnam Veterans' Memorial came to be. It is readily available today in a VHS format.

See:

Allen, Leslie. "Offerings at the Wall." *American Heritage* 46.1 (February–March 1995): 92–103.
Ashabranner, Brent K. *Always to Remember: The Story of the Vietnam Veterans Memorial*. New York: Scholastic, 1992.
Palmer, Laura. *Shrapnel in the Heart: Letters and Remembrances from the Vietnam Veterans Memorial*. New York: Viking, 1987.

M. Paul Holsinger

VIETNAM WAR STORY (Television Series). Produced for HBO by Vietnam veteran Patrick Duncan, *Vietnam War Story* was not a single film, but rather a series of twelve, approximately half-hour-long short stories. They were shown between 1989 and 1990 as four separate packages of three stories each. The directors and scriptwriters varied, although Duncan, who also directed *84 Charlie Mopic* (1989), wrote four of them. The subject matter ranges from a soldier's last night before going to Vietnam in 1963 to veterans in a military hospital stateside trying to recover from their physical and psychological wounds. Several of the shows deal with combat situations, others cover R&R, the "fragging" of officers, relationships with civilians, ARVN troops, and nurses.

Three programs focus specifically on the last days of American forces in Vietnam. One, from an enemy guerilla viewpoint, shows snipers harassing an American outpost as it is being closed down; another presents the tragic and frantic moments when the Americans evacuate the embassy in Saigon, leaving behind many Vietnamese employees and their families to certain imprisonment or death.

Altogether, *Vietnam War Story* presents a sketchbook of the war from the participants' point of view, and does so in a manner that sugarcoats nothing. It is neither an apologia nor an accusation, but rather a blunt and clear-eyed review. It offers a dramatic point-counterpoint to the excellent documentary, *Dear America: Letters Home from Vietnam*, which HBO released both theatrically and on cable in 1987.

See:

Devine, Jeremy M. *Vietnam at 24 Frames a Second: A Critical and Thematic Analysis of over 400 Films about the Vietnam War*. Jefferson, NC: McFarland, 1995, 282.

Jack Colldeweih

VIETNAM WOMEN'S MEMORIAL. During the dedication of the **Vietnam Veteran's Memorial** ("The Wall") in November 1982, a nurse who served "in country" from 1968–1969, Diane Carlson Evans, now married and the mother of four children, became convinced that the United States should also formally remember the thousands of women who volunteered to serve in that conflict. To help make her dream come true, she founded the Vietnam Women's Memorial Project in 1984.

Over the next five years, Evans and many others tirelessly raised money and lobbied Congress for permission to place a suitable monument near the popular "Wall." At first, they were repeatedly rebuffed. Members of the Commission of Fine Arts, the government agency empowered to approve or reject all memorials within the nation's capital, opposed the idea of yet another Vietnam memorial and tried to defeat what they considered the Mall's "ghettoization." Sculptor Rodger Brodin's design for the projected monument, a statue of a single army nurse in her combat fatigues, was summarily rejected in 1987. Despite such roadblocks, however, Evans persevered, and Congress finally gave approval in 1988. President George Bush signed the bill authorizing a monument early the following year.

In June 1991, New Mexico sculptor Glenna Goodacre's design for a larger-than-life-sized bronze statue of three servicewomen, one cradling a wounded soldier in her arms, another obviously looking skyward for medical assistance, the third holding the young man's helmet in her hands, was chosen for the new monument. She told reporters that, while "the memorial wall . . . is a monument to the dead," her statue was intended to convey "hope and healing." "The soldier in the sculpture isn't dead, he's going to recover," she added (Stanger, 68).

The large (six foot, eight inch; one ton) statue, begun in June 1992 and completed the following summer, was trucked across the country from Santa Fe the next fall. Placed within easy walking distance of the other two memorials that comprise the nation's commemoration to those many young Americans who fought and died in Vietnam, it was dedicated on Veteran's Day 1993 by then–Chief of Staff Colin Powell, who noted that it was "nine years in the making and over twenty years in the needing." The only national monument to any group of military women in a specific war, the Vietnam Women's Memorial today is a moving tribute to the courageous dedication of the almost twelve thousand nurses and other women who willingly served in that beleaguered country during America's first lost war.

See:

Stanger, Karen. "Glenna Goodacre Sculpts Vietnam Women's Memorial." *American Artist* 57 (August 1993): 66, 68.
Thomas, Julie Agnew, ed. *Vietnam Women's Memorial: A Commemorative.* Paducah, KY: Turner Publishing, 1993.

M. Paul Holsinger

VIET ROCK (**Musical**). Megan Terry, the author of *Viet Rock*, is an exponent of ''open theatre,'' with its constant improvisation and continual audience participation. In early 1966, based on her growing disillusion over the war in Vietnam, Terry, with the help of her Saturday morning workshop students in New York City, created this, at times, wildly irreverent attack on the United States presence in southeast Asia. Called by the author ''a folk war movie,'' the play contains rambling denunciations of everyone and everything connected with the war. It is filled with vulgarities and constant references to sexual depravity. President Lyndon Johnson is blamed for virtually everything from the Army's apparent moral decay to the expansion of syphilis within the ranks. Original, but quite undistinguished, rock-and-roll music for the play was composed by Marianne de Pury.

First performed in New York's Cafe La Mama Experimental Theatre Club and then at Yale, the play opened off-Broadway on November 10, 1966. It lasted 62 performances before closing on December 31 of the same year. Early in 1967, it was briefly staged in London, but, despite the plaudits of a small handful of critics, it quickly sank out of sight. *Viet Rock* was, however, distinguished by a number of ''firsts.'' It was the first original rock musical to be written and performed in the United States as well as the first drama in which actors left the stage to go into the audience and directly interact with the theatergoers. Widely translated into a number of foreign languages, it has become Terry's best-known work.

See:

Hughes, Catherine. ''The Theatre Goes to War.'' *America*, 20 May, 1967, 759–761.
Terry, Megan. ''Introduction to *Viet Rock*.'' *Tulane Drama Review* 11 (Fall 1966): 196–
    198.

M. Paul Holsinger

WHY VIETNAM (**Propaganda Film**). When the administration of President Lyndon Johnson determined to expand the war in Vietnam by sending hundreds of thousands of young Americans into Southeast Asia, it needed to ''sell'' the war to the public at large. *Why Vietnam* (1965), a blatantly dishonest documentary based roughly on the format first developed between 1942 and 1945 by Frank Capra in his *Why We Fight* series, was the result.

Produced by the U.S. Department of Defense to be shown to all new draftees, *Why Vietnam* was also loaned to high schools and civic clubs across the United States. For millions of citizens, it was the first full explanation they received of why the nation was fighting another Asian war. Beginning with footage of Hitler and the Nazis, the production attempted to equate them with the ''Vietnamese aggressors'' who also needed to be crushed by the forces of the United States so that freedom could live. Vietnam, it argued, was now ''our front door,'' and Americans had no choice but to keep evil from entering and infecting our families and loved ones.

Why Vietnam is filled with untruths and, occasionally, outright lies. Many historians were horrified at the picture's claim that it was the North Vietnamese who refused to allow free elections to bring about a united country when, in fact, it was the United States that purposely scuttled the vote, fearing that it would result in a communist victory. Henry Steele Commager, one of the nation's most eminent historians, noted that the film was bad history, bad scholarship, and even worse journalism

There is little positive that can be said about *Why Vietnam*. After the publication of a top-secret study of American involvement in Vietnam commissioned by the Department of Defense—the *Pentagon Papers*—in 1970, the government's attempts at deception became even clearer. When Peter Davis, the director of the later award-winning **Hearts and Minds**, created his 1971 documentary *The Selling of the Pentagon* with its clear exposé of how the Department of Defense had tried to sell the war to the American public, nearly all copies of *Why Vietnam* were withdrawn from circulation. That the nation's leaders felt that they needed such a melange of distortions to support their call for full-scale war, however, condemns everyone involved.

See:

Barnouw, Erik. *Documentary: A History of Non-Fiction Film.* 2nd ed. New York: Oxford University Press, 1993.

Barsam, Richard M. *Nonfiction Film: A Critical History.* Rev. and enlarged ed. Bloomington: Indiana University Press, 1992, 315.

M. Paul Holsinger

"THE WILLING CONSCRIPT" (Folksong). In 1963, as the war in Vietnam was about to explode into full-scale, bloody combat, Tom Paxton, one of the most original young folk song writer-performers of the day, penned "The Willing Conscript." The biting, sarcastic lyrics look at the predicament of a new draftee who needs lessons in how to kill. Though it is rumored that there is almost no difference in the enemy's appearance and our own, the pliant young man says that he is anxious to learn how to slaughter him in the most efficient way. With an almost jaunty tune that makes the words that much more ironic, "The Willing Conscript" asks how to use a bayonet properly to kill a man and questions whether one hand grenade is enough to blow his opponent to bits.

Paxton, an Oklahoman who served a tour of active duty in the Army in the late 1950s that took him no further than Fort Dix, New Jersey, recorded this new song on an album called *Ain't That News.* The following year, he sang it to great applause at the Newport Folk Festival, and, as the war in Southeast Asia expanded and more and more conscripts were called to serve, willingly or not, Paxton's composition became a tongue-in-cheek condemnation of the conflict and the entire idea of forcing young men to fight in it, or any other war.

See:

Moss, Mark. "Paxton on Paxton: An Interview." *Sing Out* 30.3 (July–August 1984): 14–24.

Pichaske, David. "The Angry No." Chapter 2 in *A Generation in Motion: Popular Music and Culture in the Sixties*. New York: Schermer, 1979, 51–89.

M. Paul Holsinger

WINNING HEARTS AND MINDS (Poetry). *Winning Hearts and Minds: War Poems by Vietnam Veterans* (1972) is important to the canon of Vietnam literature, not primarily because of its content, but rather because it was the first such anthology to emerge from a war that has produced more poetry than any since World War I.

Edited by Larry Rottmann, Jan Barry, and Basil Paquet, all members of Vietnam Veterans against the War, the slim volume of 113 short poems had a tortured publication history. Unable to find a commercial publisher for the work, which they painstakingly assembled in an apartment kitchen, the three editors, with the help of VVAW, created 1st Casualty Press, a name they selected from Aeschylus's famous dictum, "In war, truth is the first casualty," to publish privately a limited number of copies of their book. Ultimately, seeing the book's instant success—it was favorably reviewed nearly everywhere and sold out immediately—Random House put out a much larger edition.

Although much of the verse in *Winning Hearts and Minds* is raw and unfinished sounding, it nevertheless has a collective power that conveys deep anger toward a system that forced its authors into teenaged death and mayhem in the service of a hypocritical and racist ideology. The anthology contains several early poems by W. D. Ehrhart, who went on to a distinguished career as writer, editor, and educator. It also has several by Michael Casey and Paquet, both among the finest poets of the Vietnam War.

See:

Ehrhart, W. D. "Soldier-Poets of the Vietnam War." In *Tell Me Lies about Vietnam: Cultural Battles for the Meaning of the War*, ed. Alf Louvre and Jeffrey Walsh. Philadelphia: Open University Press, 1988, 149–166.
Slocock, Caroline. "Winning Hearts and Minds: The 1st Casualty Press." *Journal of American Studies* 16.1 (1982): 107–118.

Jeff Loeb

"WITH GOD ON OUR SIDE" (Folksong). In April 1963, Bob Dylan composed "With God on Our Side," a biting condemnation of the chauvinistic belief of many in the United States that its wars were always righteous because God was on "our side." A variation on Irish composer Dominic Behan's "The Patriot Game," it takes a hard, if rambling, look at this nation's warfare through the years. Beginning with the Indian Wars in the Far West and hurrying (somewhat unchronologically) through the Civil War, the Spanish-American War, World Wars I and II, and finally the Cold War, the songwriter/singer remembers all the many heroes that his teachers made him study in school, almost all of whom carried guns by their sides while claiming that they were God's special people. Their hypocrisy is clear to Dylan; if God is really on our side, he concludes, there will be no future wars.

At the Monterey (California) Folk Festival in May 1963, Dylan and already popular folk artist Joan Baez sang his new song as a duet. In late July, the two reprised their teamwork at the Newport Folk Festival, and the number brought down the house. The following month, Dylan recorded it for CBS as one cut on his new *The Times They Are-a-Changin'* album.

Some listeners, on hearing the piece for the first time, were appalled at its sentiments, since they unequivocally suggested that our government through the years had used God to push forward its militaristic goals. As the war escalated in Vietnam, however, many began to wonder if Dylan was not, perhaps, correct. The song became an antiwar standard and was frequently performed at rallies against the U.S. policies in Southeast Asia.

''With God on Our Side'' continued to be popular with many singers after the war ended. In September 1988, for instance, the Neville Brothers, a rhythm-and-blues duo, recorded it with an extra verse that updated its lyrics to include Vietnam. Dylan, who sat in on the session, liked the new stanza so much that he has subsequently added it to live performances of his own.

See:

Scheurer, Timothy E. *Born in the U.S.A. The Myth of America in Popular Culture from Colonial Days to the Present.* Jackson: University Press of Mississippi, 1991, 182–183.

Shelton, Robert. *No Direction Home: The Life and Music of Bob Dylan.* New York: DaCapo, 1997.

M. Paul Holsinger

13

The United States Military
since 1975

The withdrawal of the last American combat troops from the Republic of South Vietnam in 1973, and the even more precipitous evacuation of the U.S. embassy in Saigon when that city fell to the North Vietnamese communist forces in April 1975, represented, irrespective of the reasons, the first lost war in the nation's history. A malaise spread across the country. During the war, returning veterans were frequently damned by students and other young people opposed to U.S. intervention in Southeast Asia. Later, most were ignored as the nation hung its head in disgrace at the failure of Americans to triumph.

Things got worse long before they got better. In Cambodia, where Richard Nixon sent troops in the early 1970s during the Vietnam War, the communist Khmer Rouge won an overwhelming victory and began to soak that small nation-state in blood. Many news analysts were quick to blame the United States for once again helping to bring about the chaos. Though President Gerald Ford did successfully send in U.S. Marines to rescue the officers and crew of the USS *Mayaquez*, which the Cambodians captured in May 1975, such an action seemed to demonstrate American weakness instead of strength.

When Jimmy Carter became president after the 1976 election, he was quick to try positioning the nation as peacemaker rather than warrior. The Camp David Accords, which were drawn up after Carter brought together representatives of Egypt and Israel, seemed to indicate a breakthrough for world peace. The 1979 signing of the controversial Strategic Arms Limitation Treaty (SALT) II between the United States and the Soviet Union (an agreement that seemed to favor the USSR and give it a numerical superiority in land-based missiles) was quickly countered when Carter announced that the United States would begin building its own MX missile system.

The U.S. government was, at least since 1953, actively involved in the internal affairs of Iran. After conservative religious fundamentalists toppled the Westernized ruling monarchy in early 1979 and the Carter administration welcomed the deposed shah to the United States, an Iranian mob attacked the American embassy in Teheran and captured fifty-three hostages. Militants within that country protested daily and burned the American flag on international television for all to see. After proclaiming itself the world's strongest nation since the end of World War II, the weakened United States now seemed incapable of even protecting its embassies or citizens abroad. Under great protest, Carter finally authorized an American commando rescue attempt in April 1980, but everything went wrong, and the plan was abandoned after the mechanical malfunctioning of several of the planes in the desert and the death of eight of the rescuers. With the economy already in shambles (the inflation rate climbed to more than 12 percent and mortgage rates topped 20 percent), the embarrassment of the Democratic administration at failing to free our hostages in Iran seemed like the proverbial last straw.

That fall, voters went to the polls and overwhelmingly elected ex-motion picture actor, and former governor of California, Ronald Reagan as the nation's newest president. Reagan, a man who, above all else, understood the value of appearance, promised the public that, after so many years of seeming weakness, his main goal would be to help make "American stand tall again." Promises made are not always promises kept, unfortunately. Though the Reagan administration did negotiate the release of the Iranian hostages and moved rapidly to expand the nation's military weapons arsenal, it also began sending dozens of "military advisers" and millions of dollars in direct aid into such Latin American countries as El Salvador and Nicaragua, ostensibly to fight the takeover of Communist guerrillas in those small countries. Once again the "enemy" in Nicaragua was the so-called Sandinistas, but unlike in the 1920s and early 1930s, the United States was held in check. In the Middle East, the weakness of the United States was even more pronounced. In the midst of continuing civil war in the tiny Mediterranean nation of Lebanon, American Marines were sent into war-torn Beirut to act as "peacekeepers." In October 1983, a suicide bomber drove a truck loaded with explosives into the Marine compound; the resulting explosion killed 241 Americans and wounded an additional 80 more. When the president announced some weeks after this debacle that all American troops would be placed on warships off the coast, it was hard to argue that the nation was "standing tall."

At the point where things seemed the bleakest (and with a presidential election looming for 1984), the possibility of diverting the public's attention by beginning a military conquest became a reality. On the small West Indian island of Grenada, a communist-leaning government had negotiated a number of agreements with various Eastern bloc countries. When, in mid-1983, a radical, militarily controlled council took over that tiny nation-state, Reagan decided to intervene. More than 1,900 army paratroopers and Marines were ordered to invade Grenada, depose the ruling junta, and (officially at least) rescue a handful of American students who were enrolled in the island's lone medical college. The invasion was a total success—a great "victory" according to administration spokespersons—and many Americans, rightly or wrongly, had a sense of pride at how easily the nation's might had triumphed. Though the UN General Assembly condemned the American action and many persons wondered if it did not signal a return to the "gunboat diplomacy" of the Wilson, Harding, and Coolidge administrations earlier in the century, the "war" was popular throughout the United States. The Clint Eastwood film **Heartbreak Ridge**, one of the few motion pictures to look at the invasion, reemphasized that feeling as it contrasted the life and times of a "defeated" Marine veteran from Vietnam who now was able to train and bring the young troops under his command to total victory over the enemy.

Ronald Reagan won a second landslide victory in 1984 and, during the succeeding four years, presided over the continual growth of American military might. In contrast, the USSR, with its many satellite states, gradually weakened and began to fall apart. The "defeat" of communism left the United States, at least on the surface, the world's uncontested number one power. By the time the 1988 election elevated Vice President George Bush into the office of president, millions of citizens expressed their pride of being American in singing, with Lee Greenwood, the words of his latest hit, **"God Bless the U.S.A."**

The power of the media to control what people think has never been lost on the nation's military leaders. Officers in Vietnam had no doubt that, if reporters from the various television networks or the news media had only presented that war in a more positive light, they and their men would not only have had the backing of the American public but also have won the war. When troops invaded Grenada, the military, therefore, very consciously managed the news from the campaign, refusing all initial requests for reporters to land with the troops (as they had done in nearly every other war in the nation's history), and providing all information as the fighting progressed with an American spin. Though later revelations seemed to suggest that the campaign on that island was poorly coordinated and, in military terms at least, badly botched, the general public was kept in the dark, and the principle of controlling the news on all future armed engagements became entrenched.

Such was clearly the case on December 20, 1989, when President Bush ordered more than 24,000 army and Marine troops to invade the Central American nation of Panama. Though supposedly direct retaliation for the death of a Marine four days earlier, the motivation actually was to overthrow the military dictatorship of Panamanian General Manuel Noriega and replace it with a government that would be more congenial to the wishes of the United States. When the general was cornered and forced to surrender, all opposition to the American invasion rapidly ended. In the process, however, thousands of Panamanians were killed or wounded. Twenty-three American servicemen also died. Back home, the majority of concerned readers or television viewers got little of the real facts, as the army carefully controlled all information coming into or leaving that small country. Was the public deceived? Certainly some filmmakers and others believed so.

On August 2, 1990, the Iraqi government of Saddam Hussein opened a full-scale attack on the neighboring Islamic state of Kuwait. During both the Reagan and Bush administrations, the United States furnished Iraq with hundreds of millions of dollars worth of sophisticated military hardware. Now President Bush, buoyed by the nation's success in Panama, condemned Iraq's aggression and demanded that Hussein immediately withdraw his troops from Kuwait. When he did not, the administration began to mobilize troops, including significant numbers of National Guard units, as part of a buildup in the area that was soon designated Operation Desert Shield. In January 1991, Desert Shield became Desert Storm, as a force from twenty-eight different nations was turned against the aggressors. One hundred thirty-seven Americans died, but the loss to the Iraqi forces and Iraqi civilians was catastrophic (even the lower estimates of deaths place the number at nearly 100,000). The troops returned to the United States as great heroes. Numerous local parades took place, and, to appreciative citizens, the nation's success against a power touted as having the world's fourth largest army (albeit one that we had helped arm for many years as part of its war against Iran), marked the end of the military depression that had lasted for more than fifteen years.

The victory in Kuwait did not help George Bush politically. Though millions were euphoric after Desert Storm, problems on the home front soured many on the Republican administration and caused its defeat in the presidential election of 1992. Ironically, Bush's successor, Governor Bill Clinton of Arkansas, had consciously avoided the draft during the war in Vietnam and now became the first elected president to have refused service during the nation's many wars. Clinton's lack of military experience seemed to show. In October 1993, when American troops were sent into the east African nation of Somalia, eighteen Marines, left unprotected and forced to face a heavily armed rebel force with no backup, died. When the U.S. contingent was withdrawn in late 1994, little had been achieved. The president also finally decided to send U.S. troops into the former Yugoslavian nation of Bosnia in 1995 to enforce a hard-won cease-fire agreement made through the aegis of UN negotiators. After three years, the effort's potential for success seems very limited.

A simplistic overview of the U.S. military actions in the generation since 1975 might zero in on Grenada, Panama, and Desert Storm, stressing victories and ignoring who the enemies were. Cynics, on the other hand, might emphasize that, for all the nation's self-congratulations, it accomplished very little about which to be proud. As the twenty-first century beckons, the nation continues to pour billions of dollars into developing and perfecting new weapons of war. Whether they will ever have to be used remains to be seen.

See:

Bolger, Daniel P. *Americans at War 1975–1986: An Era of Violent Peace.* Novato, CA: Presidio, 1998.

Brands, H. W. *Since Vietnam: The United States in World Affairs, 1973–1955*. New York: McGraw-Hill, 1996.
Buckley, Kevin. *Panama: The Whole Story*. New York: Simon and Schuster, 1992.
Gordon, Michael, and Bernard E. Trainor. *The Generals' War: The Inside Story of the Conflict in the Gulf*. Boston: Little, Brown, 1995.
LeFeber, Walter. *Inevitable Revolutions: The United States in Central America*. 2nd ed. New York: Norton, 1993.

CABLE NEWS NETWORK (CNN) (Television News Network). It was Ted Turner of Atlanta, Georgia who first conceived the idea of a twenty-four-hour, seven-day-a-week news network. CNN, the Cable News Network, went on the air Sunday evening, June 1, 1980. Almost immediately, it began to "scoop" the major networks, and its in-depth reporting caught many viewers' attention. After the United States bombed Libya in 1986, CNN reporter John Donvan went on the air with the first eyewitness reports from a hotel room balcony in Tripoli. On July 13, 1987, when the network expanded to include a station featuring Headline News every half-hour, millions of Americans were already regular viewers.

CNN's greatest coup came immediately before and during the Persian Gulf War. After President George Bush ordered American planes to bomb Baghdad on the evening of January 16, 1991, CNN anchorman Bernard Shaw, John Holliman, Peter Arnett, and their crew were able to transmit the first pictures to the waiting world. Though the three major networks quickly sent reporters to the Middle East, for the rest of the war, they were outmaneuvered and certainly out-broadcast by CNN. Arnett, for instance, got the first live interview with Iraqi leader Saddam Hussein while the war was still in progress. CNN reporter Charles Jaco brought reports of the first missile attacks on Saudi Arabia and then on Israel. At the peak of the war, CNN had more than 150 broadcasters, technicians, and support people in the Gulf area, far more than any other competitor. Though some American "super-patriots" felt that the network was sympathizing with the enemy because its reporters remained in Iraq throughout the conflict, the number of admiring viewers grew steadily.

After the conclusion of the war in 1991, CNN created a colorful, glossy, and very popular book about the conflict (*War in the Gulf*) and also a dramatic videotape containing many of its action newsreels of the fighting (*Desert Storm: The Victory*). More than 500,000 copies of this 101-minute-long film and a related six-videocassette collection entitled *War in the Gulf: The Complete Story* were sold, often at supermarket checkout counters. Accompanied by upbeat, martial music in the background, *Victory* thrilled those many Americans who longed for a visual account of the short, but bloody, war.

See:

Smith, Perry M. *How CNN Fought the War: A View from Inside*. New York: Birch Lane, 1991.

M. Paul Holsinger

COURAGE UNDER FIRE (Novel-Film). Patrick Sheane Duncan, a member of the 173nd Airborne in Vietnam from 1968 to 1969, wrote and produced Home Box Office's award-winning *Vietnam War Story* (1989–1990) and the often-powerful film about cameramen during that war, *84 Charlie Mopic* (1989). However, *Courage Under Fire* (1996), a sweeping story of personal heroism during the Gulf War, is his first novel. It tells a tale filled with ambiguity. Captain Karen Emma Walden, one of the first American women to be placed in a combat command position, is killed after her Medivac helicopter is shot down over enemy territory. The army, which is conscious of the good publicity it will bring, wants to award her a Medal of Honor and appoints a tank commander from the war, Lieutenant Colonel Nat Serling, to investigate her death. Serling quickly discovers that things are not as simple as the army would like them to be; several of Walden's men praise her courage, but another claims that she was an abject coward. Serling finds that truth is many-sided, and his revelations affect the lives of nearly everyone connected with the situation, including himself. Ed Zwick, the director of the much-praised Civil War epic *Glory* (1989), wasted no time in adapting Duncan's book into the first commercial Hollywood movie to deal with the Gulf War. *Courage Under Fire* (20th Century–Fox, 1996), turns the war, which most Americans surrealistically saw each evening on their television sets, back into the often bloody conflict that it was. Faithful to the novel, as it should be since Duncan also wrote the screenplay, *Courage Under Fire* tells its story in flashbacks, as Serling (Denzel Washington), examines each conflicting account. In the end, Walden (Meg Ryan) post-humously receives her medal, much to the satisfaction of an army that values publicity almost as much as it does truth.

The Department of Defense withdrew its technical support for the film because Zwick refused to make changes in the script demanded by the Pentagon, especially where it questioned the moral and public accountability of top army officers during and after war; nonetheless, *Courage Under Fire* is a fair and honest account of how the Gulf War affected a number of lives on a very personal basis.

See:

Kilian, Michael. "Warriors Within: *Courage Under Fire*." Review of *Courage Under Fire*. Dir. Ed Zwick. *Chicago Tribune*, 9 July 1996, B1.
Wilmington, Michael. "Legends of the Gulf War." Review of *Courage Under Fire*. Dir. Ed Zwick. *Chicago Tribune*, 12 July 1996, B3.

M. Paul Holsinger

DESERT STORM: A BRIEF HISTORY (Poetry). One of the brightest young African-American poets writing in the United States today, North Carolinian (and United States Army veteran) Lenard Moore has authored a number of books and hundreds of other published poems. Shortly after the conclusion of the Gulf War in Kuwait in spring 1991, he began one of his most unconventional works, *Desert Storm: A Brief History*. Published in 1993, the fifty-seven-page poem sequentially orders almost 200 classic Japanese haiku to create a comprehensive, personal picture of a war that, to many, seemed more like a video arcade game than anything else.

Moore spans the entire chronology of the war, from the moment troops left for the Persian Gulf, in September 1990, until most came home to welcoming parades eight months later. Powerful images of combat and death are meshed with scenes of young Americans trying to cope with the boredom of days of waiting to see what their fate might be. Bombs fall, cannons boom, and blood leaks from a body bag in a helicopter, but Moore makes no attempt to force readers to accept any preconceived vision of the conflict. Instead, he vividly sets the stage and then steps aside so that each person, in his or her individual way, can begin to come to grips with what was then the nation's most recent military adventure in a land thousands of miles from home.

In the future, scholars will surely write many other books that provide a popular but comprehensive historical survey of the war in the Persian Gulf. It is hard to imagine, however, that there will be a more honest or more artistic vision of those hostilities than *Desert Storm: A Brief History*.

See:

Moore, Lenard D. "Poetry by Lenard D. Moore." *Vietnam Generation Journal* 4.3–4 (1992). Reprinted on-line. Lycos, 7 November 1997.

M. Paul Holsinger

"GOD BLESS THE U.S.A." (Song). Lee Greenwood, a sometime country-and-western singer who, in the 1980s, was fortunate enough to have nearly twenty "crossover" top ten hits, recorded the song for which he is best known, "God Bless the U.S.A.," in 1984. It immediately caught the attention of many ultrapatriotic, flag-waving Americans, and within a few weeks, it had reached the top ten charts of both main-line and country music.

When U.S. troops were sent into Panama, many disc jockeys across the country played Greenwood's recording repeatedly, and it was revived yet again during Desert Storm. It continues to be a staple of this country's political and religious right. In the late 1990s, it is still played regularly at many Republican Party rallies and conservative political conventions.

Greenwood became a personal favorite of nearly every veteran's group in the United States as a result of "God Bless the USA," winning medals of honor from such organization as the American Veterans of World War II, Korea, and Vietnam (AMVETS), the Veterans of Foreign Wars (VFW), the American Legion, the Congressional Medal of Honor Society, and the Hospitalized Veterans.

See:

McCloud, Barry. "Lee Greenwood." In *Definitive Country: The Ultimate Encyclopedia of Country Music and Its Performers*, ed. Barry McCloud. New York: Perigee Books, 1955, 345–346.

M. Paul Holsinger

HEARTBREAK RIDGE (**Film**). *Heartbreak Ridge* (Malpaso/Weston, 1986) might be described as director Clint Eastwood's homage to the classic war film. It is 1983, and Marine Sergeant Tom Highway (Eastwood), a veteran of Korea (where he won the Congressional Medal of Honor) and Vietnam, takes over an undisciplined, rebellious reconnaissance platoon by proving himself their physical and mental superior. He succeeds in getting his charges combat ready just in time to be sent to Grenada to prevent the supposed communist takeover of that West Indian island.

A hard-bitten, heavy-drinking professional, Highway finds himself at odds with his superiors and bewildered by the feminist sentiments of his former wife (Marsha Mason). His commanding officer (Everett McGill), an ambitious, corporate type, regards him as an anachronism; his platoon sees him as cold and brutal; his wife has tired of his devotion to the Marine Corps.

Heartbreak Ridge is, in many ways, an updated version of Alan Dwan's *The Sands of Iwo Jima* (1949), with Eastwood in the role made famous by John Wayne. Like Wayne's Sergeant Stryker, Highway wins the respect of his men when they realize that his demanding standards are the key to survival in battle. Though *Heartbreak Ridge* expresses a suspicion of authority certainly not found in *Sands* or any other 1940s war movie and the aging Highway does return in triumph from Grenada to his wife waiting loyally at the airport (Stryker had been struck down by a sniper's bullet at the very moment of the Marines' triumph on Iwo Jima), the two stories frequently run parallel to each other.

Heartbreak Ridge emphasizes how important the Marine victory in the Caribbean was to the corps's professional pride. Highway discovers that his fellows are no longer haunted by the defeat in Vietnam—Grenada has apparently wiped out both the stain of stalemate in Korea and defeat in Southeast Asia. The United States has, the film implies, recaptured the spirit of an earlier generation.

See:

Parish, James Robert. *The Great Combat Pictures: Twentieth-Century Warfare on the Screen.* Metuchen, NJ: Scarecrow, 1990, 204–205.

Philip J. Landon

THE PANAMA DECEPTION (**Documentary**). Operation Just Cause, the American military invasion of Panama in December 1989 was, as "small wars" go, a total success. According to information released by the U.S. Department of Defense, few persons were injured or killed and almost no one displaced when Marines Corps and army personnel attempted to capture, and then deport, Panamanian dictator General Manuel Noriega for drug smuggling. Though the U.N. General Assembly subsequently voted 75–20 to declare the prolonged attack a "flagrant violation of international law," the majority of Americans strongly supported the operation.

Two years later, a small, documentary filmmaking studio in San Diego, California, provided an entirely different version of Operation Just Cause. *The Pan-*

ama Deception (The Empowerment Project, 1992), directed by Barbara Trent and written for the screen by David Kasper, challenges the claims that few citizens of that nation were harmed during the invasion. Citing reports of more than 4,000 dead; 20,000 made homeless; and mass graves throughout the country; the ninety-four-minute-long exposé systematically offers its viewers "the other side of the story." Surveying the often less-than-just diplomatic relations between the United States and Panama, it accuses both the Reagan and Bush administrations of creating the problems that they then corrected by military might. It also takes the television networks to task for their role in supposedly deceiving the American public about the invasion.

With much nonpartisan support, *The Panama Deception* opened simultaneously in more than sixty American cities in 1992. Critically acclaimed by nearly everyone, it was selected as the year's best feature documentary by the voters of the Academy of Motion Picture Arts and Sciences.

See:

Levy, E. "The Panama Deception." *Variety*, 10 August 1992, 55.
Ryan, S. "Panama Deception." *Cineaste* 20.1 (1993): 43–44.

M. Paul Holsinger

UNITED STATES NAVY MEMORIAL. One of the nation's newest national war-related memorials sits on Pennsylvania Avenue in Washington, D.C., to honor the millions of men who, through the years, have been a part of the United States Navy. Dedicated in 1987 and featuring a seven-foot-high sculpture by Stanley Bleifeld that is intended to be emblematic of every enlisted sailor, the memorial also includes the largest map of the world, a hundred-foot diameter granite gridwork, waterfalls, a fountain, and several pools. The young *Lone Sailor*, stands on the map, hands in the pockets of his pulled up pea jacket, looking out over the oceans of the world on which he will soon be sailing. His duffel bag sits behind him, crammed full of those items that will sustain him on his voyage ahead. Though simplistic in design, the Navy memorial is touching and, in many ways, dramatic in its implications.

Bleifeld was awarded the Henry Hering Memorial Medal by the National Sculpture Society in 1990 in recognition of his distinguished use of sculpture in centering his *Lone Sailor* in the United States Navy Memorial.

See:

Coldwell, Thomas. *Granite Sea: Navigating the United States Navy Memorial.* Washington, DC: U.S. Navy Memorial, 1992.

M. Paul Holsinger

WOMEN IN MILITARY SERVICE FOR AMERICA MEMORIAL. More than 1.8 million women have served in the U.S. armed forces since the American Revolution. Though thousands of monuments to the nation's warriors have been built in every state, it was not until October 18, 1997, that a memorial was dedicated specifically to recognize America's military women. The goals of the founders of the $21.5 million structure were, from the beginning, five-fold: to recognize all the women who have served in the armed forces; to document their experiences and tell their stories; to make women's contributions visible; to show how women and men have, through the years, worked together as a team in the defense of the nation; and to hold up women military veterans as role models for generations to come. Constructed on four acres of land just inside the main entrance gate to Arlington National Cemetery, the large Women in Military Service for America Memorial is a fitting tribute to those women who served their country so faithfully.

Though Congresswoman Mary Rose Oaker of Ohio and Senator Frank Murkowski of Alaska introduced joint legislation in 1983 to allow the memorial to be built, there were many persons who openly wondered if such a single-gender monument was really needed. Not until 1986 did Congress finally pass Public Law 99-610 authorizing a privately funded memorial. Another three years passed before the project's design, submitted by the architectural team of Marion Gail Weiss and Michael Manfredi, was selected from more than 130 different entries in an international competition. Approval for the monument came in April 1995, and ground was broken on June 22, 1995.

The memorial is multidimensional. There is a large reflecting pool, a fountain, a wall of glass tablets inscribed with quotes by and about women who have served in the armed forces, and a large, two-story monument (with room inside for a museum, an education center, and a hall of honor). Four staircases allow visitors to climb from ground level to an upper terrace that provides a panoramic view of the District of Columbia just across the Potomac River.

See:

"Women in Military Service Memorial." *Women in Military Service Memorial Home Page.* On-line. Lycos, 1 November 1997.

                                                              M. Paul Holsinger

YELLOW RIBBONS (Symbols). Though historically the symbolic use of yellow ribbons in American culture goes back to the Civil War, it was during Operation Desert Storm that they gained their most visible sign of approval. Originally a sign of love and devotion worn by the wives and sweethearts of cavalrymen, they were an indication that the woman was, in a sense, "incomplete" until the return of her mate from the dangers of active duty. This practice was probably inspired by a popular early nineteenth-century British song titled "All around My Cap," which was later used as a marching song. In different musical versions, the sign of affection varied from a green willow to a purple garter, and, in a 1917 text, a yellow ribbon worn around the neck. A further adaptation appeared in John Ford's classic, *She Wore a Yellow Ribbon* (1949).

In 1973, the musical group Tony Orlando and Dawn popularized the song that gave yellow ribbons a slightly different connotation. Irwin Jesse Levine's

"Tie a Yellow Ribbon Round the Ole Oak Tree" tells of a soon-to-be-released prisoner who, feeling anxious about whether his girlfriend still loves him, asks her to put out a yellow ribbon if she wants him back. Although emotional loss, fear, and guilt are frankly explicit, there is a happy outcome, as the young man sees dozens of yellow ribbons on every tree in town. The timeliness and emotional context of the lyrics make the transition from prisoner to soldier homecoming very easy.

The use of yellow ribbons reappeared during the Iran hostage crisis of 1979–1980 and in 1991 as a sign of support for U.S. troops in Kuwait. As a show of emotive patriotism, the ribbons permeated American popular culture. They became a part of other holiday decorative displays, including Christmas, Valentine's Day, St. Patrick's Day, and Easter. Yellow ribbons were even used as a motif on issued collectible plates. Ribbons appeared in fashion advertising, and the Anheuser-Busch Company launched "Yellow Ribbon Summer," which offered veterans and their children a free visit to a Busch Garden amusement park.

See:

Heilbronn, Lisa M. "Yellow Ribbons and Remembrance: Mythic Symbols of the Gulf War." *Sociological Inquiry* 64.1 (1994): 151.

Kerstin Ketteman

Index

Page numbers in **bold type** refer to main entries in the dictionary.

Abbott, Bud, 242
Abbott, George, 288
à Becket, Thomas, 67–68
Abraham Lincoln: A History, 111
Abraham Lincoln Battalion, 223, 267
Academy Awards (Oscars), 11, 86, 100,
    104, 106, 150, 152, 156, 166, 175,
    199, 202, 213, 214, 216, 222, 229,
    235, 236, 239, 247, 259, 261, 263,
    270, 273, 279, 283, 284, 287, 290,
    299, 301, 303, 307, 309, 311, 318,
    319, 330, 341, 348, 349, 351, 355,
    363, 365, 375, 377, 383, 384, 387,
    390, 392, 394, 409, 437
Across Five Aprils, **78–79**
Action in the North Atlantic, **228–229**
Adams, Abigail, 38
Adams, Franklin, 218
Adams, Harriet Stratemeyer, 190
Adams, John, 18, 28
Adams, Samuel, 12, 13, 18, 29, 35, 38
Adamson, Harold, 250
*Admiral Porter's Fleet Running the Rebel
    Blockade of the Mississippi at Vicks-
    burg, April 16, 1863*, 69
Adoree, Renee, 198
Adventures of Buffalo Bill, The, 165
Adventures of Ozzie and Harriet, The,
    414

Aeschylus, 427
Aesthetic Papers, 66
"Affair at Coulter's Notch, The," 86
Again, 333
Agar, John, 158, 301
Agent Orange, 419
Aguinaldo, Emilio, 180, 187
Ain't That News?, 426
Air Force (Film), **229–230**
Air Force (Service Journal), 237
Air Service Boys Series, 189
Alamo, The, 62, 64, **65–66**, 68, 417
Alamo, The (Epic Poem), 65
Alamo, The (Film), 65, 68
Alamo: The Price of Freedom, 65
Alamo: 13 Days to Glory, The, 65
Albert, Eddie, 232
Alcott, Bronson, 67
Alda, Alan, 349
Aldrich, Robert, 177, 232, 255
Ali, Muhammad, **361–362**
Alice of Old Vincennes, **15–16**
Alice's Restaurant, **362**
"Alice's Restaurant," 362
"Alice's Rock and Roll Restaurant,"
    362
Alison, Joan, 247
Allen, Ethan, 14
Allen, Henry Wilson, 159–160, 168

Allen, Hervey, 111
Alley, Kirsti, 125
Alleys of Eden, The, 391
"All Quiet along the Potomac Tonight,"
   79
All Quiet on the Western Front, 284, 351,
   416
All Together Now, 326
Al Schmid—Marine, 293
Altman, Robert, 243, 250, 349, 415
Altsheler, Joseph, **57–58**
America, **16–17**, 330
American (Baltimore), 51
"American Bicentennial Series," 30
American Crisis, The, 20
American Expeditionary Force (AEF),
   194, 195, 215, 217–218
American Legion, 263, 318, 435
American Legion Monthly, The, 201
American Panorama Company, 84
Americans, The, 30
American's Home, An, 197
American Spirit, The, 114
American Theater Wing War Service,
   308
American Veterans of World War II, Ko-
   rea, and Vietnam (AMVETS), 435
Amsterdam News (New York), 257
"Anchors Aweigh," **230**
And Babies, **363**
Anderson, Judith, 111
Anderson, Maxwell, 41–42, 220, 302
Anderson Platoon, The, **363–364**
Andersonville, 42, **80–81**
Andersonville Trial, The, **81**, 420
Andre, 27
Andrew, John, 104
Andrews, Dana, 239, 294, 325
Andrews, James J., 101–102
Andrews, LaVerne, 230–231, 309, 321
Andrews, Maxene, 230–231
Andrews, Patti, 230–231
Andrews, Robert D., 234
Andrews Sisters, The, **230–231**, 242, 256,
   309, 433
And "They Thought We Wouldn't Fight,"
   205
Annakin, Ken, 279
Ansara, Michael, 153
"Answer to My Maryland," 120
"Anywhere the Bluebird Goes," 256
Apartment for Peggy, 264
Apocalypse Now, **364–365**, 379

Appomatox, 77, 89, 115
Arberg, W. H., 244
Arizona, USS, 224
Arkin, Alan, 249
Arlen, Richard, 221
Arlington National Cemetery, 185, 219–
   220, 321, 387, 422, 438
Armed Forces Radio Service, 184, 272,
   390–391
Armies of the Night, 381
Armistead, Lewis, 112
Armistice Day, 196, 219, 220
"Army Air Corps Song, The," 230, **231–
   232**, 295, 331
Army Emergency Relief Fund, 316, 331
"Army Goes Rolling Along, The," 244
Army-Navy Screen Magazine, 305
Army of the Potomac, 142
Army Specialized Training Program Re-
   serve, 284
Arnett, Peter, 433
Arnold, Benedict, 17, 37
Arnold, Elliott, 152
Arnold, Tom, 282
Arquette, Rosanna, 175
Arrow in the Sun, 174
Artist's Story of the Great War, An, 99
Art Worker's Coalition, 363
Arundel, **17**, 34, 36
ARVN (Army of the Republic of Viet-
   nam), 358, 360
Ashby, Hal, 375
Assault at Contras, 71
Assignment Home, 271
Astor, Mary, 188
As You Were, Bill, 201
Atlanta Cyclorama, 85
Atlantic Charter, 261
Atlantic Monthly, 83, 101, 107
atomic bomb, 226, 241, 268, 328, 336
Attack, **232**
Attack at Dawn, 171
Austin, Stephen, 62
Axis Sally, **232–233**

"Babylon is Fallen," 114
Bachelder, John Badger, 141
Back at the Front, 282
Back Home, 282
Back to Bataan, 393
Bacon, Lloyd, 228, 260
"Badge of Courage," 365
Baez, Joan, 346, 428

Bailey, Bill, 267
Bailey, Francis, 27
Bainter, Fay, 253, 273
Baker, Carroll, 155
Baker, George, 299–300, 333
Baker, Newton, 194
Balaban, John, 370
Balchowsky, Ed, 267
Baldwin, Faith, 264
Balin, Ina, 372–373
"Ballad of Davy Crockett, The," 68
"Ballad of Francis Powers, The," 313
"Ballad of Jane McCrea, The," 33
"Ballad of Rodger Young, The," 233
"Ballad of the Alamo," 65
"Ballad of the Green Berets, The," 365–366, 393
Band of Brothers, 339
Bangs, Edward, 43
Banjo Eyes, 329
Bankhead, Tallulah, 279
Banner, John, 270
Barbara Frietchie (Lithograph), 101
"Barbara Frietchie" (Poem), 100–101
Barbara Frietchie, The Frederick Girl, a Play, 101
Barbary Pirates, 50
Barrack Thief and Other Stories, The, 398
Barrett, James Lee, 133, 392
Barry, Jan, 427
Barrymore, Lionel, 94
Barry Wood and the Wood Nymphs, 329
Barthelmess, Richard, 116, 199
Bartlett, Sy, 319
Barton, Andrew, 43
Barton, Billy, 254
Basehart, Richard, 342, 353
Basic Training of Pavlo Hummel, The, 414
Basinger, Kim, 263
Bass, Ronald, 387
Bastard, The, 30
Bataan, 176, **234**, 269
Battle at Apache Pass, 152
Battle at Elderbush Gulch, The, **151**
Battle Cry, 227, **234–235**
"Battle Cry for Freedom, The," **81–82**
Battle Cry of Peace, The, **197–198**
battlefield reenactments, 47, **82–83**, 88, 104, 113
Battleground (Film), **235–236**, 250, 319
Battleground (Novel), 252

Battle Hymn, **339–340**
"Battle Hymn of Lt. Calley, The," **366–367**
"Battle Hymn of the Republic, The," **83–84**
Battle Hymn of the Republic, The, 84
Battle of Atlanta, The, **84–85**
Battle of Britain, The, 330
Battle of Buena Vista, 71
Battle of Cerro Gordo, 71
Battle of China, The, 330
Battle of Churubusco, 71
Battle of Gettysburg: Repulse of Long-street's Assault, July 3, 1863, The, 141
"Battle of Lexington and Concord, The," 24
Battle of Manila Bay, The, 190
Battle of Midway, The, **236–237**
Battle of Molino del Rey, 71
"Battle of New Orleans, The," **47–48**
Battle of Palo Alto, 71
Battle of Resca de la Palma, May 9, 1846, 69
Battle of Russia, The, 330
Battle of San Pietro, The, 319
Battle of Santiago Cuba, The, 181
"Battle of Trenton, The," 43
Battle Pieces and Aspects of the War, 110, 121
battles: Adobe Wells, 168; Aleutian Islands, 266; Antietam (Sharpsburg), 75, 92, 98, 103, 121, 138; Atlanta, 76, 84, 105–106, 118, 130, 135; Atlantic, The, 318; Bad Axe, 57, 58; Bataan, 14, 176, 225, 234, 253, 307, 314; Beecher Island, 168; Belleau Wood, 195, 198, 205, 218; Belloy-en-Santerre, 215; Bladensburg, 46; Blanc Mont, 218; Bloody Brook, 183; Buena Vista, 64, 66, 70, 71; Bulge, The (Ardennes Forest), 226, 232, 235, 250, 284, 389; Bull Run, First (Manassas), 74, 84, 91, 105, 140, 142; Bull Run, Second (Manassas), 75, 92, 98, 105; Bunker (Breed's) Hill, 12–13, 16, 18–19, 26, 30, 40, 43; Butte, The, 168; Camden, 14; Cantigny, 195; Cedar Creek, 132, 134; Cedar Mountain, 98; Cerro Gordo, 64; Chancellorsville, 76, 105, 115, 138; Chapultepec, 70; Charleston, 14; Chateau Thierry, 195; Chattanooga (Lookout Mountain), 76, 84, 141; Chickamauga, 78; Chippewa, 51;

Chosin Reservoir, 339, 341, 344, 352; Cold Harbor, 77, 88; Concord, 13, 16, 20, 24, 29, 30, 33, 34; Con Thien, 410; Coral Sea, 225, 229; Corregidor, 225, 295, 307, 347; Cowpens, 15, 25; Detroit, 46; Dresden, 226, 304; El Alamein, 300; Fair Oaks, 109; Fallen Timbers, 55, 59; Fetterman Massacre, 149, 167, 168, 171, 174; Fort Donelson, 75; Fort Hatteras, 142; Fort Henry, 75; Fort Wagner, 104; Fort Washington, 36; Fredericksburg, 76, 90, 105; Gettysburg, 76, 79, 82, 84, 88, 95, 102–103, 104, 111, 112, 115, 129, 141; Gilbert Islands, 259; Guadalcanal, 225, 235, 252, 260, 262, 268–269, 293, 314–315; Guam, 224; Gulf of Tonkin, 358; Hamburger Hill, 393; Horseshoe Bend, 46, 61; Hue (Tet Offensive), 359, 379, 387, 400; Ia Drang Valley, 359; Ie Shima, 296; Inchon, 337, 341, 343, 347, 350, 352; Iwo Jima, 226, 301, 321, 372; Jalapa, 64; Java Sea, 225; Kasserine Pass, 295; Khe Sanh, 341, 359; King's Mountain, 15; Kwajalein, 252; Lake Erie, 46, 49; Lee's Mills, 131; Lexington, 12, 13, 16, 20, 24, 29, 30, 34; Leyte Gulf, 226; Little Big Horn, 149, 150, 152, 153, 155, 160, 166, 167, 169, 173, 174–175, 176; Long Island, 14, 21; Lookout Mountain, 76, 84, 141; Louisbourg, 2; Makin Island, 252; Malvern Hill, 109; Manila Bay, 179, 190; Mariannas, 259; Marne, The, 199; Matamoras, 63; Maumee River, 55; Meuse-Argonne, 195, 215, 217; Midway, 225, 236, 328; Mobile Bay, 130; Monmouth, 36, 49; Monterrey, 63–64, 70; My Lai 4 (Massacre), 81, 174, 359, 366, 377, 379, 397; New Georgia, 233; New Orleans, 46, 47, 48, 49; Niagara Peninsula, 46; Ninety-Six, 34; Normandy (D-Day), 195, 225, 245, 269, 279, 318; North Africa, 225, 241, 245, 266, 272, 295, 300, 334; Ocotal, 204; Okinawa, 114, 226, 254; Oriskany, 14; Palo Alto, 109, 112; Palo Duro Canyon, 168; Pamlico Sound, 107; Paris, 225, 276; Pearl Harbor, 176, 223–224, 226, 227, 229, 242, 244, 247, 256, 260, 262–263, 272, 292, 295, 302, 305, 308, 314, 315, 318, 322, 325, 326, 327–

328, 329, 333; Peleliu, 277; Peninsula, 109, 131; Petersburg, 77, 90, 98, 125; Philippines, 226, 234, 252, 253, 266, 313–314, 347; Plattsburgh, 46; Pork Chop Hill, 351; Puebla, 64; Quebec, 14, 17, 40; Raccoon Ford, 142; Reseca la Palma, 63; Rome, 241; Ruhr, 306; Salerno, 325; Sand Creek (Massacre), 148, 166, 167, 174; Sandusky, 22; San Jacinto, 62–63, 65; San Juan Hill, 114, 179, 181, 188, 191; Saratoga, 14, 23, 32–33, 36, 40, 43; Savannah (1778), 14; Savannah (1864), 118, 135; Savo Island; 268; Seven Pines, 109; Shiloh (Pittsburg Landing), 75, 78, 84, 115, 135–136; Sicily, 225, 245, 272, 281, 295; Soissons, 218; Solomons, 225, 233, 252, 294; Spotsylvania Court House, 115; St. Mihiel, 195, 218; Summit Springs, 168, 172; Tarawa, 225, 235, 301; Thames, 60; Tippecanoe, 56, 60; Tobruk, 300; Trenton, 14, 20, 42, 43; Vera Cruz, 64; Verdun, 218; Vicksburg, 76, 84, 88, 140; Vincennes, 15; Wagon Box Incident, 174; Wake Island, 176, 224, 229, 325; Warbonnet Creek, 165; Washita, 149, 161; Wilderness, The, 77, 88, 98, 109, 115; Winchester, 107; Wounded Knee (Massacre), 85, 150, 152, 154, 162, 165; Yorktown, 15, 16, 27, 29, 34, 40, 43, 114

Battles and Leaders of the Civil War, 110, 128
Baude, Louis de (Count Frontenac), 2
Bayes, Nora, 208, 212
Beach Red, **237–238**
Beadle and Adams Dime Novels, **85**
Beals, Carleton, 204
"Beat! Beat! Drums!," 146
Beatty, Ned, 385
Beauregard, P.G.T., 91
Beautiful Rebel, The, 29
Beck, C. C., 308
Beers, Ethelinda Eliot, 79
Beery, Noah, 188
Beery, Wallace, 6, 50, 186
Beetle Bailey, 218
Behan, Dominic, 427
Behind the Lines, 252
Belasco, David, 108, 141, 162
Bell, Ulric, 355–356
Bellah, James Warner, 158, 170, 173

Bell for Adano, A, **238**
Belushi, James, 300
Bendix, William, 238, 268, 278, 325
"Beneath the Southern Cross," 323
Beneke, Tex, 256
Benet, Stephen Vincent, 65, 110–111, 174, 262
Bennett, Robert Russell, 262, 323
Benteen, Frederick W., 167
Benton, Thomas Hart, 333–334
Berenger, Tom, 112–113, 189, 409
Berg, Peter, 285
Bergen, Candice, 174, 214
Berger, Thomas, 166
Bergman, Ingrid, 247, 261
Berkey, Ralph, 353
Berlin (Germany), 226, 286
Berlin, Irving, 212, 265–266, 305, 309, 316
Bernstein, Leonard, 288–289
Berra, Yogi, 305
Berrigan, Daniel, 408, 420
Berrigan, Philip, 420
Berry, Ken, 160
Best American Short Stories, 391, 416
Best American Short Stories of the 1980s, 416
Best from Yank, The, 333
Best Years of Our Lives, The, **238–239**, 270, 374
Better Little Books, 244, 247
Betty Boop, 292
Bevan, Donald Joseph, 309
Bickford, Charles, 251
Bierce, Ambrose, **85–86**
Biggs, John, 35
Bighead, Kate, 175–176
"Big Hunt, The," 173
Big Parade, The, **198–199**, 221
Big Red One, The, 228, **239–240**
Billings, William, 19
Bill Mauldin's Army, 282
Biloxi Blues, **240–241**
Birdy, 285
Birth of a Nation, The, **86–87**, 125, 133, 142, 151, 206
Bismarck, 224
Blackburn, Tom, 30, 68
Black Elk, 151–152, 174
Black Elk Speaks, Being the Life Story of a Holy Man of the Oglala Sioux, 152, 174
Black Elk Speaks (Drama), **151–152**

Black Hawk, **58–59**
Black Hawk War, 56, 58
Black Sun, 168
Blackton, J. Stuart, 183, 190, 197
Blake, Michael, 156
Blanc, Mel, 305
Bleifeld, Stanley, 437
Bliss, P. P., 134
Blitz, The, 245, 276, 286, 295
Blondell, Joan, 253
Blood Brother, 152
Bloods: An Oral History of the Vietnam War by Black Veterans, **367–368**
Bloods of 'Nam, The, 367
Blood Song, 168
Blue and the Gray, The, **87–89**, 114
Blue Jacket (Wey-yah-pih-her-sehn-wah), 55, 59–60
Blue Jacket, **59–60**
Blum, Edwin, 310
Bob Hope, 272
Bogart, Humphrey, 228, 243, 248, 300
Boles, John, 117, 186
Bombardment of Vera Cruz, 71
Bond, Ward, 158
Bonfils, Fred, 165
Bon Homme Richard, 25
"Bonnie Blue Flag, The," **89**
"Boogie Woogie Bugle Boy of Company B," 230, 242
Boone, Pat, 254
Boonesboro, 55, 59
Booth, John Wilkes, 77
Border Watch: A Story of the Great Chief's Last Stand, The, 58
Borglum, Gutzon, 137–138, 155
Borgnine, Ernest, 255, 282
Born on the Fourth of July, 284, **368**, 398
"Born to be Wild," 381
"Born to the Sky," 231
Bosnia, 432
Boston Massacre, 13, **17–18**, 28
Boston Massacre (Engraving), 18, 24
Boston Tea Party, 7, 29
Bottoms, Timothy, 209
Boublil, Alain, 404
Boulding, Kenneth, 415
Bourke-White, Margaret, **241–242**
Bow, Clara, 222
Bowdoin, James, 18
Bowen, Robert Sidney, 327
Bowie, James, 62, 65

Bowman, Peter, 237
Boxer Rebellion, 184, 214
Boy Allies, The, **199**, 327
Boyd, James, 24–25
Boyd, Thomas, 218–219
Boyd, William, 221
"Boys in Blue," 184
Boys in Company C, The, **369**, 410
Bracken, Eddie, 242, 269
Braddock, Edward, 3, 4
Braddock: Missing in Action III, 403
"Braddock's Defeat," 4
Bradley, Omar, 290
Brady, Mathew, 98, **120–121**, 122
Bragg, Sonny, 250
brainwashing, 338, 348
Brando, Marlon, 284, 334, 364
Braugher, Andre, 104
Braun, Eva, 226
Brave Men, 295
"Break the News to Mother," **181**
Breck, Bill, 200
Breger, Dave, 264–265, 333
Brennan, Walter, 216
Bridges, Lloyd, 125, 300
Bridges at Toko-Ri, The, **340–341**
Brighton Beach Memoirs, 240
"Britannia, the Gem of the Ocean," 67–68
"British Grenadiers, The," 26
"British Prison Ship, The," 27
British War Relief Society, 308
Britt, Elton, 313
Brock, Isaac, 46
Broderick, James, 362
Broderick, Matthew, 103, 240
Broderick, William, 188
Brodie, Steve, 353
Brodin, Roger, 424
Broken Arrow, **152–153**
Brooks, Norman, 232
Brophy, John, 342
"Brother Jonathan," 53
Brown, Clarence, 273
Brown, Dee (Alexander), 154
Brown, Harry, 153, 301, 326
Brown, Lew, 256
Bruns, George, 68
Bryan, Alfred, 208
Bryan, C.D.B., 385
Bryant, William Cullen, 9, 143
Bryant's Minstrels, 97
Bryden, William, 244

Buchenwald, 286
Buckdancer's Choice, 254
Buckley, Tim, 376
Buckner, Noel, 267
Buck Privates Come Home, 242
Buck Privates/In the Navy, **242**
Buell, Don Carlos, 101
"Buena Vista," 66
Buffalo Bill's Indian Wars, 165
Buffalo Soldiers, 169, 172
Buford, John, 112
Bugles in the Afternoon, **153**
Bugs Nips the Nips, 280
Bunker Hill, or the Death of General Warren, **18–19**
Bunyan, John, 123
Burchard, Peter, 103
Burglar on the Roof, The, 190
Burgoyne, John, 14, 23, 32
Burk, John Daly, 18–19
Burke, Edwin, 117
Burnett, Carol, 385–386
Burnett, Murray, 247
"Burning the Letters," 274
Burns, Harry A., 350
Burns, Ken, 89–90, 136
Bury My Heart at Wounded Knee (Book), **154**
Bury My Heart at Wounded Knee (Drama), 154
Bush, George, 424, 431, 432, 433, 437
Butler, Robert Olen, 391
Butterfield, Roger, 70, 293
Butterworth, William, 252
Buttons, Red, 331
"Bye and Bye," 22
Byers, H. M., 135

Caan, James, 321, 387
Cable News Network (CNN), **433**
Cabot, Bruce, 6
Cady, Jerry, 268
Caesar, Adolph, 307
Cagney, James, 202–203, 221, 285
Cahn, Sammy, 273
Caine, Georgia, 270
Caine Mutiny, The, **242–243**
Caine Mutiny Court-Martial, The, 242–243
"Caissons Go Rolling Along, The," 230, **243–244**
Calhern, Louis, 350
California Gold Rush, 148

Calley, William, 363, 366–367
Call to Arms, 252
Cambodia, 360, 429
Campaigning with Crook, 164
Campaign Sketches, 109
Camp David Accords, 429
"Camptown Races," 138
"Candy-Bar Kid, The," 354
Caniff, Milton, **244–245**
Cantor, Eddie, 207, 250, 309, 329
Capa, Robert, **245–246**
Capra, Frank, 204–205, 236, 287, 326, 330, 355, 425
Captain America, **246**
Captain Blake, 164
Captain Midnight and His Secret Squadron, **247**
"Captain of the *Maine*," 188
Capture of Monterrey, 71
Caputo, Philip, 399, 407, 412
Carabatsos, Jim, 393
Carey, Harry, 229
Carey, MacDonald, 325
Carey, Timothy, 213
Caristi, Vincent, 419
Carlson, Richard, 352
Carn, John, 376
"Carolina in the Morning," 207
Carpenter, Francis Bicknell, 97–98
Carradine, David, 125
Carrying the Darkness, **369–370**
Carter, Henry, 79
Carter, Jimmy, 375, 429–430
Carter, John, 192
Carter, Lynda, 332
Caruso, Enrico, 213
Cary, Hetty, 119
Cary, Jeannie, 119
Casablanca, **247–248**, 273, 280
"Case of the Blind Pilot, The," 350
Casey, Antonio, 296
Casey, Michael, 369, 427
Cass, Lewis, 64
Casselli, Henry, Jr., **370–371**
Castillo de San Marcos, 5
Casualties of War, **371**
Catch-22, **248–249**, 323
Catholic Worker, 380
Caton-Jones, Michael, 283
Catton, Bruce, 87
Caudill, Harry, 126
Caught in the Draft, 242

"Cavalry Crossing a Ford," 146
CBI Roundup (China-Burma-India Roundup), 333
C Company, 366–367
Century Magazine, 127
Cervera, Pascual, 179
Chamberlain, Joshua, 104–105, 112–113
Chamberlain, Samuel Emery, 70–71
Champlain, Samuel de, 1, 2
Chandlee, Harry, 216
Chandler, Jeff, 152–153
Chandler, Len, 386
Channing, Carol, 253
Chapelle, Dickey, **371–372**
Chaplin, Charlie, 196, 216–217
Chaves, Richard, 419
Chennault, Claire, 266
Cherry Ames, Army Nurse, 249
Cherry Ames, Chief Nurse, 249
Cherry Ames, Flight Nurse, 249
Cherry Ames, Veterans' Nurse, 249
Cherry Ames Nurse Stories, **249–250**
Chesapeake, USS, 45, 46
"Chester," **19**
Chestnut, James, Jr., 119
Chestnut, Mary Boykin Miller, 119
Chetwynd, Lionel, 423
Cheyenne Autumn, **154–155**
Chiang Kai-shek, 255
Chicago Daily News, 276, 282
Chicago Democratic Convention (1968), 130, 306, 396, 401, 406
Chicago Evening Post, 186
Chicago World's Fair, 163
"Chickamauga," 86
Chicken Little, 326
"Chief Logan's Lament," **4–5**
Children of An Lac, The, **372–373**
China Beach, **373–374**
Chipman, N. P., 122
Christy, Howard Chandler, **181–182**
Christy Minstrels, 111, 113
Churchill, Winston (American Author), 94–95
Churchill, Winston (Prime Minister), 261, 322, 330, 408
Cimino, Michael, 377
"City of Anguish," 298
Civil Disobedience, **66–67**
Civil War, A Narrative History, The, 136
Civil War, The, **89–90**, 136
"Civilian," 399
Civil War Diary, 79

Clampett, Robert, 280, 305
Clansman, The, 86
Clark, Collenane, 296
Clark, Dane, 232
Clark, George Rogers, 15
Clark, William, 148
Clarkson, Patricia, 126
Clay, Cassius Marcellus, 361
Clay, Henry, 53
Clemens, Samuel Langhorne (Mark Twain), 127
Cliff, Montgomery, 263, 334
Clifford, Charles L., 187
Clifton, Elmer, 142
Clinton, Bill, 432
Close Combat, 252
Closing Time, 249
Clothier, William, 155
Cobb, Humphrey, 213
Cobb, Lee J., 331
Cobb, Ron, **374–375**
Cochise, 150, 152
"Code-O-Graphs," 247
Cody, William ("Buffalo Bill"), 165, 172
Cohan, George M., 212–213
Colbert, Claudette, 25, 302, 307
Cold Day in Hell, A, 168
Cold Mountain, 77, **90–91**
Cold War, 242, 243, 336, 348, 413, 427
Cole, Gary, 175
Coleman, Dabney, 239
Coleman, Horace, 369
Collier's, 245, 324
Collins, Ray, 273
Colonel Robert Potter at the Battle of Burnside's Bridge, Antietam, 132
"Colored Soldiers, The," 145
"Columbia, the Gem of the Ocean," 67–68
Combat, 160, 235, **250**
Comden, Betty, 288
"Come Up from the Fields, Father," 146
Coming Home (Film), 284, **375**, 377, 392
Coming Home (Novel), **376**
"Comin' in on a Wing and a Prayer," **250–251**
Commager, Henry Steele, 426
Command Decision, 200, **251–252**, 319
Command Performance, 272
"Command Presence," 398
Commission of Fine Arts, 424
Committee for Nuclear Disarmament, 408

Common Sense, **19–20**
"Concord Hymn," **20–21**, 33
Condon, Richard, 347
Coney, Robert J., 162
Confederate battle flag, **91–92**, 97
Confederates, **92**
"Conflict of Convictions, The," 122
Congressional Medal of Honor Society, 435
Connell, Evan S., 175
Connors, Chuck, 344
"Conquered Banner, The," **92–93**
Conrad, Joseph, 364
Conscription Act of 1863, 76, 106
Considine, Robert, 315
Constellation, USS, 46
Constitution, USS, 46, **49–50**
"Constitution and Guerriere," 50
Conte, Richard, 294
Continental Congress: First, 13; Second, 13, 17, 28, 31, 37, 38
Conway, Tim, 282
Cooke, John Esten, **93–94**
Cooke, Philip St. George, 93
Coolidge, Calvin, 431
Cooper, Chris, 126
Cooper, Gary, 100, 187, 202, 216, 222, 261
Cooper, James Fennimore, 3, 6, 11, 39, 377
Copperhead, The, **94**
Coppola, Eleanor, 365
Coppola, Francis Ford, 290, 364–365, 387
"Cops of the World," 406
Corbin, Margaret Cochran, 36
Cornell, Don, 273
Cornwallis, Charles, 14, 15, 29, 43
Corps, The, **252**
Cosmatos, George, 411
Costello, Lou, 242
Costner, Kevin, 11, 156–157
Cotton, Joseph, 302
Counterattack, 252
Counting Coup, 171
Country Joe McDonald and the Fish, 396–397
Country Music Association Awards, 407
Country of Strangers, A, 7
"Coup de Grace, The," 86
Courage Under Fire, **434**
Courier (Pittsburgh), 256–257
Couturie, Bill, 376

Cozzens, James Gould, 269
Crain, Jeanne, 264, 331
Crane, Bob, 270
Crane, Stephen, 112, 128, 191–192, 416
Crawford, Broderick, 187
Crawford, Robert M., 231, 331
Crawford, William, 22–23
Crazy Horse, 149, 150, 152, 155–156, 161, 167–168, 174, 175–176
Crazy Horse Monument, **155–156**
Creedence Clearwater Revival, 384
Crenna, Richard, 214
Crisis, The, **94–95**
Crisp, Donald, 214
Crockett, Davy, 62, 65, **68–69**
Cromwell, John, 302
Cromwell, Oliver, 43
Crook, George, 162
Crosby, Cathy Lee, 332
Crosby, Stills, Nash, and Young, 399
Cross and Sword, **5–6**
Cruise, Tom, 368
Cry Havoc, **253**
Cukor, George, 331
Cullum, John, 134
Currey, Francis, 389
Currier, Nathaniel, **69**
Curtis, Dan, 328
Curtiz, Michael, 268, 316
Custer, George Armstrong, 96, 149–159, 160–161, 162, 166, 167–168, 173, 175–177
Cycle of the West, 174
Cyclorama of the Battle of Gettysburg, **95–96**
cycloramas, 84–85, 95–96

Dachau, 343
Daffy's Southern Exposure, 329
Daffy the Commando, 280
Dafoe, Willem, 409
Dailey, Dan, 221
Daily Worker, The, 297
Daly, James A., 395–396
"Damn, Damn, Damn the Filipinos," 180
Damned to Glory, 266
Damon, Matt, 162
Dances with Wolves, 11, 150, **156–157**
Dane, Barbara, 400
Dane, Karl, 198
Danford, Robert, 244

Daniels, Jeff, 112–113
Daniels, William, 38
Dark Cloud, The, 219
Darnell, Shelby, 313
Darwell, Jane, 236
DaSilva, Howard, 38
Daugherty, Hershel, 7
Daughters of the American Revolution (DAR), 16
Daughters of the Confederacy, 97
Dave Dawson at Dunkirk, 327
Daves, Delmar, 152, 293, 309
Davidow, Ruth, 267
Davidson, Gordon, 420
Davies, Marion, 29
Davies, Peter, 399
Davis, Bette, 309
Davis, Brad, 243, 412
Davis, Britton, 162
Davis, George, 376
Davis, Gussie, 184
Davis, Henry C., 281
Davis, Isaac, 33
Davis, Jefferson, 63, 97, 125, 137
Davis, Peter, 394, 426
Davis, Richard Harding, 108, 169, 181, **182**
Davis, Theodore, 84, **96**, 107, 142
Davis, William C., 88
Davison, Bruce, 177, 311
Davy Crockett, Indian Fighter, 68
Davy Crockett, King of the Wild Frontier, 68
Davy Crockett at the Alamo, 68
Davy Crockett Goes to Congress, 68
Davy Crockett in Hearts United, 68
Dawn Patrol, The, **199–200**, 229
Day-Lewis, Daniel, 7
Day without End, 350
DC Comics, 289–290, 308
D-Day, 225, 245, 255, 269, 276, 279, 319, 389
Dead Presidents, 367
Dear America: Letters Home from Vietnam, **376–377**, 423
Dearest Enemy, **21–22**
"Dear Fatherland, Rest Quietly": A Report on the Collapse of Hitler's "Thousand Years," 241
"Dear John" (letters), **253–254**
Dear John (television show), 254
"Dear Mr. President," 413
"Death of Captain Waskow, The," 295

"Death of Colonel Crafford, The," **22–23**

Death of Jane McCrea, The, 33

Death of Tecumseh/Battle of the Thames, 69

"Death of the Ball Turret Gunner," 274

Declaration of Independence, 14, 28, 31, 37–38, 40

Decoration Day, 122

Deer Hunter, The, **377–378**, 392

Deerslayer, The, 6

"Defence of Fort M'Henry," 51

Defender (Chicago), 257

Defending the Stockade, 171

Defenseless America, 197

DeForest, John W., 123

DeGaulle, Charles, 248, 276

de Havilland, Olivia, 106, 176

de la Coste, Marie Ravenal, 136–137

Delaney, Dana, 373

de Laveleye, Victor, 322

Deliverance, 254

Del Rio, Dolores, 221

del Vecchio, John M., 417

Demarest, William, 270

DeMille, Cecil B., 142, 210

deMille, William C., 141–142

Deming, Dorothy, 249

Dempster, Carol, 16

De Niro, Robert, 377

Denker, Henry, 353

De Palma, Brian, 371

de Pury, Marianne, 425

Dere Bill: Mable's Love Letters to Her Rookie, 201

Dere Mable—Love Letters of a Rookie, **200–201**

Der Fuerher's Face, 326

Dern, Bruce, 375

de Rochemont, Louis, 259

Desert Shield, 432

Desert Storm, 272, 361, 422, 435, 438

Desert Storm: A Brief History, **434–435**

Desert Storm: The Victory, 433

Desert Victory, 319

DeVane, William, 263

Devil Dogs, 195

Devil's Backbone, 168

Devil's Disciple, The, **23–24**

de Weldon, Felix, 321

Dewey, A. Peter, 357

Dewey, George, 179, 190

Dewhurst, Coleen, 267

Diary from Dixie, A, 119

Dickey, James, **254–255**

Dickie Dare, 244

Dickinson, John, 32

Dien Cai Dau, **378**

DiFusco, John, 419

Dighton, John, 23

dime novels, 72, 85, 189

Dirty Distant War, A, 255

Dirty Dozen, The, 228, 250, **255–256**

Dirty Dozen: The Series: Danko's Dozen, 255

Dirty Dozen: Deadly Mission, The, 255

Dirty Dozen: Final Mission, The, 255

Dirty Dozen: The Next Mission, The, 255

"Dirty Gertie from Bizerte," 218

Disappointment, or the Force of Credulity, The, 43

"Disaster of the Good Ship *Maine*," 188

Disney Studios (Walt), 7, 30, 68, 102, 299, 305, 324, 326–327, 329, 417

Dispatches, **378–379**, 402

Distant Trumpet, A, **157–158**, 162

Divide and Conquer, 330

Dix, Richard, 132

"Dixie," 89, **97**

Dixon, Thomas, 86

Doddridge, Joseph, 5

Doherty, Edward, 260

domino theory, 358, 379, 395

Donald's Decision, 326

Doenitz, Karl, 226

Donlevy, Brian, 251, 325

D'Onofrio, Vincent Phillip, 387

Donohue, Troy, 158

Donovan, Robert J., 294

Don't Cry, It's Only Thunder, 373

"Don't Sit under the Apple Tree with Anyone Else But Me," 230, **256**

Donvan, John, 433

Doolittle, Amos, **24**

Doolittle, Jimmy, 294, 315–316

Doolittle Raid, 225, 294–295, 315–316, 338

Doonesbury, **379–380**

Dore, Mary, 267

Doubleday, Abner, 95

"Double V," **256–257**

Doud, Gil, 317

doughboys, 195, 201, 203, 211, 217, 219

Dougherty, Fraser, 363

Douglas, Kirk, 24, 213, 301

Douglass, Frederick, 104

Dowd, Nancy, 375
Downes, Leslie Ann, 125
"Down on the Corner," 384
Doyen, Charles, 281
draft card burning, 359, **380–381**, 406
"Draft Dodger Rag," 406
"Draft Resister," **381**
Drake, Francis, 319
Drake, Robert L., 199
Driftwood, Jimmy, 47–48
"Drinking from a Helmet," 255
"Driver, The," 255
Driver, William, 125–126
"Drop of Brandy, O!, A," 50
Dr. Strangelove, 283
Dru, Joanne, 173
Drums, **24–25**
Drums Along the Mohawk, 8, **25–26**, 155
Drum-Taps, 121, 146
Duffy, Todd, 79
Duggan, Andrew, 232
Dullea, Keir, 315
Dulles, John Foster, 338
Dull Knife, 154, 174
Dunbar, Paul Laurence, 144–145
Duncan, David Douglas, **341–342**
Duncan, Patrick Sheane, 382, 423, 434
Dunlap, William, 27
Dunmore, Lord Thomas, 4–5
Dunn, Harvey, **201**
Dunne, Finley Peter, 186–187
Durant, Will, 262
Duryea, Dan, 300
Duvall, Robert, 162, 349, 364
Dwan, Alan, 301, 344, 436
Dying Marine, 372
Dying Thunder, 168
Dylan, Bob, 150, 376, 427–428
Dymtryk, Edward, 242–243, 334
Dzunda, George, 415

Earp, Wyatt, 155
Eastwood, Clint, 157, 431, 436
EC Comics, 354
Eckert, Allan W., 60
Eddy, Nelson, 233
Edelman, Bernard, 376
Edeson, Arthur, 248
Edison, Thomas Alva, 183, 190
Edison Company, 183
Edmonds, Walter, 8, 25
Education for Death, 326
Edwards, Sherman, 37

Egan, Richard, 342, 345
Egner, Philip, 243
Ehrhart, W. D., 369–370, 427
"Eighth Air Force," 274
"Eighth of January, The," 48
84 Charlie Mopic, **382**, 423, 434
Eisenhower, Dwight David ("Ike"), 225,
    266, 279, 311, 319, 338, 358, 389
"Elegy for the Dead," 297
Ellerbrock, Charles, 119
Elliott, Sam, 112
Ellison, Richard, 421
El Salvador, 430
Emancipation Proclamation, 75, 83, 98,
    131
Emerson, Eric, 419
Emerson, Luther Orlando, 143
Emerson, Ralph Waldo, 21, 33, 66
Emery, Lee, 386
Emmett, Daniel D., 97
Emmy Award, 81, 125, 258, 286, 311,
    323, 328, 349, 365, 377, 385–386,
    399, 421
"Enclosure, The," 255
Enemy Below, The, 335
Enrico, Robert, 86
"Entry," 297
"Epitaph," 297
Epstein, Julius, 247
Epstein, Philip, 247
Ericson, John, 310
"Erie and Champlain," 49
Essanay Company, 165
Estabrook, Howard, 273
Eutaw, 39
Evans, Diane Carlson, 424
Evans, Gene, 342, 353
Evans, Linda, 125
Evans, Redd, 298
Eve, Maria Louisa, 99
Eve of St. Mark, The, 302
Everett, Edward, 103
Everybody Comes to Rick's, 247
Ewell, Tom, 282
Except for Me and Thee, 100
*Eyes of the Woods: A Story of the An-
    cient Wilderness, The*, 58

"Facing It," 378
Fairbanks, Douglas, Jr., 200
Falling Hare, 280
"Falling Soldier," 245
Fancy Free, 288

Fantastic Four, 246
Farago, Ladislas, 290
Farewell to Arms, A, **202**, 284, 397
Farewell to Manzanar, **257–258**
Farnum, William, 116
Farragut, David Glasgow, 130
Farrell, Charles, 50, 88
Faulkner, Roy, 137
Faulkner, William, 25, 135, 196
Fawcett, Farrah, 241
Fawcett Comics, 308
"Federal Offense, A," 398
Ferrar, José, 81, 243, 310
Fibber McGee and Molly, **258–259**
Fiction House, 331
Field, Connie, 298
Field, William A., 107
Fields, Barbara, 90
Fields, Herbert, 21
Fields, James T., 33
Fields, W. C., 29
Fields of Fire, **382–383**
Fighting Lady, The, **259–260**
Fighting 69th, The, **202–203**
Fighting Sullivans, The, **260**
Fighting with Our Boys in Cuba, **182–183**
Finkel, Abem, 216
"Firebombing, The," 254
First Blood, 411
1st Casualty Press, 427
First Reading of the Emancipation Proclamation of President Lincoln, The, **97–98**
"First Songs for a Prelude," 147
Fitch, Clyde, 101
Fitzgerald, F. Scott, 219
Five Women I Loved: Bob Hope's Vietnam Story, 272
Fixed Bayonets, 240, **342**
Flagg, James Montgomery, 53, 194, **203–204**
Flanders, Ed, 420
Fleming, Victor, 188
Flight, **204–205**
Flight Commander, 200
"Flight Commander, The," 199
Flowers, A. R., 376
Flying Leathernecks, 228
Flying Tigers (American Volunteer Group), 266
Flynn, Errol, 153, 176, 200, 379
Flynn, Joe, 282

Flynn, Sean, 379
Foch, Ferdinand, 215
Fogarty, John, 384
Follow the Boys, 273
Fonda, Henry, 25, 158, 236, 285, 342
Fonda, Jane, 375, 379, **383**, 386
Fontaine, Lamar, 79
Foote, Shelby, 90, 135–136
Forbes, Edward, **98–99**
Forbes, Esther, 29–30
Ford, Daniel, 392
Ford, Gerald, 318, 360, 429
Ford, Glenn, 236
Ford, John, 25, 110, 155, 158, 170, 172, 173, 221, 236, 313, 325, 438
Ford, Lena Guilbert, 209–210
Ford, Paul Leicester, 28–29
Foreign Correspondent, 279
Foreman, Carl, 276, 284
Forever in Love, 293
"Forgotten Heroes of Korea," 340, 350
Forgy, Howell, 293
Forrest, Edwin, 9
Forrest, Frederic, 241
Forrest, Nathaniel Bedford, 136
Forrest Gump, **384**, 398
Fort Apache, 155, **158–159**, 170, 173
forts: Caroline, 1; Duquense, 3; McHenry, 46, 51; Sumter, 74, 88, 108, 115, 119, 120, 125; Ticonderoga, 14; William Henry, 3, 6
For the Boys, 321
"Fortunate Son," **384–385**
Fortunate Son: The Autobiography of Lewis B. Fuller, Jr., 384–385
45th Division News, 281
For Whom the Bell Tolls, **261**
Foster, Stephen, 138, 143
4-F, 246
Four Freedoms, 261–262
Four Freedoms (Paintings), **261–262**
Four Freedoms, The (Symphony), 262
"Four Freedom Shows," 262
Four Jills in a Jeep, 275
Fourteen Points, 196
Fox, Gilbert, 48
Fox, John, Jr., 108, 116
Fox, Michael J., 371
foxhole circuit, 272
Fragile Fox, The, 232
Francis, Robert, 243
Franco, Francisco, 223, 267, 297
Frank, Pat, 344

Frankel, Ernest, 339
Frankenheimer, John, 80, 348
Frank Leslie's Illustrated Newspaper, 98, **99–100**, 124, 181, 203
Franklin, Benjamin, 19, 28, 32, 38
Frazier, Charles, 77, 90–91
"Free Americay," **26**
"Freedom from Fear," 262
"Freedom from Want," 262
"Freedom of Speech," 262
"Freedom of Worship," 262
Freedom Schools, 415
Freeman, Mona, 344
Freeman, Morgan, 104
Freleng, Isidor "Fritz," 280, 305
French, Daniel Chester, 33, 185, 328
Freneau, Philip, **26–27**
Friedberg, William, 22
Friedmann, Andre, 245
Friend, Cliff, 329
Friendly Fire, **385–386**
Friendly Persuasion, **100**
Frietchie, Barbara, **100–101**
Froeschel, George, 251
Frohman, Charles, 108, 162
From Here to Eternity, **262–263**, 314, 417
"From the Halls of Montezuma," 280
From Where the Sun Now Stands, **159–160**
Frontline Combat, 354
F.T.A., 383, **386**
F Troop, 160
Fuller, Charles, 306–307
Fuller, Samuel, 239–240, 342, 352–353
Full Metal Jacket, 379, **386–387**
Furey, Joan A., 421
Furie, Sidney J., 369, 410
Furies, The, 30
Fussell, Paul, 297
Fyles, Franklin, 162

Gable, Clark, 106, 251
Gage, Thomas, 13
Gallivan, Rick, 419
Gamson, William, 415
Gandhi, Mahatma, 67
Garcia, Calixto Iniquez, 185
Gardens of Stone, **387–388**
Gardner, Alexander, 121
Garfield, John, 229, 293, 309
Garnett, Tay, 234
Garrison's Gorillas, 250

"Garry Owen," **160–161**
Garson, Barbara, 401
Gas Attack, 200
Gates, Horatio, 14
Gatewood, Charles B., 157, 162
Gayford, Frank, 346
Gaynor, Mitzi, 312
Geary, James, 292
Geisel, Theodore ("Dr. Suess"), 305
Geld, Garry, 134
Geller, Stephen, 304
General, The, **101–102**
General Andrew Jackson/The Hero of New Orleans, 69
"General Forsyth's Fight on the Republican River, The Sioux Campaign of 1868–1869," 169
General Washington Resigning His Commission as Commander-in-Chief of the Army, 40
Genevieve de Brabant, 280
George, Chief Dan, 166
George III (King), 12, 24, 26–27, 34
"George the Third's Soliloquy," 27
George Washington Battalion, 223
Georgia Sea Islands, 113
Gerard, James W., 211–212
Geronimo, 150, 161–162, 169
Geronimo (movie), 161
Geronimo: An American Legend, **161–162**
Geronimo's Story of His Life, 161
Gershwin, Emil, 308
"Get Out and Dig, Dig, Dig," 323
Gettysburg, 82, 112–113, 115
Gettysburg: The Paintings of Mort Künstler, 115
"Gettysburg Address," **102–103**
Geyser, John, 88
Ghost Dance, 150, 151, 165
Gibbons, Floyd, **205**
Gibbons, James Sloan, 143
GI Bill, **263–264**
G.I. Joe action figure, **388–389**
G.I. Joe (book), 265
"G.I. Joe"/"Private Breger" (cartoons), **264–265**
GI Journal, 272
Gilbert, John, 198
Gillars, Mildred, 232–233
Gillette, William, 132, 181
Gilmore, Patrick Sarsfield, 145
"Gimme Shelter," 376
Gingrich, Newt, 384

Girl I Left Behind Me, The, **162–163**
Gish, Dorothy, 206
Gish, Lillian, 87, 151, 206
"Give Peace a Chance," **389**
Glackens, William, **183–184**
Glenn Miller Orchestra, 231, 256
"Glorious Seventy-Four, The," 32
Glory, 82, **103–104**, 434
Glory Brigade, The, **342–343**
Glory for Me, 238
Glory of Columbia, The, **27–28**
Glory of His Country, The, 94
Gnadenhutten, 41
"God Bless America," **265–266**, 305
"God Bless the U.S.A.," 431, **435**
Goddard, Paulette, 307
God Is My Co-Pilot, **266**
Gods and Generals, **104–105**, 113
Going after Cacciato, **389–390**, 402, 416
"Going Home," 306
Golden, Michael, 405
Golden Spur Awards (Western Writers of
    America), 153, 169
Goldstone, James, 399
Goldwyn, Samuel, 238
Gone with the Wind, 88, **105–106**
Goodacre, Glenna, 424
"Goodbye Mama, I'm Off to Yoko-
    hama," 224
Good Fight, The, **267**
Good Morning Vietnam, **390–391**
Good Scent from a Strange Mountain, A,
    391
Gordon, Bernard, 315
Gordon, Keith, 285
Go Tell the Spartans, **391–392**
Go to the Widow-Maker, 262
Gould, Elliott, 349
Goulding, Edmund, 200
Grable, Betty, 291
"Grafted into the Army," 76, **106–107**
Grand Army of the Republic (GAR), 122,
    130
Granger, Farley, 294
Grant, Rodney, 175
Grant, Ulysses S., 33, 49, 63, 75–77, 98,
    117, 122, 129, 136
Grateful Dead, The, 421
Graves, Peter, 310, 344
Graves, Ralph, 204
Gravity's Rainbow, **267–268**, 402
Great Depression, 223
Great Escape, The, 270

Great Locomotive Chase, The (1863),
    102
Great Locomotive Chase, The (1956),
    102
Greeley, Horace, 69, 134
Green, Adolph, 288
Green, Gerald, 399
Green, Paul, 5–6, 41, 60
Green Berets, 314, 365–366, 392, 406
Green Berets, The, 314, 366, 377, **392–**
    393, 412
Greene, Bette, 311–312
Greene, David, 385
Greene, Nathaniel, 14
Greene, Shecky, 250
Green Mountain Boys, 14
Greenwood, Lee, 431, 435
Grenada, 430, 432, 436
Grier, David Alan, 415
Grierson, Benjamin, 110
Griffin, W.E.B., 252–253
Griffith, D(avid) W(erk), 16, 86–87, 125,
    142, 151, 205–206, 217, 330
Grogan, Emmett, 408
Groom, Winston, 384
Gross, Larry, 161
Gruber, Edmund L., 244
Guadalcanal Diary, **268–269**
Guard of Honor, **269**
Guerriere, HMS, 46, 50
Guffey, Burnett, 263
Gulf of Tonkin Resolution, 358, 401
gunboat diplomacy, 431
Guthrie, Arlo, 362
Guthrie, Woody, 303, 304, 362
Guys and Dolls, 292
Gwynn, Edmund, 264

Hackman, Gene, 162
Haeberle, Ronald, 363
Haggard, Merle, 406
Hahne, Albert, 95
"Hail Columbia," **48–49**
Hail the Conquering Hero, **269–270**
Haines, William Wister, 251
Hale, Alan, 202, 228, 266
Hall, James, 206
Hall, Tom T., 395
Hamblen, Stuart, 184
Hamburger Hill, **393–394**
Hamilton, Guy, 24
Hamilton, Henry, 15
Hamilton, Neil, 16, 199

Hammer and Rapier, 94
Hammerstein, Jane-Howard, 311
Hammerstein, Oscar II, 312
Hammond, John, 88
Hanalis, Blanche, 372
Hancock, John, 18, 28, 29, 35
Hancock, Walker, 137
Hancock, Winfield Scott, 95, 96, 105
Hanks, Tom, 384
"Hanoi Hilton," 360
Hanser, Richard, 323
Harding, Warren G., 126, 431
"Hard Rain's Gonna Fall, A," 376
Hargrove, Marion, Jr., 301–302
Harlow, Jean, 207
Harmar, Josiah, 55, 59
Harmon, Mark, 376
Harper, Fletcher, 107
Harper's New Monthly Magazine, 121
Harper's Weekly, 53, 79, 84, 88, 96, 98, 99, **107–108**, 109, 116, 124, 134, 142, 169, 182
Harris, Charles, 181
Harris, Joel Chandler, 79
Harrison, William Henry, 47, 56, 60, 64
Harrodsborough, 55
Harron, Robert, 86, 206
Hart, Frederick, 417–418
Hart, Harry, 344
Hart, Lorenz, 21
Hart, Mickey, 421
Hart, Moss, 231, 330–331
Harvey, Lawrence, 348
Hasford, Gustav, 386
Hathaway, Henry, 187
Hawke, Ethan, 285
Hawks, Howard, 199, 216, 229, 301
Hawn, Goldie, 299
Hawthorne, Alice, 144
Hawthorne, Nathaniel, 66
Hay, John, 110, 179
Haycox, Ernest, 153
Hayden, Joe, 191
Hayden, Tom, 408
Hayes, Clair Wallace, 199
Hayes, Helen, 202
Hays, Mary Ludwig, 36
Hays, William, 36
Hayworth, Rita, 291
Hearst, William Randolph, 29, 86, 169, 178–179, 182, 192–193
Heartbreak Ridge, 393, 431, **436**
Heart of Darkness, 364

Heart of Maryland, The, **108–109**
Hearts and Minds, **394–395**, 426
Hearts of Darkness: A Filmmaker's Apocalypse, 365
"Hearts of Oak," 32
Hearts of the World, **205–206**
Hecht, Ben, 287
Hedricks, Jon, 363
Heffron, Richard, 163, 412
Heflin, Van, 235
Heggen, Thomas, 285
Heinemann, Larry, 407
Heisler, Stuart, 287
"He Kept Us Out of War," 194
"Helicopter War in South Vietnam," 372
Hell in the Pacific, 228
Heller, Joseph, 248–249, 328
Hellgenberger, Marg, 373
"Hello Vietnam," **395**, 406
Hell's Angels, **206–207**
Hemingway, Ernest, 112, 196, 202, 261, 397
Henreid, Paul, 247
Henry, Buck, 249
Henry V, 339
Henry, Patrick, 13, 29
Henry, Will (Henry William Allen), 159, 167–168
Henson, Robby, 126
"Here in My Arms," 22
Here Is Germany, 330
Here Is Your War, 295
Here We Go Again, 324
Heroes of Chancellorsville, The, 115
"Hero's Death, A," 184
Hero's Welcome, A, **395–396**
Herr, Michael, 378–379, 386, 402
Herr Meets Hare, 280
Hersey, John, 238
"He's Coming to Us Dead," **184**
"He's Got His Discharge from the Army," 107
"He Sleeps upon Havana's Shore in a Suit of Navy Blue," 188
Hess, Dean, 339–340
Hess, Erwin, 247
Heston, Charlton, 236, 421
Hewitt, John Hill, 79, 136, 144
Heyward, Leland, 238, 312
Hibbs, Jesse, 317
Hickok, "Wild" Bill, 166
Higgins, Marguerite, **343–344**
Hiker, The, **184–185**

Hill, George Roy, 304
Hill, Walter, 161
Hilt to Hilt, or Days and Nights on the Banks of the Shenandoah in the Autumn of 1864, 94
Hirohito, 226
Hiroshima, 226
History of the Conspiracy of Pontiac, 10
Hitchcock, Alfred, 278–279
Hitler, Adolph, 223, 226, 267, 308, 330, 425
Hitler Lives, 330
Hit Parade, 48, 231, 251, 256, 298
Ho Chi Minh, 255, 357, 391
Hodiak, John, 238
Hoff, Syd, 218
Hoffman, Abbie, 408
Hoffman, Dustin, 166
Hoffman, Shir, 292
Hogan's Heroes, **270–271**, 310
Hoge, Jane C., 130
Holbrook, Hal, 125, 236
Hold Back the Night, **344**
Holden, William, 110, 264, 310, 340
"Hold the Fort," 134
Holliday, Doc, 155
Holliday, Judy, 331
Holliman, John, 433
Hollywood Canteen, 230, 308–309
Hollywood Canteen (movie), 309
"Hollywood Canteen" (song), 309
Hollywood Ten, 243
Holmes, Oliver Wendell, 50
Holocaust, 92, 328
Holt, Jack, 117, 204, 210
Home, Sweet Home, 109
Home Before Morning: The True Story of an Army Nurse in Vietnam, 420
Home Defense Cartoons, 326
Home of the Brave, **271–272**
Homer, Winslow, **109–110**
Homes, Geoffrey, 153
Homestead Act, 149
Hooker, Joseph, 141
Hooker, Richard, 348–349
Hoosier Mosaics, 16
Hoover, Herbert, 52
Hoover, J. Edgar, 257, 318
Hope, Bob (Leslie Townes), 242, **272**, 377, 379, 386
Hopkinson, Francis, 32, 48
Hopkinson, Joseph, 48
Hopper, Frank, 189
Horgan, Paul, 157, 162

Hornberger, Richard, 348
Hornet, USS, 225, 315
Horse Soldiers, The, **110**
Horton, Johnny, 48
Hospitalized Veterans, 435
Hot Chocolate Band, 389
Houston, Cisco, 303
Houston, James D., 258
Houston, Jeanne Wakatsuki, 257–258
Houston, Sam, 62, 65
Howard, Bronson Crocker, 133
Howard, Ken, 38
Howard, Leslie, 106
Howard, O. O., 163
Howard, Sidney, 213
Howe, Julia Ward, 83–84
Howe, William, 13, 21, 42
Howells, William Dean, 108, 123, 133, 144
"How to Tell a True War Story," 416
"How Ya Gonna Keep 'Em Down on the Farm?," **207–208**
Hubbard, Elbert, 185
Hudson, Rock, 202, 340
Hughes, Howard, 206–207
Hull, Cordell, 224
Human Comedy, The, **273**
Humphreys, Josuha, 50
Hunt, Irene, 78–79
Hunt, Peter, 38
Hunt, Peter H., 127
Hunter, Ian McLellan, 88
Hunter, Jeffrey, 102, 172
Hunter, Kermit, 60–61
Hunter, Tab, 235
Hunters, The, **344–345**
"Hunters of Kentucky, The," **49**
Husky, Ferlin, 254
Hussein, Saddam, 432–433
Huston, Anjelica, 388
Huston, John, 128, 202, 236, 277–278, 317
Huston, Walter, 330
Hutchins, Evelyn, 267
Hutchinson, Asa, 138
Hutchinson Family Singers, 81, 138
Hutton, Marion, 256
"Hymn, Sung to the Completion of the Concord Monument," 21
"Hymn to the Alamo," 65

"I Ain't Marchin' Any More," 406
"I'd Be Proud to Be the Mother of a Soldier," 208

"I Declare the War Is Over," 406
"I Didn't Raise My Boy to Be a Coward," 208
"I Didn't Raise My Boy to Be a Soldier," 194, **208**
"I Didn't Raise My Son to Be a Soldier," 208
"I Feel Like I'm Fixin' to Die Rag," **396–397**
If I Die in a Combat Zone, **397**
"If You Love Your Uncle Sam, Bring 'Em Home," 413
"I Have a Rendezvous with Death," 215
"I Left My Heart at the Stage Door Canteen," 309, 316
"I'll Take Good Care of Mommy While You're Gone," 313
Illustrated London News, 140
"I'll Walk Alone," **273–274**
Images of the Civil War, 115
"I'm a Yankee Doodle Dandy," 212
Immortal Alamo, The, 65
Immortal Sergeant, 342
Inchon, 347
Incident at Muc Wa, 392
In Country, **397–398**
"in country," 402, 405, 412, 424
Incredible Hulk, 246
Independence Day, **28**
Independence Hall, 31
Indian Country, 407
Indians Attacking, 171
Indians on a Bluff Surveying General Miles' Troops, 171
Indian Tribes: Apache, 150, 152, 157, 158, 161–162, 172, 177; Arapahoe, 148, 149; Blackfeet, 170; Cherokee, 56, 60–61, 129; Cheyenne, 148, 149, 154–155, 175; Commanche, 148, 156; Creek, 46; Delaware, 22, 55, 59; Digger, 205; Fox, 56; Huron, 2, 6; Iroquois Confederation, 1, 26; Lakota (Sioux), 156; Mandan, 148; Miami, 59; Mingo, 4–5, 55; Mohican, 6–7; Narragansett, 2, 11; Nez Perce, 149, 159, 163; Nipmuck, 11; Oglala (Sioux), 151–152, 155, 174; Ottawa, 3, 10, 12; Pequeot, 1, 85; Powhatan, 1; Sauk (Sac), 56–57, 58; Seminole, 57, 148; Shawnee, 4, 55, 56, 59, 60; Sioux, 148, 149, 150, 151, 153, 155, 161, 163, 164, 165, 166–167, 167, 168, 169, 175, 176; Tuscarawa, 7; Wampanoag, 2, 8; Wyandot, 22, 32, 55
Indian Wars Refought, The, 165

I Never Left Home, 272
Ingraham, Joseph Holt, 72
In Pharaoh's Army, **398–399**
Interlandi, Phil, 333
In the Hands of the Seneca, 8
In the Navy, 242
In Time of Peace, 219
Intrepid, USS, 259
I Protest: Khe Sanh, Vietnam, 341
Iran Hostage Crisis, 430, 439
"Irish Jaunting Car, The," 89
Iron Triangle, The, 403
Irving, Washington, 39
"I Spoke to Jefferson on Guadalcanal," 313
"It's for God and Country and You, Mom," 406
It's Hot in Here, 324
Ives, Burl, 233
Ives, James Merritt, 69
"I Want You," 53, 194, 203
I Will Fight No More Forever, **163–164**
"I Wish I Was in Dixie's Land," 97
"I Won't Sit Under the Apple Tree with Anyone Else But You," 256

Jackknife, 398
Jackson, Andrew, 46, 47, 49, 56, 58, 61, 64
Jackson, Thomas "Stonewall," 63, 74, 75, 76, 92, 93, 100, 105, 115, 137, 138
Jaco, Charles, 433
Jagger, Dean, 319
Jakes, John, 30–31, 124
James, Henry, 108
Janice Meredith, **28–29**
Janssen, David, 317, 392
Jarman, Claude, Jr., 170
Jarre, Kevin, 103
Jarrell, Randall, **274**
Jarvis, John Wesley, 59
Jason, Rick, 250
Jeep, **274–275**
Jefferson, Martha, 38
Jefferson, Thomas, 5, 20, 28, 38, 45, 148
Jenkins, Jack, 273
Jennings, N. A., 188
Jenz, Tom, 292
Jerome, Jerry, 205
Jewison, Norman, 306, 398
"Jim Crow," 257
John Brown's Body, **110–111**
"John Brown's Body Lies a-Mouldering in the Grave," 83

John Brown's Raid, 88
"John Bull," 53
Johnny Got His Gun, **209**, 368
Johnny Tremain, **29–30**
Johnny Tremain and the Sons of Liberty,
  30
Johnson, Don, 263
Johnson, "Lady MacBird," 401
Johnson, Lyndon Baines, 358, 359, 376,
  380, 384, 395, 396, 401, 413, 415, 425
Johnson, Robert Underwood, 127
Johnson, Van, 243, 251, 273, 316, 351
Johnston, Albert Sidney, 75, 136
Johnston, Terry C., 168–169
Jolson, Al, 207
Jones, Chuck, 280, 305
Jones, James, 227, 262–263, 279, 314–
  315, 417
Jones, James Earl, 388
Jones, Jennifer, 202, 302
Jones, John Paul, 25
Jones, Robert C., 375
Jordan, Jim, 258
Jordan, Louis, 296
Jordan, Marian, 258
Jordan, Richard, 112
Joseph (Chief), 150, 159, 163–164
Juergens, Kurt, 335
Julio, Everett B. D., 115
Juneau, USS, 260
"Just Before the Battle, Mother," **111–**
  112
Justice League of America, 308

Kaiser Wilhelm II, 194, 210, 217
Kaltenborn, H. V., 286
Kanigher, Frank, 289
Kanin, Fay, 386
Kanin, Garson, 318
Kantor, MacKinley, 42, 80, 238
Karnow, Stanley, 421
Kasper, David, 437
Kay, John (Joachim Krauledat), 381
Keach, Stacy, 88, 401
Keane, Bil, 333
Keaton, Buster, 102
"Keep the Home Fires Burning," 195,
  209–210
Keighley, William, 202
Keith, Harold, 129
Keller, Daniel, 397
Kellerman, Sally, 349
Kellogg, Frank, 196

Kellogg-Briand Peace Pact, 196
Kelly, Fanny, 166–167
Kelly, Gene, 289
Kelly, Grace, 341
Kenas, Joseph, 355–356
Kendall, George Wilkins, **69–70**, 71
Keneally, Thomas, 92
Kennard, Allen, 253
Kennedy, Arthur, 155, 229
Kennedy, Edward, 393
Kennedy, John F., 294, 358, 359, 420
Kennedy, Robert, 406
Kent Family Chronicles, The, **30–31**
Kent State, 399
Kent State: What Happened and Why,
  399
Kent State Massacre, 360, **399–400**
"Kent State Massacre, The," 399
Kentucky Headhunters, 68
Keogh, Miles, 161
Kerr, Deborah, 263
Key, Francis Scott, 47, 51–52, 266
Khmer Rouge, 429
Kibbee, Roland, 23
Kiley, Richard, 100
"Killed at Resca," 86
Killer Angels, The, 90, 92, 104, **112–113**,
  115
"Kill the Bastards," 231
Kilmer, Joyce, 202
Kilpatrick, Jack Frederick, 60
Kilroy, Frank J., Jr., 275
Kilroy, James J., 275
"Kilroy Was Here," **275–276**
King, Charles (Author), 150, **164–165**,
  165
King, Charles (Singer), 212
King, Henry, 319
"Kingdom Coming," **113–114**
Kingston Trio, 413
Kirby, Jack, 246
Kirke, Lewis, 2
Kirkpatrick, Helen, **276**
Kirstein, Lincoln, 103, 296–297
Kissinger, Henry, 360
Kitchener, Horatio Herbert, 203
Kittredge, Walter, 138–139
Klemperer, Werner, 270
Kline, Wally, 176
Knight, Shirley, 100
Knox, Frank, 276
Knox, Terence, 418
Koch, Howard, 216

Komanyakaa, Yusef, 370, 378
Korda, Zoltan, 300
Korean War Veterans' Memorial, **346**
Korty, John, 258
Kotcheff, Ted, 403
Kovic, Ron, 368
Kramer, Richard, 399
Kramer, Stanley, 271, 284
K-rations, 284
Krause, Allison, 299
Kreutzmann, Bill, 421
Krueger, Kurt, 300
Kubert, Joe, 289
Kubrick, Stanley, 213, 232, 386–387
Ku Klux Klan, 87, 91, 137
Künstler, Mort, 105, **114–115**
Kurtzman, Harvey, 254
Kuwait, 432, 434, 439
Kyser, Kay, 256, 293

Ladd, Alan, 397
Ladd, Cheryl, 410
"Lafayette, We Are Here," 195
Lahti, Christine, 299
Laidlaw, William, 251
Lake, Veronica, 291, 307
Lamar, Hedy, 291
Lambert, Louis, 145
Lancaster, Burt, 23, 177, 263, 392
Landis, Frederick, 94
"Landlady of France," 50
Lansbury, Angela, 348
Lansing, Elizabeth, 249
Lantz, Paul, 8
Lasky, Jesse, 221
Last Indian Battles, The, **165–166**
Last Meeting of Lee and Jackson, The,
     115–116
"Last Night I Had the Strangest Dream,"
     346–347
Last of the Fetterman Command, The,
     171
Last of the Mohicans, The, **6–7**, 11
"Last Shot," 399
Laughton, Charles, 111
Laurents, Arthur, 271
Lawless, The, 30
Lawrence, Gertrude, 308
Lawrence, James, 46
Lawson, John Howard, 228, 300
Lawson, Ted, 315–316
Lay, Beirne, 319
Lay This Laurel, 103

Lea, Tom, **276–277**
League of Nations, 196
"Leatherstocking Tales," 6
Leaves of Grass, 146–147
Lebanon, 430
Le Duc Tho, 360
Lee, Lila, 204
Lee, Robert E., 63, 75, 76, 77, 91, 93,
     104–105, 109, 112–113, 115, 116, 120,
     131, 137, 140, 141
Lee, Robert N., 189
Lee, Stan, 246
Leigh, Vivien, 106
Lejaren, Arthur, 11
Lembeck, Harvey, 310
Lemmon, Jack, 285
Lennon, John, 389
Leopard, HMS, 45
Leopard's Spots, The, 86
Leroy, Mervyn, 316
Leslie, Frank, 99
Leslie's Weekly, 203
Les Miserables, 404
"Lesson, The," 398
"Letter from Vietnam," 365
Letters and Diary of Alan Seeger, 215
Let There Be Light, **277–278**
Lettich, Sheldon, 419
Leutze, Emanuel, 42–43
Levine, Don, 388
Levine, Irwin Jesse, 438
Levinson, Barry, 390
Levitt, Saul, 81, 420
Lewin, Frank, 59
Lewis, Jerry, 300
Lewis, Sam M., 207
Lexington, USS, 225, 275
Liberty Bell, **31**
Liberty Bonds, 329
Liberty Magazine, 205, 231
Liberty Ships, 228
"Liberty Song, The," 32
Liberty Songs, **31–32**
Libya, 433
Lichty, Lawrence, 421
Life, 70, 241, 245, 277, 293, 341, 380
Life and Times of Rosie the Riveter, The,
     298
Lifeboat, **278–279**
Life in Camp, 109
Life of Black Hawk, 58
Life Studies of the Great Army, 99
Light in the Forest, The, **7–8**

Lighton, Louis, 222
Lin, Maya, 418, 422
Lincoln, Abraham, 33, 53, 56, 58, 63, 74, 75, 77, 81, 83, 88, 94, 95, 97–98, 102–103, 108, 109, 111, 117, 118, 119–120, 121, 124, 125, 131, 143, 146, 164
Lincoln Battalion: The Story of the Americans Who Fought in Spain in the International Brigade, The, 297
Lind, Michael, 65
Line of Fire, 252
Linthicum, Charles, 52
Linville, Larry, 349
Little American, The, **210–211**
Little Big Man, **166**
Little Red Riding Rabbit, 280
Little Shepherd of Kingdom Come, The, **116**
Littlest Rebel, The, **116–117**, 186
Little Turtle, Chief, 55
Little Wolf, 154
Livermore, Mary, 130
"Lives of the Dead, The," 416
Loeb, John Jacob, 298
Loesser, Frank, 233–234, 292
Logan, Chief (Tachnechdorus), 4–5
Logan, John A., 122, 130
Logan, Josuha, 285, 312
Logan, Louise, 250
Logan, Mrs. John A., 122
Logan, The Last of the Race of Shikillemus, Chief of the Cayuga Nation, 5
Lone Ranger, The, 72
Lone Sailor, 437
Lone Star, 5
Longest Day, The, **279–280**, 335
Longfellow, Henry Wadsworth, 35
Longstreet, James, 112–113
Loo, Richard, 295
Looney Tunes, **280**, 329
"Lorena," **117–118**
Loring, Hope, 222
"Losses," 274
Lost Colony, The, 5
Lottman, George D., 230
Louis, Joe, 361
Louisbourg, 2
Louis XIV, 2
Louis Nelson Associates, 346
Love and Duty, **400**
Love and War, 124
Lovejoy, Frank, 252
Lovejoy, Owen, 98
Love Laughs at Locksmiths, 49

Lovell, Royal, 230
Lowe, Edmund, 221
Lowell, James Russell, 107
Lowell, Robert, **400–401**
Ludlow, Noah, 49
Lukeman, Augustus, 137
Lupton, John, 153
Lusitania, 210
Lyman, Will, 421
Lyon, Ben, 206
Lyrics of Lowly Life, 144

MacArthur, **347**
MacArthur, Arthur, 180
MacArthur, Douglas, 180, 226, 314, 337, 347
MacArthur, James, 7
Macarthy, Harry, 89
Macbeth, 401
MacBird!, **401–402**
MacDonald, Florence, 253
MacDonald, Philip, 300
Machine Gunner, The, 201
Mack, Marion, 102
MacKenzie, Aeneas, 176
MacLean, William, 201
Macpherson, Jeanie, 210
Macready, George, 213
Madame Butterfly, 404
Madison, James, 45–46
Mad Magazine, 354
Maguire, William, 292
Mahin, John Lee, 110
Mail Call, 272
Mailer, Norman, 227, 237, 381
Maine, USS, 53, 178–179, 187–188, 193
Malden, Karl, 331, 353
Male Call, 245
Malick, Terrence, 315
Malone, Dorothy, 100
Maloney, James, 275
Maltby, Richard, Jr., 404
Maltz, Albert, 293
"Mama, Tell Them What We're Fighting For," 395
Manchurian Candidate, The, **347–348**
Manfredi, Michael, 438
Manhattan Project, 306
Mann, Arthur, 350
Mann, Michael, 7
Mansfield, Richard, 23
Man-Who-Stands-Looking-Back, 154
Manzanar, 257–258
Maquire, William, 292

March, Fredric, 239, 340
"Marching through Georgia," 114, **118**, 135
"March of the Class of 1907," 230
March of Time, 259
"March to the Sea, The," 122
Margaret Bourke-White, 241
"Marines' Hymn, The," 230, 252, **280–281**
Marquand, John P., 237
Marsh, Dave, 362, 365
Marsh, Mae, 87, 151
Marshall, George (Film Director), 186
Marshall, George (General), 288, 316
Marshall, S.L.A., 351
Marstan, Merlin, 419
Marston, William Moulton, 332
Martin, Andrew, 279
Martin, Dean, 334
Martin, Dewey, 351
Martin, Mary, 312
Martin, Quinn, 320
Martinez, Joaquin, 177
Martinson, Leslie, 294
Martinson, Rita, 386
Marton, Andrew, 315, 350
Marvel Comics, 246, 405
Marvin, Lee, 228, 232, 240, 255, 342
Mary Chestnut's Civil War, **119**
"Maryland, My Maryland," **119–120**
*M*A*S*H*, 254, **348–349**, 373
"M*A*S*H: Binding Up the Wounds," 349
Mason, Bobbie Ann, 397
Mason, Marsha, 436
"Massachusetts Liberty Song, The," 32
"Massacre," 158
Massasoit, 2
Massey, Raymond, 111, 228, 237, 266
Matchlock Gun, The, **8**
Mather, Cotton, 9
Matheson, A. C., 137
Mathew Brady Studios, **120–121**
Mathison, Melissa, 175
Mature, Victor, 342
Mauldin, Bill, 218, **281–282**
Maxim, Hudson, 197
Maxwell, Ronald, 113
Mayaquez, USS, 429
Mayer, Frederick, 243
Mayes, Wendell, 345
Maynard, Ken, 29
Mayo, Virginia, 239
McBain, Diane, 158

McCall, Mary C., Jr., 260
McCallum, Andrew, 107
McCarthy, Eugene, 401
McCarthy, Frank, 290
McCarthy, Gerald, 370
McCarthy, Joseph, 346
McClellan, George, 75
McClure, Doug, 133
McClure's, 183
McCormack, John, 210
McCrea, Jane, **32–33**
McCurdy, Ed, 346
McDaniel, Hattie, 106, 303
McDonald, Country Joe, 396–397
McDowell, Irwin, 84, 142
McGill, Everett, 436
McGovern, George, 360, 395
McHale's Navy (Films), 282
McHale's Navy (TV Series), 160, **282**
McHale's Navy Joins the Air Force, 282
McHugh, Frank, 202
McHugh, Jimmy, 250
McIntrye and Heath Minstrels, 191
McKenna, Richard, 214–215
McKinley, William, 178–180, 186
McLaglen, Andrew V., 133
McLaglen, Victor, 158, 221
McMurray, Fred, 72, 243
McNamara, Robert, 53, 401
McNichol, Kristi, 311
McPherson, James M., 88, 115
McQueen, Steve, 214
Meade, George, 142
Me and Juliet, 323
Medal of Honor (Congressional Medal of Honor), 104, 131, 157, 195, 213, 216, 233, 305, 317, 320, 348, 384, 389, 434, 435, 436
Medicine Whip, 171
Meditations in Green, **402**
Meeker, Ralph, 213
Méliès, George, 65
Melodies, Duets, Trios, Songs and Ballads, Pastoral, Amatory, Sentimental, Patriotic, Religious, and Miscellaneous. Together with Metrical Epistles, Tales, and Presentations. By Samuel Woodsworth, 49
Melville, Herman, 110, **121–122**, 134
Memoirs of the Confederate War for Independence, 140
Memoranda during the War Days, 146
Memorial Day, **122–123**, 219, 220, 351
Memphis Belle, The, 228, **283**, 287, 319

Memphis-Nam-Sweden, **402–403**
Men, The, **283–284**
Mencow, Gus, 292
Menendez, Pedro, 1, 6
Men in War, **350**
Menjou, Adolphe, 213
Men of the Fighting Lady, 260, 340, **350–351**
Merchant Marine, U.S., 228–229, 278, 303
Meredith, Burgess, 311
Merrill, Gary, 319
Merrill's Marauders, 240
Merrimac, CSS, 84
Merry Macs, 293
Merry Tales, 127
"Message to Garcia, A," **185–186**
Metamora, **8–9**
Metz, Theodore, 191
Meyer, Kevin, 79
MIA (missing in action), 379, 403–404, 409
Michael Bonham, 39
Midler, Bette, 230, 321
Midnight Clear, A, 228, **284–285**
Midway, 236–237, 279
Miles, Alfred H., 230
Miles, Nelson, 150, 162, 165, 169
Milestone, Lewis, 294, 325, 351
Milius, John, 162, 189, 364
Milland, Ray, 153
Miller, Bob, 313
Miller, Dorrie, 227
Miller, Glenn, 231, 256
Miller, James (Actor), 239
Miller, James (Senator), 119
Miller, Jeffrey, 399
Miller, Mitch, 389
Milsome, Douglas, 387
Minter, Mary Miles, 101, 116
Minute Man, The, 13, **33–34**, 185, 328
Minute Men, 13, 16, 20, 33–34, 35, 62
"Miss Bailey's Ghost," 49
Miss Ravenal's Conversion, **123–124**
Missing in Action, **403–404**
Missing in Action 2—The Beginning, 403
"Mission with No Name," 170
Miss Saigon, **404–405**
Mister Roberts, **285–286**
Mitchell, Chad Trio, 346
Mitchell, Margaret, 105
Mitchell, Thomas, 260
Mitchener, James A., 312, 340, 350, 399
Mitchum, Robert, 236, 311, 328, 345

Mobile Army Surgical Hospitals, 338, 348–349, 410
Moby Dick, 121
"Mockingbird, The," 86
Modernaires, 256
Modine, Matthew, 283, 386
Modoc War, 168
Moffat, E. S., 117
Mohun, or The Last Days of Lee and His Paladins, 94
Monitor, USS, 84, 107
Monongahela River (Pennsylvania), 4
Montalban, Ricardo, 155
Montcalm, Louis, 3, 10
Montcalm and Wolfe, 10
Monterrey Folk Festival, 428
Montgomery, Richard, 14, 17, 40
Montgomery, Robert, 314
Moore, Lenard, 434–435
Moore, Robin, 392
Moratorium Day, 359, 389
Morgan, Dennis, 202, 266
Mormon Tabernacle Choir, 84
Morning Is a Long Time Coming, 311–312
Morrow, Vic, 250
Morse, Wayne, 401
Morton, Ed, 208
Moss, Carleton, 237
"Mother, When the War Is Over," 144
Mount Rushmore (South Dakota), 138, 156
Mount Suribachi, 226, 301, 321
Mr. Dooley in Peace and in War, **186–187**, 188
Mud, Mules, and Mountains, 281
Mudd, Roger, 368
Mullens, Gene, 385
Mullens, Peg, 385
Mulligan, Richard, 166
Mundell, W. L., 59
Murdoch, James, 134
Murkowski, Frank, 438
Murphy, Audie, 128, 317
Murphy, George, 234
Murray, Doug, 405
Murrow, Edward R., 276, **286**
Mussolini, Benito, 267
MX missiles, 429
"My Blue Heaven," 207
My Bunkie, 171
My Captivity among the Sioux Indians, **166–167**
My Confession, **70–71**

My Four Years in Germany, **211–212**
"My Mammy," 207
My Maryland, 119
"My Sweetheart Went Down with the Maine," 188

Nagasaki, 226
Naked and the Dead, The, 227, **287**
'Nam, The, **405**
napalm, 354, 420
Narita, Hiro, 258
Narrative of the Life of David Crockett of the State of Tennessee, A, 68
Narrative of the Life of Mrs. Mary Jemison, A, 11
Narrative of the Texan Sante Fe Expedition, 70
Nast, Thomas, 53, 99, 107, **124**, 134
Nathan, Rick, 369
Nathanson, E. M., 255
Nation, The, 204
National Book Awards, 90, 209, 254, 268, 311, 390, 399, 407, 416
National Farm and Home Show, 323
National Police Gazette, The, 280
National Prisoner of War Museum, 80
Natwick, Mildred, 173
Nazis Strike, The, 330
Near, Holly, 386
Nebel, Carl, 70, **71–72**
Negro Ensemble Company, 306–307
Negro Soldier, The, **287–288**, 330
Neihardt, John G., 151–152, 174
Nelson, Ralph, 173–174
Nelson, Steve, 267
Nelson, Terry, 366
Neville Brothers, 428
Nevins, Allen, 10
Newbery Awards, 7, 8, 29, 129
New England Psalm Singer, The, 19
Newly Discovered American Folk Songs, 48
Newman, Alfred, 259, 330
Newman, Allen G., 185
New Orleans Delta, 119
Newport Folk Festival, 362, 426, 428
New Sad Sack, 299
New Spirit of 1942, The, 326
New Stories from the South, 391
Newton, Wayne, 125
New York Drama Critics Circle Awards, 38, 271, 306, 312, 414, 420
New Yorker, 385
New York Evening Post, 143

New York Journal, 178–179, 187, 192–193
"New York, New York," 289
New York Tribune, 128, 134, 209
New York World, 178, 188, 192
New York World's Fair (1939), 155
Nicaragua, 196, 204
Nichols, Dudley, 229, 261
Nichols, Mike, 240, 249
nickelodeon theaters, 190
Nicolay, John G., 110
Nigh, William, 211
Nimitz, Chester W., 259
Niven, David, 187, 200
Nixon, Richard, 359–360, 367, 368, 376–377, 394, 401, 429
Noah, Mordecai, 47, 50
Nolan, Lloyd, 72, 268, 330
"No Man's Land," 195, 202, 217
"No Other Love," 323
Noreiga, Manuel, 431, 436
Norris, Chuck, 73, 361, 403
North, Edmund, 32
North, Edmund H., 290
North American Newspaper Alliance, 261
North and South, 83, **124–125**
North and South Book II, 124
North Atlantic Treaty Organization (NATO), 279
North Star, 168
Northwest Passage, 10
Norvello, Ivor, 209–210
No Survivors, **167–168**
Notebook 1967–1968, 401
Notes of a War Correspondent, 182
Notes on the State of Virginia, 5
Not in Vain, 399

Oaker, Mary Rose, 438
O'Brien, Edmond, 331
O'Brien, Pat, 202–203
O'Brien, Tim, 363, 389–390, 397, 399, 416
O'Brien, Tom, 198
"O Captain! My Captain," 146
"Occurrence at Owl Creek Bridge, An," 86
Ochs, Phil, **406**
O'Day, Molly, 184
"Ode in Memory of the American Volunteers Fallen in France," 215
O'Donnell, Cathy, 239
Offenbach, Jacques, 280
"Off We Go," 231

Oglethorpe, James, 2
O'Hara, Maureen, 170
"Oh, How I Hate to Get Up in the Morning," **212**
"Ohio," 399
"Okie from Muskogee," **406–407**
Oklahoma, 323
"Old Glory," **125–126**, 321
Old Gringo, The, 86
"Old Ironsides," **49–50**
Old Ironsides (Film), 50
"Old Oaken Bucket, The," 49
Oliver Wiswell, **34–35**
Olivier, Lawrence, 24, 347
Olsen, Theodore V., 174
"Once I Was," 376
One Gallant Rush, 102
O'Neill, James F., 318
"One of the Missing," 86
Ono, Yoko, 389
"On the Death of Captain Nicholas Biddle," 27
"On the Destruction of Cervera's Fleet," 186
On the Town, **288–289**
Operation Apache Snow, 393
Operation Just Cause, 436
Operation Pacific, 228
Operation Torch, 225
Oregon Trail, 148
Oregon Trail, The, 9
O'Reilly, Salaria Kea, 267
Orlando, Tony (and Dawn), 438
Osaka, Sono, 289
Osborn, Paul, 238, 253
O'Sullivan, Timothy, 121
"O Tannenbaum," 119
Otis, James, 18
Our Army at War, **289–290**
"Our Country Flag," 89
"Our Nation's Battle Cry, 'Remember the *Maine*,' " 188
Our Vietnam Nightmare, 343
Outcault, Richard F., 192
Over Here, 231
"Over There," 196, **212–213**

Paco's Story, **407**
Paget, Debra, 152
Paine, Thomas, 19–20
Palance, Jack, 232
Palmer, Joel Williamson, 138
Panama Deception, The, **436–437**
Papazian, Robert, 125

Papp, Joseph, 414, 419
Paquet, Basil, 370, 427
Parker, Eleanor, 293
Parker, Fess, 102
Parker, Francine, 386
"Parker Adderson, Philospher," 86
Parkman, Francis, 3, **9–10**, 58
Parsons, Charles, 99
Partch, Virgil Franklin, II (VIP), 324
Partisan: A Tale of the Revolution, The, 39
Pascal, Jefferson, 237
Pathfinder, The, 6
Paths of Glory, **213–214**, 232
Patric, Jason, 162
Patriot (Baltimore), 51
"Patriot Game, The," 427
"Patriotic Diggers," 49
Patten, Robert, 320
Patterson, Joseph, 244
Patterson, Melody, 160
Patton, **290**, 347
Patton, George Smith, 290, 389
Patton, Ordeal and Triumph, 290
Paul Revere and the World He Lived In, 29
Paul Revere's Ride (musical), 35
"Paul Revere's Ride" (poem), **35**
"Paul Vane, or Lorena's Reply," 117–118
Paxinou, Katina, 261
Paxton, Tom, 426
Payne, John, 344
Peabody, Elizabeth, 66
"Peace Committee," 396
Peace Sign/Peace Symbol, **408**
Peck, Gregory, 86, 88, 319, 347, 351
Peer, Ralph, 217
Pelham, Henry, 18
Pemberton, Samuel, 18
Penn, Arthur, 166, 362
Penn, Sean, 315, 371, 377
Pennsylvania Gazette, 32
Pennsylvania Journal, 32
Pennsylvania Magazine, 19
Pentagon Papers, 426
Peple, Edward, 117
Pepsodent Show, The, 271
"Performance, The," 254
Perkins, Anthony, 100
Perot, Ross, 417
Perry, Antoinette, 308
Perry, Oliver Hazard, 46, 49
Perry, Richard, 292

*Perry's Victory on Lake Erie Fought
  Sept. 10th, 1813*, 69
Pershing, John "Black Jack," 195, 215,
  217
Person-to-Person, 286
Peter, House, 142
Peter, Paul, and Mary, 389, 413
Peters, Donald A., 237
Petlin, Irving, 363
Pharaoh's Army, **126**
Philadelphia Centennial Exposition, 34,
  39, 99
Phile, Philip, 48
Philip ("King"), 2, 3
Philippoteaux, Paul, 95
Philistine, The, 185
Phillips, L. Z., 281
Phillips, W. A., 188
Phips, William, 2
Piantadosi, Al, 208
Picayune, The (New Orleans), 69
Pickersgill, Mary, 52
"Picket Guard, The," 79
Pickett, George, 96, 104, 141
Pickford, Jack, 116
Pickford, Mary, 141, 196, 210
Pidgeon, Walter, 251
Pierce, Franklin, 64
Pike, Albert, 97
Pilgrim's Progress, 406
pinup girls, 245, **291**
Pinza, Ezio, 312
Pirosh, Robert, 235, 250
*Pistol Packin' Mama: The Missions of a
  B-17*, **291–292**
Pitcher, Molly, **35–36**
Pittinger, William, 102
Plainsmen, The, **168–169**
Plastic Ono Band, 389
Plato, 397
Platoon, 407, **408–409**
Playboy, 314
Pleshette, Suzanne, 158
Poems, The, 27
Poems by Alan Seeger, 215
Points of Honor, 219
Polk, James, 53, 63, 64
Ponselle, Rosa, 210
*Ponteach: A Melodrama for Narrator
  and Piano*, 11
Ponteach; or the Savages of America, **10–
  11**
Pontiac (Chief), 3, 10–11, 12
Poor Little Ritz Girl, 21

Pope, John, 75
Popeye, 274
Pork Chop Hill, **351–352**
Post, Ted, 391
posttraumatic stress disorder/syndrome,
  277, 307, 421
Potter, R. M., 65
POW (prisoner of war), 80, 118, 271,
  292, 309–310, 311, 330, 348, 353, 360–
  361, 367, 379, 383, 394, 400, 403–
  404, 411, 414
Powell, Colin, 389
Powell, Dick, 242, 345
Power, Tyrone, 111
"Praise the Lord and Pass the Ammuni-
  tion," 233, **292–293**
Prelude to War, 330
Preminger, Otto, 310
Prescott, Samuel, 35
"President's March, The," 48
Presnell, Robert, 187
Preston, Robert, 325
Preston, Thomas, 18
Price, The, 277
Pride of the Marines, **293–294**
prisoner of war/missing in action (POW/
  MIA) bracelets, 404, **409–410**
"Private Breger" (cartoon), 264–265
Private Breger (book), 265
Private Breger's War, 265
Private Buckeroo, 256
"Private History of a Campaign That
  Failed, The," **127**
Proffitt, Nicholas, 387
Proof Thro' the Night, 253
propaganda, 18, 20, 33, 124, 187, 197,
  206, 210, 211, 229, 233, 236, 248,
  259, 266, 269, 295, 297, 300, 317,
  326, 330, 334, 355, 378, 387, 425
Pryce, Jonathan, 404
psychoneurosis, 277, 278
PT 109, **294**
Public Works Administration, 277
Puccini, Guillermo, 404
Puckett, Cliff, 292
Pulitzer, Joseph, 178, 192
Pulitzer Prizes, 29, 37, 80, 105, 111, 112,
  115, 119, 238, 242, 261, 269, 281–
  282, 295, 306, 312, 321, 343, 378,
  380, 385, 391, 399
Puller, Lewis B., Jr., 384–385
Purcell, Anne, 400
Purcell, Ben, 400
Purple Hearts, **410–411**

Purple Heart, The, **294–295**, 338
Putnam, Isaac, 21
Pyle, Ernie, 205, **295–296**, 310–311
Pynchon, Thomas, 267–268, 402

Quincy, Josiah, 18
Quinn, Don, 258
Quinn, Pat, 362

Rabble in Arms, 34, **36–37**
Rabe, David, 371, 413–415
Rack, The, 353
Racklin, Martin, 110
Radford, Arthur, 358
Radio Germany, 233
Radio Tokyo, 318
Raine, Norman Reilly, 238
Raine, William MacLeod, 72
Raines, Ella, 270
Rains, Claude, 247
"Raising the Flag on Iwo Jima," 321
Rambo: First Blood, Part II, **411–412**
Rambo III, 412
Randall, James Ryder, 119–120
Randolph, John, 53
Rappaport, Anatol, 415
Rathbone, Basil, 200
"Ration Blues," **296**
rationing, 227, 494–495
Ray, Aldo, 235, 287, 350
Read, Thomas Buchanan, 134
Reagan, Ronald, 305, 316, 382, 403, 409,
    417, 418, 430–432, 437
Real Glory, The, **187**
Reap the Whirlwind, 168
Reason and Emotion, 326
Rebels, The, 30
Red Badge of Courage, The, **127–128**,
    219, 317, 416
Red Cloud (Chief), 149, 174
Red Cloud's Revenge, 168
*Redeemed Captive, Returning to Zion,
    The*, 11
Redford, Robert, 355
Red Knight, The, 205
Red River, 301
Red River Dave, 313
Red Scare, 346
Reed, Carol, 318
Reed, Donna, 263, 273
Rees, Edward, 220
Reeves, George, 307
Reflections on the Civil War, 88

Register Tribune (Des Moines), 385
Reisman, Philip, Jr., 127
Remarque, Erich, 416
"Remember Pearl Harbor," 231
"Remember the *Maine*," 179, **187–188**
" 'Remember the *Maine*' Is Our Battle
    Cry," 188
Remington, Frederic, **169**, 171, 181, 192
Reno, Marcus, 153, 167
"Report from the Skull's Diorama," 378
Resistance to Civil Government, 66
Retreat, Hell!, **352**
Returning Home, 239
Reuben James, USS, 224, 303–304
Revere, Paul, 16, 18, 29, 35, 49
Rhee, Syngman, 336
Rhymes and More Rhymes of a Pfc., 297
Rhymes of a Pfc., **296–297**
Rice, Grantland, 218
Richard Carvel, 94
Richardson, Albert, **128–129**
Richmond, Kane, 308
Richter, Conrad, 7–8
Rickenbacker, Eddie, 114
Rifles for Waite, **129**
Rio Bravo, 229
Rio Grande, 158, **170**, 173
Ripley, Alexandra, 106
Ritchard, Cyril, 22
Ritchie, Douglas, 322
Ritter, Tex, 367
Robbins, Jerome, 288
Robbins, Marty, 65
Robe, Mike, 175
"Robert Gould Shaw," 145
Roberts, Kenneth, 17, 34–35, 36–37
Roberts, Paul, 313
Roberts, Stanley, 242
Robertson, Cliff, 287, 294
Robinson, Bill "Bogangles," 117
Robinson, "Sugar" Ray, 361
Rockwell, J. C., 135
Rockwell, Norman, 261–262, 298
Rodgers, Jimmie, 217
Rodgers, Richard, 21, 312, 323
Rogers, Charles "Buddy," 221
Rogers, Jimmy, 194
Rogers, Robert, 10
Rogers, Wayne, 349
ROK (Republic of Korea), 336
Roland, Gilbert, 155
Rolfe, Edwin, **297–298**
Rolle, Esther, 311

Rolling Stones, 376
Rolling Thunder, 58
Rollins, Howard, Jr., 376
Rollins, Peter C., 421
Romero, Ned, 164
Rommel, Erwin, 295
Rooney, Andy, 218
Rooney, Mickey, 273
Roosevelt, Eleanor, 269
Roosevelt, Franklin Delano (FDR), 213,
    224, 226, 261, 263, 296, 305, 313,
    328, 329, 336, 413
Roosevelt, Theodore, 172, 179, 180, 188–
    189, 191, 197
Root, George, 81, 111–112, 113, 139
Rose, Billy, 320
Rosebrook, Jeb, 164
Rosenman, Leonard, 385
Rosenthal, Joe, 226, 535
"Rosie, The Riveter" (song), 298
Rosie the Riveter, 227, **298–299**
Rosie the Riveter (film), 298
"Rosin the Bow," 135
Ross, Betsy, **37**
Ross, Harold, 218
Ross, Katherine, 133
Rossen, Robert, 326
Rottman, Larry, 427
Rough and Ready Songster, 66
Rough Riders, 114, 179, 181, 183, 188–
    189, 191
Rough Riders, The, **188–189**
Rowan, Andrew Summers, 185
Rowlandson, Mary, 3, 11
Royle, Salena, 260
Ruggles, Theo Alice, 185
Ruman, Sig, 310
Rumor of War, A, 373, 399, **412–413**
Russell, Charles, **170–171**
Russell, Harold, 239
Ryan, Abram Joseph, 92–93
Ryan, Cornelius, 270
Ryan, Meg, 434
Ryan, Robert, 255, 350

Saboteur, 279
Sacks, Michael, 304
Sadler, Barry, 365
Sad Sack, **299–300**
"Sad Sack" (cartoon), 300
Sad Sack, The (book), 299
Sad Sack, The (movie), 300
Sahara, **300**

Sahlins, Marshall, 415
Saint-Gaudens, Augustus, **130**
Saint Marie, Buffy, 175
Salomon, Henry, 323
Salonga, Lea, 404
SALT II (Treaty), 429
Salter, James, 344–345
Saludo Amigos, 327
Sam Chamberlain's Mexican War, 71
Sampson, William, 179
Sanders, Denis, 287
Sanders, Terry, 287
Sandinistas, 204, 430
Sandino, Ernesto, 204
Sandoz, Mari, 155
Sand Pebbles, The, **214–215**
Sandrich, Mark, 307
Sands of Iwo Jima, The, 228, 235, 252,
    301, 314, 319, 436
San Francisco Examiner, 86
Sanitary Commission, 130
Sanitary Fairs, **130–131**
Sansome, Leonard, 324
Santa Anna, Antonio Lopez de, 62–63,
    65, 66
Santa Fe Trail, 148
Saroyan, William, 273
Saturday Evening Post, 153, 170, 173,
    262, 264, 298, 340, 350
Saunders, John Monk, 199, 221
Savage, John, 377
Sawyer, Charles Carroll, 143
Saxon, John, 355
*Scarlett, The Sequel to Margaret Mitch-
    ell's Gone with the Wind*, 106
Schaffner, Franklin J., 290
Schenectady (New York), 2
Schermer, Jules, 260
Scheuer, Sandra, 399
Schindler's List, 92
Schlesinger, Leon, 280
Schmid, Albert, 293–294
Schoendorffer, Pierre, 363–364
Schönberg, Claude Michel, 404
Schreyvogel, Charles, 170, **171–172**
Schroeder, William, 399
Schulberg, B. P., 188
Schuyler, George S., 256–257
Schwarzkopf, Norman, 385
Scott, Allan, 307
Scott, George C., 81, 290
Scott, Julian, **131–132**
Scott, Randolph, 6

Scott, Waldo, 375
Scott, Winfield, 63–64, 70
Scott's Entrance into Mexico [City], 71
Scruggs, Jan, 422–423
Sea Chase, The, 335
Seaver, James, 11
Second Battle of Bull Run Fought August 29, 1862, 69
Second Continental Congress, 13, 17, 28, 31, 37, 38
Secret Service, **132–133**, 181
Secret Service, the Field, the Dungeon, and the Escape, The, 129
Secret Squadrons, 247
Seeds of Destiny, 300
Seeger, Alan, 194, **215**
Seeger, Pete, 304, 389, **413**
See Here, Private Hargrove, **301–302**
See It Now, 286
Seekers, The, 30
Segal, Erich, 399
Segar, E. C., 274
Seiler, Lewis, 268
Selected Poems, 274
Selective Service (Act), 194, 242, 413
Selleck, Tom, 239
Selling of the Pentagon, The, 426
Sells, Sam, 267
Selznick, David O., 106, 202
Semans, Bill, 292
Seminole Wars, 57, 148
Semper Fi, 252
Sentinels of Liberty clubs, 246
"Sequel" to *Drum-Taps*, 146
Serapis, HMS, 25
Sergeant Rutledge, **172–173**
Sergeant York, **215–216**
Sergel, Christopher, 152
Serling, Rod, 353
Sevareid, Eric, 286
1776, **37–38**
Seven Wise Dwarfs, The, 326
Sgt. Rock, 290
Shaara, Jeff, 104–105, 113
Shaara, Michael, 90, 104, 112–113
Shadow Riders, 168
Shakespeare, William, 339, 401
Shane, 397
Shannon, HMS, 46
Sharp, Alan, 177
Sharp Encounter, A, 171
Sharpshooter on Picket Duty, The, 109
Shaw, Bernard, 433

Shaw, David T., 67
Shaw, George Bernard, 23
Shaw, Irwin, 334
Shaw, Robert Gould, 103–104, 130, 145
Sheen, Charlie, 409
Sheen, Martin, 112–113, 364
shell-shock, 277
"Shenandoah," 133
Shenandoah (Drama, Film), **133**
Shenandoah (Film, Musical), **133–134**
Shenandoah Valley (Virginia), 88, 123, 133, 134
Sheridan, Ann, 291
Sheridan, Philip, 133, 134, 161,
"Sheridan at Cedar Creek," 122
"Sheridan's Ride" (Melville), 134
Sheridan's Ride (Read), **134**
Sherman, William Tecumseh, 63, 76, 84, 96, 105, 118, 130, 135
"Sherman's March to the Sea," **135**
Sherwood, Robert E., 238
She Wore a Yellow Ribbon, 155, 158, 170, **173**, 438
She Would Be a Soldier, 47, **50–51**
Shiloh, **135–136**
Shoemaker, Ann, 253
Shooting of the Russian War, 241
Shore, Dinah, 273
Short Narrative of the Horrid Massacre, A, 18
Short Timers, The, 386
Shoulder Arms, **216–217**
Sicily Sketch Book, 281
"Siegfried," 274
Silenced War Whoop, The, 171
Silverstein, Shel, 218
Simms, William Gilmore, **38–39**
Simon, Joe, 246
Simon, Neil, 22, 240–241
Sinatra, Frank, 263, 272, 273, 289, 348
Sinatra, Nancy, 364
Since You Went Away, **302–303**
Sinclair, Harold, 110
Sinese, Gary, 285
Sing Out, 346
"Sinking of the *Reuben James*, The," **303–304**
Sioux Dawn, 168
Sioux War(s), 153, 164
Sisk, Mildred Elizabeth, 233
Sitting Bull, 149, 168, 174
Six Months at the White House with Abraham Lincoln, The Story of a Picture, 98

Skinner, Cornelia Otis, 22
Slaughterhouse-Five, **304**, 328
"Sleep, Baby, Sleep," 217
Slezak, Walter, 278
Sloan, Everett, 284
Small World, 286
"Smile, Smile, Smile," 195–196
Smiling Through, 233
Smith, Albert E., 183, 190
Smith, James, 366
Smith, John Stafford, 51
Smith, Kate, 265, **305**
Smith, Oliver, 288
Smith, Oliver P., 344, 352
Snafu, **305–306**
Soldier Blue, **173–174**
Soldier's Dream, 181
soldier's heart, 277
Soldier's Play, A, **306–307**
Soldier's Secret: A Story of the Sioux War of 1890, A, 164–165
Soldier's Story, A (film), 306–307
Soldier's Story, A (non-fiction), 290
"Soldier's Sweetheart, The," **217**
"Somebody's Darling," **136–137**
Song of the Indian Wars, The, 151, **174–175**
Songs for John Doe, 413
Songs of the People, 66
Song Spinners, 251
"Son of the Gods, A," 86
Son of the Morning Star, **175–176**
Sons of Liberty, 12, 13, 30
So Proudly We Hail, 253, **307**, 373
Sothern, Ann, 253
Sousa, John Philip, 243–244
South East Asia Command (SEAC), 333
South Pacific, 312, 323
Sower, The, 333
Spanish Civil War, 223, 261, 267, 297
Spears, John R., 108
Specimen Days, 146
Spicer, Bryan, 282
Spirit of Bob Hope, The, 272
Spirit of '43, The, 326
Spirit of '76, The, **39–40**
Spotted Tail, 174
Spy, The, 6
Spy Smasher, **308**
Spy Smasher Comics, 308
Stagecoach, 158
Stage Door and Hollywood Canteens, 230, **308–309**
Stage Door Canteen (movie), 309

Stagedoor Canteen (radio show), 309
Stalag 17, 270, **309–310**
Stalin, Joseph, 336
Stalkers, The, 168
Stallings, Laurence, 198, 220
Stallone, Sylvester, 361, 411
Stamp Acts, 3, 12
Standing Bear, Henry, 155–156
Stanwyck, Barbara, 186
Starret, William, 250
Starry Night, 333
Stars and Stripes, **217–218**, 281, 299
"Stars and Stripes on Iwo Jima," 321
"Star-Spangled Banner, The," 47, **51–52**, 266, 357
Star-Spangled Banter, 281
St. Clair, Arthur, 55
Steel Helmet, The, 239, **352–353**
Steelman, John R., 355
Steichen, Edward, 259
Steinbeck, John, 278
Steiner, Max, 235
"Stellar Quartet," 210
Stephens, Harry, 419
Stephens, Henry L., 107
Steppenwolf, 381
Stept, Sam H., 256
Sterling, Robert, 22
Steve Canyon, 244
Stevens, Thaddeus, 87
Stevenson, Adlai, 338
Stevenson, Robert, 30
Stewart, James ("Jimmy"), 125, 133, 152, 155
Sticks and Bones, 371, **413–414**, 414
Stiers, David Ogden, 125
Stone, John Augustus, 8–9
Stone, Oliver, 368, 408
Stone, Peter, 37–38
Stone, Robinson, 310
Stone Mountain, 87, 137
Stone Mountain Memorial, **137–138**
"Stonewall Jackson's Way," **138**
Stop That Tank, 326
Storaro, Vittorio, 365
Storch, Larry, 160
Storming of Chapultepec (Nebel), 71
Storming of Chapultepec (Walker), 141
Storming of Chapultepec, September 13, 1847 (Currier), 69
Story of G.I. Joe, The, **310–311**
Stratemeyer, Edward, **189–190**
Strauss, Peter, 174
Strauss, Robert, 310

Strauss, Theodore, 163
Streamers, 371, **414–415**
Streeter, Edward, 200–201
Strode, Woody, 172
St. Simons Island (Georgia), 2
Stuart, J.E.B., 93
Studi, Wes, 162
Sturges, Preston, 269–270
Styne, Jule, 273
"Suicide Is Painless," 349
Sullivan, Albert, 260
Sullivan, Francis, 260
Sullivan, George, 260
Sullivan, Joseph, 260
Sullivan, Madison, 260
Sullivan, Margaret, 253
Sullivan Brothers, The (ship), 260
Sullivans, The (film), 260
Sullivans, The (ship), 260
Summer of My German Soldier, **311–312**
Summers, Florence, 201
Summit Springs Rescue—1869, The, 172
Sunset Pass, or Running the Gauntlet through Apache Land, 164
Super Rabbit, 280
Surrender of Burgoyne at Saratoga, The, 40
Surrender of Cornwallis at Yorktown, 40
Surry of Eagle Nest, or The Memories of a Staff Officer Serving in Virgina, 94
Sutherland, Donald, 255, 349, 386
Swayze, Patrick, 125
Sweeny, D. B., 387
Sweet, Blanche, 142
"Sweetheart of Song Tra Bong, The," 416
Sweetheart of the Fleet, 329
Swerdlow, Joel L., 423
Swerling, Jo, 187, 278, 288
Swing Shift, 299
Swingtime Canteen, 231
Swit, Loreta, 349

Taft, Lorado, 59
Tales of a Wayside Inn, 35
Tales of Soldiers and Civilians, 86
Tales of the South Pacific, **312–313**
Tamblyn, Russ, 352
Tammen, Harry, 165
Taradash, Daniel, 263
Target Zero, 342
Tarkington, Booth, 17, 262
Tashlin, Frank, 280

Taylor, Don, 310
Taylor, Maxwell, 358
Taylor, Robert, 234, 259
Taylor, Zachary, 63–64, 66, 70, 71, 72
Taza, Son of Cochise, 152
teach-ins, **415–416**
Tearing Down the Spanish Flag, **190–191**
Tecumseh (Tekamthi), 45, 56, 60
Tecumseh!, **60**
Television's Vietnam, 421
Temple, Shirley, 117, 158, 186, 302
"Tenting on the Old Camp Ground," **138–139**
Terkel, Studs, 227, 267
Terry, Megan, 425
Terry, Wallace, 367–368
Terry and the Pirates, 244–245
Texas Ranger, A, 72
Texas Ranger, The (Novel), 72
Texas Rangers, 63, 70, **72–73**
Texas Rangers, The (Film), 72
"Texas Rangers, The" (Folksong), 72
Texas Ruby, 184
Texians, 62
"Thanksgiving Special," 398
That's Me All Over, Mable, 201
"There'll Be a Hot Time in the Old Town Tonight," **191**
"There's a Star-Spangled Banner Waving Somewhere," **313**
"There Was a Young Soldier," 87
"These Boots Were Made for Walking," 364
They Called It "Purple Heart Valley," 241
They Died with Their Boots On, 150, 153, **176–177**
They Were Expendable, **313–314**, 325
Things They Carried, The (Book), 363, 399, **416**
"Things They Carried, The" (Short Story), 416
Thin Red Line, The, 227, 262, **314–315**, 417
13th Valley, The, **417**
Thirty Seconds over Tokyo, 225, **315–316**
Thirty Years After, An Artist's Story of the Great War, 99
This Damned Tree Leaks, 281
This Is the Army, 212, 265, 309, **316**
This Is War!, 341
Thomas, Augustus, 94
Thomas, Richard, 128

Thompson, Dave, 267
Thompson, Jim, 213
Thompson, Keene, 189
Thompson, Marshall, 317
Thompson, Maurice, 14–15
Thoreau, Henry David, 63, 66–67
Thorpe, Richard, 253
Three Cabelleros, The, 327
Three Servicemen, **417–418**
Thrifty Pig, The, 326
Through the Wheat, **218–219**
"Tie a Yellow Ribbon 'Round the Ole
    Oak Tree," 439
Tierney, Gene, 238
Tighe, Kevin, 162
"'Til the Boys Come Home," 209
Time, 367
Time Limit, **353–354**
Timely Comics, 246
Times They Are-a-Changin', The, 428
Tin Pan Alley, 195, 208
Tiomkin, Dmitri, 65, 330
Tisdale, Betty, 372–373
Titans, The, 30
"To Anacreon in Heaven," 51
Tobias, Charles, 329
Toguri d'Aquino, Iva Ikuko, 318
To Heal a Nation, 423
To Hell and Back, **317**
Tokio, Jokio, 280
Tokyo Rose, **317–318**
Tomb of the Unknowns, **219–220**
Tomei, Concetta, 373
Tonkin Gulf Resolution, 358, 401
"Tony" (Antoinette Perry) Awards, 38,
    134, 240, 312, 404, 414, 420
Tora! Tora! Tora!, 279
"To the Memory of the Brave Ameri-
    cans, under General Greene in South
    Carolina, Who Fell in the Action of
    September 8, 1781," 27
Tournier, Maurice, 6
Tour of Duty, **418–419**
Tour of Duty II: Bravo Company, 419
Tour of Duty III: The Hill, 419
Towers, Constance, 110
Tracers, **419**
Tracy, Spencer, 316
Trail of Tears, 56, 61
Trail of the Lonesome Pine, The, 116
"Tramp! Tramp! Tramp!," 130, **139–
    140**
Travis, William, 65

Treaties: Ghent, 46; Guadalupe Hidalgo,
    64; Paris (1783), 15, 40; Paris (1899),
    179
Tregaskis, Richard, 268
Trent, Barbara, 437
Trial of the Catonsville Nine, The, **420**
Trist, Nicholas, 64
Trotti, Lamar, 238, 268
Trudeau, Garry, 379–380
True Glory, The, **318–319**
*True History of the Captivity and Resto-
    ration of Mrs. Mary Rowlandson, A*,
    11
Truman, Harry S., 226, 269, 337–338,
    347, 355, 357
Trumbo, Dalton, 209, 316, 368, 386
Trumbull, John, **40–41**, 115
Trumpet in the Land, **41**
Trumpet on the Land, 168
Trzcinski, Edmund, 309–310
Tubb, Ernest, 406
Tuchner, Michael, 311
Tucker, Forrest, 160
Tucker, Henry, 143
Tucker, Sophie, 207
"Tu Do Street," 378
Turkel, Joseph, 213
Turner, J. W., 139
Turner, Kathleen, 376
Turner, Lana, 291
Turner, Nat, 58
Turner, Ted, 161, 383, 433
Tuskegee Airman, 227, 269, 389
Twain, Mark, 127
Tweed, William ("Boss"), 124
Twelve O'Clock High, 200, 235, 252, **319–
    320**
Two-Fisted Tales, **354**
Two Logs Crossing, 8
2000-Yard Stare, The, 277
Tympany Five, 296

U-boats, 210, 224, 228, 278, 303, 333
Udell, Peter, 134
Ugly Rumors, 398
Ulzana's Raid, **177**
Uncle Sam, 47, **52–53**, 124, 203, 208,
    227
"Uncle Sam Won't Go to War," 208
Uncommon Valor, 403
*Under Dewey in Manila, or The War
    Fortunes of a Castaway*, 189
underground press, 374

Unforgiven, 157
"Unfortunate Miss Bailey, The," 49
United Confederate Veterans, 93
United Daughters of the Confederacy, 137
United Nations, 336–337, 342, 431, 432, 436
United Services Organization (USO), 230, 272, 298, 299, 305, **320–321**, 372, 383, 386
United States Army Emergency Relief, 316
United States Army War Art Program, 201
United States Department of Defense, 353, 425
United States Department of the Treasury, 329
United States Department of War, 277
United States House (of Representatives) Un-American Activities Committee, 413
United States Marine Corps War Memorial, **321–322**
United States Navy Memorial, **437**
United States Office of Price Administration (O.P.A.), 296
United States Office of Special Services (O.S.S.), 357
United States Office of War Information (O.W.I), 262, 283, 293, 325, 355
"Unsung Heroes, The," 145
Unto These Hills, **60–61**
Up Front, 281–282
Uris, Leon, 227, 234–235
"U.S. Air Force, The," 231
U.S.O. Camp Shows, 320

"Vagabonding with the Tenth Horse," 169
Valley Forge (Drama), **41–42**
Valley Forge (Novel), 42
Valley Forge (Pennsylvania), 14, 41
Van Buren, Martin, 64
Vanderlyn, John, 33
Van Devanter, Lynda, **420–421**
Van Oostrum, Kees, 113, 175
van Praag, Van, 350
Van Swearingen, Marmaduke, 59
Varga Girl, 291
Vargas, Alberto, 291
"V Calls for Victory," 322
V-E (Victory in Europe) Day, 226, 251, 322

Veidt, Conrad, 247
Veterans' Administration (VA), 263, 284, 411
Veterans' Day, **220**, 417, 422
Veterans of Foreign Wars (VFW), 435
"V for Victory," **322**, 408
Victory at Sea, **323**
"Victory Cavalcade," 322
Victory gardens, 203, 322, **323–324**
Victory March, The, 326
"Victory Polka," 322
Vidor, Charles, 86
Vidor, King, 72, 198
Vietnam: A History, 421
Vietnam: A Television History, **421–422**
Vietnam Combat Art, 370
Vietnam Experience, 397
Vietnam Veterans against the War (VVAW), 427
Vietnam Veterans' Memorial, 346, 398, 417, **422–423**, 424
Vietnam Veterans of America Women Veterans Project, 421
Vietnam War Story, **423**, 434
Vietnam Women's Memorial, **424**
Vietnam Womens' Memorial Project, 424
Viet Rock, **425**
VIP, **324**
Visions of War, Dreams of Peace: Writings of Women in the Vietnam War, 421
Vitagraph, 182, 190, 197
Vitascope, 190
Vizetelley, Frank, **140**
V-J (Victory in Japan) Day, 322, 327
"V-Mail," 322
"Voice from the Army, A," 112
Voices in Vital America (VIVA), 409
Voight, Jon, 375
Volunteer for Liberty, The, 297
von Borcke, Heros, 140
Vonnegut, Kurt, Jr., 304, 328
von Richtofen, Manfred, 205
"V to Victory," 322

Wagner, Robert, 345
Wahl, Ken, 410
"Waist Deep in the Big Muddy," 413
Waite, Stand, 129
"Wait Till the War, Love, Is Over," 144
Wakatsuki, Jeanne (Houston), 257–258
Wake Island, 269, **325**
Wake Up America, 366

"Waking Early Sunday Morning," 401
Walken, Christopher, 377
Walker, Frank, 291
Walker, James, 96, **140–141**
Walker, Mort, 218
Walker, Nancy, 289
Walker, Robert, 303
Walker, Texas Ranger, 73
Walking Dead, The, 367
Walk in the Sun, A, 301, **325–326**, 374
Walsh, Raoul, 176, 221, 235, 287
Walt Disney Cartoons, **326–327**
Walter, Eugene, 116
Walthall, Henry B., 86
War Adventure Series, The, **327**
War and Remembrance, **327–328**
War Art Program, 201
War Bonds, 181, 227, 259, 262, 283, 302, 305, 321, 326, 328–329, 331
War Comes to America, 330
Warden, Jack, 315
Wardman, Ervin, 192
War Hawks, 45, **53–54**, 392
War Hunt, **354–355**
War in Korea: The Report of a Woman Combat Correspondent, 343
War in the Gulf, 433
War in the Gulf: The Complete Story, 433
War Is Kind, **191–192**
Warner, Jack, 229
"War Prayer, The," 127
Warren, Joseph, 18, 19, 26, 29, 32, 40
War Relocation (for Japanese-Americans), 227, 257–258, 288
Warrens of Virginia, The, **141–142**
Warrior Gap: A Story of the Sioux Outbreak of '68, 164
Warriors, The, 30
wars: American Revolution, 8, 12–44, 59, 64, 66, 75, 76, 90, 85, 114, 195, 389, 437; Apache, 150, 157, 161–162, 164, 172, 177; Barbary Pirates, 50; Black Hawk, 56–57, 58–59; Civil (War between the States), 15, 19, 28, 35, 38–39, 44, 49, 50, 52, 53, 57–58, 63, 66, 69, 70, 72, 74–147, 149, 154, 156, 160, 161, 164, 174, 181, 186, 195, 227, 277, 354, 389, 427, 438; Cold, 218, 236, 242, 243, 336, 346, 348, 413, 427; French and Indian, 2, 3, 4, 7, 8, 9–10, 12, 85; Grenada, 430–431,

436; King George's, 2; King Philip's, 2–3, 9, 11; King William's, 2; Korea, 184, 219, 220, 239, 252, 254, 259–260, 286, 289, 301, 324, 331–332, 336–356, 357, 372, 373, 387, 415; Lebanon, 430; Lord Dunmore's, 4–5; Mexican (and Texas), 39, 43, 62–73, 75, 85, 97, 124, 141, 148, 182, 189, 280–281, 417; Modoc, 168; Nez Perce, 149–150, 159, 163, 164; Panama (1989), 431, 432, 435, 436–437; Persian Gulf (Desert Storm), 80, 272, 361, 422, 433–436, 438; Pequot, 85; Philippine Insurrection, 127, 164, 180, 184, 186–187; Pontiac's Rebellion, 3; Queen Anne's, 2; Sandinista (Nicaragua), 196, 204, 430; Seminole, 57, 148; Sioux, 149, 153, 164–165, 168, 169, 175–176; Spanish-American, 50, 52, 53, 108, 114, 116, 146, 164, 178–93, 197, 427; Spanish Civil War, 223, 245, 261, 267, 297–298; Vietnam, 53, 67, 133, 174, 208–209, 214, 219, 248, 277, 341, 343, 357–428, 429, 432, 434; War of 1812, 39, 43, 45–54, 61, 64, 69, 75, 85, 266; World War I, 53, 57–58, 67, 95, 114, 137, 146, 164, 181, 182, 184, 186, 189, 194–222, 224, 240, 263, 265, 277, 308, 316, 327, 329, 347, 354, 427; World War II, 24, 34, 44, 65, 67, 77, 114, 118, 128, 146, 153, 156, 160, 184, 186, 197, 199, 200, 203–335, 338, 339, 340–344, 346, 347, 350, 351, 352, 352–353, 354, 355, 369, 371, 373, 379, 387, 389, 392, 393, 400, 405, 408, 409, 413, 415, 427, 430; Yamasee, 39
War Savings Stamps, 34, 203, 227, 259, 326, **328–329**
Wars for Civilization in America, The, 165
Warshaw, Jack, 399
"War Song of Dixie, The," 97
War Victory Comics, 329
War without Heroes, 341
"War Wound, The," 255
Washington, Denzel, 104, 307, 434
Washington, George, 3, 4, 13–14, 15, 20, 21, 27, 28–29, 33, 36, 37, 41–42, 42–43, 48, 51, 55, 64
Washington, Martha, 42

Washington at Monmouth, 43
Washington Crossing the Delaware, **42–43**
Water on the Brain, 324
"Water War in Vietnam," 372
Watterston, Sam, 385
Waud, Alfred, 96, 98, 99, 107, 109, **142–143**
Waud, William, 107
Wayne, David, 282, 285
Wayne, John, 65, 68, 110, 158, 170, 173, 228, 301, 314, 335, 366, 368, 369, 379, 392–393, 412, 436
Wayne, "Mad" Anthony, 55, 59
"We Are Coming, Father Abra'am," 106, **143**
Wearing of the Gray, 93
Webb, James, 382
Webster, H.D.L., 117
Webster, J. P., 117
Webster, Paul Francis, 65
"We Did It Before (and We Can Do It Again)," **329**
"Weeping, Sad and Lonely," **143–144**
Wehner, William, 841
Weigl, Bruce, 370
Weir, Robert, 107
Weiss, Marion Gail, 438
Welles, Henry C., 122
Wellman, William, 221–222, 235, 310, 325
"We'll Rally Round the Flag, Boys," 81–82
Wells, Helen, 249
"We're Tenting on the Old Camp Ground," 139
West, Benjamin, 40
West, Jessamyn, 100
"We Stand for Peace While Others War," 208
Western Writers of America, 153, 169
Westmoreland, William, 359, 376, 394
Weston, Eric, 403
Westward the Course of Empire Takes Its Way, 43
Whale, James, 207
Whaley, Frank, 285
What Next, Private Hargrove?, 302
What Price Glory?, 198, **220–221**
What's a Woman Doing Here? A Reporter's Report on Herself, 372
"When Dey 'Listed Colored Soldiers," **144–145**

"When Johnny Comes Marching Home," **145–146**
"When Lilacs Last in the Dooryard Bloom'd," 146
"When the War Is Over, Mary," 144
"When This Cruel War Is Over," 143
"When Upon the Field of Glory: An Answer to When This Cruel War Is Over," 144
"Where Have All the Flowers Gone," 413
Where's Charley?, 292
"Where the River Shannon Flows," 217
Whistle, 262, 315
White, William L., 314
Whitman, Stuart, 364
Whitman, Walt, 121, **146–147**
Whitmore, James, 163, 235
Whitmore, Stanford, 354
Whitmore, Terry, 402–403
Whitter, John Greenleaf, 100–101
Whiz Comics, 308
Why Korea?, **355–356**
Why Vietnam, **425–426**
Why We Fight, 326, **330**, 355, 425
Wicki, Bernard, 279
Widmark, Richard, 155, 353
Wild Bunch, The, 153
Wilde, Cornell, 237–238
Wilder, Billy, 310
Wilder, Margaret Buell, 302
Wilderness Clearing, 8
"Wildwood Flower," 303
Willard, Archibald M., 39–40
William I (King), 2
Williams, Bill, 205
Williams, John, 11
Williams, Robin, 390
Williamson, David, 41
"Willing Conscript, The," **426–427**
Willingham, Calder, 166, 213
Willis, Bruce, 398
Wilson, Edmund, 219
Wilson, Justin, 366
Wilson, Meredith, 233, 330
Wilson, Michael, 100
Wilson, Samuel, 52
Wilson, Woodrow, 87, 194, 196, 204, 208, 313, 320, 431
Winchell, Walter, 318
Winds of War, The, 328
Winged Victory, 231, **330–331**
Wingert, Dick, 324

"Wingman, The," 274
Wings, 199, 207, **221–222**
Wings Comics, **331–332**
"Wings, Engine, Fuselage, Tail"
   (WEFT), 326–327
Wings of America Clubs, 331
Winning Hearts and Minds, **427**
Winter, Septimus, 120, 144
Winterbotham, Russ, 247
Wise, Robert, 214
Wister, Owen, 108
Wistorm, William H., 386
"With God on Our Side," **427–428**
With the French, 182
W. J. Morgan and Co., 101
Wolcott, Alexander, 213
Wolfe, James, 3
Wolff, Tobias, 398–399
Wolf Mountain Moon, 168
Wolheim, Louis, 221
Wolper, David L., 125
Wolverton, Basil, 324
Womanhood, the Glory of a Nation, 197
Women in Military Service for America
   Memorial, **437–438**
Wonder Woman, **332**
Wood, Natalie, 263
Wood, P. J., 355
Wood, Sam, 251
Woodstock, 396
Woodstock Festival, 396
Woodward, C. Vann, 119
Woodsworth, Samuel, 49
Wooley, Monte, 303
Work, Henry Clay, 107, 113–114, 118,
   135
Works Progress Administration (WPA),
   85, 277
Wottitz, Walter, 279
Wouk, Herman, 228, 242–243, 327–328
Wright, Johnny, 395, 406
Wright, Stephen, 402
Wright, Teresa, 239, 284

Wrightson, Earl, 233
Wyckoff, Alvin, 142
Wyeth, N. C., 25
Wyler, William, 100, 238, 259, 283, 287

Yale Daily News, 379
Yalta Conference, 336
Yank, 218, 251, 264, 299, 302, **333**
Yank—The Story of the War, 333
"Yankee Doodle," **43–44**
Yankee Doodle, 39
Year from a Reporter's Notebook, A, 182
Year in Peril, The, **333–334**
"Year That Trembled and Reeled Be-
   neath Me," 146
yellow journalism, 178, **192–193**
Yellow Kid, The, 192
yellow ribbons, 155, 158, 170, 173, **438–
   439**
Yemassee, The, 39
"Yes, I Would the War Were Over,"
   144
"Yes Sir, That's My Baby," 207
Yevtushenko, Yevgeny, 399
Yip, Yip, Yaphank, 212, 265, 316
Yokel Boy, 256
York, Alvin, 215–216
Young, Gig, 229
Young, Joe, 207
Young, John Sacret, 373, 412
Young Lions, The, **334–335**
*Young Trailers: A Story of Early Ken-
   tucky, The*, 58
"You're a Grand Old Flag," 212

Zanuck, Darryl, 25, 117, 279, 331, 335
Zemeckis, Robert, 384
Zero Hour, 318
Ziegfield Follies, 29, 207
Zimmermann, Charles A., 230
Zinnemann, Fred, 263, 284
Ziolkowski, Korczak, 155–156
Ziolkowski, Ruth, 156
Zwick, Ed, 103, 434

About the Editor and Contributors

LESLIE KENNEDY ADAMS, Assistant Professor of English, Department of Languages, Houston Baptist University, Houston, Texas.

RANDAL W. ALLRED, Associate Professor of English, Division of Language, Literature, and Composition, Brigham Young University–Hawaii Campus, Laie, Hawaii.

KENT BERGER, Teacher, Wilson Intermediate School, Pekin, Illinois.

SUZANNE BRODERICK, Lecturer, Division of Humanities, Heartland Community College, Bloomington, Illinois.

MICHAEL BROWN, Assistant Professor of Communications and Mass Media, Department of Communications and Mass Media, University of Wyoming, Laramie, Wyoming.

DAN CABANISS, Instructor and Brittain Fellow, School of Literature, Communication, and Culture, Georgia Institute of Technology, Atlanta, Georgia.

CATHERINE CALLOWAY, Professor of English, Department of English and Philosophy, Arkansas State University, State University, Arkansas.

STEVE CANON, Graduate Student, Department of History, Illinois State University, Normal, Illinois.

JACK COLLDEWEIH, Professor Emeritus of Communication, Department of Communications and Speech, Fairleigh Dickinson University, Teaneck, New Jersey.

CHRISTINE DELEA, Poet, Tualatin, Oregon.

JAMES DEUTSCH, Associate Professorial Lecturer of American Civilization, American Studies Program, The George Washington University, Washington, D.C.

JAMES E. DRAINER, Director, Learning Center, Wilson School, Pekin, Illinois.

ANTHONY O. EDMONDS, Professor of History, Department of History, Ball State University, Muncie, Indiana.

KALMAN GOLDSTEIN, Professor of History, Department of History, Fairleigh Dickinson University, Teaneck, New Jersey.

J. JUSTIN GUSTAINIS, Professor of Communication, Department of Communication, State University of New York at Plattsburgh, Plattsburgh, New York.

PHILIP J. HARWOOD, Associate Professor of Communication, Department of Communication, University of Dayton, Dayton, Ohio.

D. MELISSA HILBISH, Visiting Assistant Professor of American Studies, American Studies Department, University of Maryland, College Park, Maryland.

M. PAUL HOLSINGER, Professor of History, Department of History, Illinois State University, Normal, Illinois.

COLIN L. HOPPER, Senior Teacher, American History, Lincoln-Way Community High School, Frankfort, Illinois.

KERSTIN KETTEMAN, Project Assistant, The Harvard Translations, Boston, Massachusetts.

PHILIP J. LANDON, Professor of English, Department of English, University of Maryland–Baltimore County, Baltimore, Maryland.

KARL G. LAREW, Professor of History, Department of History, Towson University, Towson, Maryland.

JEFF LOEB, Senior Teacher, The Pembroke Hill School, Kansas City, Missouri.

JAMES M. MCCAFFREY, Associate Professor of History, Department of History, University of Houston–Downtown, Houston, Texas.

ROBERT L. MCLAUGHLIN, Assistant Professor of English, Department of English, Illinois State University, Normal, Illinois.

MARTIN J. MANNING, Librarian, Bureau of Information, United States Information Agency, Washington, D.C.

CAROL MOOTS, Instructor, Social Science Department, Illinois Central College, East Peoria, Illinois.

SALLY E. PARRY, Academic Adviser, Department of English, Illinois State University, Normal, Illinois.

PHILIP L. SIMPSON, Assistant Professor of English, Brevard Community College, Palm Bay Campus, Palm Bay, Florida.

JEFFREY W. STOUT, Lecturer in History, Department of History, Illinois State University, Normal, Illinois.

ERIC D. SWEETWOOD, Senior Teacher, Social Sciences Department, Pontiac Township High School, Pontiac, Illinois.

DAVID J. TIETGE, Director, The Writing Center, Seton Hall University, South Orange, New Jersey.

DAVID K. VAUGHAN, Assistant Dean for Research and Consulting, Graduate School of Logistics and Acquisition Management, Air Force Institute of Technology, Wright-Patterson Air Force Base, Ohio.

DEVON WESTMORELAND, Teacher, Saint Ethelreda School, Chicago, Illinois.

ISBN 0-313-29908-0

90000>

EAN

9 780313 299087

HARDCOVER BAR CODE